Fodor's 2003

D1045915

Scotland

The Guide
for All Budgets

Completely
Updated

Where to Stay, Eat,
and Explore

On and Off
the Beaten Path

When to Go,
What to Pack

Maps, Travel Tips,
and Web Sites

Fodor's Travel Publications • New York, Toronto, London, Sydney, Auckland
www.fodors.com

Fodor's Scotland 2003

EDITOR: Deborah Kaufman

Editorial Contributors: Carissa Bluestone, Satu Hummasti, Beth Ingpen, Mark Porter, Brian Sheridan, David Steele, Kenneth Walton

Editorial Production: Kristin Milavec

Maps: David Lindroth Inc., Mapping Specialists, *cartographers;* Rebecca Baer and Robert Blake, *map editors*

Design: Fabrizio La Rocca, *creative director;* Guido Caroti, *art director;* Jolie Novak, *senior picture editor;* Melanie Marin, *photo editor*

Cover Design: Pentagram

Production/Manufacturing: Yexenia (Jessie) Markland

Cover Photo (Glencoe): Giovanni Simeone/DIAF

Copyright

ISBN 1–4000–1075–6

ISSN 0743–0973

Important Tip

Although all prices, opening times, and other details in this book are based on information supplied to us at this writing, changes occur all the time in the travel world, and Fodor's cannot accept responsibility for facts that become outdated or for inadvertent errors or omissions. So **always confirm information when it matters,** especially if you're making a detour to visit a specific place.

Special Sales

Fodor's Travel Publications are available at special discounts for bulk purchases for sales promotions or premiums. Special editions, including personalized covers, excerpts of existing guides, and corporate imprints, can be created in large quantities for special needs. For more information, contact your local bookseller or write to Special Markets, Fodor's Travel Publications, 1745 Broadway, New York, NY 10019. Inquiries from Canada should be directed to your local Canadian bookseller or sent to Random House of Canada, Ltd., Marketing Department, 2775 Matheson Boulevard East, Mississauga, Ontario L4W 4P7. Inquiries from the United Kingdom should be sent to Fodor's Travel Publications, 20 Vauxhall Bridge Road, London, England SW1V 2SA.

PRINTED IN THE UNITED STATES OF AMERICA

10 9 8 7 6 5 4 3 2 1

CONTENTS

ON THE ROAD WITH FODOR'S

A TRIP TAKES YOU OUT OF YOURSELF. Concerns of life at home completely disappear, driven away by more immediate thoughts—about, say, what marvels will beguile the next day, or where you'll have dinner. That's where Fodor's comes in. We make sure that you know all your options, so that you don't miss something that's around the next bend just because you didn't know it was there. Mindful that the best memories of your trip might have nothing to do with what you came to Scotland to see, we guide you to sights large and small all over the region. You might set out to tour castles and stately homes, but back at home you find yourself unable to forget that stroll across a windswept moor. With Fodor's at your side, serendipitous discoveries are never far away.

About Our Writers

Our success in showing you every corner of Scotland is a credit to our extraordinary writers. Although there's no substitute for travel advice from a good friend who knows your style, our contributors are the next best thing—the kind of people you would poll for travel advice if you knew them.

The information in these pages is largely the work of **Beth Ingpen**. A longtime editorial contributor to *Fodor's Scotland*, Beth works as a freelance editor and writer. She was previously publishing manager with the Royal Society of Edinburgh, Scotland's premier learned society, and spent lunchtimes soaking up that city's culture, particularly in its art galleries and concert halls. Close to the sea, Beth's countryside house is set in the barley fields in the rural northeast.

Mark Porter, who updated this edition's Borders and the Southwest chapter, is a regular contributor to the *Sunday Times* and other national British newspapers, including the *Scotsman*. He is a seasoned travel writer and food critic, also writing for Britain's top food magazine, *Waitrose Food Illustrated*. A former political columnist and features, arts, travel, and books editor of the *Express on Sunday*, he lives and works in Scotland and London.

David Steele, who updated the Edinburgh chapter, runs a media and public-relations business and writes widely on Scottish affairs. He spent more than 20 years as a senior writer with the *Herald* and *Evening Times*, covering a variety of subjects including politics, business, and travel. David now contributes to several publications and gives media and public-relations advice to companies and organizations across Scotland.

Glasgow updater **Kenneth Walton** is a writer and journalist based in Scotland. He is music critic for the *Scotsman* and has spent the past 20 years writing on the arts and tourism for numerous newspapers and magazines, including the *Daily Telegraph*, the *Observer*, and the *Herald*. He is author of *The Glasgow Pocket Guide*, which he completed shortly after spending a number of years as communications director for the Greater Glasgow and Clyde Valley Tourist Board.

You can rest assured that you're in good hands—and that no property mentioned in the book has paid to be included. Each has been selected strictly on its merits, as the best of its type in its price range.

How to Use This Book

Up front is Smart Travel Tips A to Z, arranged alphabetically by topic and loaded with tips, Web sites, and contact information. Destination: Scotland helps get you in the mood for your trip. Subsequent chapters in *Scotland* are arranged regionally. All city chapters begin with exploring information, with a section for each neighborhood (each recommending a good tour and listing sights alphabetically). All regional chapters are divided geographically; within each area, towns are covered in logical geographical order, and attractive stretches of road between them are indicated by the designation En Route. To help you decide what you'll have time to visit, all chapters begin with our writers' favorite itineraries. (Mix itineraries from several chapters, and you can put together a really exceptional trip.) The A to Z section that ends every chapter lists additional resources. At the end of the book

Scotland

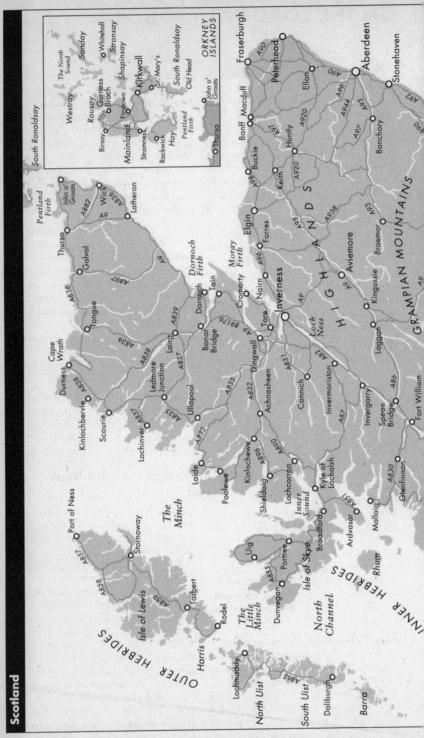

ORKNEY ISLANDS

Westray Sanday
The North Sound
Rousay Whitehall Stronsay
Birsay Gurness Stronsay
Broch Shapinsay
Mainland Finstown Kirkwall
Stromness St. Mary's
Rackwick South Ronaldsay
Hoy Old Head
Pentland Firth
Thurso John o'Groats

South Ronaldsay

Fraserburgh
Peterhead
Aberdeen
Stonehaven
A90
Banff Macduff Ellon
A920 Buckie Huntly A944 A93
Keith A96 A947 Banchory
A98 A920 A95 A93
Elgin Forres A941 A939
Moray Firth Aviemore GRAMPIAN MOUNTAINS
Inverness Kingussie Braemar
Nairn A9 Laggan A9
Cromarty A86
Tore Loch Ness
Dingwall Invermoriston Spean Bridge
Achnasheen Cannich Invergarry Fort William
A832 A831 A87 A830
Kyle of Lochalsh Glenfinnan
Lochcarron A87 Mallaig
Shieldaig Inner Sound Ardvasar
Kinlochewe Broadford
A896 A890
Poolewe Portree Isle of Skye
Laide Uig A855
Ullapool Dunvegan Rhum
A835 The Little Minch North Channel
Ledmore Junction INNER HEBRIDES
Lochinver A837
Scourie Bonar Bridge
Kinlochbervie Lairg Dornoch
A838 A839 Dornoch Firth
Durness A836 Tain
Cape Wrath A897 Bonar Bridge
Tongue A836
Golval A9
Thurso Dornoch Firth
Pentland Firth A882 Wick A836
John o'Groats Latheron A9

The Minch
Port of Ness
Stornoway A857
Tarbert A858 A859
Rodel
Isle of Lewis
Harris
OUTER HEBRIDES
Lochmaddy A865
North Uist
South Uist Daliburgh
Barra

Coll
Tiree
Tobermory
Iona
Bunessan
Mull
Lochaline
Duror
Loch Linnhe
Oban
Arduaine
Firth of Lorn
Colonsay
Jura
Port Askaig
Islay
Lochgilphead
Tarbert
Kintyre
Campbeltown

ATLANTIC OCEAN

20 mi
0
0
32 km

Montrose
Arbroath
Brechin
Forfar
Blairgowrie
Pitlochry
Dundee
St. Andrews
Cupar
Glenrothes
Kirkcaldy
Perth
Crieff
Crianlarich
Inveraray
Tarbet
Helensburgh
Kinross
Dunfermline
Stirling
Falkirk
Airdrie
Hamilton
Gourock
Greenock
Paisley
Glasgow
Motherwell
East Kilbride
Kilmarnock
Prestwick
Irvine
Largs
Rothesay
Brodick
Arran
Ardrossan
Firth of Clyde
Ayr
Girvan
Stranraer
Portpatrick
Drummore
Newton Stewart
Luce Bay
Kirkconnel
Biggar
Peebles
Moffat
Dumfries
Castle Douglas
Lockerbie
Annan
Solway Firth

North Sea

Berwick
North Berwick
Dunbar
Duns
Coldstream
Kelso
Jedburgh
Hawick
EDINBURGH
Livingston
Dalkeith
Firth of Forth
Firth of Tay

SOUTHERN UPLANDS

The Cheviot Hills

Alnwick
Hexham
Carlisle

ENGLAND

N

North Channel

NORTHERN IRELAND

SHETLAND ISLANDS
Herma Ness
Baltasound
Unst
Fetlar
Yell
Hamnavoe
Whalsay
Ulsta
Toft
Voe
Mainland
Hillswick
Brae
St. Magnus Bay
Walls
Scalloway
Lerwick
Sandwick
Sumburgh
Levenwick
Sumburgh Roost

Great Britain

SHETLAND ISLANDS

Unst

Yell

Lerwick

Mainland

Kirkwall

ORKNEY ISLANDS

Mainland

Hoy

North Sea

N

Peterhead

A90

Aberdeen

Montrose

A98

Banff

A96

A93

A90

Dundee

Firth of Tay

St. Andrew's

Firth of Forth

Berwick-on-Tweed

Newcastle

Sunderland

Middlesbrough

Whitby

ORKNEY ISLANDS

John O'Groats

Thurso

Wick

A9

A836

Dornoch

A9

A96

Inverness

Aviemore

Braemar

A93

Perth

M90

Dunfermline

Edinburgh

A68

Durham

Carlisle

A837

A838

A836

Loch Ness

A87

Fort William

A9

A85

Oban

Callander

A82

Stirling

A80

M8

Lanark

M74

Kilmarnock

Dumfries

Kirkcudbright

Keswick

SCOTLAND

Ullapool

A890

Kyle of Lochalsh

Portree

Skye

A830

A82

Mull

A83

Glasgow

Greenock

Arran

Ayr

A71

A75

Stranraer

Stornoway

Lewis

Harris

INNER HEBRIDES

Coll

Tiree

Islay

Campbeltown

Bangor

Belfast

OUTER HEBRIDES

North Uist

South Uist

ATLANTIC OCEAN

NORTHERN IRELAND

Londonderry

Portadown

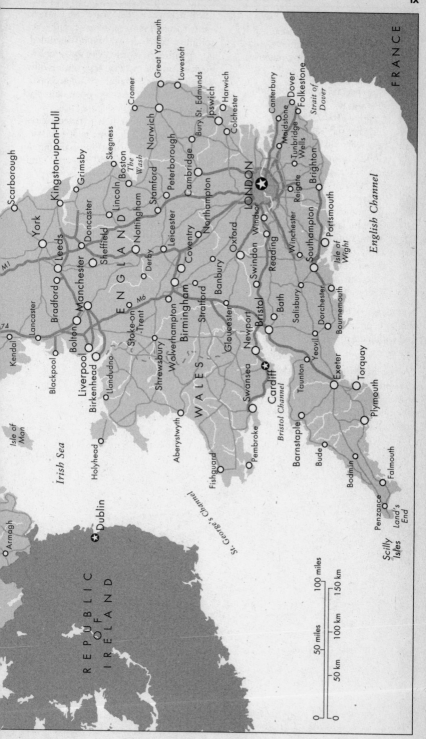

you'll find Background and Essentials, including a chronology and the Books and Movies section, which suggests enriching reading and viewing material.

Icons and Symbols

★   Our special recommendations
✕   Restaurant
🏠   Lodging establishment
✕🏠 Lodging establishment whose restaurant warrants a special trip
🦆 Good for kids (rubber duckie)
☞   Sends you to another section of the guide for more information
⊠   Address
☏   Telephone number
🕐   Opening and closing times
💰 Admission prices (those we give apply to adults; substantially reduced fees are almost always available for children, students, and senior citizens)

Numbers in white and black circles ③ ❸ that appear on the maps, in the margins, and within the tours correspond to one another.

For hotels, you can assume that all rooms have private baths (sometimes this will be a shower without a bathtub), phones, TVs, and air-conditioning unless otherwise noted. We always list a property's facili-

ties but not whether you'll be charged extra to use them, so when pricing accommodations, do ask what's included. For restaurants, it's always a good idea to book ahead; we mention reservations only when they're essential or are not accepted. All restaurants we list are open daily for lunch and dinner unless stated otherwise; dress is mentioned only when men are required to wear a jacket or a jacket and tie. Look for more information on dining in Scotland in Smart Travel Tips A to Z and in the Pleasures and Pastimes section that follows each chapter introduction.

Don't Forget to Write

Your experiences—positive and negative—matter to us. If we have missed or misstated something, we want to hear about it. We follow up on all suggestions. Contact the Scotland editor at editors@fodors.com or c/o Fodor's at 1745 Broadway, New York, New York 10019. And have a fabulous trip!

Karen Cure

Karen Cure
Editorial Director

ESSENTIAL INFORMATION

AIR TRAVEL

BOOKING

When you book **look for nonstop flights** and **remember that "direct" flights stop at least once.** Try to avoid connecting flights, which require a change of plane. Two airlines may operate a connecting flight jointly, so ask if your airline operates every segment of the trip; you may find that the carrier you prefer flies you only part of the way. To find more booking tips and to check prices and make on-line flight reservations, log on to www.fodors.com.

CARRIERS

Although a small country, Scotland has a significant air network. Contact British Airways or British Airways Express for details on flights from London's Heathrow Airport or on those from Glasgow, Edinburgh, Aberdeen, and Inverness to the farthest corners of the Scottish mainland and to the islands. Ryanair flies from London Stansted (to Prestwick, south of Glasgow); British Midland has service from Heathrow; and easyJet and GO fly between Glasgow, Edinburgh, Aberdeen, and Inverness (plus to and from Belfast and London's Luton).

➤ MAJOR AIRLINES: **British Airways** (☎ 800/247–9297). Via other carriers from London and/or Manchester: **American Airlines** (☎ 800/433–7300). **Continental** (☎ 800/525–0280). **Delta** (☎ 800/221–1212). **Northwest Airlines** (☎ 800/447–4747). **United** (☎ 800/241–6522). **Virgin Atlantic** (☎ 800/862–8621).

➤ FROM LONDON TO EDINBURGH AND GLASGOW: **British Airways** (☎ 08457/733377). **British Midland** (☎ 0870/607–0555). **easyJet** (☎ 0870/600–0000). **GO** (☎ 0870/607–6543). **Ryanair** (☎ 01292/678000).

➤ AROUND SCOTLAND: **British Airways Express** (☎ 08457/733377). **easyJet** (☎ 0870/600–0000).

CHECK-IN AND BOARDING

Always **ask your carrier about its check-in policy.** Plan to arrive at the airport about 2 hours before your scheduled departure time for domestic flights and 2½ to 3 hours before international flights. Assuming that not everyone with a ticket will show up, airlines routinely overbook planes. When everyone does, airlines ask for volunteers to give up their seats. In return, these volunteers usually get a certificate for a free flight and are rebooked on the next flight out. If there are not enough volunteers, the airline must choose who will be denied boarding. The first to get bumped are passengers who checked in late and those flying on discounted tickets, so **get to the gate and check in as early as possible,** especially during peak periods.

Always **bring a government-issued photo I.D. to the airport;** even when it's not required, a passport is best.

CUTTING COSTS

The least expensive airfares to Scotland are priced for round-trip travel and must usually be purchased in advance. Airlines generally allow you to change your return date for a fee; most low-fare tickets, however, are nonrefundable. It's smart to **call a number of airlines,** and when you are quoted a good price, **book it on the spot**—the same fare may not be available the next day. Always **check different routings** and look into using alternate airports. Also, price off-peak flights, which may be significantly less expensive than others. Travel agents, especially low-fare specialists (☞ Discounts and Deals), are helpful.

Check out discounts and passes, many of which are available during the off-season. For example, British Airways has in the past offered a Highland Rover Pass, which gave substantial savings on a total of five flights around Scotland in the winter season. Inquire before your arrival in Scotland as to what's available.

If you intend to fly to Scotland from London, **take advantage of the current fare wars** on internal routes—notably between London's four airports and Glasgow–Edinburgh. Among the cheapest are Ryanair between London Stansted (with its excellent rail links from London's Liverpool Street Station) and Glasgow Prestwick, and easyJet and GO, offering bargain fares from London Luton (with good rail links from central London) to Glasgow, Edinburgh, Aberdeen, and Inverness. Even British Airways now offers competitive fares on some flights.

Many airlines, singly or in collaboration, offer discount air passes that allow foreigners to travel economically in a particular country or region. These visitor passes usually must be reserved and purchased before you leave home. Information about passes can be difficult to track down on airline Web sites, which tend to be geared to travelers departing from a given carrier's country rather than to those intending to visit that country. Try typing the name of the pass into a search engine, or search for "pass" within the carrier's Web site.

Consolidators are another good source. They buy tickets for scheduled international flights at reduced rates from the airlines, then sell them at prices that beat the best fare available directly from the airlines. Sometimes you can even get your money back if you need to return the ticket. Carefully read the fine print detailing penalties for changes and cancellations, purchase the ticket with a credit card, and **confirm your consolidator reservation with the airline.**

When you **fly as a courier,** you trade your checked-luggage space for a ticket deeply subsidized by a courier service. There are restrictions on when you can book and how long you can stay. Some courier companies list with membership organizations, such as the Air Courier Association

and the International Association of Air Travel Couriers; these require you to become a member before you can book a flight.

➤ CONSOLIDATORS: **Cheap Tickets** (☎ 800/377–1000 or 888/922–8849, WEB www.cheaptickets.com). **Discount Airline Ticket Service** (☎ 800/576–1600). **Unitravel** (☎ 800/325–2222, WEB www.unitravel.com). **Up & Away Travel** (☎ 212/889–2345, WEB www.upandaway.com). **World Travel Network** (☎ 800/409–6753).

➤ COURIER RESOURCES: **Air Courier Association** (☎ 800/282–1202, WEB www.aircourier.org). **International Association of Air Travel Couriers** (☎ 352/475–1584, WEB www.courier.org). **Now Voyager Travel** (☎ 212/431–1616).

➤ DISCOUNT PASSES: **FlightPass, EuropebyAir** (☎ 888/387–2479, WEB www.europebyair.com).

ENJOYING THE FLIGHT

State your seat preference when purchasing your ticket, and then repeat it when you confirm and when you check in. For more legroom, you can request one of the few emergency-aisle seats at check-in, if you are capable of lifting at least 50 pounds—a Federal Aviation Administration requirement of passengers in these seats. Seats behind a bulkhead also offer more legroom, but they don't have under-seat storage. Don't sit in the row in front of the emergency aisle or in front of a bulkhead, where seats may not recline.

Ask the airline whether a snack or meal is served on the flight. If you have dietary concerns, **request special meals when booking.** These can be vegetarian, low-cholesterol, or kosher, for example. It's a good idea to pack some healthful snacks and a small (plastic) bottle of water in your carry-on bag. On long flights, try to maintain a normal routine to help fight jet lag. At night, **get some sleep.** By day, **eat light meals, drink water** (not alcohol), and **move around the cabin** to stretch your legs. For additional jet-lag tips consult *Fodor's FYI: Travel Fit & Healthy* (available at bookstores everywhere).

FLYING TIMES

Flying time is 6½ hours from New York, 7½ hours from Chicago, 9½ hours from Dallas, 10 hours from Los Angeles, and 21½ hours from Sydney.

HOW TO COMPLAIN

If your baggage goes astray or your flight goes awry, complain right away. Most carriers require that you **file a claim immediately.** The Aviation Consumer Protection Division of the Department of Transportation publishes *Fly-Rights,* which discusses airlines and consumer issues and is available on-line. At PassengerRights. com, a Web site, you can compose a letter of complaint and distribute it electronically.

➤ AIRLINE COMPLAINTS: **Aviation Consumer Protection Division** (✉ U.S. Department of Transportation, Room 4107, C-75, Washington, DC 20590, ☎ 202/366–2220, WEB www.dot.gov/airconsumer). **Federal Aviation Administration Consumer Hotline** (☎ 800/322–7873).

RECONFIRMING

Check the status of your flight before you leave for the airport. You can do this on your carrier's Web site, by linking to a flight-status checker (many Web booking services offer these), or by calling your carrier or travel agent. Always confirm international flights at least 72 hours ahead of the scheduled departure time.

AIRPORTS

The major gateway to Scotland is Glasgow Airport, about 7 mi outside Glasgow. Edinburgh Airport, 7 mi from the city, doesn't serve transatlantic flights, but does offer connections for dozens of European cities and hourly flights to London's Gatwick and Heathrow airports. It's also possible to fly into Glasgow and then take bus or train service to Edinburgh in less than two hours. Aberdeen Airport has direct flights from Amsterdam, in the Netherlands, providing a way of arriving in Scotland from the United States without first flying into London's airports. Refer to chapter A to Z sections for information on airport transfers.

➤ AIRPORT INFORMATION: **Aberdeen Airport** (☎ 01224/722331). **Edin-burgh Airport** (☎ 0131/333–1000). **Glasgow Airport** (☎ 0141/887–1111).

DUTY-FREE SHOPPING

As of July 1999, duty-free shopping allowances between the United Kingdom and other European Union member countries were abolished, although there are still numerous merchandise offers for those traveling between E.U. countries by boat, plane, and via the Channel Tunnel. Duty-free sales for travel outside the EU remain business as usual (☞ Customs and Duties).

BIKE TRAVEL

The best months for cycling in Scotland are May, June, and September, when the roads are often quieter and the weather is usually better. Winds are predominantly from the southwest, so plan your route accordingly.

Because Scotland's main roads are continually being upgraded, bicyclists can easily access the network of quieter rural roads in such areas as Dumfries and Galloway, the Borders, and much of eastern Scotland, especially Grampian. Still, care must be taken in getting from some town centers to rural riding areas, so if in doubt, ask a local. In a few areas of the Highlands, notably in northwestern Scotland, the rugged terrain and limited population have resulted in the lack of side roads, making it more difficult—sometimes impossible—to plan a minor-road route in these areas.

Several agencies now promote "safe routes" for recreational cyclists. These routes are signposted, and the agencies have produced maps or leaflets showing where they run. Perhaps best known is the Glasgow–Loch Lomond–Killin Cycleway, which makes use of former railway track beds, forest trails, quiet rural side roads, and some main roads. The Glasgow to Irvine Cycle Route runs south and west of Glasgow and links with the Johnstone and Greenock Railway Path. In Edinburgh there's the Innocent Railway Path from Holyrood Path to St. Leonards. Contact the relevant tourist board for more information.

The Scottish Tourist Board's (☞ Visitor Information) free brochure

"Cycling in Scotland" has some suggested routes and practical advice. The Ordnance Survey Landranger series of maps, available in many city bookstores, which shows gradients, is invaluable for cyclists.

BIKES IN FLIGHT

Most airlines accommodate bikes as luggage, provided they are dismantled and boxed; check with individual airlines about packing requirements. Airlines sell bike boxes, which are often free at bike shops, for about $15 (bike bags start at $100). International travelers often can substitute a bike for a piece of checked luggage at no charge; otherwise, the cost is about $100. Domestic and Canadian airlines charge $40–$80 each way.

BIKES ON BUSES

Although some rural bus services will transport cycles if space is available, **don't count on getting your bike on a bus.** Be sure to check well in advance with the appropriate bus company.

BIKES ON FERRIES

You can take bicycles on car and passenger ferries in Scotland, and it's not generally necessary to book in advance. The three main ferry service operators (☞ Boat and Ferry Travel) are Caledonian MacBrayne, which charges £1–£4 per journey for accompanied bicycles on some routes (on many routes, bicycles are carried free), and Western Ferries and Northlink Ferries, both of which carry accompanied bicycles free. **Check cycles on car ferries early** so that they can be loaded through the car entrance.

BIKES ON TRAINS

ScotRail strongly advises that you **make a train reservation for you and your bike at least one month in advance.** On several trains reservations are compulsory. A leaflet containing the latest information is available through ScotRail and can be picked up at most manned train stations within Scotland.

BIKING OFF-ROAD

Scotland's legal position on off-road cycling is complex. Cycling is covered by road traffic laws because a bike is classified as a vehicle. In a strict legal sense, cycling off-road is possible only on specifically designated cycle tracks, routes that have a common-law right-of-way for cycles, or routes that have the consent of the landowner. Legally, cyclists aren't allowed on pedestrian rights-of-way, but many landowners don't mind if cyclists use them. Nevertheless, it's best to seek local advice when planning off-road routes.

BIKING ORGANIZATIONS

The Cyclists' Touring Club actively campaigns for better cyclist facilities throughout the United Kingdom. It publishes a members magazine, route maps, and guides. Sustrans Ltd. is a nonprofit organization dedicated to providing environmentally friendly routes for cyclists, notably in and around cities.

➤ BIKE MAPS AND INFORMATION: **Cyclists' Touring Club** (⊠ National Headquarters, Cotterell House, 69 Meadrow, Godalming, Surrey GU7 3HS, England, ☎ 0870/8730060, FAX 01483/426994, WEB www.ctc.org.uk). **Sustrans Ltd.** (⊠ 162 Fountainbridge, Edinburgh EH3 9RX, ☎ 0131/624–7660, FAX 0131/624–7664, WEB www.sustrans.org.uk).

BIKING TOURS

Scottish Border Trails runs off-road mountain-bike treks in the Borders and vehicle-supported road tours on which your luggage is ferried between stops. Wildcat Bike Tours sells guided, vehicle-supported tours throughout Scotland for novices and experts.

➤ BIKE TOUR OPERATORS: **Scottish Border Trails** (⊠ Drummore, Venlaw High Rd., Peebles EH45 8RL, ☎ 01721/720336, FAX 01721/723004, arthur@trails.scottishborders.co.uk). **Wildcat Bike Tours** (⊠ Unit 111, John Player Bldg., Stirling Enterprise Park, Stirling FK7 7RP, ☎ FAX 01786/464333, WEB www.wildcat-bike-tours.co.uk).

BOAT AND FERRY TRAVEL

With so many islands, plus the great Firth of Clyde waterway, ferry services in Scotland are of paramount importance. Most ferries transport vehicles as well as foot passengers, although a few of the smaller ones are still for passengers only.

The main operator is Caledonian MacBrayne Ltd., known generally as CalMac. Services extend from the Firth of Clyde, where there's an extremely extensive network, right up to the northwest of Scotland and all of the Hebrides. Calmac sells an Island Rover runabout ticket, which is ideal for touring holidays in the islands, as well as an island-hopping scheme called Island Hopscotch.

The Dunoon–Gourock route on the Clyde is served by Western Ferries; the Islay–Jura service is operated by Serco Denholm.

Northlink Ferries operates a car ferry for Orkney between Scrabster (near Thurso) and Stromness (on the main island of Orkney, called Mainland) and between Aberdeen and Kirkwall (also on Mainland, Orkney). Northlink also runs ferries for Shetland between Aberdeen and Lerwick.

➤ BOAT AND FERRY INFORMATION: **Caledonian MacBrayne** (✉ The Ferry Terminal, Gourock PA19 1QP, ☎ 01475/650100; 08705/650000 reservations, FAX 01475/637607; 01475/635235 reservations, WEB www.calmac.co.uk). **Northlink Ferries** (✉ New Harbour Bldg., Ferry Rd., Stromness, Orkney, KW16 3BH, ☎ 01856/851144, FAX 01856/851155, WEB www.northlinkferries.co.uk). **Serco Denholm** (☎ 01475/731540). **Western Ferries** (☎ 01369/704452, FAX 01369/706020, WEB www.westernferries.co.uk).

BUS TRAVEL

The country's bus network is extensive. Bus service is comprehensive in cities, less so in country districts. Express service links main cities and towns, connecting, for example, Glasgow and Edinburgh to Inverness, Aberdeen, Perth, Skye, Ayr, Dumfries, and Carlisle; or Inverness with Aberdeen, Wick, Thurso, and Fort William. These express services are very fast, and fares are reasonable.

CUTTING COSTS

On bus routes, Tourist Trail Pass offers complete freedom of travel on any National Express or Scottish Citylink services throughout the mainland United Kingdom. Four permutations give up to 15 days of travel in 30 consecutive days. It's available from Scottish Citylink offices, most bus stations, and any National Express appointed agent.

➤ DISCOUNT PASSES: **National Express** (☎ 08705/808080, WEB www.nationalexpress.co.uk). **Scottish Citylink** (☎ 08705/505050, WEB www.citylink.co.uk).

FARES AND SCHEDULES

Contact Traveline Scotland or the Edinburgh and Scotland Information Centre for information on all public transportation and timetables.

➤ BUS INFORMATION: **Edinburgh and Scotland Information Centre** (✉ 3 Princes St., Edinburgh EH2 2QP, ☎ 0131/473–3800, FAX 0131/473–3881). **Traveline Scotland** (☎ 0870/608–2608).

PAYING

For town, suburban, or short-distance journeys, you normally buy your ticket on the bus, from a pay box, or from the driver. Sometimes you need exact change. For longer journeys— for example, Glasgow–Inverness—it's usual to reserve a seat and pay at the bus station booking office. Credit cards and traveler's checks are accepted at most bus stations.

FROM ENGLAND

Coaches (as long-distance and touring buses are usually called) usually provide the cheapest way to travel between England and Scotland; fares may be as little as a third of the rail fares for comparable trips (though rail companies have more competitive fares on some routes). About 20 companies operate service between major cities, including National Express (single class only). Journey time between London and Glasgow or Edinburgh is 8–8¼ hours. The main London terminal is Victoria Coach Station, but some Scottish companies use Gloucester Road Coach Station in west London, near the Penta Hotel. Many people travel to Scotland by coach; in summer a reservation three or four days ahead is advisable. Fares are about £32 round-trip, and credit cards are accepted.

➤ BUS LINES: **National Express** (✉ Buchanan Street Bus Station,

Killermont St., Glasgow G2 3NP,
☎ 08705/808080, WEB www.
nationalexpress.co.uk).

BUSINESS HOURS

BANKS

Banks are open weekdays 9:30–3:30,
some days to 4:45. Some banks have
extended hours on Thursday evening,
and a few are open on Saturday
morning. Some also close for an hour
at lunchtime. The major airports
operate 24-hour banking services
seven days a week.

GAS STATIONS

Service stations are at regular inter-
vals on motorways and are usually
open 24 hours a day, though stations
elsewhere usually close from 9 PM to
7 AM; in rural areas many close at 6
PM and all day on Sunday.

MUSEUMS AND SIGHTS

Most museums in cities and larger
towns are open daily, although some
may be closed on Sunday morning. In
smaller villages museums are often
open when there are visitors around—
even late on summer evenings—but
closed in poor weather, when visitors
are unlikely; there's often a contact
phone number on the door.

PHARMACIES

Pharmacies (often called "chemists"
in Scotland) usually open 9 to 5 or
5:30 Monday through Saturday,
though most large towns and cities
have either a large supermarket open
extended hours, with a pharmacy on
the premises, or have a rotation
system for pharmacists on call (there
will be a note displayed in the pharmacy's window with the number to
call). In rural areas doctors often
dispense medicines themselves. In an
emergency the police should be able
to locate a pharmacist.

SHOPS

Usual business hours are Monday
through Saturday 9 to 5 or 5:30.
Outside the main centers, most shops
observe an early closing day (they
close at 1 PM) once a week, often
Wednesday or Thursday. In small
villages many shops also close for
lunch. Department stores in large
cities and many supermarkets even in
smaller towns stay open for late-night
shopping (usually until 7:30 or 8) one
or more days a week. Apart from
some newsstands and small food
stores, many shops are closed on
Sunday except in larger towns and
cities, where main shopping malls
may be open.

CAMERAS AND
PHOTOGRAPHY

The *Kodak Guide to Shooting Great
Travel Pictures* (available at book-
stores everywhere) is loaded with tips.
➤ PHOTO HELP: **Kodak Information
Center** (☎ 800/242–2424, WEB www.
kodak.com).

EQUIPMENT PRECAUTIONS

**Don't pack film and equipment in
checked luggage,** where it is much
more susceptible to damage. X-ray
machines used to view checked luggage are becoming much more powerful and therefore are much more
likely to ruin your film. Try to **ask for
hand inspection of film,** which becomes clouded after repeated exposure to airport X-ray machines, and
**keep videotapes and computer disks
away from metal detectors.** Always
**keep film, tape, and computer disks
out of the sun.** Carry an extra supply
of batteries, and **be prepared to turn
on your camera, camcorder, or laptop**
to prove to airport security personnel
that the device is real.

VIDEOS

Remember that most video cartridges
sold in the United Kingdom do not
interface with American video players. Before purchasing any videos in
the United Kingdom ask a staff member at the store about this concern.
Happily, many attractions that have
videos also market versions specially
made for the American/overseas
market.

CAR RENTAL

If you're traveling to more than one
country, make sure your rental contract permits you to take the car
across borders and that the insurance
policy covers you in every country
you visit. Remember that unlike cars
in the United States or the rest of
Europe, British cars have the steering
wheel on the right. Therefore, you

may want to leave your rented car in Britain and pick up a left-side drive when you cross the Channel.

Rates in Glasgow begin at £35 a day and £170 a week for an economy car with a manual transmission and unlimited mileage. This does not include tax on car rentals, which is 17.5%.

➤ MAJOR AGENCIES: **Alamo** (☎ 800/522–9696, WEB www.alamo.com). **Avis** (☎ 800/331–1084; 800/879–2847 in Canada; 02/9353–9000 in Australia; 09/526–2847 in New Zealand; 0870/606–0100 in the U.K., WEB www.avis.com). **Budget** (☎ 800/527–0700; 0870/156–5656 in the U.K., WEB www.budget.com). **Dollar** (☎ 800/800–6000; 0124/622–0111 in the U.K., where it's affiliated with Sixt; 02/9223–1444 in Australia, WEB www.dollar.com). **Hertz** (☎ 800/654–3001; 800/263–0600 in Canada; 020/8897–2072 in the U.K.; 02/9669–2444 in Australia; 09/256–8690 in New Zealand, WEB www.hertz.com). **National Car Rental** (☎ 800/227–7368; 020/8680–4800 in the U.K., WEB www.nationalcar.com).

CUTTING COSTS

For a good deal, **book through a travel agent who will shop around.**

Do **look into wholesalers,** companies that do not own fleets but rent in bulk from those that do and often offer better rates than traditional car-rental operations. Prices are best during off-peak periods. Rentals booked through wholesalers often must be paid for before you leave home.

➤ WHOLESALERS: **Auto Europe** (☎ 207/842–2000 or 800/223–5555, FAX 207/842–2222, WEB www.autoeurope.com). **Destination Europe Resources** (DER; ✉ 9501 W. Devon Ave., Rosemont, IL 60018, ☎ 800/782–2424, WEB www.der.com). **Europe by Car** (☎ 212/581–3040 or 800/223–1516, FAX 212/246–1458, WEB www.europebycar.com). **Kemwel** (☎ 800/678–0678 or 800/576–1590, FAX 207/842–2124, WEB www.kemwel.com).

INSURANCE

When driving a rented car you are generally responsible for any damage to or loss of the vehicle. Collision

policies that car-rental companies sell for European rentals typically do not cover stolen vehicles. Before you rent—and purchase collision or theft coverage—see what coverage you already have under the terms of your personal auto-insurance policy and credit cards.

REQUIREMENTS AND RESTRICTIONS

Companies frequently restrict rentals to people over age 23 or under age 75.

SURCHARGES

Before you pick up a car in one city and leave it in another, **ask about drop-off charges or one-way service fees,** which can be substantial. Note, too, that some rental agencies charge extra if you return the car before the time specified in your contract. To avoid a hefty refueling fee, **fill the tank just before you turn in the car,** but be aware that gas stations near the rental outlet may overcharge. It's almost never a deal to buy the tank of gas in the car when you rent it; the understanding is that you'll return it empty, but some fuel usually remains.

CAR TRAVEL

One of the best ways to see Scotland is to rent a car and drive (on the left side of the road, of course). A car allows you to set your own pace and visit several off-the-beaten-path towns and sights.

In Scotland your own driver's license is acceptable. An International Driver's Permit is a good idea; it's available from the American or Canadian automobile associations and, in the United Kingdom, from the Automobile Association or Royal Automobile Club. These international permits, valid only in conjunction with your regular driver's license, are universally recognized; having one may save you a problem with local authorities.

AUTO CLUBS

➤ IN AUSTRALIA: **Australian Automobile Association** (☎ 02/6247–7311, WEB www.aaa.asn.au).

➤ IN CANADA: **Canadian Automobile Association** (CAA, ☎ 613/247–0117, WEB www.caa.ca).

➤ IN NEW ZEALAND: **New Zealand Automobile Association** (☎ 09/377–4660, WEB www.aa.co.nz).

➤ IN THE U.K.: **Automobile Association** (AA, ☎ 08705/500600). **Royal Automobile Club** (RAC; ☎ 08705/722–722, WEB www.rac.co.uk).

➤ IN THE U.S.: **American Automobile Association** (AAA; ☎ 800/564–6222, WEB www.aaa.com).

EMERGENCY SERVICES

For aid if your car breaks down, contact the 24-hour rescue numbers of either the Automobile Association or the Royal Automobile Club.

GASOLINE

Expect to pay a good deal more for gasoline than in the United States, about £3.18 a gallon (70p a liter) for unleaded—up to 10p a gallon higher in remote rural locations. The British imperial gallon is about 20% more in volume than the U.S. gallon—approximately 4.5 liters. Pumps dispense in liters, not gallons. Most gas stations stock unleaded, super unleaded, and LRP (replacing 4-star) plus diesel; most also accept major credit cards.

ROAD CONDITIONS

A good network of superhighways, known as motorways, and divided highways, known as dual carriageways, extends throughout Britain, though in the remoter areas of Scotland where the motorway hasn't penetrated, travel is noticeably slower. Motorways shown with the prefix M are mainly two or three lanes in each direction, without any right-hand turns. These are the roads to use to cover long distances, though inevitably you'll see less of the countryside. Service areas are at most about an hour apart. Dual carriageways, usually shown on a map as a thick red line (often with a black line in the center) and the prefix A followed by a number perhaps with a bracketed T (for example, A304[T]), are similar to motorways, except that right turns are sometimes permitted, and you'll find both traffic lights and traffic circles on them.

The vast network of other main roads, which typical maps show as either single red "A" roads, or narrower brown "B" roads, also numbered, are for the most part the old coach and turnpike roads built originally for horses and carriages. Travel along these roads is slower than on motorways because passing is more difficult. On the other hand, you'll see much more of Scotland.

Minor roads (shown as yellow or white on most maps, unlettered and unnumbered) are the ancient lanes and byways of Britain, roads that are not only living history but a superb way of discovering the real Scotland. You have to drive along them slowly and carefully. On single-track roads, found in the north and west of Scotland, there isn't room for two vehicles to pass, and you must use a passing place if you meet an oncoming car or tractor, or if a car behind wishes to overtake you. Never hold up traffic on single-track roads.

ROAD MAPS

The best general purpose touring map is the Scottish Tourist Board's Touring Map of Scotland (5 mi to the inch), widely available in bookshops, tourist information centers, and from the Scottish Tourist Board (☞ Visitor Information). Any bookshop in the main cities will usually sell good maps. For walking or getting to know a smaller area, the readily available Ordnance Survey Landranger series (1:50,000 scale) can't be beaten.

RULES OF THE ROAD

The most noticeable difference for most visitors is that when in Britain, you drive on the left and steer the car on the right. **Give yourself time to adjust to driving on the left**—especially if you pick up your car at the airport and are still suffering from jet lag.

One of the most complicated questions facing visitors to Britain is that of speed limits. In urban areas, except for certain freeways, it's generally 30 mph, but it is 40 mph on some main roads, as indicated by circular red-rimmed signs. In rural areas the official limit is 60 mph on ordinary roads and 70 mph on divided highways and motorways—and traffic police can be hard on speeders, especially in urban areas. In other respects procedures are similar to those in the United States.

CHILDREN IN SCOTLAND

On the whole, Scotland caters reasonably well to children. If you are renting a car, don't forget to **arrange for a car seat** when you reserve. For general advice about traveling with children, consult *Fodor's FYI: Travel with Your Baby* (available in bookstores everywhere).

FLYING

If your children are two or older, **ask about children's airfares.** As a general rule, infants under two not occupying a seat fly at greatly reduced fares or even for free. When booking, **confirm carry-on allowances** if you're traveling with infants. In general, for babies charged 10% of the adult fare you are allowed one carry-on bag and a collapsible stroller; if the flight is full, the stroller may have to be checked or you may be limited to less.

Experts agree that it's a good idea to use safety seats aloft for children weighing less than 40 pounds. Airlines set their own policies: U.S. carriers usually require that the child be ticketed, even if he or she is young enough to ride free, since the seats must be strapped into regular seats. Do **check your airline's policy about using safety seats during takeoff and landing.** Safety seats are not allowed everywhere in the plane, so get your seat assignments as early as possible.

When reserving, **request children's meals or a freestanding bassinet** (not available at all airlines) if you need them. But note that bulkhead seats, where you must sit to use the bassinet, may lack an overhead bin or storage space on the floor.

FOOD

Many (generally the cheaper) restaurants have a children's menu, but it's worth asking for the children's meal to be served first, so kids don't get bored waiting for more elaborate adult dishes to be prepared.

LODGING

The Scottish Tourist Board's two *Where to Stay* accommodation guides, *Hotels & Guest Houses* and *Bed & Breakfast,* indicate establishments that welcome children and have facilities for them, such as cots and high chairs. When booking, **confirm that the equipment you need will be available.** Also, **mention the age of your children when booking**—some of the more upscale country house hotels, in particular, don't allow children under a certain age (e.g., 12) to stay.

Some outstanding child-friendly lodgings are Polmaily House, at Drumnadrochit, and the Isles of Glencoe Hotel, at Ballachulish (☞ Chapter 9 for both hotels), where families definitely come first. If you have younger children (say, under 12), it's best to avoid expensive country-house hotels (as well as classy city restaurants), where staff and other guests may look askance at the sight of children.

Although there's no general policy regarding hotel rates for children in Scotland, many hotels allow children under 14 to stay for free in their parents' room: inquire when booking. Many also have adjoining family rooms.

➤ BEST CHOICES: **Isles of Glencoe Hotel** (✉ Ballachulish PA39 4HL, ☎ 01855/821582, FAX 01855/821463, WEB www.freedomglen.co.uk). **Polmaily House** (Drumnadrochit IV63 6XT, ☎ 01456/450343, FAX 01456/450813, WEB www.polmaily.co.uk).

SIGHTS AND ATTRACTIONS

Major cities, as well as many larger towns, have plenty of the usual attractions for children—zoos and aquariums, hands-on science centers, swimming pools and sports centers—as well as museums, art galleries, and historic buildings (all of which often offer activity sheets for children). Farther afield, say in the far northwest Highlands and on the remoter islands, opportunities for outdoor and cultural activities abound—walking, riding, beachcombing, exploring prehistoric cairns, scrambling over castle ramparts.

Don't forget that wherever you are in Scotland, the local tourist information center will be staffed by local people who will almost certainly have children or grandchildren themselves and will be happy to fill you in on what's best in the area for kids.

Places that are especially appealing to children are indicated by a rubber-duckie icon (🐥) in the margin.

COMPUTERS ON THE ROAD

Make sure your laptop is dual-voltage; most, but not all, laptops operate equally well on 110 and 220 volts and so require only an adapter. **Never plug your computer into any socket without first asking about surge protection**: although Scotland is computer-friendly, few hotels and B&Bs outside the major cities have built-in current stabilizers. Electrical fluctuations and surges can short your adapter or even destroy your computer, so it is worthwhile to purchase a surge protector in the United Kingdom that plugs into the socket. Also, the high winds, which can blow at any time of year (though more usually between October and March), especially in northern Scotland, often damage overhead power lines and cause power cuts: if it's a really windy day, you may want to turn off your computer.

Many hotels and some B&Bs have facilities for computer users, such as in-room data ports or even a dedicated PC room. For Internet access you need a BT-style telephone adapter (purchasable in the United Kingdom); an American one won't do.

CONSUMER PROTECTION

Whether you're shopping for gifts or purchasing travel services, **pay with a major credit card** whenever possible, so you can cancel payment or get reimbursed if there's a problem (and you can provide documentation). If you're doing business with a particular company for the first time, **contact your local Better Business Bureau and the attorney general's offices** in your state and (for U.S. businesses) the company's home state as well. Have any complaints been filed? Finally, if you're buying a package or tour, always **consider travel insurance** that includes default coverage (☞ Insurance).

➤ BBBs: **Council of Better Business Bureaus** (✉ 4200 Wilson Blvd., Suite 800, Arlington, VA 22203, ☎ 703/276–0100, FAX 703/525–8277, WEB www.bbb.org).

CRUISE TRAVEL

Many of the crossings from North America to Europe are repositioning sailings for ships that cruise the Caribbean in winter and European waters in summer. Sometimes rates are reduced, and fly-cruise packages are usually available. Check the travel pages of your Sunday newspaper or contact a travel agent for lines and sailing dates. To get the best deal on a cruise, **consult a cruise-only travel agency.**

The Scottish Tourist Board's free brochure "Sail Scotland" includes details of many charter firms operating among the islands. The National Trust for Scotland runs a regular cruise program with lectures on natural history. The destination changes each year but may well include the west coast or Northern Isles the year you wish to visit. Hebridean Island Cruises offers 4-, 6-, 7-, and 14-night luxury cruises aboard the MV *Hebridean Princess* around the Scottish islands, including all the Western Isles.

To learn how to plan, choose, and book a cruise-ship voyage, consult *Fodor's FYI: Plan & Enjoy Your Cruise* (available in bookstores everywhere).

➤ CRUISE INFORMATION: **Hebridean Island Cruises Ltd.** (✉ Griffin House, Broughton Hall, Skipton, North Yorkshire BD23 3AN, ☎ 01756/701338, FAX 01756/704794, WEB www.hebridean.co.uk). **National Trust for Scotland** (✉ National Trust for Scotland, Holiday Department, 28 Charlotte Sq., Edinburgh EH2 4ET, ☎ 0131/243–9334, WEB www.nts.org.uk).

CUSTOMS AND DUTIES

When shopping abroad, **keep receipts** for all purchases. Upon reentering the country, **be ready to show customs officials what you've bought.** If you feel a duty is incorrect, appeal the assessment. If you object to the way your clearance was handled, note the inspector's badge number. In either case, first ask to see a supervisor. If the problem isn't resolved, write to the appropriate authorities, beginning with the port director at your point of entry.

IN AUSTRALIA

Australian residents who are 18 or older may bring home A$400 worth of souvenirs and gifts (including jewelry), 250 cigarettes or 250 grams of tobacco, and 1,125 ml of alcohol (including wine, beer, and spirits). Residents under 18 may bring back A$200 worth of goods. Prohibited items include meat products. Seeds, plants, and fruits need to be declared upon arrival.

➤ INFORMATION: **Australian Customs Service** (Regional Director, ✉ Box 8, Sydney, NSW 2001; ☎ 02/9213–2000 or 1300/363263; 1800/020504 quarantine-inquiry line; FAX 02/9213–4043; WEB www.customs.gov.au).

IN CANADA

Canadian residents who have been out of Canada for at least seven days may bring in C$750 worth of goods duty-free. If you've been away fewer than seven days but more than 48 hours, the duty-free allowance drops to C$200; if your trip lasts 24 to 48 hours, the allowance is C$50. You may not pool allowances with family members. Goods claimed under the C$750 exemption may follow you by mail; those claimed under the lesser exemptions must accompany you. Alcohol and tobacco products may be included in the seven-day and 48-hour exemptions but not in the 24-hour exemption. If you meet the age requirements of the province or territory through which you reenter Canada, you may bring in, duty-free, 1.5 liters of wine *or* 1.14 liters (40 imperial ounces) of liquor *or* 24 12-ounce cans or bottles of beer or ale. If you are 19 or older you may bring in, duty-free, 200 cigarettes and 50 cigars. Check ahead of time with the Canada Customs and Revenue Agency or the Department of Agriculture for policies regarding meat products, seeds, plants, and fruits.

You may send an unlimited number of gifts (only one gift per recipient, however) worth up to C$60 each duty-free to Canada. Label the package UNSOLICITED GIFT—VALUE UNDER $60. Alcohol and tobacco are excluded.

➤ INFORMATION: **Canada Customs and Revenue Agency** (✉ 2265 St. Laurent Blvd. S., Ottawa, Ontario K1G 4K3, ☎ 204/983–3500, 506/636–5064, or 800/461–9999, WEB www.ccra-adrc.gc.ca/).

IN NEW ZEALAND

All homeward-bound residents may bring back NZ$700 worth of souvenirs and gifts; passengers may not pool their allowances, and children can claim only the concession on goods intended for their own use. For those 17 or older, the duty-free allowance also includes 4.5 liters of wine or beer; one 1,125-ml bottle of spirits; and either 200 cigarettes, 250 grams of tobacco, 50 cigars, *or* a combination of the three up to 250 grams. Meat products, seeds, plants, and fruits must be declared upon arrival to the Agricultural Services Department.

➤ INFORMATION: **New Zealand Customs** (Head office: ✉ The Customhouse, 17–21 Whitmore St., Box 2218, Wellington, ☎ 09/300–5399 or 0800/428–786, WEB www.customs.govt.nz).

IN SCOTLAND

Entering the United Kingdom from outside Europe, a traveler 17 or older can take in (a) 200 cigarettes or 100 cigarillos or 50 cigars or 250 grams of tobacco; (b) 1 liter of alcohol more than 22% volume or 2 liters of fortified wine, sparkling wine, or other liqueurs; (c) 2 liters of still table wine; (d) 60 ml of perfume and 250 ml of toilet water; (e) other goods to a value of £145 (no pooling of exemptions is allowed).

➤ INFORMATION: **HM Customs and Excise** (✉ Portcullis House, 21 Cowbridge Rd. E, Cardiff CF11 9SS, ☎ 029/2038–6423 or 0845/010–9000, WEB www.hmce.gov.uk).

IN THE U.S.

U.S. residents who have been out of the country for at least 48 hours may bring home, for personal use, $400 worth of foreign goods duty-free, as long as they haven't used the $400 allowance or any part of it in the past 30 days. This exemption may include 1 liter of alcohol (for travelers 21 and older), 200 cigarettes, and 100 non-Cuban cigars. Family members from the same household who are traveling together may pool their $400 personal exemptions. For fewer than 48 hours, the duty-free allowance drops to $200, which may include 50 cigarettes, 10 non-Cuban cigars, and 150 milliliters of alcohol (or perfume containing alcohol). The $200 allowance cannot be combined with other individuals' exemptions, and if you exceed it, the full value of all the goods will be taxed. Antiques, which the U.S. Customs Service defines as objects more than 100 years old, enter duty-free, as do original works of art done entirely by hand, including paintings, drawings, and sculptures.

You may also send packages home duty-free, with a limit of one parcel per addressee per day (except alcohol or tobacco products or perfume worth more than $5). You can mail up to $200 worth of goods for personal use; label the package PERSONAL USE and attach a list of its contents and their retail value. If the package contains your used personal belongings, mark it PERSONAL GOODS RETURNED to avoid paying duties. You may send up to $100 worth of goods as a gift; mark the package UNSOLICITED GIFT. Mailed items do not affect your duty-free allowance on your return.

➤ INFORMATION: **U.S. Customs Service** (for inquiries, ✉ 1300 Pennsylvania Ave. NW, Washington, DC 20229, WEB www.customs.gov, ☎ 202/354–1000; for complaints, ✉ Customer Satisfaction Unit, 1300 Pennsylvania Ave. NW, Room 5.5A, Washington, DC 20229; for registration of equipment, ✉ Office of Passenger Programs, 1300 Pennsylvania Ave. NW, Room 5.4D, Washington, DC 20229, ☎ 202/927–0530).

DINING

The restaurants we review in this book are the cream of the crop in each price category. Properties indicated by an ✕🏠 are lodging establishments whose restaurant warrants a special trip.

City Scots usually take their midday meals in a pub, wine bar, bistro, or department-store restaurant (which might not serve alcohol and which might ban smoking). When traveling, Scots generally eat inexpensively and quickly at a country pub or village tearoom. Places like Glasgow, Edinburgh, and Aberdeen have restaurants of cosmopolitan character and various price levels; of these, the more notable tend to open only in the evening.

MEALS AND SPECIALTIES

Some restaurants have a Taste of Scotland menu, which allows you to try traditional Scottish cuisine.

To start the day with a full stomach, try a traditional Scottish breakfast of bacon and fried eggs served with sausage, fried mushrooms and tomatoes, and usually fried bread or potato scones. Most places also serve kippers (smoked herring). All this is in addition to juice, porridge, cereal, and toast and other bread products.

MEALTIMES

In a country so involved in the tourism industry, "all-day" meal places are becoming widespread. The normal lunch period, however, is 12:30–2:30. A few places serve "high tea"—one hot dish and masses of cakes, bread and butter, and jam, served with tea only, around 5:30–6:30.

Unless otherwise noted, the restaurants listed in this guide are open daily for lunch and dinner.

PAYING

Many restaurants exclude service charges from the printed menu (which the law obliges them to display outside), then add 10%–15% to the check, or else stamp SERVICE NOT INCLUDED along the bottom, in which case you should add the 10%–15% yourself. Just **don't pay twice for service**—unscrupulous restaurateurs have been known to add service but leave the total on the credit-card slip blank.

Credit cards are widely accepted at most types of restaurants.

RESERVATIONS AND DRESS

Reservations are always a good idea; we mention them only when they're essential or not accepted. Book as far ahead as you can, and reconfirm as soon as you arrive. (Large parties should always call ahead to check the reservations policy.) We mention dress only when men are required to wear a jacket or a jacket and tie.

SERVICE

Note that most pubs do not have any waitstaff, and you're expected to go to the bar and order a beverage and your meal—this can be particularly disconcerting when you are seated in a "restaurant" upstairs but are still expected to go downstairs and get your own drinks and food.

WINE, BEER, AND SPIRITS

Most bars sell two kinds of beer—lager and ale. Lager (try Tennent's or McEwan's) is light colored, heavily carbonated, and served cold. Ale (try McEwan 80 Shilling and Caledonian 80) is dark, semicarbonated, and served just below room temperature. Many pubs, particularly city pubs, also serve "real ales"—hand-drawn beers produced by smaller breweries, which in their range of flavors are a revelation compared with the usual pub beers.

You can order Scotland's most famous beverage—whisky (here, most definitely spelled without an *e*)—at any local pub. All pubs serve any number of single-malt and blended whiskies. It's also possible to tour numerous distilleries, where you can sample a dram and purchase a bottle for the trip home. Most distilleries are concentrated in Speyside (on the Whisky Trail) and Islay.

DISABILITIES AND ACCESSIBILITY

In Scotland many hotels provide facilities for people using wheelchairs, and special carriages are available on some intercity and long-distance trains. However, since much of Scotland's beauty is found in hidden hills and corners "off the beaten track," renting a car is probably a better option.

The Royal Association for Disability and Rehabilitation (RADAR) is command central for travel information and advice on accommodations through the British Isles and Europe. Its annual publication, *Holidays in Britain and Ireland,* is a good resource.

➤ LOCAL RESOURCES: RADAR (✉ 12 City Forum, 250 City Rd., London EC1V 8AF, ☎ 020/7250–3222, WEB www.radar.org.uk).

LODGING

Though many hotels, especially the newer ones, have facilities for travelers with disabilities, this is not usually the case in B&Bs and small guest houses in Scotland. When discussing accessibility with an operator or reservations agent, **ask hard questions.** Are there any stairs, inside *or* out? Are there grab bars next to the toilet *and* in the shower/tub? How wide is the doorway to the room? To the bathroom? For the most extensive facilities meeting the latest legal specifications, **opt for newer accommodations.** If you reserve through a toll-free number, consider also calling the hotel's local number to confirm the information from the central reservations office. Get confirmation in writing when you can.

SIGHTS AND ATTRACTIONS

Many of the older castles may not be accessible to people who use wheelchairs. However, many of the recently built visitor centers must by law be accessible to people with mobility problems, and castles often have lovely gardens that may also be accessible. Most museums and galleries are wheelchair-accessible.

TRANSPORTATION

Hertz (☞ Car Rental) can provide hand controls for its cars at its rental offices in Glasgow and Edinburgh. With advance notice, ScotRail staff will assist passengers with disabilities; inquire at any ScotRail area office.

➤ COMPLAINTS: **Aviation Consumer Protection Division** (☞ Air Travel) for airline-related problems. **Departmental Office of Civil Rights** (for general inquiries, ✉ U.S. Department of Transportation, S-30, 400 7th St. SW, Room 10215, Washington, DC 20590, ☎ 202/366–4648, FAX 202/366–3571, WEB www.dot.gov/ost/docr/index.htm). **Disability Rights Section** (✉ NYAV, U.S. Department of Justice, Civil Rights Division, 950 Pennsylvania Ave. NW, Washington, DC 20530; ☎ ADA information line 202/514–0301, 800/514–0301, 202/514–0383 TTY, or 800/514–0383

TTY, WEB www.usdoj.gov/crt/ada/adahom1.htm).

TRAVEL AGENCIES

In the United States, the Americans with Disabilities Act requires that travel firms serve the needs of all travelers. Some agencies specialize in working with people with disabilities.

➤ TRAVELERS WITH MOBILITY PROBLEMS: **Access Adventures** (✉ 206 Chestnut Ridge Rd., Scottsville, NY 14624, ☎ 716/889–9096, dltravel@prodigy.net), run by a former physical-rehabilitation counselor. **CareVacations** (✉ No. 5, 5110–50 Ave., Leduc, Alberta T9E 6V4, Canada, ☎ 780/986–6404 or 877/478–7827, FAX 780/986–8332, WEB www.carevacations.com), for group tours and cruise vacations. **Flying Wheels Travel** (✉ 143 W. Bridge St., Box 382, Owatonna, MN 55060, ☎ 507/451–5005, FAX 507/451–1685, WEB www.flyingwheelstravel.com).

DISCOUNTS AND DEALS

The Scottish Explorer Ticket, available from any staffed Historic Scotland (HS) property and from many tourist information centers, allows visits to HS properties over a 3-day (£12), 7-day (£17), or 14-day (£22) period. The Trust Touring Pass, issued by the National Trust for Scotland, is also available for 7 (£18) or 14 (£26) days and allows access to all National Trust for Scotland properties. It's available to overseas visitors only and can be purchased from the National Trust for Scotland or some of the main tourist information centers.

The Great British Heritage Pass grants you access to sights administered by National Trust for Scotland and Historic Scotland as well as numerous other sights throughout Great Britain. A 7-day pass costs £35; 15-day and 30-day passes are also available. Contact the British Tourist Authority for more information.

The Royal Oak Foundation is the American affiliate of the British National Trust and the National Trust for Scotland. A $50 membership grants you free admission to National Trust for Scotland–administered sights for a year. Family memberships are also available.

Be a smart shopper and **compare all your options** before making decisions. A plane ticket bought with a promotional coupon from travel clubs, coupon books, and direct-mail offers or purchased on the Internet may not be cheaper than the least expensive fare from a discount ticket agency. And always keep in mind that what you get is just as important as what you save.

➤ DISCOUNT PASSES: **British Tourist Authority** (BTA; in the U.S.: ✉ 551 5th Ave., 7th floor, New York, NY 10176, ☎ 212/986–2200 or 800/462–2748; ✉ 625 N. Michigan Ave., Suite 1510, Chicago, IL 60611 [drop-in visits only]; in Canada: ✉ 5915 Airport Rd., Suite 120, Mississauga, Ontario L4V 1T1, ☎ 905/405–1840 or 800/847–4885; WEB www.travelbritain.com). **Royal Oak Society** (✉ 26 Broadway, Suite 950, New York, NY, 10004, ☎ 212/480–2889 or 800/913–6565, WEB www.royal-oak.org). **Trust Touring Pass** (☎ 0131/243–9300).

DISCOUNT RESERVATIONS

To save money, **look into discount reservations services** with Web sites and toll-free numbers, which use their buying power to get a better price on hotels, airline tickets, even car rentals. When booking a room, always **call the hotel's local toll-free number** (if one is available) rather than the central reservations number—you'll often get a better price. Always ask about special packages or corporate rates.

When shopping for the best deal on hotels and car rentals, **look for guaranteed exchange rates,** which protect you against a falling dollar. With your rate locked in, you won't pay more, even if the price goes up in the local currency.

➤ AIRLINE TICKETS: ☎ 800/AIR–4LESS.

➤ HOTEL ROOMS: **Hotel Reservations Network** (☎ 800/964–6835, WEB www.hoteldiscount.com). **Steigenberger Reservation Service** (☎ 800/223–5652, WEB www.srs-worldhotels.com). **Travel Interlink** (☎ 800/888–

5898, WEB www.travelinterlink.com).
Turbotrip.com (☎ 800/473–7829,
WEB www.turbotrip.com).

PACKAGE DEALS

Don't confuse packages and guided
tours. When you buy a package, you
travel on your own, just as though
you had planned the trip yourself.
Fly/drive packages, which combine
airfare and car rental, are often a
good deal. If you **buy a rail/drive
pass,** you may save on train tickets
and car rentals. All Eurail- and Eu-
ropass holders get a discount on
Eurostar fares through the Channel
Tunnel.

ELECTRICITY

To use electric-powered equipment
purchased in the U.S. or Canada,
bring a converter and adapter. The
electrical current in Scotland is 220
volts, 50 cycles alternating current
(AC); wall outlets take plugs with two
round oversize prongs and plugs with
three prongs.

If your appliances are dual-voltage,
you'll need only an adapter. Don't use
110-volt outlets marked FOR SHAVERS
ONLY for high-wattage appliances
such as blow-dryers. Most laptops
operate equally well on 110 and 220
volts and so require only an adapter.

EMBASSIES

➤ AUSTRALIA: **Australia House** (✉
Strand, London, WC2, ☎ 020/7379–
4334, WEB www.australia.org.uk).

➤ CANADA: **MacDonald House** (✉ 1
Grosvenor Sq., London, W1, ☎ 020/
7258–6600, WEB www.travelcanada.ca).

➤ NEW ZEALAND: **New Zealand
House** (✉ 80 Haymarket, London,
SW1Y 4TQ, ☎ 020/7930–8422,
WEB www.newzealandhc.org.uk).

➤ UNITED STATES: **American Consulate
General** (✉ 3 Regent Terr., Calton,
Edinburgh, ☎ 0131/556–8315). U.S.
Embassy (✉ 24 Grosvenor Sq., Lon-
don, W1A 1AE, ☎ 020/7499–9000);
for passports go to the U.S. **Passport
Unit** (✉ 55 Upper Brook St., London,
W1A 2LQ, ☎ 020/7499–9000,
WEB www.usembassy.org.uk).

EMERGENCIES

To contact the police, fire brigade,
ambulance service, or coast guard,
dial 999 from any phone. No coins
are needed for emergency calls from
public phone boxes.

ETIQUETTE AND BEHAVIOR

If you're visiting a family home, a
simple bouquet of flowers is a welcome gift. If you're invited for a meal,
bringing a bottle of wine is appropriate, if you wish, as is some candy for
the children. Kissing on greeting is
still too Continental for most Brits; a
warm handshake is just fine. The
British can never say please or thank
you too often, and to thank a host for
hospitality, either a phone call or
thank-you card is always appreciated.

BUSINESS ETIQUETTE

Punctuality is of prime importance, so
**call ahead if you anticipate a late
arrival.** Spouses do not generally
attend business dinners, unless specifically invited. If you invite someone to
dine, it is usually assumed that you
will pick up the tab. However, if you
are the visitor, your host may insist on
paying.

GAY AND LESBIAN TRAVEL

Outside the main cities, at least a
sector of Scottish society is not given
to much in the way of open expression of heterosexuality, let alone
anything else. In short, Scotland isn't
San Francisco. However, most Scots
also have an attitude of live and let
live, so it's unlikely you'll encounter
problems or any real hostility.

The British Tourist Authority has a
helpful Web site (www.gaybritain.org)
for gay and lesbian travelers in Great
Britain, including Edinburgh and
Glasgow. You'll find recommendations
for gay-friendly accommodations as
well as great tips on restaurants,
nightlife, festivals, and general travel
information in these two cities.

➤ GAY- AND LESBIAN-FRIENDLY TRAVEL
AGENCIES: **Different Roads Travel** (✉
8383 Wilshire Blvd., Suite 902, Bev-
erly Hills, CA 90211, ☎ 323/651–
5557 or 800/429–8747, FAX 323/651–
3678, lgernert@tzell.com). **Kennedy
Travel** (✉ 314 Jericho Turnpike,
Floral Park, NY 11001, ☎ 516/352–
4888 or 800/237–7433, FAX 516/354–
8849, WEB www.kennedytravel.com).
Now, Voyager (✉ 4406 18th St., San
Francisco, CA 94114, ☎ 415/626–
1169 or 800/255–6951, FAX 415/626–

8626, WEB www.nowvoyager.com).
Skylink Travel and Tour (⊠ 1006
Mendocino Ave., Santa Rosa, CA
95401, ☎ 707/546–9888 or 800/
225–5759, FAX 707/546–9891), serving lesbian travelers.

GUIDEBOOKS

Plan well and you won't be sorry.
Guidebooks are excellent tools—and
you can take them with you. You may
want to check out the RIAS (Royal
Incorporation of Architects in Scotland) guides on regional architecture,
any of the numerous local walking
guides, and the color-photo-illustrated
Fodor's Exploring Scotland.

HEALTH

No particular shots are necessary for
visiting Scotland from the United
States. If you are traveling in the
Highlands and islands in summer,
**pack some midge repellent and anti-
histamine cream** to reduce swelling:
the Highland midge is a force to be
reckoned with.

HOLIDAYS

The following dates are for public
holidays in Scotland; note that the
dates for England and Wales are
slightly different. January 1–2 (Ne'er
Day—and a day to recover), March
28 (Good Friday), May 5 (May Day),
August 4 (Summer Bank Holiday),
December 25–26. Note also that
Scottish towns and villages set their
own local holidays, on five or six
Mondays in spring and summer,
varying from town to town.

INSURANCE

The most useful travel-insurance plan
is a comprehensive policy that includes coverage for trip cancellation
and interruption, default, trip delay,
and medical expenses (with a waiver
for preexisting conditions).

Without insurance you will lose all or
most of your money if you cancel
your trip, regardless of the reason.
Default insurance covers you if your
tour operator, airline, or cruise line
goes out of business. Trip-delay
covers expenses that arise because of
bad weather or mechanical delays.
Study the fine print when comparing
policies.

If you're traveling internationally, a
key component of travel insurance is
coverage for medical bills incurred if
you get sick on the road. Such expenses are not generally covered by
Medicare or private policies. Australian citizens need extra medical
coverage when traveling abroad.

Always **buy travel policies directly
from the insurance company**; if you
buy them from a cruise line, airline,
or tour operator that goes out of
business, you probably will not be
covered for the agency or operator's
default, a major risk. Before making
any purchase, **review your existing
health and home-owner's policies** to
find what they cover away from
home.

➤ TRAVEL INSURERS: In the U.S.:
Access America (⊠ 6600 W. Broad
St., Richmond, VA 23230, ☎ 800/
284–8300, FAX 804/673–1491 or 800/
346–9265, WEB www.accessamerica.
com). **Travel Guard International**
(⊠ 1145 Clark St., Stevens Point, WI
54481, ☎ 715/345–0505 or 800/
826–1300, FAX 800/955–8785,
WEB www.travelguard.com).

➤ INSURANCE INFORMATION: In the
U.K.: **Association of British Insurers**
(⊠ 51 Gresham St., London EC2V
7HQ, ☎ 020/7600–3333, FAX 020/
7696–8999, WEB www.abi.org.uk). In
Canada: **RBC Travel Insurance**
(⊠ 6880 Financial Dr., Mississauga,
Ontario L5N 7Y5, ☎ 905/791–8700
or 800/668–4342, FAX 905/813–4704,
WEB www.rbcinsurance.com). In
Australia: **Insurance Council of Australia** (⊠ Level 3, 56 Pitt St., Sydney,
NSW 2000, ☎ 02/9253–5100, FAX 02/
9253–5111, WEB www.ica.com.au). In
New Zealand: **Insurance Council
of New Zealand** (⊠ Level 7, 111–
115 Customhouse Quay, Box 474,
Wellington, ☎ 04/472–5230, FAX 04/
473–3011, WEB www.icnz.org.nz).

LANGUAGE

"Much," said Doctor Johnson, "may
be made of a Scotchman if he be
caught young." This quote sums up,
even today, the attitude of some
English people—confident in their
English, the language of parliament
and much of the media—to the Scots
language. The Scots have long been
made to feel uncomfortable about

their mother tongue and have partly themselves to blame, for until the 1970s (and in some private schools, even today) they were actively encouraged to ape the dialect of the Thames Valley ("standard English") in order to "get on" in life.

The Scots language (that is, Lowland Scots, not Gaelic) was a northern form of Middle English and in its day was the language used in the court and in literature. It borrowed from Scandinavian, Dutch, French, and Gaelic. After a series of historical body blows—such as the decamping of the Scottish court to England after 1603 and the printing of the King James Bible in English but not in Scots—it declined as a literary or official language. It survives in various forms but is virtually an underground language, spoken at home, in shops, on the playground, the farm, or the quayside among ordinary folk, especially in its heartland, in northeast Scotland. (There they describe Scots who use the brayed diphthongs of the English Thames Valley as speaking with a *bool in the mou*—marble in the mouth!)

Plenty of Scots speak English with only an accent and virtually all will "modulate" either unconsciously or out of politeness into understandable English when conversing with a non-Scots speaker. As for Gaelic, that belongs to a different Celtic culture and, though threatened, hangs on in spite of the Highlands depopulation.

LODGING

The Scottish Tourist Board publishes two annually updated *Where to Stay* guides, *Hotels & Guest Houses* (£8.99) and *Bed & Breakfast* (£5.99), which give detailed information on facilities provided and classify and grade the accommodation (☞ Hotels). The various area tourist boards also annually publish separate accommodation listings for their areas, which can be obtained either from the Scottish Tourist Board or from the individual area tourist authority.

The lodgings we list are the cream of the crop in each price category. We always list the facilities that are available, but we don't specify whether they cost extra; when pricing accom-

modations, always ask what's included and what costs extra. Properties are assigned price categories based on the range from their least-expensive standard double room at high season (excluding holidays) to the most expensive. Properties marked ✕☑ are lodging establishments whose restaurants warrant a special trip.

Many hotels and most guest houses and B&Bs include a breakfast within the basic room rate; check if this is the case at your hotel when making reservations. All lodgings listed have private bath (which may have a shower, rather than a bathtub) unless otherwise noted.

APARTMENT AND HOUSE RENTALS

If you want a home base that's roomy enough for a family and comes with cooking facilities, **consider a furnished rental.** These can save you money, especially if you're traveling with a group. Home-exchange directories sometimes list rentals as well as exchanges.

➤ INTERNATIONAL AGENTS: **At Home Abroad** (⊠ 405 E. 56th St., Suite 6H, New York, NY 10022, ☎ 212/421–9165, FAX 212/752–1591, WEB www.athomeabroadinc.com). **Hideaways International** (⊠ 767 Islington St., Portsmouth, NH 03801, ☎ 603/430–4433 or 800/843–4433, FAX 603/430–4444, WEB www.hideaways.com; membership $129). **Hometours International** (⊠ Box 11503, Knoxville, TN 37939, ☎ 865/690–8484 or 800/367–4668, WEB http://thor.he.net/~hometour). **Interhome** (⊠ 1990 N.E. 163rd St., Suite 110, N. Miami Beach, FL 33162, ☎ 305/940–2299 or 800/882–6864, FAX 305/940–2911, WEB www.interhome.com). **Villas and Apartments Abroad** (⊠ 1270 Ave. of the Americas, 15th floor, New York, NY 10020, ☎ 212/897–5045 or 800/433–3020, FAX 212/897–5039, WEB www.ideal-villas.com). **Villas International** (⊠ 4340 Redwood Hwy., Suite D309, San Rafael, CA 94903, ☎ 415/499–9490 or 800/221–2260, FAX 415/499–9491, WEB www.villasintl.com).

BED-AND-BREAKFASTS

B&Bs, common throughout Scotland, are a special British tradition and the backbone of budget travel. They are usually in a family home, don't often have private bathrooms, and usually offer only breakfast. Guest houses are a slightly larger, somewhat more luxurious version. More upscale B&Bs, along the line of American B&Bs, can be found in Edinburgh and Glasgow especially, but other parts of Scotland as well. All provide a glimpse of everyday British life. The Scottish Tourist Board publication *Bed & Breakfast* (£5.99) grades B&Bs.

CAMPING

Camping is an economical option for budget travelers. Consult *Forestry Commission Camping and Caravan Sites* and *Cabin Sites* (both free from the Forestry Commission), or the Scottish Tourist Board publication, *Caravan & Camping Parks* (£3.99). For assistance planning a bicycle-camping trip, contact the Camping and Caravanning Club.

➤ CONTACTS: **Camping and Cara-vanning Club** (⊠ Greenfields House, Westwood Way, Coventry, England CV4 8JH, ☎ 024/7669–4995, WEB www.campingandcaravanningclub.co. uk). **Forestry Commission** (⊠ 231 Corstorphine Rd., Edinburgh, Scotland EH12 7AT, ☎ 0131/334–0303, WEB www.forestry.gov.uk).

FARMHOUSE AND CROFTING HOLIDAYS

A popular option for families with children is a farmhouse holiday, combining the freedom of B&B accommodations with the hospitality of Scottish family life. Information is available from the British Tourist Authority or the Scottish Tourist Board (☞ Visitor Information), from Scottish Farmhouse Holidays, and from the Farm Stay UK.

➤ CONTACTS: **Farm Stay UK** (⊠ National Agricultural Centre, Stoneleigh, Warwickshire, England CV8 2LZ, ☎ 024/7669–6909, WEB www.farmstayuk.co.uk). **Scottish Farmhouse Holidays** (⊠ 1 Renton Terr., Eyemouth, Berwickshire, Scotland TD14 5DF, ☎ 01890/751830, FAX 01890/751831, WEB www.scotfarmhols.co.uk).

HOME EXCHANGES

If you would like to exchange your home for someone else's, **join a home-exchange organization,** which will send you its updated listings of available exchanges for a year and will include your own listing in at least one of them. It's up to you to make specific arrangements.

➤ EXCHANGE CLUBS: **HomeLink International** (⊠ Box 47747, Tampa, FL 33647, ☎ 813/975–9825 or 800/638–3841, FAX 813/910–8144, WEB www.homelink.org; $106 per year).

HOSTELS

No matter what your age, you can **save on lodging costs by staying at hostels.** In some 4,500 locations in more than 70 countries around the world, Hostelling International (HI), the umbrella group for a number of national youth-hostel associations, offers single-sex, dorm-style beds and, at many hostels, rooms for couples and family accommodations. Membership in any HI national hostel association, open to travelers of all ages, allows you to stay in HI-affiliated hostels at member rates; one-year membership is about $25 for adults (C$35 for a two-year minimum membership in Canada, £13 in the U.K., A$52 in Australia, and NZ$40 in New Zealand); hostels run about $10–$30 per night. Members have priority if the hostel is full; they're also eligible for discounts around the world, even on rail and bus travel in some countries.

➤ ORGANIZATIONS: **Hostelling International—American Youth Hostels** (⊠ 733 15th St. NW, Suite 840, Washington, DC 20005, ☎ 202/783–6161, FAX 202/783–6171, WEB www.hiayh.org). **Hostelling International—Canada** (⊠ 400–205 Catherine St., Ottawa, Ontario K2P 1C3, ☎ 613/237–7884 or 800/663–5777, FAX 613/237–7868, WEB www.hihostels.ca). **Independent Backpackers' Hostels Scotland** (⊠ Fraoch Lodge, Deshar Rd., Boat of Garten, Inverness-shire PH24 3BN, ☎ FAX 01479/831331). **Scottish Youth Hostels Association** (⊠ 7 Glebe Crescent, Stirling FK8 2JA, ☎ 01786/891400, FAX 01786/891333, WEB www.syha.org.uk). **Youth Hostel Association of England and Wales** (⊠ Trevelyan House, Dimple Rd., Matlock, Derbyshire DE4 3YH, U.K., ☎ 0870/870–8808, FAX 0169/592–702, WEB www.yha.org.uk). **Youth Hostel Association Australia** (✉ 10 Mallett St., Camperdown, NSW 2050, ☎ 02/9565–1699, FAX 02/9565–1325, WEB www.yha.com.au). **Youth Hostels Association of New Zealand** (✉ Level 3, 193 Cashel St., Box 436, Christchurch, ☎ 03/379–9970, FAX 03/365–4476, WEB www.yha.org.nz).

HOTELS

Hotels in the larger cities are generally of good quality. Glasgow and Edinburgh have a number of superior establishments, as well as good hotels in all other price categories.

If you are touring around, you are not likely to be stranded: in recent years, even in the height of the season—July and August—hotel occupancy has run at about 80%. On the other hand, if you arrive in Edinburgh at festival time or some place where a big Highland Gathering or golf tournament is in progress, you'll have an extremely limited choice of accommodations, and your best bet will be to try for a room in a nearby village. To secure your first choice, **reserve in advance**, either through a travel agent at home, directly with the facility, or through local information centers (☞ individual city or regional chapters), making use of their "Book-a-Bed-Ahead" services. Telephone bookings made from home should be confirmed by letter. Country hotels expect you to turn up by about 6 PM.

Scotland, like the rest of the United Kingdom, runs a national star (1–5 stars) grading scheme to take some of the guesswork out of booking accommodations. When you're considering a hotel, guest house, or B&B, make sure that you pay close attention to its grading. The awards are part of the accommodations listing in the *Where to Stay* guides distributed at most tourist information centers. Not all establishments participate, but the scheme is becoming popular.

➤ RECOMMENDED HOTELS: **Scotland's Hotels of Distinction** (✉ Central Reservations Office, Box 14610, Leven, Fife, KY8 6ZA, ☎ 01333/360888, FAX 01333/360809).

➤ TOLL-FREE NUMBERS: **Best Western** (☎ 800/528–1234, WEB www.bestwestern.com). **Choice** (☎ 800/424–6423, WEB www.choicehotels.com). **Days Inn** (☎ 800/325–2525, WEB www.daysinn.com). **Hilton** (☎ 800/445–8667, WEB www.hilton.com). **Holiday Inn** (☎ 800/465–4329, WEB www.sixcontinentshotels.com). **Howard Johnson** (☎ 800/654–4656, WEB www.hojo.com). **Inter-Continental** (☎ 800/327–0200, WEB www.intercontinental.com). **Ramada** (☎ 800/228–2828; 800/854–7854 international reservations, WEB www.ramada.com or www.ramadahotels.com). **Sheraton** (☎ 800/325–3535, WEB www.starwood.com/sheraton). **Westin Hotels & Resorts** (☎ 800/228–3000, WEB www.starwood.com/westin).

MAIL AND SHIPPING

Allow at least four days for a letter or postcard to reach the United States by air mail. Surface mail service can take up to four or five weeks.

OVERNIGHT SERVICES

To find the nearest branch providing overnight mail services, contact the following agencies.

➤ MAJOR SERVICES: **DHL** (☎ 08701/100300). **FedEx** (☎ 0870/2400555 for Omega, agent for FedEx). **TNT** (☎ 0800/100600).

POSTAL RATES

Airmail letters and aerograms to the United States, Canada, Australia, and New Zealand cost 45p (under 10 grams) or 65p (under 20 grams); postcards cost 40p. Letters and postcards to Europe under 20 grams cost 37p. Within the United Kingdom first-class letters cost 27p, second-class letters and postcards 19p.

RECEIVING MAIL

If you're uncertain where you'll be staying, you can **arrange to have your mail sent to American Express.** The service is free to cardholders; all others pay a small fee. You can also collect letters at any post office by addressing them to "poste restante" at the post office you nominate. In Edinburgh a convenient central office is St. James Centre Post Office, St. James Centre, Edinburgh, EH1 3SR, Scotland.

MEDIA

NEWSPAPERS AND MAGAZINES

Scotland's major newspapers include the *Scotsman*—a conservative sheet that also self-styles itself as the journal of record—and the moderate *Glasgow Herald*, along with the tabloid *Daily Record*. The leader in terms of circulation, if not downright regional Scottish style, is the Aberdeen-based *Press and Journal*; an apocryphal tale relates that the *P&J* headlined the *Titanic* sinking as "North-East Man Drowns at Sea." The *Sunday Post*, conservative in bent, is the country's leading Sunday paper; *Scotland on Sunday* competes directly with London's *Sunday Times* for clout north of the border; and the *Sunday Herald*, an offshoot of the *Glasgow Herald*, is another major title. There are also many regional publications in Scotland; the *List*, a twice-monthly magazine with listings comparable to London's *Time Out*, covers the Glasgow and Edinburgh scenes. Many Scottish newsstands also feature editions of the leading London newspapers, such as the *London Times*, the *Evening Standard*, the *Independent*, and the *Guardian*; the *Sunday Telegraph* usually has the biggest Scotland coverage.

For magazines the selection is smaller and its purview is less sophisticated. *Heritage Scotland*, a publication of the National Trust, covers the historic preservation beat. *Scottish Homes and Interiors* is devoted to home design and style, and the *Scottish Field* covers matters dealing with the countryside. More regional in focus are the *People's Friend*, a Dundee-based publication that can be likened to a down-market *Readers' Digest*, and the *Leopard*, which covers the northeast regions around Aberdeen. For more regional coverage check out the glossy *Scottish Life*.

RADIO AND TELEVISION

The Scotland offshoot of the British Broadcasting Corporation, BBC Scotland, is based in Glasgow and has a wide variety of Scotland-based TV programming. BBC Scotland usually feeds its programs into the various BBC channels, including BBC1 and BBC2, the latter considered the more eclectic and artsy, with a higher proportion of alternative humor, drama, and documentaries. Channel 3 is used by independent channels, which can change from region to region in Scotland: Grampian, the Borders, and Scottish are three channels that are regional in focus, with Grampian beamed into the north and west of Scotland and Scottish into the southern regions. Scottish TV ranges from popular weekly shows such as *The Bill*, a detective drama, to enormous coverage of Scottish soccer and rugby matches. Originating in England, Channel 4 is a mixture of mainstream and off-the-wall programming, whereas Channel 5 has more sports and films. The Sky cable channel, along with myriad other cable channels, has increased the daily diet now available, from dawn to dusk and through till dawn again.

Radio has seen a similar explosion for every taste, from 24-hour classics on Classic FM (100–102 MHz) to rock (Richard Branson's Virgin at 105.8 MHz). BBC Radio Scotland is a leading radio station, tops for local news and useful as it provides Scottish (rather than English) weather information. Originating from England—and therefore not always received in regions throughout Scotland—the BBC channels include Channel 1 (FM 97.6) for the young and hip; 2 (FM88) for middle-of-the-roadsters; 3 (FM 90.2) for classics, jazz, and arts; 4 (FM 92.4) for news, current affairs, drama, and documentaries; and 5 Live (MW 693 kHz) for sports and news coverage, with listener phone-ins.

MONEY MATTERS

A local newspaper will cost you about 35p and a national daily, 45p. A pint of beer costs around £1.60 and a serving of whisky about the same. A cup of coffee will run from 50p to £1, depending on where you drink it; a ham sandwich, £2; lunch in a pub, £4 and up (plus your drink).

A man's haircut costs £4 and up; a woman's anywhere from £10 to £30. It costs about £1.50 to have a shirt laundered, from £5 to dry-clean a dress, and from £8 to dry-clean a man's suit.

A theater seat will cost from £5 to £30 in Edinburgh and Glasgow, less elsewhere.

Prices throughout this guide are given for adults. Substantially reduced fees are almost always available for children, students, and senior citizens. For information on taxes, see Taxes.

ATMS

ATMs are available throughout Scotland at banks and numerous other locations such as railway stations, gas stations, and department stores.

➤ ATM LOCATIONS: Cirrus (☎ 800/424–7787, WEB www.mastercard.com). Plus (☎ 800/843–7587, WEB www.visa.com).

CREDIT CARDS

MasterCard and Visa are the most widely accepted credit cards. American Express is accepted at larger department stores and hotels, but Diners Club is not widely accepted in Scotland.

Throughout this guide, the following abbreviations are used: AE, American Express; DC, Diners Club; MC, MasterCard; and V, Visa.

➤ REPORTING LOST CARDS: American Express (☎ 312/935–3600; 910/668–5309 in U.S. collect). Diners Club (☎ 303/779–1504 in U.S. collect; 0800/460800 in Scotland). MasterCard (☎ 800/964–767 toll free; 314/542–7111 in U.S. collect). Visa (☎ 800/985082 toll free; 410/581–3836 in U.S. collect).

CURRENCY

Britain's currency is the pound sterling, which is divided into 100 pence (100p). Notes are issued in the values of £50, £20, £10, and £5. Coins are issued in the values of £2, £1, 50p, 20p, 10p, 5p, 2p, and 1p. Scottish coins are the same as English ones, but Scottish notes are issued by three banks: the Bank of Scotland, the Royal Bank of Scotland, and the Clydesdale Bank. They have the same face values as English notes, and English notes are interchangeable with them in Scotland.

At this writing, the exchange rate was about Australian $2.73, Canadian

$2.35, New Zealand $3.16, and U.S. $1.55 to the pound sterling. Britain's entry into the European Union's currency—the euro—is still uncertain.

CURRENCY EXCHANGE

For the most favorable rates, **change money through banks.** Although ATM transaction fees may be higher abroad than at home, ATM rates are excellent because they are based on wholesale rates offered only by major banks. You won't do as well at exchange booths in airports or rail and bus stations, in hotels, in restaurants, or in stores. To avoid lines at airport exchange booths, **get a bit of local currency before you leave home.**

➤ EXCHANGE SERVICES: International Currency Express (☎ 888/278–6628 orders). Thomas Cook Currency Services (☎ 800/287–7362 orders and retail locations, WEB www.us.thomascook.com).

TRAVELER'S CHECKS

Do you need traveler's checks? It depends on where you're headed. If you're going to rural areas and small towns, go with cash; traveler's checks are best used in cities. Lost or stolen checks can usually be replaced within 24 hours. To ensure a speedy refund, buy your own traveler's checks—don't let someone else pay for them: irregularities like this can cause delays. The person who bought the checks should make the call to request a refund.

OUTDOORS AND SPORTS

A drive of an hour or two outside Edinburgh and Glasgow brings you to the sort of landscape you'd have to travel hours to reach in other countries. And within this landscape you can play on more than 400 golf courses; walk and hike, whether on a long-distance path or up a 3,000-ft mountain; fish in glistening lochs and rivers; and bike on dedicated cycleways. You may also find some surprises, such as surfing: the waves off the beaches of Harris and Tiree, in the west, and off Fraserburgh Beach, in the far northeast, attract aficionados from the whole of Britain. Diving is also a possibility; the wrecks of the German navy scuttled in 1919 in

Scapa Flow, Orkney, draw divers from far and wide.

With sports and the outdoors being such a large part of Scottish life and a big attraction for visitors, VisitScotland (the Scottish Tourist Board) is well prepared, with numerous books and leaflets covering each activity. Contact VisitScotland's Central Information Department, which can provide all the advice you'll need in advance, whatever your interest. If you're interested in hiking through the mountains of the north and west Highlands, visit the Walkingwild Web site (www.walkingwild.com), run by the Scottish Tourist Board.

Once you arrive in Scotland, check out the tourist information centers wherever you're staying for local information and fishing permits.

➤ INFORMATION: **VisitScotland (Scottish Tourist Board), Central Information Department** (✉ 23 Ravelston Terr., Edinburgh EH4 3EU, ☎ 0131/332–2433, WEB www.visitscotland.com).

PACKING

Travel light. Porters are more or less wholly extinct these days (and very expensive where you can find them).

In Scotland casual clothes are de rigueur, and very few hotels or restaurants insist on jackets and ties for men in the evening. For summer, lightweight clothing is usually adequate, except in the evenings, when you'll need a jacket or sweater. A waterproof coat or parka is essential. Drip-dry and wrinkle-resistant fabrics are a good bet since only the most prestigious hotels have speedy laundering or dry-cleaning service.

Many visitors to Scotland appear to think it necessary to adopt a Scottish costume. It's not. Scots themselves do not wear tartan ties or Balmoral "bunnets" (caps), and only an enthusiastic minority prefers the kilt for everyday wear.

In your carry-on luggage, **pack an extra pair of eyeglasses or contact lenses and enough of any medication** you take to last a few days longer than the entire trip. You may also ask your doctor to write a spare prescription using the drug's generic name, since brand names may vary from country to country. In luggage to be checked, **never pack prescription drugs or valuables.** And don't forget to carry with you the addresses of offices that handle refunds of lost traveler's checks. Check *Fodor's How to Pack* (available in bookstores everywhere) for more tips.

To avoid customs and security delays, carry medications in their original packaging. Don't pack any sharp objects in your carry-on luggage, including knives of any size or material, scissors, manicure tools, and corkscrews, or anything else that might arouse suspicion.

CHECKING LUGGAGE

You are allowed one carry-on bag and one personal article, such as a purse or a laptop computer. Make sure that everything you carry aboard will fit under your seat or in the overhead bin. Get to the gate early, so you can board as soon as possible, before the overhead bins fill up.

If you are flying internationally, note that baggage allowances may be determined not by piece but by weight—generally 88 pounds (40 kilograms) in first class, 66 pounds (30 kilograms) in business class, and 44 pounds (20 kilograms) in economy.

Airline liability for baggage is limited to $2,500 per person on flights within the United States. On international flights it amounts to $9.07 per pound or $20 per kilogram for checked baggage (roughly $640 per 70-pound bag) and $400 per passenger for unchecked baggage. You can buy additional coverage at check-in for about $10 per $1,000 of coverage, but it excludes a rather extensive list of items, shown on your airline ticket.

Before departure, **itemize your bags' contents** and their worth, and label the bags with your name, address, and phone number. (If you use your home address, cover it so potential thieves can't see it readily.) Inside each bag, **pack a copy of your itinerary.** At check-in, **make sure that each bag is correctly tagged** with the destination airport's three-letter code. If your bags arrive damaged or fail to arrive at all, file a written report with the airline before leaving the airport.

PASSPORTS AND VISAS

When traveling internationally, **carry your passport** even if you don't need one (it's always the best form of I.D.) and **make two photocopies of the data page** (one for someone at home and another for you, carried separately from your passport). If you lose your passport, promptly call the nearest embassy or consulate and the local police.

U.S. passport applications for children under age 14 require consent from both parents or legal guardians; both parents must appear together to sign the application. If only one parent appears, he or she must submit a written statement from the other parent authorizing passport issuance for the child. A parent with sole authority must present evidence of it when applying; acceptable documentation includes the child's certified birth certificate listing only the applying parent, a court order specifically permitting this parent's travel with the child, or a death certificate for the nonapplying parent. Application forms and instructions are available on the Web site of the U.S. State Department's Bureau of Consular Affairs (www.travel.state.gov).

ENTERING SCOTLAND

U.S., Canadian, New Zealand, and Australian citizens, even infants, need only a valid passport to enter Great Britain for stays of up to 90 days.

PASSPORT OFFICES

The best time to apply for a passport or to renew is in fall and winter. Before any trip, check your passport's expiration date, and, if necessary, renew it as soon as possible.

➤ AUSTRALIAN CITIZENS: **Australian State Passport Office** (☎ 131–232, WEB www.passports.gov.au).

➤ CANADIAN CITIZENS: **Passport Office** (to mail in applications: ✉ Department of Foreign Affairs and International Trade, Ottawa, Ontario K1A 0G3; ☎ 800/567–6868 toll free in Canada; 819/994–3500, WEB www.dfait-maeci.gc.ca/passport).

➤ NEW ZEALAND CITIZENS: **New Zealand Passport Office** (☎ 0800/22–5050 or 04/474–8100, WEB www.passports.govt.nz).

➤ U.S. CITIZENS: **National Passport Information Center** (☎ 900/225–5674, 35¢ per minute for automated service or $1.05 per minute for operator service, WEB www.travel.state.gov).

REST ROOMS

Most cities, towns, and villages have public rest rooms, indicated by signposts to WC, TOILETS, or PUBLIC CONVENIENCES. They vary hugely in cleanliness. You'll often have to pay a small amount (usually 20p) to enter public conveniences; a request for payment usually indicates a high standard of cleanliness. Gas stations, called petrol stations, also usually have rest rooms (to which the above comments also apply). In towns and cities department stores, hotels and restaurants, and pubs are usually your best bets for at least reasonable standards of hygiene.

SAFETY

WOMEN IN SCOTLAND

Don't wear a money belt or a waist pack, both of which peg you as a tourist. If you carry a purse, choose one with a zipper and a thick strap that you can drape across your body; adjust the length so that the purse sits in front of you at or above hip level. Store only enough money in the purse to cover casual spending. Distribute the rest of your cash and any valuables (including credit cards and your passport) between a deep front pocket, an inside jacket or vest pocket, and a hidden money pouch. Do not reach for the money pouch once in public.

Scotland in general is a safe country for travel, but normal rules of common sense apply. **Don't walk on your own late at night in major cities.** Note that single rooms may be hard to find in hotels and guest houses, and proprietors may not be willing to rent a double room at the single rate if it's early enough in the day to hope for a couple to book it. Booking accommodations in advance is a good idea, especially if you're traveling in rural areas.

SENIOR-CITIZEN TRAVEL

Scotland has a wide variety of discounts and travel bargains for anyone over 60. **Look into the Senior Citizen Railcard;** it's available in all major railway stations and offers one-third off most rail fares. The cost is £18. For more information on other senior-citizen rail passes, *see* Train Travel. Travelers over 50 are eligible for the Vantage 50 Coach Card (£9), available at all bus stations, which provides up to 30% off all long-distance National Express or Scottish Citylink coach fares in Britain.

Many hotels advertise off-season discounts for senior citizens, and some offer year-round savings. Budget-minded seniors may also **consider overnight accommodations at a university or college residence hall** (☞ Students in Scotland).

For discounted admission to hundreds of museums, historic buildings, and attractions throughout Britain, senior citizens need show only a passport as proof of age. Reduced-rate tickets to the theater and ballet are also available.

To qualify for age-related discounts, **mention your senior-citizen status up front** when booking hotel reservations (not when checking out) and before you're seated in restaurants (not when paying the bill). Be sure to have identification on hand. When renting a car, ask about promotional car-rental discounts, which can be cheaper than senior-citizen rates.

➤ EDUCATIONAL PROGRAMS: Elder-hostel (☒ 11 Ave. de Lafayette, Boston, MA 02111-1746, ☎ 877/426–8056, FAX 877/426–2166, WEB www.elderhostel.org). Interhostel (☒ University of New Hampshire, 6 Garrison Ave., Durham, NH 03824, ☎ 603/862–1147 or 800/733–9753, FAX 603/862–1113, WEB www.learn.unh.edu).

SHOPPING

Tartans, tweeds, and woolens may be a Scottish cliché, but nevertheless the selection, generally of high quality, and the reasonable prices of these goods make them a must-have for many visitors, whether a complete made-to-measure traditional kilt outfit or a classy designer sweater from Skye. Particular bargains can be found in Scottish cashmere sweaters; look for Johnstons of Elgin, and Ballantyne, two high-quality labels.

Food items are another popular purchase: whether shortbread, smoked salmon, boiled sweets, *tablet* (a type of hard fudge), marmalade and raspberry jams, Dundee cake, or black bun, it's far too easy to eat your way around Scotland.

For designer clothing Glasgow is the place to start; the Princes Square mall is an especially rich hunting ground. However, if you're coming from the United States you may find clothing rather expensive compared with the prices back home for similar items, such as designer jeans.

Unique jewelry is available all over Scotland but especially in some of the remote regions where get-away-from-it-all craftspeople have set up shop amid the idyllic scenery. Skye Silver, of Glendale on Skye (☞ Chapter 10), and Ola Gorrie at the Longship, of Kirkwall, Orkney (☞ Chapter 11), sell particularly attractive and unusual designs. Antique Scottish pebble jewelry is another unique style of jewelry; several specialist antique jewelry shops can be found in Edinburgh and Glasgow.

Scottish antique pottery and table silver make unusual, if sometimes pricey, souvenirs: a Wemyss-ware pig for the mantelpiece, perhaps, or Edinburgh silver candelabra for the dining table. Antiques shops and one- or two-day antiques fairs held in hotels abound all over Scotland. In general, goods are reasonably priced: shops in small communities must deal fairly if they hope for repeat business. Most dealers will drop the price a little if asked, "What's your best price?"

SIGHTSEEING GUIDES

The **Scottish Tourist Guides Association** has members throughout Scotland who are fully qualified professional guides able to conduct walking tours in the major cities, half- or full-day tours or extended tours throughout Scotland, driving tours, and special study tours. Many guides speak at least one language in addition to English. Fees are negotiable with individual guides, a list of whom can be obtained from the address below.

➤ TOURIST GUIDES ASSOCIATION: **Scottish Tourist Guides Association** (✉ Bookings Service, STGA, Old Town Jail, St. John's St., Stirling FK8 1EA, ☎ FAX 01786/451953, WEB www. stga.co.uk).

STUDENTS IN SCOTLAND

A student I.D. card can get you discounted admissions at some sights.

A Student Coach Card from National Express, available to full-time students age 17 and older, provides one-third off all long-distance coach fares in Britain; contact any National Express agent in Britain with evidence of student status. Those 16–25 are eligible for the same reduction via the National Express Young Person's Coach Card. Both passes cost £9.

A Young Person's rail card costs £18, is available to people 16–25, and provides discounts of up to one-third off the regular train ticket price. The card is available through most train stations; you'll need to show proof of student status and provide a passport photo. Contact ScotRail for more information.

➤ I.D.s AND SERVICES: **Council Travel** (✉ 205 E. 42nd St., 15th floor, New York, NY 10017, ☎ 212/822–2700 or 888/226–8624, FAX 212/822–2719, WEB www.counciltravel.com). **ScotRail** (☎ 08457/550033, WEB www.scotrail. co.uk). **Travel Cuts** (✉ 187 College St., Toronto, Ontario M5T 1P7, Canada, ☎ 416/979–2406 or 888/ 838–2887, FAX 416/979–8167, WEB www.travelcuts.com).

UNIVERSITY HOUSING

Many universities and colleges throughout Britain open their halls of residence to visitors during vacation periods—that is, from mid-March to mid-April, from July to September, and during the Christmas holidays. Campus accommodations—usually single rooms with access to lounges, libraries, and sports facilities—include breakfast and generally cost about $30 per night. Locations vary, from city centers to bucolic lakeside parks.

➤ INFORMATION: **Venuemasters Scotland** (✉ Box 808, Riccarton, Edinburgh EH14 4AS, ☎ 0131/449–4034, FAX 0131/451–3199, WEB www.venuemasters.co.uk).

TAXES

An airport departure tax of £20 (£10 for within U.K. and EU countries) per person is payable, and may be subject to more government increases, although it is included in the price of your ticket.

VALUE-ADDED TAX

The British sales tax, VAT (Value Added Tax), is 17.5%. The tax is almost always included in quoted prices in shops, hotels, and restaurants.

When making a purchase, **ask for a V.A.T. refund form** and find out whether the merchant gives refunds—not all stores do, nor are they required to. Have the form stamped like any customs form by customs officials when you leave the country or, if you're visiting several European Union countries, when you leave the EU. Be ready to show customs officials what you've bought (pack purchases together, in your carry-on luggage); budget extra time for this. After you're through passport control, take the form to a refund-service counter for an on-the-spot refund, or mail it back to the store or a refund service after you arrive home.

A refund service can save you some hassle, for a fee. Global Refund is a Europe-wide service with 130,000 affiliated stores and more than 700 refund counters—located at every major airport and border crossing. Its refund form is called a Shopping Cheque. The service issues refunds in the form of cash, check, or credit-card adjustment, minus a processing fee. If you don't have time to wait at the refund counter, you can mail in the form instead.

Further details on how to get a VAT refund and a list of stores offering tax-free shopping are available from the British Tourist Authority (☞ Visitor Information).

➤ V.A.T. REFUNDS: **Global Refund** (✉ 99 Main St., Suite 307, Nyack, NY 10960, ☎ 800/566–9828,

FAX 845/348–1549, WEB www.
globalrefund.com).

TAXIS

In Edinburgh, Glasgow, and the
larger cities, taxis with their TAXI sign
illuminated can be hailed on the
street, or booked by phone (expect a
charge). Elsewhere, most communities
of any size at all have a taxi service;
your hotel will be able to supply
telephone numbers. Very often you
will find an advertisement for the
local taxi service in public phone
booths.

TELEPHONES

Bear in mind that hotels usually levy a
hefty (up to 300%) surcharge on
calls; it's better to **use pay phones or
a calling card.**

AREA AND COUNTRY CODES

The country code for Great Britain is
44. When dialing a Scottish or British
number from abroad, drop the initial
0 from the local area code. For instance, if you are calling Edinburgh
Castle from New York City to ask
about opening hours, you first dial
011 (the international code), 44 (the
Great Britain country code), 131 (the
Edinburgh city code), then 225–9846
(the number proper). In Scotland
cellular phone numbers, the 0800 toll-
free code, and local-rate 0345 numbers do not have a 1 after the initial 0,
nor do many premium-rate numbers,
for example 0891, and special-rate
numbers, for example 08705.

DIRECTORY AND
OPERATOR ASSISTANCE

To call the operator, dial 100; directory inquiries (information), 192;
international directory inquiries, 153.

INTERNATIONAL CALLS

To make international calls *from*
Scotland, you must use the international access code 00 + the country
code + area code + number. For the
international operator, credit card, or
collect calls, dial 155. The country
code is 1 for the United States and
Canada, 61 for Australia, and 64 for
New Zealand.

LONG-DISTANCE CALLS

For long-distance calls within Britain,
dial the area code (which usually

begins with 01), followed by the
telephone number. The area code
prefix is used only when you are
dialing from outside the city. In
provincial areas the dialing codes for
nearby towns are often posted in the
booth.

LONG-DISTANCE SERVICES

AT&T, MCI, and Sprint access codes
make calling long distance relatively
convenient, but you may find the
local access number blocked in many
hotel rooms. First ask the hotel operator to connect you. If the hotel operator balks, ask for an international
operator, or dial the international
operator yourself. One way to improve your odds of getting connected
to your long-distance carrier is to
travel with more than one company's
calling card (a hotel may block Sprint,
for example, but not MCI). If all else
fails, call from a pay phone.

Note that when dialing access numbers in the United Kingdom for
AT&T and Sprint, there are different
numbers for each phone type—cable,
wireless, and British Telecom phones.

➤ ACCESS CODES: **AT&T Direct** (☎
0500/890011 for cable and wireless;
0800/890011 for British Telecom;
0800/0130011 for AT&T; 800/435–
0812 for other areas). **MCI World-
Phone** (in the U.K., dial ☎ 0800/
890222 to call the U.S. via MCI; 800/
444–4141 for other areas). **Sprint
International Access** (☎ 0500/
890877 cable and wireless; 0800/
890877 British Telecom; 800/877–
4646 for other areas).

PHONE CARDS

You can purchase BT (British Telecom) phone cards for use on public
phones from shops, post offices, or
newsstands. They are ideal for longer
calls, are composed of units of 10p,
and come in values of £3, £5, £10,
and higher. An indicator panel on the
phone shows the number of units
you've used; at the end of your call
the card is returned.

PUBLIC PHONES

There are three types of public pay
phones: those that accept only coins,
those that accept only phone cards,
and those that take British Telecom
(BT) phone cards and credit cards. For

coin-only phones, insert coins *before* dialing (minimum charge is 10p). Sometimes phones have a "press on answer" (POA) button, which you press when the caller answers.

TIME

Great Britain sets its clocks by Greenwich Mean Time, five hours ahead of the U.S. East Coast. British summer time (GMT plus one hour) requires an additional adjustment from about the end of March to the end of October.

TIPPING

Some restaurants and most hotels add a service charge of 10%–15% to the bill. In this case you aren't expected to tip. If no service charge is indicated, add 10% to your total bill, but always check first. Taxi drivers should also get 10%, hairdressers and barbers 10%–15%. You are not expected to tip theater or movie theater ushers, elevator operators, or bartenders in pubs.

TOURS AND PACKAGES

Because everything is prearranged on a prepackaged tour or independent vacation, you spend less time planning—and often get it all at a good price.

BOOKING WITH AN AGENT

Travel agents are excellent resources. But it's a good idea to collect brochures from several agencies, as some agents' suggestions may be influenced by relationships with tour and package firms that reward them for volume sales. If you have a special interest, **find an agent with expertise in that area**; the American Society of Travel Agents (ASTA; ☞ Travel Agencies) has a database of specialists worldwide.

Make sure your travel agent knows the accommodations and other services of the place being recommended. Ask about the hotel's location, room size, beds, and whether it has a pool, room service, or programs for children, if you care about these. Has your agent been there in person or sent others whom you can contact?

Do some homework on your own, too: local tourism boards can provide information about lesser-known and small-niche operators, some of which may sell only direct.

BUYER BEWARE

Each year consumers are stranded or lose their money when tour operators—even large ones with excellent reputations—go out of business. So **check out the operator.** Ask several travel agents about its reputation, and try to **book with a company that has a consumer-protection program.** (Look for information in the company's brochure.) In the United States, members of the National Tour Association and the United States Tour Operators Association are required to set aside funds to cover your payments and travel arrangements in the event that the company defaults. It's also a good idea to choose a company that participates in the American Society of Travel Agents' Tour Operator Program (TOP); ASTA will act as mediator in any disputes between you and your tour operator.

Remember that the more your package or tour includes the better you can predict the ultimate cost of your vacation. Make sure you know exactly what is covered, and **beware of hidden costs.** Are taxes, tips, and transfers included? Entertainment and excursions? These can add up.

➤ TOUR-OPERATOR RECOMMENDATIONS: **American Society of Travel Agents** (☞ Travel Agencies). **National Tour Association** (NTA; ✉ 546 E. Main St., Lexington, KY 40508, ☎ 859/226–4444 or 800/682–8886, 𝗪𝗘𝗕 www.ntaonline.com). **United States Tour Operators Association** (USTOA; ✉ 275 Madison Ave., Suite 2014, New York, NY 10016, ☎ 212/599–6599 or 800/468–7862, 𝗙𝗔𝗫 212/599–6744, 𝗪𝗘𝗕 www.ustoa.com).

TRAIN TRAVEL

Train service within Scotland is generally run by ScotRail, one of the most efficient of Britain's service providers. Trains are modern, clean, and comfortable. Scotland's rail network extends all the way to Thurso and Wick, the most northerly stations in the British Isles. Lowland services, most of which originate in Glasgow or Edinburgh, are generally fast and reliable. A shuttle makes the 50-

minute trip between the cities every half hour. Long-distance services carry buffet and refreshment cars. One word of caution: there are very few trains in the Highlands on Sunday.

For train information, prices, and schedules throughout Britain contact the National Rail Enquiries line.

CLASSES

Most trains have first-class and standard-class coaches. First-class coaches are always less crowded; they have wider seats and are often cleaner and less well-worn than standard-class cars, and they're a lot more expensive. However, on weekends you can often upgrade from standard to first class for a small fee (often £5)—ask at the time of booking.

CUTTING COSTS

If you plan to travel by train in Scotland, **consider purchasing a BritRail Pass,** which also allows travel in England and Wales. Remember that EurailPasses aren't honored in Great Britain, and be aware that if you don't plan to cover many miles, you may come out ahead by buying individual tickets. The cost of an unlimited BritRail adult pass for 8 days is $265 standard and $400 first class; for 15 days, $400 standard and $600 first class; for 22 days, $505 and $760; and for a month, $600 and $900. The Youth Pass, for those ages 16–25, provides unlimited second-class travel and costs $215 for 8 days, $280 for 15 days, $355 for 22 days, and $420 for one month. The Senior Pass, for passengers over 60, is first class only and costs $340 for 8 days, $510 for 15 days, $645 for 22 days, and $765 for one month. (These are U.S. dollar figures.)

If you want the flexibility of a car combined with the speed and comfort of the train, try BritRail/Drive (from $473 for one adult, with a $166 supplement for additional adults and $72.50 for children 5–15); this gives you a three-day BritRail Flexipass and three vouchers valid for Hertz car rental from more than 100 locations throughout Great Britain. A six-day rail pass with seven days of car rental is also available (from $958 including car, with $241 for each additional

adult, $105 for each child). Prices listed are for compact, automatic transmission cars, with first-class rail seats; other options are available at different prices. If you call your travel agency or Hertz's international desk, the car of your choice will be waiting for you at the station as you alight from your train.

The Freedom of Scotland Travelpass allows transportation on all Caledonian MacBrayne and Strathclyde ferries. You can travel any 4 days in an 8-day period ($125); 8 days in a 15-day period ($189); and 12 days in a 15-day period ($215).

Although some passes may be purchased in Scotland, you must purchase many passes in your home country; they're sold by travel agents as well as BritRail or Rail Europe.

Note that rail passes do not guarantee seats on the trains. To be assured of a seat, **reserve ahead even if you are using a rail pass.** Seat reservations are required on some European trains, particularly high-speed trains, and are a good idea on trains that may be crowded—particularly in summer on popular routes. You will also need a reservation if you purchase overnight sleeping accommodations.

FARES

Train fares vary according to class of ticket purchased and distance traveled, and you can pay with credit cards. Before you buy your ticket, stop at the Information Office/Travel Centre and request the lowest fare to your destination and information about any special offers. There's often little difference between the cost of a one-way and round-trip ticket. So if you're planning on departing from and returning to the same destination, it usually makes sense to buy a round-trip fare upon your departure, rather than purchasing two separate one-way tickets.

Note that your ticket does *not* guarantee you a seat. For that you need a seat reservation, which if made at the time of ticket purchase is usually included in the ticket price, or if booked separately, must be paid for at a cost of £1 *per train* on your itinerary.

FROM ENGLAND

There are two main rail routes to Scotland from the south of England. The first, the west-coast main line, runs from London Euston to Glasgow Central; it takes 5½ hours to make the 400-mi trip to central Scotland, and service is frequent and reliable. Useful for daytime travel to the Scottish Highlands is the direct train to Stirling and Aviemore, terminating at Inverness. For a restful route to the Scottish Highlands, take the overnight sleeper service, with soundproof sleeping carriages. It runs from London Euston, departing in late evening, to Perth, Stirling, Aviemore, and Inverness, where it arrives the following morning.

The second route is the east-coast main line from London King's Cross to Edinburgh; it provides the quickest trip to the Scottish capital, and between 8 AM and 6 PM there are 16 trains to Edinburgh, three of them through to Aberdeen. Limited-stop expresses like the *Flying Scotsman* make the 393-mi London-to-Edinburgh journey in around four hours. Connecting services to most parts of Scotland—particularly the Western Highlands—are often better from Edinburgh than from Glasgow.

Trains from elsewhere in England are good: regular service connects Birmingham, Manchester, Liverpool, and Bristol with Glasgow and Edinburgh. From Harwich (the port of call for ships from Holland, Germany, and Denmark), you can travel to Glasgow via Manchester. But it's faster to change at Peterborough for the east-coast main line to Edinburgh.

SCENIC ROUTES

Although many routes in Scotland run through extremely attractive countryside, several stand out: from Glasgow to Oban via Loch Lomond; to Fort William and Mallaig via Rannoch (ferry connection to Skye); from Edinburgh to Inverness via the Forth Bridge and Perth; from Inverness to Kyle of Lochalsh and to Wick; and from Inverness to Aberdeen.

A luxury private train, the *Royal Scotsman,* does scenic tours, partly under steam power, with banquets en route. This is a luxury experience:

some evenings require formal wear. For trips within Scotland there's a choice of a two-night (£1,390) or four-night (£2,590) tour. Contact Abercrombie & Kent for more information on these tours.

➤ TRAIN INFORMATION: **BritRail Travel** (⊠ 226 Westchester Ave., White Plains, NY 10604, ☎ 888/274–8724 or 800/677–8585, WEB www.britrail. com). **National Rail Enquiries** (☎ 08457/484950; 01332/387601 outside U.K.). **Rail Europe** (⊠ 226 Westchester Ave., White Plains, NY 10604, ☎ 800/848–7245, WEB www.raileurope. com). **ScotRail** (☎ 08457/550033, WEB www.scotrail.co.uk).

➤ TRAIN TOURS: **Abercrombie & Kent** (⊠ Sloane Square House, Holbein Pl., London, England SW1W 8NS, ☎ 0845/0700606, FAX 020/7730–9376; ⊠ 1420 Kensington Rd., Oak Brook, IL, United States 60523, ☎ 312/954–2944 or 800/323–7308; ⊠ Berkeley Hall, 1 Princes St., Box 327, St. Kilda, Melbourne, Victoria, Australia 3182, ☎ 03/9536–1800, WEB www. abercrombiekent.com).

TRANSPORTATION
AROUND SCOTLAND

If you plan to stick mostly to the cities, you will not need a car. All cities here are either so compact that all attractions are within easy walking distance of each other (Aberdeen, Dundee, Edinburgh, Inverness, and Stirling) or have an excellent local public transport system (Glasgow). And there is often good train and/or bus service from major cities to nearby day-trip destinations. Bus tours are also a good option for a day trip out of town; from Inverness, you can even catch a (quick) glance at the isles of Orkney this way. The scenic train trips mentioned under Train Travel will also let you glimpse some of the more rural parts of Scotland.

Once you leave Edinburgh, Glasgow and the Central Belt, and the other major cities, a car will make journeys faster and much more enjoyable than trying to work out public transport connections to the farther-flung reaches of Scotland (though it is possible to see much of the country by public transportation).

Traveline Scotland can provide useful information on public transport for all of Scotland.

➤ TRANSPORTATION INFORMATION: **Traveline Scotland** (☎ 0870/608–2608).

TRAVEL AGENCIES

A good travel agent puts your needs first. Look for an agency that has been in business at least five years, emphasizes customer service, and has someone on staff who specializes in your destination. In addition, **make sure the agency belongs to a professional trade organization.** The American Society of Travel Agents (ASTA)—the largest and most influential in the field with more than 24,000 members in some 140 countries—maintains and enforces a strict code of ethics and will step in to help mediate any agent-client disputes involving ASTA members if necessary. ASTA (whose motto is "Without a travel agent, you're on your own") also maintains a Web site that includes a directory of agents. (If a travel agency is also acting as your tour operator, *see* Buyer Beware *in* Tours and Packages.)

➤ LOCAL AGENT REFERRALS: **American Society of Travel Agents** (ASTA; ✉ 1101 King St., Suite 200, Alexandria, VA 22314, ☎ 800/965–2782 24-hr hot line, FAX 703/739–3268, WEB www.astanet.com). **Association of British Travel Agents** (✉ 68–71 Newman St., London W1T 3AH, ☎ 020/7637–2444, FAX 020/7637–0713, WEB www.abtanet.com). **Association of Canadian Travel Agents** (✉ 130 Albert St., Suite 1705, Ottawa, Ontario K1P 5G4, ☎ 613/237–3657, FAX 613/237–7052, WEB www.acta.ca). **Australian Federation of Travel Agents** (✉ Level 3, 309 Pitt St., Sydney, NSW 2000, ☎ 02/9264–3299, FAX 02/9264–1085, WEB www.afta.com.au). **Travel Agents' Association of New Zealand** (✉ Level 5, Tourism and Travel House, 79 Boulcott St., Box 1888, Wellington 6001, ☎ 04/499–0104, FAX 04/499–0827, WEB www.taanz.org.nz).

VISITOR INFORMATION

For general information about Scotland contact the British and Scottish tourism offices.

➤ BRITISH TOURIST AUTHORITY: **British Tourist Authority** (BTA; in the U.S.: ✉ 551 5th Ave., 7th floor, New York, NY 10176, ☎ 212/986–2200 or 800/462–2748; ✉ 625 N. Michigan Ave., Suite 1510, Chicago, IL 60611 [drop-in visits only]; in Canada: (✉ 5915 Airport Rd., Suite 120, Mississauga, Ontario L4V 1T1, ☎ 905/405–1840 or 800/847–4885); WEB www.visitbritain.com. U.K.: **The Scotland Desk, British Visitor Centre** (✉ 1 Piccadilly Circus, London [drop-in visits]; ✉ Thames Tower, Black's Rd., London W6 9EL [mail inquiries only]).

➤ SCOTTISH TOURIST BOARD: **VisitScotland** (✉ 23 Ravelston Terr., Edinburgh EH4 3EU, ☎ 0131/332–2433, FAX 0131/343–1513, WEB www.visitscotland.com; ✉ 19 Cockspur St., London SWIY 5BL [drop-in visits only]).

➤ U.S. GOVERNMENT ADVISORIES: **U.S. Department of State** (✉ Overseas Citizens Services Office, Room 4811, 2201 C St. NW, Washington, DC 20520, ☎ 202/647–5225 interactive hot line or 888/407–4747, WEB www.travel.state.gov); enclose a business-size SASE.

WEB SITES

Do check out the World Wide Web when planning your trip. You'll find everything from weather forecasts to virtual tours of famous cities. Be sure to **visit Fodors.com** (www.fodors.com), a complete travel-planning site. You can research prices and book plane tickets, hotel rooms, rental cars, vacation packages, and more. In addition, you can post your pressing questions in the Travel Talk section. Other planning tools include a currency converter and weather reports, and there are loads of links to travel resources.

For more specific information on Scotland, visit www.visitscotland.com, the Scottish Tourist Board's Web site. For stately homes and castles, try the National Trust for Scotland's site (www.nts.org.uk) or the Historic Scotland site (www.historic-scotland.gov.uk).

WHEN TO GO

The best times to visit Scotland are May–June and September–October. In these months, the weather is often dry, sunny, and warm (for Scotland, that is), all visitor attractions are open, the roads and visitor sights are less crowded, and accommodation is easy to find. Try to avoid July and August because during these months British schools are on holiday and everything will be much more crowded and possibly more expensive. Also, rainfall, especially on the west coast, is likely to be higher. That said, the Edinburgh Festival in August is a wonderful experience. A more unlikely, yet recommended, time for a good Scottish holiday would be over New Year for the celebrations on Hogmanay (New Year's Eve) just about everywhere in Scotland.

CLIMATE

The Scottish climate has been much maligned (sometimes with justification). You can be unlucky—it's possible to spend a summer week in Scotland and experience nothing but low clouds and drizzle. But on the other hand, you may enjoy calm Mediterranean-like weather even in early spring and late fall.

Generally speaking, Scotland is three or four degrees cooler than southern England. The east is drier and colder than the west; Edinburgh's rainfall is comparable to Rome's, whereas Glasgow's is more like that in Vancouver—yet the cities are only 44 mi apart. Long summer evenings grow longer still as you travel north. Dawn in Orkney and Shetland in June is around 1 AM, no more than an hour or so after sunset. Winter days are very short.

Scotland has few thunderstorms and little fog, except for local mists near coasts. But there are often variable winds that reach gale force even in summer. They blow away the hordes of gnats and midges, the curse of the western Highlands.

What follows are average daily maximum and minimum temperatures for major cities in Scotland.

➤ FORECASTS: **Weather Channel Connection** (☎ 900/932–8437), 95¢ per minute from a Touch-Tone phone.

ABERDEEN

Jan.	43F	6C	May	54F	12C	Sept.	59F	15C
	36	2		43	6		49	9
Feb.	43F	6C	June	61F	16C	Oct.	54F	12C
	36	2		49	9		43	6
Mar.	47F	8C	July	63F	17C	Nov.	47F	8C
	36	2		52	11		40	4
Apr.	49F	9C	Aug.	63F	17C	Dec.	45F	7C
	40	4		52	11		36	2

EDINBURGH

Jan.	43F	6C	May	58F	14C	Sept.	61F	16C
	34	1		43	6		49	9
Feb.	43F	6C	June	63F	17C	Oct.	54F	12C
	34	1		49	9		45	7
Mar.	47F	8C	July	65F	18C	Nov.	49F	9C
	36	2		52	11		40	4
Apr.	52F	11C	Aug.	65F	18C	Dec.	45F	7C
	40	4		52	11		36	2

HIGHLANDS

Jan.	43F	6C	May	58F	14C	Sept.	61F	16C
	32	0		43	6		49	9
Feb.	45F	7C	June	63F	17C	Oct.	56F	13C
	34	1		49	9		43	6
Mar.	49F	9C	July	65F	18C	Nov.	49F	9C
	36	2		52	11		38	3
Apr.	52F	11C	Aug.	65F	18C	Dec.	45F	7C
	40	4		52	11		34	1

FESTIVALS AND SEASONAL EVENTS

➤ DEC. 30–JAN. 1: **Hogmanay** (Edinburgh Tourist Information, ☎ 0131/473–3838) is Edinburgh's ancient, still-thriving alternative to Christmas.

➤ JAN. 25: **Burns Night** dinners and other events are held in memory of Robert Burns on his birthday in Glasgow, Ayr, Dumfries, Edinburgh, and many other towns and villages.

➤ MID-JAN.–EARLY FEB.: **Celtic Connections** (✉ Glasgow Royal Concert Hall, 2 Sauchiehall St., Glasgow, ☎ 0141/353–8000), an annual homage to Celtic music, hosts musicians from all over the world, hands-on workshops, and much more.

➤ LAST TUES. IN JAN.: During **Up Helly Aa** (Shetland Tourist Board, ☎ 01595/693434), Shetlanders celebrate their Viking heritage, culminating in the burning of a replica Viking long ship.

➤ EARLY APR.: **Edinburgh International Science Festival** (☎ 0131/473–2070, WEB www.sciencefestival.co.uk) at venues throughout the city, aims to make science accessible, interesting, and, above all, fun, especially—but not exclusively—for children.

➤ APR.: **Shetland Folk Festival** (Shetland Tourist Board, ☎ 01595/693434) is one of the biggest folk gatherings in Scotland, set in the home of fiddle playing.

➤ MID-MAY: The **Perth Festival of the Arts** (☎ 01738/475295) offers orchestral and choral concerts, drama, opera, recitals, and ballet throughout Perth, Tayside.

➤ LATE MAY: **Orkney Folk Festival** (☎ 01856/851331) brings the folkies back up to the far north in the hundreds.

➤ JUNE–AUG.: **Highland Games,** held annually in many Highland towns, include athletic and cultural events such as hammer throwing, caber tossing, Highland dancing, and pipe-band performances.

➤ THIRD WEEK IN JUNE: **St. Magnus Festival** (☎ 01856/871445, WEB www.stmagnusfestival.com) is a feast of classical and modern music, often showcasing new vocal or orchestral compositions.

➤ MID-AUG.–EARLY SEPT.: The **Edinburgh International Festival** (☎ 0131/473–2099 for information; 0131/473–2000 for tickets, WEB www.eif.co.uk), which runs for three weeks, is the world's largest festival of the arts. The **Edinburgh Festival Fringe** (☎ 0131/226–5257; 0131/226–0026 during festival only, WEB www.edfringe.com) is the refreshingly irreverent, unruly child of the Edinburgh International Festival (the two festivals take place around the same time). The **Edinburgh International Film Festival** (☎ 0131/228–4051, WEB www.edfilmfest.org.uk) concentrates on the best new films from all over the world. After dark is the **Edinburgh Military Tattoo** (✉ 32 Market St., Edinburgh EH1 1QB, ☎ 0131/225–1188, WEB www.edintattoo.co.uk), a display of military expertise.

➤ SEPT.: The **Braemar Royal Highland Gathering** (☎ 013397/55377, WEB www.braemargathering.org) hosts kilted clansmen from all over Scotland.

➤ OCT.: **Shetland Accordion and Fiddle Festival** (Shetland Tourist Board, ☎ 01595/693434) concentrates on two of the most popular instruments of folk musicians in Scotland.

1 DESTINATION: SCOTLAND

Beyond the Tartan Plaid

What's Where

Pleasures and Pastimes

Fodor's Choice

Great Itineraries

BEYOND THE TARTAN PLAID

ON SOME OLD RECORDINGS of Scottish songs still in circulation, you may run across "Roamin' in the Gloamin' " or "I Love a Lassie" or one of the other comic ditties of Harry Lauder, a star of the music halls of the 1920s. With his garish kilt, short crooked walking stick, rich rolling *R*s, and *pawky* (cheerfully impudent) humor—chiefly based on the alleged meanness of the Scots—he impressed a Scottish character on the world. But his was, needless to say, a false impression and one the Scots have been trying to stamp out ever since.

How, then, do you characterize the Scots? Temperamentally, they're a mass of contradictions. They've been likened, not to a Scotch egg, but to a soft-boiled egg: a dour, hard shell, a mushy middle. Historically, fortitude and resilience have been their hallmarks, and in their makeup there are streaks of both resignation and ferocity warring with sentimentality and love of family. Very Scottish was the instant reaction of an elderly woman of Edinburgh 200 years ago, when news arrived of the defeat in Mysore, India, and of the Scottish soldiers being fettered in irons two by two: "God help the puir chiel that's chained tae oor Davie."

The Scots are in general suspicious of the go-getter. "Whiz kid" is a term of contempt. But they're by no means plodders, though it's true they're determined and thorough, respecting success only when it has been a few hundred years in the making. Praise of some bright ambitious youngster is quenched with the sneer: "Him? Ah kent [knew] his faither."

Yet this is the nation that built commerce throughout the British Empire, opened wild territories, and was responsible for much of humankind's scientific and technological advancement; a nation boastful about things it's not too good at and shamefacedly modest about genuine achievements. Consider the following extract from a handout about the Edinburgh School of Medicine: "If one excepts a few discoveries such as that of 'fixed air' by Black, of the diverse functions of the nerve-roots by Bell, of the anaesthetic properties of chloroform by Simpson, of the invention of certain powerful drugs by Christison, and of the importance of antiseptic procedures by Lister, the influence of Edinburgh medicine has been of a steady constructive rather than a revolutionary type."

Among things that strike most newcomers to Scotland are the generosity of the Scots; their obsession with respectability; their satisfaction with themselves and their desire to stay as they are; and, above all, their passionate love of Scotland. An obstinate refusal to go along with English ideas has led to accusations that the nation has a head-in-the-sand attitude toward progress. But the Scots have their own ideas of progress, and they jealously guard the institutions that remain unique to them.

Scotland can once again celebrate its nationhood via its own parliament, elected for the first time in May 1999 and due to move into its own specially built premises at the foot of the Royal Mile in late 2003. The return of a parliament to Scottish soil, albeit one with limited powers, has generated a surge of pride in national identity, and over the next few years it will be interesting to see how the Scottish Parliament develops its role.

When it comes to education, Scotland has a proud record. The nation had four universities—St. Andrews, Aberdeen, Glasgow, and Edinburgh—when England had only two: Oxford and Cambridge. A phenomenon of Scottish social history is the *lad o' pairts* (man of talents)—the poor child of a feckless father and a fiercely self-sacrificing mother, sternly tutored by the village *dominie* (schoolmaster) and turned loose at the age of 13 with so firm a base of learning that he rose to the top of his profession. The sacrifices that boys made as a matter of course to further their education are an old Scottish tradition. "Meal Monday," the midsemester holiday at a Scottish university, is a survivor of the long weekend that once enabled students to return to their distant homes—on foot—

and replenish the sack of "meal" (oatmeal) that was their only sustenance.

Just as the Scots have their own traditions in education, so is their legal system distinct from England's. In England the police both investigate crime and prosecute suspects. In Scotland there's a public prosecutor directly responsible to the lord advocate (equivalent to England's attorney general), who is in turn accountable to parliament.

For the most part, however, you'll notice few practical differences, except in terminology. The barrister in England becomes an advocate in Scotland. Law-office nameplates designate their occupants "s. s. c." (solicitor to the Supreme Court) or "w. s." (writer to the signet); cases for prosecution go before the "procurator fiscal" and are tried by the "sheriff" or "sheriff-substitute." The terms are different in England, and procedures are slightly different, too, for Scotland is one of the few countries that still bases its legal system on the old Roman law.

Crimes with picturesque names from ancient times remain on the statute book: *hamesucken,* for example, means assaulting a person in his home. In criminal cases Scotland adds to "guilty" and "not guilty" a third verdict: "not proven." This, say the cynics, signifies "Don't do it again."

The Presbyterian Church of Scotland—the Kirk—is entirely independent of the Church of England. Until the 20th century it was a power in the land and did much to shape Scottish character. There are still those who can remember when the minister visited houses like an inquisitor and put members of the families through their catechism, punishing or reprimanding those who weren't word perfect. On Sunday morning the elders patrolled the streets, ordering people into church and rebuking those who sat at home in their gardens.

Religion in Scotland, as elsewhere, has lost much of its grip. But the Kirk remains influential in rural districts, where Kirk officials are pillars of local society. Ministers and their spouses are seen in all their somber glory in Edinburgh in springtime, when the General Assembly of the Kirk takes place, and for a week or more Scottish newspapers devote several column inches daily to the deliberations.

The Episcopal Church of Scotland has bishops, as its name implies (unlike the Kirk, where the ministers are all equal), and a more colorful ritual. Considered genteel, Episcopalianism in Scotland has been described rather sourly by the Scottish novelist Lewis Grassie Gibbon as "more a matter of social status than theological conviction . . . a grateful bourgeois acknowledgment of anglicisation."

Of the various nonconformist offshoots of the established Kirk, the Free Kirk of Scotland is the largest. It remains faithful to the monolithic unity of its forefathers, adhering to the grim discipline that John Knox promoted long ago. The Free Kirk is strong in parts of the Outer Hebrides—Lewis, Harris, and North Uist. On Sunday in these areas no buses run, and all the shops are shut. Among the fishing communities, especially those of the northeast from Buckie to Peterhead, evangelical movements, such as the Close Brethren and Jehovah's Witnesses, have made impressive inroads.

Other than religion, Scotland on the whole is mercifully free of the class consciousness and social elitism that so often amuse or disgust foreign residents in England. But its turbulent history has left Scotland a legacy of sectarian bigotry comparable to that of Northern Ireland. Scotland's large minority population of Roman Catholics is still to some extent underprivileged. Catholics tend to stick together, Protestants to mix only with Protestants. Even the two most famous soccer teams in Scotland—Rangers and Celtic—are notorious for their sectarian bias.

Finally, a word is needed on the vexed subject of nomenclature. A "scotchman" is not a native of Scotland but a nautical device for "scotching," or clamping, a running rope. Though you may find that some of those who are more conservative refer to themselves as Scotchmen and consider themselves Scotch, most prefer Scot or Scotsman and call themselves Scottish or Scots.

You may include the Scots in the broader term *British,* but they dislike the word *Brits,* and nothing infuriates them more than being called English. Nonetheless, there are a lot of Anglo-Scots, that is, people of Scottish birth who live in England or are the offspring of marriages between Scottish and English people. The term Anglo-

Scots is not to be confused with Sassenachs, the Gaelic word for "Saxon," which is applied facetiously or disdainfully to all the English. But at the same time, English people who live in Scotland remain English to their dying day, and their children after them. Similarly, the designation of "North Britain" for Scotland, which crept in during Victorian times, has now crept out again. It survives only in the names of a few "North British" hotels. Scots feel it denies their national identity, and there are some who, on receiving a letter with "N. B." or "North Britain" in the address, will cross it out and return the envelope to the sender.

WHAT'S WHERE

The organization of the following paragraphs mirrors the organization of the book, beginning with coverage of Edinburgh *in* Chapter 2.

Edinburgh

Scotland's capital makes a strong first impression—Edinburgh Castle looming from the crags of an ancient volcano, the Royal Mile stretching from the castle to the Palace of Holyroodhouse, the neoclassical monuments perched on Calton Hill, and Arthur's Seat, a small mountain with steep slopes, little crags, and spectacular vistas over the city and the Firth of Forth. Like Rome, Edinburgh is built on seven hills, and it has an Old Town district that retains striking evidence of a colorful history. The medieval Old Town, with its winding closes (narrow, stone-arched walkways) contrasts sharply with the Georgian New Town and its planned squares and streets. The New Town's squares make a perfect stage for buskers during summer's three-week-long Edinburgh International Festival, one of the world's great arts celebrations. Creative ferment abounds during this event, spilling over into the Edinburgh Festival Fringe, the unofficial, sassy offspring of the festival proper (and often an easier ticket).

Glasgow

Warm as a pint with friends, but also bold and exuberant, Glasgow used to call itself the Second City—not of Scotland but of the British Empire. It was a claim

Glaswegians could back up. Commerce hummed and prosperity ruled through Victorian times, when the City Chambers went up, a reflection of Glasgow's self-confidence—just before a long depression humbled the city's pride. These days the mood is upbeat again. Glasgow crackles with the energy of urban renaissance, complete with trendy stores and a thriving cultural life. And it's very proud of its association with and its buildings by two great homegrown architects, Charles Rennie Mackintosh and Alexander Thomson. The restaurant scene offers more surprises—from around the world and from closer to home. With Glasgow less than an hour from Loch Lomond, Burns Country, and great golf on the Clyde Coast, it's easy to crown a day trip with a sumptuous, sophisticated dinner.

The Borders and the Southwest

The Borders area comprises the great rolling fields, moors, wooded river valleys, and farmland that stretch south from Lothian, the region crowned by Edinburgh, to England. All the distinctive features of Scotland—paper currency, architecture, opening hours of pubs and stores, food and drink, and accent—start right at the border; you won't find the Borders a diluted version of England. The Dumfries and Galloway region, south of Glasgow, is a hilly and sparsely populated area, divided from England by the Solway Firth; it's a region of somber forests and radiant gardens, where in places the palm is as much at home as the pine. The county seat is Dumfries, associated with Robert Burns—he spent the last years of his life here—in much the same way that the Borders is with Sir Walter Scott.

Fife and Angus

Fife, northwest of Edinburgh, has the distinction of being the sunniest and driest part of Scotland. This area is one of sandy beaches, fishing villages, and windswept cliffs, hills, glens, and golf. Some 30 courses grace Fife, many of them seaside links with few if any windbreaks; the North Sea weather, ball-gobbling gorse, and fiendishly placed, seemingly bottomless fairway bunkers test North American golfers in ways they've only dreamed of (sometimes in nightmares). Fife is also home to the ultimate golf experience: a round on the Old Course at the Royal & Ancient Golf Club of St. Andrews. This is also an ancient university town, with romantic stone houses and seaside ruins. North of Fife is Angus, with the industrial port and main city of Dundee. Angus is renowned for its long glens, perfect for scenic hikes though secluded plateaus surrounded by hills and mountains. This area also has lovely seacoast views and a generous helping of things old, atmospheric, and quintessentially Scottish.

The Central Highlands
The main towns of Perth and Stirling are easily accessible gateways to the Central Highlands, the rugged and spectacular terrain stretching north from Glasgow. This may not be the famed Highlands of the north, but there's plenty of wild country to be experienced in the Central Highlands; here you'll find lush green woodlands and lochs (*loch* is Scots for lake). Especially in the Trossachs, deep lochs shimmer at the foot of gently sloping hills covered in birch, oak, and pine. Loch Lomond, Scotland's largest, is here; Sir Walter Scott's poems about the area, including *The Lady of the Lake,* have ensured its popularity as a tourist destination. This region also has important historical connections: this is where William Wallace, or Braveheart, battled the English and where Rob Roy MacGregor entered into legend. And Robert the Bruce won Scotland 400 years of independence on a field near Stirling Castle.

Aberdeen and the Northeast
Aberdeen, Scotland's third-largest city, is a sophisticated city built largely of glittering granite and is a main port of North Sea oil operations. The Grampian region spreads out to the west, the terrain changing from coastline—some of the United Kingdom's wildest shorelines of high cliffs and sandy beaches—to farmland to forests to hills. Here, the Grampian Mountains and the Cairngorms, beautiful regions of heather and forest, granite peaks and deep glens, are ideal terrain for hill walking in warm weather and skiing in cold weather. Here, too, is that picture-postcard land of castles called Royal Deeside, seat of Her Majesty's Balmoral Castle, plus a wealth of distilleries that make up the famous Whisky Trail.

Argyll and the Isles
Argyll, a remote, sparsely populated group of islands in western Scotland that forms part of the Inner Hebridean archipelago, is a transitional area between the Highlands and Lowlands, an environment ranging from lush landscapes to treeless islands, sea lochs to wooded hills. Oban, the hub of transportation for Argyll, is the main sea gateway for Mull and the Southern Islands. The Isle of Mull has a rolling green landscape and its capital, Tobermory, has brightly painted houses that give it a Mediterranean look. Iona, near Mull, is Scotland's most important Christian site, with an abbey and a royal graveyard. The Isle of Islay is synonymous with whisky—it produces several malts. Jura is covered with wild mountains. Sweeping southward, the long Kintyre Peninsula is a wonderland of sea views, spectacular sunsets, and prehistoric monuments. Arran is more developed than most southern isles, with mist-shrouded mountains in the north and farmland in the south.

Around the Great Glen
Rugged beauty and wide open spaces define the Great Glen—a rift valley along which the northern end of Scotland appears to be sliding southwestward and off the rest of the country by millimeters per millennium. Laced with rivers and streams, ringed by Scotland's tallest mountains, including the Cairngorms, and containing Scotland's greatest lochs, this geological tear in the southern Highlands is grand and dramatic—a fitting backdrop for red deer, golden eagles, and shaggy Highland cattle alike. The best-known beast in these parts, however, is the Loch Ness monster, and the town of Drumnadrochit is base camp for Nessie watchers. Even if you don't spot the beast, the magnificent loch should be reward enough. Inverness, on the Moray Firth, is a major shipping port and the last substantial outpost as you head north. East of Fort William, Glen Nevis has Ben Nevis, Britain's highest peak. Serious climbers come from far and wide to scale it.

The Northern Highlands
The lore of the clans, the echoes of Bonnie Prince Charlie, the wildness of the landscape, the big skies, the immensity of the rolling moors—Scotland seems richer here, in the remote and wild Northern Highlands, as if captured in concentrated form. The great surprises to many unprepared visitors are the changing terrain and the stunning effects of light and shade, cloud,

sunshine, and rainbows. In a couple of hours you may pass from heather, bracken, and springy turf to granite rock and bog, to serrated peak and snow-water lake, to the red Torridon sandstone of Wester Ross, and the flowery banks of Loch Ewe and Loch Maree. Sea inlets are deep and fjordlike. The black shapes of the isles cluster like basking whales on the skyline. Cliffs where quartzite gleams above crescents of hard sand lead around a northern shore that looks from the air as though it had been trimmed by an axe. Gaelic-speaking natives on the Isle of Skye live in villages along the coast; the varied interior has forested glens, hills of heather, rocky waterfalls, and soft mists draping haunting mountains. Before you get to Skye, stop in at Eilean Donan Castle, perhaps the most romantic of all Scottish castles. The Outer Hebrides, also known as the Western Isles, arc outward to the Atlantic; this is possibly the most rugged part of Scotland, with frequent wind and rain, and an often inhospitable landscape where anything that grows seems a gift. In between are hidden coves with white-sand beaches and turquoise waters. Westward, the next stop is North America.

The Northern Isles

The nearly unceasing wind in the Northern Isles creates a challenging climate that contributes to the feeling you've reached the end of the world. Orkney, a grouping of almost 70 islands, 20 of them inhabited, has the greatest concentration of prehistoric sites in Scotland. The treeless Mainland, Orkney's major island, strikes a peculiar mix between farmland and prominent Stone Age relics, including phenomenally well-preserved standing circles, *brochs* (circular towers), and tombs. Shetland's islands, with their dramatic vertical cliffs on the coastline and barren moors in the interior, aren't as rugged as you might think; the harshest winter weather is kept in check by the Gulf Stream. Winter days are sometimes no more than five hours long, and beautiful summer days last almost 20 hours, with a persistent twilight known as the *simmer* (summer) dim. There are few trees to be found, and no spot is farther than 3 mi from the blue-black sea. North Sea oil has brought great wealth to the Shetlands: some of Scotland's best roads are here, the buses are modern, and most homes are recently built.

PLEASURES AND PASTIMES

Biking

Cycling is an ideal way to see the country, particularly in the flat lands of Fife, with its quiet side roads. Dotted with bike rental shops, the islands of Arran and Islay are also popular cycling destinations. Don't forget that although some terrain may be flat, as in the Northern Isles, the conditions may be hazardous—strong winds or thick mist—so always bring rain gear. Roads are narrow, not to mention sparse in the more remote Northern Highlands, Hebrides, and Northern Isles, and you must often share the road with trucks and buses; always try to wear high-visibility clothing.

Castles

If you love castles, you've come to the right place. Scotland has just about every type of castle imaginable—from atmospheric medieval ruins, complete with gory tales, such as Kildrummy, to magnificent Georgian piles like Culzean, full of antiques and paintings and surrounded by parkland. The northeast of Scotland inland from Aberdeen, in particular, has a huge selection of castles to admire, helpfully strung together along the Castle Trail. Whether still in private ownership and full of family atmosphere, like Cawdor, or under the care of the National Trust for Scotland or of Historic Scotland, or just a jumble of stones atop a hill, Scotland's castles and forts vividly demonstrate the country's unsettled past and historically uneasy relationship with its southern neighbor.

Cultural Festivals

The Edinburgh International Festival is the spectacular flagship of mainstream cultural events, from theater to comedy skits. In fact, the capital suffers from Festival overkill in late August, partly because of the size of the Fringe, the less formal and more unruly offshoot of the official festival. This huge grab bag of performances spreads out of halls and theaters onto the streets of the capital. Also adding to the throng are the Edinburgh Military Tattoo and smaller events such as the Jazz Festival. Folk festivals are also held in many places at various times of the year, as are theme festivals. One of the most spectac-ular festivals is Up Helly Aa, held in Shet-land at the end of January, when Viking ceremonies culminate in the burning of a replica Viking long ship.

Dining

The best Scottish restaurants are noted for the freshest seafood, excellent red meats and game, and the use of traditional in-gredients such as oatmeal and wild berries in new, imaginative ways. Some restaurants have a Taste of Scotland menu. Initiated by the Scottish Tourist Board but now run independently, the Taste of Scotland scheme has helped to preserve some of the Scots language, especially the names for numerous traditional dishes. Most smaller towns and many villages have at least one restaurant where—certainly if a local is in charge—the service is a reminder of a Highland tradition that ensured that no stranger could travel through the coun-try without receiving a welcome.

Distillery Tours

The British government closely monitors the process of producing whisky. It is strictly commercially licensed and takes place only in Scotland's distilleries (and, in Scotland, the product is most definitely spelled *whisky*, without an *e*). Many dis-tilleries place strong emphasis on visitor facilities and attempt to inject some drama and excitement into a process that is vi-sually undramatic but nevertheless re-quires skill, method, and large-scale investment. A typical visit includes some kind of audiovisual presentation and a tour, and then a dram is usually offered. No tour of Speyside or Islay is complete without taking in at least one distillery.

Gardens

Somewhat surprisingly perhaps, Scot-land's lowland climate is very favorable to a wide variety of plants, and a highlight of a Scottish visit for any gardening en-thusiast is discovering its gardens. In the southwest, Castle Kennedy Gardens, Logan Botanic Gardens, Threave Gardens, or Arbigland Gardens are all here to enjoy. On the east coast, in addition to the im-pressive Royal Botanic Gardens in Edin-burgh, many of the stately homes, whether in private ownership or under National Trust for Scotland care, are surrounded by beautifully tended gardens and park-land. Even in the far northwestern High-lands, Inverewe defies the elements behind its shelterbelts to display luxuriant rhodo-dendrons and South American shrubs. And these are just a few of the major gar-dens; in addition, many private gardens open for one or two days each summer for charity under Scotland's Gardens Scheme: look for the yellow posters as you drive along in order to discover some nor-mally hidden delights.

Golf

Scotland is often called the home of golf and, brushing aside any suggestion that the game probably originated in the Low Countries, claims it for its own. Certainly, Scotland has a number of old established courses, often lying close to town cen-ters, where, had it not been for the early rights of golfers, the land would have been swallowed up by developments long ago. Now, with more than 400 golf courses—some world famous—Scotland is a destination for golfers the world over. St. Andrews is such a popular spot for golfers that reservations for summer play are sometimes required a year in advance. Courses are also in the major urban cen-ters: 30 courses are within or close to Ed-inburgh, and 7 courses are within Glasgow.

Hiking

Hiking is a great way of getting to know Scotland's varied landscape of low-lying glens and major mountains. From Edinburgh's Arthur's Seat to Ben Nevis, Britain's tallest peak, Scotland holds unlimited walking and hiking possibilities. However, it is es-sential to know how to use a map and compass and to be properly equipped at all times: weather conditions can change very rapidly in Scotland's hills, even at low level, and people have been known to die of exposure even in high summer.

Pubs

Whether you join in a lively political dis-cussion in a bar in Glasgow or enjoy folk music and dancing in a rural pub in the Highlands, you'll find that a public house is the perfect site to experience the Scot-tish spirit and, of course, to enjoy a pint or a wee dram. Most bars sell two kinds of beer—lager and ale. Lager (try Tennent's or McEwan's), most familiar to American drinkers, is light colored, heavily car-bonated, and served cold. Ale (try McEwan 80 Shilling and Caledonian 80) is dark, semicarbonated, and served just below room temperature. An increasing number of pubs, especially in the major cities, also serve a small selection of "real ales"— hand-drawn beers produced by smaller breweries, which in their range of flavors are a revelation compared to the usual pub beers. All pubs also carry any number of single-malt and blended whiskies.

Shopping

The best buys in Britain in general are antiques, craft items, woolen goods, china, men's shoes, books, confectionery, and toys. In Scotland many people buy tweeds, designer knitwear, Shetland and Fair Isle woolens, tartan rugs and fabrics, Edinburgh crystal, Caithness glass, malt whisky, Celtic silver, and pebble jewelry. The Scottish Highlands bristle with old *bothies* (farm buildings) that have been turned into small crafts workshops where you are welcome—but not pressured—to buy attractive handmade items of bone, silver, wood, pottery, leather, and glass. Handmade chocolates, often with whisky or Drambuie fillings, and the traditional petticoat-tail shortbread in tin boxes are popular; so, too, at a more mundane level, are boiled sweets (hard candies) in jars from particular localities—Berwick cockles, Jethart snails, Edinburgh rock, and similar crunchy items. Dundee cake, a rich fruit mixture with almonds on top, and Dundee marmalades and heather honeys are among the other eatables you can take home from Scotland.

FODOR'S CHOICE

Even with so many special places in Scotland, Fodor's writers and editors have their favorites. Here are a few that stand out.

Buildings and Monuments

Calanais Standing Stones, Calanais, Northern Highlands. This grouping of monoliths is considered second only to Stonehenge, in England, and is thought to have been used for astronomical observations.

Cawdor Castle, near Nairn, Great Glen. Shakespeare's Macbeth was Thane of Cawdor, but this 14th-century castle exudes 600 years of real, not fictional, history.

Georgian House, Edinburgh. In New Town's Charlotte Square, this house is decorated in period style to demonstrate the lifestyle of an affluent 18th-century family.

Marischal College, Aberdeen. An ornate facade, built in 1891, fronts the second-largest granite building in the world.

Torosay Castle, Isle of Mull, Argyll and the Isles. You're free to explore most of this Scottish baronial structure, one of Mull's best-known castles.

Traquair House, near Innerleithen, Borders. Secret stairs, a maze, and a bed used by Mary, Queen of Scots, are just a few of the discoveries that await inside Traquair House, which is said to be the oldest continually occupied house in Scotland.

Dining

Auchterarder House, Auchterarder, Central Highlands. This dining room, filled with sparkling glassware, is attached to a fine hotel and serves excellent international cuisine. ££££

Amaryllis, Glasgow. Celebrity chef Gordon Ramsay ensures that a modern Scottish menu, based on the best local produce, is as fresh and adventurous as the surroundings: Victorian elegance with a tasteful contemporary twist. £££–££££

Ostlers Close Restaurant, Cupar, Fife. The cuisine, including good seafood, at this simple cottage-style restaurant is imaginative without being trendy. £££

Witchery by the Castle, Edinburgh. Flickering candlelight completes the atmosphere at this spooky haunt. The lugubrious, cavernous interior is festooned with cauldrons and broomsticks—but there's nothing spooky about the Scottish-accented French food. £££

Old Monastery, Buckie, the Northeast. The setting is a Victorian former religious establishment, and the theme is ever present, from the Cloisters bar to the Chapel restaurant. Local specialties include fresh river fish and Aberdeen Angus beef. ££

Lodging

Channings, Edinburgh. This intimate, elegant hotel comprises five Edwardian terraced houses, some with wonderful views of Fife. £££–££££

Hotel Eilean Iarmain, Sleat, Isle of Skye. Wood paneling, chintz, and antiques fill this enchanting shoreside hotel. £££–££££

Kildrummy Castle Hotel, Kildrummy, Deeside. With views of Kildrummy Castle Gardens next door, this hotel offers peaceful lodgings with attentive service and fine Scottish cuisine. £££–££££

Cringletie House, Peebles, Borders. Turrets and crow-step gables lend a Scottish baronial style to this hotel with simple and comfortable accommodations; the upscale Scottish fare served in the restaurant is Cringletie's major achievement. ££–££££

Clifton House, Nairn, Great Glen. Original works of art, antique furnishings, regular musical and theatrical performances, and famed cuisine make this hotel unique. ££

22 Murrayfield Gardens, Edinburgh. An exceptionally friendly and comfortable bed-and-breakfast in a well-heeled suburb has as its hosts a couple who will be delighted to help you get the most out of your visit. ££

Museums
Auchindrain Museum, near Inveraray, Argyll. Here, an 18th-century communal tenancy farm has been restored to illustrate early farming life in the Highlands.

Burrell Collection, Glasgow. Pollock County Park has one of Scotland's finest art collections, with exhibits ranging from Egyptian, Greek, and Roman artifacts to stained glass and French impressionist paintings.

Carnegie Birthplace Museum, Dunfermline, West Lothian. The birthplace of Andrew Carnegie tells his fascinating life story.

Kilmartin House Museum, near Crinan, Argyll. This museum presents an excellent introduction to ancient Scottish history, with exhibits on stone circles, carved stones, and burial mounds.

Paisley Museum and Art Gallery, Paisley, near Glasgow. A town in the Glasgow suburbs is home to this museum, which tells the story of the woolen paisley shawl and describes the famous paisley pattern and weaving techniques.

Scottish Fisheries Museum, Anstruther, Fife. This museum illustrates the life of Scottish fisherfolk through documents, artifacts, paintings, and quayside floating exhibits.

GREAT ITINERARIES

A Heritage in Stone
7 to 10 days

Stone is a distinctive element of the Scottish landscape. On this tour you see it in many forms, on 18th-century Edinburgh streetscapes and in Aberdeen castles, in rural Angus and on Orkney in prehistoric monuments, some of Europe's finest. Distilleries flourish, too: the stony soil makes for clear, mineral-rich water that is the basis for the nation's distinctive whiskies.

South of Aberdeen (*2 or 3 days*). Head toward Dundee to spectacular 17th-century Glamis Castle, the Queen Mother's childhood home. Heading north you'll see the remarkable Aberlemno sculptured stones on your way to Brechin, a market town whose cathedral is filled with antiquities. Crathes Castle, inland, has a classic tower and a garden of clipped yews. The south Deeside road, the B976 west of Banchory, is a much quieter alternative to the busier A93 heading west toward Balmoral Castle, a Victorian fantasy designed by Prince Albert and now a beloved retreat of Queen Elizabeth II. From there go north at Dinnet and drive west through Strathdon. Nearby are the ruined 13th-century Kildrummy Castle and its gardens, and to the northeast, across rich farmland, Oyne and the fascinating Archaeolink Prehistory Park. ☞ *Dundee and Angus in* Chapter 5 *and Royal Deeside and Castle Country in* Chapter 7.

Orkney (*3 or 4 days*). From Aberdeen, take the eight-hour ferry ride north to Stromness on Mainland Orkney. North of town are reminders of the area's long history, including the huge Maes Howe burial mound (circa 2500 BC) and Ring of Brogar, with three dozen immense standing stones. Nearby Skara Brae is a Neolithic village of stone houses first occupied three millennia ago; they're complete with stone beds, cupboards, and fireplaces. The Brough of Birsay, the ruined Earl's Palace, and the Gurness Broch, an Iron Age tower, are on your way as you circle back to Kirkwall, which has a magnificent cathedral and a distillery. To the south, causeways link Orkney to the island of South Ronaldsay, site of the Italian Chapel, created by prisoners of war during World War II. From Stromness, ferry back to the mainland town of Scrabster, past the magnificent cliffs of Hoy. ☞ Around Orkney *in* Chapter 11.

South to Edinburgh (*2 or 3 days*). From Scrabster drive south toward Wick, but follow signs for the Grey Cairns of Camster, two neolithic chambered burial cairns. Proceed south to the behemoth Dunrobin Castle just south of unassuming Golspie, then on to Inverness. East of town, not far from the infamous battlefield at Culloden Moor, are the well-preserved early Bronze Age Clava Cairns, a burial complex, and Cawdor Castle, associated with Shakespeare's Macbeth. Travel south via Grantown-on-Spey over wild moorland to the main Deeside route close to the holiday resort of Ballater, where the buildings are all silver-gray stone. To the west, beyond 19th-century Balmoral Castle, is walled 17th-century Braemar Castle. Drive south from Braemar over the highest main road in Britain and down to Blairgowrie. Continue to Perth and Scone Palace, where early Scottish kings were crowned. Then head back to Edinburgh. ☞ The Northern Landscapes in Chapter 10, Speyside and Loch Ness *in* Chapter 9, Royal Deeside and Castle Country *in* Chapter 7, Perthshire *in* Chapter 6.

A Literary Tour of Scotland

8 to 10 days

Exploring the Western Highlands and Islands and the Scottish Borders—the terrain that inspired Scotland's most famous literary figures, Sir Walter Scott and Robert Louis Stevenson—reveals much about the soul of the nation. After touring Edinburgh, you and your rental car can easily escape into the Scottish countryside.

Edinburgh (*2 days*). In Edinburgh—Scott's original Heart of Midlothian and Stevenson's "precipitous city"—visit Edinburgh Castle and learn how Scott found the lost Scottish crown jewels. Down the Royal Mile, stop for a pub lunch at Deacon Brodie's Pub. (The real Deacon Brodie may have been the model for Stevenson's *Strange Case of Dr. Jekyll and Mr. Hyde*.) The Scott Monument in Princes Street, built in 1844 to commemorate the author, is an Edinburgh landmark. A superb view of the city rewards the steep climb to the top. Take a morning to tour the Palace of Holyroodhouse,

the queen's official residence in Scotland and scene of the triumphant visit by George IV in 1822, with Sir Walter Scott in charge of the publicity. Then take a bus to the pretty waterside village of Cramond, where you can visit the Cramond Inn, once the haunt of Stevenson. ☞ Exploring Edinburgh and the Lothians and Side Trips from Edinburgh *in* Chapter 2.

Into the Trossachs (*2 days*). Drive to South Queensferry for magnificent views of the bridge over the Firth of Forth, and visit the 16th-century Hawes Inn, which put in an appearance in Stevenson's *Kidnapped*. Over the Forth Road Bridge and to the west is 18th-century Culross, another setting from *Kidnapped*. At Callander you are near the Trossachs. Scott's popular *Lady of the Lake,* published in 1810, put the place firmly on the map. *Rob Roy,* on the other hand, was set in countryside you can identify from cruises aboard the steam-powered SS *Sir Walter Scott,* which has sailed from the Trossachs Pier on Loch Katrine for a century. Spend a couple of hours enjoying the peaceful scenery from the deck. To the north, past Crianlarich and Tyndrum, you cross Rannoch Moor. In Stevenson's *Kidnapped,* redcoats pursued David Balfour and Alan Breck here, amid dramatic highland scenery. ☞ Side Trips from Edinburgh *in* Chapter 2 and the Trossachs and Loch Lomond *in* Chapter 6.

Around Argyll (*2 to 3 days*). From Oban, the busy ferry port, cross over to the Isle of Mull. Near Fionnphort, to the southwest, is an area of Mull described in *Kidnapped.* The tiny Isle of Iona, accessible via ferry, was the burial place of Scottish kings in ancient times. Back on the mainland, en route to the head of Loch Awe, you'll pass ruined Kilchurn Castle. The drive south passes through beautiful countryside en route to the 18th-century planned town of Inveraray. ☞ Around Argyll and Iona and the Isle of Mull *in* Chapter 8.

Melrose and East Lothian (*2 to 3 days*). Passing through Glasgow and Lanark, visit the market town of Melrose, epicenter of Scott Country. Here you will find the famous ruined abbey that was the setting for Scott's *Lay of the Last Minstrel,* and the poet's country home, Abbotsford House. Nearby Scott's View offers a panorama of the River Tweed and Eildon Hills. Dryburgh Abbey is also a must; the author is buried in this atmospheric ruin.

The Lammermuir Hills extend north, into East Lothian, and the countryside east of Edinburgh is sometimes known as the Garden of Scotland. Stevenson set his novel *Catriona* along the coast here, around the small resort of North Berwick. ☞ Side Trips from Glasgow *in* Chapter 3, the Borders *in* Chapter 4, and Side Trips from Edinburgh *in* Chapter 2.

Island-Hopping on the Western Seaboard

7 to 9 days

This island-hopping tour takes in landfalls that are accessible even if you start your trip in Glasgow and don't have time to go farther north. Here distilleries and beaches are set amid mountain scenery, and you can experience the rhythm of island life.

Arran (*2 or 3 days*). In the port of Ardrossan catch the car ferry to Brodick. The surrounding Isle of Arran is the biggest island in the Clyde, and there's plenty to see. A mile north of the ferry pier is red-sandstone Brodick Castle, with beautiful interiors and gardens that are astonishingly yellow when rhododendrons bloom, in late spring and early summer. The road that circles the island, the String, leads to a beach and palm trees at the holiday resort of Lamlash—the climate is that mild—and on to Blackwaterfoot and the Machrie Moor Stone Circle, where there are mysterious red monoliths. The area is full of hut circles, chambered cairns, and other prehistoric sites. On Arran's northern tip is Lochranza, site of Lochranza Castle. Also on the island is Goat Fell, which at 2,866 ft is the highest mountain on Arran. Allow five hours to climb it. ☞ Arran *in* Chapter 8.

Kintyre Peninsula, Islay, Jura (*3 or 4 days*). From Lochranza take the ferry to Claonaig on the Kintyre Peninsula. The narrow B842 down the eastern shore of the peninsula is a lovely scenic drive past mountains and sea views. The main A83 heads back to Tayinloan. Take a 20-minute ferry ride from here to the balmy Isle of Gigha. The quiet roads make for great biking, and rentals are available. There are lovely beaches, and tender shrubs flourish in the gardens at Achamore. Back in Tayinloan head north to Kennacraig, where you can catch a ferry to Port Ellen on the unspoiled Isle of Islay. Beaches here are deserted, especially at Machir Bay on the west coast. You'll find good bird-watching on Islay: rare red-legged, red-beaked crows known as choughs can be found here. And there are excellent golf courses, photogenic villages such as Port Charlotte, and, most famously, distilleries that make the peaty local malt whisky. Laphroaig and Lagavulin are near Port Ellen, Bowmore is in the center of the island, and Bunnahabhain and Caol Ila are in the east, at Port Askaig.

A short ferry crossing at Port Askaig takes you to mountainous Jura, a good place for experienced walkers. Novelist George Orwell wrote *1984* while he lived on this island, in the late 1940s. The single good road takes you north past the impressive Jura House gardens and on to Craighouse, the main village, where there is a hotel and a distillery. You can catch a ferry back to Kennacraig from Port Askaig or Port Ellen. ☞ Around Argyll and Islay and Jura *in* Chapter 8.

Inveraray and Loch Lomond (*2 days*). From Kennacraig return to Glasgow via Lochgilphead and Inveraray, an 18th-century town on the shores of Loch Fyne. Here you can eat your fill of Loch Fyne oysters. A drive through Glen Croe reveals the magnificent mountains near Tarbet at the head of Loch Lomond, the largest lake in Scotland in terms of surface area. There are great views of the loch from the A82 south, and even better views from the B837 eastern-shore road, where the village of Balmaha makes a pleasant stop before the last hour's drive to Glasgow. ☞ Around Argyll *in* Chapter 8 and the Trossachs and Loch Lomond *in* Chapter 6.

2 EDINBURGH AND THE LOTHIANS

Edinburgh is to London as poetry is to prose, as Charlotte Brontë once wrote. One of the world's stateliest cities and proudest capitals, it is built—like Rome—on seven hills, making it the perfect backdrop for the ancient pageant of history. Explore its streets—peopled by the spirits of Mary, Queen of Scots, Sir Walter Scott, and Robert Louis Stevenson—marvel at brooding Edinburgh Castle, then pay your respects to the world's best-loved terrier, Greyfriars Bobby. Come evening, enjoy candlelighted restaurants or a folk *ceilidh*. And remember: you haven't earned your porridge until you've climbed Arthur's Seat.

By Gilbert
Summers

Updated by
David Steele

│ **N A SKYLINE OF SHEER DRAMA, EDINBURGH CASTLE** watches over
│ Scotland's capital city, frowning down on Princes Street, now the
│ main downtown shopping area, as if disapproving of its modern
razzmatazz. Its ramparts still echo with gunfire each day when the traditional one-o'clock gun booms out over the city, startling unwary shoppers. But nearly everywhere in Edinburgh (the *burgh* is always
pronounced *burra* in Scotland) there are spectacular buildings, whose
Doric, Ionic, and Corinthian pillars add touches of neoclassical grandeur
to the largely Presbyterian backdrop. The most notable examples perch
amid the greenery of Calton Hill, which overlooks the city center from
the east.

Large gardens and greenery are a strong feature of central Edinburgh,
where the council is one of the most stridently conservationist in Europe. Conspicuous from Princes Street is Arthur's Seat, a mountain of
bright green and yellow furze rearing up behind the spires of the Old
Town. This child-size mountain jutting 822 ft above its surroundings
has steep slopes and little crags, like a miniature Highlands set down
in the middle of the busy city. Appropriately, these theatrical elements
give a unique identity to Edinburgh's skyline—after all, the city has
been a stage that has seen its fair share of romance, violence, tragedy,
and triumph.

In fact, the curtain is currently going up on a spectacular new act, as
nearly 300 years after the Union of Parliaments, Edinburgh is once again
the seat of a Scottish parliament. Of course, the first-time visitor to Scotland may be surprised that the country still has a capital city, perhaps
believing the seat of government was drained of its resources and
power after the union with England in 1707—far from it. The Union
of Parliaments brought with it a set of political partnerships—such as
separate legal, ecclesiastical, and educational systems—that Edinburgh
assimilated and integrated with its own surviving institutions.

But Scotland now has significantly more control over its government
than at any time since 1707. The first 129 Members of the Scottish
Parliament (MSPs) were elected on May 6, 1999, and have extensive
powers in Scotland over education, health, housing, transport, training, economic development, the environment, and agriculture (foreign
policy, defense, and economic policy remain with the U.K. government
at Westminster, London). The parliament now sits in temporary accommodations at the Assembly Hall of the Church of Scotland, on the
Mound, but in late 2003 is scheduled to move into a brand-new structure, designed by the late Spanish architect Enric Miralles, at the foot
of the Royal Mile, adjacent to the Palace of Holyroodhouse.

Towering above the parliament building, as it does nearly everywhere
throughout the city, is Edinburgh Castle, the symbolic heart of the country. This structure was actually built over the plug of an ancient volcano. Many thousands of years ago, an eastward-grinding glacier
encountered the tough basalt core of the volcano and swept around
it, scouring steep cliffs and leaving a trail of matter, like the tail of a
comet. This material formed a ramp gently leading down from the rocky
summit. On this *crag* and *tail*—now the setting for the city castle—
would grow Edinburgh.

The lands that rolled down to the sea were for centuries open country, sitting between Castle Rock and the tiny community clustered by
the shore that grew into Leith, Edinburgh's seaport. By the 12th century Edinburgh had become a walled town, still perched on the hill.
Its shape was becoming clearer: like a fish with its head at the castle,

its backbone running down the ridge, and its ribs leading briefly off on either side. The backbone gradually became the continuous thoroughfare now known as the Royal Mile, and the ribs became the closes (alleyways), some still surviving, that were the scene of many historic incidents.

By the early 15th century Edinburgh had become the undisputed capital of Scotland. The bitter defeat of Scotland at Flodden in 1513, when Scotland aligned itself with France against England, caused a new defensive city wall to be built. Though the castle escaped destruction, the city was burned by the English earl of Hertford under orders from King Henry VIII (1491–1547) of England. By 1561, when Mary, Queen of Scots (1542–87), returned from France already widowed, the guest house of the Abbey of Holyrood had grown to become the Palace of Holyroodhouse. Mary's legacy to the city included the destruction of most of the earliest buildings of Edinburgh Castle, held by her supporters after she was forced to flee her homeland.

In the trying decades after the union with England in 1707, many influential Scots, both in Edinburgh and elsewhere, went through an identity crisis, but out of the 18th-century difficulties grew the Scottish Enlightenment, during which educated Scots made great strides in medicine, economics, and science.

Changes, too, came to the cityscape itself. By the mid-18th century it had become the custom for wealthy Scottish landowners to spend the winter in the Old Town of Edinburgh, in town houses huddled between the high Castle Rock and the Royal Palace below. In the tall, crowded buildings of old Edinburgh, the well-to-do tended to have their rooms on the middle floors, whereas the "lower orders" occupied dwellings on the top and ground floors. Uniquely cross-fertilized in the coffeehouses and taverns, intellectual notions flourished among a people determined to remain Scottish despite their parliament having voted to dissolve itself. One result was a campaign to expand and beautify the city, to give it a look worthy of its future nickname, the Athens of the North. Thus was the New Town of Edinburgh built, whose broad streets and gracious buildings created a harmony that even today's throbbing traffic cannot obscure.

Today's Edinburgh is the second-most important financial center in the United Kingdom, one of many reasons its residents come from all over Britain. Not the least of these reasons is the city's regularly being ranked near the top in surveys measuring "quality of life"; thus New Town apartments on fashionable streets sell for considerable sums. In some senses the city is showy and materialistic, but Edinburgh still supports learned societies, some of which have their roots in the Scottish Enlightenment: the Royal Society of Edinburgh, for example, established in 1783 "for the advancement of learning and useful knowledge," is still an important forum for interdisciplinary activities, both in Edinburgh and in Scotland as a whole.

Hand in hand with the city's academic and scientific life is a rich cultural force, with the Edinburgh International Festival attracting lovers of all the arts. Running for three weeks from mid-August into September, this is the biggest arts festival in the world. It attracts talent from all parts of the globe: first-tier orchestras and conductors, international dance troupes and ballet companies, and leading opera and theater performers.

But even as Edinburgh moves through the 21st century, the guardian castle remains the focal point of the city and its venerable history. Princes Street—a master stroke in city planning—was built up on only one side, allowing magnificent views of the great rock on which the fortress stands. Turn a corner off, say, George Street, and you will see not an endless cityscape, but blue sea and a patchwork of fields. This is the county of Fife, beyond the inlet of the North Sea called the Firth of Forth—a reminder, like the mountains to the northwest, which can be glimpsed from Edinburgh's highest points, that the rest of Scotland lies within easy reach.

Pleasures and Pastimes

Dining

Although Edinburgh's restaurants now serve a sophisticated, diverse mix of foreign cuisines, from Mexican and Thai to Greek and Russian, perhaps the most exotic of all is genuine Scottish cuisine. When in Edinburgh, look out for the traditional and nouvelle versions of the classic favorites, such as marvelous salmon and venison, and of course the spicy haggis, usually served with *neeps and tatties* (mashed turnips and potatoes).

Other culinary delights await—including variations on old Scottish dishes such as *partan bree* (a rich crab soup) and Loch Fyne herring. Scotland is traditionally the "land o' cakes," so be sure to enjoy some of these delicious buns, pancakes, scones, and biscuits for breakfast or high tea.

Not so long ago the standards of cooking and service too often betrayed that puritanical Scottish conviction that enjoying yourself is a sin. Today Scottish game and seafood are often presented with great flair; all the best restaurants deal directly with local boats and producers, so freshness is guaranteed. After the feast, other delicacies await: handmade chocolates, often with whisky or Drambuie fillings, and the traditional "petticoat tail" shortbread are good choices, or try some of the boiled sweets in jars, such as Edinburgh rock. Oatmeal, local cheeses, and even malt whisky (turning up in any course) amplify the Scottish dimension. And speaking of whisky, be sure to try a "wee dram" of a single malt—the pale, unblended spirit—when you visit Scotland's capital.

Lodging

From grand hotel suites done up in tartan fabrics to personal-touch bed-and-breakfasts, Edinburgh is splendidly served by a wide variety of guest accommodations. Many of the best are in lovely traditional Georgian or Victorian properties, some of which are even in the New Town, only a few minutes from downtown. The downtown area also has a number of upscale hotels, each with an international flavor.

Nightlife and the Arts

Edinburgh's nightlife is quite varied and includes dinner dances, dance clubs, Scottish musical evenings, and *ceilidhs* (a mix of country dancing, music, and song; pronounced *kay*-lees). Jazz and folk music in general are wide-ranging. Edinburgh is world renowned for its flagship arts event, the Edinburgh International Festival, and there is no escaping a theater buzz if you visit the city from August to early September. The annual festival has attracted all sorts of international performers since its inception in 1947. Even more obvious to the casual stroller during this time is the refreshingly irreverent Edinburgh Festival Fringe, unruly child of the official festival, which spills out of halls and theaters and onto the streets all over town. Film and book festivals are also regulars on the calendar. At other times throughout the year, professional and amateur groups alike offer diverse cultural performances appropriate to a capital city, even if Edinburgh's neighbor and rival city, Glasgow, has the reputation of being more lively.

Outdoor Activities and Sports

Edinburgh is a fairly compact, if hilly, city, and biking is a good way to get around. A network of cycle lanes and dedicated tracks allows you to avoid the traffic. The East Lothian countryside, with its miles of twisting roads and light traffic, is within cycling distance of the city.

You won't have to go far for golf: about 30 courses, many of which welcome visitors, lie within or close to the city (not including the easily accessible East Lothian courses).

Shopping

To make the most of shopping in Edinburgh, you'll need at least two days, in part because the city's most interesting shops are scattered among several districts. Edinburgh's downtown has the usual chain stores, lined up shoulder to shoulder and selling identical goods. But within a few yards, along some of the side streets, you'll find shops carrying more exclusive wares, such as designer clothing, unique craft items, 18th-century silverware, and wild-caught, smoked Scottish salmon.

As the capital city and an important tourist center, Edinburgh has a cross section of Scottish specialties, such as tartans and tweeds, rather than products peculiar to the Edinburgh area. Once you venture into Edinburgh's "villages"—perhaps Stockbridge, Bruntsfield, Morningside, or even the Old Town itself—you'll find many unusual stores specializing in single items, such as antique clocks or designer knitwear using the finest Scottish wool or cashmere. In many cases the goods sold in these stores are unavailable elsewhere in Scotland.

Edinburgh is a fruitful hunting ground for antiques. Scotland has a strong tradition of distinctive furniture makers, silversmiths, and artists; top-quality examples of their work can still be found, but at a price. Most reputable dealers can arrange transport abroad for your purchases if you buy something too bulky to fit into your luggage.

EXPLORING EDINBURGH AND THE LOTHIANS

The Old Town, which bears a great measure of symbolic weight as the "heart of Scotland's capital," is a boon for lovers of atmosphere and history. In contrast, if you appreciate the unique architectural heritage of Edinburgh's Enlightenment, then the New Town's for you. If you belong to both categories, don't worry—the Old and the New towns are only yards apart. The Princes Street Gardens roughly divide Edinburgh into two areas: the winding, congested streets of Old Town, to the south, and the orderly, Georgian architecture of New Town, to the north. Princes Street runs east–west along the north edge of the Princes Street Gardens. Explore the main thoroughfares but also don't forget to get lost among the tiny *wynds* and *closes*: old medieval alleys that connect the winding streets. Away from Edinburgh's central core, Victorian expansion and urban sprawl have greatly increased the city's dimensions, but Edinburgh, as cities go, is still compact, and much of the city center can be covered on foot.

The hills, green fields, beaches, and historic houses and castles in the countryside outside Edinburgh—Midlothian, West Lothian, and East Lothian, collectively called the Lothians—can be reached quickly by bus or car, a welcome escape from the festival crush at the height of summer.

Numbers in the text correspond to numbers in the margin and on the Edinburgh, West Lothian and the Forth Valley, and Midlothian and East Lothian maps.

Great Itineraries

Edinburgh's spectacular setting usually makes a good first impression. You can be here for a day and think you know the place, as even a cursory bus tour will enable you to grasp the layout of the castle, Royal Mile, Old Town, New Town, and so on. However, if your taste is more for leisurely strolling through the nooks and crannies of the Old Town closes, then allow three or four days for exploring.

IF YOU HAVE 2 DAYS

To start off, make your way to Edinburgh Castle—not just the battlements—and spend some time here, if only to revel in its sense of history. Certainly, take a city bus tour as well. Your list of must-sees should also include the National Gallery of Scotland and, unless it's January or February, the Georgian House for an idea of life in the New Town.

IF YOU HAVE 5 DAYS

Five days allow plenty of time for Old Town exploration, including the important museums of Huntly House and the People's Story (in the Canongate Tolbooth), and for a walk around the New Town, with its Scottish National Portrait Gallery and the Scottish National Gallery of Modern Art. You should also have plenty of time for shopping, not only in areas close to the city center, such as Rose Street and Victoria Street, but also in some of the less touristy areas, such as Bruntsfield. Head to Leith to visit the former royal yacht *Britannia;* then check out Leith's numerous eating places. You could also get out of town: hop on a bus out to Midlothian to see the stunning stone carving in Rosslyn Chapel, at Roslin, and visit the Edinburgh Crystal Visitor Centre, at Penicuik, for crystal bargains. Consider spending another half day traveling out to South Queensferry to admire the Forth road and rail bridges; then visit palatial Hopetoun House, with its wealth of portraits and fine furniture.

IF YOU HAVE 8 DAYS

In eight days, in addition to a thorough exploration of Edinburgh's Old and New towns, museums, galleries, and a shopping trip or two, you will not only have time to explore Leith, Roslin, and South Queensferry but will also be able to take a couple of side trips from the city. Allow at least a day for each trip so you have time to enjoy stately homes, such as Dalmeny House for its Rothschild collection of sumptuous French furniture; a historic ruin such as Linlithgow Palace, with its Mary, Queen of Scots, connection; or the magnificently sited Castle Campbell. At Gullane, with its splendid East Lothian beach, you can walk in the footsteps of Robert Louis Stevenson. The Andrew Carnegie Birthplace Museum, at Dunfermline; Dunbar, with its John Muir Country Park; and the delightful market town of Haddington, with the nearby Lennoxlove House, are other gems beyond the city limits. If it's festival time, however, you can probably take in shows, concerts, and exhibitions for eight solid days and hardly stray from the city center.

Old Town

Eastward of Edinburgh Castle, the historic castle ramp turns into the street known as the Royal Mile, the backbone of the Old Town, leading from the castle down to the Palace of Holyroodhouse. The Mile, as it's called, is actually made up of one thoroughfare that bears, in consecutive sequence, different names—the Esplanade, Castlehill, Lawnmarket, Parliament Square, High Street, and Canongate. The streets and passages winding into their tenements, or "lands," and crammed onto the ridge in back of the Mile really *were* Edinburgh until the 18th century saw expansions to the south and north. Everybody lived here, the richer folk on the lower floors of houses, with less well-to-do fam-

Edinburgh

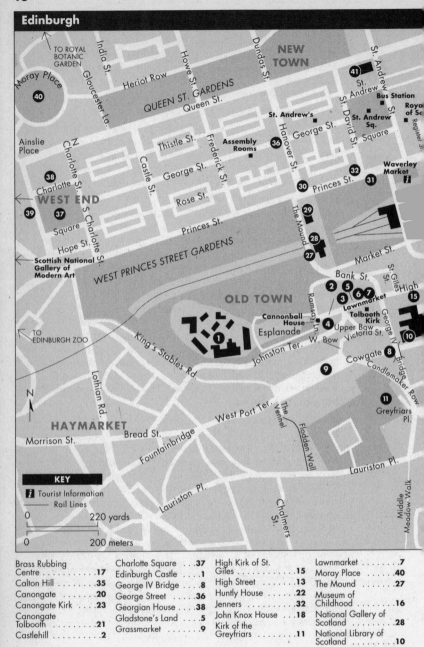

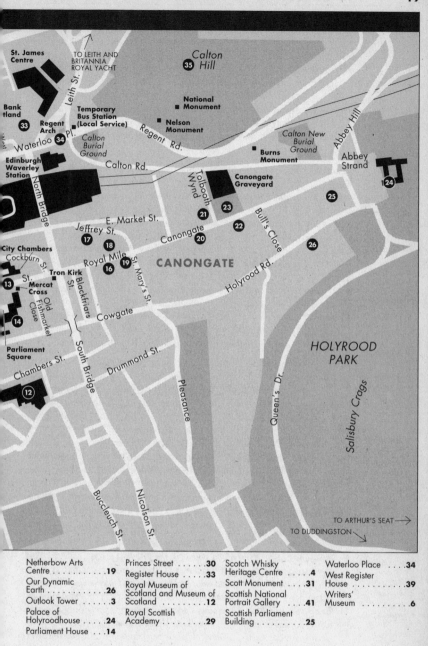

St. James
Centre

TO LEITH AND
BRITANNIA
ROYAL YACHT

Calton
35 *Hill*

Leith St.

Bank
tland

33 Regent
Arch

34 Waterloo Pl.

West

Temporary
Bus Station
(Local Service)

Calton
Burial
Ground

Regent Rd.

Calton Rd.

■ National
  Monument

■ Nelson
  Monument

Calton New
Burial
Ground

Abbey Hill

■ Burns
  Monument

Edinburgh
Waverley
Station

North Bridge

E. Market St.

Jeffrey St.

17

18

City Chambers

Cockburn St.

■ Tron Kirk

St.

13

Mercat
Cross

Old
Fishmarket
Close

14

Parliament
Square

Chambers St.

Blackfriars St.

Royal Mile

16

19

St. Mary's St.

Cowgate

South Bridge

Drummond St.

12

Tolbooth
Wynd

21

23

Canongate
Graveyard

20

22

CANONGATE

Bull's Close

Holyrood Rd.

25

26

Abbey
Strand

24

HOLYROOD
PARK

Pleasance

Queen's Dr.

Salisbury Crags

Buccleuch St.

Nicolson St.

TO ARTHUR'S SEAT →

TO DUDDINGSTON ↘

ilies on the middle floors—the higher up, the poorer. Time and progress (of a sort) have swept away some of the narrow closes and tall tenements of the Old Town, but enough survive for you to be able to imagine the original profile of Scotland's capital, and there is now refurbishment under way to make many of these surviving closes more inviting to explore. Sir Walter Scott (1771–1832), David Hume (1711–76), the painter Allan Ramsay (1713–84), and many other well-known names are associated with the Old Town. But perhaps three are more famous than any others—John Knox (circa 1514–72); Mary, Queen of Scots (1542–87); and Prince Charles Edward Stuart (1720–88).

A Good Walk

A perfect place to begin your exploration of the Old Town is **Edinburgh Castle** ①. After exploring its extensive complex of buildings and admiring the armchair-worthy view from the battlements, set off down the first part of Royal Mile, stopping en route at your choice of museums and other interesting ports of call. To the left of **Castlehill** ②, the **Outlook Tower** ③ affords more splendid views of the city from its camera obscura. Opposite, the **Scotch Whisky Heritage Centre** ④ provides an unusual opportunity to discover Scotland's liquid gold—stop off for a sample. The six-story tenement known as **Gladstone's Land** ⑤, a survivor of 16th-century domestic life, is on the left as you head east. Near Gladstone's Land, down yet another close, stands the **Writers' Museum** ⑥, housed in a fine example of 17th-century urban architecture. Farther down on the right are the Tolbooth Kirk (a *tolbooth* was a town hall or prison, and *kirk* means "church") and Upper Bow.

From the **Lawnmarket** ⑦ you can start your discovery of the Old Town closes, the alleyways that spread like ribs from the Royal Mile backbone. For a worthwhile shopping diversion, turn right down **George IV Bridge** ⑧, then to the right down Victoria Street, a 19th-century addition to the Old Town. Its shops carry antiques, old prints, clothing, and quality giftware. Down in the historic **Grassmarket** ⑨, where parts of the old city walls still stand, the shopping continues. Retrace your steps to George IV Bridge, then detour again southward to see the **National Library of Scotland** ⑩, the **Kirk of the Greyfriars** ⑪, and the little statue of faithful Greyfriars Bobby. On Chambers Street, at the foot of George IV Bridge, are the impressive galleries of the **Royal Museum of Scotland and Museum of Scotland** ⑫, housed in a lavish Victorian building.

Returning to the junction of George IV Bridge with the Royal Mile, turn right (eastward) down **High Street** ⑬ to visit the old **Parliament House** ⑭; the **High Kirk of St. Giles** ⑮; the Mercat Cross, still the site of royal proclamations; and the elegant City Chambers, bringing a flavor of the New Town's neoclassicism to the Old Town's severity. Farther down on the right stands the Tron Kirk, with the **Museum of Childhood** ⑯ and **Brass Rubbing Centre** ⑰ beyond, providing the opportunity for an unusual souvenir. **John Knox House** ⑱, associated with Scotland's severe 16th-century religious reformer, and the **Netherbow Arts Centre** ⑲ are on this section of the Royal Mile, which immediately afterward becomes **Canongate** ⑳.

A short distance down Canongate on the left is **Canongate Tolbooth** ㉑. **Huntly House** ㉒ stands opposite, and the **Canongate Kirk** ㉓ and Acheson House are nearby. This walk draws to a close, as it started, on a high point: the **Palace of Holyroodhouse** ㉔, full of historic and architectural interest and some fine paintings, tapestries, and furnishings to admire, in Holyrood Park. Being erected nearby is the new **Scottish Parliament Building** ㉕, scheduled to be completed by late 2003. And **Our Dynamic Earth** ㉖, which uses state-of-the-art technology to educate and entertain, makes a nice stop for those interested in science.

TIMING

This walk could be accomplished in a day, but to give the major sights—the castle, Palace of Holyroodhouse, and Royal Museum of Scotland—the time they deserve and also to see at least some of the other attractions properly, you should allow two days. Consider ending the first day with an afternoon in the Royal Museum of Scotland and devoting the second afternoon to Holyroodhouse.

Sights to See

🐣 **⑰** **Brass Rubbing Centre.** No experience is necessary for this delightfully hands-on way to explore the past by creating do-it-yourself replicas from original Pictish stones and markers, rare Scottish brasses, and medieval church brasses. All the materials are here, and children find the pastime quite absorbing. It's down a close opposite the Museum of Childhood. ✉ *Trinity Apse, Chalmers Close, Old Town,* ☎ *0131/556–4364.* ▦ *Free, rubbings 90p–£15 each.* ☉ *Mon.–Sat. 10–5, Sun. during festival noon–5.*

⑳ **Canongate.** This section of the Royal Mile takes its name from the canons who once ran the abbey at Holyrood (in Scots, *gate* means "street"). Canongate itself was originally an independent *burgh,* another Scottish term used to refer to a community with trading rights granted by the monarch. Here you'll find the ☞ **Canongate Kirk** and Graveyard, ☞ **Canongate Tolbooth,** ☞ **Huntly House,** and Acheson House. ✉ *Section of Royal Mile from end of High St. to Abbey Strand at entrance to Palace of Holyroodhouse, Old Town.*

㉓ **Canongate Kirk.** The graveyard of the Canongate Kirk, built in 1688, is the burial place of some notable Scots, including economist Adam Smith (1723–90), author of *The Wealth of Nations* (1776), who once lived in the nearby 17th-century Panmure House. You can also visit the grave of the undervalued Scots poet Robert Fergusson (1750–74). That Fergusson's grave is even marked is the result of efforts by the much more famous Robert Burns (1759–96). On a visit to the city Burns was dismayed to find the grave had no headstone, so he commissioned an architect—by the name of Robert Burn—to design one. (Burn reportedly took two years to complete the commission, so Burns, in turn, took two years to pay.) Burn also designed the Nelson Monument, the tall column on Calton Hill to the north, which you can see from the graveyard.

Against the eastern wall of the graveyard is a bronze sculpture of the head of Mrs. Agnes McLehose, the "Clarinda" of the copious correspondence in which Robert Burns engaged while confined to his lodgings with an injured leg in 1788. Burns and McLehose—a talented woman who had been abandoned by her husband—exchanged passionate letters for some six weeks that year, Burns signing his name "Sylvander," Mrs. McLehose "Clarinda." The missives were dispatched across town by a postal service that delivered them within the hour for one penny. The curiously literary affair ended when Burns left Edinburgh in 1788 to take up a farm tenancy and to marry Jean Armour.

Opposite the Canongate graveyard stands **Acheson House** (circa 1633), once a fine town mansion, which, like so much of the property in the Canongate, fell on hard times. It has been restored, as has the 1628 **Moray House** a little farther up the street. ✉ *Canongate, Old Town,* ☎ *0131/662–9025.* ☉ *Daily.*

㉑ **Canongate Tolbooth.** Nearly every city and town in Scotland once had a tolbooth. Originally a customhouse where tolls were gathered, a tolbooth came to mean "town hall" and later "prison" because detention cells were housed in the basement. The building where Canongate's town council once met now houses a museum, the **People's Story,**

which focuses on the lives of "ordinary" people from the 18th century to today. Exhibits describe how this in some ways rather sterile street, Canongate, once bustled with the activities of the various tradesmen needed to supply life's essentials in the days before superstores. Special displays include a reconstruction of a cooper's workshop and a 1940s kitchen. ⊠ *Canongate, Old Town,* ☎ *0131/529–4057.* 🎟 *Free.* ⊙ *Mon.–Sat. 10–5, Sun. during festival 2–5.*

NEED A BREAK?	You can get a good cup of tea and a sticky cake, a quintessentially Scottish indulgence, from **Clarinda's** (⊠ 69 Canongate, Old Town, ☎ 0131/557–1888).

❷ **Castlehill.** In the late 16th century witches were brought to what is now a street in the Royal Mile to be burned at the stake, as a bronze plaque here recalls. The cannonball embedded in the west gable of Castlehill's **Cannonball House** was, according to legend, fired from the castle during the Jacobite Rebellion of 1745, led by Charles Edward Stuart (also known as Bonnie Prince Charlie, 1720–88), the most romantic of the Stuart pretenders to the British throne. Most authorities agree on a more prosaic explanation, however; they say it was a height marker for Edinburgh's first piped-water supply system, installed in 1681. Atop the Gothic **Tolbooth Kirk**, built in 1842–44 for the General Assembly of the Church of Scotland, is, at 240 ft, the tallest spire in the city. It houses the Edinburgh Festival offices, the **Festival Centre.**

The **Upper Bow,** running from Lawnmarket to Victoria Street, was once the main route westward from the town and castle. Before Victoria Street was built in the late 19th century, the Upper Bow led down into a narrow dark thoroughfare coursing between a canyon of tenements. All traffic struggled up and down this steep slope from the Grassmarket, which joins the now-truncated West Bow at its lower end. ⊠ *East of the Esplanade and west of Lawnmarket, Old Town.*

NEED A BREAK?	Several atmospheric pubs and restaurants bustle on this section of the Royal Mile. Try the friendly pub **Jolly Judge** (⊠ James Ct., Old Town, ☎ 0131/225–2669), where firelight brightens the dark-wood beams.

OFF THE BEATEN PATH	**DUDDINGSTON –** Tucked behind Arthur's Seat, and about a one-hour walk from Princes Street via Holyrood Park, this little community, formerly of brewers and weavers, has the interesting Duddingston Kirk, with a Norman doorway and a watchtower that was built to keep body snatchers out of the graveyard. The church overlooks Duddingston Loch, popular with bird-watchers, and moments away is an old-style pub called the Sheep's Heid Inn, which serves a wide selection of beers and has the oldest skittle (bowling) alley in Scotland. ⊠ *Take Lothian Bus 42 or 46, Duddingston.*

★ ❶ **Edinburgh Castle.** The crowning glory of the Scottish capital, Edinburgh Castle is popular not only because of its symbolic value as the heart of Scotland but also because of the views from its battlements: on a clear day the vistas—stretching to the "kingdom" of Fife—are of breathtaking loveliness. Clear days are frequent now; Edinburgh is officially smokeless, and the nickname "Auld Reekie" no longer applies.

The castle opens the chronicle of Scottish history. Archaeological investigations have established that the rock on which the castle stands was inhabited as far back as 1000 BC, in the latter part of the Bronze Age. There have been fortifications here since the mysterious people called the Picts first used it as a stronghold in the 3rd and 4th centuries

AD. The Picts were dislodged by Saxon invaders from northern England in AD 452, and for the next 1,300 years the site saw countless battles and skirmishes. You'll hear the story of how Randolph, earl of Moray, nephew of freedom-fighter Robert the Bruce, scaled the heights one dark night in 1313, surprised the English guard, and recaptured the castle for the Scots. At the same time he destroyed every one of its buildings except for St. Margaret's Chapel, dating from around 1076, so that successive Stewart kings had to rebuild the place bit by bit.

The castle has been held over time by Scots and Englishmen, Catholics and Protestants, soldiers and royalty. In the 16th century Mary, Queen of Scots, chose to give birth here to the future James VI of Scotland (1566–1625), who was also to rule England as James I. In 1573 it was the last fortress to support Mary's claim as the rightful Catholic queen of Britain, causing the castle to be virtually destroyed by English artillery fire.

You enter across the **Esplanade,** the huge forecourt, which was built in the 18th century as a parade ground and now serves as the castle parking lot. It comes alive with color each August when it is used for the Tattoo, a magnificent military display, with the massed pipes and drums of the Scottish regiments beating retreat on the floodlighted heights. Heading over the drawbridge and through the gatehouse, past the guards, you'll find the rough stone walls of the **Half-Moon Battery,** where the one-o'clock gun is fired every day in an impressively anachronistic ceremony; these curving ramparts give Edinburgh Castle its distinctive appearance from miles away. Climb up through a second gateway and you come to the oldest surviving building in the complex, the tiny 11th-century **St. Margaret's Chapel,** named in honor of Saxon queen Margaret (1046–93), who had persuaded her husband, King Malcolm III (circa 1031–93), to move his court from Dunfermline to Edinburgh. Edinburgh's environs—the Lothians—were occupied by Saxon settlers with whom the queen felt more at home, or so the story goes (Dunfermline was surrounded by Celts). The chapel was the only building spared when the Scots razed the castle in 1313, having won it back from their English foes. The **Crown Room** contains the "Honours of Scotland"—the crown, scepter, and sword that once graced the Scottish monarch. Upon the **Stone of Scone,** in the Crown Room, Scottish monarchs once sat to be crowned. In the section now called **Queen Mary's Apartments,** Mary, Queen of Scots, gave birth to James VI of Scotland. The **Great Hall** displays arms and armor under an impressive vaulted, beamed ceiling. Scottish parliament meetings were conducted here until 1840. During the Napoleonic Wars in the early 19th century, the castle held French prisoners of war, whose carvings can still be seen on the vaults under the Great Hall.

Military features of interest include the **Scottish National War Memorial,** the **Scottish United Services Museum,** and the famous 15th-century Belgian-made cannon *Mons Meg.* This enormous piece of artillery has been silent since 1682, when it exploded while firing a salute for the duke of York; it now stands in an ancient hall behind the Half-Moon Battery. Contrary to what you may hear from locals, it is not *Mons Meg* but the battery's time gun that goes off with a bang every weekday at 1 PM, frightening visitors and reminding Edinburghers to check their watches. ☎ *0131/225–9846 for Edinburgh Castle; 0131/225–7393 for War Memorial.* ✒ *£8.* ⊙ *Apr.–Sept., daily 9:30–5:15; Oct.–Mar., daily 9:30–4:15.*

NEED A BREAK?   **Edinburgh Castle Café** (✉ Edinburgh Castle, Old Town, ☎ 0131/668–8800) serves coffee, light lunches, and afternoon tea in a bright location with panoramic views over the city.

⑧ George IV Bridge. It's not immediately obvious that this is in fact a bridge, as buildings are closely packed most of the way along both sides. But these buildings descend several stories below street level, as you can see by looking over the short lengths of parapet.

At the corner of George IV Bridge and Candlemaker Row, near the Greyfriars Church, stands one of the most photographed sculptures in Scotland, *Greyfriars Bobby.* This statue pays tribute to the famous Skye terrier who kept vigil beside his master's grave in the churchyard for 14 years, after 1848, leaving only for a short time each day to be fed at a nearby pub after the one-o'clock salute from the castle. Make a point of renting a video of the memorable 1961 Walt Disney film *Greyfriars Bobby*—it shows the poverty of Scottish life back then (unusual for a Disney presentation), and is a moving interpretation of an enthralling story. ⊠ *Between Bank St. and intersection with Candlemaker Row, Old Town.*

⑤ Gladstone's Land. A standout for those in search of the authentic atmosphere of old Edinburgh, this narrow, six-story tenement, next to the Assembly Hall on Lawnmarket, is a survivor from the 17th century. Typical Scottish architectural features are on show here, including an arcaded ground floor (believe it or not, even here—in the city center—livestock sometimes inhabited the ground floor). The house itself is furnished in the style of a 17th-century merchant's home and displays magnificent painted ceilings. ⊠ *477B Lawnmarket, Old Town,* ☎ *0131/226–5856.* ☜ *£3.50.* ☉ *Easter–Oct., Mon.–Sat. 10–5, Sun. 2–5; last admission at 4:30.*

⑨ Grassmarket. An area that was for centuries an agricultural market now hosts numerous shops, bars, and restaurants, making it a hive of activity at night. Sections of the Old Town wall can be traced approximately on the north (castle) side by a series of steps that run steeply up from Grassmarket to Johnston Terrace above. By far the best-preserved section of the wall, however, can be found by crossing to the south side and climbing the steps of the lane called the Vennel. Here you can see a section of the 16th-century **Flodden Wall,** which comes in from the east and turns southward at Telfer's Wall, a 17th-century extension. From here there are outstanding views northward to the castle. Grassmarket's history is long and fabulous. Nineteenth-century body snatchers Burke and Hare lived here, and the **cobbled cross** marks the site of the town gallows. Among those hanged here were many 17th-century Covenanters. Judges were known to issue the death sentence for these religious reformers with the words, "Let them glorify God in the Grassmarket."

From the northeast corner of the Grassmarket, **Victoria Street,** a 19th-century addition to the Old Town, leads up to George IV Bridge. Shops here sell antiques, designer clothing, and high-quality gift items.

⑮ High Kirk of St. Giles. This is one of the city's principal churches, sometimes called St. Giles's Cathedral (it was briefly a cathedral in the mid-17th century), but anyone expecting a rival to Paris's Notre Dame or London's Westminster Abbey will be disappointed: St. Giles is more like a large parish church than a great European cathedral. There has been a church here since AD 854, although most of the present structure dates from 1829. The spire, however, was completed in 1495. Outside, the building is dominated by this stone crown, towering 161 ft above the ground; inside, the atmosphere is dark and forbidding. At the far end of the church you'll find a life-size bronze statue of the Scot whose spirit still dominates the place, the great religious reformer and preacher John Knox, before whose zeal all Scotland once trembled. The most elaborate feature is the **Chapel of the Order of the Thistle,** bearing the belligerent national motto NEMO ME IMPUNE LACESSIT ("No one provokes me with impunity"), which was added in 1911. The church lies about one-third of the way along the Royal Mile from Edinburgh Castle. ⊠ *High St., Old Town,* ☎ *0131/225–9442,* WEB *www.stgiles.net.* ▧ *Kirk free, Thistle Chapel suggested donation £1.* ☉ *Easter–mid-Sept., Mon.–Sat. 9–7, Sun. 1–5; mid-Sept.–Easter, Mon.–Sat. 9–5, Sun. 1–5.*

🔞 **High Street.** Some of Old Town's most impressive buildings and sights can be found on High Street, one of the four streets making up the Royal Mile. There are also other, less obvious historic relics to be seen. Near Parliament Square, look on the west side for a **heart** set in cobbles. This marks the site of the vanished Tolbooth, the center of city life from the 15th century until the building's demolition in 1817. This ancient civic edifice, which formerly housed the Scottish parliament and was used as a prison from 1640 onward, inspired Sir Walter Scott's novel *The Heart of Midlothian.*

Just outside Parliament House is the **Mercat Cross** (*mercat* means "market"), a focus of public attention for centuries. A great landmark of Old Town life, this was an old mercantile center, and in the early days this area also saw executions and was the spot where royal proclamations were—and are still—read. Most of the present cross is comparatively modern, dating from the time of William Ewart Gladstone (1809–98), the great Victorian prime minister and rival of Benjamin Disraeli (1804–81). Across High Street from St. Giles's Cathedral stands the **City Chambers,** now the seat of local government. Built by John Fergus, who adapted a design of John Adam in 1753, the chambers were originally known as the Royal Exchange and intended to be where merchants and lawyers could conduct business. Note how the building drops 11 stories to Cockburn Street on its north side.

A *tron* is a weigh beam used in public weigh houses, and the **Tron Kirk** was named after a salt tron that used to stand nearby. The kirk itself was built after 1633, when St. Giles's became an Episcopal cathedral for a brief time. In this church in 1693, a minister offered an often-quoted prayer for the local government: "Lord, hae mercy on a' [all] fools and idiots, and particularly on the Magistrates of Edinburgh."

You would once have passed out of the safety of the town walls through a gate called the **Netherbow Port.** Look for the brass studs in the street cobbles that mark its location. A plaque outside the Netherbow Arts Centre depicts the gate. ⊠ *Between Lawnmarket and Canongate, Old Town.*

🟢 **Huntly House.** A must-see if you're interested in the details of Old Town life, this attractive timber-front building, dating from 1570, houses a fascinating museum of local history, displaying Scottish pottery and Edinburgh silver and glassware. ⊠ *142 Canongate, Old Town,* ☎ *0131/ 529–4143,* WEB *www.cac.org.uk.* ▧ *Free.* ☉ *Mon.–Sat. 10–5, Sun. during festival 2–5.*

🔞 **John Knox House.** It's not certain that Scotland's severe religious reformer John Knox ever lived here, but mementos of his life are on view inside. This distinctive dwelling affords a glimpse of what Old Town life was like in the 16th century. The projecting upper stories were once commonplace along the Royal Mile, darkening and further closing in the already narrow passage. Look for the initials of former owner James Mossman and his wife, carved into the stonework on the "marriage lintel." Mossman was goldsmith to Mary, Queen of Scots, and was hanged in 1573 for his allegiance to her. ⊠ *45 High St., Old Town,* ☎ *0131/556–2647,* WEB *www.johnknoxhouse.org.uk.* ▧ *£2.25.* ☉

July, Mon.–Sat. 10–5, Sun. noon–4; Aug., Mon.–Sat. 10–7, Sun. noon–4; Sept.–June, Mon.–Sat. 10–5 (last admission ½ hr before closing).

⑪ Kirk of the Greyfriars. The Gothic Greyfriars Church, built circa 1620 on the site of a medieval monastery, was where the National Covenant, declaring the independence of the Presbyterian Church in Scotland from government control, was signed in 1638. The covenant plunged Scotland into decades of civil war. Informative panels tell the story, and there's a visitor center on-site. Be sure to search out the graveyard—one of the most evocative in Europe. Nearby, at the corner of George IV Bridge and Candlemaker Row, stands one of the most photographed sites in Scotland, the Greyfriars Bobby statue. ⊠ *Greyfriars Pl., Old Town,* ☎ *0131/225–1900.* 🎫 *Free.* ☉ *Easter–Oct., weekdays 10:30–4:30, Sat. 10:30–2:30; Nov.–Easter, Thurs. 1:30–3:30; groups by appointment.*

❼ Lawnmarket. The second of the streets that make up the Royal Mile was formerly the site of the produce market for the city, with a once-a-week special cloth sale of wool and linen. Now it's home to ☞ **Gladstone's Land** and the ☞ **Writers' Museum.** At different times the Lawnmarket Courts housed James Boswell, David Hume, and Robert Burns. In nearby Brodie's Close in the 1770s lived the infamous Deacon Brodie, pillar of society by day and a murdering gang leader by night. Robert Louis Stevenson (1850–94) may well have used him as the inspiration for his *Strange Case of Dr. Jekyll and Mr. Hyde.* ⊠ *Between Castlehill and High St., Old Town.*

🖐 ⑯ Museum of Childhood. Even adults tend to enjoy this cheerfully noisy museum—a cacophony of childhood memorabilia, vintage toys, and dolls, as well as a reconstructed schoolroom, street scene, fancy-dress party, and nursery—the first in the world to be devoted solely to the history of childhood. It's two blocks past the North Bridge–South Bridge junction on High Street. ⊠ *42 High St., Old Town,* ☎ *0131/529–4142.* 🎫 *Free.* ☉ *Mon.–Sat. 10–5, Sun. during festival 2–5.*

⑩ National Library of Scotland. The National Library, founded in 1689, houses a superb collection of books and manuscripts on the history and culture of Scotland, and also mounts regular exhibitions. Genealogists investigating family trees come here, and even amateur family sleuths will find the staff helpful in their research. ⊠ *George IV Bridge, Old Town,* ☎ *0131/226–4531,* 🌐 *www.nls.uk.* 🎫 *Free.* ☉ *Mon., Tues., Thurs., Fri. 9:30–8:30; Wed. 10–8:30; Sat. 9:30–1; exhibitions Mon.–Sat. 10–5; festival hrs weekdays 10–8, Sat. 10–5, Sun. 2–5.*

⑲ Netherbow Arts Centre. The gallery and theater here host a regular program of exhibitions and productions. The café serves breakfast coffee with home-baked goods, full lunches, and afternoon teas. ⊠ *43 High St., Old Town,* ☎ *0131/556–9579,* 🌐 *www.johnknoxhouse.org.uk.* 🎫 *£2.25.* ☉ *Mon.–Sat. 10–5 and for evening performances.*

㉖ Our Dynamic Earth. Using state-of-the-art technology, Our Dynamic Earth educates and entertains as it brings to life the wonders of the planet. From the big bang to the unknown future, you'll travel through every environment on Earth and encounter creatures you probably never even knew existed—and that's just at the parking lot. ⊠ *Holyrood Rd., Holyrood,* ☎ *0131/550–7800,* 🌐 *www.dynamicearth.co.uk.* 🎫 *£7.95.* ☉ *Easter–Oct., daily 10–6; Nov.–Easter, Wed.–Sun. 10–5; last entry 1 hr and 15 mins before closing.*

❸ Outlook Tower. Want to view Edinburgh as Victorian travelers once did? Then head for the 17th-century Outlook Tower's **camera obscura,** where you'll find an optical instrument—a sort of projecting telescope—that affords bird's-eye views of the whole city (on a clear day, that is) illuminated onto a concave table. The structure was significantly altered in the 1840s and 1850s with the installation of the telescopic "magic lantern." ⊠ *Castlehill, Old Town,* ☎ *0131/226–3709.* ☒ *£4.50.* ☉ *Apr.–Oct., weekdays 9:30–6, weekends 10–6; Nov.–Mar., daily 10–5.*

★ ㉔ **Palace of Holyroodhouse.** Once the haunt of Mary, Queen of Scots, and the setting for high drama—including at least one notorious murder, a spectacular funeral, several major fires, and centuries of the colorful lifestyles of larger-than-life, power-hungry personalities—this is now Queen Elizabeth's official residence in Scotland. A doughty and impressive palace standing at the foot of the Royal Mile in a hilly public park, it is built around a graceful, lawned central court at the end of Canongate. When the queen or royal family is not in residence, you can take a guided tour. Many monarchs, including Charles II, Queen Victoria, and George V, have left their mark on its rooms, but it is Mary, Queen of Scots, whose spirit looms largest. For some visitors the most memorable room here is the little chamber in which in 1566 David Rizzio, secretary to Mary, Queen of Scots, met an unhappy end. In part because Rizzio was hated at court for his social-climbing ways, Mary's second husband, Lord Darnley (known as Henry Stewart, 1545–65), burst into the queen's rooms with his henchmen, dragged Rizzio into an antechamber, and stabbed him more than 50 times; a bronze plaque marks the spot. Darnley himself was murdered in Edinburgh the next year to make way for the queen's marriage to her lover, Bothwell.

The **King James Tower** is the oldest surviving section, containing the rooms of Mary, Queen of Scots, on the second floor, and Lord Darnley's rooms below. Though much has been altered, there are fine fireplaces, paneling, plasterwork, tapestries, and 18th- and 19th-century furniture throughout. Along the front of the palace, between the two main towers, are the duchess of Hamilton's room and the Adam-style dining room. Along the south side of the palace are the **Throne Room** and other drawing rooms now used for social and ceremonial occasions.

At the back of the palace is the **King's Bedchamber.** The 150-ft-long **Great Picture Gallery** displays the portraits of 111 Scottish monarchs. These were commissioned by Charles II, who was eager to demonstrate his Scottish ancestry—some of the royal figures here are fictional and the likenesses of others imaginary. All the portraits were painted by a Dutch artist, Jacob De Witt, who signed a contract in 1684 with the queen's cash keeper, Hugh Wallace, that bound him to deliver 110 pictures within two years, for which he received an annual stipend of £120. Surely one of the most desperate scenes in the palace's history is that of the artist feverishly turning out potboiler portraits at the rate of one a week for two years.

The palace came into existence originally as a guest house for the Abbey of Holyrood, which was founded in 1128 by Scottish king David I (1082–1153). Look for the brass letters sss set into the road at the beginning of Abbey Strand (the continuation of the Royal Mile beyond the traffic circle). The letters stand for "sanctuary" and recall the days when the former abbey served as a retreat for debtors, which it was until 1880, when the government stopped imprisoning people for debt. Curiously, the area of sanctuary extended across what is now Holyrood Park, so debtors could get some fresh air without fear of being caught by their creditors. Oddest of all, however, was the agreement that after debtors checked in at Holyrood they were able to go anywhere in the city on Sunday. This made for great entertainment on Sunday evening as midnight approached: the debtors raced back to

Holyrood before the stroke of 12, often hotly pursued by their creditors. The poet Thomas de Quincey (1785–1859) and the comte d'Ar-
tois (known as Charles X, 1757–1836), brother of the deposed king
of France, Louis XVIII (1755–1824), were two of the more famous of
Holyrood's denizens.

After the Union of the Crowns in 1603, when the Scottish royal court
packed its bags and decamped for England, the building fell into decline. Oliver Cromwell (1599–1658), the Protestant Lord Protector of
England who had conquered Scotland, ordered the palace rebuilt after
a fire in 1650, but the work was poorly carried out. When the monarchy was restored with the ascension of Charles II (1680–1685) to the
British throne in 1660, Holyrood was rebuilt in the architectural style
of Louis XIV (known as the Sun King, 1638–1715), and this is the style
you see today.

In 1688 an anti-Catholic faction ran riot within the palace, and in 1745,
during the last Jacobite campaign, Charles Edward Stuart occupied the
palace. After the 1822 visit of King George IV (1762–1830), at a more
peaceable time, the palace sank into decline once again. But Queen Victoria (1819–1901) and her grandson King George V (1865–1936) re-
newed interest in the palace: the buildings were once more refurbished
and made suitable for royal residence. Behind the palace lie the open
grounds and looming crags of Holyrood Park, the hunting ground of
early Scottish kings. At Edinburgh's minimountain, **Arthur's Seat** (822
ft), views are breathtaking. ⊠ *Abbey Strand, Holyrood,* ☎ *0131/556–
7371; 0131/556–1096 for recorded information,* WEB *www.royal.gov.uk.*
☎ *£6.50.* ⊙ *Apr.–Oct., daily 9:30–5:15; Nov.–Mar., daily 9:30–3:45;
closed during royal visits.*

NEED A
BREAK?

Near the gates of the Palace of Holyrood house is the **Abbey Strand
Tearoom** (⊠ The Sanctuary, Abbey Strand, Holyrood, ☎ no phone),
a good spot for a cup of tea or a Scottish sticky cake.

⓮ **Parliament House.** The seat of Scottish government until 1707, when
the governments of Scotland and England were united, Parliament House
now contains the Supreme Law Courts of Scotland. The structure is
partially hidden by the bulk of St. Giles's. Parliament Hall, inside, is
remarkable for its hammer-beam roof and its display of portraits by
major Scottish artists. ⊠ *Parliament Sq., Old Town,* ☎ *0131/225–2595,*
WEB *www.scotcourts.gov.uk.* ☎ *Free.* ⊙ *Weekdays 10–4.*

★ ⓬ **Royal Museum of Scotland and Museum of Scotland.** Occupying an imposing Victorian building on Chambers Street is the Royal Museum
of Scotland, which covers a broad spectrum; from natural history and
archaeology to scientific and industrial history. The great Main Hall,
with its soaring roof and "bird-cage" design, is architecturally interesting in its own right. The striking building next door houses the **Museum of Scotland**, with displays concentrating on Scotland's own
heritage. This state-of-the-art, no-expense-spared modern museum is
full of playful models, intricate reconstructions, and paraphernalia
stretching from the Bronze Age to the latest Scottish pop stars. More
than 300 exhibits reflect modern life through the eyes of ordinary Scots.
⊠ *Chambers St., Old Town,* ☎ *0131/225–7534,* WEB *www.nms.ac.uk.*
☎ *Free.* ⊙ *Mon. and Wed.–Sat. 10–5, Tues. 10–8, Sun. noon–5.*

❹ **Scotch Whisky Heritage Centre.** The mysterious process that turns
malted barley and spring water into one of Scotland's most important
exports is revealed in this museum. Although whisky-making is not in
itself packed with drama, the center manages an imaginative presentation using models and tableaux viewed while riding in low-speed bar-

rel-cars. At one point you'll find yourself inside a huge vat surrounded by bubbling sounds and malty smells. ⊠ *354 Castlehill, Old Town,* ☎ *0131/220–0441,* WEB *www.whisky-heritage.co.uk.* ⊠ *£6.50.* ⊙ *Daily 10–6; last tour at 5; call for extended hrs in summer.*

㉕ Scottish Parliament Building. After many years of construction and a cost of many millions of pounds, this building at the foot of the Royal Mile will house the 129 MSPs of Scotland's parliament when it's completed in late 2003. The structure was designed by Barcelona architect Enric Miralles, in association with Edinburgh's RMJM Architects. Donald Dewar, Scotland's very first and highly respected first minister, chose the site amid great controversy. Both Dewar and Miralles died in 2000, before witnessing the completion of the controversial structure. **The Parliament Visitor Centre** (⊠ Committee Chambers, ground floor, George IV Bridge, Old Town, ☎ 0131/348–5000, WEB www. scottish.parliament.uk), open Monday through Saturday from 9:30 to 5, provides general information about the role of parliament and its impact on the public. There's information about the development of the new structure, including a detailed architect's model.

❻ Writers' Museum. Down a close off Lawnmarket is Lady Stair's House, built in 1622 and a good example of 17th-century urban architecture. The museum housed here evokes Scotland's literary past with exhibits on Sir Walter Scott, Robert Louis Stevenson, and Robert Burns. The entertaining and dramatic **McEwan's Edinburgh Literary Pub Tour** (☎ 0131/225–6665 or 0131/225–6667), which brings Scotland's literary greats to life, makes a wonderful complement for a visit to the museum. ⊠ *Off Lawnmarket, Old Town,* ☎ *0131/529–4901,* WEB *www.cac.org.uk.* ⊠ *Free.* ⊙ *Mon.–Sat. 10–5, Sun. during festival 2–5.*

New Town

It was not until the Scottish Enlightenment, a civilizing time of expansion in the 1700s, that the city fathers decided to break away from the Royal Mile's rocky slope and create a new Edinburgh below the castle, a little to the north. This was to become the New Town, with elegant squares, classical facades, wide streets, and harmonious proportions. Clearly, change had to come. For at the dawn of the 18th century, Edinburgh's unsanitary environment—primarily a result of the crowded conditions in which most people lived—was becoming notorious. The well-known Scots fiddle tune "The Flooers (flowers) of Edinburgh" was only one of many ironic references to the capital's unpleasant environment, which greatly embarrassed the Scot James Boswell (1740–95), biographer and companion of the English lexicographer Dr. Samuel Johnson (1709–84). In his *Journal of a Tour of the Hebrides,* Boswell recalled that on retrieving the newly arrived Johnson from his grubby inn in the Canongate, "I could not prevent his being assailed by the evening effluvia of Edinburgh. . . . Walking the streets at night was pretty perilous and a good deal odoriferous."

To help remedy this sorry state of affairs, in 1767 James Drummond, the city's lord provost (the Scots term for mayor), urged the town council to hold a competition to design a new district for Edinburgh. The winner was an unknown young architect named James Craig (1744–95). His plan called for a grid of three main east–west streets, balanced at either end by two grand squares. These streets survive today, though some of the buildings that line them have been altered by later development. Princes Street is the southernmost, with Queen Street to the north and George Street as the axis, punctuated by St. Andrew and Charlotte squares. A look at the map will reveal a geometric symmetry unusual in Britain. Even Princes Street Gardens are balanced by Queen

Street Gardens, to the north. Princes Street was conceived as an exclusive residential address, with an open vista facing the castle. It has since been altered by the demands of business and shopping, but the vista remains.

The New Town was expanded several times after Craig's death and now covers an area about three times larger than Craig envisioned. Indeed, some of the most elegant facades came later and can be found by strolling north of Queen Street Gardens.

A Good Walk

Start your walk on **The Mound** ㉗, the sloping street that joins the Old and New towns. Two galleries immediately east of this great linking ramp, the **National Gallery of Scotland** ㉘ and the **Royal Scottish Academy** ㉙, are the work of William Playfair (1789–1857), an architect whose neoclassical buildings contributed greatly to Edinburgh's title: the Athens of the North.

At the foot of the Mound is Edinburgh's most famous street, **Princes Street** ㉚, the humming center of modern-day Edinburgh—a ceaseless promenade of natives and visitors alike patter along its mile or so of retail establishments. Residents lament the disappearance of the dignified old shops that once lined this street; now a long sequence of chain stores on the north side has replaced them, although the south side still affords a grand vista of the castle to the south. Walk east until you reach the soaring Gothic spire of the **Scott Monument** ㉛. Opposite is that most Edinburgh of institutions, **Jenners** ㉜ department store. **Register House** ㉝, an elegant neoclassical treasure designed by Robert Adam (1728–92), stands opposite the main post office and marks the east end of Princes Street. Immediately west of Register House is the Café Royal, at 17 Register Street, one of the city's most interesting pubs. It has good beer and great character, with ornate tiles and stained glass contributing to the atmosphere.

The monuments on Calton Hill, growing ever more noticeable ahead as you walk east along Princes Street, can be reached by first continuing along **Waterloo Place** ㉞, the eastern extension of Princes Street, from which you can get to the Regent Bridge. Waterloo Place then continues in a single sweep through the Calton Burial Ground to the screen walling at the base of **Calton Hill** ㉟. On the left you'll see steps that lead to the hilltop. If you're walking and don't feel up to the steep climb, take the road farther on to the left, which loops up the hill at a more leisurely pace.

Leaving Calton Hill, you may wish to continue east along Regent Road, perhaps as far as the Burns Monument, to admire the views westward of the castle and of the facade of the former Royal High School directly above you. Then retrace your steps to the Waterloo Place traffic lights and make your way to St. Andrew Square by cutting through the St. James Centre shopping mall, taking in the designer stores on the street known as The Walk, including the upscale Harvey Nichols store. After admiring the lavish interior of the Royal Bank of Scotland, on the eastern side of the square—the building was originally the town house of the immensely rich Sir Lawrence Dundas, one of Chippendale's most lavish patrons—walk west along **George Street** ㊱, with its variety of shops.

The essence of the New Town spirit survives in **Charlotte Square** ㊲, at the west end of George Street, and especially in the beautiful **Georgian House** ㊳ and **West Register House** ㊴. To explore further, choose your own route northward, down to the wide and elegant streets centering on **Moray Place** ㊵, a fine example of an 1820s development. Then make your way back eastward along Queen Street to visit the **Scottish National Portrait Gallery** ㊶, which has exceptional paintings and a fine restaurant. Another attraction within reach of the New Town is the 70-acre **Royal Botanic Garden.** Walk down Dundas Street, the continuation of Hanover Street, and turn left and across the bridge over the Water of Leith, Edinburgh's small-scale river. This path leads to the gardens, still one of the most cherished spots for residents as well as an important center for scientific research.

TIMING

This walk could be done in a morning if you start early, but if you want to get the most out of the National Gallery of Scotland and the Scottish National Portrait Gallery, take the whole day and allow at least an hour for each museum. The Portrait Gallery has a good restaurant, so one option is to arrive in time for lunch, then spend the afternoon there.

Sights to See

㉟ **Calton Hill.** Robert Louis Stevenson's favorite view of his beloved city was from the top of this hill. The architectural styles represented by the extraordinary collection of monuments here include mock Gothic—the Old Observatory, for example—and neoclassical. Under the latter category falls William Playfair's (1789–1857) monument to his talented uncle, the geologist and mathematician John Playfair (1748–1819), as well as his cruciform **New Observatory.** The piece that commands the most attention, however, is the so-called **National Monument,** often referred to as "Edinburgh's [or Scotland's] Disgrace." Intended to mimic Athens's Parthenon, this monument for the dead of the Napoleonic Wars was started in 1822 to the specifications of a design by Playfair. But in 1830, only 12 columns later, money ran out, and the columned facade became a monument to high aspirations and poor fund-raising. The tallest monument on Calton Hill is the 100-ft-high **Nelson Monument,** completed in 1814 in honor of Britain's naval hero Horatio Nelson (1758–1805). The **Burns Monument** is the circular Corinthian temple below Regent Road. Devotees of Robert Burns may want to visit one other grave—that of Mrs. Agnes McLehose, or "Clarinda," in the Canongate Graveyard. ⊠ *Bounded by Leith St. to the west and Regent Rd. to the south, Calton,* ☎ *0131/556–2716,* WEB *www.cac.org.uk.* ⊠ *Nelson Monument £2.50.* ☉ *Apr.–Sept., Mon. 1–6, Tues.–Sat. 10–6; Oct.–Mar., Mon.–Sat. 10–3.*

㊲ **Charlotte Square.** At the west end of George Street is the New Town's centerpiece—an 18th-century square that is home to one of the proudest achievements of Robert Adam, Scotland's noted neoclassical architect. On the north side, Adam designed a palatial facade to unite three separate town houses of such sublime simplicity and perfect proportions that architects come from all over the world to study it. Happily, the Age of Enlightenment grace notes continue within, as the center town house is now occupied by the ☞ **Georgian House** museum, and to the west stands ☞ **West Register House.** ⊠ *West end of George St., New Town.*

OFF THE BEATEN PATH **EDINBURGH ZOO** – Edinburgh's zoo holds traditional zoo delights, with more than 1,000 species, animal contact and handling sessions in the main season, as well as its ever-popular Penguin Parade (held daily in summer). The zoo spreads out over an 80-acre site on the slopes of Corstorphine Hill. ⊠ *Corstorphine Rd., next to Holiday Inn Edinburgh, 4 mi west of city, Corstorphine,* ☎ *0131/334–9171,* WEB *www.edinburghzoo.org.uk.* ⊠ *£7.* ☉ *Apr.–Sept., daily 9–6; Oct. and Mar., daily 9–5; Nov.–Feb., daily 9–4:30.*

36 George Street. With its upscale shops and handsome Georgian frontages, this is a more pleasant, less crowded street for wandering than Princes Street. The **statue of King George IV**, at the intersection of George and Hanover streets, recalls the visit of George IV to Scotland in 1822. He was the first British monarch to do so since King Charles II, in the 17th century. By the 19th century Scotland was perceived at Westminster, the distant English seat of parliament, as being almost civilized enough for a monarch to visit safely.

The ubiquitous Sir Walter Scott turns up farther down the street. It was at a grand dinner in the **Assembly Rooms,** between Hanover and Frederick streets, that Scott acknowledged having written the *Waverley* novels (the name of the author had hitherto been a secret). You can meet Scott once again, in the form of a plaque just downhill, at 39 Castle Street, where he lived from 1797 until his death in 1832. ⊠ *Between Charlotte and St. Andrew Sqs., New Town.*

★ **38 Georgian House.** The National Trust for Scotland has furnished this house in period style to show the elegant domestic arrangements of an affluent family of the late 18th century. The hallway was designed to accommodate sedan chairs, in which 18th-century grandees were carried through the streets. ⊠ *7 Charlotte Sq., New Town,* ☎ *0131/225–2160,* WEB *www.nts.org.uk.* 🖃 *£5.* ☉ *Late Mar.–late Oct., daily 10–6; late Oct.–late Dec. and late Jan.–late Mar., daily 11–4 (last admission ½ hr before closing).*

32 Jenners. Edinburgh's equivalent of London's Harrods department store, Jenners is noteworthy not only for its high-quality wares and good restaurants, but also because of the building's interesting architectural detail—baroque on the outside, with a mock-Jacobean central well inside. It was one of the earliest department stores ever to be established, in 1838. The caryatids decorating the exterior were said to have been placed in honor of the store's predominantly female customers. ⊠ *48 Princes St., New Town,* ☎ *0131/225–2442,* WEB *www.jenners.com.* ☉ *Mon., Wed., Fri., Sat. 9–5:30, Tues. 9:30–5:30, Thurs. 9–7:30.*

OFF THE
BEATEN PATH

LEITH – Edinburgh's ancient seaport has been revitalized with the restoration of those fine commercial buildings that survived an earlier, and insensitive, redevelopment phase. It's worth exploring the lowest reaches of the Water of Leith, an area where pubs and restaurants now proliferate. The major attraction for visitors here, however, is the former royal yacht *Britannia,* moored outside the huge Ocean Terminal shopping mall (it costs £7.75 and is open daily 9:30–4:30), where you can wander around the ship that Queen Elizabeth called "the one place where I can truly relax," then check in at the shore-based visitor center, which tells the ship's sometimes fabled story. ⊠ *Reach Leith by walking down Leith St. and Leith Walk, from east end of Princes St. (20- to 30-min); or take Bus 7, 10, 14, 16, 17, 22, 25, 32/52, 34/35, 42/46, or 87, Circle Rte. 87 or 2/12, or special Britannia Bus X50 from Waverley Bridge.*

40 Moray Place. Twelve-sided Moray Place—with its "pendants," Ainslie Place and Randolph Crescent—was laid out in 1822 by the earl of Moray. It's a fine example of an 1820s development, with imposing porticos and a central secluded garden (for residents only). From the start the houses were planned to be of particularly high quality, and the curving facades are still pleasant today. ⊠ *Between Charlotte Sq. and the Water of Leith, New Town.*

27 The Mound. The Mound originated from the need for a dry-shod crossing of the muddy quagmire left behind when Nor' Loch, the body of water below the castle, was drained (the railway now cuts through this area). The work is said to have been started by a local tailor, George Boyd, who tired of struggling through the mud en route from his New Town house to his Old Town shop. The building of a ramp was under way by 1781, and by the time of its completion, in 1830, "Geordie Boyd's mud brig [bridge]," as the street was first known, had been built up with an estimated 2 million cartloads of earth dug from the foundations of the New Town.

★ ㉘ **National Gallery of Scotland.** Opened to the public in 1859 in a grand neoclassical building designed by William Playfair, the National Gallery was renovated in the late 1980s at vast expense to show the original gilding and rich color schemes of reds and greens within the galleries. A wide selection of paintings, from the Renaissance to the Postimpressionist period, is on display here. Most famous are the old-master paintings bequeathed by the duke of Sutherland, including Titian's *Three Ages of Man.* All the great names are here; works by Velázquez, El Greco, Rembrandt, Goya, Poussin, Clouet, Turner, Degas, Monet, and van Gogh, among others, complement a fine collection of Scottish art, including Sir Henry Raeburn's *Reverend Robert Walker Skating on Duddingston Loch* and other masterworks by Ramsay, Raeburn, and Wilkie. ⊠ *The Mound, Old Town, on the border with New Town,* ☎ *0131/332–2266,* WEB *www.natgalscot.ac.uk.* ☎ *Free.* ☉ *Mon.–Sat. 10–5, Sun. noon–5; extended hrs during festival. Print Room, weekdays 10–12:30 and 2–4:30 by appointment.*

㉚ **Princes Street.** The south side of this well-planned street is occupied by the well-kept Princes Street Gardens, which act as a wide green moat to the castle on its rock. Unfortunately, the north side is now one long sequence of chain stores with unappealing modern fronts that can be seen in almost any large British town. ⊠ *Running east–west from Waterloo Pl. to Lothian Rd., East End to West End.*

NEED A BREAK?	Visit any of the excellent sandwich shops in the neighborhood, pick up a snack, and head for Princes Street Gardens. Sit on a bench and watch the world go by, with the castle brooding above and the squirrels scampering around your feet.

㉝ **Register House.** Scotland's first custom-built archives depository, Register House, designed by the great Robert Adam, was partly funded by the sale of estates forfeited by Jacobite landowners after their last rebellion in Britain (1745–46). Work on the Regency-style building, which marks the end of Princes Street, started in 1774. The statue in front is of the first duke of Wellington (1769–1852). It's possible to conduct genealogical research here; call ahead for more information. ⊠ *Princes St., New Town,* ☎ *0131/535–1314.* ☎ *Free.* ☉ *Weekdays 9–4:30.*

NEED A BREAK?	Immediately west of Register House is the **Café Royal** (⊠ 17 W. Register St., New Town, ☎ 0131/557–4792), which has good beer and lots of character, with ornate tiles and stained glass.

OFF THE BEATEN PATH	**ROYAL BOTANIC GARDEN –** This 70-acre garden, just north of the city center, is second only to Kew Gardens in London for the variety of plants it contains and for the charm of its setting. An immense array of species is on show, from tropical to Nordic, including Britain's largest rhododendron and azalea collection. A highlight is an impressive Chinese garden. A convenient cafeteria and a shop are on the premises. To reach the gardens, only a 10- to 15-minute walk from the New Town, walk down Dundas Street, the continuation of Hanover Street, and turn

left across the bridge over the Water of Leith, Edinburgh's small-scale river. ⊠ *Inverleith Row, Inverleith,* ☎ *0131/552–7171,* WEB *www.rbge. org.uk.* ⊠ *Free; donation for greenhouses appreciated.* ☉ *Gardens Nov.–Jan., daily 9:30–4; Feb. and Oct., daily 9:30–5; Mar. and Sept., daily 9:30–6; Apr.–Aug., daily 9:30–7. Shop, cafeteria, and exhibition areas Mar.–Oct., daily 10–5; Nov.–Feb., daily 10–3:30.*

㉙ Royal Scottish Academy. The William Playfair–designed Academy, closed at this writing (autumn 2002) for major refurbishment, was scheduled to reopen in summer 2003 with a world-class exhibition of the works of Monet. It's worth visiting this imposing neoclassic temple overlooking Princes Street for the architecture alone. ⊠ *Princes St., Old Town,* ☎ *0131/558–7097,* WEB *www.royalscottishacademy.org. Closed for refurbishment until August 2003.*

㉛ Scott Monument. What appears to be a Gothic cathedral spire chopped off and planted in the east end of the Princes Street Gardens is the nation's tribute to Sir Walter—a 200-ft-high monument looming over Princes Street. Built in 1844 in honor of Scotland's most famous author, Sir Walter Scott, the author of *Ivanhoe, Waverley,* and many other novels and poems, it's centered on a marble statue of Scott and his favorite dog, Maida. It's worth taking the time to explore the immediate area, Princes Street Gardens, one of the prettiest city parks in Britain. In the open-air theater, amid the park's trim flower beds, stately trees, and carefully tended lawns, brass bands occasionally play. Here, too, is the famous **monument to David Livingstone,** whose African meeting with H. M. Stanley is part of Scot-American history. ⊠ *Princes St., Old Town,* ☎ *0131/529–4068.* ⊠ *£2.50.* ☉ *Mar.–May and Oct., Mon.–Sat. 9–6, Sun. 10–6; June–Sept. Mon.–Sat. 9–8, Sun. 10–6; Nov.–Feb., Mon.–Sat. 9–4, Sun. 10–4.*

OFF THE
BEATEN PATH

SCOTTISH NATIONAL GALLERY OF MODERN ART – This handsome former school building on Belford Road, close to the New Town, displays paintings and sculpture, including works by Pablo Picasso, Georges Braque, Henri Matisse, and André Derain. The gallery also has an excellent restaurant in the basement. ⊠ *Belford Rd., Dean Village,* ☎ *0131/ 556–8921.* ⊠ *Free.* ☉ *Mon.–Sat. 10–5, Sun. noon–5; extended hrs during the festival.*

★ **㊶ Scottish National Portrait Gallery.** A magnificent red-sandstone Gothic building dating from 1889 on Queen Street houses this must-visit institution. The gallery contains a superb Thomas Gainsborough painting and portraits by the Scottish artists Allan Ramsay and Sir Henry Raeburn, among many others. You can see portraits of classic literary figures such as Robert Burns and Sir Walter Scott, and modern portraits depict actors, sports stars, and living members of the royal family. The building's beautiful William Hole murals representing Scots from the Stone Age to the 19th century are themselves worthy of study. ⊠ *Queen St., New Town,* ☎ *0131/624–6200.* ⊠ *Free; charge for special exhibitions.* ☉ *Mon.–Sat. 10–5, Sun. 2–5.*

㉞ Waterloo Place. The fine neoclassically inspired architecture on this street was designed as a piece by Archibald Elliot (d. 1823) in 1815. Waterloo Place extends over Regent Bridge, bounded by the 1815 **Regent Arch,** a simple, triumphal Corinthian-column war memorial at the center of Ionic screens bordering the bridge. ⊠ *Eastern extension of Princes St., East End.*

㊴ West Register House. The former St. George's Church, in the middle of the west side of Charlotte Square, today fulfills a different role, as an extension of the original Register House on Princes Street. It contains modern records that are available to view for a fee, but call ahead if you wish to carry out extensive genealogical research. ⊠ *Charlotte Sq., New Town,* ☎ *0131/535–1400.* ⌨ *Free.* ☉ *Weekdays 9–4:30.*

DINING

As befits one of the richest cities in Britain, Edinburgh has a huge number of restaurants, including the predictable cosmopolitan range, but there's also a strong emphasis on traditional style. This tends to mean the Scottish-French style that harks back to the historical "Auld Alliance," founded on a shared loathing for the English. The Scots element is the preference for plain and fresh foodstuffs; the French supply the sauces, often to be poured on after cooking. This equation has now been elevated to a high art in many Edinburgh eateries.

On the whole, restaurants tend to be fairly small to medium size, so it's best to make reservations at the more popular ones, even on weekdays and definitely at festival time. As Edinburgh is an unusually small capital, most of the good restaurants are within easy walking distance of the main streets, Princes Street and the Royal Mile.

It's possible to eat well in Edinburgh without spending a fortune. Even at those restaurants ranked in the top price category, two people can often squeeze by for under £30 if they order prudently. A service charge of 10% or more may be added to your bill, though this practice is not adhered to uniformly. If no charge has been added and you are satisfied with the service, a 10% tip is appropriate. Dining in Edinburgh is slightly different from much of Britain because the city council has relaxed outdated British licensing laws: people often eat a bit later into the evening in Scotland than in England, or rather they finish eating and then drink on in a leisurely Scottish fashion.

CATEGORY	COST*
££££	over £22
£££	£16–£22
££	£9–£15
£	under £9

per person for a main course at dinner, including VAT

Old Town

French

££££ ★ ✕ **Witchery by the Castle.** Centuries of fascinating history and the hundreds of "witches" who were executed on Castlehill, just yards from where you will be seated, are the inspiration for this atmospheric restaurant. The cavernous interior, complete with flickering candlelight, is festooned with cabalistic insignia and tarot-card characters. Gilded ceilings with heraldic paintings reflect the close links of the "Auld Alliance" between France and Scotland—an alliance reflected in the food. Fine venison, duck, lamb, salmon, and fillet steak are among the specialties. Pre- and post-theater (5:30–6:30 and 10:30–11:30) £9.95 two-course specials are a great and inexpensive way to sample the exceptional food. ⊠ *352 Castlehill, Royal Mile, Old Town,* ☎ *0131/225–5613. Reservations essential. AE, DC, MC, V.*

££–£££ ✕ **Merchants.** This is a bustling, cheery cavern of bright scarlet walls, mirrors, plants, and a nonstop jazz sound track, all set beneath the dramatic arch of George IV Bridge and only moments from the Grassmarket. The menu ranges from simple haggis and beef to a mille-feuille of scallops and lamb chops with raspberry-and-mint sauce. Its ambitious dishes are reminiscent of old-fashioned nouvelle, but Merchants really does the basics best. Set lunches run from £8.50; set dinners start at £16.50. ✉ *17 Merchant St., Old Town*, ☎ *0131/225–4009. AE, DC, MC, V.*

££ ✕ **Le Sept.** Tucked discreetly down a cobbled lane off the Royal Mile, this low-arched restaurant in the city center is a refined gem and an understated local institution. It's friendly, lively, unfussy, and famed for its crepes with adventurous fillings, but the daily changing menu also lists simple staples such as delicately cooked salmon fillets and succulent lamb stew. The wine list is similarly select, and the service is always delightful. Set lunches offer an unbeatable value, with three courses costing £6. ✉ *7 Old Fishmarket Close, Old Town*, ☎ *0131/ 225–5428. AE, MC.*

Scottish

£££–££££ ✕ **Number One.** Set within the Edwardian splendor of the Balmoral Hotel is this grand and stylish restaurant, with a menu that highlights the best of Scottish seafood and game. A smooth-as-velvet celeriac velouté is served over scallops, fillet of turbot is paired with a pesto-potato puree and spinach, and risotto takes its flavor from mushrooms and truffles. The wine list is extensive, the service impeccable. All in all, this is an intimate dining experience for those special-occasion evenings. ✉ *Princes St., Old Town*, ☎ *0131/556–2414. Reservations essential. Jacket and tie. AE, DC, MC, V.*

££–£££ ✕ **The Tower.** Housed in the Museum of Scotland, this rooftop restaurant serves up a feast of contemporary aesthetics and pleasant distractions before you even get to the menu. The modern architecture affords one of the finest vistas in Edinburgh. The Tower has a high-powered ambience and an intelligible menu with an exquisite oyster and shellfish selection, Aberdeen Angus beef, roast saddle of wild red venison, and more. The two-course theater supper, available from 4 to 6, is an especially good value, but be careful not to miss curtain time because the lovely Edinburgh skyline is working its ancient charm. ✉ *Museum of Scotland, Chambers St., Old Town*, ☎ *0131/225–3003. Reservations essential. AE, DC, MC, V.*

££ ✕ **Beehive Inn.** The Beehive snuggles in the Grassmarket, under the majestic shadow of the castle. Some 400 years ago the Beehive was a coaching inn, and outside the pub's doors once stood the main city gallows. Bar suppers and snacks are served throughout the day, within the inn or in the beer garden. Upstairs, Rafters Restaurant has a dinner menu. Try the grilled salmon steaks. Don't be put off by the noisy bar; there's usually a quieter spot to be found. You can book literary lunch and supper packages in conjunction with the McEwan's Edinburgh Literary Pub Tour, which departs from here. ✉ *18–20 Grassmarket, Old Town*, ☎ *0131/225–7171. AE, DC, MC, V. No lunch at Rafters.*

££ ✕ **Doric Tavern.** Beyond this café-bistro bar's rather tatty entrance staircase plastered with posters and playbills, the stripped wood floor, dark-wood tables, and navy velvet curtains create a subdued, languid environment. The menu always lists a daily special—such as roast-pigeon salad with raspberry-vinegar dressing—and a selection of fresh fish and meat dishes, always accompanied by vegetarian options. Try the lavish choices from the fixed-price lunch (£13.50) or dinner (£19.50), both excellent values. ✉ *15/16 Market St., Old Town*, ☎ *0131/225–1084. Reservations essential. AE, MC, V.*

Vegetarian

££ ✕ **Bann UK.** Just off the Royal Mile, in the heart of the Old Town, is Bann UK, where you can dine on vegetarian fare in a light and airy room with sturdy wooden furniture. Sip a cup of coffee with a decadent piece of cake from the selection delivered daily by a local French patisserie, or dine on enchiladas or a phyllo basket of cream cheese, herbs, and vegetables. Allow plenty of time for lunch, as service can be slow. ⊠ *5 Hunter Sq., Old Town,* ☎ *0131/226–1112. AE, DC, MC, V.*

New Town

Chinese

££ ✗ **Kweilin.** Highlights such as deep-fried crispy chicken on the bone and meat-stuffed eggplant on a hot plate make this pleasant family-run restaurant popular with the city's Chinese community. The lunchtime special menu is a pricey-sounding £10 but worth it, and the special menus tailored for two, three, or four evening diners are an even better value; they start at £18 per person. Amid the traditional Chinese decor are several large paintings depicting scenes from the Kwangsi Province, of which Kweilin is the capital. ⊠ *19–21 Dundas St., New Town,* ☎ *0131/ 557–1875. AE, MC, V. Closed Mon. Jan.–Nov.*

Eclectic

£££–££££ ✗ **Oloroso.** In the heart of the New Town and close to main shopping streets, Oloroso makes the perfect spot for a revitalizing lunch or dinner after exploring the city. You'll find well-prepared and -presented contemporary international cooking, efficient and friendly service, and a comfortable bar. Try the roasted duck breast with braised red cabbage, apples, and tarragon jus, or the aubergine *galette* (eggplant tart) with a tomato-and-cinnamon sauce. The private dining room and roof terrace afford stunning views across the Firth of Forth to the hills of Fife on one side, and the castle and city rooftops on the other side. ⊠ *33 Castle St., New Town,* ☎ *0131/226–7614. AE, DC, MC, V.*

££–£££ ✗ **The Dome.** The splendid interior of this former bank with painted plasterwork and a central dome provides an elegant backdrop for relaxed dining. Or you could just opt for a drink at the central bar, a favored spot where sophisticates wind down after work. The toasted BLT sandwiches are almost big enough for two, but if you're ravenous the eclectic menu offers many other options: try the penne sautéed in a basil cream with fresh mussels, or the char-grilled chicken salad with nan bread. ⊠ *14 George St., New Town,* ☎ *0131/624–8624. AE, MC, V.*

££ ✗ **Rick's.** There's no *Casablanca* theme, and Sam doesn't play it even once, but the local office crowd provides a lively ambience after 5 at this restaurant-bar within a hotel. The minimalist design is ultra-Manhattan and ultrachic. An imaginative contemporary menu includes duck breast with arugula salad, seafood tagliatelle, fresh tuna with coriander mashed potatoes, and a chocolate tart with pear puree. The bright lobby bar serves cocktails amid brash music and chrome-and-stone decor. Service is erratic. ⊠ *55 Fredrick St., New Town,* ☎ *0131/ 622–7800. AE, MC, V.*

French

£££–££££ ✗ **Pompadour.** As might be expected of a restaurant named after the
★ king's mistress, Madame de Pompadour, the dining room here is inspired by the court of Louis XV, with subtle plasterwork and rich murals. The cuisine is also classic French, with top-quality Scottish produce completing the happiest of alliances. The extensive, well-chosen wine list complements such dishes as sea bass with crispy leeks and caviar-butter sauce, whole lobster with mustard and cheese, and loin of venison with potato pancakes. This is the place to go if you want a festive night out, and it's ideal for the formal lunch that needs lightening up. ⊠ *Caledonian Hilton Hotel, Princes St., West End,* ☎ *0131/459– 9988. Reservations essential. AE, DC, MC, V. No lunch weekends.*

£££ ✗ **Le Café St. Honoré.** Quintessentially Parisian in style, this restaurant smacks of all that is charming about French dining. From the

Edinburgh Dining and Lodging

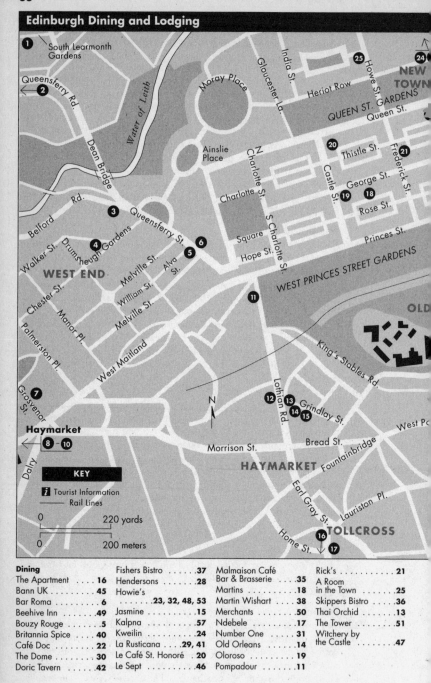

Dining

The Apartment **16**	Fishers Bistro **37**	Malmaison Café	Rick's **21**
Bann UK **45**	Hendersons **28**	Bar & Brasserie **35**	A Room
Bar Roma **6**	Howie's	Martins **18**	in the Town **25**
Beehive Inn **49**	. . . . **23, 32, 48, 53**	Martin Wishart . . . **38**	Skippers Bistro **36**
Bouzy Rouge **5**	Jasmine **15**	Merchants **50**	Thai Orchid **13**
Britannia Spice **40**	Kalpna **57**	Ndebele **17**	The Tower **51**
Café Doc **22**	Kweilin **24**	Number One **31**	Witchery by
The Dome **30**	La Rusticana **29, 41**	Old Orleans **14**	the Castle **47**
Doric Tavern **42**	Le Café St. Honoré . **20**	Oloroso **19**	
	Le Sept **46**	Pompadour **11**	

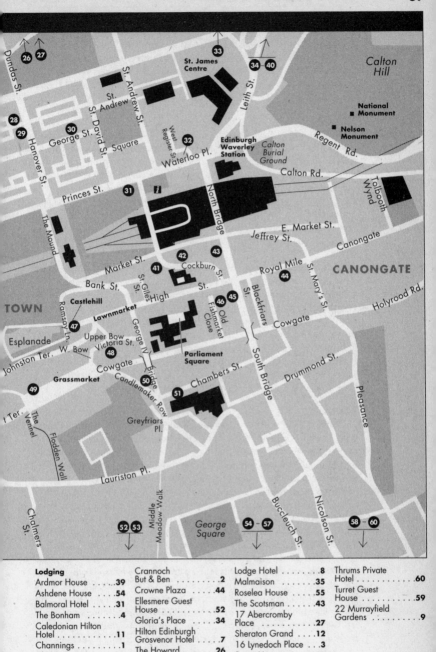

Lodging

Ardmor House **39**
Ashdene House **54**
Balmoral Hotel **31**
The Bonham **4**
Caledonian Hilton
Hotel **11**
Channings **1**
Classic Guest
House **56**

Crannoch
But & Ben **2**
Crowne Plaza **44**
Ellesmere Guest
House **52**
Gloria's Place **34**
Hilton Edinburgh
Grosvenor Hotel **7**
The Howard **26**
Kew House and
Apartments **10**

Lodge Hotel **8**
Malmaison **35**
Roselea House **55**
The Scotsman **43**
17 Abercromby
Place **27**
Sheraton Grand **12**
16 Lynedoch Place . . .**3**
Stuart House **33**
Teviotdale House . . .**58**

Thrums Private
Hotel **60**
Turret Guest
House **59**
22 Murrayfield
Gardens **9**

moment you enter this beautifully lighted room you are transported into a decadently stylish belle epoque. A concise and varied menu leaves more time for chat. Start off with a warm salad of scallops, monkfish, chorizo, and pine nuts, followed by lamb confit or panfried turbot cooked with cider, green peppercorns, and prawns. The wine list is extensive. ⊠ *34 N.W. Thistle Street La., New Town,* ☎ *0131/226–2211. AE, DC, MC, V. Closed Sun.*

Italian

££–£££ ✕ **Café Doc.** An authentic Italian treasure is tucked away on Thistle Street. Don't be deceived by the café front and pine furniture, although you're assured of a great cappuccino—you can expect fine Italian cuisine here. The restaurant at the back of the café comes to life in the evening, with an eclectic menu of northern Italian cuisine prepared with fresh local Scottish produce. The linguine with lobster is a house specialty, and the risotto bursts with flavor and character, much like the Venetian owner Massimo, who given the chance will regale you with lively banter. ⊠ *49A Thistle St., New Town,* ☎ *0131/220–6846. MC, V.*

££ ✕ **La Rusticana.** Hanover Street exists to delight lovers of Italian food;
★   some of the best pasta and pizza restaurants compete here, but La Rusticana usually wins the day. Stronger on pasta than pizza, this cellar restaurant does the taste-bud trick best, while being only marginally above average in price. Along with its sister restaurant in the Old Town, on Cockburn Street, it is a fundamental part of Edinburgh's food culture, a favorite for business meetings, and a generous patron of charity events. It's in the city center, two minutes from Princes Street. ⊠ *90 Hanover St., New Town,* ☎ *0131/225–2227;* ⊠ *25 Cockburn St., Old Town,* ☎ *0131/225–2832. AE, DC, MC, V.*

Scottish

££–£££ ✕ **Martins.** Don't be put off by the off-the-beaten-path location of this spot, tucked away in a little back alley between Frederick and Castle streets, for it's well worth finding. The menu emphasizes organically grown local products and wild-caught foods. Typical modern Scottish dishes include fillet of turbot, panfried with fennel and green peppercorn sauce, or charred lamb fillet with couscous, spinach, and an anise sauce. The cheese board, famed far and wide, has a sampling of Scottish and Irish cheeses. Lunches are an excellent value. The wine list includes an excellent choice of half bottles. Smoking is not permitted. ⊠ *70 Rose St. North La., New Town,* ☎ *0131/225–3106. Reservations essential. AE, DC, MC, V. Closed Sun. and Mon. No lunch Sat.*

££ ✕ **A Room in the Town.** At this relaxed and friendly bistro serving Scots-French fare, there's a strong emphasis on local fresh meat, with the Scottish touch accounting for slightly sweeter-than-usual sauces. The somewhat high prices are offset by a BYOB policy (there's an excellent wine shop a block away), but wine is also available at standard restaurant prices, along with very nice brandy. Scottishly plain but Continentally cheerful, it's perfect for a sociable night out with friends. Note that it can get a bit smoky when full. ⊠ *18 Howe St., New Town,* ☎ *0131/225–8204. Reservations essential. MC, V.*

Vegetarian

£ ✕ **Hendersons.** This was Edinburgh's original vegetarian restaurant long before it was fashionable to serve healthful, meatless creations. Tasty options include eggplant, tomato, and chickpea curry, or leek-and-Stilton pie. If you haven't summoned the courage to try an authentic haggis while in Scotland, come here to sample a vegetarian version. The Bistro Bar, owned by the same proprietors, around the corner on Thistle Street, is also open daily in the evening. ⊠ *94 Hanover St., New*

Town, ☎ *0131/225–2131. AE, DC, MC, V. Closed Sun. except during festival.*

Haymarket

Cajun

££　✕ **Old Orleans.** The finest Cajun cooking in Edinburgh—no, it's not the *only* Cajun cooking here—Old Orleans serves up its dishes with real southern United States extravagance. There are also Mexican and regional American dishes that with the Cajun items include red snapper, swordfish, smothered turkey, traditional jambalaya, and spareribs (they come with a large bib and finger bowl). The music is blues and jazz, and the walls display amusing New Orleans kitsch: trellis- and metalwork, brass instruments, and travel-related mementos. The constantly changing lunchtime menu is equally welcoming, coming in at less than £8. ⊠ *30 Grindlay St., Haymarket,* ☎ *0131/229–1511. AE, DC, MC, V.*

Chinese

£　✕ **Jasmine.** Seafood is the specialty of this small, friendly, candlelighted Cantonese restaurant, with rapid service to deal with the constant stream of customers, even on weekdays. The subdued cream interior with wooden screens is relaxing, although tables are quite closely spaced. Delicious dishes include crispy monkfish with honey sauce, baked crabs in black bean sauce, and fried oysters with ginger and spring onions. For two or more people, the set menus are a good value. A take-out menu is available. ⊠ *32 Grindlay St., Haymarket,* ☎ *0131/229–5757. AE, MC, V.*

Thai

£　✕ **Thai Orchid.** The theme is green at this bowfront restaurant, where green walls and brightly colored Thai silks set off Thai statues and gold masks. The food is a genuine taste of Thailand: the first king of Thailand once enjoyed *gaeng masaman* (beef or chicken slow cooked with roasted peanuts and potatoes), the same dish you'll find here at Thai Orchid. Other menu options include *goong nung* (king prawns steamed with lemongrass, white wine, lime juice, and coriander), and *gai yang* (chicken breast marinated with ground rice, garlic, soy sauce, and ground herbs, char-grilled and served with sticky rice and chili-pepper dip). ⊠ *44 Grindlay St., Haymarket,* ☎ *0141/228–4438. AE, MC, V. Closed Sun. No lunch Sat.*

West End and Points West

Eclectic

££–£££　✕ **Bouzy Rouge.** The dining room of this fashionable restaurant is cheery and simple—wooden tables, bright tiles, and modern art—and the food is exceptional. The imaginative combinations can sound pretentious, but they are actually a treat. For a strangely satisfying meal try the saddle of Perthsire venison with blueberry and cinnamon coulis followed by butterscotch-stuffed pear poached in red wine and served with citrus sorbet. ⊠ *1 Alva St., West End,* ☎ *0131/225–9594. AE, DC, MC, V.*

££　✕ **The Apartment.** A wacky, whirlwind affair, The Apartment is a popular restaurant with a varied and fun menu that always results in huge portions at very reasonable prices. Choose from one of four menu categories: CHL (Chunky Healthy Lines), Fish Things, Other Things, and The Slab. Sample dishes include fabulous mussels in a creamy sauce, North African spicy marinated lamb patties, *merguez* (spicy sausage) and grilled basil-wrapped goat cheese, and such huge salads as *tiede* piquant (spicy olives, potatoes, roasted peppers, and chorizo, topped with a poached egg). ✉ *7–13 Barclay Pl., near King's Theatre, Toll-cross,* ☏ *0131/228–6456. MC, V.*

Italian

££ ✕ **Bar Roma.** Bar Roma serves up a genuine Italian experience, even if most of the waiters hail from places more local than Roma or Torino. The food tastes great, the place is noisy and fun, the chatty waiters are full of energy, and the hosts are always willing to squeeze you in, no matter how crowded the place may be. If you want to dine in peace and quiet, however, avoid early evening when the office crowd warms up for a night on the town. Specialties include bumper calzone and seafood linguine. Bar Italia, owned by the same people, is only a few hundred yards away in Lothian Road. ✉ *39a Queensferry St., West End,* ☏ *0131/226–2977. AE, MC, V.*

South Side

African

£ ✕ **Ndebele.** This small, very friendly café—named after the tribe from South Africa and Zimbabwe that has maintained the customs and language of its Zulu ancestors—is ideally placed for a snack before a trip to the Cameo cinema opposite. The large selection of interesting sandwiches on a choice of breads, the tasty *boerewors* (South African sausage), or smoked ostrich can be eaten on the spot or ordered out. There's also a large selection of deli products for sale, including *biltong* (strips of cured, air-dried meat). African art hangs on the wood-paneled, geometric-patterned walls in bright shades of purple and orange. ✉ *57 Home St., Tollcross,* ☏ *0131/221–1141. No credit cards.*

Indian

£ ✕ **Kalpna.** The unremarkable facade of this vegetarian Indian restau-
★ rant, amid an ordinary row of shops, and the low-key interior, enlivened by Indian prints and fabric pictures, belie the food—unlike anything you are likely to encounter elsewhere in the city. *Dam aloo Kashmiri* is a medium-spicy potato dish with a sauce made from honey, pistachios, and almonds. *Bangan mirch masala* is spicier, with eggplant and red chili peppers. For the unsure palate, a lunchtime buffet allows you to pick and mix for only £5 and to do it again on Wednesday evening for £8.95. ✉ *2–3 St. Patricks Sq., South Side,* ☏ *0131/667–9890. MC, V. Closed Sun. except in summer.*

Scottish

££–£££ ✕ **Howie's.** This chain consists of lively neighborhood bistros, all fun but each with its own character. The steaks are tender Aberdeen beef, and the Loch Fyne herring is sweet-cured to Howie's own recipe. All five restaurants are licensed, but you can bring your own bottle if you want to. ✉ *29 Waterloo Pl., East End,* ☏ *0131/556–5766;* ✉ *10–14 Victoria Street, Old Town,* ☏ *0131/225–1271;* ✉ *208 Bruntsfield Pl., Bruntsfield,* ☏ *0131/221–1777;* ✉ *63 Dalry Rd., Fountainbridge,* ☏ *0131/313–3334. AE, MC, V. No lunch Mon. at Dalry Rd. location.*

Leith

French

£££ ✕ **Martin Wishart.** Slightly out of town but worth every penny of the
★ taxi fare, this rising culinary star woos diners with an impeccable and varied menu of French-influenced and beautifully presented dishes. Terrine of foie gras, compote of Agen prunes, and sole Murat (glazed fillet of lemon sole with baby onions, artichoke, parsley, and lemon) with *pommes en cocotte* (potatoes cooked in a casserole) typify the cuisine served here. This intimate and contemporary restaurant nestles mod-

estly on the shore of the Water of Leith. Reservations are essential on
weekends. ⊠ *54 The Shore, Leith,* ☎ *0131/553–3557. MC, V. Closed
Sun.–Mon. No lunch Sat.*

££–£££ ✗ **Malmaison Café Bar and Brasserie.** Freshly made soups, crunchy
salads, inventive sandwiches (try the roasted red pepper and pesto),
and gooey pastries are the choices in this eatery, part of the stylish Malmaison Hotel in Edinburgh's rejuvenated dockside area. Extremely popular are the Malmaison fish cakes with chips, buttered spinach, and
parsley sauce. If you fancy something more substantial (and more expensive), try the Brasserie, which serves traditional French and modern British cuisine. ⊠ *1 Tower Pl., Leith,* ☎ *0131/555–6868.
Reservations essential at Brasserie. AE, DC, MC, V.*

Pan-Asian

££ ✗ **Britannia Spice.** A few hundred yards from the former Royal Yacht
from which it gets its name, this restaurant is a good place to recover
from the Ocean Terminal shopping experience. Britannia Spice serves
a large selection of dishes from India, Bangladesh, Thailand, and
Nepal. Try the Thai beef or the Nepalese trout with vegetables and green
chilies. The waitstaff is friendly and attentive. ⊠ *150 Commercial St.,
Britannia Way, Leith,* ☎ *0131/555–2255. AE, DC, MC, V.*

Seafood

££–£££ ✗ **Fishers Bistro.** Both locals and visitors flock to this laid-back pub-
cum-bistro down on the waterfront in Leith. Bar meals are served, but
for more comfort and elegance sit in the cozy green-walled dining room.
Seafood is a specialty—the Loch Fyne oysters are wonderful. Watch
the blackboard for the daily special, perhaps spicy sweet-potato and
turnip soup followed by seared swordfish steak with sweet chili-pepper sauce. The staff is friendly and efficient. It's a good idea to reserve
ahead for the bistro. ⊠ *1 The Shore, Leith,* ☎ *0131/554–5666. AE,
DC, MC, V.*

££–£££ ✗ **Skippers Bistro.** Don't miss this superb seafood restaurant, tucked
away in a corner of Leith. It has a traditional, snug, cluttered interior,
with dark wood, shining brass, and lots of pictures and seafaring
ephemera. For a starter, try traditional *Cullen skink,* a creamy fish soup
full of surprises. Main dishes change daily but might include halibut,
salmon, monkfish, or sea bass in delicious sauces. ⊠ *1A Dock Pl., Leith,*
☎ *0131/554–1018. Reservations essential. AE, MC, V. No dinner Sun.*

LODGING

It used to be that Scottish hotels were considered either rather better
or much worse than their English counterparts; the good ones were
very good, and the bad ones horrid. Today these distinctions no longer
exist, and Scotland's capital has a large selection of delightful hotel accommodations. The inexpensive Scottish hotel, once reviled, is now at
least the equal of anything that might be found in England. If you're
planning to stay in Edinburgh during the annual summer arts festival,
be sure to reserve several months in advance. Also note that weekend
rates in the larger hotels are always much cheaper than midweek rates,
so if you want to stay in a plush hotel, come on the weekend.

CATEGORY	COST*
££££	over £170
£££	£120–£170
££	£70–£120
£	under £70

*All prices are for a standard double room, including service, breakfast, and
VAT.*

Old Town

££££   🖪 **The Scotsman.** When the *Scotsman* newspaper moved from these
★   premises in 1999, it left behind a magnificent turn-of-the-20th-century
gray sandstone building, with a marble staircase and a fascinating social history. A modern, luxurious hotel has been created within the shell
of the old structure. Dark wood, earthy colors, tweeds, and contemporary furnishings decorate the guest rooms and public spaces. ✉ *20
N. Bridge, Old Town, EH1 1YT,* ☎ *0131/556–5565,* FAX *0131/652–3652,*
WEB *www.thescotsmanhotelgroup.co.uk. 56 rooms, 12 suites. 2 restaurants, indoor pool, health club, spa, bar, nightclub, meeting rooms. AE,
DC, MC, V.*

£££–££££   🖪 **Crowne Plaza.** Although it was built late in the 1980s, this central
modern hotel blends into its surroundings among the ancient buildings on the Royal Mile. Guest rooms are spacious, neat, and plain—
practical rather than luxurious. ✉ *80 High St., Royal Mile, Old
Town EH1 1TH,* ☎ *0131/557–9797,* FAX *0131/557–9789,* WEB
*www.crowneplazaed.co.uk. 238 rooms. Restaurant, indoor pool, health
club, meeting rooms, parking (fee). AE, DC, MC, V.*

New Town

££££   🖪 **Balmoral Hotel.** The attention to detail in the elegant rooms and the
★   sheer élan of a re-created Edwardian heyday contribute to the popularity of this grand former railroad hotel. Staying here, below the impressive clock tower marking the east end of Princes Street, gives you
a strong sense of being at the center of Edinburgh life. The hotel's main
restaurant is the plush and stylish Number One, serving the best of Scottish seafood and game. ✉ *1 Princes St., East End, EH2 2EQ,* ☎
0131/556–2414, FAX *0131/557–3747,* WEB *www.roccofortehotels.com.
168 rooms, 2 suites. 2 restaurants, in-room data ports, indoor pool,
health club, hair salon, bar, parking (fee). AE, DC, MC, V.*

££££   🖪 **The Howard.** The Howard, close to Drummond Place, is a classic
★   New Town building, elegant and superbly proportioned. It's also small
enough to offer personal attention. You'll like it if you enjoy a swank
private-club atmosphere. Antiques and original works of art fill the spacious guest rooms, some of which overlook the garden. ✉ *34 Great
King St., New Town, EH3 6QH,* ☎ *0131/557–3500,* FAX *0131/557–
6515,* WEB *www.thehoward.com. 19 rooms. Restaurant, free parking;
no a/c. AE, DC, MC, V.*

£££–££££   🖪 **Caledonian Hilton Hotel.** "The Caley," a conspicuous block of red
★   sandstone beyond the west end of West Princes Street Gardens, was
built between 1898 and 1902 as the flagship hotel of the Caledonian
Railway, and its imposing Victorian decor has been faithfully preserved. The public area has marbled green columns and an ornate stair-
well with a burnished-metalwork balustrade. Rooms are exceptionally
large and well appointed, and the generous width of the corridors testifies that this establishment was designed in a more sumptuous age.
✉ *Princes St., West End, EH1 2AB,* ☎ *0131/222–8888,* FAX *0131/225–
6632,* WEB *www.hilton.com. 249 rooms. 2 restaurants, cable TV, meeting rooms, parking (fee). AE, DC, MC, V.*

££   🖪 **17 Abercromby Place.** Shuttered windows and antique furniture and
★   rugs (some used as wall hangings) characterize the decor of this Georgian terraced house with stunning views from the top-floor rooms. This
B&B sets a high standard, with a host who enjoys meeting guests and
can be a very helpful guide. Dinner can be provided by prior arrangement. This house is unusual for the area, in that it has parking spaces
for seven cars. ✉ *17 Abercromby Pl., New Town, EH3 6LB,* ☎ *0131/
557–8036,* FAX *0131/558–3453,* WEB *www.abercrombyhouse.com. 9*

rooms. *Dining room, in-room data ports, refrigerators, cable TV, free parking; no a/c. MC, V.*

£–££ 🏠 **Ardmor House.** A relaxed and comfortable guest house combines the original features of a Victorian home with contemporary furnishings. Rooms are fresh and modern, with an occasional carefully chosen antique. The friendly owners, Robin and Colin, extend a warm welcome to both gay and straight visitors. They'll indulge your every whim, and they offer a thoroughly efficient concierge service with a twist—lots of personal opinions and recommendations thrown in. ⊠ *74 Pilrig St., Pilrig, EH6 5AS,* ☎ FAX *0131/554–4944,* WEB *www. ardmorhouse.freeserve.co.uk. 5 rooms. Dining room, some pets allowed; no a/c. MC, V.*

£–££ 🏠 **Gloria's Place.** This luxurious Georgian B&B is a 10-minute walk from the city center. The bedrooms are well equipped, with direct-dial phones and laptop computer outlets, and the comfortable sitting room has a wall of books. ⊠ *20 London St., New Town, EH3 6NA,* ☎ *0131/ 557–0216,* FAX *0131/315–3375,* WEB *www.scotland.org. 3 rooms. In-room data ports, some pets allowed; no a/c, no smoking. AE, MC, V.*

£–££ 🏠 **Stuart House.** A Victorian terraced house with some fine plaster-
★   work houses this B&B, just a 15-minute walk from the city center. The decor suits the structure: bold colors, floral fabrics, and generously curtained windows combine with antique and traditional-style furniture and chandeliers to create an opulent interior. ⊠ *12 E. Claremont St., Canonmills, EH7 4JP,* ☎ *0131/557–9030,* FAX *0131/557–0563,* WEB *www. stuartguesthouse.co.uk. 7 rooms. Some pets allowed; no a/c, no smoking. AE, DC, MC, V.*

Haymarket

£££–££££ 🏨 **Hilton Edinburgh Grosvenor Hotel.** Several terrace houses have been converted into this attractive, comfortable hotel, distinguished by an elegant Victorian facade. From the moment you enter the large reception area, furnished with ample Chesterfield armchairs, you'll be pampered. The single rooms are fairly small, and the doubles are just adequate. Bright peach curtains, floral bedspreads, and dark-wood furniture decorate the rooms. First- and second-floor bedrooms have high ceilings with attractive plaster cornices. Just a short walk from the West End's shopping district, the hotel is also convenient to Haymarket railway station. ⊠ *Grosvenor St., Haymarket, EH12 5EF,* ☎ *0131/226–6001,* FAX *0131/220–2387,* WEB *www.hilton.com. 189 rooms. Restaurant, 2 bars, meeting rooms. AE, DC, MC, V.*

£–££ 🏨 **Lodge Hotel.** Spacious rooms at this detached Georgian stone house
★   are furnished in period style, with swagged curtains and canopy beds, and are stocked with fresh flowers and fruit as well as a decanter of sherry. Downstairs, you can relax at the cocktail bar and peaceful gold-and-blue sitting room. The dining room has well-spaced tables covered with crisp white cloths and a menu heavy on fresh Scottish produce. The hotel, a 15-minute walk from Princes Street, is easy to find on the main A8 Edinburgh–Glasgow road. ⊠ *6 Hampton Terr., West Coates, Haymarket, EH12 5JD,* ☎ *0131/337–3682,* FAX *0131/ 313–1700,* WEB *www.thelodgehotel.co.uk. 11 rooms. Dining room; no a/c, no smoking. AE, DC, MC V.*

West End and Points West

££££ 🏨 **Sheraton Grand.** Beyond the reception area and sweeping grand staircase, you'll find the guest rooms, which are well above average size. Many are traditionally decorated, with tartan furnishings and prints of old Edinburgh. The grandest rooms face the castle. This property has two fine restaurants: the brasserie-style Terrace, overlooking

Edinburgh Castle and Festival Square, and the intimate Grill Room, serving fine fish, game, and Scottish beef. The hotel is popular with locals, especially after work and in the evening before and after concerts at Usher Hall. ⊠ *1 Festival Sq., Lothian Rd., West End, EH3 9SR,* ☎ *0131/229–9131,* FAX *0131/228–4510,* WEB *www.sheraton.com. 260 rooms. 2 restaurants, indoor pool, gym, spa, bar, meeting rooms, free parking. AE, DC, MC, V.*

£££–££££ 🖪 **The Bonham.** This contemporary hotel in a traditional town-house space boldly mixes sleek design with state-of-the-art business accommodation. Beyond unassuming white hallways, each room is done in a unique minimalist concept, with modern pieces from local artists, geometric furnishings, and attractive lighting. The modern restaurant—in chic unadorned style with oversize mirrors and a central catwalk of light—serves Scottish specialties with Californian twists. The service at the hotel is thorough, yet unobtrusive. ⊠ *35 Drumsheugh Gardens, West End, EH3 7RN,* ☎ *0131/226–6050; 0131/623–6060 reservations,* FAX *0131/226–6080,* WEB *www.thebonham.com. 50 rooms. Restaurant, in-room data ports, meeting rooms. AE, DC, MC, V.*

£££–££££ 🖪 **Channings.** Five Edwardian terraced town houses make up this in-
★ timate, elegant hotel in an upscale West End neighborhood just minutes from Princes Street. Beyond the clubby, oak-paneled lobby lounge are the quiet guest rooms, with restrained colors, antiques, marble baths, and great views of Fife (from those facing north), setting a stylish, refined tone. The Brasserie offers excellent value in traditional Scottish and Continental cooking, especially at lunchtime; try the hot smoked salmon with coriander and saffron risotto. ⊠ *12–16 S. Learmonth Gardens, West End, EH4 1EZ,* ☎ *0131/315–2226 or 0131/332–3232,* FAX *0131/332–9631,* WEB *www.channings.co.uk. 46 rooms. 2 restaurants, lobby lounge, meeting rooms. AE, DC, MC, V.*

££ 🖪 **16 Lynedoch Place.** You'll find considerate hosts in Andrew and Susie Hamilton (and Gertrude, the lovable dog), who have opened up their beautiful Georgian terraced house as a B&B, a five-minute walk from the center of town. Rosy pinks, cool yellows, terra-cotta oranges, and floral patterns decorate the tasteful rooms. Susie goes all out for breakfast, which is served in a magnificent hunter green dining room with antiques and family pictures. In a pinch, they will open up two of the guest rooms upstairs for a family. ⊠ *16 Lynedoch Pl., West End, EH3 7PY,* ☎ *0131/225–5507,* FAX *0131/226–4185,* WEB *www. 16lynedochplace.co.uk. 3 rooms. Dining room, library, free parking; no a/c, no smoking. MC, V.*

££ 🖪 **22 Murrayfield Gardens.** A handsome stone house in an upscale res-
★ idential area called Murrayfield, this is an impressive B&B on all counts, with particularly friendly owners. Warm yellows decorate the elegant first-floor lounge, the sunny dining room, and the bedrooms. With prior notice, dinner will be provided. There's easy parking in this neighborhood, and it's only a 10-minute bus ride from downtown. ⊠ *22 Murrayfield Gardens, Murrayfield, EH12 6DF,* ☎ *0131/337–3569,* FAX *0131/337–3803,* WEB *www.number22.co.uk. 3 rooms. Dining room, free parking; no a/c. MC, V. Closed during Christmas and 2 wks in Feb.*

£–££ 🖪 **Kew House and Apartments.** This establishment is about as sump-
★ tuous as a guest house can be without being classified a full-service hotel. Inside the elegant terrace, dating from 1860, are six tastefully modernized rooms with all the usual luxuries—hair dryer, pants press, and fresh flowers—plus chocolates, shortbread, and a decanter of sherry on arrival. There is also, unusual for a guest house, a bar and a restaurant. It's a 15-minute stroll from the center of town. ⊠ *1 Kew Terr., New Town, EH12 5JE,* ☎ *0131/313–0700,* FAX *0131/313–0747. 6 rooms, 2 apartments. Restaurant, bar, free parking; no a/c, no smoking. AE, DC, MC, V.*

£ ⊞ **Crannoch But & Ben.** This tip-top B&B offers private baths, a comfortable lounge, and good hearty breakfasts. Only 3 mi from the city and on a good bus route, it's also particularly convenient for the airport. ⊠ *467 Queensferry Rd., Barnton, EH4 7ND,* ☎ *0131/336–5688. 2 rooms. Free parking; no a/c, no smoking. MC, V.*

South Side

££ ⊞ **Ashdene House.** On a quiet residential street on the South Side, only 10 minutes from the city center by bus, sits this Edwardian house, a first-class B&B. Country-style reproduction pine furniture and vividly colored fabrics decorate the guest rooms. In the downstairs public areas, turn-of-the-20th-century shades of pink complement the age of the house. The owners are particularly helpful in arranging tours and evening theater entertainment, and they will recommend local restaurants. There's ample parking on the street and in a nearby lot. ⊠ *23 Fountainhall Rd., Sciennes, EH9 2LN,* ☎ *0131/667–6026,* WEB *welcome.to/ashdene_house. 5 rooms. Free parking; no a/c, no smoking. MC, V.*

££ ⊞ **Roslea House.** "A touch of tartan" and bold colors decorate this Victorian B&B guest house. After a tough day of sightseeing, you can unwind in the sitting room. On the main route from the south, the Roselea is easy to find. ⊠ *11 Mayfield Rd., Sciennes, EH9 2NG,* ☎ *0131/ 667–6115,* FAX *0131/667–3556,* WEB *www.roselea-guesthouse.com. 5 rooms. Dining room, free parking; no a/c. AE, MC, V.*

£–££ ⊞ **Classic Guest House.** Stripped pine floors throughout, elegant chinoiserie in the dining room, and pastel florals in the warm bedrooms fill the modern classic interior of this Victorian terraced house. Note that three of the four rooms have en suite showers only. It's easy to find this guest house, on a main route into Edinburgh from the south. ⊠ *50 Mayfield Rd., Sciennes, EH9 2NH,* ☎ *0131/667–5847,* FAX *0131/662–1016. 4 rooms. Dining room; no a/c, no smoking. MC, V.*

£–££ ⊞ **Ellesmere Guest House.** The first-class rooms in this Victorian terraced house have modern furniture with pleasant pastel floral bedspreads and curtains; one room has a four-poster bed. You can relax in the comfortable sitting room, but the owners prefer that you not smoke there. Ellesmere sits close to the King's Theatre and several good restaurants, and the place is stocked with brochures covering things to do in Edinburgh. ⊠ *11 Glengyle Terr., Tollcross, EH3 9LN,* ☎ *0131/229–4823,* FAX *0131/229–5285,* WEB *www.edinburghbandb.co.uk. 6 rooms. No a/c. No credit cards.*

£–££ ⊞ **Thrums Private Hotel.** There is a pleasing mix of the modern and traditional in this detached Georgian house. It's small, cozy, and quiet, yet surprisingly close to downtown—handy for walks in Holyrood Park and perhaps an ascent of Arthur's Seat. The family that runs the hotel is very welcoming and more than willing to advise you on what to see and do in and around Edinburgh. ⊠ *14–15 Minto St., Newington, EH9 1RQ,* ☎ *0131/667–5545,* FAX *0131/667–8707. 15 rooms. Restaurant, bar, free parking, some pets allowed; no a/c. MC, V.*

£ ⊞ **Teviotdale House.** The friendly Thiebauds are the hosts at this small family-run and -owned hotel, and the house is a warm retreat on a tree-lined street away from but within reach of city-center bustle (a 10-minute bus ride). Individually decorated rooms and innovative, appetizing home cooking for breakfast make this a pleasant, reasonable budget alternative to city-center hotels. Note that six of the rooms have showers, but no bathtubs. ⊠ *53 Grange Loan, Sciennes, EH9 2ER,* ☎ *0131/ 667–4376,* FAX *0131/667–4763. 7 rooms. Dining room; no a/c, no smoking. AE, MC, V.*

£ ⊞ **Turret Guest House.** Cheerful and cozy, this B&B has modern furnishings, but many of the building's Victorian cornices, paneled doors, and high ceilings remain, and one of the rooms has a four-poster bed. On a quiet residential street on the South Side, it's close to bus routes as well as the Commonwealth Pool and Holyrood Park. ⊠ *8 Kilmaurs Terr., Prestonfield, EH16 5DR,* ☎ *0131/667–6704,* FAX *0131/668–1368,* WEB *www.turret.clara.net. 7 rooms, 5 with bath. Dining room; no a/c. MC, V.*

Leith

££–£££   🏨 **Malmaison.** Once a seamen's hostel, the Malmaison, in the heart of Leith, now has good-value yet stylish digs only 10 minutes by bus from the city center. A dramatic black, cream, and taupe color scheme prevails in the public areas. King-size beds, CD players, and satellite TV are standard in all bedrooms, which are decorated in a bold, modern style. The French theme of the hotel, sister to the Malmaison in Glasgow, is emphasized in the Café Bar and Brasserie, which serves all day. ⊠ *1 Tower Pl., Leith, EH6 7DB,* ☎ *0131/468–5000,* FAX *0131/468–5002. 60 rooms. Restaurant, café, cable TV, bar, free parking. AE, DC, MC, V.*

NIGHTLIFE AND THE ARTS

The Arts

To those who think Edinburgh's arts scene consists of just the elegiac wail of a bagpipe and the twang of a fiddle or two, hundreds of performing arts options will prove them wrong. The jewel in the crown, of course, is the famed Edinburgh International Festival of Music, Drama, and Art, which now attracts the best in music, dance, theater, painting, and sculpture from all over the globe during three weeks from mid-August to early September.

The *List,* available from newsstands throughout the city, and the *Day by Day Guide* and *Events 2003* available from the **Edinburgh and Scotland Information Centre** (⊠ 3 Princes St., East End, ☎ 0131/473–3800, WEB www.edinburgh.org), carry the most up-to-date details about cultural events. The *Herald* and *Scotsman,* Scotland's leading daily newspapers, also carry listings and reviews in their arts pages every day, with special editions during the festival. Tickets are generally available from box offices in advance; in some cases they are also available from certain designated travel agents or at the door, although concerts by national orchestras often sell out long before the day of the performance.

Dance

Edinburgh has no ballet or modern dance companies of its own, but visiting companies perform from time to time at the Festival Theatre or Royal Lyceum.

Festivals

The **Edinburgh International Festival** (⊠ The Hub, Edinburgh Festival Centre, Castlehill, Old Town, EH1 2NE, ☎ 0131/473–2099 for information; 0131/473–2000 for tickets, FAX 0131/473–2003, WEB www.eif.co.uk), the premier arts event of the year and the biggest arts festival in the world, has since 1947 attracted performing artists of international caliber to a celebration of music, dance, drama, and artwork. The festival runs from mid-August to the beginning of September.

The **Edinburgh Festival Fringe** (⊠ Edinburgh Festival Fringe Office, 180 High St., Old Town, EH1 1QS, ☎ 0131/226–5257 for information; 0131/226–0026 during festival only, FAX 0131/226–0016, WEB www.edfringe.com) presents many theatrical and musical events, some by amateur groups (you have been warned), and is more of a grab bag than the official festival. During festival time—roughly the same as the International Festival—it's possible to arrange your own entertainment program from morning to midnight and beyond, if you don't feel overwhelmed by the variety available.

The **Edinburgh International Film Festival** (✉ Edinburgh Film Festival Office, at the Filmhouse, 88 Lothian Rd., West End, EH3 9BZ, ☎ 0131/228–4051, FAX 0131/229–5501, WEB www.edfilmfest.org.uk) is yet another aspect of the busy summer festival logjam in Edinburgh.

The **Edinburgh Military Tattoo** (✉ Edinburgh Military Tattoo Office, 32 Market St., Old Town, EH1 1QB, ☎ 0131/225–1188, FAX 0131/225–8627, WEB www.edintattoo.co.uk) may not be art, but it is certainly entertainment. It's sometimes confused with the festival itself, partly because the dates overlap. This celebration of martial music and skills with bands, gymnastics, and stunt motorcycle teams is set on the castle esplanade, and the dramatic backdrop augments the spectacle. Dress warmly for late-evening performances. Even if it rains, the show most definitely goes on.

Jazz enthusiasts delight in the August **International Jazz Festival** (✉ 29 St. Stephen St., Stockbridge, EH3 5AN, ☎ 0131/467–5200), which attracts international top performers and brings local enthusiasts out of their living rooms and into the pubs and clubs to listen and play.

The **Edinburgh International Science Festival** (for information: ✉ Roxburgh's Court, off 323 High St., Edinburgh EH1 1PW, ☎ 0131/473–2070, WEB www.sciencefestival.co.uk; tickets: ✉ The Hub, Castlehill, Edinburgh EH1 2NE), held around Easter each year, aims to make science accessible, interesting, but above all fun. Children's events turn science into entertainment and are especially popular.

Film

Apart from cinema chains, Edinburgh has the excellent three-screen **Filmhouse** (✉ 88 Lothian Rd., West End, ☎ 0131/228–2688 box office), the best venue for modern, foreign-language, offbeat, or simply less-commercial films. Its diverse monthly program is available from the box office and at several other locations throughout the city (at the Tourist Centre, for example, or in theater lobbies).

The **Cameo** (✉ 38 Home St., Tollcross, ☎ 0131/228–4141) has three extremely comfortable theaters, a bar, and late-night specials. The family-owned and -run **Dominion** (✉ Newbattle Terr., Morningside, ☎ 0131/447–4771) is a pleasant alternative to the larger commercial cinemas.

Music

The **Festival Theatre** (✉ 13–29 Nicolson St., Old Town, ☎ 0131/529–6000) hosts ballet, opera, and concerts, including performances by the Royal Scottish National Orchestra in season. The **Playhouse** (✉ Greenside Pl., East End, ☎ 0870/606–3424) leans toward popular artists and musicals. The intimate **Queen's Hall** (✉ Clerk St., Old Town, ☎ 0131/668–2019) hosts small recitals. **Usher Hall** (✉ Lothian Rd., East End, ☎ 0131/228–1155) is Edinburgh's grandest venue, and international performers and orchestras, including the Royal Scottish National Orchestra, perform here.

Theater

MODERN

The **Netherbow Arts Centre** (✉ 43 High St., Old Town, ☎ 0131/556–9579) includes modern plays in its program of music, drama, and cabaret. The **Theatre Workshop** (✉ 34 Hamilton Pl., Stockbridge, ☎ 0131/226–

5425) hosts fringe events during the Edinburgh Festival and modern, community-based theater year-round. The **Traverse Theatre** (✉ 10 Cambridge St., Old Town, ☎ 0131/228–1404) has developed a solid reputation for new, stimulating Scottish plays, performed in a specially designed flexible space.

TRADITIONAL

Edinburgh has three main theaters. The **Festival Theatre** (✉ 13–29 Nicolson St., Old Town, ☎ 0131/529–6000) presents opera and ballet, along with the occasional excellent tour. The **King's** (✉ 2 Leven St., Tollcross, ☎ 0131/529–6000) has a program of contemporary and traditional dramatic works. The **Royal Lyceum** (✉ Grindlay St., Old Town, ☎ 0131/248–4848) shows traditional plays and contemporary works, often transferred from or prior to their London West End showings.

At Musselburgh, on the eastern outskirts of Edinburgh, the **Brunton Theatre** (✉ Ladywell Way, Musselburgh, ☎ 0131/665–2240) presents a regular program of repertory, touring, and amateur performances. At the **Church Hill Theatre** (✉ Morningside Rd., Morningside, ☎ 0131/447–0111), local dramatic societies mount productions of a high standard. The **Playhouse** (✉ Greenside Pl., East End, ☎ 0870/606–3424) hosts mostly popular artists and musicals.

Nightlife

The **Edinburgh and Scotland Information Centre** (✉ 3 Princes St., East End, ☎ 0131/473–3800, WEB www.edinburgh.org), above Princes Mall, can supply information on various types of nightlife, especially on spots hosting dinner dances. The *List*, available from newsstands throughout the city, provides information on the music scene.

Bars and Pubs

Edinburgh's 400-odd pubs are a study in themselves. In the eastern and northern districts of the city you'll find some grim, inhospitable-looking places that proclaim that drinking is no laughing matter. But throughout Edinburgh many pubs have deliberately traded in their old spit-and-sawdust images for atmospheric revivals of the warm, oak-paneled, leather-chaired *howffs* of a more leisurely age. Most pubs and bars are open weekdays and Saturday from 11 AM to midnight, and from 12:30 to midnight on Sunday.

OLD TOWN

Stop in at **Deacon Brodie's Pub** (✉ 435 Lawnmarket, Old Town, ☎ 0131/225–6531), named for the infamous criminal who may have inspired Robert Louis Stevenson's *Strange Case of Dr. Jekyll and Mr. Hyde,* for a traditional pub meal or a pint.

NEW TOWN

Abbotsford (✉ 3 Rose St., New Town, ☎ 0131/225–1894) has an ever-changing selection of five real ales, bar lunches, and lots of Victorian atmosphere. **Cask and Barrel** (✉ 115 Broughton St., New Town, ☎ 0131/556–3132) is a spacious, busy pub in which to sample hand-pulled ales at the horseshoe bar, reflected in a collection of brewery mirrors. **Cumberland Bar** (✉ 1–3 Cumberland St., New Town, ☎ 0131/558–3134) has 11 ales on tap, wood trim, typical pub mirrors, and a comfy sitting room. **80 Queen Street** (✉ 80 Queen St., New Town, ☎ 0131/538–8111), with cozy dark-wood booths and a muted color scheme, is just the place for soup-and-sandwich lunches with a pint of draft beer.

Guildford Arms (✉ 1 W. Register St., east end of Princes St., New Town, ☎ 0131/556–4312) is worth a visit for its interior alone: ornate plasterwork, cornices, friezes, and wood paneling form the backdrop for some excellent draft ales, including Orkney Dark Island. **Harry's Bar** (✉ 7B Randolph Pl., New Town, ☎ 0131/539–8100), an Americana-decorated basement bar with disco music, is hugely popular with locals. **Kay's Bar** (✉ 39 Jamaica St., New Town, ☎ 0131/225–1858), a friendly, comfortable New Town spot, is a good place for a bar lunch. Don't miss the selection of 50 single-malt whiskies in addition to the real ales on draft. **Milne's Bar** (✉ 35 Hanover St., New Town, ☎ 0131/225–6738) is known as the poets' pub because of its popularity with the Edinburgh literati. Pies and baked potatoes go well with seven real ales and varying guest beers (beers not of the house brewery). Victorian advertisements and photos of old Edinburgh give the place an old-time feel.

Standing Order (✉ 62–66 George St., New Town, ☎ 0131/225–4460), in a former banking hall with a magnificent painted-plasterwork ceiling, is one of the popular and expanding J. D. Wetherspoon chain of pubs, priding itself on friendly, music-free watering holes with cheap beer and ample nonsmoking areas—you can even lounge on leather sofas. **Tiles** (✉ 1 St. Andrew Sq., New Town, ☎ 0131/558–1507), which is closed Sunday, in a converted banking hall, gets its name from the wealth of tiles covering the walls, which are topped by elaborate plasterwork. The large selection of real ales complements a choice of bar meals or a table d'hôte menu specializing in fresh Scottish poultry, game, and fish. Sip a martini or cosmopolitan at **Tonic** (✉ 34A Castle St., New Town, ☎ 0131/225–6431), one of Edinburgh's reliable cocktail bars. This is a stylish basement bar with bouncy stools and comfy sofas, pale wood, and chrome.

WEST END

Cloisters (✉ 26 Brougham St., Tollcross, West End, ☎ 0131/221–9997), a West End pub, prides itself on the absence of music, gaming machines, and any other modern pub gimmicks; it specializes instead in real ales, malt whiskies, and good food, all at reasonable prices.

SOUTH SIDE

Leslie's Bar (✉ 45 Ratcliffe Terr., South Side, ☎ 0131/667–7205) is convenient to the hotels and guest houses of Newington, with superb Victorian decor in its small saloon and public bars. **Southsider** (✉ 3–7 W. Richmond St., South Side, ☎ 0131/667–2003), convenient to the antiques and junk shops of Causewayside, is a busy, sometimes smoky bar popular with locals and students.

LEITH

The 260-year-old **Malt and Hops** (✉ 45 The Shore, Leith, ☎ 0131/555–0083), with its own ghost and a choice of real ales, overlooks the waterfront down in Leith.

Casinos

The following casinos are private, but membership can be granted with 24 hours' notice. All have American roulette, poker, blackjack, and slot machines and are open from afternoon or evening to the wee hours of the morning. You must be at least 18 years old to enter. **Stanley Berkeley** (✉ 2 Rutland Pl., West End, ☎ 0131/228–4446). **Stanley Edinburgh** (✉ 5B York Pl., New Town, ☎ 0131/624–2121). **Stanley Martell** (✉ 7 Newington Rd., Newington, ☎ 0131/667–7763).

Ladbrokes Maybury Casino (✉ 5 S. Maybury Rd., Corstorphine, ☎ 0131/338–4444) has a highly rated restaurant in addition to gaming tables.

Ceilidhs and Scottish Evenings

For those who feel a trip to Scotland is not complete without hearing the "Braes of Yarrow" or "Auld Robin Gray," several hotels present traditional Scottish-music evenings in the summer season, including the **Carlton Highland Hotel** (✉ North Bridge, Old Town, ☎ 0131/556–7277). The **Edinburgh Thistle Hotel** (✉ Leith St., New Town, ☎ 0131/556–0111) produces Jamie's Scottish Evening.

Try **The Caledonian Brewery** (✉ 42 Slateford Rd., Dalry, ☎ 0131/623–8066) for foot-stomping fun. The brewery organizes about three ceilidhs per month, with loads of space and plenty of beer.

Folk Clubs

You can usually find folk musicians performing in various pubs throughout Edinburgh, although of late there's been a decline in the live music scene because of dwindling profits and the predominance of popular theme bars. The **Ensign Ewart** (✉ 521 Lawnmarket, Old Town, ☎ 0131/226–1928), by the castle, is a cozy, intimate pub with live folk music most nights. The **Tron** (✉ Hunter Sq., Old Town, ☎ 0131/220–1591) is well known for its performances of folk music. For a bit of *wellie* (volume, energy) put your head round the door of **Whistle Binkies Pub** (✉ 4–6 Niddry St., Old Town, ☎ 0131/557–5114), a friendly basement bar with great music.

Nightclubs

For the young and footloose, many Edinburgh dance clubs offer reduced admission and/or less expensive drinks for early revelers. Consult the *List* for special events.

L'Attaché Nightclub (✉ Beneath the Rutland Hotel, 3 Rutland St., West End, ☎ 0131/229–3402), which is open Friday and Saturday, has DJs spinning mainstream sounds from the '60s through the '90s. **CC Blooms** (✉ 23 Greenside Pl., East End, ☎ 0131/556–9331) is a popular gay club. The well-liked **Club Mercado** (✉ 36–39 Market St., Old Town, ☎ 0131/226–4224) has theme nights covering the full spectrum of musical sounds; it's open Friday through Sunday. The **Honeycomb** (✉ 36–38 Blair St., off High St., Old Town, ☎ 0131/220–4381), a hot spot with a live DJ, gets a mixed gay and straight crowd; it's open Friday through Sunday. The **Opal Lounge** (✉ 51a George St., New Town, ☎ 0131/226–2275), a casual but stylish nightspot, evolves by a subtle change of mood and lighting from a restaurant to a club for drinks and dancing to soul or funk. **Po Na Na Souk Bar** (✉ 43B Frederick St., New Town, ☎ 0131/226–2224) is a dance club where you can hear yourself think and where the ages range from teens to people who could be their parents. Laid-back yet very slickly run, the place gets rather crowded on weekend evenings. The **Venue** (✉ 15–21 Calton Rd., New Town, ☎ 0131/557–3073) blares varying beats, including techno and progressive house.

OUTDOOR ACTIVITIES AND SPORTS

Participant Sports

Biking

Rates in summer are about £50 per week for up to a 21-speed and £60 for a mountain bike. You can rent bicycles through **Bike Trax** (✉ 13 Lochrin Pl., Tollcross, ☎ 0131/228–6333). **Recycling** (✉ 276 Leith Walk, Leith, ☎ 0131/553–1130) runs a sell-and-buy-back scheme for extended periods (say, more than two weeks), which can save you money, and also has especially good deals on weekly rates.

Golf

For the courses listed below, *SSS* indicates the "standard scratch score," or average score.

The Scottish Tourist Board provides a free leaflet on golf in Scotland, available from the **Edinburgh and Scotland Information Centre** (✉ 3 Princes St., East End, ☎ 0131/473–3800, WEB www.edinburgh.org).

Braids (✉ Braids Hill Rd., Braidburn, 3 mi south of city, ☎ 0131/447–6666): Course 1, 18 holes, 5,865 yards, SSS 67; Course 2, 18 holes, 4,744 yards, SSS 63. **Bruntsfield Links** (✉ 32 Barnton Ave., Davidson's Mains, 2 mi south of city, ☎ 0131/336–4050, FAX 0131/336–5538): 18 holes, 6,407 yards, SSS 71. **Craigentinny** (✉ Craigentinny Ave., Craigentinny, 3 mi east of city, ☎ 0131/554–7501): 18 holes, 5,407 yards, SSS 67. **Duddingston** (✉ Duddingston Rd. W, Duddingston, 4 mi east of city, ☎ FAX 0131/661–4301): 18 holes, 6,420 yards, SSS 71.

Liberton (✉ Kingston Grange, 297 Gilmerton Rd., Liberton, 4 mi south of city, ☎ 0131/664–8580, FAX 0131/666–0853): 18 holes, 5,412 yards, SSS 69. **Lothianburn** (✉ Biggar Rd., Fairmilehead, 6 mi south of city, ☎ 0131/445–5067): 18 holes, 5,568 yards, SSS 68. **Portobello** (✉ Stanley St., Portobello, 2 mi north of city, ☎ 0131/669–4361): 9 holes, 2,410 yards, SSS 32. **Silverknowes** (✉ Silverknowes Pkwy., Silverknowes, 4 mi northwest of city, ☎ 0131/336–3843): 18 holes, 6,210 yards, SSS 71. **Torphin Hill** (✉ Torphin Rd., Colinton, 3 mi west of city, ☎ 0131/441–1100): 18 holes, 4,580 yards, SSS 66.

Health Clubs

Some of the larger Edinburgh hotels have their own fitness centers. Most facilities are free to guests, though there may be a charge for snooker and squash. You can use the pool and gym for £8.50 a day at **Fitness First** (✉ 111 Glasgow Rd., Corstorphine, ☎ 0131/334–9191).

Running and Track Sports

At **Holyrood Park,** at almost any time of day or night, joggers run the circuit around Arthur's Seat. **Meadowbank Stadium** (✉ London Rd., Lochend, ☎ 0131/661–5351) has facilities for more than 30 track and indoor sports.

Skiing

Hillend (✉ Biggar Rd., Fairmilehead, ☎ 0131/445–4433), on the southern edge of the city, is the longest artificial ski slope in the United Kingdom—go either to ski (equipment can be rented on the spot) or to ride the chairlift, which costs £1.30, for fine city views. It's open year-round from 9:30 to 9 Monday through Saturday and from 9:30 to 7 on Sunday.

Swimming

The **Royal Commonwealth Pool** (✉ Dalkeith Rd., Prestonfield, ☎ 0131/667–7211), the largest swimming pool in the city, is part of a complex that includes a fitness center and a cafeteria. It costs £2.40–£5.80 to use the pool, and it's open daily 6–9:30.

Spectator Sports

Rugby

At Murrayfield Stadium, home of the **Scottish Rugby Union** (☎ 0131/346–5000), Scotland's international rugby matches are played in early spring. During that time of year, crowds of good-humored rugby fans from Ireland and Wales add greatly to the sense of excitement in the streets of Edinburgh.

Soccer

Like Glasgow, Edinburgh is soccer-mad, and there's an intense rivalry between the city's two professional teams. The **Heart of Midlothian Football Club ("Hearts")** plays in maroon and white and is based at Tynecastle (☎ 0131/200–7255). The green-bedecked **Hibernian ("Hibs")** club plays its home matches at Easter Road (☎ 0131/661–2159).

SHOPPING

Arcades and Shopping Centers

Like most large towns, Edinburgh has succumbed to the fashion for under-one-roof shopping. **Cameron Toll** shopping center (✉ Bottom of Dalkeith Rd., Mayfield), in the city's South Side, caters to local residents, with food stores and High Street brand names. If you don't want to be distracted by wonderful views between shops—or if it's raining— try the upscale **Princes Mall** (✉ East end of Princes St., East End), with a fast-food area, designer-label boutiques, and shops that sell Scottish woolens and tweeds, whisky, and confections. The **Ocean Terminal** (✉ Ocean Dr., Leith) houses a large collection of shops as well as bars and eateries. Here you can also visit the former royal yacht *Britannia*. The **St. James Centre** (✉ East end of Princes St., East End) has Dorothy Perkins, HMV, and numerous other chain stores. **South Gyle** (✉ On outskirts of city, off A720, near airport, Gyle) is based on a typical U.S.-style shopping mall. Here you'll find the usual High Street brand names, including a huge Marks & Spencer.

Department Stores

In contrast to other major cities, Edinburgh has few true department stores. If you plan on a morning or a whole day of wandering from department to department, trying on beautiful clothes, buying crystal or china, or stocking up on Scottish food specialties, with a break for lunch at an in-store restaurant, then Jenners is your best bet.

Aitken and Niven (✉ 77–79 George St., New Town, ☎ 0131/225–1461) is an Edinburgh institution: a small department store where the well-heeled come to buy upscale clothing, shoes, and accessories. **British Home Stores** (✉ 64 Princes St., East End, ☎ 0131/226–2621), also known as Bhs, carries typical department-store goods: clothes, household gadgets, linens, and foodstuffs. **Frasers** (✉ West end of Princes St., West End, ☎ 0131/225–2472) is a part of Britain's largest chain of department stores. In the city center is **Jenners** (✉ 48 Princes St., New Town, ☎ 0131/225–2442), which specializes in traditional china and glassware and Scottish clothing (upscale tweeds and tartans). Its justly famous food hall sells shortbreads and Dundee cakes (a light fruit cake with a distinctive pattern of split almonds arranged in circles on the top), honeys, and marmalades, as well as high-quality groceries. **John Lewis** (✉ 69 St. James Centre, East End, ☎ 0131/556–9121), part of a United Kingdom–wide chain, specializes in furniture and household goods, and pledges it is "never knowingly undersold." **Marks & Spencer** (✉ 54, 91, and 104–106 Princes St., New Town, ☎ 0131/225–2301) sells well-priced, stylish everyday clothes and basic accessories. You can also buy food items and household goods here.

Shopping Districts

Despite its renown as a shopping street, **Princes Street** in the New Town may disappoint some visitors with its dull, anonymous modern architecture, average chain stores, and fast-food outlets. It is, however, one of the best spots to shop for tartans, tweeds, and knitwear, especially if your time is limited. One block north of Princes Street, **Rose Street** has many smaller specialty shops; part of the street is a pedestrian zone, so it's a pleasant place to browse. The shops on **George Street** tend to be fairly upscale. London names, such as Laura Ashley and Waterstones bookstore, are prominent, though some of the older independent stores continue to do good business.

The streets crossing George Street—Hanover, Frederick, and Castle—are also worth exploring. **Dundas Street,** the northern extension of Hanover Street, beyond Queen Street Gardens, has several antiques shops. **Thistle Street,** originally George Street's "back lane," or service area, has several boutiques and more antiques shops. As may be expected, many shops along the **Royal Mile** sell what may be politely or euphemistically described as tourist-ware—whiskies, tartans, and tweeds. Careful exploration, however, will reveal some worthwhile establishments. Shops here also cater to highly specialized interests and hobbies.

Close to the castle end of the Royal Mile, just off George IV Bridge, is **Victoria Street,** with specialty shops grouped in a small area. Follow the tiny West Bow to **Grassmarket** for more specialty stores. North of Princes Street, on the way to the Royal Botanic Garden, is **Stockbridge,** an oddball shopping area of some charm, particularly on St. Stephen Street. To get here, walk north down Frederick Street and Howe Street, away from Princes Street, then turn left onto North West Circus Place. **Stafford and William streets** form a small, upscale shopping area in a Georgian setting. Walk to the west end of Princes Street and then along its continuation, Shandwick Place, then turn right onto Stafford Street. William Street crosses Stafford halfway down.

Specialty Shops

Antiques

Antiques dealers tend to cluster together, so it may be easiest to concentrate on one area—St. Stephen Street, Bruntsfield Place, Causewayside, or Dundas Street, for example—if you are short on time. Try **The Courtyard Antiques** (⊠ 108A Causewayside, Sciennes, ☎ 0131/662–9008) for a fascinating mixture of high-quality antiques, toys, and militaria.

Books, Paper, Maps, and Games

As a university city and cultural center, Edinburgh is endowed with excellent bookstores. All stock guides and books detailing information about every aspect of Edinburgh life, and all have extended opening hours (until 10 PM on certain nights), including Sunday. Waterstone's has some of the most central locations. **Waterstones** (⊠ 83 George St., New Town, ☎ 0131/225–3436; ⊠ 13–14 Princes St., East End, ☎ 0131/556–3034; ⊠ 128 Princes St., West End, ☎ 0131/226–2666).

Carson Clark Gallery (⊠ 181–183 Canongate, Old Town, ☎ 0131/556–4710) specializes in antique maps, sea charts, playing cards, and prints.

Try **George Waterston** (⊠ 35 George St., New Town, ☎ 0131/225–5690) not only for stationery but also for an excellent selection of small gift items.

Clothing Boutiques

Edinburgh is home to several top-quality designers—although, it must be said, probably not as many as are found in Glasgow, Scotland's fashion center—some of whom make a point of using Scottish materials in their creations. **Bill Baber** (⊠ 66 Grassmarket, Old Town, ☎ 0131/225–3249) is one of the most imaginative of the many Scottish knitwear designers, and a long way from the conservative pastel "woolies" sold at some of the large mill shops. Well-heeled Edinburgh has a branch of **D**

and B by Angela Holmes (✉ 37–39 Frederick St., New Town, ☎ 0131/ 225–1019), which carries distinctive clothing—from silk ball gowns and wedding dresses to flowing corduroy skirts with matching jackets and pretty cotton print summer dresses. **Judith Glue** (✉ 60 and 64 High St., Old Town, ☎ 0131/558–1866) carries brilliantly patterned Orkney knitwear, as well as distinctive crafts, cards, jewelry, and paintings.

If you're shopping for children, especially those who fit the tousled-tomboy mold, try **Baggins** (✉ 12 Deanhaugh St., Stockbridge., ☎ 0131/ 315–2011) for practical, reasonably priced clothes made from natural fibers, as well as toys and fancy dress items. All clothes here are made to the owner's design in the store's on-site workshop.

The **Extra Inch** (✉ 12 William St., West End, ☎ 0131/226–3303) stocks a full selection of clothes in European size 38 (U.S. size 8) and up.

Jewelry

Clarksons (✉ 87 West Bow, Old Town, ☎ 0131/225–8141), a family firm, handcrafts a unique collection of jewelry, including Celtic styles. The jewelry here is made with silver, gold, and precious gems, with a particular emphasis on diamonds. The jeweler **Hamilton and Inches** (✉ 87 George St., New Town, ☎ 0131/225–4898), established in 1866, is a silver- and goldsmith worth visiting not only for its modern and antique gift possibilities, but also for its late-Georgian interior, designed by David Bryce in 1834—all gilded columns and elaborate plasterwork. **Joseph Bonnar** (✉ 72 Thistle St., New Town, ☎ 0131/226–2811), in the heart of New Town, specializes in antique jewelry.

Linens, Textiles, and Home Furnishings

Head to **And So To Bed** (✉ 30 Dundas St., New Town, ☎ 0131/652– 3700) for a wonderful selection of embroidered and embellished bed linens, cushion covers, and the like. **In House** (✉ 28 Howe St., New Town, ☎ 0131/225–2888) sells designer furnishings and collectibles at the forefront of modern design for the home. **Studio One** (✉ 10–16 Stafford St., New Town, ☎ 0131/226–5812) has a well-established and comprehensive inventory of kitchen goods and gift articles.

Outdoor Sports Gear

If you plan to do a lot of hiking or camping in the Highlands or the Islands, you may want to look over the selection of outdoor clothing, boots, jackets, and heavy- and lightweight gear at **Tiso** (✉ 123–125 Rose St., New Town, ☎ 0131/225–9486; ✉ 41 Commercial St., Leith, ☎ 0131/554–0804). The Leith store is the larger of the two branches.

Scottish Specialties

If you want to identify a particular tartan, several shops on Princes Street will be pleased to assist. The **Clan Tartan Centre** (✉ 70–74 Bangor Rd., Leith, ☎ 0131/553–5100) has extensive displays of various aspects of tartanry. At the **Edinburgh Old Town Weaving Company** (✉ 555 Castlehill, Old Town, ☎ 0131/226–1555), you can watch and even talk to the cloth- and tapestry weavers as they work, then buy the products. **Geoffrey (Tailor) Highland Crafts** (✉ 57–59 High St., Old Town, ☎ 0131/557–0256) can clothe you in full Highland dress, with kilts made in its own workshops. The affiliated **21st Century Kilts** crafts contemporary kilts in leather, denim, and even camouflage. **Edinburgh Crystal** (✉ Eastfield, Penicuik, ☎ 01968/675128) makes fine glassware stocked by many large stores and gift shops in the city center, but you can also visit its premises—visitor center, restaurant, and shops, including a seconds and discontinued-lines store for real bargains—in Penicuik, 10 mi south of Edinburgh.

SIDE TRIPS FROM EDINBURGH

If you stand on an Edinburgh eminence—the castle ramparts, Arthur's Seat, Corstorphine Hill—you can plan a few Lothian excursions without even the aid of a map. The Lothians is the collective name given to the swath of countryside south of the Firth of Forth and surrounding Edinburgh. Many courtly and aristocratic families lived here, and the region still has the castles and mansions to prove it. The rich arrived and with them, deer parks, gardens in the French style, and Lothian's fame as a seed plot for Lowland gentility. Although the region has always provided rich pickings for historians, it also used to offer even richer pickings for coal miners—for a century after the industrial revolution, gentle streams in fairy glens (so the old writings describe them) steamed and stank with pollution. Although some black spots still remain, most of the rural countryside is now once again a fitting setting for excursions. When the coal miners left, admirals came here to retire, and today the "land of Lud" happily affords many delights. The 70-mi round-trip exploration of the historic houses and castles of West Lothian and the Forth Valley and some territory north of the River Forth can be accomplished in a full day with select stops. Stretching east to the sea and south to the Lowlands from Edinburgh, the sights in Midlothian and East Lothian are no more than one hour from Edinburgh. The inland river valleys, hills, and castles of Midlothian and East Lothian's delightful waterfronts, dunes, and golf links offer a taste of Scotland close to the capital.

West Lothian and the Forth Valley

West Lothian skirts the edge of the Central Highlands and comprises a good bit of Scotland's central belt. The River Forth snakes across a widening floodplain on its descent from the Highlands, and by the time it reaches the western extremities of Edinburgh, it has already passed below the mighty Forth bridges and become a broad estuary. Castles and stately homes sprout thickly on both sides of the Forth.

Cramond

42 At this compact settlement on the coast west of the city (4 mi northwest of the city center), you can watch summer sunsets over the Firth of Forth, joined by the River Almond. The river's banks, once the site of mills and industrial works, now have pleasant, leafy walks.

DINING

£–££ ✕ **Cramond Inn.** In this dark 17th-century village inn—once the haunt of Robert Louis Stevenson—you can stop for a pint at the bar or a selection from the small but varied pub menu, with such dishes as grilled halibut and new potatoes, sole and salmon rolls, chicken with mango chutney and rice, and steak. ⊠ *Cramond Glebe Rd., Cramond Village,* ☎ *0131/336–2035. DC, MC, V.*

Dalmeny House

43 Dalmeny House, the first of the stately houses clustered on the western edge of Edinburgh, is the home of the earl and countess of Rosebery. This 1815 Tudor Gothic mansion displays among its sumptuous contents the best of the family's famous collection of 18th-century French furniture. Highlights include the library, the Napoléon Room, the Vincennes and Sevres porcelain collections, and the drawing room, with its tapestries and highly wrought French furniture. ⊠ *B924, by South Queensferry, 7 mi west of city center,* ☎ *0131/331–1888,* WEB *www. dalmeny.co.uk.* 🖾 *£4.* ☉ *July–Aug., Sun.–Tues. 2–5:30; last admission at 4:30.*

West Lothian and the Forth Valley

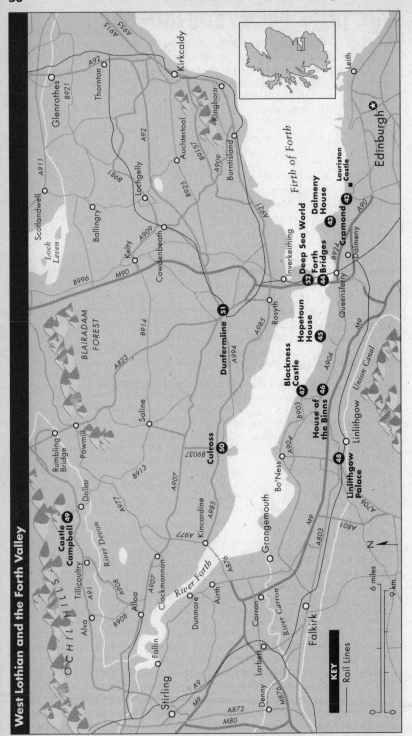

Kirkcaldy

Glenrothes

Thornton

Kinghorn

Auchtertool

Burntisland

Lochgelly

Kelty

Ballingry

Scotlandwell

Loch
Leven

Cowdenbeath

BLAIRADAM
FOREST

Dunfermline 51

Rosyth

Inverkeithing

Forth
Bridges 52

Deep Sea World 44

Firth of Forth

Dalmeny
House 43

Lauriston
Castle

Cramond 42

Edinburgh

Leith

Queensferry

Dalmeny

Hopetoun
House 45

Blackness
Castle 47

House of
the Binns 46

Culross 50

Saline

Powmill

Rumbling
Bridge

Dollar

Castle
Campbell 49

Tillicoultry

OCHIL HILLS

Alva

River Devon

Clackmannan

Alloa

Fallin

Stirling

Dunmore

Airth

Kincardine

Bo'Ness

Grangemouth

Linlithgow

Linlithgow
Palace 48

Union Canal

Carron

Larbert

Falkirk

Denny

River Forth

River Carron

N

6 miles

9 km

South Queensferry

★ ④④ This pleasant little waterside community, a former ferry port 9 mi west of the city, is completely dominated by the **Forth Bridges,** dramatic structures of contrasting architecture that span the Firth of Forth at this historic crossing point. The **Forth Rail Bridge** was opened in 1890 and at the time hailed as the eighth wonder of the world, at 2,765 yards long, except on a hot summer's day when it expands by about another yard! Its neighbor is the 1,993-yard-long **Forth Road Bridge,** in operation since 1964.

DINING

£–££ ✕ **The Hawes Inn.** In his novel *Kidnapped,* Robert Louis Stevenson describes a room at this inn as "a small room, with a bed in it, and heated like an oven by a great fire of coal." The dramatic setting and history alone are well worth the trip to the inn, which is 10 mi from the city center of Edinburgh and 1 mi from Dalmeny Railway station. A recurring nautical theme and fireplaces at this 1638 pub create a sense of comfort and coziness. You'll find traditional pub fare here, such as haggis and fish-and-chips. ⊠ *Newhalls Rd.,* ☎ *0131/331–1990. AE, MC, V.*

Hopetoun House

④⑤ The palatial premises of Hopetoun House, probably Scotland's grandest courtly seat and home of the marquesses of Linlithgow, are considered to be among the Adam family's finest designs. The enormous house was started in 1699 to the original plans of Sir William Bruce (1630–1710), then enlarged between 1721 and 1754 by William Adam (1689–1748) and his son Robert. There's a notable painting collection, and the house has decorative work of the highest order, plus all the trappings to keep you entertained: a nature trail, a restaurant in the former stables, and a museum. Much of the wealth that created this sumptuous building came from the family's mining interests in the surrounding regions. ⊠ *6 mi west of South Queensferry, off A904,* ☎ *0131/331–2451,* WEB *www.hopetounhouse.com.* ⊡ *£5.30.* ☉ *Apr.–Sept., daily 10–5:30, last admission at 4:30; Oct., daily 11–4, last admission at 3:30.*

House of the Binns

④⑥ The 17th-century general "Bloody Tam" Dalyell (circa 1599–1685) transformed a fortified stronghold into a gracious mansion, the House of the Binns (the name derives from *ben,* the Scottish word for *hill*). The present exterior dates from around 1810 and shows a remodeling into a kind of mock fort with crenellated battlements and turrets. Inside, there are magnificent plaster ceilings done in the Elizabethan style. The house is cared for by the National Trust for Scotland. ⊠ *Off A904, 4 mi east of Linlithgow,* ☎ *01506/834255,* WEB *www.nts.org.uk.* ⊡ *£5.* ☉ *House May–Sept., Sat.–Thurs. and Sun. 1–5. Parkland late Mar.– late Oct., daily 10–7; Jan.–late Mar. and late Oct.–Dec., daily 10–4.*

Blackness Castle

④⑦ The castle of Blackness stands like a grounded gray hulk on the very edge of the Forth. A curious 15th-century structure, it has had a varied career as a strategic fortress, state prison, powder magazine, and youth hostel. The countryside is gently green and cultivated, and open views extend across the blue Forth to the distant ramparts of the Ochil Hills. The castle is run by Historic Scotland, a government organization that looks after many historic properties in Scotland. ⊠ *B903, 4 mi northeast of Linlithgow,* ☎ *0131/668–8800,* WEB *www.historic-scotland.net.* ⊡ *£1.80.* ☉ *Apr.–Sept., daily 9:30–6; Oct.–Mar., Mon.–Wed. and Sat. 9:30–4, Thurs. 9:30–noon, Sun. 2–4.*

Linlithgow Palace

48 On the edge of Linlithgow Loch stands the splendid ruin of **Linlithgow Palace,** birthplace of Mary, Queen of Scots, in 1542. Burned, perhaps by accident, by Hanoverian troops during the last Jacobite rebellion in 1746, this impressive shell stands on a site of great antiquity, though nothing for certain survived an earlier fire in 1424. The palace gatehouse was built in the early 16th century, and the central courtyard's elaborate fountain dates from around 1535. The halls and great rooms are cold, echoing stone husks now in Historic Scotland's care. ✉ *A706, south shore of Linlithgow Loch,* ☎ *01506/842896,* WEB *www. historic-scotland.gov.uk.* 🎫 *£2.80.* ☼ *Apr.–Sept., daily 9:30–6; Oct.– Mar., Mon.–Sat. 9:30–4, Sun. 2–4.*

En Route From the M9 you'll begin to gain tempting glimpses of the Highland hills to the northwest and the long, humped wall of the Ochil Hills, across the river plain to the north. The **River Carron,** which flows under the M9, gave its name to the *carronade,* a kind of cannon manufactured in Falkirk, a few minutes to the southwest. You'll also pass the apocalyptic complex of Grangemouth Refinery (impressive by night), which you may also smell if the wind is right—or wrong! The refinery processes North Sea crude oil but was originally sited here because of the now-extinct oil-shale extraction industry of West Lothian, pioneered by a Scot, James "Paraffin" Young. This landscape may not be the most scenic in Scotland, but it has certainly played its role in the nation's industrial history.

Ochil Hills

The scarp face of the Ochil Hills looms unmistakably. It is an old fault line that yields up hard volcanic rocks and contrasts with the quantities of softer coal immediately around the River Forth. The steep Ochils provided grazing land and water power for Scotland's second-largest textile area. Some mills still survive in the so-called Hillfoots towns, on the scarp edge east of Stirling. Several hikers' routes run into the narrow chinks of glens here. Behind Alva sits **Alva Glen,** a park near the converted Strude Mill, at the top and eastern end of the little town. East of Alva Glen is the **Ochil Hills Woodland Park,** which provides access to Silver Glen. The **Mill Glen,** behind Tillicoultry (pronounced tilly-*coot*-ree), with its giant quarry, fine waterfalls, and interesting plants, is a good hiking option for energetic explorers.

Dollar

This *douce* (Scots for well-mannered or gentle) and tidy town below the Ochil Hills slopes lies at the mouth of Dollar Glen. With green woods below, bracken hills above, and a view that on a clear day stretches right across the Forth Valley to the tip of Tinto Hill near Lanark, **Castle Campbell** is certainly the most atmospheric fortress within easy reach of Edinburgh. Formerly known as Castle Gloom, Castle Campbell stands out among Scottish castles for the sheer drama of its setting. The sturdy square of the tower house survives from the 15th century, when this site was first fortified by the first earl of Argyll (died 1493). Other buildings and enclosures were subsequently added, but the sheer lack of space on this rocky eminence ensured that there would never be any drastic changes. The castle is associated with the earls of Argyll, as well as with John Knox, the fiery religious reformer, who preached here. It also played a role in the religious wars of the 17th century, having been captured by Oliver Cromwell in 1654 and garrisoned with English troops. It is now cared for by Historic Scotland. To get here you'll have to follow a road off the A91 that angles sharply up the east side of the wooded defile. The narrow road ends in a parking lot from which it's only a short walk to Castle Campbell, high on a great sloping mound in the center of the glen. ⊠ *Dollar Glen, 1 mi north of Dollar, 30 mi north-west of Edinburgh,* ☏ *0131/668–8800,* WEB *www.historic-scotland.gov.uk.* 🖭 *£2.80.* ⊙ *Apr.–Sept., daily 9:30–6:30; Oct.–Mar., Mon.–Wed. 9:30–4:30, Thurs. noon–4:30, Sat. 9:30–noon, Sun. 2–4:30.*

Culross

50 With its Mercat Cross, cobbled streets, tolbooth, and narrow wynds, Culross, on the muddy shores of the Forth, is now a living museum of a 17th-century town and one of the most remarkable little towns in all of Scotland. It once had a thriving industry and export trade in coal and salt (the coal was used in the salt-panning process). It also had, curiously, a trade monopoly in the manufacture of baking *girdles* (griddles). But as local coal became exhausted, the impetus of the industrial revolution passed Culross by, and other parts of the Forth Valley prospered. Culross became a backwater town, and the merchants' houses of the 17th and 18th centuries were never replaced by Victorian developments or modern architecture. In the 1930s the then-new and also very poor National Trust for Scotland started to buy up the decaying properties. With the help of several other agencies, these buildings were conserved and brought to life. Today ordinary citizens live in many of the National Trust properties. A few—the Palace, Study, and Town House—are open to the public. ⊠ *25 mi northwest of Edinburgh,* ☏ *01383/880359,* WEB *www.nts.org.uk.* 🖭 *Palace, Study, and Town House £5.* ⊙ *Palace, Study, and Town House July–Aug., daily 10–6; late Mar.–late June and Sept.–late Oct., daily noon–5; last admission 1 hr before closing.*

Dunfermline

51 Dunfermline, 16 mi northwest of Edinburgh, was once the world center for the production of damask linen, but the town is better known today as the birthplace of millionaire philanthropist Andrew Carnegie (1835–1919). Undoubtedly Dunfermline's most famous son, Carnegie endowed the town with a library, health and fitness center, spacious park, and, naturally, a Carnegie Hall, still the focus of culture and entertainment. The 1835 weaver's cottage in which Carnegie was born

★ is now the **Andrew Carnegie Birthplace Museum.** Don't be misled by the cottage's exterior. Inside it opens into a larger hall, where documents, photographs, and artifacts relate Carnegie's fascinating life story. You'll learn such obscure details as the claim that Carnegie was one of only three men in the United States then able to translate Morse code by ear as it came down the wire. ⊠ *Moodie St.,* ☏ *01383/724302.* 🖭 *£2.* ⊙ *Apr.–Oct., Mon.–Sat. 11–5, Sun. 2–5.*

The **Dunfermline Museum** tells the full story of the town's history as a producer of damask linen. ⊠ *Viewfield Terr.,* ☏ *01383/313838.* 🖭 *Free.* ⊙ *Weekdays 11–5.*

The **Dunfermline Abbey and Palace** complex was founded in the 11th century by Queen Margaret, the English wife of the Scots king Malcolm III. Some Norman work can be seen in the present church, where Robert the Bruce (1274–1329) lies buried. The palace grew from the abbey guest house and was the birthplace of Charles I (1600–1649). Dunfermline was the seat of the royal court of Scotland until the end of the 11th century, and its central role in Scottish affairs is explored by means of display panels dotted around the drafty but hallowed buildings. ⊠ *Monastery St.,* ☏ *0131/668–8800.* 🖭 *£2.20.* ⊙ *Apr.–Sept., daily 9:30–6:30; Oct.–Mar., Mon.–Wed. and Sat. 9:30–4:30, Thurs. 9:30–noon, Sun. 2–4:30; last admission ½ hr before closing.*

Deep Sea World

52 The former ferry port in North Queensferry on the north side of the Forth dropped almost into oblivion after the Forth Road Bridge opened but was dragged abruptly back into the limelight when the hugely popular Deep Sea World arrived in the early 1990s. This sophisticated "aquarium"—for want of a better word—on the Firth of Forth offers a fascinating view of underwater life. Go down a clear acrylic tunnel for a diver's-eye look at more than 5,000 fish, including a posse of 9-ft sharks, and visit the exhibition hall, which has an audiovisual presentation on local marine life, an Amazon jungle display, and various other creatures. Nervous ichthyophobes will feel more at ease in the adjacent café and gift shop. ⊠ *North Queensferry,* ☎ *01383/411880,* WEB *www.deepseaworld.com.* ⊒ *£6.95.* ⊙ *Daily 10–6; last admission 45 min before closing.*

West Lothian and the Forth Valley A to Z

BUS TRAVEL

First Midland Bluebird bus services link most of this area, but working out a detailed itinerary by bus is best left to your travel agent or guide.
➤ BUS INFORMATION: **First Midland Bluebird** (☎ 01324/613777).

CAR TRAVEL

Leave Edinburgh by Queensferry Road—the A90—and follow signs for the Forth Bridge. Beyond the city boundary at Cramond take the slip road, B924, for South Queensferry, watching for signs to Dalmeny House. From Dalmeny follow the B924 for the descent to South Queensferry. The B924 continues westward under the approaches to the suspension bridge and then meets the A904. On turning right onto A904, follow signs for Hopetoun House, House of the Binns, and Blackness Castle. From Blackness take the B903 to its junction with the A904. Turn left for Linlithgow on the A803. At this point it's best to join the M9, which will speed you westward. Follow Kincardine Bridge signs off the motorway, cross the Forth and take the A977 north from Kincardine, formerly a trading port and distillery center. Take the A907 to Alloa, get on the A908 (marked TILLICOULTRY) for a short stretch, and then pick up the B908 (marked ALVA).

At this point you'll be leaving the industrial northern shore of the Forth behind and entering the Ochil Hills, which you can explore by following the A91 eastward at Alva; squeezed between the gentle River Devon and the steep slopes above, the road continues to Dollar, where you should follow signs to Castle Campbell. From the castle, retrace your route to A91 and turn left. A few minutes outside Dollar, turn right onto a minor road (signposted RUMBLING BRIDGE). Then turn right onto the A823. Follow A823 through Powmill (follow the signs for Dunfermline); turn right off A823, following the signs for Saline, and take an unclassified road due south to join the A907. Turn right, and then within a mile go left on the B9037, which leads down to Culross. Take the B9037 east to join the A994, which leads to Dunfermline. From here follow the Edinburgh signs to the A823 and return via North Queensferry and the Forth Road Bridge (toll 60p traveling north into Fife only).

TRAIN TRAVEL

Dalmeny, Linlithgow, and Dunfermline all have rail stations and can be reached from Edinburgh Waverley station. For information call the National Train Enquiry Line.
➤ TRAIN INFORMATION: **National Train Enquiry Line** (☎ 08457/ 484950).

VISITOR INFORMATION

The tourist information office in the Mill Trail Visitor Centre, at Alva, can provide information on the region's textile establishments as well as a *Mill Trail* brochure, which directs you to mill shops selling bargain woolen and tweed goods.

➤ TOURIST INFORMATION: **Mill Trail Visitor Centre** (✉ W. Stirling St., Alva, ☎ 01259/769696).

Midlothian and East Lothian

In spite of the finest stone carving in Scotland at Rosslyn Chapel, associations with Sir Walter Scott, outstanding castles, and miles of varied rolling countryside, Midlothian, the area immediately south of Edinburgh, for years remained off the beaten tourist path. Perhaps a little in awe of sophisticated Edinburgh to the north and the well-manicured charm of the stockbroker belt of nearby upmarket East Lothian, Midlothian was quietly preoccupied with its own workaday little towns and dormitory suburbs.

As for East Lothian, it started with the advantage of golf courses of world rank, most notably Muirfield, plus a scattering of stately homes and interesting hotels. Red-pantiled and decidedly middle class, it is an area of glowing grain fields in summer and quite a few discreetly polite STRICTLY PRIVATE signs at the end of driveways. Still, it has plenty of interest, including photogenic villages, active fishing harbors, and vistas of pastoral Lowland Scotland, seemingly a world away (but much less than an hour by car) from bustling Edinburgh.

Roslin

★ ⓝ This pretty little U-shape miners' village, with its rows of stone-built terraced cottages, is famous for the extraordinary **Rosslyn Chapel.** Conceived by Sir William Sinclair (circa 1404–80) and dedicated to St. Matthew in 1450, the chapel is outstanding for the quality and variety of the stone carving inside. Covering almost every square inch of stonework are human figures, animals, and plants. The chapel was actually never finished. The original design called for a cruciform structure, but only the choir and parts of the east transept walls were completed. ✉ *Roslin, off A703, 7½ mi south of Edinburgh,* ☎ *0131/440–2159,* WEB *www. rosslyn-chapel.com.* 🎫 *£4.* ☉ *Mon.–Sat. 10–5, Sun. noon–4:45.*

Edinburgh Crystal Visitor Centre

ⓝ There are fine views of the Pentland Hills beyond the town of Penicuik, but its chief attraction is the Edinburgh Crystal Visitor Centre, with crystal pieces and an audiovisual exhibition on the production of crystal. Guided tours reveal the stages involved in the manufacture of cut crystal. In addition, groups of 6 to 10 people can prebook a VIP tour (adults over 18 only), which includes an opportunity for you to blow a glass bubble and cut your own piece of glass, later polished and given to you as a keepsake. Advance booking is essential for this tour. The Visitor Centre also has a coffee shop and gift shops. ✉ *Eastfield, Penicuik, 10 mi south of Edinburgh,* ☎ *01968/675128,* WEB *www.edinburgh-crystal.com.* 🎫 *Center free, tours £3, VIP tour £10.* ☉ *Tours available Mon.–Sat. 9– 4, Sun. 11–4.*

The Pentlands

This unmistakable range of hills immediately south of Edinburgh has the longest artificial ski slope in Britain, at Hillend, and an all-year chairlift that provides magnificent views, even for nonskiers. There are several other access points along the A702 running parallel to the hills—the best is Flotterstone, where you'll find a parking lot, pub, and quiet roads for walking.

DINING

£–££ ✕ **The Old Bakehouse.** Here you'll find home-cooked fare in quaint, wood-beamed rooms. Danish open sandwiches are the specialty, but

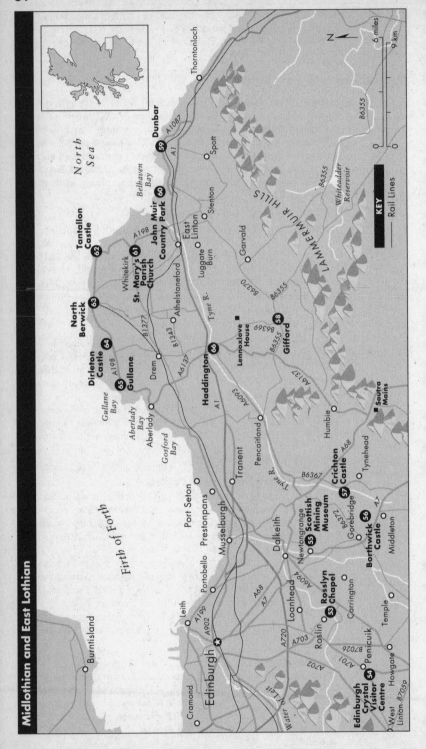

Midlothian and East Lothian

homemade soups and hot main courses are also available. ⊠ *West Linton, southwest of Penicuik on A702,* ☎ *01968/660830. MC, V. Closed Mon. and Tues. No dinner Sun.*

Scottish Mining Museum

55 The Scottish Mining Museum, in the former mining community of Newtongrange, provides a good introduction to the history of Scotland's mining industry and its mining communities. Go on shift as a coal miner and experience life at the (virtual reality) coal face. There are also interactive displays and "magic helmets" that bring the tour to life and relate the power that the mining company had over the lives of the individual workers in a frighteningly autocratic system that survived well into the 1930s—the mining company owned the houses, shops, and even the pub. Newtongrange was in fact the largest planned mining village in Scotland. The scenery is no more attractive than you would expect, though the green Pentland Hills hover in the distance. ⊠ *A7, Newtongrange, 9 mi south of Edinburgh,* ☎ *0131/663–7519,* WEB *www.scottishminingmuseum.com.* ☞ *£4.* ☉ *Mar.–Oct., daily 10–5; Nov.–Feb., daily 10–4; last admission 1½ hrs before closing.*

Borthwick Castle

56 Set in green countryside with scattered woods and lush hedgerows, the little village of Borthwick is dominated by Borthwick Castle, which dates from the 15th century and is still occupied. This stark, tall, twin-towered fortress is associated with Mary, Queen of Scots. She came here on a kind of honeymoon with her ill-starred third husband, the earl of Bothwell. Their already-dubious bliss was interrupted by Mary's political opponents, often referred to as the Lords of the Congregation, a confederacy of powerful nobles who were against the queen's latest liaison and who instead favored the crowning of her young son, James. Rather insensitively, they laid siege to the castle while the newlyweds were there. The history books relate that Mary subsequently escaped disguised as a man. She was not free for long, however. It was only a short time before she was defeated in battle and imprisoned. She languished in prison for 21 years before Queen Elizabeth I of England (1558–1603) signed her death warrant in 1587. Bothwell's fate was equally gloomy: he died insane in a Danish prison. ⊠ *North Middleton, 13 mi southeast of Edinburgh, near Gorebridge,* ☎ *01875/820514.* ☞ *Free.* ☉ *Tours occasionally available between noon and 4; call ahead.*

LODGING

£££–££££ 🏨 **Borthwick Castle.** There are hotels with castle names, and hotels inside what once were castles, and then there is Borthwick, which is still first a castle and only second a place where you can stay. This 15th-century fortress was taking guests half a century before Columbus sailed to the Americas. Nowhere else in Scotland offers the extraordinary experience of living a part of history. Your "bedchamber" is warm and comfortable, equipped with bath or shower. You dine not in a restaurant but in the Great Hall, lit by candles and the gleam of a log fire. ⊠ *North Middleton, Midlothian EH23 4QY,* ☎ *01875/820514,* FAX *01875/821702. 10 rooms. Fishing, horseback riding; no a/c. AE, DC, MC, V. Closed Jan.–mid-Mar.*

Crichton Castle

57 Crichton Castle, a Historic Scotland property, stands amid attractive, rolling Lowland scenery, interrupted here and there by patches of woodland. Crichton was a Bothwell family castle; Mary, Queen of Scots, attended the wedding here of Bothwell's sister, Lady Janet Hepburn, to Mary's brother, Lord John Stewart. The curious arcaded range reveals diamond-faceted stonework; this particular geometric pattern is unique in Scotland and is thought to have been inspired by Renaissance styles on the Continent, particularly Italy. The oldest part of the work is the 14th-century keep (square tower). You can reach this castle from Borthwick Castle by taking a peaceful walk through the woods (there are signposts along the way). ✉ *B6367, near Pathhead, 7 mi southeast of Dalkeith,* ☎ *0131/668–8800,* WEB *www.historic-scotland.gov.uk.* ☞ *£2.* ☉ *Apr.–Sept., daily 9:30–6.30.*

En Route   Follow the A68 5 mi south, away from Edinburgh, to the very edge of the Lammermuir Hills. Just beyond the junction with the A6137 you'll come to a spot called **Soutra Mains.** There's a small parking lot here, from which you can enjoy glorious unobstructed views extending northward over the whole of the Lothian plain.

Gifford

58   With its 18th-century kirk and Mercat Cross, Gifford, 25 mi east of Edinburgh, is a good example of a tweedily respectable, well-scrubbed, red-pantile-roofed East Lothian village.

Dunbar

59   In the days before tour companies started offering package deals to the Mediterranean, Dunbar was a popular holiday beach resort. Now a bit faded, the town is lovely for its spacious Georgian-style properties, characterized by the astragals, or fan-shape windows, above the doors; the symmetry of the house fronts; and the parapeted roof lines. Though not the popular seaside playground it once was, Dunbar, 30 mi east of Edinburgh, does still have an attractive beach and a picturesque harbor.

John Muir Country Park

60   Taking in the estuary of the River Tyne winding down from the Moorfoot Hills, the John Muir Country Park holds varied coastal scenery: rocky shoreline, golden sands, and the mixed woodlands of Tyninghame, teeming with wildlife. Dunbar-born conservationist John Muir (1838–1914), whose family emigrated to the United States when he was a child, helped found the Yosemite and Sequoia national parks. ✉ *Off the A1087, 28 mi east of Edinburgh.*

St. Mary's Parish Church

61   The unmistakable red-sandstone St. Mary's Parish Church, with its Norman tower, stands on a site occupied since the 6th century. It was a place of pilgrimage in medieval times because of its healing well. Behind the kirk, in a field, stands a tithe barn. Tithe barns originated with the practice of giving to the church a portion of local produce, which then required storage space. At one end of the structure stands a 16th-century tower house, which at one point in its history accommodated visiting pilgrims. The large three-story barn was added to the tower house in the 17th century. ✉ *A198, Whitekirk, 27 mi east of Edinburgh.* ☞ *Free.* ☉ *Daily, early morning–late evening.*

Tantallon Castle

62   Rising on a cliff beyond the flat fields east of North Berwick, Tantallon Castle is a substantial ruin defending a headland with the sea on three sides. The red sandstone is pitted and eaten by time and sea spray, with the earliest surviving stonework dating from the late 14th century. The fortress was besieged in 1529 by the cannons of King James V (1512–42). Rather inconveniently, the besieging forces ran out of gunpowder. Cannons were used again, to deadlier effect, in a later siege during the Civil War in 1651. Twelve days of battering with the heavy guns of Cromwell's General Monk greatly damaged the flanking towers. However, much of the curtain wall of this former Douglas stronghold, now cared for by Historic Scotland, survives. ✉ *A198, 3 mi east of North Berwick,* ☎ *0131/668–8800,* WEB *www.historic-scotland.gov.uk.*

🖾 *£2.80.* ☺ *Apr.–Sept., daily 9:30–6:30; Oct.–Mar., Mon.–Wed. and Sat. 9:30–4:30, Thurs. 9:30–noon, Sun. 2–4:30; last admission ½ hr before closing.*

North Berwick

63 The pleasant little seaside resort of North Berwick, 26 mi northeast of Edinburgh, manages to retain a small-town personality even when it's thronged with city visitors on warm summer Sunday afternoons. Munching on ice cream, the city folk stroll on the beach and in the narrow streets or gape at the sailing craft in the small harbor. An observation deck, exhibits, and films at the **Scottish Seabird Centre** provide a good introduction to the world of the gannets and puffins that nest on nearby Bass Rock. Live interactive cameras let you take an even closer look at the bird. ⊠ *The Harbour,* ☎ *01620/890202,* WEB *www. seabird.org.* 🖾 *£4.95.* ☺ *Apr.–Sept., daily 10–6; Oct.–Mar. weekdays 10–4, weekends 10–5:30.*

LODGING

£ 🏠 **Glebe House.** This 18th-century former manse sits amid its own secluded grounds, yet it's within the heart of town, convenient to the train station and only minutes from the beach. It's also close to 18 golf courses, including nearby Muirfield. The elegant bedrooms, one of which has a four-poster bed, are in keeping with the Regency style of the house. Grand period furniture, paintings, and ornaments fill the sitting and dining rooms. ⊠ *Law Rd., EH39 4PL,* ☎ *01620/892608,* FAX *01620/ 829608. 4 rooms. No a/c, no-smoking rooms. No credit cards.*

Dirleton

64 Right in the center of this small village sits the 12th-century **Dirleton Castle,** surrounded by a high outer wall. Within the wall you'll find a 17th-century bowling green, set in the shade of yew trees and surrounded by a herbaceous flower border that blazes with color in high summer. Dirleton Castle, now in Historic Scotland's care, was occupied in 1298 by King Edward I of England as part of his campaign for the continued subjugation of the unruly Scots. ⊠ *A198, 22 mi northeast of Edinburgh,* ☎ *01620/850330,* WEB *www.historic-scotland.gov.uk.* 🖾 *£2.80.* ☺ *Apr.– Sept., daily 9:30–6; Oct.–Mar., Mon.–Sat. 9:30–4, Sun. 2–4.*

Gullane

65 Very noticeable along this coastline are the golf courses of East Lothian, laid out wherever there is available links space. Gullane, surrounded by them, is ultrarespectable, its inhabitants often clad in expensive golfing sweaters. **Muirfield,** venue for the Open Championship, is nearby, as is **Greywalls,** now a hotel but originally a private house, designed by Sir Edwin Lutyens (1869–1944). Apart from golf, at **Gullane's beach,** well within driving distance of the city, you can enjoy restful summer evening strolls.

LODGING

££££ 🏠 **Greywalls.** This is the ideal hotel for a golfing vacation: comfortable, with attentive service and fine modern British cuisine that makes the most of local produce. The turn-of-the-20th-century house itself, designed by Sir Edwin Lutyens in the shape of a crescent and with a walled garden, is an architectural treasure. Edward VII used to stay here, as have Nicklaus, Trevino, Palmer, and a host of other golfing greats. Shades of restful green predominate in the stylish fabrics from the likes of Nina Campbell, Colefax and Fowler, and Osborne and Little. A separate lodge house can accommodate up to eight people. ⊠ *Muirfield, Gullane EH31 2EG,* ☎ *01620/842144,* FAX *01620/842241,* WEB *www.greywalls.co.uk. 23 rooms, 1 lodge. Restaurant, putting green, tennis court. AE, DC, MC, V. Closed Nov.–Mar.*

Haddington

One of the best-preserved medieval street plans in the country can be explored in Haddington, 15 mi east of Edinburgh. Among the many buildings of architectural or historical interest is the Town House, designed by William Adam in 1748 and enlarged in 1830. A wall plaque at the Sidegate recalls the great heights of floods from the River Tyne. Beyond is the medieval Nungate footbridge, with the Church of St. Mary a little way upstream.

Just to the south of Haddington stands **Lennoxlove House,** the grand ancestral home of the very grand dukes of Hamilton and Lennox, which displays items associated with Mary, Queen of Scots. A turreted country house, part of it dating from the 15th century, Lennoxlove is a cheerful mix of family life and Scottish history. The beautifully decorated rooms house collections of portraits, furniture, and porcelain. ✉ *B6369, 1 mi south of Haddington,* ☎ *01620/823720,* WEB *www. lennoxlove.org.* ☞ *£4.* ☉ *Tours Easter–Oct., Wed., Thurs., and weekends 2–4:30; call ahead to confirm tour times.*

Midlothian and East Lothian A to Z

BUS TRAVEL

City bus services run out as far as Swanston and the Pentland Hills. First Lowland buses run to towns and villages throughout Midlothian and East Lothian. For details of all services, inquire at the St. Andrew Square bus station in Edinburgh.

➤ BUS INFORMATION: **First Lowland** (☎ 0131/663–9233).

CAR TRAVEL

Leave Edinburgh via the A701 (Liberton Road). At the former mining community of Bilston, turn left to Roslin on the B7006. From Roslin return to the A701 for Penicuik and the Edinburgh Crystal Visitor Centre. From Penicuik take the A766 to A702, which runs beneath the Pentland Hills to West Linton. Then follow the B7059 and the A701 to Leadburn and then Howgate. Get onto the A6094 for a few minutes, then turn right onto the B6372, and continue past Temple, an attractive village on the edge of the Moorfoot Hills, toward Gorebridge.

At the junction of B6372 with A7, just before Gorebridge, you have a choice. If your interests tend toward social history, turn left and drive 2 mi to reach Newtongrange and the Scottish Mining Museum. If your interests lie elsewhere, turn right instead, and after a few moments' travel south you will see a sign for Borthwick. Take a left onto an unclassified road off A7, and a few minutes later Borthwick Castle appears. From Borthwick take the B6372 and turn right onto the A68. Just beyond the village of Pathhead you'll see signs to Crichton Castle. Having detoured to the castle, follow the A68 south, away from Edinburgh, to the very edge of the Lammermuir Hills. Just beyond the junction with the A6137, at Soutra Mains, there's a small parking lot from which to enjoy the view. Make your way back to the A6137 and turn right onto it; turn right again onto the B6355, go through Gifford, and head east for the junction with the B6370, which leads to Dunbar.

West of Dunbar, on the way back to Edinburgh, the A1087 leads to the sandy reaches of Belhaven Bay, signposted from the main road, and to the John Muir Country Park. From the park drive north on the A198 (a right turn off the A1), to reach St. Mary's Parish Church at Whitekirk, Tantallon Castle, North Berwick, Dirleton, and Gullane. A198 eventually leads to Aberlady, from which you can take the A6137 south to the former county town of Haddington and, by way of the B6369, to Lennoxlove House. Return to the A1 at Haddington and head west back to Edinburgh. From Haddington it's about 15 mi back to the city center.

TRAIN TRAVEL

There is no train service in Midlothian. In East Lothian, the towns of North Berwick, Drem, and Dunbar have train stations with regular service from Edinburgh.

EDINBURGH AND THE LOTHIANS A TO Z

To research prices, get advice from other travelers, and book travel arrangements, visit www.fodors.com.

AIR TRAVEL

Airlines serving Edinburgh include Aer Lingus, Air France, British Airways, British Midland, Crossair, easyJet, Euroscot, Gill Air, KLM, Servisair, and Scott Airways. No transatlantic flights come through Edinburgh; you must instead fly into Glasgow, 50 mi away.

Ryanair and easyJet have sparked a major price war on the Anglo-Scottish routes. They offer unbeatable, no-frills airfares on routes connecting Edinburgh Airport, Glasgow International, Prestwick Airport (near Glasgow), and London's major airports.
➤ CARRIERS: **easyJet** (☎ 0870/600–0000). **Ryanair** (☎ 08701/569569).

AIRPORTS

At present, Edinburgh Airport, 7 mi west of the city center, offers no transatlantic flights. It does, however, have air connections throughout the United Kingdom—London (Heathrow, Gatwick, Stansted, Luton, and City), Aberdeen, Birmingham, Bournemouth, Bristol, Dundee, East Midlands, Kirkwall (Orkney), Leeds–Bradford, Manchester, Norwich, Shetland, Southampton, and Belfast (in Northern Ireland)—as well as with a number of European cities, including Amsterdam, Brussels, Copenhagen, Dublin, Dusseldorf, Munich, Paris, and Zurich. Flights take off for Edinburgh Airport virtually every hour from London's Gatwick and Heathrow airports; it's usually faster and less complicated to fly through Gatwick, which has excellent rail service from London's Victoria Station.

Glasgow Airport, 50 mi west of Edinburgh, serves as the major point of entry into Edinburgh for transatlantic flights.

Prestwick Airport, 30 mi southwest of Glasgow, after some years of eclipse by Glasgow Airport, has grown in importance, not least because of the activities of Ryanair.
➤ AIRPORT INFORMATION: **Edinburgh Airport** (☎ 0131/333–1000). **Glasgow Airport** (☎ 0141/887–1111). **Prestwick Airport** (☎ 01292/511006).

AIRPORT TRANSFERS BETWEEN EDINBURGH AIRPORT AND DOWNTOWN

There are no rail links to the city center, despite the fact that the airport sits between two main lines. By bus or car you can usually make it to Edinburgh in a comfortable half hour, unless you hit the morning or evening rush hours (7:30–9 and 4–6).

Lothian Buses and Guide Friday run buses between Edinburgh Airport and the city center and within easy reach of several hotels. The buses run every 15 minutes daily (9–5) and less frequently (roughly every hour) during off-peak hours. The trip takes about 30 minutes, or about 45 minutes during rush hour. A single-fare ticket on a Lothian Bus costs £3.30, on Guide Friday £3.60.

You can arrange for a chauffeur-driven limousine to meet your flight at Edinburgh Airport through David Grieve Chauffeur Drive for about £55; Little's Chauffeur Drive, £46 plus VAT; and Sleigh Ltd., £50 plus VAT.

Several car-rental companies operate from the terminal building. The cost starts at about £40 a day, depending on the firm. If you choose to plunge yourself into Edinburgh's traffic system, take care on the first couple of traffic circles (called roundabouts) you encounter on the way into town from the airport—even the most experienced drivers find them challenging. By car the airport is about 7 mi west of Princes Street downtown and is clearly marked from A8. The usual route to downtown is via the suburb of Corstorphine.

Taxis are readily available outside the terminal. The trip takes 20–30 minutes to the city center, 15 minutes longer rush hour. The fare is roughly £15. Note that because of a local regulation, airport taxis picking up fares from the terminal are any color, not the typical black cabs, although these also take fares going to the airport.
➤ CONTACT: **David Grieve Chauffeur Drive** (✉ 9/7 Lower Gilmore Pl., Tollcross, ☎ 0131/229–8666). **Guide Friday** (☎ 0131/556–2244). **Little's Chauffeur Drive** (✉ 5 St. Ninian's Dr., Corstorphine, ☎ 0131/334–2177). **Lothian Buses** (☎ 0131/555–6363). **Sleigh Ltd.** (✉ 6 Devon Pl., West End, ☎ 0131/337–3171).

AIRPORT TRANSFERS BETWEEN GLASGOW AIRPORT AND EDINBURGH

Scottish Citylink buses leave Glasgow Airport every 15 minutes to travel to Glasgow's Buchanan Street (journey time is 25 minutes), where you can transfer to an Edinburgh bus (leaving every 20 minutes). The trip to Edinburgh takes 70 minutes and costs £7 round-trip and £4.50 oneway. A somewhat more pleasant option is to take a cab from Glasgow Airport to Glasgow's Queen Street train station (lasts 20 minutes and costs about £15) and then take the train to Waverley Station in Edinburgh. Trains leave about every 30 minutes; the trip takes 50 minutes and costs £7.30. Check times on weekends. Another, less expensive alternative—best for those with little luggage—is to take the bus from Glasgow Airport to Glasgow's Buchanan bus station, walk five minutes to the Queen Street train station, and catch the train to Edinburgh.

Taxis from Glasgow Airport to downtown Edinburgh take about 70 minutes and cost around £70–£80.
➤ TAXIS AND SHUTTLES: **Scottish Citylink** (☎ 08705/505050, WEB www.citylink.co.uk). **Taxis** (☎ 0141/848–4900).

BUS TRAVEL

National Express provides bus service to and from London and other major towns and cities. The main terminal, St. Andrew Square bus station, is only a couple of minutes (on foot) north of Waverley station, immediately east of St. Andrew Square. Long-distance coaches must be booked in advance from the booking office in the terminal. Edinburgh is approximately eight hours by bus from London.

First Lowland, operating green-and-cream buses, provides much of the service between Edinburgh and the Lothians and conducts day tours around and beyond the city. First Bus Company also runs buses out of Edinburgh into the surrounding area.
➤ BUS LINES: **First Bus Company** (☎ 0131/663–1945). **First Lowland** (☎ 08706/082608). **National Express** (☎ 08705/808080, WEB www. nationalexpress.co.uk).

BUS TRAVEL WITHIN EDINBURGH

Lothian Buses, with its burgundy-and-white buses, is the main operator within Edinburgh. You can buy tickets on the bus. The Day Saver Ticket (£2.20), allowing unlimited one-day travel on the city's buses, can be purchased in advance or from the driver on any Lothian bus (exact fare is required when purchasing on a bus). The Rider Card (for which you will need a photo) is valid on all buses for seven days (beginning Sunday through Saturday night) and costs £10.50; the four-week Rider costs £30.50.

➤ INFORMATION: **Lothian Buses** (✉ 27 Hanover St., New Town, ☎ 0131/555–6363; ✉ Waverley Bridge, Old Town, ☎ 0131/555–6363 or 0131/554–4494; WEB www.lothian-buses.co.uk).

CAR RENTAL

Major companies have booths at the airport. Rates start at about £40 per day.

➤ AGENCIES: **Avis** (☎ 0131/333–1866). **Europcar** (☎ 0131/344–3114). **Hertz** (☎ 0131/333–1019). **National Car Rentals** (☎ 0131/344–3250).

CAR TRAVEL

Downtown Edinburgh centers on Princes Street, which runs east–west and is closed to all but taxis and buses for most of its length. If you're driving from the east coast you'll come in on A1, with Meadowbank Stadium serving as a landmark. The highway bypasses the suburbs of Musselburgh and Tranent; therefore, any bottlenecks will occur close to downtown. From the Borders the approach to Princes Street is by A7/A68 through Newington. From Newington the east end of Princes Street is reached by North Bridge and South Bridge. Approaching from the southwest, you'll join the west end of Princes Street (Lothian Road) via A701 and A702; if you're coming west from Glasgow or Stirling you'll meet Princes Street from M8 or M9, respectively. A slightly more complicated approach is via M90—from Forth Road Bridge/Perth/east coast; the key road for getting downtown is Queensferry Road, which joins Charlotte Square close to the west end of Princes Street.

Driving in Edinburgh has its quirks and pitfalls, but competent drivers should not be intimidated. Metered parking in the city center is scarce and expensive, and the local traffic wardens are a feisty, alert bunch. Note that illegally parked cars are routinely towed away, and getting your car back will be expensive. After 6 PM the parking situation improves considerably, and you may manage to find a space quite near your hotel, even downtown. If you park on a yellow line or in a resident's parking bay, be prepared to move your car by 8 the following morning, when the rush hour gets under way. Parking lots are clearly signposted; overnight parking is expensive and not permitted in all lots.

CONSULATES

The London office of the Canadian High Commission can provide local information for visitors.

➤ CANADA: **Canadian High Commission** (☎ 0207/258–6316).
➤ UNITED STATES: **American Consulate General** (✉ 3 Regent Terr., Calton, ☎ 0131/556–8315).

EMERGENCIES

In an emergency dial **999** for an ambulance or for the police or fire departments (no coins are needed for emergency calls made from pay phones). Edinburgh Royal Infirmary lies 6 mi southeast of the city center in an area known as Little France.

You can find out which pharmacy is open late on a given night by looking at the notice posted on every pharmacy door. A pharmacy—or dispensing chemist, as it is called here—is easily identified by its sign, showing a green cross on a white background. Boots is open weekdays 8 AM–9 PM, Saturday 8–6, Sunday 10:30–4:30.

To retrieve lost property, try the Lothian and Borders police headquarters.
➤ HOSPITAL: **Edinburgh Royal Infirmary** (⊠ Dalkeith Rd., Little France, ☎ 0131/536–1000).
➤ LATE-NIGHT PHARMACY: **Boots** (⊠ 48 Shandwick Pl., west end of Princes St., West End, ☎ 0131/225–6757).
➤ LOST AND FOUND: **Lothian and Borders police headquarters** (⊠ Fettes Ave., Inverleith, ☎ 0131/311–3131).

MAIL AND SHIPPING
The post office in St. James Centre is the most central and is open Monday 9–5:30, Tuesday–Friday 8:30–5:30, and Saturday 8:30–6. There are two other main post offices in the city center. Many newsagents also sell stamps.
➤ POST OFFICES: **City Center post offices** (⊠ 40 Frederick St., New Town; ⊠ 7 Hope St., West End). **St. James Centre** (⊠ St. Andrew Sq., New Town, ☎ 0131/556–0478).

MONEY MATTERS
Most city-center banks have a bureau de change (usual banking hours are weekdays 9:30–4:45). The bureau de change at the Tourist Centre, Waverley Market, is open daily. There are also bureaux de change at Waverley Station, Edinburgh Airport, and Frasers department store, at the west end of Princes Street.

SIGHTSEEING TOURS
DAY TRIPS
Lothian Buses and limousine companies (☞ Airports and Transfers) offer day trips to destinations such as St. Andrews and Fife or the Trossachs and Loch Lomond.

ORIENTATION TOURS
Guide Friday, Ltd., conducts an orientation tour (£8.50) in cheerful open-top double-decker buses providing hop-on/hop-off service. Their commentaries tend to be more colorful than accurate. The minimum tour time is one hour, and buses leave from Waverley Bridge. This company also operates a shuttle bus service to see the former royal yacht *Britannia,* moored beside the Ocean Terminal at Leith; the bus runs every 40 minutes from Waverley Bridge (cost 50 pence).

Lothian Buses runs the Edinburgh Classic Tour, a worthwhile introduction to the Old and New Towns. The £7.50 ticket is a bargain because it's valid on any other Classic Tour bus for the rest of the day. There are frequent departures from Waverley Bridge (outside the rail station) and other points around the city. Open-top buses operate in suitable weather. This is a flexible, show-up-and-hop-on service, meaning that you can get off the bus at any attractions you may want to see more closely and then get on another open-top bus later. Allow an hour for the complete tour. You can buy tickets from the Lothian Regional Transport offices on Hanover Street or Waverley Bridge, or you can buy them from the driver.

Scottish Tourist Guides, endorsed by the Scottish Tourist Board, provides knowledgeable guides appropriate for an individual or a group. The tours are wide-ranging and flexible, and there's even a "Nightlife" tour.
➤ CONTACT: **Guide Friday, Ltd.** (⊠ 133–135 Canongate, Old Town, ☎ 0131/556–2244). **Lothian Buses** (☎ 0131/555–6363). **Scottish Tourist Guides** (contact Doreen Boyle, ⊠ Old Jail, St. John St., Stirling FK8 1EA, ☎ 01786/451953).

PERSONAL GUIDES

Scottish Tourist Guides can supply guides (in 19 languages) who are fully qualified and will meet clients at any point of entry into the United Kingdom or Scotland. They can also tailor tours to your interests.
➤ CONTACT: **Scottish Tourist Guides** (contact Doreen Boyle, ✉ Old Jail, St. John St., Stirling FK8 1EA, ☎ 01786/451953).

WALKING TOURS

Cadies and Witchery Tours, a fully qualified member of the Scottish Tourist Guides Association, has built a reputation for combining entertainment and historical accuracy in its lively and enthusiastic Ghosts and Gore Tour and Murder and Mystery Tour (£7 each), which take you through the narrow Old Town alleyways and closes, with costumed guides and other theatrical characters showing up en route.

The McEwan's Edinburgh Literary Pub Tour takes you on a memorable journey through 300 years of Scottish literary history, fact, and fiction. From the Old Town to the New, the action is well-paced across four charming pubs of literary merit. All tours leave from the Beehive Inn, in the Grassmarket, and by arrangement can include a literary lunch or supper.
➤ CONTACT: **Cadies and Witchery Tours** (✉ 352 Castlehill, Old Town, ☎ 0131/225–6745, WEB www.witcherytours.com). **The McEwan's Edinburgh Literary Pub Tour** (✉ 97B W. Bow, Suite 2, Old Town, ☎ 0131/226–6665 or 0131/226–6667).

TAXIS

Taxi stands can be found throughout the downtown area. The following are the most convenient: the west end of Princes Street; South St. David Street, and North St. Andrew Street (both just off St. Andrew Square); Waverley Market; Waterloo Place; and Lauriston Place. Alternatively, hail any taxi displaying an illuminated FOR HIRE sign.

TRAIN TRAVEL

Edinburgh has no urban or suburban rail systems.

Edinburgh's main train hub, Waverley Station, is downtown, below Waverley Bridge and around the corner from the unmistakable spire of the Scott Monument. Travel time from Edinburgh to London by train is as little as 4½ hours for the fastest service.

Edinburgh's other main station is Haymarket, about four minutes (by rail) west of Waverley. Most Glasgow and other western and northern services stop here. Haymarket can be slightly more convenient if you're staying in hotels beyond the west end of Princes Street.

For information call the National Train Enquiry Line.
➤ TRAIN INFORMATION: **National Train Enquiry Line** (☎ 08457/484950).

TRAVEL AGENTS

➤ LOCAL AGENT REFERRALS: **American Express** (✉ 139 Princes St., West End, ☎ 08706/001060).

VISITOR INFORMATION

Several excellent city maps are available at bookstores. Particularly recommended is the *Bartholomew Edinburgh Plan*, with a scale of approximately 4 inches to 1 mi, by the long-established Edinburgh cartographic company John Bartholomew and Sons, Ltd.

The Edinburgh and Scotland Information Centre, adjacent to Waverley Station (follow the TIC signs in the station and throughout the city), offers an accommodations service (Book-A-Bed-Ahead) in addition to the more typical services. It's open May–June and September, Monday–Saturday 9–7, Sunday 10–7; July–August, Monday–Saturday 9–8, Sunday 10–8; October–April, Monday–Saturday 9–6, Sunday 10–6.

Complete information is also available at the airport information desk at the Edinburgh Airport.

The *List,* a publication available from city-center bookstores and newsstands, and the *Day by Day Guide* and *Events 2003,* from the Edinburgh and Scotland Information Centre, list information about all types of events, from movies and theater to sports. The *Herald* and *Scotsman,* national newspapers published in Glasgow and Edinburgh, are good for both national and international news coverage, as well as for reviews and notices of upcoming events throughout Scotland.

➤ TOURIST INFORMATION: **Edinburgh and Scotland Information Centre** (✉ 3 Princes St., East End, ☎ 0131/473–3800, FAX 0131/473–3881, WEB www.edinburgh.org).

3   GLASGOW

If Edinburgh is proud, age-of-elegance, and reserved, Glasgow is feisty, industrial-revolution, and exuberant—and never more so than now, since cultural renewal has restored much of Glasgow's 19th-century grandeur. Today a busy metropolis with a thriving artistic life and cityscape à la Charles Rennie Mackintosh and Alexander "Greek" Thomson, Scotland's largest city is also its most fashionable and fun-loving, and more vibrant than ever.

By John
Hutchinson

Updated
by Kenneth
Walton

IN THE DAYS WHEN BRITAIN still ruled over an empire, Glasgow pronounced itself the Second City of the Empire. Its people were justifiably proud of Glasgow, as it was here that Britain's great steamships,
including the 80,000-ton *Queen Elizabeth,* were built. The term "Clyde-
built" (from Glasgow's River Clyde) became synonymous with good
workmanship and lasting quality. Scots engineers were to be found wherever there were engines—Glaswegians built the railway locomotives that
opened up the Canadian prairies, the South African veldt, the Australian
plains, and the Indian subcontinent. The world's greatest industrial and
scientific thinkers, such as Lord Kelvin and James Watt, tested their
groundbreaking theories and discoveries as young men in Glasgow.

A 16th-century traveler described Glasgow as "a flourishing cathedral
city reminiscent of the beautiful fabrics and florid fields of England."
Daniel Defoe in 1727 described it as "one of the cleanliest and most
beautiful and best-built of cities." Massive industrialization in the
19th century, however, was soon to create a Glasgow less clean and
less beautiful.

Stretching along the heavily industrialized banks of the River Clyde,
Glasgow had fallen into a severely depressed state by the early 20th
century. By the middle of the century its dockland slums were notorious seedbeds of inner-city decay. "All Glasgow needs," said an architecture pundit then, "is a bath and a little loving care." During the last
two decades of the 20th century, happily, the city received both. Modern Glasgow has undergone an urban renaissance: trendy downtown
stores, a booming and diverse cultural life, stylish restaurants, and an
air of confidence make it Scotland's most exciting city.

The city's development has been unashamedly commercial, tied up with
the wealth of its manufacturers and merchants, who constructed a vast
number of civic buildings throughout the 19th century. Many of these
have been preserved, and Glasgow has a justifiable claim to being
Britain's greatest Victorian city. Among those who helped shape Glasgow's unique Victorian cityscape during that great period of civic expansion was the local-born architect Alexander "Greek" Thomson
(1817–75). Many of his buildings have only recently begun to be appreciated and are still in disrepair. Side by side with the overly Victorian, Glasgow, always at the forefront of change, has an architectural
vision of the future in the work of Charles Rennie Mackintosh (1868–
1928). The Glasgow School of Art, the Willow Tearoom, the *Glasgow
Herald* building (now home to the Lighthouse architecture and design
center), and the churches and schools he designed point clearly to the
clarity and simplicity of the best of 20th-century design.

Glasgow first came into prominence in Scottish history somewhere
around 1,400 years ago, and typically for this rambunctious city it all
had to do with an argument between a husband and his wife. When
the king of Strathclyde gave his wife a ring, she was rash enough to
present it to an admirer. The king, having surreptitiously repossessed
it, threw it into the Clyde before quizzing his wife about its disappearance.
In her distress, the queen turned to her confessor, St. Mungo, for advice. He instructed her to fish in the river and—surprise—the first salmon
she landed had the ring in its jaws. Glasgow's coat of arms is dominated by three salmon, one with a ring in its mouth. Not surprisingly,
Mungo became the city's patron saint. His tomb lies in the mighty medieval cathedral that bears his name.

Glasgow flourished quietly during the Middle Ages. Its cathedral was
the center of religious life, its university a center of serious academia.

Although the city was made a burgh (i.e., granted trading rights) in 1175 by King William the Lion, its population never numbered more than a few thousand people. What changed Glasgow irrevocably was the Treaty of Union between Scotland and England, in 1707, which allowed Scotland to trade with the essentially English colonies in America. Glasgow, with its advantageous position on Scotland's west coast, prospered. In came cotton, tobacco, and rum; out went various Scottish manufactured goods and clothing. The key to it all was tobacco. The prosperous merchants known as tobacco lords ran the city, and their wealth laid the foundation for the manufacturing industries of the 19th century.

As Glasgow prospered, its population grew. The "dear green place" (the literal meaning of the Gaelic *Glas Cu,* from which the name "Glasgow" purportedly derives) expanded beyond recognition, extending westward and to the south of the original medieval city, which centered around the cathedral and High Street. The 18th-century Merchant City, now largely rejuvenated, lies just to the south and east of George Square, where all but a few of the original merchants' houses remain in their original condition. As the merchants moved to quieter areas in the west of the city, the beaux arts elegance of their mansions and quiet streets gave way to larger municipal buildings and commercial warehouses. Today Glasgow is infinitely more famous for its Victorian cityscapes. During the 19th century the population grew from 80,000 to more than 1 million, and along with this enormous growth there developed a sense of exuberance and confidence that's still reflected in the city's public buildings. The City Chambers, built in 1888, are a proud statement in marble and gold sandstone, a clear symbol of the wealthy and powerful Victorian industrialists' hopes for the future.

Today, as always, Glasgow's eye is trained on the future. Still, it has learned to take the best of its past and adapt it for the needs of the present day. The dear green places still remain in the city-center parks; the medieval cathedral stands proud, as it has done for 800 years; the Merchant City is revived and thriving; the Victorian splendor has been cleansed of its grime; and the cultural legacy of museums and performing arts is stronger than ever. To cap it all, Glasgow is a nexus of rail routes and motorways that can deliver you in less than an hour to Edinburgh, Stirling, Loch Lomond, the Burns Country, and the Clyde coast golfing resorts. The city is an excellent place to get out of—but, of course, is also a great place to get into.

Pleasures and Pastimes

Dining
You'll find Chinese, Italian, and Indian food in addition to the usual French and Scottish offerings. Glasgow also has a strong café culture: visit one or two to get a feel for this important feature of the city. Pubs are good bets for cheap lunches and friendly chats.

Lodging
Glasgow is Scotland's major business destination, with the Scottish Exhibition and Conference Centre serving as the hub of activity. Several big city-center hotels of both expensive and moderate character serve business travelers, and you'll find some good and reasonable small hotels and guest houses with a more pronounced character in the suburbs, convenient to the city by public transport.

Shopping
Glaswegians love to dress up, and you'll find some of the world's best clothes at the many stores and malls that have helped to make Glasgow

the biggest and most popular U.K. retail center outside of London. Princes Square is the in place to enhance your wardrobe—if you're willing to break the bank to do so. Buchanan Galleries is also very popular with serious shoppers.

EXPLORING GLASGOW

You can't read Glasgow's layout in a single glance. However, the city center is relatively flat and set along a straightforward grid of streets, making it easy to walk around Glasgow Cathedral and Provand's Lordship, High Street, and the Merchant City. The River Clyde, on which Glasgow's trade across the Atlantic developed, runs through the center of the city—literally cutting it in two and offering intriguing views of buildings on the south side. In Glasgow always look up: your reward is much ornate detailing visible above eye level.

In the quieter, slightly hillier western part of the city is Glasgow University and the often forgotten bohemian side of Glasgow.

Numbers in the text correspond to numbers in the margin and on the Glasgow and Glasgow Excursions: Ayrshire and the Clyde Valley maps.

Great Itineraries

To take advantage of Glasgow's wealth of cultural sites and shopping, you could easily spend four or five days, but you can see the city's greatest hits in only two days.

IF YOU HAVE 2 DAYS

Glaswegians are justifiably proud of the Burrell Collection in Pollok Country Park, so it should top your list of must-sees. On the first day explore the core of historic Glasgow—the medieval area, dominated by Glasgow's cathedral, and Merchant City. Buchanan Street, including the Princes Square development and the Buchanan Galleries, has the best shopping. On the second day, see the West End, including the artwork and Charles Rennie Mackintosh furniture at the Hunterian Art Gallery. If you haven't yet seen the city-center parks, venture to Glasgow Green, the art collections at Pollok Country Park, or the House for an Art Lover, at Bellahouston Park. Remember that Glasgow's pubs and clubs serve up entertainment until late in the evening.

IF YOU HAVE 5 DAYS

Five days will allow enough time to enjoy more of Glasgow's key museums and cultural attractions: the Glasgow Gallery of Modern Art, in the city center, or the St. Mungo Museum of Religious Life and Art, to the east. You could easily take a full day to see the cluster of West End museums by Kelvingrove Park (Hunterian Art Gallery and Hunterian Museum, Museum of Transport, and the Glasgow Art Gallery and Museum, Kelvingrove). For a good day trip take the hour-long train ride to Wemyss Bay, and from there take the ferry to the Isle of Bute, where you can visit Mount Stuart, a spectacular, stately Victorian home.

IF YOU HAVE 10 DAYS

Ten days will allow you to thoroughly explore all the museums (you may want to visit the Burrell Collection more than once). Shopping in Princes Square can easily occupy a morning; Buchanan Street, Sauchiehall Street, and Argyle Street will also reward inveterate shoppers. Make time for at least one side trip. Ayrshire and the Clyde coast need at least two days, possibly three if you want to see everything: Mount Stuart House, on the Isle of Bute; Ayr and Alloway, which will delight Robert

Burns enthusiasts; and the cliff-top Culzean Castle, whose Georgian elegance provides sharp contrast to the Victorian Gothic spirit of Mount Stuart. Travel up the Clyde Valley to Lanark for a morning at New Lanark, the restored World Heritage Site that was Robert Owen's 18th-century social experiment in improving the lives of mill workers. Here you can also enjoy beautiful walks along the waterfall-dotted River Clyde. Biggar will fill an afternoon or more with its fascinating museums, including Moat Park, which has a fine embroidery collection.

Medieval Glasgow and the Merchant City

In this central part of the city, alongside the relatively few surviving medieval buildings, are some of the best examples of the architectural confidence and exuberance that so characterized the burgeoning Glasgow of the turn of the 20th century.

A Good Walk

George Square ①, the focal point of Glasgow's business district, is the natural starting point. It's in the very heart of Glasgow and is convenient to the Buchanan Street bus and underground stations and parking lot, as well as the two main railway stations, Queen Street and Glasgow Central. After viewing the **City Chambers** ②, on the square's east side, leave by the northeast corner and head eastward through a not particularly pretty part of the city along George Street, past Strathclyde University. Turn left at High Street, then go up the hill to **Glasgow Cathedral** ③, the **St. Mungo Museum of Religious Life and Art** ④, and the fascinating if macabre **Necropolis** ⑤, just off Cathedral Square.

Opposite the cathedral, across Castle Street, stands **Provand's Lordship** ⑥, Glasgow's oldest house. Retrace your steps down Castle Street and walk south down High Street. Look for the Greek goddess Pallas atop the imposing gray-sandstone building on the right, the former Bank of Scotland, before reaching the Tolbooth Steeple at **Glasgow Cross** ⑦. Continue southeast along London Road (under the bridge) about a quarter of a mile, and you'll come to the **Barras** ⑧, Scotland's largest indoor market. Turn right down Greendyke Street from London Road to reach **Glasgow Green** ⑨ by the River Clyde, with the **People's Palace** ⑩ museum of social history as its centerpiece.

Take the walkway west through Glasgow Green to the prominent McLennan Arch, and then head northeast via Saltmarket toward Tolbooth Steeple. Continue westward along Trongate. On the right is Candleriggs, which leads through to the ancient Ramshorn Church cemetery, where, among the opulent tombstones, are those of Glasgow's rich merchants. On the left, jutting out into Trongate, is the Tron Steeple, all that remains of a church burned down in 1793 when a joke by the local chapter of the Hell-Fire Club (young aristocratic troublemakers) got out of hand. The rebuilt church is the Tron Theatre.

Continue along the Trongate, then turn right on Hutcheson Street. This is Glasgow's **Merchant City,** with many handsome restored Georgian and Victorian buildings. At the end of the street, just south of George Square, look for **Hutcheson's Hall** ⑪, a National Trust for Scotland visitor center and shop. Continue up John Street, take a left on Cochrane Street, and a right on South Frederick Street; on the west side of George Square, on the corner with West George Street and opposite the magnificent City Chambers, is the **Merchants' House** ⑫. Return to Ingram Street and walk down Glassford Street; on the right is the Trades House, whose 1791 facade was designed by Robert Adam. Turn right along Wilson Street to reach Virginia Street, another favorite haunt of Glasgow's tobacco merchants. Walk northward up Virginia Street

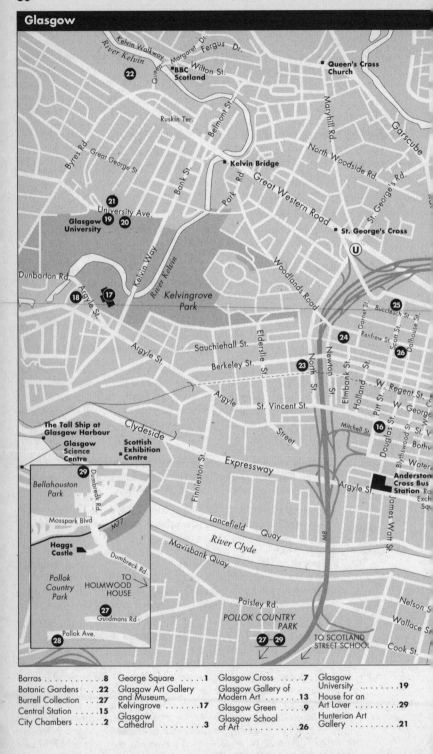

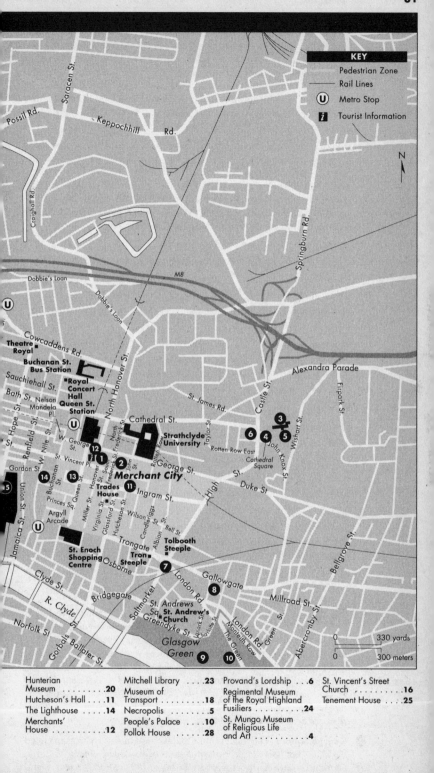

KEY

Pedestrian Zone

Rail Lines

Ⓤ Metro Stop

🛈 Tourist Information

N

Saracen St.

Possil Rd.

Keppochhill Rd.

Craighall Rd

Dobbie's Loan

M8

Dobbie's Loan

Springburn Rd.

Alexandra Parade

Elipark St.

Ⓤ

Cowcaddens Rd.

Theatre Royal

Buchanan St. Bus Station

Sauchiehall St.

Royal Concert Hall

Bath St.

Nelson Mondela Pl.

Queen St. Station

North Hanover St.

Cathedral St.

St. James Rd.

Castle St.

Hope St.

St.

Renfield St.

W. Nile St.

Ⓤ

W. George St.

St. Vincent Pl.

North Frederick St.

Strathclyde University

Taylor St.

3

6 **4** **5**

John Knox St.

Wishart St.

St. Vincent St.

12

1

2

Rotten Row East

Cathedral Square

Gordon St.

14

13

George St.

Raiten Row

Frederick St.

John St.

Merchant City

Ingram St.

Duke St.

High St.

15

Union St.

Jamaica St.

Buchanan St.

Queen St.

Miller St.

Virginia St.

Glassford St.

Hutcheson St.

Princes Sq.

11

Trades House

Wilson St.

Candleriggs

Bell St.

Albion

Bellgrove St.

Argyll Arcade

Ⓤ

St. Enoch Shopping Centre

Trongate

Tron Steeple

Osborne

Tolbooth Steeple

7

London Rd.

Gallowgate

8

Millroad St.

Abercromby St.

Clyde St.

Bridgegate

R. Clyde

Saltmarket

St. Andrews Sq.

St. Andrew's Church

London Rd.

The Green

Monteith Row

Greendyke St.

Norfolk St.

Gorbals

Ballater St.

Glasgow Green

9

10

330 yards

300 meters

back to Ingram Street. To the left you'll have a good view down to the elegant Royal Exchange Square and the former Royal Exchange building. Once a meeting place for merchants and traders, it's now the **Glasgow Gallery of Modern Art** ⑬. Royal Exchange Square leads you westward to the pedestrian-zone shopping area of Buchanan Street. The Princes Square shopping mall, on the east side, has a good selection of specialty shops. Just off Buchanan Street to the west, in Mitchell Lane, is **The Lighthouse** ⑭, a showcase center for architecture and design, housed in a Charles Rennie Mackintosh–designed building.

Make your way down to Argyle Street. Looking to the west, you'll see the large railway bridge supporting the tracks going into **Central Station** ⑮. Head north up Union Street, past Alexander Thomson's Egyptian Halls on the right before the Gordon Street junction, to St. Vincent Street. To see a famous example of Alexander Thomson's Greek revival churches, walk west on St. Vincent Street about eight blocks to Pitt Street and the **St. Vincent's Street Church** ⑯.

TIMING

This walk covers a lot of ground, but can be done comfortably in a day, leaving time to browse in Glasgow Cathedral, the People's Palace, and the Glasgow Gallery of Modern Art. Start after the morning rush hour, say at 10, and finish before the evening rush starts, about 4. Remember that the Barras is open only on weekends and the City Chambers only on weekdays.

Sights to See

❽ **Barras.** Scotland's largest indoor market—named for the barrows, or pushcarts, formerly used by the stall holders—is a must-see for anyone addicted to searching through piles of junk for bargains. The approximately 80-year-old institution, open weekends only, consists of nine markets. The atmosphere is always good-humored, and you can find just about anything here, in any condition, from old model railroads to quality jewelry. Haggling is compulsory! You can reach the Barras by walking from ScotRail's Argyle Street station, or take any of the various buses to Glasgow Cross at the foot of the Gallowgate. ⊠ *¼ mi east of Glasgow Cross on London Rd., Glasgow Cross,* ☎ *0141/552–7258.* ⊡ *Free.* ☉ *Weekends 9–5.*

⑮ **Central Station.** The railway bridge supporting the tracks going into the station is known as the Highlandman's Umbrella because it was the traditional gathering place for immigrant Highlanders looking for work in Glasgow in the early 20th century. The depot is the main station for trains to England and the Ayrshire coast and has interesting shops. ⊠ *Bounded by Gordon, Union, Argyle, Jamaica, Clyde, Oswald, and Hope Sts., City Center.*

★ ❷ **City Chambers.** Dominating the east side of George Square, this exuberant expression of Victorian confidence, built by William Young in Italian Renaissance style, was opened by Queen Victoria (1819–1901) in 1888. Among the interior's outstanding features are the entrance hall's vaulted ceiling, the marble-and-alabaster staircases, and the banqueting hall. Several smaller suites are furnished in different woods. ⊠ *George Sq., City Center,* ☎ *0141/287–2000,* WEB *www.glasgow.gov. uk.* ⊡ *Free guided tours weekdays at 10:30 and 2:30; may be closed for occasional civic functions.* ☉ *Weekdays 9–4:30.*

❶ **George Square.** The focal point of Glasgow's business district is lined with an impressive collection of statues of worthies: Queen Victoria; Scotland's national poet, Robert Burns (1759–96); the inventor and developer of the steam engine, James Watt (1736–1819); Prime Minister William Gladstone (1809–98); and towering above them all, Scotland's great historical novelist, Sir Walter Scott (1771–1832). The column was intended for George III (1738–1820), after whom the square is named, but when he was found to be insane toward the end of his reign, his statue was never erected. On the square's east side stands the magnificent Italian Renaissance–style ☞ **City Chambers**; the handsome ☞ **Merchants' House** fills the corner with West George Street.

Off and around George Square, several streets—Virginia Street, Miller Street, Glassford Street—recall the yesterdays of mercantile wealth. The French-style palaces, with their steep mansard roofs and cupolas, were once tobacco warehouses. Inside them are shops and offices; here and there you may trace the elaborately carved mahogany galleries where auctions once took place. ⊠ *Between St. Vincent and Argyle Sts., City Center.*

★ ❸ **Glasgow Cathedral.** The most complete of Scotland's cathedrals (it would have been more complete had 19th-century vandals not pulled down its two rugged towers), this is an unusual double church, one above the other, dedicated to Glasgow's patron saint, St. Mungo. Begun in the 12th century, consecrated in 1136, and completed about 300 years later, it was spared the ravages of the Reformation—which destroyed so many of Scotland's medieval churches—mainly because Glasgow's trade guilds defended it. In the lower church is the splendid crypt of St. Mungo, who was originally known as St. Kentigern (*kentigern* means "chief word,") but who was nicknamed St. Mungo (meaning "dear one") by his early followers in Glasgow. The site of the tomb has been revered since the 6th century, when St. Mungo founded a church here. Mungo features prominently in local legends; one such legend is about a pet bird that he nursed back to life, and another tells of a bush or tree, the branches of which he used to miraculously relight a fire. Tree, bird, and the salmon with a ring in its mouth (from the famous tale related in the introduction above) are all to be found on the city of Glasgow's coat of arms, together with a bell that Mungo brought from Rome. ⊠ *Cathedral St., City Center,* ☎ *0131/668–8800,* WEB *www. historic-scotland.net.* 🎟 *Free.* ☉ *Apr.–Sept., Mon.–Sat. 9:30–6, Sun. 1–5; Oct.–Mar., Mon.–Sat. 9:30–4, Sun. 1–4 and for services.*

❼ **Glasgow Cross.** This crossroads was the center of the medieval city. The Mercat Cross (*mercat* means "market"), topped by a unicorn, marks the spot where merchants met, where the market was held, and where criminals were executed. Here, too, was the *tron,* or weigh beam, installed in 1491 and used by merchants to check weights. The Tolbooth Steeple dates from 1626 and served as the civic center and the place where travelers paid tolls. ⊠ *Intersection of Saltmarket, Trongate, Gallowgate, and London Rd., Glasgow Cross.*

❸ **Glasgow Gallery of Modern Art.** One of Glasgow's boldest galleries occupies the former Royal Exchange building. The Exchange, designed by David Hamilton (1768–1843) and finished in 1829, was a meeting place for merchants and traders; later it became Stirling's Library. It incorporates the mansion built in 1780 by William Cunninghame, one of the wealthiest tobacco lords. The modern art, craft, and design collections contained within this handsome building include Scottish figurative art, works by Scottish artists such as Peter Howson and John Bellany, and also paintings and sculpture from around the world, including Papua New Guinea, Ethiopia, and Mexico. The display scheme is designed for each floor to reflect the elements—air, fire, and water—which creates some unexpected juxtapositions and also allows for various interactive exhibits. ⊠ *Queen St., City Center,* ☎ *0141/229–1996.* 🎟 *Free.* ☉ *Mon.–Thurs. and Sat. 10–5, Fri. and Sun. 11–5.*

❾ Glasgow Green. Glasgow's oldest park, on the northeast side of the River Clyde, has a long history as a favorite spot for public recreation and political demonstrations. Note the Nelson Column, erected long before London's; the McLennan Arch, originally part of the facade of the old Assembly Halls in Ingram Street; and the Templeton Business Centre, a former carpet factory built in the late 19th century in the style of the Doge's Palace in Venice. The most significant building in the park is the ☞ **People's Palace.**

★ ⓫ Hutcheson's Hall. Now a visitor center and shop for the National Trust for Scotland, this elegant neoclassical building was designed by David Hamilton in 1802. The hall was originally a hospice founded by two brothers, George and Thomas Hutcheson; you can see their statues in niches in the facade. ⊠ *158 Ingram St., Merchant City,* ☎ *0141/552–8391,* 🕸 *www.nts.org.uk.* ⌸ *£2.* ⊙ *Mon.–Sat. 10–5.*

⓮ The Lighthouse. Charles Rennie Mackintosh designed these former offices of the *Glasgow Herald* newspaper in 1893. Mackintosh's building now serves as a fitting setting for Scotland's **Centre for Architecture, Design and the City,** which celebrates all facets of the architectural profession. The **Mackintosh Interpretation Centre** is a great starting point for discovering more about his other buildings in the city. ⊠ *11 Mitchell La., City Center,* ☎ *0141/225–8414,* 🕸 *www.thelighthouse.co.uk.* ⌸ *£2.50 charge for Mackintosh Interpretation Centre; £1 charge for temporary exhibitions.* ⊙ *Mon. and Wed.–Sat. 10:30–5; Tues. 11–5; Sun. noon–5.*

Merchant City. Among the preserved Georgian and Victorian buildings in this area bounded by High, Argyle, Buchanan, and George streets, are elegant designer boutiques. The **City and County buildings,** on Ingram Street, were built in 1842 to house civil servants; note the impressive arrangement of bays and Corinthian columns. To see more interesting architecture, take time to explore the roads off of Ingram Street—including Candleriggs, Wilson, and Glassford.

⓬ Merchants' House. A golden sailing ship, a reminder of the importance of sea trade to Glasgow's prosperity, tops this handsome 1874 Victorian building, home to Glasgow's chamber of commerce. Inside is the fine **Merchants' Hall,** embellished with stained-glass windows and many portraits. ⊠ *West side of George Sq., City Center,* ☎ *0141/221–8272.* ⌸ *Free.* ⊙ *Hall and anterooms, weekdays 10–noon, and 2–5 unless closed for meetings, or by appointment.*

❺ Necropolis. A burial ground since the beginning of recorded history, the Necropolis, modeled on the famous Père-Lachaise Cemetery in Paris, contains some extraordinarily elaborate Victorian tombs. A statue of John Knox (circa 1514–72), leader of the Scottish Reformation, watches over the cemetery, which includes the tomb of 19th-century Glasgow merchant William Miller (1810–72), author of the "Wee Willie Winkie" nursery rhyme. ⊠ *Behind Glasgow Cathedral, City Center.*

★ ⓾ People's Palace. An impressive Victorian red-sandstone building dating from 1894 houses an intriguing museum dedicated to the city's social history. Included among the exhibits is one devoted to the ordinary folk of Glasgow, called the *People's Story.* Also on display are the writing desk of John McLean (1879–1923), the "Red Clydeside" political activist who came to Lenin's notice, and the famous "banana boots" worn on stage by well-known Glasgow-born comedian Billy Connolly. Behind the museum are the well-restored Winter Gardens, a relatively sheltered spot where you can escape the often chilly winds whistling across the green. ⊠ *Glasgow Green, Glasgow Cross,* ☎ *0141/*

554–0223, WEB *www.glasgow.gov.uk.* ✉ *Free.* ☉ *Mon.–Thurs. and Sat. 10–5, Fri. and Sun. 11–5.*

⑥ Provand's Lordship. Glasgow's oldest house was built in 1471 by Bishop Andrew Muirhead as a residence for churchmen. Mary, Queen of Scots (1542–87) is said to have stayed here. After her day, however, the house fell into decline and was used as a sweets shop, a soft-drink factory, the home of the city hangman, and a junk shop. The city finally rescued it and turned it into a museum. Exhibits show the house as it might have looked in its heyday, with period rooms and a spooky re-creation of the old hangman's room. ✉ *3 Castle St., City Center,* ☎ *0141/553–2557.* ✉ *Free.* ☉ *Mon.–Thurs. and Sat. 10–5, Fri. and Sun. 11–5.*

④ St. Mungo Museum of Religious Life and Art. An outstanding collection of artifacts speaks for the many religious groups that have settled throughout the centuries in Glasgow and the west of Scotland. The centerpiece is surrealist Salvador Dalí's (1904–89) magnificent painting *Christ of St. John of the Cross.* Inside are a gift shop and a café. ✉ *2 Castle St., City Center,* ☎ *0141/553–2557.* ✉ *Free.* ☉ *Mon.–Thurs. and Sat. 10–5, Fri. and Sun. 11–5.*

⑯ St. Vincent's Street Church. Dating from 1859, this church, the work of Alexander Thomson, exemplifies his Greek revival style, replete with Ionic temple, sphinx-esque heads, Greek ornamentation, and rich interior color. ✉ *Pitt and St. Vincent Sts., City Center.*

The West End

Glasgow's West End has a stellar mix of education, culture, art, and parkland. The neighborhood is dominated by Glasgow University, founded in 1451, making it the third-oldest in Scotland, after St. Andrews and Aberdeen, and at least 130 years ahead of the University of Edinburgh. It has thrived as a center of educational excellence, particularly in the sciences. The university buildings sit amid parkland, reminding you that Glasgow is a city with more green space per citizen than any other in Europe. You'll also be reminded in the West End that Glasgow is a city of museums and art galleries, having benefited from the generosity of industrial and commercial philanthropists and from the deep-seated desire of the city founders to place Glasgow at the forefront of British cities.

A Good Walk

Start at the city's main art museum, the **Glasgow Art Gallery and Museum, Kelvingrove** ⑰, in Kelvingrove Park, west of the M8 beltway, at the junction of Sauchiehall (pronounced *socky*-hall) and Argyle streets. There are free parking facilities, and plenty of buses come here from downtown. (Note that the Kelvingrove may close starting in March 2003 for renovations, so call ahead.) Across Argyle Street and next to the Kelvin Hall Sports Arena is the **Museum of Transport** ⑱.

As you walk up tree-lined Kelvin Way, the skyline to your left is dominated by the Gilbert Scott Building, **Glasgow University**'s ⑲ main edifice. Turn left onto University Avenue and walk past the Memorial Gates, which were erected in 1951 to celebrate the university's 500th birthday. On either side of the road are two important galleries, both maintained by the university. On the south side of University Avenue, in the Victorian part of the university, is the **Hunterian Museum** ⑳. Across University Avenue, in an unremarkable building from the 1970s, is the even more interesting **Hunterian Art Gallery** ㉑.

The walk from the university to the **Botanic Gardens** ㉒ isn't very exciting, but it's worth the effort. Continue west along University Avenue, turn right at Byres Road, and walk as far as Great Western Road and the Hilton Glasgow Grosvenor Hotel. The 40 acres of gardens are across the busy Great Western Road.

After leaving the gardens, cross the River Kelvin on Queen Margaret Drive and walk past the BBC Scotland building, just after Hamilton Drive. Turn right, then right again down the steps to the Kelvin Walkway, on the north bank of the river. (Farther upstream the Kelvin Walkway connects with the West Highland Way, an official long-distance footpath leading to Fort William, approximately 100 mi away.) The walkway that heads downstream toward the city center first crosses a footbridge, then passes old mill buildings, and then goes under Belmont Street and the Great Western Road at Kelvinbridge. Here it passes the Kelvinbridge underground station and goes under the Gibson Street Bridge, then back into Kelvingrove Park.

At this point, you can choose to take one of the paths up the hill and explore the stately Victorian crescents and streets of the park area, or you can take the lower road past the fountain and head directly back to Sauchiehall Street. Whichever way you choose, you should end up, having walked eastward, at the point where Sauchiehall Street crosses the M8 motorway. Down North Street to your right (southward) you'll see the front of **Mitchell Library** ㉓. Cross the M8 motorway and continue down Sauchiehall Street to the **Regimental Museum of the Royal Highland Fusiliers** ㉔. Turn left onto Garnet Street and walk to the top, then left on Buccleuch (pronounced buck-*loo*) Street. On the left stands the **Tenement House** ㉕, tucked away from normal tourist routes. Coming out of the Tenement House, head east on Buccleuch Street to Scott Street. As you turn south on Scott Street, notice the mural that reflects the name of the area, Garnethill, then turn left onto Renfrew Street and walk to Charles Rennie Mackintosh's masterpiece, the **Glasgow School of Art** ㉖. Nearby is his equally celebrated Willow Tearoom, where you can enjoy a cup of Earl Grey. To return to the city center, either continue down Scott Street, then east on Sauchiehall Street, or turn south down Blythswood Street, noting the elegant Blythswood Square, constructed between 1823 and 1829.

TIMING

You need at least a day for this walk, and even then you won't manage to do justice to the Hunterian museums and the Glasgow Art Gallery and Museum, Kelvingrove; if you anticipate lingering at the museums and galleries, plan at least two days since each could take up an enjoyable day in itself.

Sights to See

㉒ **Botanic Gardens.** The displays here were begun by the Royal Botanical Institute of Glasgow in 1842 and include an herb garden, tropical plants, and a world-famous collection of orchids. The most spectacular building in the complex is the **Kibble Palace,** built in 1873 and originally the conservatory of a Victorian eccentric named John Kibble. Its domed, interlinked greenhouses contain tree ferns, palm trees, temperate plants, and the Tropicarium, where you can experience the lushness of a tropical rain forest. Elsewhere on the grounds are more conventional greenhouses, as well as well-maintained lawns and colorful flower beds. ✉ *Great Western Rd., West End,* ☎ *0141/334–2422.* ✉ *Free.* ☉ *Gardens daily 7–dusk; Kibble Palace and other greenhouses daily 10–4:45. All close at 4:15 in winter (approximately Oct.–Feb.).*

★ ⑰ **Glasgow Art Gallery and Museum, Kelvingrove.** Looking like a combination of cathedral and castle, this magnificently ornamented redsandstone edifice dating from the early 20th century contains Glasgow's main museum and art gallery. There has always been debate as to which facade is the front and which is the back. However you enter, the Kelvingrove gallery houses what's claimed to be Britain's finest civic collection of British and Continental paintings, with 17th-century Dutch art, a selection from the French Barbizon school, French impressionism, Scottish art from the 17th century to the present, silver, ceramics, European armor, and even Egyptian archaeological finds. Be sure to pause at Rembrandt's *The Man in Armor.* At press time the museum was considering closing for extensive renovations starting March 2003, so call ahead. The Burrell Collection in the South Side will exhibit some of the gallery's artwork during the renovation. ✉ *Kelvingrove Park, West End,* ☎ *0141/287–2699,* WEB *www.glasgow.gov.uk.* 🎟 *Free.* ⏲ *Mon.–Thurs. and Sat. 10–5, Fri. and Sun. 11–5.*

★ 26 **Glasgow School of Art.** The exterior and interior, structure, furnishings, and decoration of this art nouveau building form a unified whole, reflecting the inventive genius of Charles Rennie Mackintosh, who was only 28 years old when he won the competition for its design. Architects and designers from all over the world come to admire it, but because it's a working school of art, general access is sometimes limited. Guided tours are available; it's best to make reservations. The art-school shop has an interesting selection of Mackintosh prints, postcards, and books, together with a selection of contemporary art by students and graduates. A block away is Mackintosh's Willow Tearoom. ✉ *167 Renfrew St., City Center,* ☎ *0141/353–4500,* WEB *www.gsa.ac.uk.* 🎟 *£5.* ⏲ *Tours weekdays at 11 and 2, Sat. at 10:30 and 11:30.*

NEED A BREAK?

The **Willow Tearoom** (✉ 217 Sauchiehall St., City Center, ☎ 0141/332–0521) has been restored to its original, archetypal Charles Rennie Mackintosh art nouveau design, right down to the decorated tables and chairs. The building was designed by Mackintosh in 1903 for Kate Cranston, who ran a chain of tearooms. The tree motifs reflect the street address—*sauchie* is an old Scots word for willow.

OFF THE BEATEN PATH

GLASGOW SCIENCE CENTRE – This family attraction, on the former Glasgow Garden Festival site, consists of an IMAX theater, a fun-packed Science Mall, and the 417-ft Glasgow Tower, a unique viewing point for the whole city. The Science Mall focuses its state-of-the-art displays on exploration, discovery, and the environment. Set aside half a day to make the most of it. ✉ *50 Pacific Quay, South Side,* ☎ *0141/420–5000,* WEB *www.gsc.org.uk.* 🎟 *Glasgow Tower £5.50, IMAX films £5.50; Science Mall £6.50.* ⏲ *Daily 10–6.*

19 **Glasgow University.** The architecture, grounds, and great views of Glasgow below all warrant a visit to the university. The Gilbert Scott Building, the university's main edifice, was built more than a century ago and is a good example of the Gothic Revival style. **Glasgow University Visitor Centre** has exhibits on the university, a coffee bar, and a gift shop and is the starting point for one-hour guided walking tours of the campus. ✉ *University Ave., West End,* ☎ *0141/330–5511.* 🎟 *Free; guided tour £2.* ⏲ *May–Sept., Mon.–Sat. 9:30–5, Sun. 2–5; Oct.–Apr., Mon.–Sat. 9:30–5. Tours: May–Sept., Mon.–Sat. at 2; Oct.–Apr., Wed. at 2.*

★ 21 **Hunterian Art Gallery.** This Glasgow University gallery houses Glasgow-doctor William Hunter's (1718–83) collection of paintings (his antiquarian collection is housed in the nearby Hunterian Museum), together with prints and drawings by Tintoretto, Rembrandt, Sir Joshua Reynolds, and Auguste Rodin, as well as a major collection of paintings by James McNeill Whistler, who had a great affection for the city that bought one of his earliest paintings. Also in the gallery is a replica of **Charles Rennie Mackintosh's town house,** which used to stand nearby. The rooms contain Mackintosh's distinctive art nouveau chairs, tables, beds, and cupboards, and the walls are decorated in the equally distinctive style devised by him and his artist wife, Margaret. ⊠ *Glasgow University, Hillhead St., West End,* ☏ *0141/330–5431,* WEB *www. hunterian.gla.ac.uk.* 🎫 *Free.* ◷ *Mon.–Sat. 9:30–5. Mackintosh house closed for lunch 12:30–1:30.*

㉚ Hunterian Museum. The city's oldest museum (1807) and part of Glasgow University, the Hunterian showcases part of the collections of William Hunter, an 18th-century Glasgow doctor who assembled a staggering quantity of valuable material. (The doctor's art treasures are housed in the nearby Hunterian Art Gallery.) The museum displays Hunter's hoards of coins, manuscripts, scientific instruments, and archaeological artifacts in a striking Gothic building. ⊠ *Glasgow University, West End,* ☏ *0141/330–4221,* WEB *www.hunterian.gla.ac.uk.* 🎫 *Free.* ◷ *Mon.–Sat. 9:30–5.*

Kelvingrove Park. This peaceful retreat, purchased by the city in 1852, takes its name from the River Kelvin, which flows through it. Among the numerous statues of prominent Glaswegians is one of Lord Kelvin (1824–1907), the Scottish mathematician and physicist who pioneered a great deal of work in electricity. The park also has a massive fountain commemorating a lord provost of Glasgow from the 1850s, a duck pond, a play area, a small open-air theater, and lots of exotic trees. ⊠ *Northwest of city center, bounded roughly by Sauchiehall St., Woodlands Rd., and Kelvin Way, West End.*

㉓ Mitchell Library. The largest public reference library in Europe houses more than a million volumes, including what's claimed to be the world's largest collection on Robert Burns. A bust in the entrance hall commemorates the library's founder, Stephen Mitchell, who died in 1874, the same year the library was founded. Minerva, goddess of wisdom, looks down from the library's dome, encouraging the library's users and frowning at the drivers thundering along the motorway just in front of her. The western facade (at the back), with its sculpted figures of Mozart, Beethoven, Michelangelo, and other artistic figures, is particularly beautiful. ⊠ *North St., City Center,* ☏ *0141/287–2931.* 🎫 *Free.* ◷ *Mon.–Thurs. 9–8, Fri.–Sat. 9–5.*

★ ⑱ Museum of Transport. Here Glasgow's history of locomotive building is dramatically displayed with full-size exhibits. The collection of Clyde-built ship models is world famous. Anyone who remembers Britain in the 1930s will wax nostalgic at the re-created street scene from that era. ⊠ *Kelvin Hall, 1 Bunhouse Rd., West End,* ☏ *0141/ 287–2720,* WEB *www.glasgow.gov.uk.* 🎫 *Free.* ◷ *Mon.–Thurs. and Sat. 10–5, Fri. and Sun. 11–5.*

- -

OFF THE
BEATEN PATH

QUEEN'S CROSS CHURCH – To learn about the Glasgow-born designer Mackintosh, head for the Charles Rennie Mackintosh Society Headquarters, housed in a church that he designed. Although one of the leading lights in the turn-of-the-20th-century art nouveau movement, Mackintosh died in 1928 with his name scarcely known. Today he's widely accepted as a brilliant innovator. This off-the-beaten-track center provides further insight into Glasgow's other Mackintosh-designed buildings, which include Scotland Street School, the Martyrs Public School, the Glasgow School of Art, and reconstructed interiors in the Hunterian Art Gallery. The church sits on the corner of Springbank Street at the junction of Garscube Road with Maryhill Road; a cab ride can get you here, or take a bus toward

Queen's Cross from stops along Hope Street. ⊠ *870 Garscube Rd.,
West End,* ☎ *0141/946–6600,* WEB *www.crmsociety.com.* 🎫 *£2.*
⊙ *Weekdays 10–5, Sun. 2–5, or by appointment.*

㉔ **Regimental Museum of the Royal Highland Fusiliers.** Exhibits of medals,
badges, and uniforms relate the history of a famous, much-honored
regiment and the men who served in it. ⊠ *518 Sauchiehall St., City
Center,* ☎ *0141/332–0961.* 🎫 *Free.* ⊙ *Mon.–Thurs. 9–4:30, Fri. 9–
4, weekends by appointment only.*

OFF THE
BEATEN PATH

THE TALL SHIP AT GLASGOW HARBOUR – This maritime attractions centers
around the restored tall ship the *Glenlee,* a former cargo ship originally
built in Glasgow in 1896, purchased by the Spanish navy, and bought
back by Glasgow in the 1990s. The ship itself is fascinating, but take
time to explore the Pumphouse Exhibition and Gallery, which has films
of the restoration process and interactive exhibits. A bus (No. 100) runs
every half hour from the Buchanan Street bus station. ⊠ *100 Stobcross
Rd., West End,* ☎ *0141/222–2513,* WEB *www.thetallship.com.*
🎫 *£4.50.* ⊙ *Mar.–Oct., daily 10–5; Nov.–Feb., daily 11–4.*

★ **㉕** **Tenement House.** An ordinary, simple city-center apartment is anything
but ordinary inside: it was occupied from 1911 to 1965 by Agnes
Toward, who seems never to have thrown anything away. Her legacy
is a fascinating time capsule, painstakingly preserved with her everyday furniture and belongings. The red-sandstone building dates from
1892 and can be found in the Garnethill area north of Charing Cross
station. ⊠ *145 Buccleuch St., City Center,* ☎ *0141/333–0183,* WEB *www.
nts.org.uk.* 🎫 *£3.50.* ⊙ *Mar.–Oct., daily 2–5, last admission 4:30.*

The South Side: Art-Filled Parks West

Just southwest of the city center in the South Side are two of Glasgow's
dear green places—Bellahouston Park and Pollok Country Park—
which have important art collections: Charles Rennie Mackintosh's
House for an Art Lover, the Burrell Collection, and Pollok House. A
respite from the buzz of the city can also be found in the parks, where
you can have a picnic or ramble through greenery and gardens. Both
parks are off Paisley Road, about 3 mi southwest of the city center.
You can take a taxi or car, city bus, or a train from Glasgow Central
Station to Pollokshaws West Station or Dumbreck.

A Good Tour

Traveling either by car, taxi, bus, or train, start your art exploration
at the **Burrell Collection** ㉗, with its diverse works displayed in a su-
permodern structure. Repair to the museum's good café-restaurant for
a bite, or plan to pack a picnic lunch to enjoy in one of the parks. **Pollok House** ㉘, with the Stirling Maxwell Collection of painting and fine
art, is just a walk of a few hundred yards beyond the Burrell. Head
north on Haggs Road and Dumbreck Road to Bellahouston Park and
the fascinating **House for an Art Lover** ㉙, built based on Charles Rennie Mackintosh's art nouveau design entry for a 1901 competition.

TIMING

Allow the good part of a day for seeing the three collections, strolls
through the parks, and a picnic or lunch. Note that the House for an
Art Lover is usually open only on weekends (and some weekdays).

Sights to See

★ **㉗** **Burrell Collection.** A custom-built, ultramodern (1983), elegant building of pink sandstone and stainless steel houses thousands of items of
all descriptions, from ancient Egyptian, Greek, and Roman artifacts

REDISCOVERING CHARLES RENNIE MACKINTOSH

NOT SO LONG AGO, the furniture of Glasgow-born architect Charles Rennie Mackintosh (1868–1928) was broken up for firewood. Today his major bookcases and chairs go for hundreds of thousands of pounds at auction, art books are devoted to his astonishingly elegant Arts and Crafts interiors, and artisans around the world look to his theory that "decoration should not be constructed, rather construction should be decorated" as holy law. Mackintosh's stripped-down designs slammed the door on Victorian antimacassars and floral chintz, ushering in the modern age with their deceptively stark style. Ironically, Scotland's most innovative designer had an extensive influence on European design, but failed to receive recognition as a true original in his native country until well after his death.

Mackintosh trained in architecture at the Glasgow School of Art and was apprenticed to the Glasgow firm of John Hutchison at the age of 16. During his training, he was awarded several prizes in recognition of his exceptional talent. In 1889 he joined the Glasgow firm Honeyman and Keppie. Early influences on his work included the Pre-Raphaelites, James McNeill Whistler (1834–1903), Aubrey Beardsley (1872–98), and Japanese art, but by the 1890s a distinct Glasgow style had been developed by Mackintosh and others. The building for the *Glasgow Herald* newspaper, which he designed in 1893 and which is now the Lighthouse Centre for Architecture, Design and the City, was soon followed by other major Glasgow buildings: Queen Margaret's Medical College; the Martyrs Public School; tearooms for Catherine Cranston, including the famous Willow Tearoom that can still be seen today; the Hill House, Helensburgh, now owned by the National Trust for Scotland; and Queen's Cross Church, completed in 1899 and now the headquarters of the Charles Rennie Mackintosh Society. In 1897 Mackintosh began work on a new home for the Glasgow School of Art, now recognized as one of his major achievements; it still retains original fittings, furnishings, ornamentation, and documents.

Mackintosh married Margaret Macdonald in 1900, and in later years her decorative work enhanced the interiors of his buildings. Over the next few years he worked abroad as well as in Scotland, being especially successful in Germany and Austria. In 1904 he became a partner in Honeyman and Keppie and designed Scotland Street School, now the Museum of Education, in the same year. Until 1913, when he left Honeyman and Keppie and moved to England, Mackintosh's various projects included work on buildings and/or interiors over much of Scotland, but especially in the Central Belt: Comrie, Bridge of Allan, Kilmacolm, and many other places. He preferred whenever possible to include interiors—furniture and fittings—as part of his overall design (a talent demonstrated clearly at the Hill House). He believed that building design should be "a total work of art, to the wholeness of which each contrived detail contributes."

Commissions in England after 1913 included a variety of design challenges not confined to buildings, including fabrics, furniture, and even bookbindings for the publishers Blackie and Sons. In 1923 Mackintosh settled in France, but he returned to London in 1927 and died there in 1928.

Glasgow must be the best place in the world to admire Mackintosh's work: in addition to the buildings mentioned above, most of which can be visited, the Hunterian Art Gallery contains magnificent reconstructions of the principal rooms at 78 Southpark Avenue, Mackintosh's Glasgow home, and original drawings, documents, and records, plus the re-creation of a room at 78 Derngate, Northampton.

to Chinese ceramics, bronzes, and jade. You'll also find medieval tapestries, stained glass, Rodin sculptures, and exquisite French impressionist paintings—Degas's *The Rehearsal* and Sir Henry Raeburn's *Miss Macartney,* to name a few. Eccentric millionaire Sir William Burrell (1861–1958) donated the magpie collection to the city in 1944. The exterior and interior were designed with large glass walls so that the items on display could relate to their surroundings in Pollok Country Park: art and nature, supposedly in perfect harmony. The Burrell will host major exhibitions of works from the Glasgow Art Gallery and Museum, Kelvingrove, when the latter museum closes for renovations, as is expected in spring 2003. ⊠ *2060 Pollokshaws Rd., Buses 45, 48, and 57 from Union St., South Side,* ☎ *0141/287–2550.* 🎫 *Free.* ☉ *Mon.–Thurs. and Sat. 10–5, Fri. and Sun. 11–5.*

OFF THE BEATEN PATH   **HOLMWOOD HOUSE** – The National Trust for Scotland has undertaken the restoration of this large mansion house, designed by Alexander "Greek" Thomson for the wealthy owner of a paper mill. Its classical Greek architecture and stunningly ornamented wood and marble features are among Thomson's finest. You can witness the ongoing restoration process one or two days a week. ⊠ *61–63 Netherlee Rd., South Side,* ☎ *0141/637–2129,* ᵂᴱᴮ *www.nts.org.uk.* 🎫 *£3.50.* ☉ *Apr.–Oct., daily 1:30–5:30, last admission at 5.*

㉙ **House for an Art Lover.** Within Bellahouston Park is a "new" Mackintosh house: based on a competition entry Charles Rennie Mackintosh submitted to a German magazine in 1901, but which was never built in his lifetime, it was completed in 1996. The building houses Glasgow School of Art's postgraduate study center and exhibits of designs for the various rooms and decorative pieces Mackintosh and his wife, Margaret, created. ⊠ *Bellahouston Park, Dumbreck Rd.; Buses 9, 53, and 54 from Union St., South Side,* ☎ *0141/353–4770.* 🎫 *£3.50.* ☉ *Apr.–Sept., Sat.–Thurs. 10–4; Oct.–Mar., weekends 10–4.*

㉘ **Pollok House.** The classic Georgian Pollok House, dating from the mid-1700s, contains the Stirling Maxwell Collection of paintings, including works by El Greco, Murillo, Goya, Signorelli, and William Blake. Fine 18th- and early 19th-century furniture, silver, glass, and porcelain are also on display. The house has fine gardens and looks over the White Cart River and Pollok Country Park, where, amid mature trees and abundant wildlife, the city of Glasgow's own highland cattle peacefully graze. ⊠ *Pollok Ave., Buses 45, 45A, 56, and 57 to the Gate of Pollok County Park, South Side,* ☎ *0141/616–6410,* ᵂᴱᴮ *www.nts.org.uk.* 🎫 *Apr.–Oct., £5; Nov.–Mar., free.* ☉ *Apr.–Oct., daily 10–5; Nov.–Mar., daily 11–4.*

OFF THE BEATEN PATH   **SCOTLAND STREET SCHOOL** – A former school designed by Charles Rennie Mackintosh, this building houses a fascinating museum of education. Classrooms re-create school life in Scotland during Victorian times and World War II, and a cookery room recounts a time when education for young Scottish girls consisted of little more than learning how to become a perfect housewife. An exhibition space and café are also here. The building sits opposite Shields Road underground station. ⊠ *225 Scotland St., South Side,* ☎ *0141/287–0500,* ᵂᴱᴮ *www.glasgow.gov.uk.* 🎫 *Free.* ☉ *Mon.–Thurs. and Sat. 10–5, Fri. and Sun. 11–5.*

DINING

Until the 1980s Glaswegians were famously unfussy about the vittles they ate—many of them wound up eating fast food, and, not surprisingly, newspaper surveys determined they had the shortest life span in the United Kingdom. Then something strange quietly occurred: Glasgow became acquainted with the concept of discerning taste buds and then eagerly welcomed one of the liveliest and most varied dining scenes in the country. No longer were hot curries, for which Glasgow is deservedly famous, and anything fried in batter enough. Today gastronomes no longer need approach Glasgow with trepidation and, more important, the local life expectancy has risen by six years.

The key to Glaswegian cuisine is not Glasgow. It's the flurry of foreign restaurants that abound—from late-night crepe stalls and *pakora* (Indian fried chickpea cakes) bars to elegant restaurants with worldly menus. Glasgow restaurants tend to be larger than their Edinburgh counterparts, so getting a table at the establishment of your choice shouldn't be a problem, though making reservations for a Friday or Saturday night is still advisable.

CATEGORY	COST*
££££	over £22
£££	£16–£22
££	£9–£15
£	under £9

per person for a main course at dinner, including VAT

Victorian Glasgow and Merchant City

Chinese

££ ✕ **Amber Regent.** This may not be the cheapest Chinese restaurant in town, but it's certainly one of the finest and most formal. For a start, the meticulously sculpted vegetables that accompany the hors d'oeuvres seem almost too artful to eat. Succulent Szechuan king prawns, and duck with mashed prawns in an oyster sauce readily attest to Amber Regent's long-standing reputation for serving excellent Cantonese and Szechuan cuisine. But this reputation also means that the restaurant can get very busy. For really top value, arrive before 6:45 PM, when the main courses are half price. ⊠ *50 West Regent St., City Center*, ☎ *0141/331–1655. AE, DC, MC, V. Closed Sun.*

££ ✕ **Loon Fung.** The pleasant, efficient staff at this popular Cantonese restaurant guides you enthusiastically through the house specials, including the famed dim sum. If you like seafood, try the deep-fried wonton with prawns, crispy stuffed crab claws, or lobster in garlic-and-cheese sauce. The three-course business lunch is first class and only £7.90. ⊠ *417 Sauchiehall St., City Center*, ☎ *0141/332–1240. AE, MC, V.*

Eclectic

£££–££££ ✕ **Rogano.** The spacious art deco interior, modeled after the style of the *Queen Mary* ocean liner—maple paneling, chrome trim, and dramatic ocean murals—is enough to recommend this restaurant. Portions are generous in the main dining area, where impeccably prepared specialties include roast rack of lamb and classic seafood dishes like seared scallops. Downstairs in the Café Rogano (£–££), the brasserie-style food is more modern and imaginative; the always-changing menu might list clam chowder or Mediterranean grilled swordfish. The theater menu provides early evening and late-night bargains, and the fixed-price lunch menu is popular upstairs. There's also an oyster bar. ⊠ *11 Exchange Pl., City Center*, ☎ *0141/248–4055. AE, DC, MC, V.*

££–££££ ✕ **ArtHouse Grill.** Many of Glasgow's greatest treasures lie hidden in basements. This elusive mix of grill restaurant and oyster bar is no exception. Take the trouble to find it and you'll discover that underground doesn't necessarily mean understated. The slick and upbeat interior—

with oak, stained glass, and burgundy and bright blue fabrics—is bold but tasteful, and never over the top. So is an eclectic menu that includes everything from marinated tuna to quality burgers and steak dishes. ⊠ *129 Bath St., City Center,* ☎ *0141/572–6002. AE, DC, MC, V.*

£££ ✕ **Khublai Khan Barbecue.** This sincerely Mongolian effort is about as exotic as you can get in this city. Wild boar and things you probably haven't heard of feature strongly, as you'll discover when you order the only option available, the Mongolian Feast (£15.50), which includes an unlimited barbecue main course. The massive space is festooned with handwoven rugs and a huge mural of Mongolian warriors advancing threateningly. Don't worry: the service is friendly. You may be too full for dessert, but don't pass up the unique *ristretto*—a miniature coffee that packs a giant punch. ⊠ *26 Candleriggs St., Merchant City,* ☎ *0141/552–5646. AE, DC, MC, V. No lunch.*

££–£££ ✕ **City Café.** On the rim of the city center, but with one of the best riverside locations in Glasgow, this contemporary, sunlight-filled restaurant is convenient for the adjacent Scottish Exhibition and Conference Centre and the south bank's Glasgow Science Centre. The menu dresses up traditional dishes with modern touches: roast salmon wrapped in prosciutto and served with a fennel compote, for example, or fillet of lamb with caramelized onions, broad beans, and a morel sauce. In good weather you can dine outside by the banks of the Clyde, and in the shadow of the mighty Finnieston Crane. ⊠ *Finnieston Quay, City Center,* ☎ *0141/227–1010. AE, DC, MC, V.*

££–£££ ✕ **Gordon Yuill and Company.** This busy restaurant's bright, modern
★ surroundings echo its fresh and exciting approach to dishes based on the best of Scottish produce. Excellent seafood options, such as steamed mussels with lemongrass, and several meat dishes, such as calves liver with crispy pancetta, are matched with imaginative Asian-influenced vegetarian dishes. A breakfast menu, available every day from 8, ranges from boiled eggs and bacon rolls to Loch Fyne kippers. Service is personal and friendly. ⊠ *257 West Campbell St., City Center,* ☎ *0141/ 572–4052. Reservations essential. AE, DC, MC, V.*

££–£££ ✕ **Groucho Saint Jude's.** You don't have to be young and "with it" to dine here, but it helps. With glitzy, modern appeal, Groucho's is the fashionable spot for the young Glasgow executive set after office hours. Even if this is not your crowd, don't let that stop you from tackling the extensive cocktail selection and equally diverse menu. Away from the bar, the quieter, more traditional dining room serves a daunting selection of dishes, but everything from the wild-mushroom risotto to the char-grilled sirloin of Aberdeen Angus is beautifully prepared and swiftly served. Celebrity-spotting is also part of the experience, but only if you know the local football stars. ⊠ *190 Bath St., City Center,* ☎ *0141/352–8800. Reservations essential. AE, DC, MC, V.*

££–£££ ✕ **78 St. Vincent.** Originally a bank, with slender interior Doric columns and strikingly carved griffins on the outside, this is now a stylish place to enjoy contemporary French-influenced Scottish cuisine. As your eyes feast on the wall-length modern mural by Glasgow artist Donald McLean, your palate can relish the Highland venison with gin-scented jus, or smoked duck salad with egg, scallops, prawns, and soy-sauce dressing. ⊠ *78 St. Vincent St., City Center,* ☎ *0141/248–7878. AE, DC, MC, V.*

££ ✕ **Brasserie.** A hotel basement fitted with wooden booths provides a quiet, relaxed environment in which to appreciate a varied modern European menu. The fish cakes are a traditional favorite here but also good are the spaghetti with mussels and clams for a starter, and the char-grilled rib-eye steak for a main course. Be sure to leave room for desserts such as the pineapple mille-feuille and homemade coconut sorbet. ⊠ *Malmaison Hotel, 278 W. George St., City Center,* ☎ *0141/ 572–1001. Reservations essential. AE, DC, MC, V. No lunch Sat.*

Glasgow Dining and Lodging

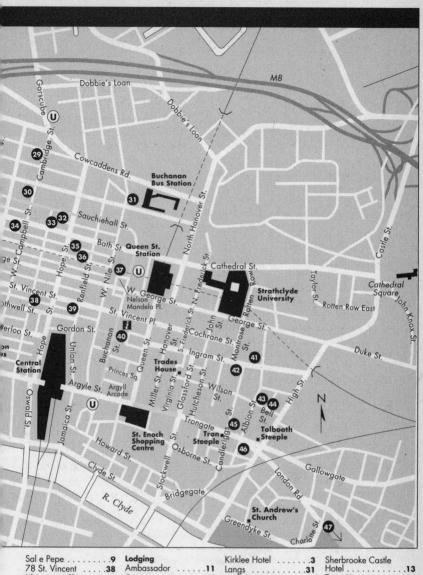

££   ✕ **Drum and Monkey.** A glorious Victorian former bank houses this
busy and friendly bar-restaurant. The food ranges from acceptable-
enough pub fodder to some Scottish-French delights, served up in an
adjacent bistro. Try the excellent fish cakes, the smoked salmon with
spinach and lemon-butter sauce, or the chicken stuffed with smoked
cheese and rosemary. ⊠ *93–95 St. Vincent St., City Center,* ☎ *0141/
221–6636. AE, DC, MC, V. Restaurant closed Sun. Jan.–Mar.*

£–££ ✕ **Café Gandolfi.** Once the offices of the former Glasgow cheese market, this trendy café is now popular with the design-conscious under-
30 crowd. Wooden tables and chairs crafted by Scottish artist Tim Stead
are so fluidly shaped it's hard to believe they're inanimate. The café
opens early for breakfast, serving croissants, eggs *en cocotte* (casserole
style), and espresso. The rest of the day the menu lists interesting
soups, salads, and local specialties, all made with the finest Scottish
produce. Don't miss the smoked venison or the finnan haddie (smoked
haddock). Evenings are livened up with good beers and decent wines.
⊠ *64 Albion St., Merchant City,* ☎ *0141/552–6813. MC, V.*

Indian

£–££ ✕ **Mr. Singh's.** One of Glasgow's most popular eateries serves superb
Indian and international cuisine backed by three generations of family experience. The restaurant is a restful haven in creams and blues
with plenty of beech wood, rather quirkily combined with Indian waiters in kilts and a menu including haggis *pakora* (deep-fried haggis
parcels). Meats and vegetables can be cooked in a number of deliciously
different sauces: try the lamb Mazadar—hot and spicy, with Rémy Martin—or the pistachio *korma* (curried meat with onions and vegetables).
⊠ *149 Elderslie St., City Center,* ☎ *0141/204–0186 or 0141/221–1452.
AE, DC, MC, V.*

Italian

£–££ ✕ **Pavarotti Trattoria.** Despite the somewhat silly name, no doubt aris-
ing from the restaurant's proximity to Scottish Opera's Theatre Royal,
this is not a kitsch affair but a sincerely Italian restaurant run by the
Scala family. The menu changes regularly because chef-owner Federico
will purchase only the freshest ingredients. Consequently, the standard
meat and fish dishes are unusually succulent. The lunch and pretheater set menus—only £8.90 each—are exceptionally good values. ⊠
91 Cambridge St., City Center, ☎ *0141/332–9713. AE, DC, MC, V.
No lunch Sun.*

£   ✕ **Fazzi Café Bar.** With its red tablecloths, tile floor, and bentwood chairs,
this inexpensive Italian café-bar is a cheerful place for a quick plate-
ful of gnocchi *alla Emiliana* (with tomato, basil, and cheese sauce) or
spinach-and-ricotta ravioli. The delicatessen here sells takeout. ⊠ *65–
67 Cambridge St., City Center,* ☎ *0141/332–0941. AE, DC, MC, V.*

Japanese

£–££ ✕ **OKO.** Sit by the conveyor belt and pick off the dishes that take your
★   fancy: tempura, sushi, and teriyaki preparations are among the classic minidishes that are both filling and reasonably priced. The interior
has a metallic avant-garde design. ⊠ *68 Ingram St., Merchant City,*
☎ *0141/572–1500. AE, MC, V. No lunch Sun.*

Pan-Asian

£–££ ✕ **Ruby.** The menu at this friendly restaurant starts with a Chinese base
and layers on Thai and Indonesian specialties. It then mixes the three
together, and the resulting taste sensations attract a cultlike clientele.
The menu has something for everyone. You can even get local fish-and-
chips, but far more tempting is the *ho mok talag* (mixed seafood in
herbs and a coconut sauce) or *dading rendang* (Spice Islands beef). The
menu prices can be deceptive, for although most main courses are under

£10, adding side dishes, starters, and dessert means you're likely to spend more than £20 a head. ⊠ *377 Sauchiehall St., City Center*, ☎ *0141/ 331–1277. AE, DC, MC, V.*

Russian

£–££ ✕ **Café Cossachok.** Near the Tron Theatre, this is a willfully arty
★ place: the tables are hand-carved, the lighting courtesy of candles, and the decor is a sea of shawls. The Russian owner pays further homage to his homeland with live music, at 8:30 Sunday, and a nicely chilled selection of vodkas. The menu includes delicious Petrushka blintzes and trout à la Pushkin (in a thirst-rousing salty sauce). This fun venue is fashionable among the fashionable, from actors to politicians, so it's best to book ahead. ⊠ *10 King St., Merchant City*, ☎ *0141/553–0733. AE, MC, V. Closed Mon. No lunch Sun.*

Scottish

££–££££ ✕ **City Merchant.** In Glasgow a purely Scottish restaurant is almost a novelty, and few can compare with this venue. The cooking is plain and simple, but makes use of the best ingredients. You can sample the freshest venison and steak in the land, but seafood remains the real attraction. The mussels and oysters from Loch Etive are wondrous, and the sea bass is renowned. There's a nice and relatively inexpensive selection of wines. Given the simple preparations, it may seem pricey (two-course set menus cost £10.50) but if you have a penchant for fresh and honest cuisine, this place is a joy. ⊠ *97–99 Candleriggs St., Merchant City*, ☎ *0141/553–1577. AE, DC, MC, V. No lunch Sun.*

££–£££ ✕ **Yes.** The basement location belies this restaurant's fine sense of
★ style, with careful lighting and mirrors that set off the dramatic red, purple, and cream color scheme. Widely spaced tables enhance the relaxed ambience in which you can enjoy contemporary Scottish cuisine. Try the Surprise Menu: an eclectic four-course selection incorporating the best fresh produce available, which might include rack of lamb with a wild-mushroom risotto or seared chicken breast on a bed of spinach. The ground-floor café-bar serves Mediterranean-Italian specialties in flashy digs. Reservations are advised. ⊠ *22 W. Nile St., City Center*, ☎ *0141/221–8044. AE, DC, MC, V. Closed Sun.*

££ ✕▣ **The Inn on the Green.** The Scottish-flavored à la carte menu at this warm and friendly basement restaurant ranges from layered haggis, and neeps (turnips) and mash, to hot Hebridean oak-smoked salmon. Live, relaxing nightly jazz accompanies your meal. You can purchase any of the delightful original works of art that clutter the walls. ⊠ *25 Greenhead St., Glasgow Cross*, ☎ *0141/554–0165. AE, MC, V.*

£ ✕ **Willow Tearoom.** There are two branches of this restaurant, but
★ Sauchiehall Street is the authentic one. Conceived by the great Charles Rennie Mackintosh, the Room De Luxe (the original tearoom) is kitted out with his trademark furniture, including those high-back chairs with elegant long lines and subtle curves. The St. Andrew's Platter is an exquisite selection of trout, salmon, and prawns. Scottish and Continental breakfasts are available throughout the day, and the scrambled eggs with Scottish salmon is traditional Scots food at its finest. The in-house baker guarantees fresh scones, cakes, and pastries. ⊠ *217 Sauchiehall St., City Center*, ☎ *0141/332–0521. MC, V. No dinner.*

West End and Environs

Eclectic

£–££ ✕ **Cul De Sac.** At the end of a quiet cobbled lane, this is one of the most relaxing of Glasgow's trendy West End eateries, right on the edge of the Glasgow University campus. It's a nice alternative to the more formal restaurants in the area, and large French windows add to the friendly street-café atmosphere. The menu includes everything from affordable pastas to red snapper to seared medallion of pork. ✉ *44–46 Ashton La., West End,* ☎ *0141/334–4749. AE, DC, MC, V.*

Indian

£–££ ✕ **Ashoka West End.** This Punjabi restaurant consistently outperforms
★   its many competitors in quality, range, and taste. All portions are large enough to please the ravenous, but there's nothing heavy-handed about the cooking here: vegetable *samosas* (stuffed savory deep-fried pastries) are crisp and light, the selection of breads is superb, and the spicing for the lamb, chicken, and prawn dishes is fragrant. The eclectic decor—involving a bizarre mixture of plants, murals, rugs, and brass lamps—and inappropriate Western music simply emphasize Ashoka's idiosyncrasy. Reservations are advised on weekends. ✉ *1284 Argyle St., West End,* ☎ *0800/454817. AE, MC, V. No lunch Sat.–Tues.*

£–££ ✕ **Killermont Polo Club.** Though not the most likely setting for an Indian restaurant, this former Victorian church manse on the outskirts of Glasgow's West End has the restful and romanticized atmosphere of colonial India. It specializes in the rather unique *Dum Puhkt* cooking tradition, which for a time was held secret by the Mughal royal family. The appetizer *shammi kebab badami* consists of firm patties of minced lamb shot through with cinnamon, coriander, and almonds. The gently prepared *chandi kaliyan* main course mixes lamb with a gravy of poppy seeds, cashews, and saffron. Finish off with the gorgeous sponge dessert, *gulab jamin.* ✉ *2022 Maryhill Rd., West End,* ☎ *0141/946–5412. AE, DC, MC, V.*

Italian

£–££ ✕ **Sal e Pepe.** Behind the inconsequential facade here are three floors of homey atmosphere and homey cooking, making it all seem like a very effortless Little Italy. Seafood is a specialty, but the half-price pizza and pasta dishes are perfect for value-conscious diners; they're available weekdays from 3 to 6, when everyone else is at work. There's also a supremely filling three-course pretheater special in the evening for only £8.95. ✉ *18 Gibson St., West End,* ☎ *0141/341–0999. MC, V.*

Japanese

£–£££ ✕ **Fusion.** This Japanese sushi bar serves a refreshing mix of dishes in
★   an equally refreshing modern setting. Try the sushi *kombis* or salmon, beef, or chicken teriyaki. The prawn-and-vegetable tempura is delicious. ✉ *41 Byres Rd., West End,* ☎ *0141/339–3666. MC, V.*

Latin

££ ✕ **Cottier's.** A converted Victorian church decorated by Glasgow artist Daniel Cottier is the unusual setting for this theater-bar-restaurant (the Arts Theatre is attached). Red walls and beamed ceilings warm the downstairs bar, where the pub grub on offer has Tex-Mex flavors. In the restaurant try the spicy lamb cooked with coconut, lime, cilantro, and beans, or the tuna and snapper fillets with anchovy, chili, and citrus butter—two excellent choices from the South American dishes on the menu. Weekend reservations are advised. ✉ *93 Hyndland St., West End,* ☎ *0141/357–5825. AE, MC, V.*

Middle Eastern

£ ✕ **Bay Tree.** A small delight in the university area, this café serves wonderful Middle Eastern vegetarian dishes. Egyptian *phool* (broad beans dressed with spices and herbs), Turkish *mulukia* (fried, sliced eggplant with a tomato-and-herb sauce), and *kurma* (stew with spinach, herbs, and beans) are among its delights. ✉ *403 Great Western Rd., West End,* ☎ *0141/334–5898. No credit cards.*

Scottish

£££–££££ ✕ **Amaryllis.** Set within the plush One Devonshire Gardens hotel is one
★ of Glasgow's most stylish restaurants. Amaryllis thrives on the reputation of its owner and celebrity chef Gordon Ramsay, and on a concise menu that contrasts sautéed sea bream and *pomme boulangère* (sliced
potatoes cooked in broth) with poached pigeon from Bresse. The spacious Victorian dining rooms, in bright creams and blues, match the
splendor of the original town house. ⊠ *1 Devonshire Gardens, West
End,* ☎ *0141/337–3434. Reservations essential. AE, MC, V. Closed
Mon. and Tues. No lunch Sat.*

£££ ✕ **Ubiquitous Chip.** In a converted mews stable behind the Hillhead
★ underground station is a restaurant that is an institution among members of Glasgow's media and thespian communities. The service is
friendly, and the interior very outdoorsy, with a glass roof, much greenery, and a fishpond. The menu specializes in game; Scotch-smoked salmon
in Darjeeling tea is typical of the chef's clever blending of Scots fare
with unusual elements. The wines are excellent. There are specially priced
two- and three-course meals, from £20 to £35; the Sunday special comes
in at £17.50 for four courses and a glass of bubbly. ⊠ *12 Ashton La.,
West End,* ☎ *0141/334–5007. AE, DC, MC, V.*

Vegetarian

£ ✕ **Grassroots Café.** One of Glasgow's most relaxing eateries, Grass Roots
provides vegetarian cooking that is wholesome, fresh, and above all,
interesting. Unlike the food, which includes its specialty Thai potatoes
and vegetarian chili, the interior is simple and plain. The list of fruit
juices is exhaustive, and organic ingredients are guaranteed, including
the wine. Set aside plenty of time, though, as nothing is hurried, especially for the popular weekend breakfasts. ⊠ *97 St. George's Rd.,
West End,* ☎ *0141/333–0534. AE, MC, V.*

South Side

Seafood

£–££ ✕ **Harry Ramsdens.** The traditional British fish supper comes with a
touch of class in Glasgow's biggest and most popular fish-and-chips
restaurant. This massive modern temple to cholesterol, complete with
sentimental stained glass and basic tearoom-style seating, offers much
more than the standard cod. Scallop of chicken in a light batter is just
one of the many deep-fried delights on a menu that spares less thought
for the waistline than the taste buds. You'll probably have to join the
inevitable queue in the bar area, but slick service means you rarely have
to wait long. ⊠ *251 Paisley Rd., opposite Springfield Quay, South Side,*
☎ *0141/429–3700. AE, DC, MC, V.*

LODGING

Central Glasgow never really goes to sleep, so downtown hotels will
be noisier than those in the leafy and genteel West End, convenient for
museums and art galleries, or southern suburbs, convenient for the Burrell Collection. The flip side is that most downtown hotels are within
walking distance of all the main sights, whereas you will need to make
use of the (excellent) bus service if you stay in the suburbs. Most
smaller hotels and all guest houses and bed-and-breakfasts include breakfast in the room rate. Larger hotels usually charge extra for breakfast.
Facilities are equal to those offered at accommodations in any other
major city—as elsewhere, you pay for what you get, with room service standard in most hotels (you may also get sports and leisure facilities in the largest), although rarer in guest houses and nonexistent
in B&Bs.

CATEGORY	COST*
££££	over £170
£££	£120–£170
££	£70–£120
£	under £70

All prices are for a standard double room, including service, breakfast, and VAT.

Medieval Glasgow and Merchant City

££££ 🏨 **Glasgow Hilton.** This is a typical, very professional international hotel on first impression, but Glasgow friendliness permeates its upscale image. Three theme restaurants—Cameron's, a Highland shooting lodge; Minsky's, a New York–style deli; and Shimla Pinks, an Indian restaurant—serve superb food, as does Raffles bar, with its colonial Singapore theme. ✉ *1 William St., City Center, G3 8HT,* ☎ *0141/204–5555,* FAX *0141/204–5004,* WEB *www.hilton.com. 319 rooms. 3 restaurants, health club, hair salon, bar, meeting room, free parking. AE, DC, MC, V.*

£££–££££ 🏨 **Malmaison.** The small, modern Malmaison, housed in a converted church, prides itself on personal service and outstanding amenities: each room has puffy down comforters and CD players. The art deco interior employs bold colors—eggplant, navy, cream, red—in playful prints and geometric shapes all balanced out by traditional fabrics and furniture. The lobby's splendid staircase has a wrought-iron balustrade illustrating Napoléon's exploits (the hotel takes its name from his home). The warm Brasserie offers traditional British-French cooking. Café Mal serves savory pizzas and pasta in an airy terra-cotta-hued room with iron fixtures and a spiral staircase. ✉ *278 W. George St., City Center, G2 4LL,* ☎ *0141/572–1000,* FAX *0141/572–1002,* WEB *www.malmaison.com. 72 rooms, 8 suites. 2 restaurants, minibars, gym, bar, meeting room. AE, DC, MC, V.*

££ 🏨 **Langs.** Langs's sophisticated and ultramodern character fits perfectly with its proximity to Glasgow Royal Concert Hall and the Buchanan Galleries shopping mall. It has a Japanese minimalist look that extends from the bright, wooden reception bar to bedrooms so imaginatively furnished they verge on the eccentric—soothing night-lights glow into the bedrooms through glass bricks in the bathroom, for example. Large windows add to the overall brightness, especially in the foyer areas. Mediterranean cuisine is the specialty of the Las Brisas restaurant. The Oshi restaurant serves excellent Japanese three-course pre- and post-theater menus for around £10. Japanese body treatments are available in the Oshi Spa. ✉ *2 Port Dundas St., City Center, G2 3LD,* ☎ *0141/333–1500,* FAX *0141/333–5700,* WEB *www.langshotels.com. 70 rooms, 30 suites. 2 restaurants, gym, spa, bar, meeting room; no a/c. AE, DC, MC, V.*

££ 🏨 **Babbity Bowster's.** There's a lively atmosphere at this intimate hotel in a restored 18th-century Robert Adam town house. Modern European furniture and simple, white bed linens fill the rooms, and the first-floor gallery displays many works by Glaswegian artists. The restaurant's teak tables, upholstered chairs, wooden floor, and gray-and-white color scheme complement the handsome hotel. ✉ *16–18 Blackfriars St., Merchant City, G1 1PE,* ☎ *0141/552–5055,* FAX *0141/552–7774. 6 rooms. Restaurant, café, bar; no a/c. AE, MC, V.*

££ 🏨 **The Inn on the Green.** Each spacious and bright room at this small, highly individual hotel has uniquely designed furniture—solid wood and metal creations, described by the owner as "designer rustic." Request one of the rooms with open views over Glasgow Green, Glasgow's oldest public park. The hotel, which is a convenient cab ride from downtown, has a lively restaurant that dishes up Scottish fare along with live jazz music. ✉ *25 Greenhead St., Glasgow Cross G40 1ES,* ☎ *0141/554–0165,* FAX *0141/556–4678,* WEB *www.theinnonthegreen. co.uk. 18 rooms. Restaurant, bar; no a/c. AE, MC, V.*

£ 🏨 **Bewley's.** With an emphasis on city-center convenience and practical budgets, Bewley's has simple, modern appeal: no frills, just clean-cut comfort and rich fabrics. And it's all just a stone's throw away from busy Sauchiehall Street. If the hotel doesn't have the facilities you need, staff can often still help you out: the hotel has an affiliation, for example, with a neighboring fitness center that charges a reduced fee of £8 per session. Loop restaurant serves breakfast, lunch, and dinner, with specialties such as Thai chicken with mint couscous. ✉ *110 Bath St., City Center, G2 2EN,* ☎ *0141/353–0800,* FAX *0141/353–0900,* WEB *www.bewleyshotels.com. 103 rooms. Restaurant, bar; no a/c. AE, DC, MC, V.*

West End and Environs

£££–££££ 🏨 **One Devonshire Gardens.** Celebrities such as Luciano Pavarotti ★ and Elizabeth Taylor name this hotel, which comprises a group of Victorian houses on a sloping tree-lined street, their favorite. Elegance is the theme, from the sophisticated drawing room to the sumptuous guest rooms with rich drapery and traditional mahogany furnishings; 10 of the rooms have four-poster beds. The hotel restaurant is equally stylish, with a different menu each month. Specialties include paupiette of sole filled with organic salmon and served with champagne sauce. Don't confuse the hotel restaurant with the privately run Amaryllis restaurant. ✉ *1 Devonshire Gardens, West End, G12 0UX,* ☎ *0141/339– 2001,* FAX *0141/337–1663,* WEB *www.one-devonshire-gardens.co.uk. 40 rooms. Restaurant, free parking; no a/c. AE, DC, MC, V.*

££ 🏨 **Town House.** A handsome old terraced house in a quiet cul-de-sac ★ serves as a B&B. The owners are welcoming, and the Town House thrives on repeat business. Restrained cream-and-pastel-stripe decor, stripped pine doors, and plain fabrics complement the high ceilings, plasterwork, and other original architectural features of the house. There's a comfortable sitting room with books, a coal-burning fireplace, and informative leaflets. ✉ *4 Hughenden Terr., West End, G12 9XR,* ☎ *0141/ 357–0862,* FAX *0141/339–9605,* WEB *www.thetownhouseglasgow.com. 10 rooms. No a/c. MC, V.*

£–££ 🏨 **Angus.** The biggest plus at this cozy yet spacious city-center hotel is the friendly staff with a knack for detail. All the rooms have the tasteful Victorian ambience. ✉ *966–970 Sauchiehall St., West End, G3 7TH,* ☎ *0141/357–5155,* FAX *0141/339–9469,* WEB *www.angushotelglasgow. co.uk. 19 rooms. Cable TV; no a/c. AE, MC, V.*

£ 🏨 **Ambassador.** Opposite the West End's peaceful Botanic Gardens, ★ and convenient for cab, bus, and underground travel to the city center, the Ambassador forms part of an elegant terrace of town houses on the banks of the River Kelvin. The interior echoes the peacefulness of the location and the traditional Victorian ethos of the spacious former family home. Though largely traditional, the rooms have a contemporary edge, with rich red and gold fabrics and beech furniture. ✉ *7 Kelvin Dr., West End, G20 8QG,* ☎ *0141/946–1018,* FAX *0141/ 945–5377,* WEB *www.glasgowhotelsandapartments.co.uk. 17 rooms. No a/c. MC, V.*

£ 🏨 **Kirklee Hotel.** This West End B&B near the university is in a small ★ and cozy Edwardian town house replete with home-away-from-home comforts. A bay window in the lounge overlooks a garden, and the Victorian morning room is adorned with embroidered settees and silk-wash wallpapers. Engravings and a large library offer decorative touches that any university don would appreciate. The owners are friendly and helpful. ⊠ *11 Kensington Gate, West End G12 9LG,* ☏ *0141/334–5555,* 𝙵𝙰𝚇 *0141/339–3828,* 𝚆𝙴𝙱 *www.scotland2000.com/ kirklee. 9 rooms. Library; no a/c. AE, DC, MC, V.*

£   🏨 **Manor Park Hotel.** On a quiet street close to Victoria Park, one of
★ Glasgow's most idyllic West End parks, this hotel combines urban spaciousness with proximity to city action. Each of the neat and airy bedrooms, even the bright attic ones, in this stately terraced town house bears the name in Gaelic of a Scottish island. The friendly owners themselves are Gaelic speakers, and tartan plays its part subtly in the homey decor. Local rail and bus services make travel into the city flexible and quick. ⊠ *28 Balshagray Dr., West End, G11 7DD,* ☏ *0141/339–2143,* 𝙵𝙰𝚇 *0141/339–5842,* 𝚆𝙴𝙱 *www.manorparkhotel.com. 10 rooms. Lounge, free parking; no a/c. AE, MC, V.*

£   🏨 **Number Thirty Six.** A Victorian terraced house in the West End, this B&B is convenient to the Hunterian museums and the Glasgow Art Gallery and Museum, Kelvingrove. A Continental-style breakfast is served in your room. ⊠ *36 St. Vincent Crescent, West End, G3 8NG,* ☏ *0141/248–2086,* 𝙵𝙰𝚇 *0141/221–1477. 5 rooms. No a/c, no smoking. MC, V.*

£   🏨 **The Sandyford.** The Sandyford is more an upscale B&B than a hotel, with a fine Victorian exterior, burgundies and greens inside, and pine furniture. On the west end of famous Sauchiehall Street, the hotel is convenient to all city-center facilities, including the Scottish Exhibition Centre and many art galleries. ⊠ *904 Sauchiehall St., West End, G3 7TF,* ☏ *0141/334–0000,* 𝙵𝙰𝚇 *0141/337–1812. 55 rooms. No a/c. MC, V.*

£   🏨 **Victorian House.** This B&B on a quiet residential street is only a block from the Charles Rennie Mackintosh–designed Glasgow School of Art. Although the staff is welcoming, the plain bedrooms are disappointing after the dramatic bright yellow used in the entrance hall and reception area. There are plenty of restaurants on nearby Sauchiehall Street. ⊠ *212 Renfrew St., City Center, G3 6TX,* ☏ *0141/332–0129,* 𝙵𝙰𝚇 *0141/353–3155. 57 rooms. No a/c. MC, V.*

South Side

£££–££££   🏨 **Sherbrooke Castle Hotel.** Come to the Sherbrooke for a flight of Gothic fantasy. Its cavernous rooms hark back to grander times when the South Side of Glasgow was home to the immensely wealthy tobacco barons, whose homes boasted turrets and towers. The spacious grounds are far from the noise and bustle of the city yet only a 10-minute drive from the city center. Like the tobacco barons, the hotel's proprietor insists on tasteful decor and good traditional cooking; the restaurant serves fine food made with fresh ingredients prepared on the premises, including the breads. Locals flock to the busy bar. ⊠ *11 Sherbrooke Ave., Pollokshields, South Side, G41 4PG,* ☏ *0141/427–4227,* 𝙵𝙰𝚇 *0141/427–5685. 25 rooms. Restaurant, bar; no a/c. AE, DC, MC, V.*

£–£££   🏨 **Ewington Hotel.** This quiet row of former Victorian town houses opposite Queen's Park has an open and traditional look. Victorian-style furniture, ornately decorated bedrooms with heavy and elaborate pink-and-green floral fabrics, and an open fire in the spacious lobby all add to the relaxed out-of-town character. The hotel has its own bar and restaurant. Downtown Glasgow is only a short bus or train ride away. ⊠ *132 Queen's Dr., South Side, G42 8QW,* ☏ *0141/423–1152,* 𝙵𝙰𝚇 *0141/422–2030. 43 rooms. Restaurant, bar, meeting room, free parking; no a/c. AE, DC, MC, V.*

NIGHTLIFE AND THE ARTS

Celtic Connections (✉ Glasgow Royal Concert Hall, 2 Sauchiehall St., City Center, G2 3NY, ☎ 0141/353–8000), held in the second half of January, is an ever-expanding annual homage to Celtic music, with musicians from Africa, France, Canada, Ireland, and Scotland playing and conducting hands-on workshops on such topics as harp-making and -playing.

The Arts

Concerts

Glasgow's **Royal Concert Hall** (✉ 2 Sauchiehall St., City Center, ☎ 0141/353–8000) has 2,500 seats and is the main venue of the Royal Scottish National Orchestra (RSNO), which performs winter and spring. The **Royal Scottish Academy of Music and Drama** (✉ 100 Renfrew St., City Center, ☎ 0141/332–5057) is one of the main small venues for concerts, recitals, and theater productions. The **Scottish Exhibition and Conference Centre** (✉ Finnieston, West End, ☎ 0141/248–3000) regularly hosts pop concerts.

Dance and Opera

Glasgow is home to the Scottish Opera and Scottish Ballet, both of which perform at the the **Theatre Royal** (✉ Hope St., City Center, ☎ 0141/332–9000). Visiting dance companies from many countries appear here as well.

Film

The **Glasgow Film Theatre** (✉ 12 Rose St., City Center, ☎ 0141/332–8128), an independent public cinema, screens the best new-release films from all over the world. The **Grosvenor** (✉ Ashton La., West End, ☎ 0141/339–4298) is a popular, compact cinema in Glasgow's West End. The **Odeon Film Centre** (✉ Renfield St., City Center, ☎ 0870/505–0007), an intimate movie theater, screens all the latest releases. **UGC Cinemas** (✉ 7 Renfrew St., City Center, ☎ 0870/907–0789), an 18-screen multilevel facility, is Glasgow's busiest movie complex and the world's tallest cinema building, at 170 ft.

Theater

Tickets for theatrical performances can be purchased at theater box offices or by telephone through the **Ticket Center** booking line (☎ 0141/287–5511).

The **Arches** (✉ 253 Argyle St., City Center, ☎ 0901/022–0300) stages new and controversial drama from around the world. Some of the most exciting theatrical performances take place at the internationally renowned **Citizens' Theatre** (✉ 119 Gorbals St., South Side, ☎ 0141/429–0022), where productions, and their sets, are often of hair-raising originality. Contemporary works are staged at **Cottier's Arts Theatre** (✉ 93 Hyndland St., West End, ☎ 0141/357–3868), in a converted church. The **King's Theatre** (✉ Bath St., City Center, ☎ 0141/287–5511) puts on drama, light entertainment, variety shows, musicals, and amateur productions. The **Pavilion** (✉ 121 Renfield St., City Center, ☎ 0141/332–1846) hosts family variety entertainment along with rock and pop concerts.

The **Royal Scottish Academy of Music and Drama** (✉ 100 Renfrew St., City Center, ☎ 0141/332–5057) stages international and student performances. The **Theatre Royal** (✉ Hope St., City Center, ☎ 0141/332–9000) hosts performances of major dramas, including an occasional season of plays by international touring companies, as well as opera and ballet. The **Tron Theatre** (✉ 63 Trongate, Merchant City, ☎ 0141/552–4267) puts on Scottish and international contemporary theater.

Nightlife

Consult the biweekly magazine the *List,* available at newsstands and bookstores, and the *Scotsman, Herald,* and *Evening Times* newspapers for up-to-date listings.

Bars and Pubs

Glasgow's pubs were once known for serious drinkers who demanded few comforts. Times have changed, and many pubs have been turned into smart wine bars. Most pubs are open daily from 11 AM to 11 PM.

If you visit only one pub in Glasgow, make it the **Horseshoe Bar** (✉ 17–21 Drury St., City Center, ☎ 0141/229–5711), which offers a sentimental, sepia-tinted glimpse of all the friendlier Glasgow myths and serves that cheerful distillation over what is purported to be the world's longest bar. Refurbishment would be a curse on its original tiling, stained glass, and deeply polished woodwork. Almost as intriguing as the decor is the clientele—a complete cross section of the city's populace. The upstairs lounge, with a bargain three-course lunch for £3, serves the steak pie for which Britain is famous.

Babbity Bowster's (✉ 16–18 Blackfriars St., Merchant City, ☎ 0141/552–5055), a busy, friendly spot, serves interesting beers and good food. The **Bon Accord** (✉ 153 North St., City Center, ☎ 0141/248–4427) is famous for its large selection of traditional ales. Despite its former austere existence as a Victorian church, the always-busy **Cottiers** (✉ Hyndland St., West End, ☎ 0141/357–5825) is a famous haunt of the young. The best seat is outside in the popular beer garden. The classic Victorian **Drum and Monkey** (✉ 93 St. Vincent St., City Center, ☎ 0141/221–6636) attracts an after-work crowd of young professionals.

There's good live music in the **Halt** (✉ 160 Woodlands Rd., West End, ☎ 0141/564–1527), which attracts a mixed-age clientele. **King Tut's Wah Wah Hut** (✉ St. Vincent St., City Center, ☎ 0141/221–5279), which hosts live music most nights, claims to have been the venue that discovered the U.K. pop band Oasis. This is a favorite with students, but its cozy and traditional pub setting draws people of all ages. **Nico's** (✉ 375 Sauchiehall St., City Center, ☎ 0141/332–5736), designed along the lines of a Paris café, is a favorite with art students and young Glaswegian professionals. The **Riverside Club** (✉ Fox St. off Clyde St., City Center, ☎ 0141/248–3144) hosts traditional *ceilidh* (a mix of country dancing, music, and song; pronounced *kay*-lee) bands on Friday and Saturday evenings; get there early, as it's very popular.

The **Scotia Bar** (✉ 112 Stockwell St., Merchant City, ☎ 0141/552–8682) serves up a taste of an authentic Glasgow pub, with some traditional folk music occasionally thrown in. **Tennants** (✉ 191 Byres Rd., West End, ☎ 0141/334–9122), a spacious street-corner bar, prides itself on a comprehensive selection of beers, lively conversation, and a refreshing lack of loud music. The best Gaelic pub is **Uisge Beatha** (✉ 232–246 Woodlands Rd., West End, ☎ 0141/564–1596), pronounced *oos*-ki *bee*-ha, which means "water of life" and is the origin of the word *whisky* (the term is a phonetic transliteration of the Gaelic word *uisge*). It serves *fraoch* (heather beer) in season and has live music on Wednesday and Sunday.

Nightclubs

As in most of Britain's clubs, electronic music—from house to techno to drum and bass—is par for the course in dance clubs. **Archaos** (✉

25 Queen St., City Center, ☎ 0141/204–3189), Glasgow's biggest club, has three dance floors blasting house, garage, indie, R&B, soul, and hip-hop music. It's open Wednesday through Sunday from 11 PM to 4 AM. The **Arches** (✉ 253 Argyle St., City Center, ☎ 0901/022–0300) is one of the city's largest arts venues, for both its own and touring theater groups, but on Friday (from 11 PM to 3 AM) and Saturday (from 10:30 PM to 4 AM) it thumps with house and techno and welcomes big music names. The **Polo Lounge** (✉ 84 Wilson St., Merchant City, ☎ 0141/553–1221) is Glasgow's largest gay club, with three bars and two dance floors for '70s, '80s, '90s, and '00s sounds—something for everyone. The festivities run Monday through Thursday from 5 PM to 1 AM, Friday from 5 PM to 3 AM, and weekends from noon to 3 AM.

OUTDOOR ACTIVITIES AND SPORTS

The **Greater Glasgow and Clyde Valley Tourist Board** (✉ 11 George Sq., near Queen Street station, City Center, ☎ 0141/204–4400) can provide more information on the following outdoor activities.

Biking and Running

The tourist board can provide a list of cycle paths and of the 70 parks and gardens in Glasgow where you can jog or pedal around the pathways.

Fishing

With loch, river, and sea fishing available, the area is popular with anglers. Details of fishing permits and locations are available from the tourist board.

Golf

Several municipal courses are operated within Glasgow proper by the local authorities. Bookings are relatively inexpensive and should be made directly to the course 24 hours in advance to ensure prime tee times (courses open at 7 AM). A comprehensive list of contacts, facilities, and greens fees of the 30 or so other courses near the city is available from the tourist board.

Kings Park (✉ Croftpark Ave., South Side, ☎ 0141/630–1597): 9 holes, 2,071 yards, SSS 30. **Lethamhill** (✉ 1240 Cumbernauld Rd., North City, ☎ 0141/770–6220): 18 holes, 5,836 yards, SSS 68. **Linn Park** (✉ Simshill Rd., South Side, ☎ 0141/637–5871): 18 holes, 5,132 yards, SSS 65. **Littlehill** (✉ Auchinairn Rd., North City, ☎ 0141/772–1916): 18 holes, 6,240 yards, SSS 70. **Ruchill** (✉ Brassey St., North City, ☎ 0141/946–8793): 9 holes, 2,217 yards, SSS 31.

Health Clubs

There are 19 municipal sports centers, including the three mentioned below, ranging from fairly basic swimming pools to facilities for a wide array of sports. See the brochure available from the tourist board for details. The larger hotels also have sports and leisure facilities, usually free of charge, for their guests. **Bellahouston Leisure Center** (✉ 31 Bellahouston Dr., South Side, ☎ 0141/287–5454). **Kelvin Hall International Sports Arena** (✉ Kelvin Hall, Argyle St., West End, ☎ 0141/357–2525). **Scotstoun Leisure Centre** (✉ Danes Dr., Scotstoun, West End, ☎ 0141/959–4000).

Sailing and Water Sports

The Firth of Clyde and Loch Lomond, each about a 30-minute drive southwest and north of Glasgow, respectively, both have water-sports facilities for sailing, canoeing, windsurfing, and rowing, with full equipment rental. Details are available from the tourist board.

Soccer

The city has been sports mad, especially for football (soccer), for more than 100 years, and the rivalry between its two main clubs, the Rangers and the Celtic, is legendary. Matches are held usually on Saturday in winter, and Glasgow has in total four teams playing in the Scottish Leagues. Admission prices start at about £17. Don't go looking for the family-day-out atmosphere of many American football games; soccer remains a fiercely contested game attended mainly by males, though the stadiums at Ibrox and Celtic Park are fast becoming family-friendly. Rangers wear blue and play at **Ibrox** (pronounced *eye*-brox; ✉ Edmiston Dr., South Side, ☎ 08706/001993), to the west of the city. The Celtic wear green and play in the east at **Celtic Park** (✉ 95 Kerrydale St., East End, ☎ 0141/551–8653).

SHOPPING

Glasgow has long been famous for its clothes shopping, and you can cover its main shopping centers and streets at small expense by bus, *provided* you don't get off. No one has yet discovered any way of keeping shop-'til-you-droppers on the buses, however, and considering the range, value, and attractiveness of the goods in the city's boutiques, no one can blame them.

Arcades and Shopping Centers

The **Buchanan Galleries** (✉ 220 Buchanan St., City Center, ☎ 0141/333–9898), at the top end of Buchanan Street next to the Royal Concert Hall, is packed with high-quality shops; its magnet attraction is the John Lewis department store. By far the best complex is **Princes Square** (✉ 48 Buchanan St., City Center, ☎ 0141/204–1685), with high-quality shops in an art-nouveau setting, along with cafés and restaurants. Look particularly for the Scottish Craft Centre, which carries an outstanding collection of work created by some of the nation's best craftspeople. **St. Enoch's Shopping Centre** (✉ 55 St. Enoch Sq., City Center, ☎ 0141/204–3900) is eye-catching if not especially pleasing— it's a modern glass building that resembles an overgrown greenhouse. It houses various stores, but most could be found elsewhere.

Department Stores

British Home Stores (✉ 67–81 Sauchiehall St., City Center, ☎ 0141/332–0401) carries typical department-store goods: clothes, household gadgets, linens, and foodstuffs. **Debenham's** (✉ 97 Argyle St., also accessed from St. Enoch Centre, City Center, ☎ 0141/221–0088) is one of Glasgow's principal department stores, with china and crystal as well as women's and men's clothing. **Frasers** (✉ 21–45 Buchanan St., City Center, ☎ 0141/221–3880), a Glasgow institution, stocks wares that reflect many of Glasgow's new and traditional images—leading European designer clothes and fabrics combined with home-produced articles, such as tweeds, tartans, glass, and ceramics. The magnificent interior, set off by the grand staircase rising to various floors and balconies, is itself worth a visit.

Marks & Spencer (✉ 2–12 Argyle St., City Center, ☎ 0141/552–4546; ✉ 172 Sauchiehall St., City Center, ☎ 0141/332–6097) sells sturdy, practical clothes and basic accessories at moderate prices; you can also buy food items and household goods here. **John Lewis** (✉ Buchanan Galleries, 220 Buchanan St., City Center, ☎ 0141/353–6677) is a favorite for its good-value mix of clothing and household items.

Shopping Districts

On the main, often-crowded pedestrian area of **Argyle Street,** you'll find chain stores such as Debenham's. An interesting diversion off Argyle Street is **Argyll Arcade,** a covered street that has the largest collection of jewelers under one roof in Scotland. This L-shape arcade, built in 1904, houses several locally based jewelers and a few shops specializing in antique jewelry. **Buchanan Street,** off the Argyll Arcade, is Glasgow's premier shopping street and almost totally a pedestrian area. The usual suspects are here: Laura Ashley, Burberry's, Jaeger, and other household names, some with premises in Buchanan Galleries, at the top end of the street. **St. Enoch Square,** which is also the main underground station, houses the St. Enoch Shopping Centre.

The huge **Barras** indoor market, on London Road in the Glasgow Cross neighborhood, prides itself on selling everything "from a needle to an anchor"; stalls hawk antique (and not-so-antique) furniture, bric-a-brac, good and not-so-good jewelry, and textiles—you name it, it's here. Many of Glasgow's young and upwardly mobile make their home in **Merchant City,** on the edge of the city center. Shopping here is expensive, but the area is worth visiting if you're seeking the young Glasgow style. The university dominates the area around **West End,** and the shops cater to local and student needs. The easiest way to get here is by the underground system to Hillhead. If you're an antiques connoisseur and art lover, a walk along **West Regent Street** is highly recommended, as there are various galleries and shops, some specializing in Scottish antiques and paintings.

Specialty Shops

Antiques and Fine Art

The **Compass Gallery** (⊠ 178 W. Regent St., City Center, ☎ 0141/221–6370) hosts interesting fine-art exhibitions. **Cyril Gerber Fine Art** (⊠ 148 W. Regent St., City Center, ☎ 0141/221–3095 or 0141/204–0276) specializes in British paintings from 1880 to the present; they will export, as will most galleries. **De Courcys** (⊠ 5–21 Cresswell La., West End), an antiques and crafts arcade, has quite a few shops to visit, and lots of goods, including paintings and jewelry, are regularly auctioned here. De Courcys is on one of the cobblestone lanes to the rear of Byres Road.

Books and Paper

Borders Books, Music and Café (⊠ 98 Buchanan St., City Center, ☎ 0141/222–7700), set in a former bank building, has a particularly friendly Glasgow air and carries a wide selection of Scottish books. The **Glasgow School of Art** (⊠ 167 Renfrew St., City Center, ☎ 0141/353–4526) has the Mackintosh Shop, selling various books, cards, jewelry, and ceramics. Students often sell their work during the degree show in June. **Papyrus** (⊠ 374 Byres Rd., West End, ☎ 0141/334–6514; ⊠ 296–298 Sauchiehall St., City Center, ☎ 0141/353–2182) carries designer cards and small gifts, as well as a good selection of books.

Clothing Boutiques

At Princes Square there are several famous designer names. **Ted B** (⊠ Unit 19, The Glasshouse, Princes Sq., City Center, ☎ 0141/ 9664) stocks men's and women's designer wares—lots of clothi accessories—at designer prices. **Strawberry Fields** (⊠ 517 Grea ern Rd., City Center, ☎ 0141/339–1121), sells colorful childre

Food

Peckham's Delicatessen (⊠ 100 Byres Rd., West End, ☎ 0 1454; ⊠ 43 Clarence Dr., West End, ☎ 0141/357–2909;

Station, City Center, ☎ 0141/248–4012; ✉ Glassford St., Merchant City, ☎ 0141/553–0666) is *the* place for Continental sausages, cheeses, and anything else you'd need for a delicious picnic.

Home Furnishings and Textiles
Casa Fina (✉ 1 Wilson St., Merchant City, ☎ 0141/552–6791) stocks stylish modern furniture and giftware. **In House** (✉ 24–26 Wilson St., Merchant City, ☎ 0141/552–5902) has top-quality, contemporary designer furniture as well as glassware, china, and textiles. **Linens Fine** (✉ The Courtyard, Princes Sq., City Center, ☎ 0141/248–7082) carries wonderful embroidered and embellished bed linens and other textiles. At the **National Trust for Scotland**'s shop (✉ Hutcheson's Hall, 158 Ingram St., Merchant City, ☎ 0141/552–8391) many of the items for sale, such as china, giftware, textiles, toiletries, and housewares, are designed exclusively for trust properties and are often handmade. Wander around **Stockwell Bazaar** (✉ 67–77 Glassford St., Merchant City, ☎ 0141/552–5781) to view a huge selection of fine china and earthenware, glass, and ornaments. Items will be packed and sent overseas for you, if requested.

Scottish Specialties
For high-quality giftware in Charles Rennie Mackintosh style, head to **Catherine Shaw** (✉ 24 Gordon St., City Center, ☎ 0141/204–4762; ✉ 32 Argyll Arcade, City Center, ☎ 0141/221–9038). **Hector Russell Kiltmakers** (✉ 110 Buchanan St., City Center, ☎ 0141/221–0217) specializes in Highland outfitting, Scottish gifts, woolens, cashmere, and women's fashions. **MacDonald MacKay Ltd.** (✉ 161 Hope St., City Center, ☎ 0141/204–3930) makes, sells, and exports Highland dress and accessories for men and custom-made kilts and skirts for women.

Sports Gear
You'll find good-quality outerwear at **Tiso Sports** (✉ 129 Buchanan St., City Center, ☎ 0141/248–4877), handy if you're planning some Highland walks.

Tobacco
Robert Graham (✉ 71 St. Vincent St., City Center, ☎ 0141/221–6588) carries a tremendous variety of tobaccos and pipes. Much of Glasgow's wealth was generated by the tobacco lords during the 17th and 18th centuries; at Graham's you'll experience a little of that colorful history.

SIDE TRIPS FROM GLASGOW: IN AND AROUND ROBERT BURNS COUNTRY

Those grand solitudes you see when flying into Glasgow Airport, that jigsaw puzzle of firths and straits and interlocking islands, harbors numerous one-day excursion destinations. Here you can travel south to visit the fertile farmlands of Ayrshire—Robert Burns country—or west to the Firth of Clyde, or southeast to the Clyde Valley, all by car or, in a modified form, by public transportation. You may want to begin with the town of Paisley. Once a distinct burgh but now part of the Glasgow suburban area, it has plenty of gritty character, largely from vestiges of its industrial heritage. It was once famous for its paisley shawl manufacturing, and its museum displays a fine collection of these garments. Palatial treasures are also en route—the Hamilton Mausoleum, Marquess of Bute's Mount Stuart House on the Isle of Bute, and Castle, a favored retreat for Eisenhower and Churchill that for its Robert Adam (1728–92) design and spectacular sea-ing.

The highlight of this region is Robert Burns country. English children learn that Burns (1759–96) is a good minor poet. But Scottish children know that he's Shakespeare, Dante, Rabelais, Mozart, and Karl Marx rolled into one. As time goes by, it seems that the Scots have it more nearly right. As poet and humanist, Burns increases in stature. When you plunge into Burns country, don't forget that he's held in extreme reverence by Scots of all backgrounds. They may argue about Sir Walter Scott and Bonnie Prince Charlie, but there's no disputing the merits of the poet of "Bonnie Doon."

Paisley

30 The industrial prosperity of Paisley came from textiles and, in particular, from the woolen paisley shawl. The internationally recognized paisley pattern is based on the shape of a palm shoot, an ancient Babylonian fertility symbol brought to Britain by way of Kashmir. The full story of the pattern and of the innovative weaving techniques introduced in
★ Paisley is told in the **Paisley Museum and Art Gallery,** which has a world-famous shawl collection. ✉ *High St.,* ☎ *0141/889–3151.* 🎟 *Free.* ☉ *Tues.–Sat. 10–5, Sun. 2–5.*

To get an idea of the life led by textile industry workers, visit the **Sma' Shot Cottages.** These re-creations of mill workers' houses contain displays of linen, lace, and paisley shawls. An 18th-century weaver's cottage is also open to visitors. ✉ *11–17 George Pl.,* ☎ *0141/889–1708.* 🎟 *Free.* ☉ *Apr.–Sept., Wed. and Sat. 12–4; Oct.–Mar. by appointment only.*

Paisley's 12th-century Cluniac **Abbey** dominates the town center. Almost completely destroyed by the English in 1307, the abbey was not totally restored until the early 20th century. It is associated with Walter Fitzallan, the high steward of Scotland, who gave his name to the Stewart monarchs of Scotland (Stewart is a corruption of "steward"). Outstanding features include the vaulted stone roof and stained glass of the choir. Paisley Abbey is today a busy parish church; if you're visiting with a large group you should call ahead. ☎ *0141/889–7654.* 🎟 *Free.* ☉ *Mon.–Sat. 10–3:30, Sun. services 11, 12:15, and 6:30.*

DINING AND LODGING

££ ✕🏠 **Glynhill Hotel.** This extended former mansion house combines elegant living with modern hotel convenience. Stylish and bright contemporary furnishings make the bedrooms cheerful and comfortable. Two established restaurants provide several lunch and dinner options. The buffet-style Palm Court Carverie serves a three-course dinner for £17.95. Le Gourmet, with its table d'hôte and à la carte menus, is a favorite with locals. The hotel is just off the M8 motorway (Junction 27) and close to Glasgow Airport and Paisley town center. ✉ *169 Paisley Rd., Renfrew, PA4 8XB,* ☎ *0141/886–5555,* WEB *www.glynhill.co.uk,* FAX *0141/885–2838. 125 rooms. Restaurant, indoor pool, bar, meeting room, free parking; no a/c. AE, DC, MC, V.*

Paisley A to Z

BUS TRAVEL
There's regular service to Paisley from the Buchanan Street bus station in Glasgow. Traveline Scotland can provide information on schedules and fares.

➤ BUS INFORMATION: **Buchanan Street bus station** (☎ 0141/333–3708). **Traveline Scotland** (☎ 0870/608–2608).

CAR TRAVEL
Take the M8 westbound and turn off at Junction 27, which is clearly signposted to Paisley.

TRAIN TRAVEL

Service runs every 5–10 minutes throughout the day from Glasgow Central Station.

➤ TRAIN INFORMATION: **Glasgow Central Station** (☎ 0845/748–4950 for information on national train service).

VISITOR INFORMATION

The tourist information center, which is open daily from 10 to 5, except on Sundays from October through March, is near Paisley Gilmour Street Railway Station.

➤ TOURIST INFORMATION: **Tourist information center** (✉ 9A Gilmour St., ☎ 0141/889–0711).

Ayrshire and the Clyde Coast

Robert Burns is Scotland's national and best-loved poet. His birthday is celebrated with speeches and dinners, feasting, and singing (Burns Suppers) on January 25, in a way in which few other countries celebrate a poet. He was born in Alloway, beside Ayr, just an hour or so south of Glasgow, and the towns and villages where he lived and loved make for an interesting day out.

On your way here you'll travel beside the estuary and firth of the great River Clyde and will be able to look across to Dumbarton and its Rock, a nostalgic farewell point for emigrants leaving Glasgow. The river is surprisingly narrow here, considering that the *Queen Elizabeth II* and the other great ocean liners sailed these waters from the place of their birth. Farther along the coast, the views north and west to Loch Long, Holy Loch, and the Argyll Forest Park are outstanding on a clear day. Two high points of the trip, in addition to the Burns connections, are Mount Stuart House, on the Isle of Bute, and south of Ayr, Culzean Castle, flagship of the National Trust for Scotland.

Wemyss Bay

③ From the old Victorian village of Wemyss Bay there's ferry service to the Isle of Bute, once a favorite holiday spot for Glaswegians. The many handsome buildings, especially the station and its covered walkway between platform and steamer pier, with its exuberant wrought ironwork, are a reminder of the Victorian era's grandeur and style and of the generations of visitors who used trains and ferries for their summer holidays. South of Wemyss Bay, you can look across to the island of Arran, another Victorian holiday favorite, and then to the island of Great Cumbrae, a weighty name for a tiny island.

Isle of Bute

③ The Isle of Bute affords a host of relaxing walks and scenic vistas. **Rothesay,** a faded but appealing resort, is the main town. Bute's biggest draw
★ is spectacular **Mount Stuart,** ancestral home of the marquesses of Bute, about 5 mi south of Rothesay. The massive Victorian Gothic palace built in red sandstone has ornate interiors, including the Marble Hall, with star-studded vault, stained glass, arcaded galleries, and magnificent tapestries woven in Edinburgh in the early 20th century. The paintings and furniture throughout the house are equally outstanding. ✉ *Isle of Bute,* ☎ *01700/503877,* WEB *www.mountstuart.com.* ✉ *Joint ticket for house and gardens, £7; gardens only, £3.50.* ☉ *Gardens May–Sept., Mon., Wed., and Fri.–Sun. 10–6; house May–Sept., Mon., Wed., Fri.–Sun. 11–5.*

DINING AND LODGING

££ ✕🔟 **Ardmory House Hotel.** This garden-surrounded hotel in a peaceful residential area evokes a modern home away from home, with Bute fabric (woven on the island) covering the chairs and a cozy bar with an open fire downstairs. Muted colors decorate the plainly furnished but comfortable bedrooms. The staff is exceptionally friendly and attentive. Standard bar meals such as homemade soup, lasagna, and chili are on offer, and the restaurant serves more elaborate creations—breast of duck with spiced mandarin orange and cherry mulled-wine sauce or salmon on a nest of fettuccine vegetables with saffron-butter sauce. ⊠ *Ardmory Rd., Ardbeg, Isle of Bute, PA20 0PG,* ☎ *01700/ 502346,* FAX *01700/505596. 5 rooms. Restaurant, bar; no a/c. MC, V.*

Largs

㉝ At the coastal resort of Largs, the community makes the most of the town's Viking history. This was the site in 1263 of a major battle that finally broke the power of the Vikings in Scotland, and every September a commemorative Viking Festival is held. **Vikingar! the Viking Heritage Centre** tells the story of the Viking influence in Scotland by way of film, tableaux, and displays. ⊠ *Barrfields, Greenock Rd.,* ☎ *01475/ 689777.* 🎫 *£4.* ☉ *Mar.–Oct., weekdays and Sun. 10:30–5:30, Sat. 12:30–3:30; Feb. and Nov., Sat. 12:30–3:30, Sun. 10:30–3:30.*

If you're in Largs on the seafront on a summer's afternoon, take time to visit the **Clark Memorial Church** (⊠ Bath St., ☎ 01475/675186), which has a particularly splendid array of Glaswegian Arts and Crafts stained glass of the 1890s in its windows. Among the studios involved in their design were those of Stephen Adam (1848–1910) and his contemporary Christopher Wall.

☝ Just south of Largs is **Kelburn Castle and Country Park,** the historic estate of the earl of Glasgow. There are walks and trails through the mature woodlands, including the mazelike Secret Forest, which leads deep into the thickets. The adventure center and commando-assault course wear out even the most overexcited of children. They tell a tale here of rescuing an elderly woman from halfway around the assault course, who commented, "Well, I did think it was rather a *hard* nature trail." Make sure you read the signposts. ⊠ *Fairlie, Ayrshire,* ☎ *01475/568685.* 🎫 *Grounds and castle £6; castle tour is an additional £1.50; grounds only £4.50.* ☉ *Grounds Easter–Oct., daily 10–6; Nov.–Easter, daily 11–5. Castle July–Sept., daily tours at 1:30, 2:45, and 4.*

Irvine

㉞ Robert Burns puts in an appearance at Irvine. Founded in 1826, the Irvine Burns Club is one of the oldest in the world. The poet came here to learn to dress flax (the raw material for linen), and the heckling (flax-dressing) shed where he worked and the house where he lived are museums known as the **Vennel Art Gallery.** ⊠ *4 and 10 Glasgow Vennel,* ☎ *01294/275059.* 🎫 *Free.* ☉ *Fri.–Sun. 10–1 and 2–5.*

Troon

㉟ The small coastal town of Troon is famous for its international golf course, Royal Troon. You can easily see golf is popular here: at times, the whole 60-mi-long Ayrshire coast seems one endless course.

DINING AND LODGING

££–£££ ✗ **MacCallums Oyster Bar.** The main ingredients at MacCallums come
★ straight from the sea, and the menu varies depending on the day's catch. You can usually count on lobster in garlic butter; seared scallops; or grilled langoustines. Excellent light white wines match the freshness of the food. Simple furnishings and solid wooden tables and floorboords decorate the dining room. Hidden among the boatyards and customs buildings of Troon Harbour, this top-class restaurant is easy to miss; it's right next to the Seacat Ferry Terminal. ⊠ *The Harbour, Troon,* ☎ *01292/319339. AE, DC, MC, V. Closed Mon.*

Glasgow Excursions: Ayrshire and the Clyde Valley

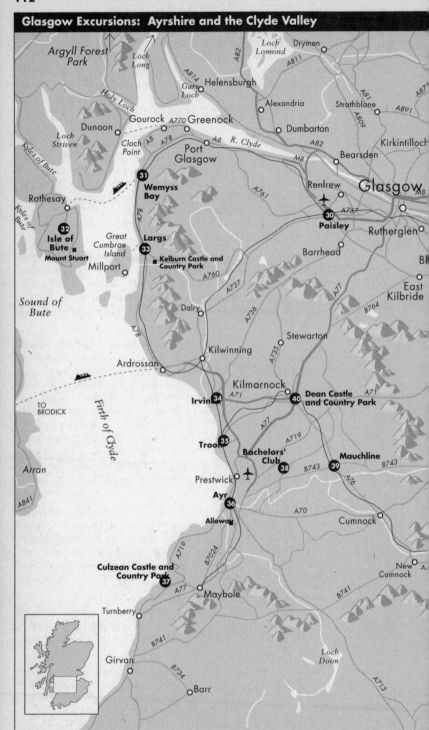

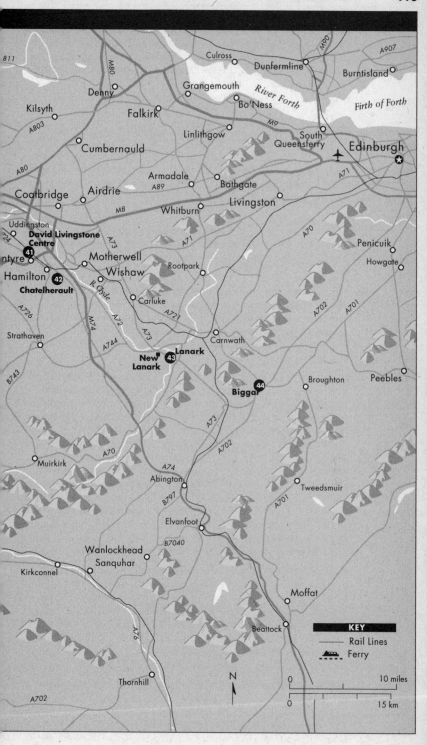

811

Culross

Dunfermline

Burntisland

Grangemouth

River Forth

Bo'Ness

Firth of Forth

A907

M90

Denny

M80

Kilsyth

Falkirk

A803

Linlithgow

M9

South
Queensferry

Edinburgh ✪

Cumbernauld

A80

Armadale

A89

Bathgate

Livingston

A71

✈

Coatbridge

Airdrie

M8

Whitburn

Uddingston

A724

**David Livingstone
Centre**

A73

Penicuik

Howgate

A70

ntyre

㊶

Motherwell

Rootpark

Wishaw

Hamilton

㊷

Chatelherault

R. Clyde

Carluke

Carnwath

A702

A701

A726

M74

A72

A721

A73

Strathaven

A744

**New
Lanark**

Lanark ㊸

Broughton

Peebles

B743

A73

Biggar ㊹

A70

Muirkirk

A74

Abington

A702

Tweedsmuir

B797

A701

Elvanfoot

Wanlockhead
Sanquhar

B7040

Moffat

Kirkconnel

Beattock

A76

KEY

—— Rail Lines

🚢 Ferry

N

0   10 miles

Thornhill

A702

0   15 km

£££   ✕🏨 **Piersland House Hotel.** This hotel is set in a late-Victorian mansion, formerly the home of a whisky magnate. All the bedrooms are furnished in traditional style. Oak paneling and log fires in the restaurant provide a warm backdrop for traditional Scottish cuisine, including specialties such as beef medallions in pickled walnut sauce. ⊠ *15 Craigend Rd., just north of Ayr, KA10 6HD,* ☎ *01292/314747,* 𝖥𝖠𝖷 *01292/315613. 28 rooms. Restaurant; no a/c. AE, DC, MC, V.*

GOLF

Royal Troon (⊠ Craigend Rd., ☎ 01292/311555), a club founded in 1878, has two 18-hole courses: the Old, or Championship (7,107 yards, SSS 74), and the Portland (6,289 yards, SSS 70). Access for nonmembers is limited between May and October to Monday, Tuesday, and Thursday only; day tickets cost £150 and include two rounds and a buffet lunch.

SHOPPING

Many Glaswegians frequent **Regalia Fashion Salon** (⊠ 44 Church St., ☎ 01292/312162) for its unusual collection of designer clothing for women.

Ayr

36   The commercial port of Ayr is Ayrshire's chief town, a peaceful and elegant place with an air of prosperity and some good shops. Robert Burns was baptized in the Auld Kirk (Old Church) here and wrote a humorous poem about the Twa Brigs (Two Bridges), which cross the river nearby. He described Ayr as a town unsurpassed "for honest men and bonny lasses."

If you're on the Robert Burns trail, head for **Alloway,** on B7024 in Ayr's southern suburbs. In Alloway, among the middle-class residences, you'll find the one-room thatched **Burns Cottage,** where Scotland's national poet was born in 1759 and which his father built; a museum of Burnsiana is next door. Not many outside Scotland appreciate the depth of affection Scotland has for Burns. To his fellow Scots he's more than a great lyric bard; he's the champion of the underdog, the lover of noble causes, the hater of pomposity and cant, the prophet of social justice. "A man's a man for a' that"—such phrases have exalted the Scottish character, while his love songs warm the coldest hearts. January 25, Burns Night, is an anniversary of importance in Scotland. ☎ *01292/441215.* 🎟 *£3; £5 ticket also includes admission to Tam o' Shanter Experience and Burns Monument, plus an audio guide.* ☉ *Apr.– Oct., daily 9–6; Nov.–Mar., Mon.–Sat. 10–4, Sun. noon–4.*

Find out all about Burns at the **Tam o' Shanter Experience.** Here you can first enjoy a 10-minute audiovisual journey through his life and times, then watch as one of Burns's most famous poems, "Tam o' Shanter," is brought to life on a three-screen theatrical set. It's down the road from Burns Cottage and around the corner from Alloway's ruined church. ☎ *01292/443700.* 🎟 *£1.50; £5 ticket also includes admission to Burns Cottage and Burns Monument, plus an audio guide.* ☉ *Apr.–Sept., daily 9–5:30; Oct.–Mar., daily 10–5.*

Auld Alloway Kirk is where Tam o' Shanter, in Burns's eponymous poem, unluckily passed a witches' revel—with Old Nick himself playing the bagpipes—on his way home from a night of drinking. Tam, in flight from the witches, managed to cross the **Brig o' Doon** (*brig* is Scots for *bridge*) just in time. His gray mare, Meg, lost her tail to the closest witch. (Any resident of Ayr will tell you that witches cannot cross running water.)

The **Burns Monument** overlooks the Brig o' Doon. ☎ *No phone.* 🎟 *£1, or as part of £5 ticket for Burns Cottage and Tam o' Shanter Ex-*

perience. ☼ *Apr.–Oct., daily 9–6; Nov.–Mar., Mon.–Sat. 10–4, Sun. noon–4*

££–£££ ✕ **Fouter's Bistro.** Fouter's is in a long and narrow cellar, yet its white
★ walls and decorative stenciling create a sense of airiness. The cuisine
is also light and skillful—no heavy sauces here. Try the roast Ayrshire
lamb with pan juices and red wine and mint, or sample the "Taste of
Scotland" appetizer—smoked salmon, trout, and other goodies. This
is modern Scottish and French cooking at its best. ⊠ *2A Academy St.,*
☎ *01292/261391. AE, DC, MC, V. Closed Sun. and Mon.*

Ayr has a good mixture of traditional and new shops. You can watch
craftspeople at work at the **Diamond Factory** jewelry workshop (⊠ 26
Queen's Court, ☎ 01292/280476). Particularly coveted are the handmade Celtic wedding bands. The store will export your purchases if
you don't have time to wait for the work to be completed. The **Mill
Shop, Begg of Ayr** (⊠ Viewfield Rd., ☎ 01292/267615) sells a good
selection of scarves, stoles, plaids, and travel rugs handmade on-site.

Culzean Castle and Country Park

★ ③⑦ The dramatic cliff-top Culzean (pronounced ku-*lain*) Castle and Country Park is the National Trust for Scotland's most popular property,
yet it remains unspoiled. Robert Adam designed the neoclassical mansion, complete with a walled garden, in 1777. In addition to its marvelous interiors, it contains the National Guest Flat, donated by the
people of Scotland in appreciation of General Eisenhower's (1890–1969)
services during World War II. As president he stayed here once or twice,
and his relatives still do so occasionally. Between visits it's used by the
National Trust for official entertaining. The rooms on the approach
to this apartment evoke the atmosphere of World War II: mementos
of Glenn Miller (1904–44), Winston Churchill (1874–1965), and other
personalities of the era all help create a suitably 1940s mood. On the
estate grounds, shrubberies reflect the essential mildness of this coast,
though some visitors, meeting the full force of a westerly gale, might
think otherwise. Culzean's perpendicular sea cliff affords views across
the Firth of Clyde to Arran and the Irish coast. Not a stone's throw
away, it seems, the pinnacle of Ailsa Craig rears from midchannel. ☎
01655/884400, WEB *www.nts.org.uk.* ⊠ *Park and castle £9; park only
£4.50.* ☼ *Park, daily 9:30–sunset; castle, Mar.–Oct., daily 10–5, last
admission at 4:30. Guided tours July–Sept., daily 11:30 and 3:30;
Oct.–June, daily 3:30.*

Bachelors' Club

③⑧ At Tarbolton is the Bachelors' Club, the 17th-century house where Robert
Burns learned to dance, founded a debating and literary society, and
became a Freemason. ☎ *01292/541940,* WEB *www.nts.org.uk.* ⊠
£2.50. ☼ *Mar.–Oct., daily 1–5.*

Mauchline

③⑨ Mauchline has strong connections with the poet Robert Burns. There's
a **Burns House** here, four of his daughters are buried in the churchyard,
and **Poosie Nansie's Pub,** where he used to drink, is still serving pints
today. The village is also famous for making curling stones.

Kilmarnock

This industrial town, home of Johnny Walker whisky, has more enjoyment for Burns enthusiasts: the Dick Institute, which houses the Burns
④⓪ Museum and the Burns Federation. **Dean Castle and Country Park** is
a 14th-century castle with a wonderful collection of medieval arms and
armor and an attractive visitor center. Burns also inevitably gets a men-

tion. ⊠ *Off Glasgow Rd.,* ☎ *01563/522702.* 🎟 *Free.* ☉ *Apr.–Oct., daily noon–5; Nov.–Mar., weekends 12–4.*

Ayrshire and the Clyde Coast A to Z

BUS TRAVEL

From Glasgow, take the bus to Largs for Cumbrae; Ardrossan for Arran; Ayr and Kilmarnock for the Burns Heritage Trail; and Troon, Prestwick, and Ayr to play golf. Bus companies also operate one-day guided excursions; for details contact the tourist information center in Glasgow, Strathclyde Passenger Transport (SPT) Travel Centre.

➤ BUS INFORMATION: **Strathclyde Passenger Transport (SPT) Travel Centre** (☎ 08706/082608).

CAR TRAVEL

Begin your trip from the Glasgow city center westbound on the M8, signposted for Glasgow Airport and Greenock. Join the A8 and follow it from Greenock to Gourock and around the coast past the Cloch Lighthouse. Head south on the A78 to the old Victorian village of Wemyss Bay and take the ferry over to Bute to see Mount Stuart (leave your car behind: a bus service takes you to the house from the ferry). Then continue down the A78 through Largs, Irvine, Troon, and on to Ayr and Alloway. Head to Culzean Castle, then return to Ayr and turn eastward on the B743, the Mauchline Road; but before you get here, turn left on a little road to Tarbolton and the Bachelors' Club. Return to the B743, visit Mauchline, and then head north on A76 to Kilmarnock. Glasgow is only a half hour away on the fast A77.

TRAIN TRAVEL

You can travel via train to Largs for Cumbrae; Ardrossan for Aryan; Ayr and Kilmarnock for the Burns Heritage Trail; and Troon, Prestwick, and Ayr to play golf.

➤ TRAIN INFORMATION: **National Rail Enquiry Line** (☎ 0845/748–4950).

VISITOR INFORMATION

All of the visitor centers in the area can provide you with brochures on the Burns Heritage Trail.

➤ TOURIST INFORMATION: **Ayr** (⊠ 22 The Sandgate, ☎ 01292/678100). **Irvine** (⊠ New St., ☎ 01292/678100). **Kilmarnock** (⊠ 62 Bank St., ☎ 01292/678100). **Largs** (⊠ Promenade, ☎ 01292/678100). **Rothesay** (⊠ The Winter Gardens, Rothesay, Isle of Bute, ☎ 01292/678100).

Clyde Valley

The River Clyde is (or certainly was) famous for its shipbuilding and heavy industries, yet its upper reaches flow through some of Scotland's most fertile farmlands, rich with tomato crops. It's an interesting area, with ancient castles as well as museums that tell the story of manufacturing and mining prosperity.

Blantyre

④ In the not-very-pretty town of Blantyre, look for signs to the **David Livingstone Centre,** a park area around the tiny (tenement) apartment where the great explorer of Africa (1813–73) was born. Displays tell of his journeys, of his meeting with Stanley ("Dr. Livingstone, I presume"), of Africa, and of the area's industrial heritage. ☎ *01698/823140,* WEB *www. nts.org.uk.* 🎟 *£3.50.* ☉ *Apr.–Sept., Mon.–Sat. 10–5, Sun. 12:30–5; Oct.– Mar., Mon.–Sat. 10:30–4, Sun. 12:30–4; call to confirm in winter.*

Bothwell Castle, with its well-preserved walls, dates to the 13th century and stands above the River Clyde. It's close to the David Livingstone Centre. ☎ *0131/668–8800.* 🎫 *£2.* ⊙ *Apr.–Sept., daily 9:30–6; Oct.–Mar., Mon.–Wed. and Sat. 9:30–4, Sun. 2–4, Thurs. 9:30–noon.*

Hamilton

The **Hamilton Mausoleum,** in Strathclyde Country Park near the industrial town of Hamilton, was built in the 1840s as an extraordinary monument to the lavish eccentricities of the dukes of Hamilton, who ❹❷ had more money than sense. Near Hamilton is **Chatelherault** (pronounced *shat*-lerro), a unique one-room-deep facade—part shooting lodge, part glorified dog kennel—designed in elegant Georgian style by William Adam (1689–1748) for the dukes of Hamilton. Within Chatelherault is an exhibition describing the glories of estate life. ☎ *01698/426213.* 🎫 *Free.* ⊙ *Visitor center Apr.–Sept., Mon.–Sat. 10–5, Sun. noon–5:30; Oct.–Mar., Mon.–Sat. 10–5, Sun. noon–5 (house has same hours as visitor center, but is closed Fri. year-round).*

Lanark

❹❸ Set in pleasing, rolling countryside, Lanark is a typical old Scottish town. It's now most often associated with its unique neighbor New Lanark, a World Heritage Site that was home to a social experiment—a model community with well-designed workers' homes, a school, and public buildings. The River Clyde powers its way through a beautiful wooded gorge, and its waters were harnessed to drive textile mill machinery before the end of the 18th century. The owner, David Dale (1739–1806), was noted for his caring attitude toward the workers, unusual for that era. Later, his son-in-law, Robert Owen (1771–1858), took this attitude even further, founding a benevolent doctrine known as Owenism and eventually crossing the Atlantic to become involved in a similar project in Indiana, called New Harmony, which, unlike New Lanark, failed. (Robert Owen's son Robert Dale Owen, 1801–77, helped found the Smithsonian Institution.)

After many changes of fortune the mills eventually closed and were converted into a hotel and private residential properties. As a result, residents have moved in and New Lanark has maintained its unique environment, where those leading normal everyday lives mix easily with the tourists. One of the mills has been converted into an **interpretative center,** which tells the story of this brave social experiment. Upstream, the Clyde flows through some of the finest river scenery anywhere in Lowland Scotland, with woods and spectacular waterfalls. ☎ *01555/665876,* 🌐 *www.newlanark.org.* 🎫 *£4.95.* ⊙ *Daily 11–5.*

LODGING

££ 🏨 **New Lanark Mill Hotel.** Housed in a converted cotton mill at the 18th-century model village of New Lanark, this hotel is decorated in a spare, understated style that allows the impressive architecture of barrel-vaulted ceilings and elegant Georgian windows to speak for itself. Right next to the river in the heart of the village, the hotel has all the attractions—visitor center, shops, Falls of Clyde Wildlife Reserve—at its doorstep. ✉ *New Lanark ML11 9DB,* ☎ *01555/667200,* FAX *01555/667222,* 🌐 *www. newlanark.org. 38 rooms, 8 cottages No a/c. AE, DC, MC, V.*

SHOPPING

Lanark has an interesting selection of shops within walking distance of each other. **McKellar's the Jewellers** (✉ 41 High St., ☎ 01555/661312) sells Charles Rennie Mackintosh–inspired designs in gold and silver. **Strands** (✉ 8 Bloomgate, ☎ 01555/665757) carries yarns and knitwear, including Aran designs and one-of-a-kind creations by Scottish designers.

Biggar

❹❹ A pleasant town built of stone, Biggar is a rewarding place to spend an hour or two, out of all proportion to its size. At Biggar you are near the headwaters of the Clyde, on the moors in the center of southern Scotland. The Clyde flows west toward Glasgow and the Atlantic Ocean, and the Tweed, only a few miles away, flows east toward the North Sea. There are fine views around Biggar: to Culter Fell and to the Border Hills in the south.

Gladstone Court Museum paints a fascinating picture of life in the town in years past, with reconstructed Victorian shops, a bank, a phone exchange, and a school. ⊠ *Gladstone Court,* ☎ *01899/221050.* ☑ *£2.* ⊘ *Apr.–Oct., Mon.–Sat. 10:30–5, Sun. 2–5.*

For Biggar's geology and prehistory, plus an interesting embroidery collection (including samplers and fine patchwork coverlets), visit the **Moat Park Heritage Centre,** also in the town center, in a former church. ⊠ *Moat Park Church, Moat Park,* ☎ *01899/221050.* ☑ *£2.* ⊘ *Easter–mid-Oct., Mon.–Sat. 10:30–5, Sun. 2–5.*

The **Gasworks,** built in 1839, is a fascinating reminder of the efforts once needed to produce gas for light and heat. ⊠ *Moat Park,* ☎ *01899/221050.* ☑ *£1.* ⊘ *June–Sept., daily 2–5.*

The **Greenhill Covenanters' House** is a farmhouse with Covenanting relics, 17th-century furnishings, costume dolls, and rare farm breeds. The Covenanters were breakaway supporters of Presbyterianism in the 17th century. ⊠ *Moat Park,* ☎ *01899/221050.* ☑ *£1.* ⊘ *May–Sept., daily 2–5.*

🅒 **Biggar Puppet Theatre** regularly presents performances by Purves Puppets. Before and after performances, two half-hour hands-on tours led by the puppeteers are available. One tour goes backstage with the puppets being demonstrated on stage; the other tours the puppet museum. The theater also has games and a picnic area. ⊠ *B7016, east of Biggar,* ☎ *01899/220631.* ☑ *Performances £5, tours £2.50.* ⊘ *Sept.–Easter, Mon.–Sat. 10–5; Easter–Aug., Mon.–Sat. 10–5, Sun. 2–5. Call for additional opening times and details.*

LODGING

£££–££££ 🄷 **Shieldhill Castle.** This foursquare Norman manor has stood on this spot since 1199, though it was greatly enlarged in 1560. It's in an ideal location for touring the Borders—just 27 mi from Edinburgh and 31 mi from Glasgow. The rooms are named after great Scottish battles—Culloden, Glencoe, Bannockburn—and are furnished with great comfort, with miles of Laura Ashley fabrics and wallpaper. ⊠ *Quothquan, near Biggar, ML12 6NA,* ☎ *01899/220035,* FAX *01899/221092,* WEB *www.shieldhill.co.uk. 16 rooms. 2 restaurants; no a/c. MC, V.*

Clyde Valley A to Z

BUS TRAVEL

Buses run between Glasgow and Hamilton. Inquire at the Buchanan Street bus station for details. Traveline Scotland can provide information on schedules and fares.

➤ Bus Information: **Buchanan Street bus station** (☎ 0141/333–3708). **Traveline Scotland** (☎ 0870/608–2608).

CAR TRAVEL

Take A724 east out of Glasgow, south of the river through Rutherglen toward Hamilton; it's not a very pretty route. In Blantyre look for signs to the David Livingstone Centre. From Blantyre take the main road to Hamilton. Then travel on the A72 past Chatelherault toward Lanark. You pass the ruins of medieval Craignethan Castle, lots of greenhouses for tomatoes, plant nurseries, and gnarled old orchards running down to the Clyde. Before reaching Lanark, follow the signs down a long winding hill, to New Lanark. A72 continues south of Lanark to join A702 near Biggar. At the end of a full day of touring you can return to Glasgow the quick way by joining the M74 from the A744 west of Lanark (the Strathaven road). Or take a more scenic route through Strathaven (pronounced *stra*-ven) itself, A726 to East Kilbride, and enter Glasgow from south of the river.

TRAIN TRAVEL

Service runs from Glasgow Central Station to Hamilton and Lanark; for details call the National Train Enquiry Line. There are no trains to Biggar, but there's a connecting bus from Hamilton to Biggar.
➤ TRAIN INFORMATION: **National Rail Enquiry Line** (☎ 0845/748–4950).

VISITOR INFORMATION

➤ TOURIST INFORMATION: **Abington** (✉ Welcome Break Services, M74 Junction 13, ☎ 01864/512436). **Biggar** (✉ 155 High St., ☎ 01899/221066). **Hamilton** (✉ Road Chef Services, M74 Northbound, ☎ 01698/285590). **Lanark** (✉ Horsemarket, Ladyacre Rd., ☎ 01555/661661).

GLASGOW A TO Z

To research prices, get advice from other travelers, and book travel arrangements, visit www.fodors.com.

AIR TRAVEL

Airlines operating through Glasgow Airport to Europe and the rest of the United Kingdom include Aer Lingus, Air Malta, British Airways, British Midland, easyJet, Icelandair, KLM UK, and GO. Several carriers fly from North America, including Air Canada, American Airlines, Continental, and Icelandair (service via Reykjavík).

Ryanair, easyJet, and GO have sparked a major price war on the Anglo-Scottish routes (e.g., between London and Glasgow). Ryanair offers unbeatable no-frills, rock-bottom air fares between Prestwick and London's Stansted Airport. GO and easyJet operate similar services from Glasgow to Stansted and Luton, respectively.
➤ CARRIERS: **Aer Lingus** (☎ 0845/973–7747). **Air Canada** (☎ 0870/524–7226). **Air Malta** (☎ 0845/607–3710). **American Airlines** (☎ 0845/778–9789). **British Airways** (☎ 0845/773–3377). **British Midland** (☎ 0870/607–0555). **Continental** (☎ 0800/776464). **easyJet** (☎ 0870/600–0000). **GO** (☎ 0870/607–6543). **Icelandair** (☎ 0845/758–1111). **KLM UK** (☎ 0870/507–4074). **Ryanair** (☎ 0870/156–9569).

AIRPORTS

Glasgow Airport is about 7 mi west of the city center on the M8 to Greenock. The airport serves international and domestic flights, and most major European carriers have frequent and convenient connections (some via airports in England) to many cities on the Continent. There's frequent shuttle service from London, as well as regular flights from Birmingham, Bristol, East Midlands, Leeds/Bradford, Manchester, Southampton, Isle of Man, and Jersey. There are also flights from Wales (Cardiff) and Ireland (Belfast, Dublin, and Londonderry). Local Scottish connections can be made to Aberdeen, Barra, Benbecula, Campbeltown, Inverness, Islay, Kirkwall, Shetland (Sumburgh), Stornoway, and Tiree.

Prestwick Airport, on the Ayrshire coast about 30 mi southwest of Glasgow and for some years eclipsed by Glasgow Airport, has grown in importance, not least because of the activities of Ryanair.

➤ AIRPORT INFORMATION: **Glasgow Airport** (☎ 0141/887–1111 for information; 0141/848–4440 for tourist information desk and accommodations-booking service). **Prestwick Airport** (☎ 01292/511006).

Glasgow Airport: Though there's a railway station about 2 mi from Glasgow Airport (✉ Paisley Gilmour St.), most people travel the short distance to the city center by bus or taxi. Journey time is about 20 minutes, longer at rush hour.

Express buses run from Glasgow Airport (terminal forecourt, outside departures lobby) to near the Central railway station, to Queen Street railway station, and to the Buchanan Street bus station. There's service every 15 minutes throughout the day. The fare is £3.50 on both Scottish Citylink and Fairline buses.

The drive from Glasgow Airport into the city center is normally quite easy, even if you're used to driving on the right. The M8 motorway runs beside the airport (Junction 29) and takes you straight into the Glasgow city center. Thereafter Glasgow's streets follow a grid pattern, at least in the city center, but a map is useful and can be supplied by the car-rental company.

Most companies that provide chauffeur-driven cars and tours will also do limousine airport transfers. Companies that are currently members of the Greater Glasgow and Clyde Valley Tourist Board are Charlton Chauffeur Drive, Corporate Travel, Little's, Peter Holmes, and Robert Neil.

Metered taxis are available outside domestic arrivals. The fare should be £15–£18.

Prestwick: An hourly coach service operates to Glasgow but takes much longer than the frequent train service. There's a rapid half-hourly train service (hourly on Sundays) direct from the terminal building to Glasgow Central. By car the city center is reached via the fast A77 in about 40 minutes (longer in rush hour). Metered taxi cabs are available at the airport. The fare to Glasgow is about £40.

➤ CONTACT: **Charlton Chauffeur Drive** (☎ 0141/570–2000). **Corporate Travel** (☎ 0141/639–8057). **Little's Chauffeur Drive** (☎ 0141/883–2111). **Peter Holmes** (☎ 01389/830688). **Robert Neil** (☎ 0141/641–2125).

BUS TRAVEL

Glasgow's bus station is on Buchanan Street. The main intercity operators are National Express and Scottish Citylink, which serve numerous towns and cities in Scotland, Wales, and England, including London (8½–9 hours); there's also service to Edinburgh. Buchanan Street is close to the underground station of the same name and to the Queen Street station. Traveline Scotland can provide information on schedules and fares.

➤ BUS INFORMATION: **Buchanan Street bus station** (☎ 0141/333–3708). **National Express** (☎ 0870/580–8080, WEB www.nationalexpress.co.uk). **Scottish Citylink** (☎ 0870/505050, WEB www.citylink.co.uk). **Traveline Scotland** (☎ 0870/608–2608).

BUS TRAVEL WITHIN GLASGOW

Bus service is reliable within Glasgow, and connections are convenient from buses to trains and the underground. Note that buses require exact fare, which varies by the destination.

The many bus companies cooperate with the underground and Scot-Rail to produce the Family Day Tripper Ticket (£13), which is a great way to get around the whole area, from Loch Lomond to Ayrshire. Tickets are a good value and are available from Strathclyde Passenger Transport (SPT) Travel Centre and at main railway and bus stations. ➤ INFORMATION: **Strathclyde Passenger Transport (SPT) Travel Centre** (✉ St. Enoch Sq., City Center, ☎ 0870/608–2608).

CAR RENTAL
Costs vary according to the size of the car but average about £30–£40 per day.
➤ AGENCIES: **Avis** (✉ 161 North St., City Center, ☎ 0141/221–2827; ✉ Glasgow Airport, Paisley, ☎ 0141/887–2261 or 0141/842–7599; ✉ Prestwick Airport, Prestwick, ☎ 01292/477218). **Budget Rent-a-Car** (✉ 101 Waterloo St., City Center, ☎ 0845/960–6060; ✉ Glasgow Airport, Paisley, ☎ 0845/960–6060). **Europcar** (✉ 38 Anderson Quay, West End, ☎ 0141/248–8788; ✉ Glasgow Airport, Paisley, ☎ 0141/887–0414; ✉ Prestwick Airport, Prestwick, ☎ 01292/678198). **Hertz** (✉ 138 Hyde Park St., City Center, ☎ 0141/248–7736; ✉ Glasgow Airport, Paisley, ☎ 0141/887–2451). **National Alamo Car Rental** (✉ Glasgow Airport, Paisley, ☎ 0141/887–7915; ✉ Prestwick Airport, Prestwick, ☎ 01292/671222).

CAR TRAVEL
If you come to Glasgow from England and the south of Scotland, you'll probably approach the city from the M6, M74, and A74. The city center is clearly marked from these roads. From Edinburgh the M8 leads to the city center and is the route that cuts straight across the city center and into which all other roads feed. From the north either the A82 from Fort William or the A/M80 from Stirling also feed into the M8 in the Glasgow city center. From then on you only have to know your exit: Exit 16 serves the the northern part of the city center, Exit 17/18 leads to the northwest and Great Western Road, and Exit 18/19 takes you to the hotels of Sauchiehall Street, and the Scottish Exhibition and Conference Centre.

You don't need a car in the city center, and you're probably better off without one; though most new hotels have their own lots, parking here can be trying. More convenient are the park-and-ride operations at underground stations (Kelvinbridge, Bridge Street, and Shields Road), which will bring you into the city center in a few minutes. The West End museums and galleries have their own lots, as does the Burrell. Parking wardens are constantly on patrol, and you'll be fined (upward of £26) if you park illegally. Multistory garages are open 24 hours a day at the following locations: Anderston Centre, George Street, Waterloo Place, Mitchell Street, Cambridge Street, and Concert Square. Rates run between £1 and £2 per hour.

EMERGENCIES
In case of any emergency, dial **999** to reach an ambulance or the police or fire departments (no coins are needed for emergency calls from public phones).

Note that pharmacies generally operate on a rotating basis for late-night opening; hours are posted in storefront windows. Munro Pharmacy is open daily 9–9.
➤ DENTISTS: **Glasgow Dental Hospital** (✉ 378 Sauchiehall St., City Center, ☎ 0141/211–9600 weekdays 9–3).
➤ HOSPITALS: **Glasgow Royal Infirmary** (✉ Castle St., near cathedral, City Center, ☎ 0141/211–4000). **Glasgow Western Infirmary** (✉ Dumbarton Rd., near university, West End, ☎ 0141/211–2000). **Southern General Hospital** (✉ 1345 Govan Rd., south side of Clyde Tunnel, South Side, ☎ 0141/201–1100). **Stobhill Hospital** (✉ 133 Balornock

Rd., near Royal Infirmary and Bishopriggs, North City, ☎ 0141/201–3000).
➤ PHARMACY: **Munro Pharmacy** (✉ 693 Great Western Rd., West End, ☎ 0141/339–0012).

MAIL AND SHIPPING

The main post office is at St. Vincent Street, and there are many smaller post offices around the city.
➤ POST OFFICE: **Main post office** (✉ St. Vincent St., City Center, ☎ 0845/722–3344).

SIGHTSEEING TOURS

BOAT TOURS

Cruises are available on Loch Lomond and to the islands in the Firth of Clyde; contact the Greater Glasgow and Clyde Valley Tourist Board for details. Contact the *Waverley* paddle steamer from June through August, and Clyde Marine Cruises from May through September.
➤ CONTACT: **Clyde Marine Cruises** (✉ Greenock, Greenock, ☎ 01475/721281). **Greater Glasgow and Clyde Valley Tourist Board** (✉ 11 George Sq., near Queen Street station, City Center, ☎ 0141/204–4400). ***Waverley*** (☎ 0141/221–8152).

BUS TOURS

City Sightseeing bus tours leave daily from the west side of George Square. The Greater Glasgow and Clyde Valley Tourist Board can give further information and arrange reservations. Details of longer tours northward to the Highlands and islands can be obtained from the tourist board or Strathclyde Passenger Transport (SPT) Travel Centre.

Classic Coaches operates restored coaches from the 1950s, '60s, and '70s on tours to the north and west and to the islands. The following Glasgow companies run regular bus tours around the region: Scotguide Tours, Southern Coaches, and Weirs Tourlink.
➤ CONTACT: **Classic Coaches** (☎ 0141/889–4050). **Greater Glasgow and Clyde Valley Tourist Board** (✉ 11 George Sq., near Queen Street station, City Center, ☎ 0141/204–4400). **Scotguide Tours** (☎ 0141/204–0444). **Southern Coaches** (☎ 0141/876–1147). **Strathclyde Passenger Transport (SPT) Travel Centre** (✉ St. Enoch Sq., City Center, ☎ 0870/608–2608). **Weirs Tourlink** (☎ 0141/944–6688).

PRIVATE GUIDES

Little's Chauffeur Drive arranges personally tailored car-and-driver tours, both locally and throughout Scotland. The Scottish Tourist Guides Association also provides an all-around service. Taxi firms offer city tours. If you allow the driver to follow a set route, the costs are £15 for one hour, £30 for two hours, and £45 for three hours for up to five people; they take American Express, MasterCard, and Visa. If you wish the driver to follow your own route, the charge will be £15 an hour or the reading on the meter, whichever is greater. You can book tours in advance and be picked up and dropped off wherever you like. Contact the Glasgow-wide TOA Taxis.
➤ CONTACT: **Little's Chauffeur Drive** (✉ 1282 Paisley Rd. W, South Side, ☎ 0141/883–2111). **Scottish Tourist Guides Association** (☎ FAX 0131/453–1297). **TOA Taxis** (☎ 0141/429–7070 or 0141/429–2900).

WALKING TOURS

The Greater Glasgow and Clyde Valley Tourist Board can provide information on special walks on a given day.
➤ CONTACT: **Greater Glasgow and Clyde Valley Tourist Board** (✉ 11 George Sq., near Queen Street station, City Center, ☎ 0141/204–4400).

SUBWAY

Glasgow is the only city in Scotland that has a subway, or underground, as it's called here. It was built at the end of the 19th century and takes the simple form of two circular routes, one going clockwise and the other counterclockwise. All trains eventually bring you back to where you started, and the complete circle takes 24 minutes. This extremely simple and efficient system operated relatively unchanged in ancient carriages (cars) until the 1970s, when it was modernized. The tunnels are small, so the trains themselves are tiny (by London standards), and this, together with the affection in which the system is held and the bright orange paint and circular routes of the trains, gave it the nickname the Clockwork Orange.

Flat fares (90 pence) and the Discovery Ticket one-day pass (£1.60, after 9:30) are available. Trains run regularly from Monday through Saturday from early morning to late evening, with a limited Sunday service, and connect the city center with the West End (for the university) and the city south of the River Clyde. Look for the orange U signs marking the 15 stations. Further information is available from Strathclyde Passenger Transport (SPT) Travel Centre.
➤ INFORMATION: **Strathclyde Passenger Transport (SPT) Travel Centre** (✉ St. Enoch Sq., City Center, ☎ 0870/608–2608).

TAXIS

You'll find metered taxis (usually black and of the London sedan type) at stands all over the city center. Most have radio dispatch. Some have also been adapted to take wheelchairs. You can hail a cab on the street if its FOR HIRE sign is illuminated. A typical ride from the city center to the West End or the South Side costs £5.50 to £6.
➤ CONTACT: **Radio dispatch** (☎ 0141/429–7070).

TRAIN TRAVEL

Glasgow has two main rail stations: Central and Queen Street. Central is the arrival and departure point for trains from London's Euston station (five hours), which come via Crewe and Carlisle in England, as well as via Edinburgh from King's Cross. It also serves other cities in the northwest of England and towns and ports in the southwest of Scotland: Kilmarnock, Dumfries, Ardrossan (for the island of Arran), Gourock (for Dunoon), Wemyss Bay (for the Isle of Bute), and Stranraer (for Ireland). The Queen Street station has frequent connections to Edinburgh (50 minutes) and onward by the east-coast route to Aberdeen or south via Edinburgh to Newcastle, York, and London's King's Cross. Other services from Queen Street go to Stirling, Perth, and Dundee; northward to Inverness, Kyle of Lochalsh, Wick, and Thurso; along the Clyde to Dumbarton and Balloch (for Loch Lomond); and on the scenic West Highland line to Oban, Fort William, and Mallaig. Oban and Mallaig have island ferry connections. For details contact the National Rail Enquiry Line.

A regular bus service links the Queen Street and Central stations. Both are close to stations on the Glasgow underground. At Queen Street go to Buchanan Street, and at Central go to St. Enoch. Black city taxis are available at both stations.

The Glasgow area has an extensive network of suburban railway services. Locals still call them the Blue Trains, even though most are now painted maroon and cream. Look for signs to LOW LEVEL TRAINS at the Queen Street and Central stations. For more information and a free map, call Strathclyde Passenger Transport (SPT) Travel Centre or the National Rail Enquiry Line. Details are also available from the Greater Glasgow and Clyde Valley Tourist Board.

➤ TRAIN INFORMATION: **Greater Glasgow and Clyde Valley Tourist Board** (✉ 11 George Sq., near Queen Street station, City Center, ☎ 0141/ 204–4400). **National Rail Enquiry Line** (☎ 0870/748–4950). **Strathclyde Passenger Transport (SPT) Travel Centre** (✉ St. Enoch Sq., City Center, ☎ 0870/608–2608).

TRANSPORTATION AROUND GLASGOW

The Glasgow city center—the area defined by the M8 motorway to the north and west, the River Clyde to the south, and Glasgow Cathedral and High Street to the east—is relatively compact. Glaswegians themselves walk a good deal, and the streets are designed for pedestrians. The streets are relatively safe, even at night, but be sensible. Good street maps are available from bookstores and the helpful Greater Glasgow and Clyde Valley Tourist Board. Most streets follow a grid plan; if you get lost, though, just ask the locals.

To go farther afield, to the West End or to the South Side, some form of transportation is required. Glasgow is unusual among British cities in having an integrated transport network, and information about all options is available from Strathclyde Passenger Transport (SPT) Travel Centre.

➤ CONTACT: **Greater Glasgow and Clyde Valley Tourist Board** (✉ 11 George Sq., near Queen Street station, City Center, ☎ 0141/204– 4400). **Strathclyde Passenger Transport (SPT) Travel Centre** (✉ St. Enoch Sq., City Center, ☎ 0870/608–2608).

TRAVEL AGENCIES

➤ LOCAL AGENT REFERRALS: **American Express** (✉ 115 Hope St., City Center, ☎ 0141/222–1405). **Thomas Cook** (✉ 15–17 Gordon St., City Center, ☎ 0141/201–7200).

VISITOR INFORMATION

The Greater Glasgow and Clyde Valley Tourist Board provides information and has an accommodations-booking service, a bureau de change, a Western Union money transfer service, city bus tours, guided walks, boat trips, and coach tours around Scotland. Books, maps, and souvenirs are also available. The office is open September through June, Monday through Saturday 9 to 6, and July through August, Monday through Saturday 9 to 8 and Sunday 10 to 6. The tourist board's branch office at the airport is open Monday through Saturday 7:30 to 5, Sunday 8 to 3:30 (Sunday 7:30 to 5, April through September).

➤ TOURIST INFORMATION: **Greater Glasgow and Clyde Valley Tourist Board** (✉ 11 George Sq., near Queen Street station, City Center, ☎ 0141/204–4400, FAX 0141/221–3524).

4 THE BORDERS AND THE SOUTHWEST

DUMFRIES, GALLOWAY, SIR WALTER SCOTT COUNTRY

One of Scotland's icon regions, the Borders is the heartland of minstrelsy, ballad, and folklore—the homeland of the tweed suit and cashmere sweater, of medieval abbeys, of the lordly Tweed and its salmon, and the native soil of Sir Walter Scott, who created so much of the aura of Scotland's historical romance. Hilly and sparsely populated, the Dumfries and Galloway region, south of Glasgow, is a riot of green pastures, brooding forests, and radiant gardens, where the palm, in places, is as much at home as the pine.

By Gilbert
Summers

Updated by
Mark Porter

I F YOU ARE COMING TO SCOTLAND from England, the Borders is the first region you're likely to encounter. Although you'll find no checkpoints or customs outposts, the Scottish tourist authorities firmly promulgate the message that it is indeed Scottish land you've entered. All the idiosyncrasies that distinguish Scotland—from the myriad different names for things to the seemingly unpredictable local holidays—start as soon as you reach the first Scottish signs by the main roads north.

The region embraces the whole 90-mi course of one of Scotland's greatest rivers, the Tweed, and its tributaries. By mill chimneys and peel (a small fortified tower common to this region) fortresses and woodlands luxuriant with game birds and stately homes, in a series of fast-rushing torrents and dark serpentine pools, the rivers flow through the history of two nations. For at different times the region has been in English hands, just as slices of northern England have been in Scottish hands (just to the east is that large English city, Berwick-upon-Tweed). All the main routes from London to Edinburgh traverse the Borders region, whose hinterland of undulating pastures, woods, and valleys is enclosed within three lonely groups of hills: the Cheviots, Moorfoots, and the Lammermuirs. Most towns are overgrown villages and often so full of history that their everyday life and provincial Victorian Gothic style may disappoint you. Innumerable hamlets dot the land, so valley slopes have quite a lived-in look; yet the total population is still relatively sparse. Sheep still outnumber human beings by 14 to 1—which is just as Sir Walter Scott, the Borders region's most famous resident, would have wanted it. His pseudo-monastic, pseudo-baronial home at Abbotsford is the most visited of Scottish literary landmarks.

Although most visitors inevitably pass this way, the Borders and especially Galloway, to the west, are unfortunately often overlooked. So strong is the tartan-ribboned call of the Highlands that many people rush on, pause for breath at Edinburgh, then plunge northward, thus missing this scenic portion of upland Scotland. And that's a shame because the Borders and the Dumfries and Galloway regions have as broad a selection of stately homes and fortified castles as you'll encounter just about anywhere in Scotland. Galloway, west of the town of Dumfries and the surrounding area called Dumfrieshire, has the advantage of a coastline facing south, made even more appealing by the North Atlantic Drift (Scotland's part of the Gulf Stream), which bathes the coastal lands with warmer water. With its coastal farmlands giving way to woodlands, high moors, and some craggy hills, Galloway may not be the Highlands, but it gives a convincing impression to those seeking the authentic Scotland.

Pleasures and Pastimes

Biking

In the rural farming areas and upland stretches you'll have a wide choice of quiet side roads to avoid the heavy traffic on A routes, the main arteries. The Craik Forest is typical of Forestry Commission properties, with bike routes in mountains and trails in the network of forestry access roads.

Dining

The Borders is reasonably well served by hotels ranging from budget to luxury, and most good restaurants are found usually within hotels rather than as independent establishments. Despite being slightly off the beaten tourist path, the region of Dumfries and Galloway offers a good selection of relatively inexpensive options for dining, though once again most are within hotels.

CATEGORY	COST*
££££	over £22
£££	£16–£22
££	£9–£15
£	under £9

per person for a main course at dinner, including VAT

Fishing

The Solway Firth is noted for sea fishing, particularly at the Isle of Whithorn, Port William, Portpatrick, Stranraer, and Loch Ryan. The wide range of game-fishing opportunities extends from the expensive salmon beats of the River Tweed—sometimes known by its nickname, the Queen of Scottish Rivers—to undiscovered hill *lochans* (small lakes). You can buy permits at tourist offices, tackle shops, newsstands, and post offices.

Lodging

In the Borders you'll have several lodging options from which to choose, from top-quality hotels to cozy 18th-century drovers' inns to quaint bed-and-breakfasts. Dumfries and Galloway tend to be a little cheaper, and here farmhouse bed-and-breakfasts are good options. You're likely to get a hearty farm breakfast, but keep in mind that many of these B&Bs are *working* farms, where early morning activity and the presence of animals are an inescapable part of the scene. Unless otherwise indicated, all rooms have private baths.

CATEGORY	COST*
££££	over £140
£££	£110–£140
££	£65–£110
£	under £65

All prices are for a standard double room, including service, breakfast, and VAT.

Shopping

The Borders in particular has a fairly affluent population, which is reflected in the upscale shops in Peebles, for example, and other towns. The Borders is well known for its knitwear industry, and mill shops are in abundance. Throughout the Borders region also look for the specialty peppermint or fruit-flavor boiled sweets (hard candies)—Jethart Snails, Hawick Balls, Berwick Cockles, and Soor Plums—which, with tablet (a solid caramel-like candy) and fudge, are available at most local confectioners.

Exploring the Borders and the Southwest

The Scottish Borders is largely characterized by upland moors and hills, with fertile, farmed, and forested river valleys. The textile towns of the Borders have plenty of personality—Borders folk are sure of their own identity and are fiercely partisan toward their own native towns. The Southwest, also known as Dumfries and Galloway, shares the upland characteristics and, if anything, has a slightly wilder air—the highest hill in Dumfries and Galloway is the Merrick, at 2,765 ft. Easygoing and peaceful, towns in this region are usually very attractive, with wide streets and colorful frontages.

The best way to explore the region is to get off the main arterial roads—the A1, A697, A68, A7, M74/A74, and A75—for the little back roads. You may occasionally be delayed by a herd of cows on their way

The Borders

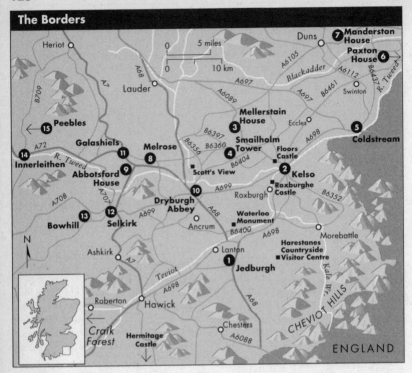

to the milking parlor, but this is often far more pleasant than, for example, tussling on the A75 with heavy-goods vehicles rushing to make the Irish ferries.

Numbers in the text correspond to numbers in the margin and on the Borders and Dumfries and Galloway maps.

Great Itineraries

To travel at a leisurely pace through the Borders and spend time at some of the region's grand mansions, you could easily allow three days, although the total driving distance between each town is not great: in the Borders there are several points of interest quite close to one another.

Owing to the high ground and forests at the heart of Dumfries and Galloway, a linear itinerary that keeps largely to the coast might be best. Once again, distances between towns are not large, but traveling on narrow country roads can take a little longer than you might expect. If you particularly enjoy sketching or taking photographs, this is not an area to be rushed, in which case three days is the minimum time needed to sample an abbey or two and see the settings of Dumfries and Galloway towns.

IF YOU HAVE 2 DAYS

If you have only two days, then you will have to concentrate on either the Borders or the Southwest. **Jedburgh** ① is the best place to get an idea of how important the Borders abbeys were. If you cross the border to the west, head for someplace like **Kirkcudbright** ㉖ for a flavor of Dumfries and Galloway.

IF YOU HAVE 5 DAYS

Plan to divide your time between the Borders (three days) and Dumfries and Galloway (two days); you'll have to be selective about which abbeys and stately homes you can fully explore. Jedburgh Abbey, in **Jedburgh** ①, is a must-see, as is the abbey at **Melrose** ⑧. Melrose also has gardens to enjoy, several museums, and famous stately homes nearby, including **Abbotsford House** ⑨, home of Sir Walter Scott. Finish up at **Peebles** ⑮, where you should allow plenty of time to shop.

In Dumfries and Galloway, two days will give you time to visit **Sweetheart Abbey** ㉑, in New Abbey, then **Arbigland Gardens** ㉒, in Kirkbean, an excellent example of the lush gardens for which the area is famous. Try to fit in Castle Douglas and **Threave Gardens** ㉕, with the nearby gaunt Threave Castle, on a river island and reached by boat, providing a gritty contrast. **Kirkcudbright** ㉖ is also worth even a quick visit for its artistic connections.

IF YOU HAVE 10 DAYS
In five days in the Borders, such jewels as **Floors Castle, Mellerstain House** ③, and **Paxton House** ⑥ can all be enjoyed (though you may get stately home indigestion), and you will also have time to admire the views and soak up the historic atmosphere at **Smailholm Tower** ④ or **Dryburgh Abbey** ⑩. One of the most unlikely attractions, Robert Smail's Printing Works, at **Innerleithen** ⑭, is also one of the most historically interesting, and it's close to Traquair House, acknowledged as the oldest lived-in house in Scotland. You'll also have time for an essential shopping visit to **Peebles** ⑮.

Five days in Dumfries and Galloway will also minimize the problem of choosing what to see—you'll have time for nearly everything. Still, at the top of your list should be **Threave Gardens** ㉕, Threave Castle, and **Kirkcudbright** ㉖. Explore the hills above Gatehouse of Fleet, with its **Cardoness Castle** ㉗ and heritage center; meander around the southern coastline; penetrate the wild and wooded **Glen Trool** ㉚; and travel deep into the Machars to **Whithorn** ㉜, a site of early religious importance. Complete your Galloway gardens experience with **Castle Kennedy Gardens** ㉝ and the Logan Botanic Gardens.

When to Tour the Borders and the Southwest

Because many properties are privately owned and shut down from early autumn until early April, the area is less well suited to off-season touring than some other parts of Scotland. The region does look magnificent in autumn, however, especially along the wooded river valleys of the Borders. Late spring is the time to see the rhododendrons of the gardens in Dumfries and Galloway.

THE BORDERS

Although the Borders has many attractions, it is most famous for being the home base for Sir Walter Scott (1771–1832), the early 19th-century poet, novelist, and creator of *Ivanhoe*, who single-handedly transformed Scotland's image from that of a land of brutal savages to one of romantic and stirring deeds and magnificent landscapes. One of the best ways to approach this district is to make the theme of your tour the life and works of Scott. The novels of Scott are not read much nowadays—in fact, frankly, some of them are difficult to wade through—but the mystique that he created, the aura of historical romance, has outlasted his books and is much in evidence in the ruined abbeys, historical houses, and grand vistas of the Borders.

In addition to the Scott heritage, Borders folk take great pride in the region's fame as Scotland's main woolen-goods manufacturing area. To this day the residents possess a marked determination to defend their towns and communities. Changing times have allowed them to reposition their priorities: instead of guarding against southern raiders, they now concentrate on maintaining a fiercely competitive rugby team for the popular intertown rugby matches. The Borders is a stronghold of this European counterpart to American football.

Borders communities have also reestablished their identities through the curious affairs known as the Common Ridings. Long ago it was essential that each town be able to defend its area, and over the centuries this need became formalized in mounted gatherings to "ride the boundaries." The observance of the tradition lapsed in certain places but has now been revived. Leaders and attendants are solemnly elected each year, and Borderers who now live away from home make a point of attending their town's event. (You are welcome to watch and enjoy the excitement of clattering hooves and banners proudly displayed, but this is essentially a time for native Borderers.) The Common Ridings possess at least as much authenticity and historic significance as the concocted Highland Games, so often taken to be the essence of Scotland. The little town of Selkirk, in fact, claims its Common Riding is the largest mounted gathering anywhere in Europe.

The Borders towns cluster around and between the two great rivers, the Tweed and the Teviot. They encompass all four of the great ruined Borders abbeys. The monks in these long-abandoned religious foundations were the first to work the fleeces of their sheep flocks, thus laying the foundation for what is still the area's main manufacturing industry.

Jedburgh

❶ *50 mi south of Edinburgh, 95 mi southeast of Glasgow.*

The town of Jedburgh (*-burgh* is always pronounced *burra* in Scots) was for centuries the first major Scottish target of invading English armies. In more peaceful times it developed textile mills, most of which have since languished. The large landscaped area around the town's tourist information center was once a mill but now provides an encampment for the armies of modern tourists. The past still clings to this little town, however. The ruined abbey dominates the skyline and is compulsory visiting if you're interested in acquiring a feeling of the former role of the Borders abbeys.

★ **Jedburgh Abbey,** the most impressive of the Borders abbeys, was nearly destroyed by the English earl of Hertford's forces in 1544–45, during the destructive time known as the Rough Wooing. This was English king Henry VIII's (1491–1547) armed attempt to persuade the Scots that it was a good idea to unite the kingdoms by the marriage of his young son to the infant Mary, Queen of Scots (1542–87); the Scots disagreed and sent Mary to France instead. The full story is explained in vivid detail at the **Jedburgh Abbey Visitor Centre,** which also provides information on interpreting the ruins. Ground patterns and foundations are all that remain of the once-powerful religious complex. ✉ *High St.,* ☎ *0131/668–8800.* 🎟 *£3.30.* ☉ *Apr.–Sept., daily 9:30–6:30; Oct.–Mar., Mon.–Sat. 9:30–4:30, Sun. 2–4:30.*

The **Mary, Queen of Scots House,** a *bastel* (from the French *bastille*), was the fortified town house in which, some say, Mary stayed before embarking on her famous 20-mi ride to visit her wounded lover, the earl of Bothwell (circa 1535–78), at Hermitage Castle. An interpretative center in the building relates the tale. ✉ *Queen St.,* ☎ *01835/863331.* 🎟 *£2.50.* ☉ *Mon.–Sat. 10–4:30, Sun. 11–4:30.*

Jedburgh Castle Jail re-creates life in a Howard Reform Prison, with prison cells to inspect. The history of the Royal Burgh of Jedburgh is told through room settings in period style, costumed figures, and audiovisuals. ⊠ *Castlegate,* ☎ *01835/864750.* ☜ *£1.50.* ☉ *Easter–Oct., Mon.–Sat. 10–4:30, Sun. 1–4.*

☙ The **Harestanes Countryside Visitor Centre,** 2 mi north of Jedburgh, conveys life in the Borders. The Discovery Room has changing displays on the countryside, wildlife, and crafts, plus you'll find a wooden games and puzzles room, and a tearoom and gift shop. Outside are a play area, marked trails, and guided walks. ⊠ *Monteviot, at junction of A68 and B6400,* ☎ *01835/830306.* ☜ *Free.* ☉ *Apr.–Oct., daily 10–5.*

In view on the skyline is the **Waterloo Monument,** an imposing tower that is another reminder of the power of the landowning gentry: a marquis of Lothian built the monument in 1815, with the help of his tenants, in celebration of the victory of Wellington at Waterloo. If you have time, you can walk to the tower from the Harestanes Countryside Visitor Centre in about an hour. ⊠ *Off B6400, 5 mi north of Jedburgh.*

OFF THE
BEATEN PATH

HERMITAGE CASTLE – To appreciate the famous 25-mi ride of Mary, Queen of Scots, to visit her wounded lover, the earl of Bothwell, travel southwest from Jedburgh to this, the most complete remaining example of the bare and grim medieval border castles, full of gloom and foreboding. Restored in the early 19th century, it was built in the 14th century (replacing an earlier structure) to guard what was at the time one of the important routes from England into Scotland. The original owner, Lord Soulis, notorious for diabolical excess, was captured by the local populace, which wrapped him in lead and boiled him in a cauldron—or so the tale goes. The castle lies on an unclassified road between the A7 and B6399, about 15 mi south of Hawick, in the desolate Borders hills. ⊠ *Liddesdale,* ☎ *0131/668–8800.* ☜ *£2.* ☉ *Apr.–Sept., daily 9:30–6:30.*

Dining and Lodging

£–££
★

✕ **Cross Keys, Ancrum.** A national treasure, this traditional pub specializes in local produce, from fish to game. A splendid array of Scottish beers—real ale, as it is known here—is served. This is the quintessential village inn, right down to the quaint green outside the front door. ⊠ *The Green, Ancrum, 3 mi northeast of Jedburgh,* ☎ *01835/830344. DC, MC, V.*

£

🏠 **Hundalee House.** This tastefully furnished 300-year-old B&B—with a dark-wood interior and blazing fires—sits among 14 acres of gardens and woodland. There are stunning views across to the English border at Carter Bar and to the Cheviot hills in the southeast. Two of the four bedrooms have four-poster beds. The house is about a mile south of Jedburgh on the A68. ⊠ *Jedburgh, Roxburghshire TD8 6PA,* ☎ 📠 *01835 863011. 4 rooms. No a/c, no room phones, no room TVs. No credit cards. Closed Jan.–Feb.*

£

🏠 **Spinney Guest House.** Two unpretentiously converted and modernized farm cottages make up this B&B offering the highest standards for the price. Three additional log cabins each sleep three, with self-catering or B&B service. ⊠ *Langlee, Jedburgh TD8 6PB,* ☎ *01835/863525,* 📠 *01835/864883. 3 rooms, 3 log cabins. No a/c, no room phones, no room TVs. MC, V.*

Bicycling

Christopher Rainbow Tandem & Bike Hire (⊠ 8 Timpendean Cottages, ☎ 01835/830326 or 07799/525123, 🌐 www.btinternet.com/~christopher.rainbow) rents tandems, mountain bikes, and touring bikes and is ideally placed for the four Borders abbeys, Tweed, and Borderloop cycleways. The company provides recovery service, luggage forwarding, tour itineraries, and lodging bookings. It's on the A698, near the junction with the A68, between Jedburgh and Ancrum.

Kelso

② *12 mi northeast of Jedburgh.*

One of the most charming Borders burghs, Kelso is often described as having a Continental flavor—some people think it resembles a Belgian market town. The town has a broad, paved Market Square and fine examples of Georgian and Victorian Scots town architecture.

Kelso Abbey is the least intact ruin of the four great Borders abbeys—just a bleak fragment of what was once the largest of the group. On a main invasion route, the abbey was burned three times in the 1540s alone, on the last occasion by the English earl of Hertford's forces in 1545, when the 100 men and 12 monks of the garrison were butchered and the structure all but destroyed. ⊠ *Bridge St.,* ☎ *0131/668–8800.* 🎟 *Free.* ⊙ *Apr.–Sept., daily 9:30–6:30; Oct.–Mar., Mon.–Sat. 9:30–4:30, Sun. 2–4:30.*

★ On the bank of the River Tweed, just on the outskirts of Kelso, stands the palatial **Floors Castle,** the largest inhabited castle in Scotland. The ancestral home of the dukes of Roxburghe, Floors is an architectural extravagance bristling with pepper-mill turrets and towers that stand on the "floors," or flat terrain, of the Tweed bank opposite the barely visible ruins of Roxburghe Castle. The enormous home was built by William Adam (1689–1748) in 1721 and modified in the 1840s by William Playfair (1789–1857), using mock-Tudor touches. A holly tree in the deer park marks the place where King James II of Scotland (1430–60) was killed in 1460 by a cannon that "brak in the shooting." ⊠ *A6089,* ☎ *01573/223333.* 🎟 *Joint ticket for castle and grounds, £5.50; grounds only, £3.* ⊙ *Apr.–Oct., daily 10–4.*

Don't confuse 12th-century **Roxburghe Castle** with the comparatively youthful Floors Castle nearby. Only traces of rubble and earthworks remain of this ancient structure. The modern-day village of **Roxburgh** is young; the original Roxburgh, one of the oldest burghs in Scotland, has virtually disappeared, though its name lives on in the duke's title and in the name of the old county of Roxburghshire. ⊠ *Off A699, 4 mi southwest of Kelso.*

Dining and Lodging

££   ✕▥ **Edenwater House.** This handsome and restful stone house, a for-
★   mer manse, overlooks Edenwater in the hamlet of Ednam, 2 mi north of Kelso. Four luxurious guest rooms afford superb views of the river and the Cheviot hills. The tasteful inn is filled with antiques and serves what connoisseurs regard as the best food in the Borders. Roast saddle of hare with foie gras, pork fillet with a ginger-and-honey glaze, and fillet of monkfish crusted with basil and coriander in beurre blanc are some of dishes on the refined but simple menu. The restaurant (£££) is open Friday through Saturday for nonguests. ⊠ *Off the B6461, Ednam, TD5 7QL,* ☎ *01573/224070,* FAX *01573/226615,* WEB *www. edenwaterhouse.co.uk. 3 rooms, 1 suite. Restaurant, golf privileges, fishing; no a/c. DC, MC, V. Closed Jan. 1–14.*

££–£££   ▥ **Ednam House Hotel.** People return again and again to this large, ap-
★   pealing hotel on the banks of the River Tweed, close to Kelso's grand abbey and old Market Square. The open fire in the hall, sporting paintings, and cozy armchairs impart a homey air. The restaurant's three glass walls afford views of the garden and river; the Scottish fare here includes

fresh local vegetables, fresh wild Scottish salmon, Borders beef, and home-made ice cream and traditional puddings. ☒ *Bridge St., TD5 7HT,* ☎ *01573/224168,* ⒻⒶⓍ *01573/226319,* ⓌⒺⒷ *www.ednamhouse.com. 30 rooms. Restaurant, golf privileges, fishing, horseback riding; no a/c. MC, V. Closed late Dec.–early Jan.*

Mellerstain House

❸ *7 mi northwest of Kelso.*

One fine example of the Borders area's fine ornate country homes is Mellerstain House. Begun in the 1720s, it was finished in the 1770s by Robert Adam (1728–92) and is considered one of his finest creations. Sumptuous plasterwork covers almost all interior surfaces, and there are outstanding examples of 18th-century furnishings. The beautiful terraced gardens are as renowned as the house. ☒ *Off A6089,* ☎ *01573/410225.* ▣ *£5.50.* ☉ *House: Easter and May–Sept., Sun.–Fri. 12:30–5; Oct., weekends noon–4:30. Restaurant, antiques shop, and plant sales: Easter and May–Sept., Sun.–Fri. 11:30–5:30.; Oct., weekends 11:30–5.*

Smailholm Tower

★ ❹ *6 mi south of Mellerstain House, 8 mi northwest of Kelso.*

This characteristic Borders structure stands uncompromisingly on top of a barren, rocky ridge in the hills south of Mellerstain, providing a contrast to the luxury of Mellerstain House. Built solely for defense, this 16th-century Borders peel affords memorable views. If you let your imagination wander in this windy spot, you can almost see the flapping pennants and rising dust of an advancing raiding party and hear the anxious securing of doors and bolts. Sir Walter Scott found this an inspiring spot. His grandfather lived at nearby Sandyknowe Farm (not open to the public), and the young Scott visited the tower often during his childhood. A museum here displays costumed figures and tapestries relating to Scott's Borders folk ballads. ☒ *Off B6404,* ☎ *0131/668–8800.* ▣ *£2.* ☉ *Apr.–Sept., daily 9:30–6:30.*

Coldstream

❺ *9 mi east of Kelso.*

Three miles west of Coldstream, the England–Scotland border comes down from the hills and runs beside the Tweed for the rest of its journey to the sea. Coldstream itself, like the town of Gretna, was once a marriage place for runaway couples from the south at a time when the marriage laws of Scotland were more lenient than those of England; a plaque on the former bridge tollhouse recalls this fact. The town is also celebrated in military history: in 1659 General Monck raised a regiment of foot guards here on behalf of his exiled monarch, Charles II (1630–85). Known as the Coldstream Guards, the successors to this regiment have become an elite corps in the British army.

★ The **Coldstream Museum,** in the Coldstream Guards' former headquarters, examines the history of the community of Coldstream, past and present. A special exhibition recalls the history of the Coldstream Guards. ☒ *Market Sq.,* ☎ *01890/882630.* ▣ *Free.* ☉ *Apr.–Sept., Mon.–Sat. 10–4, Sun. 2–4; Oct., Mon.–Sat. 1–4.*

Dignified houses and gardens line the stretch of the Tweed near Coldstream. The best-known house is the **Hirsel,** where a complex of farmyard buildings now serves as a crafts center and museum, with interesting walks on the extensive grounds. It's a favorite spot for bird-watchers, and superb rhododendrons bloom here in late spring. The house itself is not open to the public. ✉ *A697, immediately west of Coldstream,* ☎ *01890/882834.* ✆ *Free; parking £2.* ⊙ *Grounds daily sunrise–sunset; museum and crafts center weekdays 10–5, weekends noon–5.*

Dining and Lodging

£–££ ✕▥ **Wheatsheaf Hotel and Restaurant.** The Wheatsheaf is a restau-
★   rant that also provides accommodation—an important distinction ac-
       cording to the chef-owner. This country inn serves outstanding food
       in both the black-beamed bar and the restaurant. The sheer class of
       the Scottish cuisine, whether the meal is beef, salmon, or venison, has
       won widespread praise, yet neither the food nor the small but care-
       fully chosen wine list is overpriced. If you don't want to leave after
       your meal, stay in one of the seven country-style bedrooms. The inn
       sits on the main street of Swinton, midway between Coldstream and
       Duns. ✉ *Swinton TD11 3JJ,* ☎ *01890/860257.* ☏ *01890/860688. 7
       rooms. Restaurant, bar; no a/c. MC, V.*

Paxton House

❻ *15 mi northeast of Coldstream.*

Stately Paxton House is a comely Palladian mansion, with interiors designed by Robert Adam, and Chippendale and Trotter furniture. The
splendid Regency picture gallery, an outstation of the National Galleries of Scotland, houses a magnificent collection of paintings. The garden is delightful, with an ice house, squirrel hide, and a restored
boathouse with a museum of salmon net fishing. A crafts shop and a
tearoom are adjacent to the house. ✉ *Paxton, 15 mi northeast of Coldstream (take A6112 and B6461),* ☎ *01289/386291.* ✆ *Joint ticket for
house and garden, £5; garden only, £2.50.* ⊙ *House and garden Apr.–
Oct., daily 11–5, last tour at 4:15; tearoom daily 10–5:30.*

Manderston House

❼ *15 mi north of Coldstream.*

Manderston House is a good example of the grand, no-expense-spared
Edwardian country house. The family that built it made its fortune selling herring to Russia. An original 1790s Georgian house on the site
was completely rebuilt from 1903 to 1905 to the specifications of John
Kinross. The silver-plated staircase was modeled after the one in the
Petit Trianon, at Versailles. There's much to see downstairs in the
kitchens, and outside, among a cluster of other buildings, is the one-
of-a-kind marble dairy. You can reach the house by traveling northwest from Coldstream along the A6112 to Duns, then taking the
A6105 east. ✉ *2 mi east of Duns,* ☎ *01361/882636.* ✆ *Joint ticket
for house and grounds, £6; grounds only, £3.50.* ⊙ *Mid-May–Sept.,
Thurs. and Sun. 2–5, grounds open until dusk; also Bank Holiday Mon.
2–5, grounds open until dusk.*

Melrose

❽ *15 mi west of Coldstream.*

In the center of the handsome community of Melrose sits **Melrose Abbey,**
one of the four Borders abbeys. "If thou would'st view fair Melrose
aright, go visit it in the pale moonlight," wrote Scott in *The Lay of the
Last Minstrel,* and so many of his fans took the advice literally that a
sleepless custodian begged him to rewrite the lines. Today the abbey
is still impressive: a red-sandstone shell with slender windows in the
Perpendicular style and some delicate tracery and carved capitals, carefully maintained. Among the carvings high on the roof is one of a bag-

pipe-playing pig. An audio tour is included in the admission price. ⊠ *Main Sq.,* ☎ *0131/668–8800.* ⛶ *£3.30.* ⊙ *Apr.–Sept., daily 9:30–6:30; Oct.–Mar., Mon.–Sat. 9:30–4:30, Sun. 2–4:30.*

The National Trust for Scotland's **Priorwood Gardens,** next to Melrose Abbey, specializes in flowers for drying. Next to the gardens is an orchard with some old apple varieties. Dried flowers are on sale in the shop. ⊠ *Main Sq.,* ☎ *01896/822493.* ⛶ *£2.* ⊙ *Apr.–Sept., Mon.–Sat. 10–5, Sun. 1–5; Oct.–Dec., Mon.–Sat. 10–5, Sun. 1–4.*

The **Trimontium Exhibition,** in the Square, displays artifacts from the largest Roman settlement in Scotland, which was at nearby Newstead. The display includes tools and weapons, a blacksmith's shop, pottery, and scale models of the fort. A guided 5-mi, four-hour walk to the site takes place each Thursday afternoon (also on Tuesday in July and August); phone ahead for details. ⊠ *Ormiston Institute, The Square,* ☎ *01896/822651.* ⛶ *£1.50.* ⊙ *Apr.–Oct., weekdays 10:30–4:30, weekends 10:30–1 and 2–4:30.*

OFF THE BEATEN PATH

THIRLESTANE CASTLE – In the nursery in this 17th-century castle, children are invited to play with Victorian-style toys and masks and to dress up in costumes. Thirlestane lies 10 mi north of Melrose off the A68. ⊠ *Lauder,* ☎ *01578/722430.* ⛶ *Joint ticket for castle and grounds, £5.30; grounds only, £1.50.* ⊙ *Apr.–Oct., Sun.–Fri. 10:30–5, last admission 4:15; grounds open until 6.*

Dining and Lodging

££ ✕ **Hoebridge Inn.** Whitewashed walls, oak-beamed ceilings, and an open fire create a homey welcome at this popular restaurant. Colorful oil-on-glass paintings decorate the walls, and in summer the no-smoking conservatory comes into its own. The cuisine is modern Scottish with Australian and Mediterranean influences. Typical dishes are chargrilled saddle of Hebridean lamb with cassoulet, and venison bourguignon with parsley mash. The inn lies in the village of Gattonside, just next to Melrose but a 2-mi drive along the B6360, thanks to the intervention of the Tweed; you can also reach the inn from Melrose by taking a 10-minute walk over the footbridge. ⊠ *Gattonside,* ☎ *01896/823082. MC, V. Closed Feb.*

££–£££ ✕▥ **Dryburgh Abbey Hotel.** Mature woodlands and verdant lawns surround this civilized hotel on a sweeping bend of the River Tweed and right next to the abbey ruins. The restrained decor and earthy, muted colors throughout create a sense of peace in keeping with the location. The restaurant (££, no-smoking) specializes in traditional Scottish fare. ⊠ *St. Boswells, TD6 0RQ,* ☎ *01835/822261,* ⛶ *01835/823945,* ⬚ *www.dryburgh.co.uk. 38 rooms. Restaurant, golf privileges; no a/c. AE, MC, V.*

££ ✕▥ **Burts Hotel.** Built in 1722, this quiet hotel retains a considerable amount of its period style. It has a particularly welcoming bar, with a cheerful open fire and a wide selection of fine malt whiskies, ideal for a quiet dram before or after a meal. The elegant restaurant has dark-green-stripe wallpaper, high-back upholstered chairs, and white-linen tablecloths. Cannon of venison and roast duck terrine are typical entrées on the Scottish menu with Continental overtones. Reproduction antiques and floral pastels fill the bedrooms and public areas. Fishing can be arranged. ⊠ *Market Sq., TD6 9PL,* ☎ *01896/822285,* ⛶ *01896/822870,* ⬚ *www. burtshotel.co.uk. 20 rooms. Restaurant; no a/c. AE, DC, MC, V.*

Nightlife and the Arts

The Wynd Theatre (⊠ 3 Buccleuch St., ☎ 01896/823854) has a monthly program of four nights of drama from national touring companies, two concerts of folk, blues, jazz, or oratorio from touring national and international companies, plus classic film on two Fridays. There's also an art gallery highlighting top contemporary Scottish artists, plus a bar and nearby parking. Tickets cost £8 for performances, £6 for films.

Abbotsford House

❾ *2 mi west of Melrose.*

In 1811 Sir Walter Scott, already an established writer, bought a farm on this site named Cartleyhole, which was a euphemism for the real name, Clartyhole (*clarty* is Scots for "muddy" or sticky"). The name was surely not romantic enough for Scott, who renamed the property Abbotsford House and eventually had it entirely rebuilt in the Romantic style, emulating several other Scottish properties. The result was called "the most incongruous pile that gentlemanly modernism ever devised" by art critic John Ruskin. That was Mr. Ruskin's idiosyncratic take: most people have found this to be one of the most fetching of all Scottish abodes. A gently seedy pseudo-baronial mansion chock-full of Scottish curios, Ramsay portraits, and mounted deer heads, this is an appropriate domicile for a man of such an extraordinarily romantic imagination. It's worth visiting just to feel the atmosphere that the most successful writer of his day created and to see the condition in which he wrote, driving himself to pay off his endless debts (for more on his life and history, *see* the Close-Up box, "Sir Walter Scott: A Voice from the Borders"). To Abbotsford came most of the famous poets and thinkers of Scott's day, including Wordsworth and Washington Irving. With some 9,000 volumes in the library, Abbotsford is the repository for the writer's collection of Scottish memorabilia and historic artifacts. Scott died here in 1832, and the house is today owned by his descendants. ✉ *B6360,* ☎ *01896/752043.* 🎫 *£4.* ⊙ *June–Sept., daily 9:30–5; Mar.–Oct., Mon.–Sat. 9:30–5, Sun. 2–5.*

Dryburgh Abbey

★ **❿** *8 mi southeast of Melrose.*

Sir Walter Scott's final resting place and the most peaceful and secluded of the Borders abbeys, Dryburgh Abbey sits on gentle parkland in a loop of the Tweed. The abbey suffered from English raids until, like Melrose, it was abandoned in 1544. The style is transitional, a mingling of rounded Romanesque and pointed early English. The side chapel, where the Haig and Scott families lie buried, is lofty and pillared and detached from the main buildings. ✉ *Off A68,* ☎ *0131/668–8800.* 🎫 *£2.80.* ⊙ *Apr.–Sept., daily 9:30–6:30; Oct.–Mar., Mon.–Sat. 9:30–4:30, Sun. 2–4:30.*

OFF THE
BEATEN PATH

SCOTT'S VIEW – There's no escaping Sir Walter in this part of the country: 3 mi north of Dryburgh is possibly the most photographed rural view in the south of Scotland. (Perhaps the only view used more often to summon a particular interpretation of Scotland is Eilean Donan Castle, far to the north.) The sinuous curve of the River Tweed and the gentle landscape unfolding to the triple peaks of the Eildons and then rolling out into shadows beyond are certainly worth seeking. You arrive at this peerless vista, where Scott often came to meditate, by taking the B6356 north from Dryburgh. A poignant tale is told about the horses of Scott's funeral cortege: on their way to Dryburgh Abbey they stopped here out of habit as they had so often in the past.

SIR WALTER SCOTT: A VOICE FROM THE BORDERS

SIR WALTER SCOTT (1771–1832) was probably Scottish tourism's best propagandist. Thanks to his fervid "Romantik" imagination, his long narrative poems—such as *The Lady of the Lake*—and a truly long string of historical novels, including *Ivanhoe, Waverley, Rob Roy, Redgauntlet,* and *The Heart of Midlothian,* the world fell in love with the image of heroic Scotland. Seriously told and thoroughly documented, his works lifted fiction high above the Gothic romances of his contemporaries. As part of the Romantic movement in Britain (the English poets William Wordsworth and Samuel Taylor Coleridge were his near-contemporaries), Scott wrote of Scotland as a place of Highland wilderness and clan romance, shaping outsiders' perceptions of Scotland in a way that to a certain extent survives even today.

Scott was born in College Wynd, Edinburgh. A lawyer by training, he was an assiduous collector of old ballads and tales. As a young boy recovering from illness, Scott was sent to his grandfather's farm, near Smailholm in the Borders, where he first heard the stirring tales of Borders history. After qualifying as an advocate in 1792 and after his marriage in 1797 to Margaret Charlotte Charpentier, daughter of a French refugee, Scott seriously began to devote his spare time to writing. *The Lay of the Last Minstrel,* a romantic poem published in 1805, brought him fame and was soon followed by further romantic verse narratives.

In 1811 Scott bought the house that was to become Abbotsford, his Borders mansion near Melrose, which he rebuilt and which gradually became a storehouse of Scottish history: Bonnie Prince Charlie's *quaich* (drinking bowl), library ceiling plaster casts from Rosslyn Chapel, Rob Roy's broadsword, and an entrance porch copied from Linlithgow Palace are examples of the wealth of artifacts he amassed, all of which can still be seen today.

Scott started on his series of Waverley novels in 1814, at first anonymously, and by 1820 had produced *Waverley, Guy Mannering, The Antiquary, Tales of My Landlord* (three series), and *Rob Roy.* Between 1820 and 1825 there followed an additional 11 titles, including *Ivanhoe* and *The Pirate,* which was partly written during a voyage around Scotland with lighthouse builder Robert Stevenson, grandfather of novelist Robert Louis Stevenson. Many of his verse narratives and novels focused on real-life settings, in particular the Trossachs, west of Stirling, which rapidly became and still remain extremely popular with visitors.

In 1826 Ballantyne's publishing house, in which Scott was a partner, went bankrupt, and Scott took it as a matter of honor to personally clear the debts. Until his death six years later, he produced a copious amount of work, including additional novels, a biographical *Life of Napoleon,* and translations of German works. Scott's health started to fail under the pressure of work (and those mounting bills), and he died on September 21, 1832.

Apart from his writing, Scott is also remembered as the discoverer, in 1819, of the Honours of Scotland—the crown, scepter, and sword of state of the Scottish monarchs—which had been wrapped up, dumped in the bottom of a chest in Edinburgh Castle, and forgotten since 1707, when Scotland lost its independence. Today these historic symbols of Scotland's sovereignty are on display in the castle.

Abbotsford can be visited in spring and summer, and other houses associated with Scott can be seen (from the outside only) in Edinburgh: 25 George Square, which was his father's house, and 39 Castle Street. The site of his birthplace, in College Wynd, is marked with a plaque. The most obvious structure associated with Scott is the Scott Monument on Princes Street, which looks for all the world like a Gothic rocket ship with a statue of Scott and his pet dog as passengers.

Galashiels

⑪ *5 mi northwest of Melrose.*

A busy gray-stone Borders town, Galashiels is still active with textile mills and knitwear shops. The **Lochcarron of Scotland Cashmere and Wool Centre** houses a museum of the town's history and industry, where you can go on a mill tour and learn about the manufacture of tartans and tweeds. ⊠ *Waverley Mill, Huddersfield St.,* ☎ *01896/752091.* ⊠ *£2.50.* ☉ *June–Sept., Mon.–Sat. 9–5, Sun. noon–5; Oct.–Dec. and Jan.–May, Mon.–Sat. 9–5. Guided year-round tours Mon.–Thurs. at 10:30, 11:30, 1:30, and 2:30; Fri. at 10:30 and 11:30.*

Dating from 1583, **Old Gala House,** a short walk from the town center, is the former home of the lairds (landed proprietors) of Galashiels. It now serves as a museum with displays on the building's history and the town of Galashiels, as well as a contemporary art gallery and exhibition space. You can trace your family history through a comprehensive genealogy facility. ⊠ *Scott Cres.,* ☎ *01750/20096.* ⊠ *Free.* ☉ *Apr.–Sept., Tues.–Sat. 10–4; Oct., Tues.–Sat. 1–4.*

Shopping
Lochcarron of Scotland Cashmere and Wool Centre (⊠ Waverley Mill, ☎ 01896/752091) sells a wide selection of woolens and tweeds.

Selkirk

⑫ *7 mi south of Galashiels.*

Selkirk is a hilly outpost with a smattering of antiques shops and an assortment of bakers selling the Selkirk Bannock (fruited sweet breadcake) and other cakes. Sir Walter Scott was sheriff (judge) of Selkirkshire from 1800 until his death in 1832, and his statue stands in Market Place. **Sir Walter Scott's Courtroom,** where he presided, contains a display examining Scott's life, his writings, and his time as sheriff, and it includes an audiovisual presentation. ⊠ *Market Pl.,* ☎ *01750/20096.* ⊠ *Free.* ☉ *Apr.–May and Sept., Mon.–Sat. 10–4; June–Aug., Mon.–Sat. 10–4, Sun. 2–4; Oct., Mon.–Sat. 1–4.*

Halliwell's House Museum, tucked off the main square in Selkirk, was once an ironmonger's shop, now re-created downstairs. Upstairs, an exhibit tells the town's tale, with useful background information on the Common Ridings as well as an audiovisual presentation. ⊠ *Market St.,* ☎ *01750/20096.* ⊠ *Free.* ☉ *Apr.–June and Sept.–Nov., Mon.–Sat. 10–5, Sun. 2–4; July–Aug., Mon.–Sat. 10–6, Sun. 2–6.*

Bowhill

⑬ *3 mi west of Selkirk.*

Bowhill, one of the stately homes in the Borders, dates from the 19th century and houses an outstanding collection of works by Gainsborough, Van Dyck, Canaletto, Reynolds, and Raeburn, as well as porcelain and period furniture. The house is open in July only (parties, however, can book at other times); the grounds and playground have more friendly hours. ⊠ *Off A708,* ☎ *01750/22204.* ⊠ *Joint ticket for house and grounds and playground, £4.50; grounds and playground only, £2.* ☉ *House July, daily 1–4:30. Grounds and playground Easter–June and Aug., Sat.–Thurs. noon–5; July, daily noon–5.*

Innerleithen

⑭ *15 mi northwest of Selkirk.*

The main reason to come to the linear community of Innerleithen is
to see **Robert Smail's Printing Works.** The fully operational, restored
print shop with a reconstructed waterwheel fascinates adults and older
children, who can try their hand at old-fashioned typesetting. ⊠ *7–9
High St.,* ☎ *01896/830206.* ⊡ *£2.50.* ☉ *Easter and May–Sept., Mon.–
Sat. 10–1 and 2–5, Sun. 2–5; Oct., Sat. 10–1 and 2–5, Sun. 2–5; last
admission 45 mins before closing, morning and afternoon.*

★ Near the town of Innerleithen stands **Traquair House,** said to be the
oldest continually occupied house in Scotland (since 1107). Secret
stairs, intricate embroidery, more than 3,000 books, a maze, and a bed
used by Mary, Queen of Scots, in 1566 are just a few of the discoveries. Ale is still brewed in the 18th-century brew house here, and it's
recommended. It's even possible to stay overnight here. ⊠ *Traquair,
1 mi from Innerleithen,* ☎ *01896/830323.* ⊡ *£5.50.* ☉ *Easter–May
and Sept.–Oct., daily 12:30–5:30; June–Aug., daily 10:30–5:30; last
admission at 5.*

Lodging

££££ **⊡ Traquair House.** A stay in the private quarters at Traquair will let
you experience the unique atmosphere of this ancient house for yourself. Antiques and chintz-draped canopy beds fill the guest rooms.
You can savor a glass of the house's own ale in the 18th-century Lower
Drawing Room. A three-course dinner is also available for a hefty £41.
⊠ *Innerleithen, Peeblesshire, EH44 6PW,* ☎ *01896/830323,* FAX *01896/
830639. 3 rooms. No a/c. MC, V.*

Shopping

The **Mill Shop** (⊠ Walkerburn, 2 mi east of Innerleithen, ☎ 01896/
870619) has a large mill store selling a wealth of styles, as well as an
adjacent museum of woolen textiles.

Peebles

⑮ *6 mi west of Innerleithen.*

Thanks to its excellent though pricey shopping, Peebles gives the impression of catering primarily to leisured country gentlefolk. Architecturally the town is nothing out of the ordinary, a very pleasant Borders
burgh. Don't miss the splendid dolphins ornamenting the bridge crossing the River Tweed.

Neidpath Castle, a 15-minute walk upstream along the banks of the Tweed
from Peebles, perches artistically above a bend in the river, and comes
into view through the tall trees. The castle is a medieval structure remodeled
in the 17th century, with dungeons hewn from solid rock. You can return on the opposite riverbank after crossing an old, finely skewed railroad viaduct. ⊠ *Near Peebles,* ☎ FAX *01721/720333.* ⊡ *£3.* ☉ *Easter
week and June 17–Sept. 9, Mon.–Sat. 10:30–4.30, Sun. 12:30–4.30.*

Lodging

££–££££ ✕⊡ **Cringletie House.** Despite the grand turrets and crow-step gables
★ in traditional baronial style, this spacious property still manages to come
across as homey. A British-country-house style pervades the hotel, and
bedrooms are individually themed. From an elaborately ceilinged first-
floor drawing room you can enjoy pretty views of the valley. An old-
fashioned walled garden surrounds the building, and the produce
grown here is used in the restaurant. Locals dine here for such upscale
Scottish fare as boned quail stuffed with trompette mushrooms, fol-

lowed by loin of deer from the neighboring estate. The afternoon tea, served in the conservatory, is especially recommended. ⊠ *Edinburgh Rd., Off A703, EH45 8PL,* ☎ *01721/730233,* ℻ *01721/730244,* Ⓦᴱᴮ *www.cringletie.com. 14 rooms. Restaurant, putting green, tennis court, croquet; no a/c. AE, MC, V.*

££–££££ ✕🖬 **Park Hotel.** You'll find comfort and tranquillity at this hotel, on the banks of the River Tweed at the northern tip of the Ettrick Forest. Rooms have striped or floral wallpaper and pastel fabrics. The restaurant serves superior Scottish cuisine; many of the dishes use local salmon and trout. ⊠ *Innerleithen Rd., EH45 8BA,* ☎ *01721/720451,* ℻ *01721/723510. 24 rooms. Restaurant; no a/c. AE, DC, MC, V.*

££–££££ ✕🖬 **Peebles Hydro.** Not only does the Hydro have something for
  ★   everyone, but it has it in abundance: archery, snooker, pony trekking, a whirlpool, and a sauna are just a few of the diversions here. The elegant Edwardian building, reminiscent of a French château, sits on 30 acres. High ceilings give the public areas an airy, spacious feel. Bedrooms are comfortably furnished, though room sizes and decorative standards vary. The restaurant has a Scottish menu with local salmon, lamb, and beef. ⊠ *Innerleithen Rd., EH45 8LX,* ☎ *01721/720602,* ℻ *01721/722999,* Ⓦᴱᴮ *www.peebleshotelhydro.co.uk. 132 rooms. Restaurant, tennis court, pool, health club, sauna, bicycles, baby-sitting, children's programs (ages infant–16), playground, laundry service; no a/c. AE, DC, MC, V.*

£   🖬 **Drummore.** This hillside B&B, set in an acre of wild gardens full of bird life, is well positioned both for touring the Borders and for visiting Edinburgh. The house is modern and clean, and the guest lounge has a vast picture window that overlooks the River Tweed. ⊠ *Venlaw High Rd., EH45 8RL,* ☎ *01721/720336,* ℻ *01721/723004. 2 rooms. No a/c, no room TVs. MC, V. Closed Nov.–Mar.*

Bicycling

Scottish Border Trails (⊠ Drummore, Venlaw High Rd., Peebles EH45 8RL, ☎ 01721/720336) rents bicycles and also organizes cycling and walking holidays, including lodging.

Shopping

You can easily spend a day browsing on High Street and in the courts and side streets leading off it, but be prepared for temptations at every turn.

GIFTS

Head to Toe (⊠ 43 High St., ☎ 01721/722752) stocks natural beauty products of all descriptions and a variety of linens—from lace doilies to patchwork quilts, silk flowers, handmade pine furniture, candles, and cards. If you need a rest after a heavy day of shopping, repair to the **Country Shop** (⊠ 56 High St., ☎ 01721/720630), a gift store with souvenirs aplenty and a coffee shop upstairs, with views over the town and bustling High Street.

HARDWARE

Scott's Hardware Store (⊠ 48 High St., ☎ 01721/720262) has every kind of tool, implement, fixture, fitting, and garden gadget (even mousetraps) spread in glorious array over floors, walls, and ceiling.

JEWELRY AND ANTIQUES

The German-born and Swiss-trained watchmaker Jurgen Tubbecke sells antiques alongside his handcrafted chronometers at the **Clockmaker** (⊠ 3 High St., ☎ 01721/723599).

Among the many craftspeople and jewelers on High Street is **Keith Walter** (⊠ 28 High St., ☎ 01721/720650), a gold- and silversmith who makes items on the premises and stocks jewelry made by other local designers.

GALLOWAY HIGHLANDS

The region of Galloway embraces the southwest portion of Scotland, west of the main town of Dumfries. The area's terrain is diverse—from its gentle coastline and breezy uplands to areas gradually disappearing below blankets of conifers. Use caution when negotiating the A75: although this main trunk road has been improved in recent years, you are liable to find aggressive trucks bearing down on you as these commercial vehicles race for the Irish ferries at Stranraer and Cairnryan (anything as environmentally sensible as a direct east–west railway link was closed years ago). Trucks notwithstanding, once you are off the main roads, Dumfries and Galloway have some of the most pleasant touring roads in Scotland—though the occasional herd of cows on the way to be milked is a potential hazard.

Gretna

16 *10 mi north of Carlisle, 87 mi south of Glasgow, 92 mi southwest of Edinburgh.*

Gretna and **Gretna Green** are, quite simply, an embarrassment to native Scots. What else can you say about a place that advertises "amusing joke weddings," as does one of the visitor centers here? These strange goings-on are tied to the reputation this community developed as a refuge for runaway couples from England, who once came north to take advantage of Scotland's more lenient marriage laws. This was the first place they reached on crossing the border. At one time anyone could perform a legal marriage in Scotland. Often the village blacksmith did the honors, presumably because he was conveniently situated near the main road.

Ruthwell

21 mi west of Gretna, 83 mi south of Glasgow, 88 mi southwest of Edinburgh.

The landscape is not impressive around the flat fields of the Upper Solway Firth, but as you progress west, you'll find more of interest. In-
17 side **Ruthwell Parish Church** is the 8th-century **Ruthwell Cross**, a Christian sculpture admired for the quality of its carving. Considered an idolatrous monument, it was removed and demolished by Church of Scotland zealots in 1640 but was later reassembled. The **Savings Banks Museum,** near the church in Ruthwell, tells the story of the savings-bank movement, founded by the Reverend Dr. Henry Duncan in 1810. ✉ *6½ mi west of Annan,* ☎ *01387/870640.* 🎫 *Free.* ☉ *Easter–Oct., daily 10–1 and 2–5; Nov.–Easter, Tues.–Sat. 10–1 and 2–5.*

18 At Clarencefield, less than a mile from Ruthwell, is **Comlongon,** a more recent mansion house that adjoins a well-preserved 15th-century border keep. You can avail yourself of the 12-bedroom B&B at the castle (£££; price includes food and accommodation). ✉ *B724, 8 mi west of Annan,* ☎ *01387/870283.* 🎫 *£3.* ☉ *Daily 10–1.*

Caerlaverock Castle

★ **19** *5 mi west of Ruthwell.*

Caerlaverock Castle overlooks a nature reserve on a coastal loop of the B725. Built in a triangular design unique in Britain, this 13th-century moated fortress has solid-sandstone masonry and an imposing double-tower gatehouse. King Edward I of England (1239–1307) besieged the castle in 1300, when his forces occupied much of Scotland as the

Dumfries and Galloway

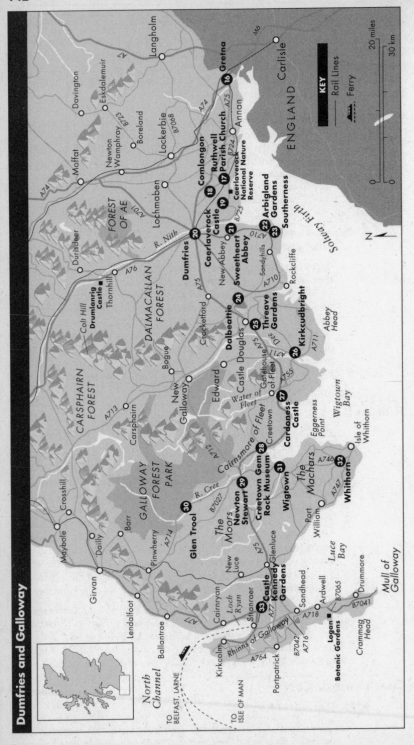

Wars of Independence commenced. The castle suffered many times in Anglo-Scottish skirmishes, as the video presentation attests. ⊠ *Off B725, 5 mi west of Ruthwell,* ☎ *01387/770244.* ⊡ *£2.80.* ☉ *Apr.–Sept., daily 9:30–6; Oct.–Mar., Mon.–Sat. 9:30–4, Sun. 2–4.*

The **Caerlaverock National Nature Reserve** lets you observe wintering wildfowl from blinds and a visitor center. ⊠ *Off B725, east of Caerlaverock Castle,* ☎ *01387/770275.* ⊡ *Free.* ☉ *Bird-watching year-round, daily 24 hrs; visitor center May–Sept., daily 10–5.*

Dumfries

20 *15 mi northwest of Ruthwell, 76 mi south of Glasgow, 81 mi southwest of Edinburgh.*

The town of Dumfries, where Scotland's national poet Robert Burns (1759–96) spent the last years of his short life, is a no-nonsense, red-sandstone community. The playwright J. M. Barrie (1860–1937) spent his childhood in Victoria Terrace here in the 1870s, and the garden of Moat Brae House is said to be the playground that inspired his boyish dreams in *Peter Pan.* The **River Nith** meanders through Dumfries, and the pedestrians-only town center makes shopping a pleasure. The town also contains Robert Burns's favorite *howff* (pub), the Globe Inn; one of the houses he lived in; and his mausoleum.

Not surprisingly, in view of its close association to the poet, Dumfries has a **Robert Burns Centre,** housed in a sturdy former mill overlooking the river. The center has an audiovisual program and an extensive exhibit on the life of the poet. ⊠ *Mill Rd.,* ☎ *01387/264808.* ⊡ *Free; small charge for audiovisual show.* ☉ *Apr.–Sept., Mon.–Sat. 10–8, Sun. 2–5 (café, daily 11–4); Oct.–Mar., Tues.–Sat. 10–1 and 2–5.*

OFF THE BEATEN PATH
DRUMLANRIG CASTLE – This spectacular estate is as close as Scotland gets to the treasure houses of England—which is not surprising, since it's owned by the dukes of Buccleuch, one of the wealthiest British peerages. Ornate, square built, and resplendent with romantic turrets, this pink-sandstone palace was constructed in 1689 by the first duke of Queensbury, who, after nearly bankrupting himself building the place, found it disappointing on his first overnight stay and never returned. The Buccleuchs inherited the palace and soon filled the richly decorated rooms with Louis Quatorze furniture and a valuable collection of paintings by Holbein, Rembrandt, da Vinci, Reynolds, Murillo, and many family portraits. There are also crafts workshops, a working forge, a playground, a gift shop, and a tearoom adorning the parklands, which form a breathtaking backdrop for the house. ⊠ *Near Thornhill, about 15 mi northwest of Dumfries off A76,* ☎ *01848/330248.* ⊡ *Joint ticket for castle and park, £6; park only, £3.* ☉ *Castle: May–Aug., Mon.–Sat. 11–4, Sun. noon–5, last entry at 4; country park, gardens, and adventure playground: May–Sept., daily 11–4.*

MUSEUM OF LEAD MINING – There are underground trips for the stout-hearted at this museum devoted to one of Scotland's lesser-known industries. The Miners' Library not only shows how the miners educated themselves but also has a genealogical computer database. To reach the museum follow the Mennock Pass through rounded moorland hills to Wanlockhead, a fairly bleak village at Scotland's highest elevation. ⊠ *Goldscaur Rd., Wanlockhead, on B797 northeast of Sanquhar, 27 mi northwest of Dumfries,* ☎ *01659/74387,* WEB *www.leadminingmuseum. co.uk.* ⊡ *£3.95.* ☉ *Apr.–Oct., daily 10–4:30, last guided tour at 4.*

Nightlife and the Arts

Gracefield Arts Centre (⊠ 28 Edinburgh Rd., ☎ 01387/262084) has public art galleries and studios with a constantly changing exhibition program. The **Dumfries and Galloway Arts Festival** is usually held at the end of May at several venues throughout the region. Contact the Gracefield Arts Centre for more information. The **Robert Burns Centre Film Theatre** (⊠ Mill Rd., ☎ 01387/264808) screens special-interest, foreign, and other films not widely released.

Outdoor Activities and Sports

Cycles can be rented from **Greirson and Graham** (⊠ 10 Academy St., ☎ 01387/259483).

Shopping

Dumfries is the main shopping center for the region, with all the big-name chain stores as well as specialty shops.

GIFTS AND CRAFTS

Greyfriars Crafts (⊠ 56 Buccleuch St., ☎ 01387/264050) sells mainly Scottish goods, including glass, ceramics, and jewelry.

If you are visiting Drumlanrig Castle, don't miss the **crafts center** (☎ 01848/331555) in the stable block, chock-full of all types of crafts, including leather goods, landscape and portrait works, stainless-steel jewelry, and cutlery. The center is open May through August, daily 9 to 5; September through April, by appointment.

POSTCARDS

For a souvenir that's easy to pack, try **David Hastings** (⊠ Marying, Shieldhill, Lockerbie, ☎ 01387/710451; visitors by appointment), with more than 100,000 old postcards.

New Abbey

7 mi south of Dumfries, 83 mi south of Glasgow, 88 mi southwest of Edinburgh.

㉑ The village of New Abbey has at its center **Sweetheart Abbey,** which provides a mellow red and roofless backdrop to the village. It was founded in 1273 by Devorgilla Balliol in memory of her husband, John. The couple's son, also named John (1250–1315), was the puppet king installed in Scotland by Edward of England when the latter claimed sovereignty over Scotland. After John's appointment the Scots gave him a scathing nickname that would stay with him for the rest of his life: Toom Tabard (Empty Shirt). ⊠ *A710 at New Abbey,* ☎ *0131/668–8800.* 💷 *£1.80.* ☉ *Apr.–Sept., daily 9:30–6:30; Oct.–Mar., Mon.–Wed. and Sat. 9:30–4:30, Thurs. 9:30–noon, Sun. 2–4:30.*

Arbigland Gardens

㉒ *5 mi south of New Abbey, 88 mi south of Glasgow, 94 mi southwest of Edinburgh.*

The little community of Kirkbean (blink and you've missed it) set in a bright green landscape is the backdrop for Arbigland Gardens; follow signs from the village. An Arbigland local named John Paul, the son of a gardener, left Scotland and became the founder of the U.S. navy. This seafaring son, John Paul Jones (1747–92), returned to his native coast in a series of daring raids in 1778. A museum will brief you on the history. The gardens tended by Jones's father are typical of the area: lush and sheltered, with blue water visible through the protecting trees. The walled garden dating from 1745 has been restored using plantings of roses typical of the 18th century. ⊠ *Off A710 by Kirkbean,* ☎ *01387/880613.* ⊑ *£2.* ☉ *Apr.–Sept., Tues.–Sun. 10–5.*

Southerness

㉓ *3 mi south of Kirkbean, 91 mi south of Glasgow, 97 mi southwest of Edinburgh.*

The road to Southerness (A710) ends in a welter of recreational vehicles and trailer homes in the shadow of one of Scotland's earliest lighthouses, built in 1749 by the port authorities of Dumfries who were anxious to make the treacherous River Nith approaches safer.

En Route The road to Southerness turns west and becomes faintly Riviera-like. You can take a brisk walk from Sandyhills to Rockcliffe, two of the sleepy coastal communities overlooking the creeping tides and endless shallows of the Solway coast.

Dalbeattie

㉔ *12 mi northwest of Southerness, 89 mi south of Glasgow, 95 mi southwest of Edinburgh.*

Like the much larger Aberdeen, far to the northeast, Dalbeattie contains buildings constructed with local gray granite from the town's quarry. The predominance of granite, with its well-scrubbed gray glitter, makes Dalbeattie atypical of Galloway towns, where housefronts are predominantly painted in pastels.

Lodging

££ 🏠 **Auchenskeoch Lodge.** This quaint and informal Victorian shooting
★ lodge, now a small-scale country-house hotel, has three bedrooms and delicious food (for residents only). The antique furnishings have a comfortable, faded elegance. The sitting room houses crammed bookshelves and an open fire, and in the games room is a full-size billiards table. A private loch and croquet lawn provide outdoor entertainment. Many of the vegetables and herbs used in the set dinner menu—prepared to a high standard in traditional Scottish style—are grown on the 20 acres of gardens and woodland surrounding the hotel. ⊠ *By Dalbeattie, DG5 4PG,* ☎ 𝖥𝖠𝖷 *01387/780277. 3 rooms. Dining room, croquet; no a/c. MC, V. Closed Nov.–Easter.*

Outdoor Activities and Sports

Barend Riding School and Trekking Centre (⊠ Sandyhills, by Dalbeattie, Kirkcudbrightshire, ☎ 01387/780632 or 01387/780533) helps you to a "horse-high" view of the beautiful coast and countryside of this region.

Castle Douglas

6 mi west of Dalbeattie, 94 mi south of Glasgow, 99 mi southwest of Edinburgh.

This is a pleasant town, with a long main street where the home bakeries vie for business. Castle Douglas's main attraction is its proximity to **Threave Gardens.** As Scotland's best-known charitable conservation agency, the National Trust for Scotland cares for several garden properties. This horticultural undertaking demands the employment of many gardeners—and it is at Threave that the gardeners train, thus ensuring there is always some fresh development or experimental planting here. This gives lots of vigor and interest to the sloping parkland around the mansion house of Threave. There's a good visitor center as well. ⊠ *South of A75, 1 mi west of Castle Douglas,* ☎ *01556/502575,*

WEB *www.nts.org.uk.* ⊠ *£5.* ⊙ *Gardens daily 9:30–sunset; walled garden and greenhouses daily 9:30–5; visitor center, plant center, exhibition, and shop Apr.–Oct., daily 9:30–5:30; restaurant daily 10–5.*

Threave Castle, not to be confused with the mansion house in Threave Gardens, was an early home of the Black Douglases, the earls of Nithsdale, and lords of Galloway. The castle was dismantled in the religious wars of the mid-17th century, though enough of it remains to have housed prisoners from the Napoleonic Wars of the 19th century. It's a few minutes from Castle Douglas by car and is signposted from the main road. To get there, you must leave your car in a farmyard and walk the rest of the way. Make your way down to the reeds by the river on an occasionally muddy path. At the edge of the river you can then ring a bell, and, rather romantically, a boatman will come to ferry you across to the great stone tower looming from a marshy island in the river. ⊠ *North of A75, 3 mi west of Castle Douglas,* ☎ *0131/668–8800.* ☎ *£2.20, includes ferry.* ⊙ *Apr.–Sept., daily 9:30–6:30.*

Outdoor Activities and Sports

BIKING

You can rent bicycles from **Ace Cycles** (⊠ Church St., ☎ 01556/504542).

WATER SPORTS

The **Galloway Sailing Centre** (⊠ Loch Ken, ☎ 01644/420626, WEB www.lochken.co.uk) rents dinghies, windsurfing equipment, and canoes. It also runs residential sailing, windsurfing, and canoeing courses.

Shopping

BOOKS

It's well worth the short drive north from Castle Douglas (A75 then B794) to visit **Benny Gillies Books, Maps and Prints** (⊠ 31–33 Victoria St., Kirkpatrick Durham, ☎ 01556/650412), which stocks an outstanding selection of secondhand and antiquarian Scottish books, hand-colored antique maps, and prints depicting areas throughout Scotland.

GIFTS

The **Posthorn** (⊠ 26–30 St. Andrew St., ☎ 01556/502531) is renowned for its display of figurines by Border Fine Art as well as Scotland's biggest display of Moorcroft enameled pottery.

JEWELRY

Galloway Gems (⊠ 130–132 King St., ☎ 01556/503254) sells silver jewelry and also stocks mineral specimens, polished stone slices, and art materials.

Kirkcudbright

26 *11 mi southwest of Castle Douglas, 103 mi south of Glasgow, 109 mi southwest of Edinburgh.*

Kirkcudbright is an 18th-century town of unpretentious houses, some of them color-washed in pastel shades and roofed with the blue slates of the district. For much of this century it has been known as an artists' town, and its L-shape main street is full of crafts and antiques shops. Conspicuous in the town center is **MacLellan's Castle,** the shell of a once-elaborate castellated mansion dating from the 16th century. ⊠ *Off High St.,* ☎ *0131/668–8800.* ☎ *£2.* ⊙ *Apr.–Sept., daily 9:30–6.*

The 18th-century **Broughton House** was once the home of the artist E. A. Hornel, one of the "Glasgow Boys" of the late 19th century. Many of his paintings hang in the house, which is furnished in period style and contains an extensive library specializing in local history. There's also a Japanese garden. ⊠ *12 High St.,* ☏ *01557/330437.* 🎫 *£3.50.* ☉ *Apr.–June and Sept.–Oct., daily 1–5:30; July–Aug., daily 11–5:30; last admission at 4:45.*

Stuffed with all manner of local paraphernalia, the delightfully old-fashioned **Stewartry Museum** allows you to putter and absorb as much or as little as takes your interest in the display cases. ⊠ *St. Mary St.,* ☏ *01557/331643.* 🎫 *£1.50.* ☉ *Oct.–Apr., Mon.–Sat. 11–4; May, Mon.–Sat. 11–5; June–Sept., Mon.–Sat. 10–6, Sun. 2–5.*

The **Tolbooth Arts Centre,** in the old tolbooth, gives a history of the town's artists' colony and its leaders E. A. Hornel, Jessie King, and Charles Oppenheimer, and displays some of their paintings as well as works by modern artists and craftspeople. ⊠ *High St.,* ☏ *01557/ 331556.* 🎫 *£1.50.* ☉ *Oct.–Apr., Mon.–Sat. 11–4; May, Mon.–Sat. 11–5; June and Sept., Mon.–Sat. 11–5, Sun. 2–5; July–Aug., Mon.–Sat. 10–6, Sun. 2–5.*

Gatehouse of Fleet

9 mi west of Kirkcudbright, 108 mi southwest of Glasgow, 114 mi southwest of Edinburgh.

㉗ A peaceful, pleasant backwoods sort of place, Gatehouse of Fleet has a castle guarding its southern approach from the A75. **Cardoness Castle** is a typical Scottish tower house, severe and uncompromising. The 15th-century structure once was the home of the McCullochs of Galloway, then the Gordons—two of the area's important and occasionally infamous families. ⊠ *A75, 1 mi southwest of Gatehouse of Fleet,* ☏ *0131/668–8800.* 🎫 *£2.20.* ☉ *Apr.–Sept., daily 9:30–6:30; Oct.–Mar., Sat. 9:30–4:30, Sun. 2–4:30.*

The **Mill on the Fleet** heritage center is a converted cotton mill in which you can learn the history behind this pretty little town's involvement in this industry. Here you can see a changing program of arts and crafts exhibitions. The tearoom serves light lunches and delicious home-baked goods. ⊠ *High St.,* ☏ *01557/814099.* ☉ *Easter–Oct., daily 10:30–4:30.*

Lodging

£££–££££ 🏠 **Cally Palace.** Many of the public rooms in this Georgian hotel, built in 1763 as a private mansion, retain their original grandeur, with elaborate plaster ceilings and marble fireplaces. The bedrooms are individually decorated and well equipped. Surrounding the house are 150 acres of gardens, loch, and parkland, including an 18-hole golf course; an indoor leisure center has a pool, solarium, and sauna. Scottish produce stars in the restaurant in such dishes as seared medallions of Kirroughtree venison. The staff is exceptionally friendly and prepared to spoil you. ⊠ *Off the A75, DG7 2DL,* ☏ *01557/814341,* 📠 *01557/ 814522,* 🌐 *www.mcmillanhotels.co.uk. 56 rooms. Restaurant, 18-hole golf course, putting green, tennis court, pool, hot tub, sauna, fishing, croquet, bar; no a/c. MC, V. Closed Jan.–Feb.*

£ 🏠 **High Auchenlarie Farmhouse.** This 300-year-old working beef farm, set high on a hillside overlooking Wigtown Bay, offers bed and breakfast. There are tremendous views, and on a clear day you can see all the way to the Isle of Man. ⊠ *DG7 2HB,* ☏ *01557/840231. 3 rooms. No a/c. No credit cards.*

Shopping

The merchandise shop at **Galloway Lodge Preserves** (⊠ 24–28 High St., ☏ 01557/814357) sells its own marmalades and mustards, plus

Scottish pottery. There's a well-stocked gift and crafts shop at the **Mill on the Fleet** heritage center (⊠ High St., ☎ 01557/814099).

En Route   If you avoid the A75, then your route will loop to the northwest on the way to Creetown. Take a right by the Anwoth Hotel, in Gatehouse of Fleet, where the signpost points to Gatehouse Station. This route will provide you with a taste of the Dumfries and Galloway hinterland. Beyond the wooded valley where the Water of Fleet runs (local rivers are often referred to as "Water of [name of river]"), dark hills and conifer plantings lend a brooding, empty air to this lonely stretch.

Creetown Gem Rock Museum

㉘   *12 mi west of Gatehouse of Fleet, 95 mi southwest of Glasgow, 112 mi southwest of Edinburgh.*

The low-ground community of Creetown is noted for its Gem Rock Museum. The museum has an eclectic mineral collection, a dinosaur egg, an erupting volcano, and a crystal cave. Also here are an Internet café, an audiovisual display, and a tearoom. ⊠ A75, Creetown, ☎ 01671/820357. ⊡ £2.90. ⊙ *Easter–Sept., daily 9:30–5:30; Oct.–Nov., daily 10–4; early–mid-Dec. and Feb., weekends 10–4; Mar.–Easter, daily 10–4 and by appointment; last admission 30 mins before closing.*

Shopping
The **Creetown Gem Rock Museum** (⊠ A75, Creetown, ☎ 01671/820357) sells extraordinary mineral and gemstone crystals—both loose and in settings—in its gift shop.

Newton Stewart

㉙   *8 mi northwest of Creetown, 89 mi southwest of Glasgow, 108 mi southwest of Edinburgh.*

The solid and bustling little town of Newton Stewart makes a good touring base for the western region of Galloway. One possible excursion to the north from Newton Stewart takes you to the **Galloway Forest Park.** Take the A714 north from town along the wooded valley of the **River Cree,** which has a nature reserve called the Wood of Cree on the far bank.

Glen Trool

★ **㉚**   *12 mi north of Newton Stewart, 77 mi southwest of Glasgow, 96 mi southwest of Edinburgh.*

Glen Trool is one of Scotland's best-kept secrets. With high purple-and-green hilltops shorn rock-bare by glaciers and with a dark, winding loch and thickets of birch trees sounding with birdcalls, the setting almost looks more highland than the real Highlands, to the north. Note **Bruce's Stone,** just above the parking lot, marking the site where in 1307 Scotland's champion Robert the Bruce (King Robert I, 1274–1329) won his first victory in the Scottish Wars of Independence. To get here, follow the A714 north and turn right at the signpost for Glen Trool. This road leads you toward the hills that have thus far been the backdrop for the woodlands. Watch for another sign for Glen Trool. Follow this little road through increasingly wild woodland scenery to its terminus at a parking lot. Only after you have left the car and climbed for a few minutes onto a heathery knoll does the full, rugged panorama become apparent.

En Route   The **Machars** is the name given to the triangular promontory south of Newton Stewart. This is an area of gently rolling farmlands, yellow-gorse hedgerows, rich grazing for dairy cattle, and stony prehistoric sites. Most of the glossy, green expanse is used for dairy farming. Fields are bordered by dry *stane dykes* (dry walling) of sharp-edge stones, and small hills and hummocks give the area its characteristic frozen-wave look, a reminder of the glacial activity that shaped the landscape.

Wigtown

31 *8 mi south of Newton Stewart, 96 mi southwest of Glasgow, 114 mi southwest of Edinburgh.*

Twenty bookshops have sprung up on the brightly painted main street of the sleepy hamlet of Wigtown, which has been voted Scotland's national Book Town. Down by the muddy shores of Wigtown Bay there's a monument to the Wigtown Martyrs, two women who were tied to a stake and left to drown in the incoming tide during the anti-Covenant witch-hunts of 1685. Although much of Dumfries and Galloway's history is linked with Borders feuds, it is associated even more with the ferocity of the so-called Killing Times, when the Covenanters were persecuted for their belief that the king should be second to the church. Wigtown's **Bladnoch distillery** is Scotland's southernmost malt whisky producer. It has a visitor center and a gift shop, and tours are available. ☎ *01988/402605 or 01988/402235,* WEB *www.bladnoch.co.uk.* ⊙ *Weekdays 9–5, tours weekdays 10–4:15.*

Whithorn

32 *11 mi south of Wigtown, 107 mi southwest of Glasgow, 125 mi southwest of Edinburgh.*

The Machars are well known for their early Christian sites. The road that is now the A746 was a pilgrims' way and a royal route that ended at **Isle of Whithorn,** which is not a true island but was a place that early Scottish kings and barons sought to visit at least once in their lives. The pilgrimage was often prescribed as a penance, but these pleasant shores impose no penance today. The goal was St. Ninian's Chapel, the 4th-century cell of Scotland's premier saint. Some pilgrims headed for Whithorn village and others for the spit-of-sand "isle." Both places claimed to be the site of the original stone church of the saint. As you approach Whithorn's 12th-century priory, observe the royal arms of pre-1707 Scotland—that is, Scotland before the Union with England—carved and painted above the arch of the *pend* (covered way).

The **Whithorn Dig and Visitor Centre** explains the significance of what is claimed to be the site of the earliest Christian community in Scotland. The museum includes a collection of early Christian crosses. The dig site itself is beside the shell of the priory. ⊠ *Main St., Whithorn,* ☎ *01988/500508.* 🎫 *£2.70.* ⊙ *Apr.–Oct., daily 10:30–5; last tour at 4.*

Lodging

££ **Corsemalzie House.** This attractive 19th-century mansion stands among 44 acres of peaceful grounds 5 mi from the fishing village of Port William, west of Whithorn. Sporting pursuits are the hotel's main draw, with sea and game fishing, and golf on tap. The restaurant (£23.50 for four courses) has a Scottish menu with hearty venison stew or steak Auld Alliance (with red-wine sauce), and the public rooms and bedrooms are in keeping with the country-house style of the hotel. ⊠ *Corsemalzie Hotel, by Port William, Newton Stewart, Wigtownshire DG8 9RL,* ☎ *01988/860254,* FAX *01988/860213,* WEB *www.corsemalzie-house.ltd.uk. 15 rooms. Golf privileges, fishing; no a/c. AE, MC, V. Closed late Jan.–Feb.*

Stranraer

34 mi northwest of Whithorn, 89 mi southwest of Glasgow via A77, 133 mi southwest of Edinburgh.

The town of Stranraer is not a very scenic place itself, but nearby are Castle Kennedy Gardens, the highlight of this region. Stranraer is also the main ferry port to Northern Ireland—if you happen to make a purchase in one of its shops, you may wind up with some Irish coins in your change.

★ ㉝ The **Castle Kennedy Gardens** surround the shell of the original Castle Kennedy, which was burned out in 1716. The current property owners, the earl and countess of Stair, live on the grounds, at Lochinch Castle, built in 1864 (not open to the public). Pleasure grounds dispersed throughout the property were built by the second earl of Stair in 1733. The earl was a field marshal and used his soldiers to help with the heavy work of constructing banks, ponds, and other major landscape features. When the rhododendrons are in bloom, the effect is kaleidoscopic. There's also a pleasant tearoom. ⊠ *North of A75, 3 mi east of Stranraer,* ☎ *01776/702024.* ⊡ *£3.* ☉ *Apr. (or Easter, if earlier)–Sept., daily 10–5.*

Portpatrick

8 mi southwest of Stranraer, 97 mi southwest of Glasgow, 143 mi southwest of Edinburgh.

The holiday town of Portpatrick lies across the Rhinns of Galloway from Stranraer. Once an Irish ferry port, Portpatrick's exposed harbor eventually proved too risky for larger vessels. Today the village is the starting point for Scotland's longest official long-distance footpath, the **Southern Upland Way,** which runs a switchback course for 212 mi to Cockburnspath, on the east side of the Borders. Just south of Portpatrick are the lichen-yellow ruins of 16th-century **Dunskey Castle,** accessible by a cliff-top path.

The southern half of the Rhinns of Galloway has a number of interesting places to visit, all easily reached from Portpatrick. Among them is **Ardwell House Gardens,** a pleasant retreat on a domestic scale. ⊠ *Ardwell, 11 mi south of Portpatrick,* ☎ *01776/860227.* ⊡ *£2.* ☉ *Apr.–Sept., daily 10–5.*

★ The spectacular **Logan Botanic Gardens,** one of the National Botanic Gardens of Scotland, are a must-see for garden lovers. Displayed here are plants that enjoy the prevailing mild climate, especially tree ferns, cabbage palms, and other southern-hemisphere exotica. ⊠ *Off B7065 at Port Logan,* ☎ *01776/860231.* ⊡ *£3.* ☉ *Mar.–Oct., daily 9:30–6.*

If you wish to visit the southern tip of the Rhinns of Galloway, called the **Mull of Galloway,** follow the B7065/B7041 until you run out of land. The cliffs and seascapes here are rugged, and there is a lighthouse and a bird reserve.

THE BORDERS AND THE SOUTHWEST A TO Z

To research prices, get advice from other travelers, and book travel arrangements, visit www.fodors.com.

AIR TRAVEL
The nearest Scottish airports are at Edinburgh, Glasgow, and Prestwick (outside of Glasgow).

BOAT AND FERRY TRAVEL

P&O European Ferries runs a service from Larne, in Northern Ireland, to Cairnryan several times daily, with a crossing time of one hour. Seacat operates a fast-speed catamaran service once a day, which takes only 90 minutes to cross from Belfast to Stranraer.

➤ BOAT AND FERRY INFORMATION: **P&O European Ferries** (✉ Cairnryan Port, Cairnryan, near Stranraer, ☎ 0870/242–4666). **Seacat** (☎ 0990/523523).

BUS TRAVEL

From the south the main bus services use the M6 or A1, with appropriate feeder services into the hinterland; contact Scottish Citylink or National Express. For bus links from Edinburgh and Glasgow contact First Edinburgh or Stagecoach Western.

First Edinburgh offers the flexible tickets Reiver Rover (£28 weekly, £8 daily) and Waverley Wanderer (£33.50 weekly, £11.50 daily), which provide considerable savings for travel in the Borders. Stagecoach Western serves towns and villages in Dumfries and Galloway.

➤ BUS INFORMATION: **First Edinburgh** (☎ 01896/752237). **National Express** (☎ 08705/808080, WEB www.nationalexpress.co.uk). **Scottish Citylink** (☎ 08705/505050, WEB www.citylink.co.uk). **Stagecoach Western** (☎ 01563/525192, 01387/253496, or 01776/704484).

CAR TRAVEL

The main route into both the Borders and Galloway from the south is the M6, which becomes the A74. Or you can take the scenic and leisurely A7 northeastward through Hawick toward Edinburgh or the A75 and other parallel routes westward into Dumfries and Galloway and to the ferry ports of Stranraer and Cairnryan.

There are, however, several alternative routes: starting from the east, the A1 brings you from the English city of Newcastle to the border in about an hour. The A1 has the added attraction of Berwick-Upon-Tweed, on the English side of the border, but traffic on the route is heavy. Moving west, the A697, which leaves the A1 beside Alnwick (in England) and crosses the border at Coldstream, is a leisurely back-road option with a view of the countryside. The A68 is probably the most scenic route to Scotland: after climbing to Carter Bar, it reveals a view of the Borders hills and windy skies before dropping into the ancient town of Jedburgh, with its ruined abbey.

EMERGENCIES

Dial **999** for an ambulance, the police, or the fire department (no coins are needed for emergency calls from public telephone booths).

All towns in the region have at least one pharmacy. Pharmacies are not found in rural areas, where general practitioners often dispense medicines. The police will provide assistance in locating a pharmacist in an emergency.

OUTDOORS AND SPORTS

FISHING

Scottish Borders Angling Guide is the best way to find your way around the many Borders waterways. *Fishing in Dumfries and Galloway* covers the Southwest. The tourist boards for Dumfries and Galloway and the Borders carry these and other publications, including a comprehensive information pack.

GOLF

There are more than 30 courses in Dumfries and Galloway and 19 in the Borders. The Freedom of the Fairways Pass (five-day pass, £75; three-day pass, £50, no play on weekends) allows play on all 19 Borders courses and is available from the Scottish Borders Tourist Board. The Gateway to Golf Pass (five-day pass, £95; three-day pass, £65) is accepted by most clubs in Dumfries and Galloway and is available from the Dumfries and Galloway Tourist Board. The tourist boards supply comprehensive leaflets.

TOURS
The bus companies mentioned above also run orientation tours in the area.

Tours to the area are primarily conducted by Edinburgh- and Glasgow-based companies (☞ Chapters 2 and 3). James French runs coach tours in the summer. Ramtrad Holidays arranges custom-tailored chauffeur-driven tours, as well as golf and fishing packages.
➤ CONTACT: **James French** (✉ French's Garage, Coldingham, ☎ 01890/771283). **Ramtrad Holidays** (✉ 54 Edinburgh Rd., Peebles, ☎ FAX 01721/720845).

TRAIN TRAVEL
Both the Borders and the Southwest suffered badly in the shortsighted contraction of Britain's rail network in the 1960s, but there are now moves to reintroduce a Borders line. For now there is no train service in the Borders, and there's only limited service in the Southwest. You can use services from London's Euston to Glasgow; these trains stop at Carlisle, just south of the border, and some also stop at Lockerbie. There are direct trains from Carlisle to Dumfries, stopping at Gretna Green. You can pick up trains from Carlisle to Stranraer, which also has a direct link to Ayr and Glasgow. There's also a service twice daily between Dumfries and Stranraer.

On the east coast, which has a more regular and better service (London's King's Cross to Edinburgh), many trains stop at Berwick-Upon-Tweed, just south of the border. For more information call the National Train Enquiry Line.

The Scottish Borders Rail Link is actually a bus service linking Hawick, Selkirk, and Galashiels with rail services at Carlisle, Edinburgh, and Berwick.
➤ TRAIN INFORMATION: **National Train Enquiry Line** (☎ 0345/484950). **Scottish Borders Rail Link** (☎ 01896/752237).

VISITOR INFORMATION
Seasonal information centers are at Castle Douglas, Coldstream, Eyemouth, Galashiels, Gatehouse of Fleet, Gretna Green, Hawick, Kelso, Kirkcudbright, Langholm, Melrose, Moffat, Newton Stewart, Sanquhar, and Selkirk.
➤ THE BORDERS: **Jedburgh** (✉ Murray's Green, ☎ 01835/863435, FAX 01835/864099). **Peebles** (✉ High St., ☎ 01721/720138, FAX 01721/724401).
➤ DUMFRIES AND GALLOWAY: **Dumfries** (✉ Whitesands, ☎ 01387/253862, FAX 01387/245555). **Stranraer** (✉ Harbour St., ☎ 01776/702595, FAX 01776/889156).

5 FIFE AND ANGUS

ST. ANDREWS, DUNDEE,
AND GLAMIS CASTLE

The sunniest and driest part of Scotland,
Fife is famed for the ancient town of St.
Andrews, home to the Old Course—but
there's much more hereabouts than just a
round of *gowf* at the Royal & Ancient: East
Neuk villages filled with Dutch-inspired
steeples, sandy beaches, and the town that
gave birth to Robinson Crusoe lie beyond.
Heading north across the Firth of Tay,
Dundee—once famous for "jute, jam,
and journalism"—is the gateway to the
windswept glens of Angus and marvels like
Glamis Castle, one of Scotland's most
magnificent castles.

By Gilbert Summers

Updated by Beth Ingpen

THE REGIONS OF FIFE AND ANGUS sandwich Scotland's fourth-largest—and often overlooked—city, Dundee. This is typical eastern-seaboard country: open beaches, fishing villages, and breezy cliff-top walkways. Scotland's east coast has only light rainfall throughout the year; northeastern Fife, in particular, may claim the record for the most sunshine and the least rainfall in Scotland, which all adds to the enjoyment when you're touring the East Neuk (*neuk*, pronounced nyook, is Scots for corner) or exploring St. Andrews's nooks and crannies.

"Farewell Scotland, I'm awa' to Fife," cried the fishwife of Newhaven, setting sail for the opposite shore of the Firth of Forth. It was all of 6 mi away, but she expressed what many Lothian people used to feel: that Fife was a foreign place. It proudly styles itself as a "kingdom," and its long history lends some substance to the boast. From medieval times its earls were first among Scottish nobility and crowned her kings. Within its confines many great monasteries were founded, and nearly every village has some remnant of history, which really began here when the Romans went home in the 4th century AD and the Picts—the word derives from the tattoos that adorned this tribe—moved in. For many, however, the most historic event in this region was the birth of golf, in the 15th century, which, legend has it, occurred in St. Andrews, an ancient university town with romantic stone houses and seaside ruins. Here, at the Royal & Ancient Club, the ruling body of the game worldwide still has its headquarters.

Not surprisingly, fishing and seafaring have also played a role in the history of the East Neuk coastal region. From the 16th through 19th centuries, a large population lived and worked in the small ports and harbors that form a continuous chain around Fife's coast, which James V once called "a beggar's mantle fringed with gold." Although some fancy it a Scottish equivalent of the Italian Riviera, James V's golden fringe—today a series of waterfront villages darkened by the shrubbery of masts and rigging—is not all that golden in terms of sand or sunshine. The outlook of black rocks and seaweed may seem rather dreary to some, but the villages, with no two windows or chimney pots alike, have character, with brownstone or color-washed fronts, rusty charm, fishy weather vanes, outdoor stone stairways to upper floors, and crude carvings of anchors and lobsters on their lintels—all crowded on steep, narrow *wynds* (narrow streets) and hugging pint-size harbors that in the golden era supported village fleets of 100 ships apiece.

North, across the Firth of Tay, lies the region of Angus, whose particular charm is its variety: in addition to its seacoast and pleasant Lowland market centers, there's also a hinterland of lonely rounded hills with long glens running into the typical Grampian Highland scenery beyond. One of Angus's interesting features, which it shares with the eastern Lowland edge of Perthshire, is its fruit-growing industry. Seen from roadside or railway, what at first sight appear to be sturdy grapevines on field-length wires turn out to be soft-fruit plants, mainly raspberries. The chief fruit-growing area is Strathmore, the broad vale between the northwesterly Grampian Mountains and the small coastal hills of the Sidlaws behind Dundee. Striking out from this valley—the heart of the Angus region—you can make a number of day trips to uplands or seacoast.

Pleasures and Pastimes

Dining

With an affluent population, St. Andrews supports several stylish hotel restaurants. Because it is a university town and popular tourist destination, there are also many good-value cafés and bistro-style restaurants. In Ceres is the Peat Inn, a restaurant that many hold to be one of the very best in Scotland. The coastal communities serve up fine seafood. In some of the West Fife towns, such as Kirkcaldy and Dunfermline, and in Dundee, restaurants serve not only traditional Scottish fare, but also Italian, Indian, and Chinese specialties. There are also numerous small cafés of all kinds. Bar lunches are the rule in large and small hotels throughout the region, and in seaside places the "carry *oot*" (to go) meal is an old tradition.

CATEGORY	COST*
££££	over £22
£££	£16–£22
££	£9–£15
£	under £9

per person for a main course at dinner, including VAT

Golf

What serious golfer doesn't dream of playing at world-famous St. Andrews? Once you're in Fife, that dream can be easily realized. Six St. Andrews courses, all part of the St. Andrews Club, are open to visitors, and more than 40 other courses in the region offer golf by the round or by the day. Many area hotels have golfing packages or will arrange a day of golf. A round on a municipal course costs very little, and most clubs, apart from some pretentious spots, demand only comparatively modest greens fees.

Lodging

If you're staying in Fife, the obvious base is St. Andrews, with ample accommodations of all kinds. Other towns also have a reasonable selection, and you'll find good hotels and guest houses at Dunfermline and Kirkcaldy. Along the coastal strip and in the Howe of Fife between Strathmiglo and Cupar are some superior country-house hotels, many with their own restaurants.

CATEGORY	COST*
££££	over £140
£££	£110–£140
££	£65–£110
£	under £65

All prices are for a standard double room, including service, breakfast, and VAT.

Exploring Fife and Angus

Fife lies north of the Firth of Forth, stretching far up the Forth Valley (which is west and a little north of Edinburgh), with St. Andrews on its eastern coast. Northwest of Fife and across the Firth of Tay, the city of Dundee and its rural hinterland, Angus, stretch still farther north and west toward the foothills of the Grampian Mountains.

Numbers in the text correspond to numbers in the margin and on the Fife Area, St. Andrews, and Angus Area maps.

Great Itineraries

This is not a huge area, so getting around is straightforward. Treat it as a series of excursions off the main north–south artery, the A90/M90,

156

Fife Area

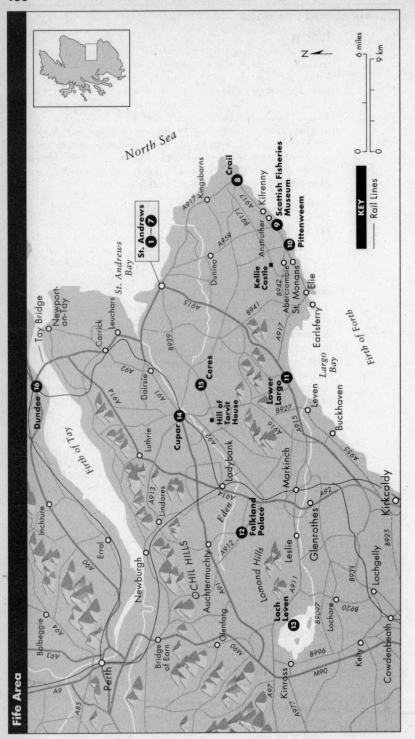

KEY

— Rail Lines

6 miles
9 km

North Sea

St. Andrews 1–7

Crail 8

Scottish Fisheries Museum 9

Pittenweem 10

Kilrenny

Anstruther

Kellie Castle

Abercrombie

St. Monans

Elie

Earlsferry

Firth of Forth

Kingsbarns

Dunino

St. Andrews Bay

Leuchars

Newport-on-Tay

Tay Bridge

Carrick

Dairsie

Luthrie

Lindores

Inchture

Errol

Balbeggie

Perth

Bridge of Earn

Newburgh

Auchtermuchty

Glenfarg

Kinross

OCHIL HILLS

Lomond Hills

Loch Leven 13

Leslie

Glenrothes

Falkland Palace 12

Ladybank

Markinch

Cupar 14

Hill of Tarvit House

Ceres 15

Lower Largo

Largo Bay

Leven

Buckhaven

Largo 11

Kirkcaldy

Lochgelly

Lochore

Kelty

Cowdenbeath

Dundee 16

Firth of Tay

which leads from Edinburgh to Aberdeen. Fife has a pleasant but not spectacular rural hinterland—in fact, it feels a long way from the hills. Angus is different, with a strong sense of a looming massif always to the north. When it comes to exploring, you can take your pick of the glens of Angus—especially the Glens Prosen or Clova—or, farthest north, Esk, all of which are delightfully out of the way. They represent probably one of the most overlooked corners of Scotland.

IF YOU HAVE 2 DAYS

Two days allow you to sample the extremes of the area in every sense. Make your way to ⌖ **St. Andrews** ①–⑦ to take in this most attractive of Scottish east-coast Lowland towns. The next day travel north of ⌖ **Dundee** ⑯ to visit **Kirriemuir** ㉑, a typical Angus town, where J. M. Barrie (the author of *Peter Pan*) was born, and to see the castle at **Glamis** ㉓—and perhaps to explore the hills via the glens of Angus west of Kirriemuir.

IF YOU HAVE 5–6 DAYS

This allows plenty of time to spend two or three days sampling not just ⌖ **St. Andrews** ①–⑦ but also the rest of the East Neuk, with its characteristic pantile-roof fishing villages—**Crail** ⑧, Anstruther and its **Scottish Fisheries Museum** ⑨, **Pittenweem** ⑩, and, just inland, Kellie Castle—all strung along the south-facing coast. Also worth exploring are the inland communities of **Falkland** (its **palace** ⑫ was once a royal hunting lodge); **Cupar** ⑭, close to Hill of Tarvit House; and the Fife Folk Museum, at ⌖ **Ceres** ⑮ (for a real treat have a meal and stay overnight at The Peat Inn). If you golf, you could allocate a day on a golf course as well. In Angus you can first travel along the breezy coast toward **Arbroath** ⑰ and **Montrose** ⑱, where the sharply contrasting Adam-designed **House of Dun** ⑲ lies within easy reach. Staying overnight near ⌖ **Forfar** ㉒ will bring the inland communities of **Kirriemuir** ㉑, **Glamis** ㉓, and **Meigle** ㉔, with its outstanding collection of early medieval sculpture, within easy reach the next day.

When to Tour Fife and Angus

Spring in the Angus glens can be quite captivating, with the high tops still snow covered. Similarly, the moorland colors of autumn are appealing. In autumn and winter, some hotels in rural Angus get busy with foreign sportspeople intent on marauding the local wildfowl. However, Fife and Angus are really spring and summer destinations, when sights are open to visitors.

ST. ANDREWS AND THE EAST NEUK VILLAGES

In its western parts, Fife still bears the scars of heavy industry, especially coal mining, but these signs are less evident as you move east. Northeastern Fife, around the university-and-golf town of St. Andrews, seems to have played no part in the industrial revolution; instead, its residents earned a living from the grain fields or from the sea. Fishing has been a major industry, and in the past a string of Fife ports traded across the North Sea. Today the legacy of Dutch-influenced architecture—crow-step gables (the stepped effect on the ends of the roofs) and distinctive town houses, for example—is still plain to see and gives these East Neuk villages a distinctive character.

St. Andrews is unlike any other Scottish town. Once Scotland's most powerful ecclesiastical center as well as the seat of the country's oldest university and then, much later, the very symbol and spiritual home of golf, the town has a comfortable, well-groomed air, sitting almost smugly apart from the rest of Scotland. This air of superiority has received a huge boost from Prince William's presence here, since 2001, as a student at the university.

St. Andrews

52 mi northeast of Edinburgh, 83 mi northeast of Glasgow.

It may have a ruined cathedral and a grand university—the oldest in Scotland—but the modern claim to fame for St. Andrews is mainly its status as the home of golf. Forget that Scottish kings were crowned here, or that John Knox preached here, or that Reformation reformers were burned at the stake here. Thousands flock to St. Andrews to play at the Old Course, home of the Royal & Ancient Club, and to follow in the footsteps of Hagen, Sarazen, Jones, and Hogan. Of course, nongolfers can tread the city streets to take in historic sights. In fact, St. Andrews's layout is still pure Middle Ages: its three main streets—North, Market, and South—converge on the city's earliest religious site, near the cathedral. Like most of the town's ancient monuments, the cathedral ruins are impressive in their desolation—but this is no dusty museum-city. The streets are busy, the shops are stylish, the gray houses sparkle in the sun, and the scene is particularly brightened during the academic year by bicycling students in scarlet gowns. You may want to take a cue from their mode of transport: car parking in St. Andrews is notoriously difficult. If possible, visit without a car, as the town is small enough to explore on foot or by bicycle.

Local legend has it that St. Andrews was founded by one St. Regulus, or Rule, who, acting under divine guidance, carried relics of St. Andrew by sea from Patras in Greece. He was shipwrecked on this Fife headland and founded a church. The holy man's name survives in the
❶ square-shape **St. Rule's Tower,** consecrated in 1126 and the oldest surviving building in St. Andrews. You can enjoy dizzying views of town from the top of the tower, accessed via a steep set of stairs. ⊠ *Off Pends Rd.,* ☎ *0131/668–8800,* WEB *www.historic-scotland.gov.uk.* ⌫ *£2.20, includes admission to cathedral.* ☉ *Apr.–Sept., daily 9:30–6; Oct.–Mar., daily 9:30–4.*

❷ **St. Andrew's Cathedral,** near St. Rule's Tower, is today only a ruined, poignant fragment of what was formerly the largest and most magnificent church in Scotland. Work on it began in 1160, and consecration was finally celebrated in 1318 after several setbacks. The cathedral was subsequently damaged by fire and repaired, but finally fell into decay in the 16th century, during the Reformation. Only ruined gables, parts of the nave south wall, and other fragments survive. The on-site museum helps you interpret the remains and gives a sense of what the cathedral must once have been like. ⊠ *Off Pends Rd.,* ☎ *0131/668–8800,* WEB *www.historic-scotland.gov.uk.* ⌫ *£2.20, includes admission to St. Rule's Tower; combined admission to cathedral, tower, and St. Andrews Castle, £4.* ☉ *Apr.–Sept., daily 9:30–6; Oct.–Mar., daily 9:30–4.*

❸ On the shore north of the cathedral stands **St. Andrews Castle,** which was started at the end of the 13th century. Although now a ruin, the remains include a rare example of a cold and gruesome bottle dungeon, in which many prisoners spent their last hours. Even more atmospheric is the castle's mine and countermine. The former was a tunnel dug by besieging forces in the 16th century; the latter, a tunnel dug by castle defenders in order to meet and wage battle below ground. You can stoop and crawl into this narrow passageway—an eerie experience, despite the addition of electric light. The visitor center has a good audiovisual

---

St. Andrews

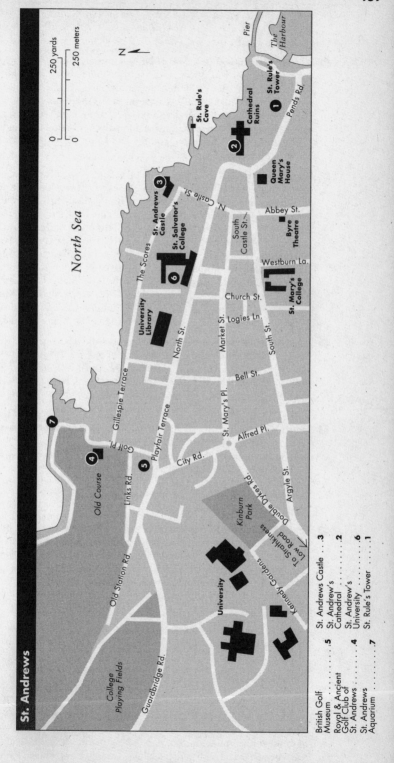

North Sea

The Harbour

Pier

St. Rule's Tower **1**

Cathedral Ruins **2**

St. Rule's Cave

Queen Mary's House

Pends Rd.

N. Castle St.

Abbey St.

South Castle St.

Byre Theatre

Westburn La.

St. Andrews Castle **3**

St. Salvator's College

University Library

The Scores

North St.

Church St.

Logies Ln.

Market St.

St. Mary's College

South St.

University **6**

Bell St.

Gillespie Terrace

Playfair Terrace

St. Mary's Pl.

Alfred Pl.

Argyle St.

City Rd.

Double Dykes Rd.

Golf Pl.

Links Rd.

5

4

Old Course

Kinburn Park

Old Station Rd.

Guardbridge Rd.

College Playing Fields

University

Kennedy Gardens

Low Road

To Strathkinness

7

0   250 yards
0   250 meters

N

presentation on the castle's history. ⊠ *End of North Castle St.,* ☎ *0131/ 668–8800,* WEB *www.historic-scotland.gov.uk.* ⊑ *£2.80; castle and cathedral, £4.* ☉ *Apr.–Sept., daily 9:30–6; Oct.–Mar., daily 9:30–4.*

❹ The **Royal & Ancient Golf Club of St. Andrews** on The Scores, the ruling house of golf worldwide, is the spiritual home of all who play or follow the game. Its clubhouse on the dunes—a dignified building open to club members only—is adjacent to St. Andrews's famous Old Course. The town of St. Andrews prospers on golf, golf schools, and golf equipment (the manufacture of golf balls has been a local industry for more than 100 years), and the Old Course is associated with the greatest players of the game.

As to the game and its origins on the Royal & Ancient's course, golf was perhaps originally played with a piece of driftwood, a shore pebble, and a convenient rabbit hole on the sandy, coastal turf. It has been argued that golf came to Scotland from Holland, but historical evidence points to Scotland as the cradle, if not the birthplace, of the game. Citizens of St. Andrews were playing golf on the town links (public land) as far back as the 15th century. Rich golfers, instead of gathering on the common links, formed themselves into clubs by the 18th century. Arguably, the world's first golf club was the Honourable Company of Edinburgh Golfers, founded in Leith in 1744, which is now at Muirfield in East Lothian. The Society of St. Andrews Golfers, founded in 1754, became the Royal & Ancient Golf Club of St. Andrews in 1834.

❺ The **British Golf Museum** explores the centuries-old relationship between St. Andrews and golf and displays golf memorabilia. It's just opposite the Royal & Ancient Golf Club. ⊠ *Bruce Embankment,* ☎ *01334/ 460046,* WEB *www.britishgolfmuseum.co.uk.* ⊑ *£4.* ☉ *Easter–mid-Oct., daily 9:30–5:30; mid-Oct.–Easter, call or check Web site for opening hrs.*

❻ Aside from being the home of golf, St. Andrews is also the site of Scotland's oldest university. Founded in 1411, **St. Andrew's University** now consists of two stately old colleges in the middle of town and some modern buildings on the outskirts. A third, weatherworn college, originally built in 1512, has become a girls' school. The handsome university buildings can be explored on guided walks, sometimes led by students in scarlet gowns. ☎ *01334/462245.* ⊑ *£4.* ☉ *Tours: June– Aug., weekdays at 11 and 2:30.*

❼ At the **St. Andrews Aquarium,** seals, fish, crustaceans, and many other forms of marine life inhabit various aquariums and pool gardens designed to simulate their natural habitats. ⊠ *The Scores, West Sands,* ☎ *01334/474786.* ⊑ *£4.95.* ☉ *Easter–Oct., daily 10–6; Nov.–Easter, daily 10–5; last admission 1 hr before closing.*

Leuchars, about 6 mi northwest of St. Andrews's famous Old Course on the A919, has a 12th-century church with some of the finest Norman architectural features to be seen anywhere in Scotland. Note in particular the blind arcading (arch shapes on the wall) and the beautifully decorated chancel and apse.

Dining and Lodging

£££   ✕ **Balaka.** The handsome gray-stone premises here hide a 1-acre garden of herbs, vegetables, and flowers used in this restaurant's Bangladeshi dishes. The Rouf family displays its exceptional cookery prowess amid a restrained dusty pink interior with crisp white tablecloths and vases of roses. Popular dishes include *mas bangla* (marinated Scottish salmon fried in mustard oil with garlic, scallions, and eggplant) and green-herb chicken, enhanced by fresh coriander from the garden. ⊠ *Alexandra Place,* ☎ *01334/474825. AE, MC, V. No lunch Sun.*

££££   ✕🏨 **Rufflets Country House Hotel.** Ten acres of formal and informal gardens surround this creeper-covered country house just outside St. Andrews. All the rooms are beautifully decorated and comfortable, with the amenities you would expect of a top-class hotel. Dinner is served in the roomy Garden Restaurant, famous for its use of local produce to create memorable Scottish dishes. Try the the Tay salmon or the pan-seared collop of Rannoch venison in a raspberry-tea-syrup glaze served with fresh asparagus. Lighter and less expensive bar meals are also available at lunch and in the evening. ✉ *Strathkinness Low Rd., KY16 9TX,* ☎ *01334/472594,* FAX *01334/478703,* WEB *www.rufflets.co.uk. 22 rooms. Restaurant, bar; no a/c. AE, DC, MC, V.*

£   🏨 **Aslar Guest House.** This Victorian terraced house stands close to shops, golf courses, and historic attractions such as the castle. All the rooms are individually decorated—one with a four-poster bed—and have private bath and shower (unusual for bed-and-breakfasts). ✉ *120 North St., KY16 9AF,* ☎ *01334/473460,* FAX *01334/477540,* WEB *www. aslar.com. 5 rooms. No a/c, no room phones. MC, V.*

£   🏨 **University of St. Andrews.** For accommodation within walking distance of all attractions, it's hard to beat the university for value and convenience. Room sizes—mainly singles—vary from adequate in the New Hall building to happily spacious in the older buildings. The newer rooms have private bathrooms. Self-catering accommodation is also available, at Albany Park. ✉ *79 North St., KY16 9AD,* ☎ *01334/ 462000,* FAX *01334/462500,* WEB *www.st-andrews.ac.uk. 120 rooms, 72 with shower. Restaurant, bar, lounge, laundry facilities; no a/c, no room phones, no room TVs. MC, V. Closed early Sept.–early June.*

Nightlife and the Arts

PUBS

Chariots (✉ The Scores, ☎ 01334/472451), inside the Scores Hotel, is popular with locals in their thirties and forties.

THEATER

Byre Theatre (✉ Abbey St., ☎ 01334/476288, WEB www.byretheatre. com) has a main auditorium seating 220 plus a studio theater space. The theater puts on its own productions, working with various theater groups, and also hosts visiting productions. Experimental and youth theater, small-scale operatic performances, contemporary dance, and Sunday night jazz (in the foyer) also take place regularly. There's also an excellent café-bar.

Golf

One 9-hole and five 18-hole courses, all part of the St. Andrews Links Trust, are open to visitors. For details of availability—there's usually a waiting list, which varies according to the time of year—contact the **Reservations Department** (✉ St. Andrews Links Trust, Pilmour House, St. Andrews KY16 9SF, ☎ 01334/466666, FAX 01334/477036, WEB www.standrews.org.uk or www.golfagent.com).

Balgove Course (1993): 9 holes, 1,520 yards, par 30. **Eden Course** (1914): 18 holes, 6,162 yards, par 70. **Jubilee Course** (1897): 18 holes, 6,805 yards, par 72. **New Course** (1895): 18 holes, 6,604 yards, par 71. **Old Course** (15th century): 18 holes, 6,566 yards, par 72, handicap certificate required year-round. **Strathtyrum Course** (1993): 18 holes, 5,094 yards, par 69.

Shopping

Bonkers (✉ 80 Market St., ☎ 01334/473919) carries a huge selection of books, cards, pottery, soft toys, and gift items. **Renton Oriental Rugs** (✉ 72 South St., ☎ 01334/476334) is the best place in the region, if not in all Scotland, to buy Oriental rugs and carpets of all colors, patterns, and sizes—many of them antiques. **St. Andrews Fine Art** (⊠ 84A Market St., ☎ 01334/474080) is the place to go for Scottish paintings—oils, watercolors, drawings, and prints—from 1800 to the present. The **St. Andrews Pottery Shop** (⊠ Church Sq. between South St. and Market St., ☎ 01334/477744) sells decorative domestic stoneware, porcelain, ceramics, enamel jewelry, and terra-cotta pots.

Crail

★ ❽ *10 mi south of St. Andrews via A917.*

One of numerous fishing communities along the Fife coast, Crail is the oldest, most palatial by local standards, and most aristocratic of East Neuk burghs, where fish merchants retired and built cottages. The town landmark is a picturesque Dutch-influenced town house, or *tolbooth,* which contains the oldest bell in Fife, cast in Holland in 1520. As you head into East Neuk from this tiny port, look about for tolbooths, market crosses, and merchant houses and their little *doocots* (dovecotes, where pigeons were kept for winter meat)—typical picturesque touches of this region. Full details on the heritage and former trading links of Crail can be found in the **Crail Museum and Heritage Center.** ⊠ 62–64 Marketgate, ☎ 01333/450869. ☞ Free. ☉ Easter and June–Sept., Mon.–Sat. 10–1 and 2–5, Sun. 2–5; after Easter–end of May, weekends and holidays 2–5.

Anstruther

4 mi southwest of Crail via A917.

Anstruther, locally called Anster, has a picturesque waterfront with a few shops brightly festooned with children's pails and shovels, a ges-
★ ❾ ture to seaside vacationers. Facing Anstruther harbor is the **Scottish Fisheries Museum,** housed in a colorful cluster of buildings, the earliest of which dates from the 16th century. The museum illustrates the difficult life of Scottish fisherfolk, past and present, through documents, artifacts, ship models, paintings, and tableaux. These displays, complete with the reek of tarred rope and net, have been known to induce nostalgic tears in not a few old deckhands. There are also floating exhibits at the quayside. ⊠ Anstruther harbor, ☎ 01333/310628, WEB www.scottish-fisheries-museum.org. ☞ £3.50. ☉ Apr.–Oct., Mon.–Sat. 10–5:30, Sun. 11–5; Nov.–Mar., Mon.–Sat. 10–4:15, Sun. noon–4:15; last admission 45 mins before closing.

Dining

££££ ✕ **The Cellar.** Specializing in fish but with a selection of Scottish beef and lamb as well, the Cellar is devoted to serving top-quality ingredients cooked simply in modern Scottish style, preserving all their natural flavors. The crayfish-and-mussel bisque is famous, and the wine list reflects high standards. You enter this unpretentious, old-fashioned restaurant through a small courtyard. It's popular with the locals, but its fame is widespread. ⊠ 24 E. Green, ☎ 01333/310378. AE, DC, MC, V. Closed Sun. and Mon. Nov.–Easter.

Nightlife and the Arts

The **Dreel Tavern** (⊠ 16 High St. W, ☎ 01333/310727) is a 16th-century coaching inn famous for its hand-drawn ales.

Bicycling

The back roads of Fife make pleasant biking terrain. You can rent bicycles from **East Neuk Outdoors** (⊠ Cellardyke Park, ☎ 01333/311929), which also has archery, rappeling, climbing, orienteering, and canoeing equipment and provides instruction.

Pittenweem

🔟 *1½ mi southwest of Anstruther via A917.*

Many examples of East Neuk architecture serve as the backdrop for the working harbor at Pittenweem. Look for the crow-step gables, white *harling* (Scots for roughcasting, the rough mortar finish on walls), and red pantiles (S-shape in profile). The *weem* part of the town's name comes from the Gaelic *uaime,* or cave. This town's particular cave is **St. Fillan's Cave,** which contains the shrine of St. Fillan, a 6th-century hermit who lived inside it. It's up a close (alleyway) behind the waterfront. ⊠ *Cove Wynd, near harbor,* ☎ *01333/311495 (Gingerbread Horse Craft Shop has key).* ⌦ *£1.* ◷ *Mon.–Sat. 10–5, Sun. noon–5.*

Kellie Castle, dating from the 16th and 17th centuries and restored in Victorian times, stands among the grain fields and woodlands of northeastern Fife. Four acres of pretty gardens surround the castle, which is looked after by the National Trust for Scotland. ⊠ *B9171, 3 mi northwest of Pittenweem,* ☎ *01333/720271.* ⌦ *Garden and grounds £2; combined ticket to castle and gardens £5.* ◷ *Castle Apr.–Sept., Thurs.–Mon. noon–5; garden and grounds year-round, daily 9:30–sunset.*

Lower Largo

⓫ *10 mi west of Pittenweem via A917 and A915.*

Lower Largo's main claim to fame is that it was the birthplace of Alexander Selkirk (1676–1721), the Scottish sailor who was the inspiration for Daniel Defoe's (1660–1731) *Robinson Crusoe.* Once a juvenile delinquent, he grew up to terrorize the region and then departed to sail the seas. In 1704, having quarreled with his captain, Selkirk was put ashore on the isle of Juan Fernandez off the coast of Chile. Four years later a British privateer picked him up; his rescuers found him dressed in goatskins and surrounded by tame goats. Piratical adventures on the way home earned him a fortune, and he returned to Largo so richly dressed his mother didn't recognize him. His statue can be seen above the doorway of the house on Main Street, where he was born.

Shopping

At nearby Upper Largo, in a converted barn, **Scotland's Larder** (⊠ Upper Largo, ☎ 01333/360414) is a shop-restaurant that sells a huge assortment of Scottish preserves, baked goods, and seasonal produce—anything from Dundee cakes (a light fruit cake with a distinctive, circular pattern of split almonds on the top) and shortbread to smoked salmon and oysters. It also has tastings, talks, and cooking demonstrations, all of which show off the savory foods of Scotland.

Falkland

★ *14 mi northwest of Lower Largo.*

One of the loveliest communities in Fife, Falkland is a royal burgh of twisting streets and crooked stone houses. The National Trust for
★ ⓬ Scotland's **Falkland Palace,** a former hunting lodge of the Stuart monarchs and one of the earliest examples in Britain of the French Renaissance style, dominates the town. Overlooking the main street is the palace's most impressive feature—the walls and chambers on its south side, all rich with Renaissance buttresses and stone medallions, built for King James V (1512–42) in the 1530s by French masons. He died here, and the palace was a favorite resort of his daughter, Mary, Queen of Scots (1542–87). The gardens behind the palace contain a most unusual survivor: a royal tennis court—not at all like its modern counterpart—built in 1539. In the beautiful gardens, overlooked by the palace

turret windows, you may easily imagine yourself back at the solemn hour when James on his deathbed pronounced the doom of the house of Stuart: "It cam' wi' a lass and it'll gang wi a lass." ⊠ *Main St., Falkland,* ☎ *01337/857397.* ⊠ *Palace and gardens £7; gardens only, £3.* ☉ *Mar.–Oct., Mon.–Sat. 10–6, Sun. 1–5.*

Loch Leven

⑬ *10 mi southwest of Falkland via A911.*

Scotland's largest Lowland loch, Loch Leven is famed for its fighting trout. The area is also noted for abundant bird life, particularly its wintering wildfowl. Mary, Queen of Scots, was forced to sign the deed of abdication in her island prison in the loch. On the southern shore overlooking the lock, **Vane Farm Nature Reserve,** a visitor center run by the Royal Society for the Protection of Birds, provides information about Loch Leven's ecology. ⊠ *Vane Farm, Rte. B9097, just off M90 and B996,* ☎ *01577/862355.* ⊠ *£3.* ☉ *Daily 10–5.*

Cupar

⑭ *21 mi northwest of Loch Leven via M90 and A91, 10 mi west of St. Andrews via A91.*

With a station on the Edinburgh–Aberdeen line, Cupar is a busy market town, and many of its shops are privately owned (as opposed to chain stores). On rising ground near the town stands the National Trust for Scotland's **Hill of Tarvit House.** Originally a 17th-century mansion, the house was altered in the high-Edwardian style in the late 1890s and early 1900s by the Scottish architect Sir Robert Lorimer (1864–1929). Inside the house are fine collections of antique furniture, Chinese porcelain, bronzes, tapestries, and Dutch paintings. Lorimer also designed the formal Edwardian gardens. A tearoom is also on the premises. ⊠ *2 mi south of Cupar off A916,* ☎ *01334/653127.* ⊠ *£5 house and gardens; gardens only, £2.* ☉ *House Apr.–Oct., daily noon–5. Tearoom Apr.–Sept., daily noon–5; Oct., weekends noon–5. Garden and grounds daily 9:30–sunset.*

At the **Scottish Deer Centre,** red deer can be seen at close quarters on ranger-guided tours. There are also nature trails, a winery, falconry displays, an adventure playground (a wood and tire fortress suitable for older children), five shops, and a coffee bar. ⊠ *A91, near Rankelour Farm, just outside Cupar,* ☎ *01337/810391.* ⊠ *£4.50.* ☉ *Easter–Oct., daily 10–6; Nov.–Easter, daily 10–5.*

OFF THE BEATEN PATH   **DAIRSIE BRIDGE** – A few minutes east of Cupar at Dairsie, an unclassified road goes off to the right from the A91 and soon runs by the River Eden. The Dairsie Bridge, which goes over the river, is 450 years old and has three arches, one above the other. Above the trees rises the spire of Dairsie Church, dating from the 17th century. The stark ruin of Dairsie Castle, often overlooked, stands gloomily over the river nearby. With wild-rose hedges, grazing cattle, and pheasants calling from the woody thickets, this is the very essence of rural Lowland Fife, yet it's only about 15 minutes from the Old Course.

Dining

£££   ✕ **Ostlers Close Restaurant.** This long-established, unpretentious, cottage-style restaurant, with plain painted walls and stick-back chairs, ★   has earned a well-deserved reputation for top-quality cuisine that is imaginative without being trendy. Wild mushrooms in season are a particular favorite with the chef, and the fish and shellfish dishes are especially good. Ostlers Close is tucked away up an alleyway off of Cupar's main street. It's a good idea to reserve ahead, particularly for lunch. ⊠ *Bonnygate,* ☎ *01334/655574,* WEB *www.ostlersclose.co.uk. AE, MC, V. Closed Sun. and Mon. No lunch Tues.–Thurs.*

Outdoor Activities and Sports
Cupar Sports Centre (⊠ Carselogie Rd., ☎ 01334/412290) houses a swimming pool, sports hall, fitness rooms, squash, and steam bath.

Shopping
With its wide selection of British and international designer-clothing labels, **Margaret Urquhart** (⊠ 13–17 Lady Wynd, ☎ 01334/652205) attracts customers from as far away as Edinburgh and Glasgow.

Ceres

⑮ *3 mi southeast of Cupar via A916 and B939, 9 mi southwest of St. Andrews.*

To learn more about the history and culture of rural Fife, visit the **Fife Folk Museum,** in the town of Ceres. The life of local rural communities is reflected in artifacts and documents, all housed in suitably authentic buildings, including a former weigh house and adjoining weavers' cottages. ⊠ *High St.,* ☎ *01334/828180.* 🎫 *£2.50.* ☉ *Easter and mid-May–Sept., daily 2–5.*

Dining and Lodging
££££ ✕🏠 **The Peat Inn.** This popular inn is best known for its outstanding
★ modern Scottish-style restaurant, generally considered one of the finest in Scotland. Mouthwatering entrées might include roast scallops with potatoes and leeks and a pea puree, or medallions of monkfish and lobster with artichoke hearts in a lobster sauce. Book well in advance. A detached building houses eight comfortable suites. ⊠ *Jct. B940 and B941, 6 mi southwest of St. Andrews (Peat Inn, Cupar, Fife, KY15 5LH),* ☎ *01334/840206,* FAX *01334/840530,* WEB *www.thepeatinn.co.uk. 8 suites. Restaurant, bar; no a/c. AE, MC, V. Closed Sun.–Mon.*

DUNDEE AND ANGUS

The industrial city of Dundee, once famed for its economic reliance on "jute, jam, and journalism," contrasts dramatically with the farmlands and glens of its rural hinterland, Angus, and the coastal links northward. Angus combines coastal agriculture on rich, red soils with dramatic inland glens that pierce their way into the foothills of the Grampian mountain ranges to the northwest. Although the peaceful back roads in this area are uncluttered, the main road from Perth/Dundee to Aberdeen—the A90—requires special care, with its mix of fast cars, lorries, and unexpectedly slow farm traffic.

Dundee

⑯ *14 mi northwest of St. Andrews, 58 mi north of Edinburgh, 79 mi northeast of Glasgow.*

The city of Dundee makes a good base at any time of year for exploring Fife and Angus, and it holds many interesting sights in its own right. Dundee's urban renewal program—its determination to shake off its grimy industrial past—was motivated in part by the arrival of the **RRS (Royal Research Ship)** *Discovery,* the vessel used by Captain Robert Scott (1868–1912) on his polar explorations. The steamer was originally built and launched in Dundee; now it's a permanent tourist exhibit. An onboard exhibition allows you to sample life as it was aboard the intrepid

Angus Area

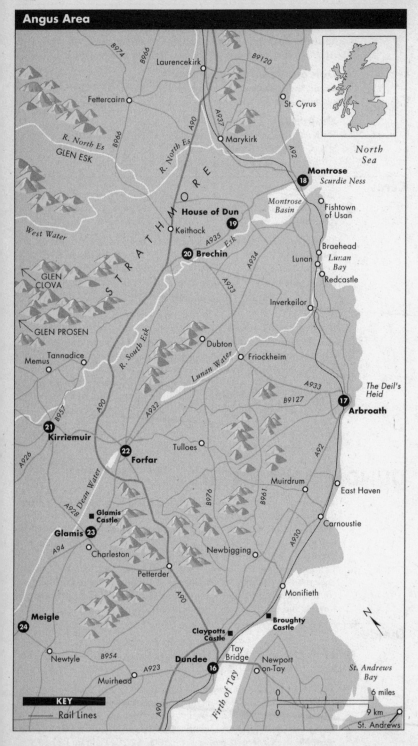

B974
B966
Laurencekirk
B9120
Fettercairn
St. Cyrus
A937
A90
Marykirk
A92
R. North Es
GLEN ESK
R. North Esk
North
Sea
West Water
House of Dun **19**
Keithock
A935
Montrose **18**
Scurdie Ness
Montrose
Basin
Fishtown
of Usan
20 Brechin
A934
Braehead
Lunan
Lunan
Bay
Redcastle
A933
GLEN
CLOVA
Inverkeilor
GLEN PROSEN
R. South Esk
Dubton
Friockheim
Lunan Water
A933
Memus
Tannadice
A932
The Deil's
Heid
B9127
17
Arbroath
21
Kirriemuir
B957
Tulloes
A90
A926
22 Forfar
Muirdrum
A92
East Haven
B976
B961
Glamis
Castle
Carnoustie
Glamis **23**
A94
Charleston
Newbigging
A930
Petterder
Dean Water
A928
Monifieth
Meigle
24
N
Claypotts
Castle
Broughty
Castle
Newtyle
B954
Tay
Bridge
St. Andrews
Bay
Muirhead
A923
Dundee
16
Newport
on-Tay
A90
Firth of Tay
St. Andrews

KEY
—— Rail Lines

0   6 miles
0   9 km
St. Andrews

Discovery, and the *Polarama* exhibit lets you experience life in Antarctica hands-on and heads-in—you'll feel the temperature and the wind chill as if you were there. ⊠ *Discovery Point, Discovery Quay,* ☎ 01382/201245, WEB *www.rrsdiscovery.com.* £6.25. ☉ *Apr.–Oct., Mon.–Sat. 10–5, Sun. 11–5; Nov.–Mar., Mon.–Sat. 10–4, Sun. 11–4.*

At Victoria Dock lies berthed the frigate **Unicorn,** a 46-gun wooden warship. The *Unicorn* has the distinction of being the oldest British-built warship afloat (it's also the fourth-oldest in the world), having been launched at Chatham, England, in 1824. On board, you can clamber right down into the hold, or discuss the models and displays about the Royal navy's history with the friendly staff. ⊠ *Victoria Dock, just east of Tay Rd. bridge,* ☎ 01382/200900 or 01382/200893. £3.50. ☉ *Apr.–Oct., daily 10–5; Nov.–Mar., Wed.–Sun. 10–4, last admission 20 mins before closing; call ahead to confirm hrs in winter.*

In a former jute mill, the **Verdant Works** houses a multifaceted exhibit on the story of jute and Dundee's historical involvement in the jute trade. Restored machinery, audiovisuals, and tableaux all vividly re-create the hard, noisy life of the jute worker. ⊠ *W. Hendersons Wynd,* ☎ 01382/225282. £5.95. ☉ *Apr.–Oct., Mon.–Sat. 10–5, Sun. 11–5; Nov.–Mar., Wed.–Sat. 10:30–4:30, Sun. 11–4:30.*

You'll see the world upside down when you're strapped into the gyroscope at **Sensation,** a hands-on science center focusing on the five senses. Although the general noise level testifies to the child-friendly nature of the place, enthusiastic staff members persuade visitors of all ages to participate. Among the many experiments and activities, you can "age" yourself (or making yourself look younger) on computer screens or practice your balance on wobble boards. ⊠ *Greenmarket,* ☎ 01382/228800, FAX 01382/868602, WEB *www.sensation.org.uk* £5.50. ☉ *Apr.–Oct., daily 10–6; Nov.–Mar., daily 10–5.*

Dundee's principal museum and art gallery is the **McManus Galleries,** which has displays on a range of subjects, including local history, trade, and industry. ⊠ *Albert Sq.,* ☎ 01382/432084. *Free.* ☉ *Mon.–Wed. and Fri.–Sat. 10–5, Thurs. 10–7, Sun. 12:30–4.*

An innovative building designed by architect Richard Murphy houses the city's most exciting artistic venue, the **Dundee Contemporary Arts.** Its galleries specialize in the best works of both Scottish and international artists. Creative facilities include a print studio and a visual research center linked to the University of Dundee. The presence of working artists encourages many meet-the-artist events year-round. There are also two movie theaters, a gift shop, and a café. ⊠ *152 Nethergate,* ☎ 01382/909900. *Free.* ☉ *Tues.–Sat. 10:30–midnight, Sun. 10:30 AM–11 PM; galleries close at 5:30 Tues.–Wed. and weekends, at 8 Thurs.–Fri.; limited print-studio hrs so call ahead.*

The **University Botanic Gardens** are a well-landscaped collection of native and exotic plants. Also on the premises are tropical and temperate greenhouses, a visitor center, and a coffee shop. ⊠ *Riverside Dr.,* ☎ 01382/647190. £2. ☉ *Mar.–Oct., daily 10–4:30; Nov.–Feb., daily 10–3:30.*

Mills Observatory is the only full-time public observatory in Britain, with a resident astronomer. There are displays on astronomy, space exploration, scientific instruments, and a 10-inch refracting telescope for night viewing of the stars and planets. ⊠ *Balgay Hill,* ☎ 01382/435846. *Free.* ☉ *Oct.–Mar., weekdays 4–10, weekends 12:30–4; Apr.–Sept., Tues.–Fri. 11–5, weekends 12:30–4.*

OFF THE
BEATEN PATH

CLAYPOTTS CASTLE – In the eastern suburbs of Dundee, away from the surviving Victorian architecture of the city center, lies a well-preserved 16th-century tower house laid out in a Z plan. You can view the castle from the outside only. ✉ *South of A92, 3 mi east of city center.*

BROUGHTY CASTLE – Originally built to guard the Tay estuary, Broughty Castle is now a museum focusing on fishing, ferries, and the history of the town of Broughty Ferry's whaling industry. There's also a display of arms and armor. The castle lies about a mile east of Claypotts Castle. ✉ *Broughty Ferry, 4 mi east of city center,* ☎ *01382/436916.* ▣ *Free.* ☉ *Apr.–Sept., Mon.–Sat. 10–4, Sun. 12:30–4; Oct.–Mar., Tues.–Sat. 10–4, Sun. 12:30–4.*

Dining and Lodging

£   ✗ **Het Theatercafe.** At the lively Rep Theatre, you have a choice of the café-bar upstairs, with drinks, snacks, and good coffee, or the downstairs restaurant with its internationally inspired menu. Dishes at the restaurant include chicken *satay* (grilled on skewers) and Cajun chicken or fish cakes. Theater posters of past productions and stills of actors hang on the walls. ✉ *Dundee Repertory Theatre, Tay Sq.,* ☎ *01382/ 206699. MC, V. Closed Sun.*

££££ ✗▥ **Kinnaird.** A luxurious country house set in extensive grounds above the Tay Valley northwest of Dundee, Kinnaird has elegant, individually decorated bedrooms with king-size beds and antique furniture. Reception rooms welcome you with open fires and fresh flowers, and imaginative Scottish cuisine rounds out a memorable experience. ✉ *Kinnaird Estate, PH8 0LB,* ☎ *01796/482440,* ℻ *01796/482289,* 🌐 *www.kinnairdestate.com. 9 rooms. 2 restaurants, tennis court, fishing, croquet; no a/c, no kids under 12. MC, V.*

£££–££££ ✗▥ **Hilton Dundee.** A central, yet riverside, situation convenient for many attractions plus the usual high standards of this international hotel chain are reason enough to stay here. Green and blue bedspreads and curtains and wooden furniture fill the bedrooms. Add the fine international Unicorn Restaurant and the river views, and this modern hotel is hard to resist. ✉ *Earl Grey Place, DD1 4DE,* ☎ *01382/ 229271,* ℻ *01382/200072,* 🌐 *www.hilton.com. 129 rooms. Restaurant, indoor pool; no a/c. AE, DC, MC, V.*

£££–££££ ✗▥ **Queen's Hotel.** This handsome Victorian, former railway hotel in the lively west end of Dundee is thoroughly up-to-date inside, though it still retains its architectural charm. Modern oak furniture, green carpets, and simple burgundy, gold, or yellow curtains and bedspreads decorate the spacious rooms. Nosey Parkers Bistro (£–££) is popular with locals for its international dishes or a quick drink after work. White tablecloths play nicely against the bright primary colors of the restaurant. ✉ *160 Nethergate, DD1 4DU,* ☎ *01382/322515,* ℻ *01382/ 202668,* 🌐 *www.queenshotel-dundee.com. 52 rooms, 1 suite. Restaurant; no a/c. AE, DC, MC, V.*

££–£££ ✗▥ **Swallow Hotel.** This Victorian mansion sits among 5 acres of landscaped gardens, which is unusual for the city of Dundee. The fairly spacious bedrooms are done in pink or yellow, with geometric- or floral-patterned curtains and modern wooden furniture. The Conservatory Restaurant (£–££) serves Scottish-influenced international fare and gives the impression that you are actually sitting in the garden. ✉ *Kingsway West, Invergowrie, DD2 5JT,* ☎ *01382/631200,* ℻ *01382/ 631201. 104 rooms, 3 suites. Restaurant, pool, gym, sauna, steam room; no a/c. AE, DC, MC, V.*

Nightlife and the Arts

DANCE CLUBS

Dundee is well supplied with dance clubs. **Fat Sam's Disco** (✉ 31 S. Ward Rd., ☎ 01382/228181) attracts clubbers of all ages to its Thursday rock-and-indie night, Friday funk, and Saturday house sounds. The younger set (18–23) chooses **Mardi Gras** (✉ 21 S. Ward Rd., ☎ 01382/205551) for mainstream chart toppers and a sprinkling of '60s and '70s music. **Oasis Night Club** (✉ St. Andrews La., ☎ 01382/221061) is strictly for those over 25, with a musical medley covering the 1960s to the 1990s.

MUSIC

Bonar Hall (✉ Park Pl., ☎ 01382/345466) hosts classical, jazz, and rock concerts, as well as chamber music. **Caird Hall** (✉ City Sq., ☎ 01382/434451) is one of Scotland's finest concert halls, staging a wide range of music. **West Port Bar** (✉ Henderson's Wynd, ☎ 01382/200993) hosts folk music on Monday and jazz and poetry on Sunday afternoon. It's also a regular haunt for local bands.

THEATER

The **Dundee Repertory Theatre** complex (✉ Tay Sq., ☎ 01382/223530) includes an exhibition gallery and is home to a resident theater group as well as a dance company. Both offer diverse programs. **Whitehall Theatre** (✉ 12 Bellfield St., ☎ 01382/322684) has mostly musical entertainment, including light opera.

Outdoor Activities and Sports

Dundee Olympia Leisure Centre (✉ Earl Grey Pl., ☎ 01382/434173) has four swimming pools, a diving pool, sauna, water slides, exercise equipment, a climbing wall, and a restaurant.

Shopping

COFFEE AND TEA

J. Allan Braithwaite (✉ 6 Castle St., ☎ 01382/322693) carries 13 freshly roasted coffees and more than 30 blended teas, including mango and apricot. (Remember that such specialty teas can usually be taken home without import restriction if you purchase them as gifts.)

SCOTTISH SPECIALTIES

Dundee is lucky to have a particularly impressive branch of **Hector Russell** (✉ 6a Castle St., ☎ 01382/206805, WEB www.hector-russell.com), kiltmakers extraordinaire, where every item necessary for correct Highland dress can be purchased, made-to-measure or off the rack. The staff is knowledgeable and helpful.

SHOPPING MALLS

Overgate (✉ Overgate, ☎ 01382/314201) is a modern shopping mall housing upscale chain stores. Many of the major retail chains can be found at **Wellgate Shopping Centre** (✉ Off Panmure St., ☎ 01382/225454).

For bargain hunting, try **City Quay** (✉ Victoria Docks, Camperdown St., ☎ 01382/220583), where factory and designer outlet shops cluster conveniently together.

Arbroath

 15 mi north of Dundee via A92.

You'll find traditional boatbuilding in the holiday resort and fishing town of Arbroath. It also has several small curers and processors, and shops sell the town's most famous delicacy, "Arbroath smokies"—whole haddock gutted and lightly smoked.

Arbroath Abbey, founded in 1178, is an unmistakable presence in the town center; it seems to straddle whole streets, as if the town were simply ignoring the red-stone ruin in its midst. Surviving today are remains of the church, as well as one of the most complete examples in existence of an abbot's residence. From here in 1320 a passionate plea was sent by King Robert the Bruce (1274–1329) and the Scottish Church to Pope John XXII (circa 1245–1334) in far-off Rome. The pope had until then sided with the English kings, who adamantly refused to acknowledge Scottish independence. The Declaration of Arbroath stated firmly, "For as long as but a hundred of us remain alive, never will we on any conditions be brought under English rule. It is in truth not for glory, nor riches, nor honours that we are fighting, but for freedom— for that alone, which no honest man gives up but with life itself." Some historians describe this plea, originally drafted in Latin, as the single most important document in Scottish history. The pope advised English king Edward II (1284–1327) to make peace, but warfare was to break out along the border from time to time for the next 200 years. The excellent visitor center recounts this history in its well-planned displays. ✉ *Arbroath town center,* ☎ *0131/668–8800,* WEB *www. historic-scotland.gov.uk.* 🎫 *£2.50.* ☉ *Apr.–Sept., daily 9:30–6; Oct.– Mar., Mon.–Wed. and Sat. 9:30–4, Thurs. 9:30–12:30, Sun. 2–4.*

Arbroath was the shore base for the construction of the Bell Rock lighthouse on a treacherous, barely exposed offshore rock in the early 19th century. A signal tower was built to facilitate communication between the mainland and the builders working offshore. In the tower now is the **Signal Tower Museum,** which tells the story of the lighthouse, built by Robert Stevenson (1772–1850) in 1811. (The name Stevenson is strongly associated with the building of lighthouses throughout Scotland, though the most famous son of that family is remembered for another talent: Robert Louis Stevenson [1850–94] gravely disappointed his family by choosing to be a writer instead of an engineer.) The museum also houses a collection of items related to the history of the town, its folk life, and the local fishing industry. ✉ *Ladyloan, west of harbor,* ☎ *01241/875598,* WEB *www.angus.gov.uk.* 🎫 *Free.* ☉ *Sept.–June, Mon.–Sat. 10–5; July–Aug., Mon.–Sat. 10–5, Sun. 2–5.*

Nightlife and the Arts

For a good pint, seek out the **Foundry Bar** (✉ E. Mary St., ☎ 01241/ 872524), a spartan bar frequented by locals and enlivened by impromptu music sessions on Wednesday and Friday—customers often bring along their fiddles and accordions, and all join in.

Montrose

⑱ *14 mi north of Arbroath via A92.*

An unpretentious and attractive town with a museum and a selection of shops, Montrose is also noted for its beach. Behind Montrose the River Esk forms a wide estuary known as the Montrose Basin. The **Montrose Basin Wildlife Centre,** run by the Scottish Wildlife Trust, is a nature reserve, with a good number of geese, ducks, and swans. ✉ *Rossie Braes,* ☎ *01674/676336,* WEB *www.montrosebasin.org.uk.* 🎫 *£2.50.* ☉ *Reserve daily, 24 hrs. Visitor center Apr.–Oct., daily 10:30–5; Nov.– Mar., daily 10:30–4.*

House of Dun

★ ⑲ *4 mi west of Montrose via A935.*

The National Trust for Scotland's leading attraction in this area is the House of Dun, which overlooks the Montrose Basin. This 1730s mansion, built by architect William Adam (1689–1748), is particularly noted for its ornate plasterwork. ✉ *A935,* ☎ *01674/810264.* 🎫 *House and garden, £7; garden only, £1.* ☉ *House Apr.–June and Sept.–Oct., Fri.– Tues. noon–5; July–Aug., Fri.–Tues. 11–6. Garden and grounds daily 9:30–sunset. Restaurant daily 11–6.*

Brechin

㉓ *10 mi southwest of Montrose.*

The small market town of Brechin, in Strathmore, has a cathedral that was founded circa 1200 and contains an interesting selection of antiquities. The town's 10th-century **Round Tower,** next to the cathedral, is one of only two on mainland Scotland (they are more frequently found in Ireland). It was originally built for the local Culdee monks. ✉ *Free.* ☉ *Daily 9–5.*

The first arrivals in this part of Scotland were the Picts, who came sometime in the first millennium AD. **Pictavia** explores what is known about this race of Celts using actual artifacts, replicas, and interactive exhibits. ✉ *Brechin Castle Centre, off the A90,* ☎ *01356/626241,* WEB *www. pictavia.org.uk.* ✉ *£3.25.* ☉ *Apr.–Oct., Mon.–Sat. 9–6, Sun. 10–6; Nov.– Mar., Mon.–Sat. 9–5, Sun. 10–5.*

Nightlife and the Arts

Arena (✉ 79–81 High St., ☎ 01356/624313) has a mix of live bands and DJs and attracts young people from a wide area.

En Route   You can rejoin the hurly-burly of the A90 for the return journey south; the more pleasant route, however, leads southwesterly on minor roads (there are several options) that go along the face of the Grampians, following the fault line that separates Highland and Lowland. The **glens of Angus** extend north from various points on Route A90. Known individually as the glens of Isla, Prosen, Clova, and Esk, these long valleys run into the high hills of the Grampians and offer a choice of clearly marked walking routes. Those in Glen Clova are especially appealing.

Kirriemuir

㉑ *15 mi southeast of Brechin.*

Kirriemuir stands at the heart of Angus's red-sandstone countryside and was the birthplace of the writer and dramatist Sir James Barrie (1860–1937), best known abroad as the author of *Peter Pan.* **Barrie's birthplace** now has upper floors furnished as they might have been in Barrie's time, with manuscripts and personal mementos displayed. The outside washhouse is said to have been Barrie's first theater. Next door, at 11 Brechin Road, is an exhibition called *The Genius of J. M. Barrie,* which provides literary and theatrical information on the author. ✉ *9 Brechin Rd.,* ☎ *01575/572646 or 01575/572353,* WEB *www. nts.org.uk.* ✉ *£3.50; combined ticket with Camera Obscura £5.* ☉ *Apr.–Oct., Sat.–Wed. noon–5.*

J. M. Barrie donated the **Camera Obscura,** housed in a cricket pavilion on Kirriemuir Hill, just northeast of Kirriemuir, to the town—one of only three in the country. It affords magnificent views of the surrounding area on a clear day. ✉ *Kirriemuir Hill,* ☎ *no phone.* ✉ *£3.50; combined ticket with Barrie's birthplace £5.* ☉ *Apr.–Sept., daily noon–5.*

Dining and Lodging

£–££ ✗ **Drovers Inn.** The Drovers, set in the heart of the Angus farmlands, ★   is a rare find in Scotland, with more the feeling of an English country pub than a Scottish inn. Plain but friendly surroundings, decorated with old farm implements and historic photographs, form the backdrop for simple bar food: pies and nourishing soups. The restaurant serves a Scottish menu of venison and other local delights, including an excellent Aberdeen Angus steak. Everything is homemade, from bread to sorbets, and only local produce is used. The inn is popular with locals;

weekends it's best to make reservations, even for bar meals. ⊠ *Off A90, Memus, near Kirriemuir,* ☎ *01307/860322. MC, V.*

Forfar

㉒ *7 mi east of Kirriemuir.*

Forfar goes about its business of being the center of a farming hinterland without being preoccupied with tourism. This means it's an everyday, friendly, and pleasant-enough Scottish town, bypassed by the A90 on its way north. A high point of the town is the **Meffan Museum and Art Gallery,** which displays an impressive collection of Pictish carved stones and frequently changing art exhibitions. ⊠ *20 W. High St.,* ☎ *01307/464123.* 🖼 *Free.* ⊘ *Mon.–Sat. 10–5.*

OFF THE
BEATEN PATH
ABERLEMNO – High-quality examples of Pictish stone carvings can be seen about 5 mi northeast of Forfar alongside the B9134. Carvings of crosses, angels, serpents, and other animals adorn the stones, which date to the 7th–early 9th centuries. Note the stone in the nearby churchyard—one side is carved with a cross and the other side depicts the only known battle scene in Pictish art, with horsemen and foot soldiers.

Dining and Lodging

££   ✕🖼 **Royal Hotel.** Now fully modernized, this former coaching inn in the center of Forfar serves as a welcoming base for exploring or golfing. The bedrooms are well equipped, though those in the more modern part of the hotel are on the small side. All have a green-and-peach color scheme, with stained-wood finishes and floral fabrics. The public rooms have retained their 19th-century charm. The leisure complex has a pool, gym, and roof garden. The restaurant turns out well-cooked standard international fare—such as fish-and-chips and lasagna—served by a friendly staff. ⊠ *Castle St., DD8 3AE,* ☎ 𝐅𝐀𝐗 *01307/462691. 19 rooms. Restaurant, pool, gym, sauna; no a/c. AE, DC, MC, V.*

£   🖼 **Redroofs.** This former cottage hospital, now a hospitable private
★   home, has superb bed-and-breakfast accommodations in spacious surroundings set among trees. Redroofs is very comfortable, and the hosts go out of their way to help you plan your sightseeing and enjoy the area. Curios collected by the owners on their travels decorate the unique sitting room. Evening meals can be provided by prior arrangement. ⊠ *Balgavies, Guthrie, by Forfar, DD8 2TH,* ☎ 𝐅𝐀𝐗 *01307/ 830268. 3 rooms. Refrigerators; no a/c, no room phones, no-smoking rooms. No credit cards.*

Glamis

★ **㉓** *5 mi southwest of Forfar, 6 mi south of Kirriemuir via A928.*

Set in pleasantly rolling countryside is the village of Glamis (pronounced Glahms), with a village green, a line of cottages, a folk museum, and Glamis Castle. The latter is the second-most visited residence in Scotland, after Balmoral Castle in Deeside. A row of 19th-century cottages with unusual stone-slab roofs makes up the **Angus Folk Museum,** whose exhibits focus on the crafts and tools of domestic and agricultural life in the region during the past 200 years. ⊠ *Off A94,* ☎ *01307/840288.* 🖼 *£3.50.* ⊘ *Apr.–Oct., Sat.–Wed. noon–5.*

★ **Glamis Castle,** one of Scotland's best-known and most beautiful castles, connects Britain's royalty through 10 centuries, from Macbeth ("thane of Glamis") to the late Princess Margaret, who was born here in 1930—the first royal princess born in Scotland in 300 years—because the castle was the ancestral home of her mother. The property of the earls of Strathmore and Kinghorne since 1372, the castle was largely reconstructed in the late 17th century; the original keep, which is much older, is still intact. One of the most famous rooms in the castle is Duncan's Hall, the legendary setting for Shakespeare's *Macbeth*. Guided tours allow you to see fine collections of china, tapestries, and furniture. Other facilities include shops, a produce stall, and a restaurant. ✉ *A94, 1 mi north of Glamis*, ☎ *01307/840393.* ✑ *Castle and grounds, £6.50; grounds only, £3.20.* ☉ *Apr.–June and Sept.–Oct., daily 10:30–5:30; July–Aug., daily 10–5:30; last tour at 4:45.*

Meigle

㉔ *7 mi southwest of Glamis, 15 mi west of Dundee.*

The town of Meigle, in the wide swath of Strathmore, has one of the most notable medieval collections in Western Europe, housed at the **Meigle Museum.** This magnificent collection consists of some 25 sculptured monuments from the Celtic Christian period (8th to 10th centuries), nearly all of which were found in or around the local churchyard. ✉ *A94*, ☎ *0131/668–8800.* ✑ *£2.* ☉ *Apr.–Nov., daily 9:30–6.*

FIFE AND ANGUS A TO Z

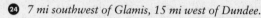

To research prices, get advice from other travelers, and book travel arrangements, visit www.fodors.com.

AIRPORTS

Glasgow Airport, 50 mi west of Edinburgh, is a major point of entry for international flights. Passengers landing in Glasgow have easy access to Edinburgh and Fife and Angus. Edinburgh Airport, 7 mi west of downtown Edinburgh, provides connections throughout the United Kingdom, as well as to a number of cities on the Continent.

BUS TRAVEL

Buses connect Edinburgh's St. Andrew Square bus station and Glasgow's Buchanan Street bus station to Fife and Angus. Scottish Citylink operates hourly service to Dundee from both Glasgow and Edinburgh. Stagecoach Fife Buses serves Fife and St. Andrews.

Local service connects St. Andrews and Dundee to many of the smaller towns throughout Fife and Angus. A Day Rover ticket (£5 with Strathtay Scottish; £10 with Stagecoach Fife) is a good value. The Strathtay pass covers Dundee and Angus, and Stagecoach covers all of Fife.
➤ Bus Information: **Scottish Citylink** (☎ 08705/505050, WEB www. citylink.co.uk). **Stagecoach Fife Buses** (☎ 01592/261461). **Strathtay Scottish** (☎ 01382/228345).

CAR RENTAL

➤ Agencies: **Arnold Clark** (✉ E. Dock St., Dundee, ☎ 01382/225382). **Avis** (c/o DIS, ✉ Old Glamis Rd., Dundee, ☎ 01382/832264). **Hertz** (✉ 18 W. Marketgate, Dundee, ☎ 01382/223711).

CAR TRAVEL

The M90 motorway from Edinburgh takes you to within a half hour of St. Andrews and Dundee. If you're coming from Fife, you can use the A91 and the A914 and then cross the Tay Bridge to reach Dundee, though the quickest way is to use the fast-paced, less-scenic M90/A90. Travel time from Edinburgh to Dundee is about one hour, from Edinburgh to St. Andrews, 1½ hours.

Fife is an easy area to get around—although it can be difficult to find a place to park in St. Andrews. Most roads are quiet and uncongested.

The most interesting sights are in the east, which is served by a network of cross-country roads. Angus is likewise an easy region to explore because it's serviced by a fast main road, the A90, which travels through the middle of the Strathmore valley and then on to Aberdeen; the A92, another, gentler road that runs to the east near the coast; and a network of rural roads between the Grampians and Route A90.

EMERGENCIES

Dial 999 in case of an emergency to reach an ambulance, or the fire or police departments (no coins are needed for emergency calls made from public phone booths).

Consult your hotel, a tourist information center, or the yellow pages of the telephone directory for listings of local doctors and dentists. Late-night pharmacies are not found outside the larger cities. In St. Andrews, Dundee, and other larger centers, pharmacies use a rotating system for off-hours and Sunday prescription service.

TOURS

Travel Greyhound runs several general orientation bus tours of the main cities and the region from late July to early August. Fishers Tours has bus tours year-round both within and outside the region. Lochs and Glens operates bus tours of Scotland year-round.

Heritage Golf Tours Scotland specializes in golf vacations that include hotel and car rental and course reservations. Links Golf St. Andrews tailors tours to individual requirements.

➤ Bus Tours: **Fishers Tours** (⌧ 16 West Port, Dundee, ☎ 01382/227290). **Lochs and Glens** (⌧ Gartocharn, West Dunbartonshire, ☎ 01389/713713, WEB www.lochsandglens.com). **Travel Greyhound** (⌧ Unit 56, The Forum Centre, Commercial St., Dundee, ☎ 01382/340006 or 01382/340007).

➤ Golf Tours: **Heritage Golf Tours Scotland** (⌧ Swilken House, 21 Loch Dr., Helensburgh, G84 8PY, ☎ 01436/674630, WEB www.golftours-scotland.co.uk). **Links Golf St. Andrews** (⌧ 7 Pilmour Links, St. Andrews, KY16 9JG, ☎ 01334/478639, WEB www.linksgolfstandrews.com).

TRAIN TRAVEL

ScotRail stops at Kirkcaldy, Markinch (for Glenrothes), Cupar, Leuchars (for St. Andrews), Dundee, Arbroath, and Montrose. For details of the various services, call National Rail Enquiries.

➤ Train Information: **National Rail Enquiries** (☎ 08457/484950).

VISITOR INFORMATION

The Arbroath, Dundee, Forth Bridges, Kirkcaldy, and St. Andrews tourist offices are open year-round. Smaller tourist information centers operate seasonally in the following towns: Anstruther, Brechin, Carnoustie, Crail, Forfar, Kirriemuir, and Montrose.

➤ Tourist Information: **Arbroath** (⌧ Market Pl., Arbroath, DD11 1HR, ☎ 01241/872609). **Dundee** (⌧ 7–21 Castle St., Dundee, DD1 3AA, ☎ 01382/527527, WEB www.angusanddundee.co.uk). **Forth Bridges** (⌧ c/o Queensferry Lodge Hotel, St. Margaret's Head, North Queensferry, KY11 1HP, ☎ 01383/417759). **Kirkcaldy** (⌧ 19 Whytescauseway, Kirkcaldy, KY1 1XF, ☎ 01592/267775). **St. Andrews** (⌧ 70 Market St., St. Andrews, KY16 9NU, ☎ 01334/472021, WEB www.standrews.com).

6 THE CENTRAL HIGHLANDS

STIRLING, THE TROSSACHS
AND LOCH LOMOND, PERTHSHIRE

Memories of Rob Roy MacGregor, Robert
the Bruce, and that brave heart William
Wallace abound in the Central Highlands.
Here, in Scotland's wasp waist, Perth and
Stirling are the main gateways to rugged
and spectacular wild country, including the
fabled Trossachs, where deep, wandering
lochs—including Loch Lomond—shimmer
under hills cloaked in the browns and
purples of bracken and heather. No matter if
"ye'll take the high road and I'll tak' the low
road"—this region is a must for many.

By Gilbert
Summers

Updated by
Beth Ingpen

STAND ON STIRLING CASTLE ROCK TO SURVEY the whole Central
Highland region, and you will see Scotland coast to coast. This is
where Scotland draws in her waist, from the Clyde in the west to
the Forth in the east. You can judge just how near the area is to the well-
populated Midland Valley by looking out from the ramparts of Edinburgh Castle: the Highland hills, which meander around the Trossachs
region and above Callander, are clearly visible. Similarly, the high-tower
blocks of some of Glasgow's peripheral housing developments are noticeable from many of the countryside's higher peaks, particularly Ben
Lomond. Today the old county seats of Perth and Stirling still play important roles as the primary administrative centers of the counties of
Perthshire and Stirlingshire, respectively, which make up the Central Highlands. Geographically, it's no surprise that this region has been a favorite
vacation getaway for Edinburghers and Glaswegians for centuries.

As early as 1794 the local minister in Callander, on the very edge of
the Highlands, wrote: "The Trossachs are often visited by persons of
taste, who are desirous of seeing nature in her rudest and unpolished
state." What these early visitors came to see was a series of lochs and
hills, whose crags and slopes were hung harmoniously with shaggy birch,
oak, and pinewoods. The tops of the hills are high but not too sav-
age—real wilderness would have been too much for these fledgling nature lovers. The Romantic poets, especially William Wordsworth
(1770–1850), sang the praises of such locales. Though Wordsworth is
more closely associated with the Lake District in England, his travels
through Scotland and the Trossachs inspired several of his poems. But
it was Sir Walter Scott (1771–1832) who definitively put this area on
the tourist map by setting his 1810 dramatic verse narrative, *The Lady
of the Lake,* in the landscape of the Trossachs. Scott's verse was an immediate and huge success, and visitors flooded in to trace the events
of the poem across the region. The poem mentions every little bridge
and farmhouse and is still the most comprehensive guide to the area.
Various engineering schemes of the Glasgow Water Department, however, have rendered some of the topography out of date.

Just as the Trossachs have long attracted those with discriminating tastes,
so has Loch Lomond, Scotland's largest loch in terms of surface area.
The hard rocks to the north confine it to a long thin ribbon, and the
more yielding Lowlands allow it to spread out and assume a softer,
wider form. Here the Lowlands' fields and lush hedgerows quickly give
way to dark woods and crags—just a half hour's drive north from Glasgow. The song, "The Banks of Loch Lomond," said to have been written by a Jacobite prisoner incarcerated in Carlisle, England, captures
beautifully a particular style of Scottish sentimentality, resulting in the
popularity of the "bonnie, bonnie banks" around the world, especially
wherever Scots are to be found.

Scots, in particular, prize the sights of this region, for they are some of
the most hallowed in their history. "Scots Wha He Wi' Wallace Bled,"
a rousing pipe-band tune generally regarded as the Scottish national
anthem, is played much about here. It deals with William Wallace who,
like Robert the Bruce, waged war against England in the 13th and 14th
centuries. At Stirling Bridge and Bannockburn, respectively, the most
notable battles of Wallace and Bruce were fought. In nearby Callander, Rob Roy MacGregor, the Scottish Robin Hood, lived (and looted
and terrorized) his way into the storybooks.

Within the region the physical contrast between Lowland and Highland is quite pronounced because of the Highland boundary fault. This

geological divide also marked the boundary between Scotland's two languages and cultures, Gaelic and Scots, with the Gaels ensconced northwest behind the mountain barrier. In the Central Highlands the fault runs through Loch Lomond, close to Callander, to the northeast above Perth, and into the old county of Angus. Remember that even though the Central Highlands are easily accessible, there is still much high, rough country in the region. Ben Lawers, near Killin, is the ninth-highest peak in Scotland, and the moor of Rannoch is as bleak and empty a stretch as can be seen anywhere in the northlands. But if the glens and lochs prove to be too lonely or intimidating, it's only a short journey to the softer and less harsh Lowlands.

Pleasures and Pastimes

Biking

The big attraction for cyclists is the dedicated Glasgow–Killin cycleway. This route runs along former railroad track beds, as well as otherwise private and minor roads, to reach well into the Central Highlands by way of the Trossachs and Callander. Away from the cycleway, the main roads can be busy with holiday traffic.

Dining

Regional country delicacies—loch trout, river salmon, mutton, and venison—appear regularly on even modest menus in Central Highlands restaurants. The urban areas south and southwest of Stirling, in contrast, lack refined dining spots. Here you will find simple pubs, often crowded and noisy, but serving substantial food at lunchtime (eaten balanced on your knee, perhaps, or at a shared table). Three sturdy courses at one of these pubs will cost you about £10.

CATEGORY	COST*
££££	over £22
£££	£16–£22
££	£9–£15
£	under £9

per person for a main course at dinner, including VAT

Fishing

Coarse and game fishing, loch and river fishing, and sea angling are among the fishing options in the area. There are statutory fishing seasons for salmon and sea trout (January 15 through October 15 on the Tay River system). Coarse fishing for grayling, pike, perch, and roach on the Earn River system is reserved February through October. In some cases, Sunday fishing is illegal. Visitor information centers have publications, updated annually, that show the best locations.

Golf

There are many excellent courses in the region. Visitor information centers can supply details of local courses.

Hiking

Hill walking and "Munro-bagging" (climbing all the mountains more than 3,000 ft high; so-called in honor of the mountaineer who first listed them) are popular, so even in the wilder parts of the Highlands, you will find locals able to give advice on routes. For high-level routes, it is essential to be properly supplied with boots and safety equipment. Visitor centers carry information on local routes. The publications *Walk Loch Lomond and the Trossachs* and *Walk Perthshire*, available at bookstores or visitor information centers, are invaluable for hikers and trekkers.

Lodging

In Stirling and Callander, as well as in the small towns and villages throughout the region, you'll find a selection of tourist accommodations out of all proportion to the size of the communities (industrial towns are the exceptions). Standards of less expensive establishments have improved in recent years and are still improving. The grand hotels, though few, were brought into existence by the carriage trade of the 19th century, when travel in Scotland was the fashion. The level of service at these places has, by and large, not slipped; you'll also find many country hotels that are a match for the grand hotels in comfort. Unless otherwise indicated, all rooms have private baths.

CATEGORY	COST*
££££	over £140
£££	£110–£140
££	£65–£110
£	under £65

All prices are for a standard double room, including service, breakfast, and VAT.

Exploring the Central Highlands

The main towns of Stirling and Perth serve as roadway hubs for the area, making both places natural starting points for Highland tours. Stirling itself is worth covering in some detail on foot. The successive waves of development of this important town can easily be traced—from castle and Old Town architecture to Victorian developments and urban and industrial sprawl.

The Trossachs are a short distance from Stirling, all easily covered in a loop. You can get to Loch Lomond from either Glasgow or Stirling, and there are two other routes to take. The main road up the west bank (A82) is not recommended for leisurely touring, as the traffic is heavy and it's not a relaxing drive. Do use this road, however, if you are on your way to Oban, Kintyre, or Argyll. Loch Lomond is best seen from one of two cul-de-sac roads: by way of Drymen at the south end, up to Rowardennan, or if you are pressed for time, west from Aberfoyle to reach Loch Lomond near its northern end, at Inversnaid. Note that in the Trossachs, the road that some maps show going all the way around Loch Katrine is a private road belonging to the Strathclyde Water Board and is open only to walkers and cyclists.

Getting around Perthshire is made interesting by the series of looped tours accessible from the A9, a fast main artery. Exercise caution while driving the A9 itself, however; there have been many auto accidents in this area. The entire route can be completed in a single day, but if you have time on your hands and are seeking a little spontaneity, you may want to overnight in villages along the way.

Numbers in the text correspond to numbers in the margin and on the Central Highlands and Stirling maps.

Great Itineraries

This is excellent touring country. The glens, in some places, run parallel to the lochs, including those along Lochs Earn, Tay, and Rannoch, making for satisfying loops and round-trips.

IF YOU HAVE 2 DAYS

There's enough to see in ⊞ **Stirling** ①–⑱ to fill up at least a day. The second day, cover the Trossachs loop, which includes **Loch Venachar** ㉓, Loch Achray, and **Loch Katrine** ㉔, and the historic towns of **Dunblane** ⑲, **Doune** ⑳, **Callander** ㉑, and **Aberfoyle** ㉕.

IF YOU HAVE 6 OR 7 DAYS

Spend a day in ☷ **Stirling** ①–⑱. (Don't overlook the Mill Trail country, east of Stirling, if you are shopping for Scottish woolens.) Then visit **Dunblane** ⑲ and **Doune** ⑳, staying overnight at ☷ **Callander** ㉑ to explore the fine country northward toward **Balquhidder Glen** ㉒. Spend a day in the **Trossachs** around ☷ **Loch Venachar** ㉓ and **Loch Katrine** ㉔, and take a boat ride to see the landscape at its best. The next day travel to **Drymen** ㉖ for a morning around **Loch Lomond** ㉗ before driving into Perthshire. Spend a night at ☷ **Auchterarder** ㊱, with its antiques shops, or travel straight to ☷ **Perth** ㉘, where you should base yourself for two or three days while exploring Perthshire. Go west for **Crieff** ㉟ and Drummond Castle Garden or north for Highland resort towns such as **Dunkeld** ㉙, with its cathedral; **Pitlochry** ㉚, close to the historic Pass of Killiecrankie; impressive **Blair Castle** ㉛; and **Aberfeldy.** Between Pitlochry and Aberfeldy, make time for the bleak landscapes of **Loch Rannoch**—a great contrast to the generally pastoral Perthshire countryside.

When to Tour the Central Highlands

The Trossachs and Loch Lomond can get quite busy and crowded in high summer, so the area makes a good choice for off-season touring. You're near enough to the Lowland edge to take advantage of any good weather in winter in order to enjoy the dramatic Highland light; fall colors are also spectacular.

STIRLING

26 mi northeast of Glasgow, 36 mi northwest of Edinburgh.

In some ways, Stirling is a little Edinburgh with similar "crag-and-tail" foundations and a royal half mile. Its castle, built on a steep-sided plug of rock, dominates the landscape, and its esplanade affords views of the surrounding valley plain of the River Forth. Stirling's strategic position, commanding the lowest bridge on the Forth, was appreciated by the Stewart kings, and they spent a lot of time at its castle—a fact that, together with the relics of freedom fighters in the neighborhood, has led some Scottish nationalists to declare that Stirling, not Edinburgh, should really be the capital city.

Exploring Stirling

The historic part of town is tightly nestled around the castle—everything is within easy walking distance. You can either take a taxi or walk—if you're feeling energetic—out to Bannockburn Heritage Centre or the National Wallace Monument, on the town's outskirts.

A Good Tour

Stirling is one of Britain's great historic towns. An impressive proportion of the old town walls remain and can be seen from Dumbarton Road, as soon as you step outside the tourist information center. If you're an art lover, make a foray west along Dumbarton Road to visit the **Smith Art Gallery and Museum** ①. Back near the information center, on Corn Exchange Road, is a modern statue of Robert MacGregor (1671–1734), better known as Rob Roy, notorious cattle dealer and drover, part-time thief and outlaw, Jacobite (most of the time), and hero of Sir Walter Scott's namesake novel (1818). Rob is practically inescapable if you visit Callander and the Trossachs, where he had his home.

About 25 yards up the hill on Corn Exchange from Rob Roy's statue is another statue, of Campbell Bannerman, where you should make a sharp left on to the upper **Back Walk** ②. This gentle but relentless up-

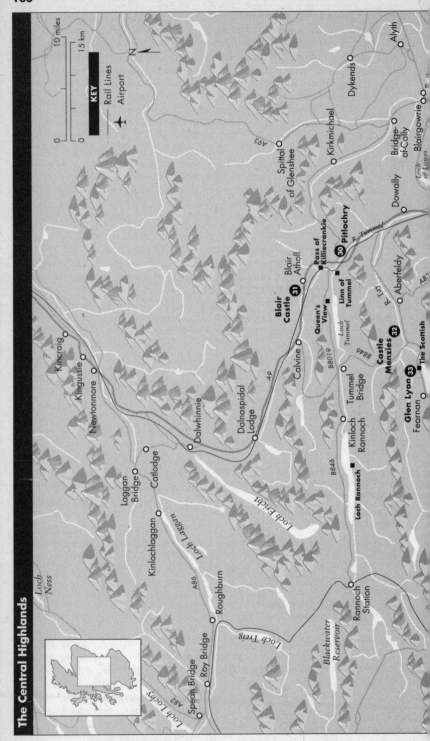

The Central Highlands

Loch Ness

Loch Lochy

Spean Bridge

Roy Bridge

Roughburn

A86

Loch Laggan

Kinlochlaggan

Loch Treig

Blackwater Reservoir

Rannoch Station

Catlodge

Laggan Bridge

Loch Ericht

Kinloch Rannoch

Loch Rannoch

B846

Dalwhinnie

Dalnaspidal Lodge

Newtonmore

Kingussie

Kincraig

A9

A86

Calvine

B8019

B846

Tummel Bridge

Fearnan

Glen Lyon **33**

The Scottish

Castle Menzies **32**

Loch Tummel

Linn of Tummel

Queen's View

Blair Atholl

Blair Castle **31**

Pass of Killiecrankie

30 **Pitlochry**

R. Tummel

Aberfeldy

R. Tay

A827

Dowally

Spittal of Glenshee

A93

Kirkmichael

Dykends

Alyh

Bridge-of-Cally

Blairgowrie

Loch of Lowes

KEY

Rail Lines

✈ Airport

0 — 10 miles

0 — 15 km

N ←

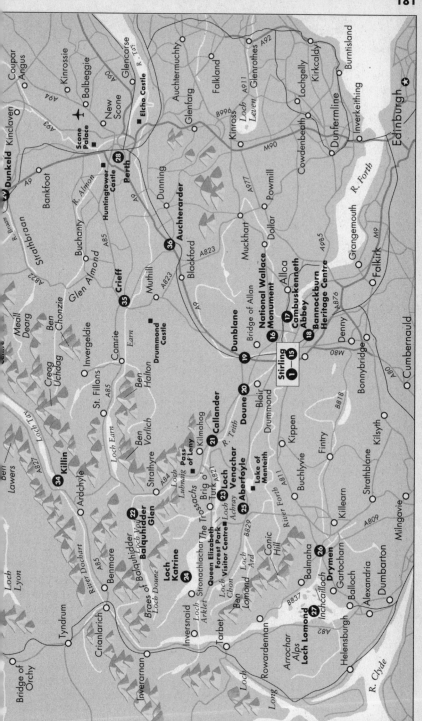

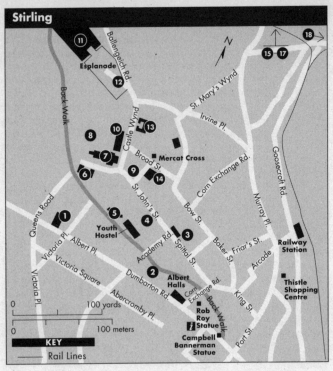

hill path follows the old-town walls, eventually leading to the castle. After
about 110 yards north, at a junction, follow the sign to the right for the
Old Town Jail along Academy Road, which passes behind the Stirling
Highland Hotel, formerly the Old High School, built in 1854 on the site
of the former Greyfriars Monastery. At the junction of Academy Road
and Spittal Street/St. John's Street, look across to **Darrow House** ③, a
fine example of Scottish domestic architecture, now a private home.

Turn left on to St. John's Street and walk uphill, passing another typical town house, **Bothwell Ha** ④, on the left-hand side. Behind Bothwell Ha and accessed by a path from St. John's Street is the **Old Town
Jail** ⑤, the former military detention barracks. It now contains exhibits
on life in a 19th-century Scottish prison. Adjacent to the Old Town
Jail and accessed from St. John's Street is the Youth Hostel, housed in
Erskine Marykirk, a neoclassical church built in 1824. Walk a little
farther north on St. John's Street; at the junction with Castle Wynd is
a path to your left. Walk up this path to find **Cowane's Hospital** ⑥,
which was built as almshouses in 1639. The medieval **Church of the
Holy Rude** ⑦ is on your right, and straight ahead is the **cemetery** ⑧,
with some unusual monuments.

Walk back down the path to St. John's Street. Directly across the road
from the end of the path is **Mar Place House** ⑨, a restored Georgian
town house. Turn left onto Castle Wynd, and immediately on your left
is the long and ornate facade of the distinctively Renaissance **Mar's
Wark** ⑩. Continue up the hill, following signs to **Stirling Castle** ⑪ and
the **Royal Burgh of Stirling Visitor Centre** ⑫. At this point you can appreciate the strategic position of the castle and the wonderful views
toward the Highlands. You can also see the Wallace Monument and
Old Stirling Bridge from here. After exploring the castle, walk back
down Castle Wynd. On your left-hand side is **Argyll's Lodging** ⑬.

Turn left onto Broad Street; 100 yards down on the right-hand side is the **Tolbooth** ⑭. The Mercat Cross, where proclamations were made, stands opposite. Continue down Broad Street, and turn right onto Bow Street, following it around to the left downhill toward the more modern part of Stirling, with its many shops. Alternatively, walk a few minutes down from the castle (via Barn Road, Castlehill, and Lower Bridge Street) to see the medieval **Old Stirling Bridge** ⑮. Drive north–northeast down Causewayhead Road from the castle to get to the Gothic pencil that is the **National Wallace Monument** ⑯, commemorating Scotland's great freedom fighter. Due east of the castle and most easily reached from the monument are the ruins of **Cambuskenneth Abbey** ⑰, in an idyllic riverside setting. The historic battle site of **Bannockburn Heritage Centre** ⑱—rather incongruously set in the middle of a housing development—is south of town, off Glasgow Road (A80).

TIMING

Stirling is a compact town, and this tour, though it has many sights to admire, can be done at high speed in a day or in a more leisurely fashion over two days.

Sights to See

⑬ **Argyll's Lodging.** A nobleman's town house built in three phases from the 16th century onward, this building is actually older than the name it bears—that of Archibald, the ninth earl of Argyll (1629–85), who bought it in 1666. It was for many years a military hospital, then a youth hostel. It has now been refurbished to show how the nobility lived in 17th-century Stirling. Specially commissioned reproduction furniture and fittings are based on the original inventory of the house's contents at that time. ⊠ *Castle Wynd,* ☎ *0131/668–8800,* WEB *www. historic-scotland.gov.uk.* ☞ *£3; £7 ticket includes admission to Stirling Castle.* ⊙ *Apr.–Sept., daily 9:30–5:15; Oct.–Mar., daily 9:30–4:15.*

② **Back Walk.** The upper Back Walk will take you along the outside of the city's walls, past a watchtower and the grimly named Hangman's entry, carved out of the great whinstone boulders that once marked the outer defenses of the town. One of several access areas is off Dumbarton Road, opposite the tourist information center. ⊠ *Runs from Dumbarton Rd. to Castle Rock.*

★ ⑱ **Bannockburn Heritage Centre.** In 1298, the year after William Wallace's victory, Robert the Bruce (1274–1329) materialized as the nation's champion, and the final bloody phase of the Wars of Independence began. Bruce's rise resulted from the uncertainties and timidity of the great lords of Scotland (ever unsure of which way to jump and whether to bow to England's demands). This tale is recounted at the Bannockburn Heritage Centre, hidden among the sprawl of housing and commercial development on the southern edge of Stirling. This was the site of the famed Battle of Bannockburn in 1314. In Bruce's day the Forth had a shelved and partly wooded floodplain. So he cunningly chose this site, noting the boggy ground on the lower reaches in which the heavy horses of the English would founder. The events of this time have been re-created within the center by means of an audiovisual presentation, models and costumed figures, and an arresting mural depicting the battle in detail (look closely for some particularly unsavory goings-on). ⊠ *Off A80,* ☎ *01786/812664,* WEB *www.nts.org.uk.* ☞ *£3.50.* ⊙ *Site daily. Heritage Centre mid-Mar.–late Oct., daily 10–6; mid-Jan.–mid-Mar. and late Oct.–mid-Dec., daily 10:30–4.*

④ **Bothwell Ha.** This 16th-century hall (*ha* is Scots for *hall*) is said to have been owned by the earl of Bothwell (circa 1535–78), the third husband of Mary, Queen of Scots (1542–87). ⊠ *St. John's St. Closed to public.*

⑰ Cambuskenneth Abbey. On the south side of the Abbey Craig, the scanty remains of this 13th-century abbey lie in a sweeping bend of the River Forth, with the dramatic outline of Stirling Castle as a backdrop. Important meetings of the Scottish Parliament were once held here, and King Edward I (1239–1307) of England visited in 1304. The abbey was looted and damaged during the Scots Wars of Independence in the late 13th and early 14th centuries. The reconstructed tomb of King James III (1452–88) can be seen near the outline of the high altar. ⊠ *Ladysneuk Rd.,* ☎ *0131/668–8800,* WEB *www.historic-scotland.gov.uk.* ⊠ *Free.* ☉ *Daily, 24 hrs.*

⑧ Cemetery. Among the most notable of the many unusual monuments in the cemetery near the Church of the Holy Rude is the **Star Pyramid** of 1858. Also look for the macabre, glass-walled **Martyrs Monument,** erected in memory of two Wigtownshire girls who were drowned in 1685 for their Covenanting faith. The castle dominates the foreground, and from **Ladies' Rock,** a high perch within the cemetery, there are excellent views of the looming fortress. ⊠ *Top of St. John's St.*

⑦ Church of the Holy Rude. The nave of this handsome church survives from the 15th century, and a portion of the original medieval timber roof can also be seen. This is the only Scottish church still in use to have witnessed the coronation of a Scottish monarch—James VI (1566–1625) in 1567. ⊠ *Top of St. John's St.*

⑥ Cowane's Hospital. Built in 1639 for *decayed breithers* (unsuccessful merchants), this building has above its entrance a small, cheery statue of the founder himself, John Cowane, which is said to come alive on Hogmanay Night (December 31) to walk the streets with the locals and join in their New Year's revelry. ⊠ *St. John's St.*

③ Darrow House. Dating from the 17th century, this house displays the characteristic crow-step gables, dormer windows, and projecting turnpike stair of the period. ⊠ *Spittal St. Closed to the public.*

⑨ Mar Place House. This handsome Georgian building was saved from dereliction and painstakingly restored through the town council's ongoing Old Town renovation program. ⊠ *Mar Pl. Closed to public.*

⑩ Mar's Wark. These distinctive windowless and roofless ruins are the stark remains of a Renaissance palace built in 1570 by Lord Erskine (died 1572), earl of Mar and Stirling Castle governor. The name means "Mar's work," or building. Look for the armorial carved panels, the gargoyles, and the turrets flanking a railed-off *pend* (archway). During the 1745 Jacobite rebellion, Mar's Wark was laid siege to and severely damaged, but its admirably worn shell survives. ⊠ *Castle Wynd,* ☎ *0131/668–8800,* WEB *www.historic-scotland.gov.uk. View from outside only.*

⑯ National Wallace Monument. It was near Old Stirling Bridge that the Scottish freedom fighter William Wallace (circa 1270–1305) and a ragged army of Scots won a major victory in 1297. The movie *Braveheart,* directed by and starring Mel Gibson, was based on Wallace's life. A more accurate version of events is told in an exhibition and audiovisual presentation at this pencil-thin museum on the Abbey Craig. Up close, this Victorian shrine to William Wallace, built between 1856 and 1869, becomes less slim and soaring, revealing itself to be a substantial square tower with a creepy spiral stairway. To reach the monument, follow the Bridge of Allan signs (A9) northward, crossing the River Forth by Robert Stephenson's (1772–1850) New Bridge of 1832, next to the historic old one. The National Wallace Monument is signposted at the next traffic circle. ⊠ *Abbey Craig,* ☎ *01786/472140.* ⊠ *£3.95.* ☉ *Mar.–*

May and Oct., daily 10–5; June and Sept., daily 10–6; July–Aug., daily 9:30–6:30; Nov.–Feb. daily 10:30–4.

⑮ Old Stirling Bridge. North of Stirling Castle, on the edge of town, is a narrow, humped 15th-century bridge, now open only to pedestrians. ⊠ *Off Drip Rd., A84.*

⑤ Old Town Jail. The original town jail, now restored, has living exhibitions about life in a 19th-century Scottish prison. Furnished cells, models, and staff—dressed as prisoners, wardens, and prison reformers—bring the past vividly to life. From October through March, these living-history performances take place only on weekends. ⊠ *Access from St. John's St.,* ☎ *01786/450050,* WEB *www.visitscotland.com.* ⊠ *£3.95.* ☉ *Apr.–Sept., daily 9:30–6; Oct. and Mar., daily 9:30–5; Nov.–Feb., daily 9:30–4; last admission 1 hr before closing.*

⑫ Royal Burgh of Stirling Visitor Centre. This visitor center standing at the foot of the Castle Esplanade houses a shop and exhibition hall with an audiovisual presentation on the town and surrounding area. ⊠ ☎ *01786/462517.* ⊠ *Free.* ☉ *Apr.–Oct., daily 9:30–6; Nov.–Mar., daily 9:30–5.*

❶ Smith Art Gallery and Museum. This community art gallery, founded in 1874 with the bequest of a local collector, showcases a varied exhibition program of paintings and sculpture. ⊠ *Albert Pl./Dumbarton Rd.,* ☎ *01786/471917.* ⊠ *Free.* ☉ *Tues.–Sat. 10:30–5, Sun. 2–5.*

★ **⑪ Stirling Castle.** Its magnificent strategic position made Stirling Castle the grandest prize in the Scots Wars of Independence in the late 13th and early 14th centuries. The Battle of Bannockburn in 1314 was fought within sight of its walls, and the victory by Robert the Bruce yielded both the castle and freedom from English subjugation for almost four centuries.

The daughter of King Robert I (Robert the Bruce), Marjory, married Walter Fitzallan, the high steward of Scotland. Their descendants included the Stewart dynasty of Scottish monarchs (Mary, Queen of Scots, was a Stewart, though she preferred the French spelling, *Stuart*). The Stewarts were mainly responsible for many of the works that survive within the castle walls today. They made Stirling Castle their court and power base, creating fine Renaissance-style buildings that were not completely obliterated, despite subsequent reconstruction for military purposes.

You'll enter the castle through its outer defenses, which consist of a great curtain wall and batteries that date from 1708, built to bulwark earlier defenses by the main gatehouse. From this lower square the most conspicuous feature is the **palace,** built by King James V (1512–42) between 1538 and 1542. The decorative figures festooning the ornately worked outer walls of this edifice show the influence of French masons. Overlooking the upper courtyard is the **Great Hall,** built by King James IV (1473–1513) in 1503. Before the Union of Parliaments in 1707, when the Scottish aristocracy sold out to England, this building had been used as one of the seats of the Scottish Parliament. After 1707 it sank into decline, becoming a riding school, then a barracks. It has since been restored to its original splendor.

Among the later works built for regiments stationed here, the **King's Old Building** stands out; it is a 19th-century baronial revival on the site of an earlier building. The oldest building on the site is the **Mint,** or **Coonzie Hoose,** perhaps dating as far back as the 14th century. Below is an arched passageway leading to the westernmost section of the ramparts, the **Nether Bailey.** You'll have the distinct feeling here of being in the bow of a warship sailing up the *carselands* (valley plain) of the

Forth Valley, which fans out before the great superstructure of the castle. Among the gun platforms and the crenellations of the ramparts, you may find yourself pondering the strategic significance of Stirling. To the south lies the hump of the Touch and the Gargunnock hills (part of the Campsie Fells), which diverted potential direct routes from Glasgow and the south. For centuries all roads into the Highlands across the narrow waist of Scotland led to Stirling. If you look carefully northward, you can still see the Old Stirling Bridge, once the lowest and most convenient place to cross the river. For all these geographic reasons, the castle was perhaps the single most important fortress in Scotland. ⊠ *Castlehill,* ☎ *0131/668–8800,* WEB *www.historic-scotland.gov.uk.* ⌖ *£7, including admission to Argyll's Lodging.* ⊘ *Apr.–Sept., daily 9:30–5:15; Oct.–Mar., daily 9:30–4:15.*

⑭ **Tolbooth.** The Tolbooth, built in 1705, has a traditional Scottish steeple and gilded weathercock. For centuries the Burgh Court handed down sentences here, and the Tolbooth also served as a jail. ⊠ *Broad St.*

Dining and Lodging

£££   ✕ **Hermann's Brasserie.** A simple, light, and airy interior—including a conservatory area—is the setting for highly recommended modern Scottish cuisine such as *Cullen skink* (an archetypal Scottish soup made with smoked fish and potato) or seared salmon fillet with pink-peppercorn sauce. ⊠ *58 Broad St.,* ☎ *01786/450632. AE, MC, V.*

£   ✕ **Berties Restaurant.** Berties serves coffees and light lunches in the impressive Victorian-style Albert Halls, by the Rob Roy statue. Try the Brie melted over a bacon baguette, or salmon fish cakes with red-pepper coulis. In summer you can sit outside on the cobblestones; on Sunday there are live Scottish music sessions. ⊠ *Albert Halls, Dumbarton Rd.,* ☎ *01786/473544. MC, V. No dinner.*

£££–££££   ✕🏠 **Stirling Highland Hotel.** The attractive 1854 building this hotel occupies was once the Old High School, and many original architectural features remain. Furnishings are old-fashioned, with solid wood, tartan, florals, and low-key, neutral color schemes. The hotel has two restaurants: the Italian Rizzio's and the modern-Scottish Scholars, with outstanding seafood. ⊠ *Spittal St., FK8 1DU,* ☎ *01786/272727,* FAX *01786/272829,* WEB *www.paramount-hotels.co.uk. 96 rooms. 2 restaurants, pool, health club, sauna, bar; no a/c. AE, DC, MC, V.*

££   ✕🏠 **Park Lodge Hotel.** A French family runs this elegant 18th-century establishment. The interior is all fanlights, antique furniture, and candles. The Heritage Restaurant (£££) highlights French classics such as *filet au poivre* (pepper beef steak) and *magret de canard* (duck breast). ⊠ *32 Park Terr., FK8 2JS,* ☎ *01786/474862,* FAX *01786/449748,* WEB *www.parklodge.net. 10 rooms. Restaurant; no a/c. MC, V.*

£–££   ✕🏠 **Terraces Hotel.** This central hotel with plenty of parking is a good base for exploring Stirling and the region. A comfortable Georgian town house, it is comparatively small, with friendly and attentive service. The restaurant (£££) serves traditional Scottish dishes; steak is a specialty. ⊠ *4 Melville Terr., FK8 2ND,* ☎ *01786/472268,* FAX *01786/450314,* WEB *www.hotelnet.co.uk/terraceshotel. 17 rooms. Restaurant; no a/c. AE, DC, MC, V.*

£   🏠 **Castlecroft.** Tucked beneath Stirling Castle, with fine views over the plain of the River Forth toward the Highland hills, this warm and comfortable modern house is very central for sightseeing in the Old Town. ⊠ *Ballengeich Rd., FK8 1TN,* ☎ *01786/474933,* FAX *01786/466716. 6 rooms. No room phones, no a/c. MC, V.*

£   🏠 **Lochend Farm.** Extensive country views, wholesome farm cooking, and a pleasantly relaxing pace are the hallmarks of this peaceful working farm. Only 5 mi from the M9/M80, southwest of Stirling, it also makes a good touring base. The traditionally furnished—and very comfortable—bedrooms have sinks and share a bathroom. ☒ *Carronbridge, Denny, Stirlingshire FK6 5JJ,* ☎ *01324/822778,* WEB *www.lochendfarm.com. 2 rooms without bath. No room phones, no a/c. No credit cards.*

£ ⊡ **Stirling Youth Hostel.** A former neoclassical church houses this hostel, with high-grade four- and six-bed rooms (and a few doubles) with in-room bath facilities. Use of the television room, the dining room, and the self-service, fully equipped kitchen is included in the bargain price of £11 (£12.50 in July and August) per person, including breakfast. ☒ *Erskine Marykirk, St. John's St., FK8 1EA,* ☎ *01786/473442,* WEB *www.syha.org.uk. 126 beds. No room phones, no a/c. MC, V.*

£ ⊡ **West Plean.** This handsome rambling, early Georgian house is part
★ of a working farm, with a walled garden and woodland walks. Well-prepared food and spacious rooms make this bed-and-breakfast an excellent bargain. ☒ *Denny Rd., FK7 8HA,* ☎ *01786/812208,* FAX *01786/480550. 3 rooms. No a/c. No credit cards.*

Nightlife and the Arts

The **Macrobert Arts Centre** (☒ Stirling University, ☎ 01786/461081, WEB www.macrobert.stir.ac.uk) has a theater, art gallery, and studio with programs that range from films to pantomime.

Shopping

Though in a nondescript 1970s building, the downtown **Thistle Shopping Centre** nevertheless has a good selection of stores. Many locals travel to the nearby town of **Bridge of Allan,** which has interesting specialty shops, including **Glass Works** (☒ The Avenue, ☎ no phone), for original glassware made on the premises, and **Fotheringham Gallery** (☒ The Avenue, ☎ 01786/832861), for special gifts and paintings.

Ceramics

South of Stirling, at Larbert (and signposted off the A9), is **Barbara Davidson's pottery studio** (☒ Muirhall Farm, ☎ 01324/554430), run by one of the best-known potters in Scotland, in an 18th-century farm setting. It's open Monday–Saturday 10–5 and Sunday noon–5. In July and August you can even try throwing your own pot for a small fee.

Knitwear

East of Stirling is **Mill Trail** country, along the foot of the Ochil Hills. A leaflet from any local tourist information center will lead you to the delights of a real mill shop and low mill prices—even on cashmere—at Tillicoultry, Alva, and Alloa.

Scottish Specialties

House of Henderson (☒ 6–8 Friars St., ☎ 01786/473681), a Highland outfitters, sells tartans, woolens, and accessories and offers a made-to-measure kilt service.

THE TROSSACHS AND LOCH LOMOND

Immortalized by Wordsworth and Sir Walter Scott, the Trossachs (the name means "bristly country") may contain some of Scotland's loveliest forest, hills, and glens. The area has a very peculiar charm: it combines the wildness of the Highlands with the prolific vegetation of an old Lowland forest. The Trossachs' open ground is a dense mat of bracken and heather, and its woodland is of silver birch, dwarf oak, and hazels—trees that fasten their roots into every crevice of the rocks and stop short on the very brink of the lochs. The most colorful season is fall, particularly October, a lovely time when most visitors have departed and the hares, deer, and game birds have taken over. Even in rainy weather the Trossachs of "darksome glens and gleaming lochs" are memorable: the water filtering through the rocks comes out so pure and clear that the lochs are like sheets of crystal glass.

Inspired by the views of mountainous terrain seen from the ramparts of Stirling Castle, you can use this northward route to explore areas west and north to the Highland line. Distances are not great if you go by car. If you travel the classic Trossachs loop, you will share the route with plenty of day-trippers.

Dunblane

★ ⑲ *7 mi north of Stirling.*

The oldest part of Dunblane—with its twisting streets and lovely town houses—huddles around the square where the partly restored ruins of **Dunblane Cathedral** stand. Bishop Clement oversaw construction of the cathedral in the early 13th century on the site of St. Blane's tiny 8th-century cell. It is contemporary with the Borders abbeys but more mixed in its architecture—part early English and part Norman. Dunblane ceased to be a cathedral, as did most others in Scotland, at the time of the Reformation, in the mid-16th century. ☎ *0131/668–8800,* WEB *www.historic-scotland.gov.uk.* ⌧ *Free.* ☉ *Apr.–Sept., daily 9:30–6; Oct.–Mar., Mon.–Sat. 9:30–4, Sun. 2–4.*

Dining and Lodging

££££ ✕⊡ **Cromlix House Hotel.** Cherished furniture and paintings, the original conservatory, and a library enhance the period atmosphere of this Victorian former hunting lodge. Food is served in two elegant, country-house-style dining rooms. Specialties include game and lamb from the hotel estate. Try the delicious confit of guinea fowl as a starter, followed by beef with pickled walnuts. ⌧ *Kinbuck, on B8033, 3 mi northeast of Dunblane, 10 mi northeast of Stirling, FK15 9JT,* ☎ *01786/822125,* FAX *01786/825450,* WEB *www.cromlixhouse.com. 6 rooms, 8 suites. Restaurant, tennis court, fishing, library; no a/c. AE, DC, MC, V.*

Doune

★ ⑳ *5 mi west of Dunblane.*

The Highland-edge community of Doune was once a center for pistol making. No self-respecting Highland chief's attire was complete without a prestigious and ornate pair of pistols. Today Doune is more widely known for one of the best-preserved medieval castles in Scotland. **Doune Castle** looks like an early castle is supposed to look: grim and high-walled, with echoing, drafty stone vaults. Construction of the fortress began in the early 15th century on a now-peaceful riverside tract. The best place to photograph this squat, walled fort is from the bridge, a little way upstream, west on A84. The castle is signposted to the left as you enter the town from the Dunblane road. ⌧ *Off A84,* ☎ *0131/668–8800,* WEB *www.historic-scotland.gov.uk.* ⌧ *£2.80.* ☉ *Apr.–Sept., daily 9:30–6; Oct.–Mar., Mon.–Wed. and Sat. 9:30–4, Sun. 2–4.*

Callander

⑳ *8 mi northwest of Doune.*

A traditional Highland-edge resort, Callander bustles throughout the year—even during off-peak times—simply because it is a gateway to the Highland scenery that's within easy reach of Edinburgh and Glasgow. As a result, there's plenty of window-shopping here, plus nightlife in pubs and a good selection of accommodations.

Callander's **Rob Roy and Trossachs Visitor Centre** provides another encounter with the overly romanticized "tartan Robin Hood," Rob Roy MacGregor. A man of great physical strength and courageous energy, MacGregor is known as a defender of the downtrodden and scourge of authorities. He was, in fact, a medieval throwback, a cattle thief, an embezzler of lairds' rents, and the operator of a vicious protection racket among poor farmers. You can learn more about his high jinks from the high-tech account—replete with displays and tableaux—in the modern visitor center. Hollywood paid homage to this local folk legend with the 1995 film *Rob Roy*, starring actors Liam Neeson and Jessica Lange. ⊠ *Ancaster Sq.,* ☎ *01877/330342,* WEB *www.visitscotland. com.* 🖾 *£3.25.* ☉ *July–Aug., daily 9–6; Mar.–June and Sept.–Dec., daily 10–5; Jan.–Feb., daily 10:30–3:30.*

A walk is signposted from the east end of the main street to the **Bracklinn Falls,** over whose lip Sir Walter Scott once rode a pony to win a bet. For the fit and well-shod only is a 1½-mi walk through the woods up to the **Callander Crags,** with views of the Lowlands as far as the Pentland Hills behind Edinburgh. The walk begins at the west end of the main street.

Dining and Lodging

£ ✕ **Pip's Coffee House.** Come to this cheerful little place just off the main street for light meals, soups, and salads, as well as Scottish home baking. ⊠ *Ancaster Sq.,* ☎ *01877/330470. Closed Wed. Oct.–Feb. No credit cards.*

£££–££££ ✕🏠 **Roman Camp.** This former hunting lodge, dating to 1625, has 20
★   acres of gardens with river frontage, yet is within easy walking distance of Callander's town center. The antiques-filled sitting rooms and library are more reminiscent of a stately family home than a hotel. The restaurant has a good reputation for its salmon, trout, and other seafood, all cooked in an imaginative, modern Scottish style. Also delicious is the fillet of Scotch beef with an herb-potato scone and wild-mushroom mousseline. ⊠ *Callander, Perthshire FK17 8BG,* ☎ *01877/330003,* FAX *01877/331533,* WEB *www.roman-camp-hotel.co.uk. 14 rooms. Restaurant, fishing, library; no a/c. AE, DC, MC, V.*

Outdoor Activities and Sports

BIKING, HIKING, AND CANOEING

Wheels/Trossachs Backpackers (⊠ Invertrossachs Rd., ☎ 01877/331100, WEB www.scottish-cycling.co.uk) is a friendly firm that can help with route planning and also arranges hostel accommodations, organized walks, and canoe trips.

GOLF

The **golf course** at Callander (⊠ Aveland Rd., ☎ 01877/330090) was designed by Tom Morris and has fine views and a tricky moorland layout. The course is 18 holes, 5,151 yards, and par 66.

Shopping

A vast selection of woolens is on display at three mill shops in and near Callander. All the stores, which are part of the Edinburgh Woollen Mill Group, provide overseas mailing and tax-free shopping. **Callander Woollen Mill** (⊠ 12–18 Main St., ☎ 01877/330273). **Kilmahog Woollen Mill** (⊠ North of town at Trossachs Turning, ☎ 01877/330268). **Trossachs Woollen Mill** (⊠ North of town at Trossachs Turning, ☎ 01877/330178).

En Route   Callander is the gateway to the Trossachs, but because it is on the main road, the A84, it also attracts overnight visitors on their way to Oban, Fort William, and beyond. All this traffic enters the proper Highlands just north of Callander, where the slopes squeeze both the road and rocky river into the narrow **Pass of Leny.** An abandoned railway—now a pleasant walking or bicycling path—also goes through the pass, past Ben Ledi Mountain and Loch Lubnaig.

Balquhidder Glen

❷❷ *12 mi north of Callander.*

A 20-minute drive from Callander, through the Pass of Leny and beyond Strathyre, is Balquhidder Glen (pronounced *bal*-whidd-*er*), a typical Highland glen that runs westward. The glen has characteristics seen throughout the north: a flat-bottom U-shape profile, formed by prehistoric glaciers; extensive Forestry-Commission plantings replacing much of the natural woodlands above; a sprinkling of farms; and farther up the glen, hill roads bulldozed into the slopes to provide access for foresters. You may notice a boarded-up look of some of the area's houses, many of which are second homes for affluent residents of the south. The glen is also where Loch Voil and Loch Doune spread out, adding to the stunning vistas. This area is often known as the Braes (Slopes) of Balquhidder and was once the home of the MacLarens and the MacGregors. **Rob Roy MacGregor's** grave is signposted beside Balquhidder village. The site of his house, now a private farm, is beyond the parking lot at the end of the road up the glen. The glen has no through road, though there is a right-of-way (on foot) from the churchyard where Rob Roy is buried, through the plantings in Kirkton Glen and then on to open windy grasslands and a blue *lochan* (little lake). This path eventually drops into the next valley, Glen Dochart, and rejoins the A84.

The Trossachs

10 mi west of Callander.

With its harmonious scenery of hill, loch, and wooded slopes, the Trossachs has been a popular touring region since the late 18th century, at the dawn of the age of the Romantic poets. Influenced by the writings of Sir Walter Scott, early visitors who strayed into the Highlands from the central belt of Scotland admired this as the first "wild" part of Scotland they encountered. The Trossachs represent the very essence of what the Highlands are supposed to be: birch wood and pine forests, vistas down lochs where the woods creep right to the water's edge, and in the background, peaks that rise high enough to be called mountains, though they're not as high as those to the north and west. The Trossachs are almost a Scottish visual cliché. They're popular right through the year, drawing not only first-time visitors from all around the world, but also Scots out for a Sunday drive.

❷❸ The A821 runs west together with the first and gentlest of the Trossachs lochs, **Loch Venachar.** A sturdy gray-stone building, with a small dam at the Callander end, controls the water that feeds into the River Teith (and, hence, into the Forth) to compensate for the Victorians having tinkered with the water supply. A few minutes after it passes Loch Venachar the A821 becomes muffled in woodlands and twists gradually down to the village of **Brig o' Turk.** (*Turk* is Gaelic for the Scots *tuirc*, meaning wild boar, a species that has been extinct in this region since about the 16th century.)

Loch Achray, stretching west of Brig o' Turk, dutifully fulfilling expectations of what a verdant Trossachs loch should be: small, green, reedy meadows backed by dark plantations, rhododendron thickets, and lumpy, thickly covered hills. The parking lot by Loch Achray is the place to begin the ascent of steep, heathery **Ben An,** which affords some of the best Trossachs' views. The climb requires a couple of hours and good lungs.

★ ❷⁴ At the end of Loch Achray, a side road turns right into a narrow pass, leading to **Loch Katrine,** the heart of the Trossachs. During the time of Sir Walter Scott, the road here was narrow and almost hidden by the overhanging crags and mossy oaks and birches. Today it ends at a slightly anticlimactic parking lot with a shop, café, and visitor center. To see the finest of the Trossachs lochs properly, you must—even for just a few minutes—go westward on foot; the road beyond the parking lot (open only to Strathclyde Water Board vehicles) is well paved and level. Loch Katrine's water is taken by aqueduct and tunnel to Glasgow—a Victorian feat of engineering that has ensured the purity of the supply to Scotland's largest city for more than 100 years.

The steamer SS *Sir Walter Scott* embarks on cruises of Loch Katrine every summer. Take the cruise if time permits, as the shores of Katrine remain undeveloped and scenic. This loch is the setting of Scott's narrative poem, *The Lady of the Lake,* and Ellen's Isle is named after his heroine. ⊠ *Trossachs Pier,* ☎ *01877/376316,* WEB *www.lochkatrine.org.uk.* ⊠ *£6.50 Apr.–June and Sept.–late Oct.; £7 July–Aug.* ☉ *Cruises Apr.–late Oct., Thurs.–Tues. at 11, 1:45, and 3:15, Wed. at 1:45 and 3:15.*

En Route For more exquisite nature viewing after your visit to Loch Katrine, drive back through the pass to the main A821 and turn right, heading south to higher moorland blanketed with conifer plantations—some of which have near-mature timber planted in the 1940s by the Forestry Commission. The conifers hem in the views of Ben Ledi and Ben Venue, which can be seen over the spiky green waves of trees as the road snakes around heathery knolls and hummocks. There's another viewing area at the highest point here in a small parking lot on the right. Soon the road swoops off the Highland edge and leads downhill. Near the start of the descent, the **Queen Elizabeth Forest Park Visitor Centre** can be seen on the left. The center has displays on the life of the forest, a summer-only café, some fine views over the Lowlands to the south, and a network of footpaths. The Trossachs end here.

Aberfoyle

❷⁵ *11 mi south of Loch Katrine, in the Trossachs.*

Aberfoyle has numerous souvenir shops and an attraction that appeals ☺ mainly to children. The **Scottish Wool Centre** tells the story of Scottish wool "from the sheep's back to your back." The Sheep Amphitheatre has live specimens of the main breeds, and in the Textile Display Area you can try spinning and weaving. You will also find a Kids' Farm (with lambs and kids) and a Sheepdog Training Display (weekends in summer only). The shop stocks a huge selection of woolen garments and knitwear. Live sheep shows take July through August. ⊠ *Off Main St.,* ☎ *01877/382850.* ⊠ *£3.* ☉ *Apr.–Sept., daily 9:30–6; Oct.–Dec. and Feb.–Mar., daily 10–5; Jan., daily 10–4:30.*

The tiny island of **Inchmahome,** on the Lake of Menteith, was a place of refuge in 1547 for the young Mary, Queen of Scots. The loch lies a short distance to the east of Aberfoyle.

OFF THE
BEATEN PATH

ALONG THE B829 – From Aberfoyle you can take a trip to see the more enclosed northern portion of **Loch Lomond.** During the off-season the route has an untamed and windswept air when it extends beyond the shelter of trees. Take the B829 (signposted INVERSNAID and STRONACHLACHAR), which runs west from Aberfoyle and offers outstanding views of **Ben Lomond,** especially in the vicinity of Loch Ard. The next loch, where the road narrows and bends, is **Loch Chon,** which appears dark and forbidding. Its ominous reputation is further enhanced by the local legend: the presence of a dog-headed monster prone to swallowing passersby. Beyond Loch Chon, the road climbs gently from the plantings to open moor with a breathtaking vista over **Loch Arklet** to the Arrochar Alps, the name given to the high hills west of Loch Lomond. Hidden from sight in a deep trench, Loch Arklet is dammed to feed Loch Katrine. Go left at the road junction (a right will take you to the town of Stronachlachar) and take the open road along Loch Arklet. These deserted green hills were once the rallying grounds of the Clan Gregor. Near the dam on Loch Arklet, on your right, **Garrison Cottage** recalls the days when the government had to billet troops here to keep the MacGregors in order. From Loch Arklet the road zigzags down to Inversnaid, where you will see a hotel, house, and parking lot, with Loch Lomond stretching out of sight above and below. The only return to Aberfoyle is by retracing the same route.

Dining and Lodging

££££ ✕☷ **Macdonald Forest Hills Hotel.** A traditional-Scottish-country-house theme pervades this hotel, from the rambling white building itself to the wood-paneled lounges, log fires, and numerous sporting activities. More than 20 acres of gardens and grounds surround the building, which sits on a grassy hillside overlooking Loch Ard. Chintz drapes and reproduction antiques fill the bedrooms. The restaurant's tartan decor makes an appropriate backdrop for excellent Scottish cuisine—sometimes prepared with a Mediterranean touch. The menu emphasizes game, salmon, shellfish, and the best Scottish beef and lamb. ⊠ *Kinlochard, FK8 3TL,* ☎ *01877/387277,* FAX *01877/387307,* WEB *www.foresthills-hotel.co.uk. 56 rooms. Restaurant, tennis court, indoor pool, gym, sauna, boating, fishing, bicycles, horseback riding, children's programs (ages 5–12); no a/c. AE, DC, MC, V.*

Outdoor Activities and Sports

BIKING

Trossachs Cycle Hire (⊠ Trossachs Holiday Park, ☎ 01877/382614, WEB www.trossachsholidays.co.uk) rents out bicycles.

WALKING

The long-distance walkers' route, the **West Highland Way,** which runs 95 mi from Glasgow to Fort William, follows the bank of Loch Lomond at Inversnaid, which you can reach from the B829. The brief stroll up the path is very pleasant, particularly if you're visiting during the spring, when birdsong fills the oak-tree canopy. You may get an inkling of why Scots wax so romantic about their bonnie, bonnie banks.

Drymen

🜲 *11 mi southwest of Aberfoyle.*

Drymen is a respectable and cozy town in the Lowland fields, with stores, tea shops, and pubs catering to the well-to-do Scots who have moved here from Glasgow. For the most outstanding Loch Lomond view from the south end, drive west from Drymen and take just a few minutes to clamber up bracken-covered **Duncryne Hill.** At dusk you may be rewarded by a spectacular sunset. You can't miss this distinctive dumpling-shape hill, south of Gartocharn on the Drymen–Balloch road, the A811.

Shopping

The Rowan Gallery (⊠ 36 Main St., ☎ 01360/660996) displays original paintings and prints and specializes in contemporary work by Scottish artists. Also here is a fine selection of ceramics, woodwork, cards, and jewelry.

Loch Lomond

27 *3 mi west of Drymen via B837, signposted* ROWARDENNAN *and* BALMAHA; *14 mi west of Aberfoyle.*

The upper portion of Loch Lomond, Scotland's largest loch in terms of surface area, is a sparkling ribbon of water snaking into the hills. Toward the south, the more yielding Lowlands allow the loch to spread out into a softer, wider form. Wooded islands, some of which can be visited, dot this portion of the lake.

At the little settlement of **Balmaha,** the versatile recreational role filled by Loch Lomond is clear: cruising craft are at the ready, hikers appear out of woodlands on the West Highland Way, and day-trippers stroll at the loch's edge. The heavily wooded offshore islands look alluringly close. One of the best ways to explore them is by taking a cruise or renting a boat. The island of **Inchcailloch** (*inch* comes from *innis,* Gaelic for island), just offshore, can be explored in an hour or two. Pleasant pathways thread through oak woods planted in the 18th century, when the bark was used by the tanning industry.

Conic Hill, behind Balmaha, is a wavy ridge of bald, heathery domes above the pine trees. If you have a regional map, note how Inchcailloch and the other islands line up with Conic Hill. This geographic line is indicative of the Highland boundary fault, which runs through Loch Lomond and the hill.

Loch Lomond is seldom more than a narrow field's length away from the B837 as the road runs northwest to the town of **Rowardennan.** Where the drivable road ends, in a parking lot crunchy with pinecones, you can ramble along one of the marked loch-side footpaths or make your way toward not-so-nearby Ben Lomond, 3½ mi away.

Dining and Lodging

££££ ✕⌂ **Cameron House.** This luxury hotel combines top-quality service ★ with country-club facilities, all on the shores of Loch Lomond. Pastel shades and antique reproductions decorate the bedrooms. The outstanding restaurants serve excellent Scottish-French cuisine, such as poached salmon with hollandaise sauce. There's also a nautical-style diner called Breakers. ✉ *Loch Lomond, Alexandria, Dumbartonshire G83 8QZ,* ☎ *01389/755565,* FAX *01389/759522,* WEB *www.cameronhouse.co.uk. 96 rooms, 7 suites. 3 restaurants, golf privileges, 2 pools, health club, fishing, squash, bar; no a/c. AE, DC, MC, V.*

Outdoor Activities and Sports

MacFarlane and Son (✉ Boatyard, Balmaha, Loch Lomond, ☎ 01360/870214) runs cruises on Loch Lomond. They also run a mail boat to the islands that takes passengers; it operates July through August, Monday through Saturday at 11:30; April through June and September through October, Monday, Thursday, and Saturday at 11:30; and November through March, Monday and Thursday at 10:50. You can even rent a rowboat or a small powerboat from MacFarlane's if you prefer to do your own exploration. From Tarbet, on the western shore, **Cruise Loch Lomond** (✉ Boatyard, Tarbet, ☎ 01301/702356, WEB www.cruiselochlomondltd.com) runs tours all year.

Shopping

At **Thistle Bagpipe Works** (✉ Luss, Dunbartonshire, ☎ 01436/860250), on the western shore of Loch Lomond, you can commission your own made-to-order set of bagpipes. You can also order a complete Highland outfit, including kilt and jacket.

PERTHSHIRE

Although Perth has an ancient history dating to the Dark Ages, it has been rebuilt and recast innumerable times, and sadly, no trace remains of the pre-Reformation monasteries that once dominated the skyline. In fact, modern Perth has swept much of its colorful history under a grid of bustling shopping streets. The town serves a wide rural hinterland and has a well-off air, making it one of Scotland's most interesting shopping towns outside of Edinburgh and Glasgow.

Perth's rural hinterland is grand in several senses. On the Highland edge, prosperous-looking farms are scattered across heavily wooded countryside, and even larger properties are screened by trees and parkland. All this changes as the mountain barrier is penetrated, giving rise to grouse moors and deer forest (in this case, *forest* has the Scots meaning of, paradoxically, *open hill*). Parts of Perthshire are quite remote without ever losing their cozy feel.

Perth

28 *36 mi northeast of Stirling, 43 mi north of Edinburgh, 61 mi northeast of Glasgow.*

Perth has long been a focal point in Scottish history, and several critical events took place here, including the assassination of King James I of Scotland (1394–1437) and John Knox's (1514–72) preaching in St. John's Kirk in 1559. Later, the 17th-century religious wars in Scotland saw the town occupied, first by the marquis of Montrose (1612–50), then later by Oliver Cromwell's (1599–1658) forces. The Jacobites also occupied the town in the 1715 and 1745 rebellions.

Perth's attractions—with the exception of the shops—are scattered and take time to reach on foot. Some, in fact, are far enough away to necessitate the use of a car, bus, or taxi. A modest selection of castles is within easy reach of Perth.

The cruciform-plan **St. John's Kirk,** dating from the 12th century, was internally divided into three parts at the Reformation, but was restored to something closer to its medieval state by Sir Robert Lorimer in the 1920s. ⊠ *St. John St.,* ☎ *01738/626159.* ⌨ *£1 donation.* ⊙ *Weekdays 10–2 and 2–4, and for Sun. services.*

The **Perth Art Gallery and Museum** has a wide-ranging collection of natural history, local history, and archaeology, plus a rotating exhibit program. ⊠ *78 George St.,* ☎ *01738/632488.* ⌨ *Free.* ⊙ *Mon.–Sat. 10–5.*

On the North Inch of Perth, look for **Balhousie Castle** and the **Regimental Museum of the Black Watch.** Some will tell you the Black Watch was a Scottish regiment whose name is a reference to the color of its tartan. An equally plausible explanation, however, is that the regiment was established to keep an undercover watch on rebellious Jacobites. *Black* is the Gaelic word *dubh,* meaning, in this case, "hidden" or "covert," used in the same sense as the word *blackmail.* ⊠ *Facing North Inch Park (entrance from Hay St.),* ☎ *0131/310–8530.* ⌨ *Free.* ⊙ *May–Sept., Mon.–Sat. 10–4:30; Oct.–Apr., weekdays 10–4. Closed last Sat. in June.*

The Round House contains the **Fergusson Gallery,** displaying a selection of 6,000 works—paintings, drawings, and prints—by the Scottish artist J. D. Fergusson (1874–1961). ⊠ *Marshall Pl.,* ☎ *01738/441944.* ⌨ *Free.* ⊙ *Mon.–Sat. 10–5.*

Off the A9 west of town is **Caithness Glass,** where you can watch glassworkers creating silky-smooth bowls, vases, and other glassware. Also here are a small museum, restaurant, and shop. ⊠ *Inveralmond,* ☎ *01738/492320.* 🖭 *Free.* ☉ *Factory weekdays 9–4:30. Shop Easter–Nov., Mon.–Sat. 9–5, Sun. 10–5; Dec.–Easter, Mon.–Sat. 9–5, Sun. noon–5.*

Huntingtower Castle, a curious double tower that dates from the 15th century, is associated with an attempt to wrest power from the young James VI in 1582. Some early painted ceilings survive, offering the vaguest hint of the sumptuous interiors, once found in many such ancient castles, that are now reduced to bare and drafty rooms. ⊠ *Off A85,* ☎ *0131/668–8800,* 𝖶𝖤𝖡 *www.historic-scotland.gov.uk.* 🖭 *£2.20.* ☉ *Apr.–Sept., daily 9:30–6; Oct.–Mar., Mon.–Wed. and Sat. 9:30–4, Thurs. 9–noon, Sun. 2–4.*

Elcho Castle, a fortified mansion on the east side of Perth, is the abandoned 15th-century seat of the earls of Wemyss. All that remains is a shell. ⊠ *On River Tay,* ☎ *0131/668–8800,* 𝖶𝖤𝖡 *www.historic-scotland.gov.uk.* 🖭 *£2.* ☉ *Apr.–Sept., daily 9:30–6; Oct.–Nov., daily 9:30–4.*

★ ☾ **Scone Palace** is much more cheerful and vibrant than Perth's other castles. The palace is the current residence of the earl of Mansfield but is open to visitors. Although it incorporates various earlier works, the palace today has mainly a 19th-century theme, with mock castellations that were fashionable at the time. There's plenty to see if you're interested in the acquisitions of an aristocratic Scottish family: magnificent porcelain, furniture, ivory, clocks, and 16th-century needlework. A coffee shop, restaurant, gift shop, and play area are on-site, and the extensive grounds have a pine plantation.

The palace has its own mausoleum nearby, on the site of a long-gone abbey on **Moot Hill,** the ancient coronation place of the Scottish kings. To be crowned, they sat on the Stone of Scone, which was seized in 1296 by Edward I of England, Scotland's greatest enemy, and placed in the coronation chair at Westminster Abbey, in London. It was returned to Scotland in November 1996 and is now on view in Edinburgh Castle. Some Scots hint darkly that Edward was fooled by a substitution and that the real stone is hidden, waiting for Scotland to regain its independence. ⊠ *Braemar Rd.,* ☎ *01738/552300,* 𝖶𝖤𝖡 *www. scone-palace.co.uk.* 🖭 *£6.20.* ☉ *Apr.–Oct., daily 9:30–5:15; last admission at 4:45.*

Dining and Lodging

££–£££ ✕🏠 **Parklands.** This top-quality hotel, a stylish Georgian town house overlooking lush woodland, is perhaps best known for its restaurant, Acanthus Restaurant and Colourist Bistro (£–££), serving Scottish fish, game, and beef. A sense of elegance permeates the interior, with its restrained decor and modern furniture. ⊠ *2 St. Leonard's Bank, PH2 8EB,* ☎ *01738/622451,* 𝖥𝖠𝖷 *01738/622046. 14 rooms. 2 restaurants; no a/c. AE, DC, MC, V.*

££ ✕🏠 **Sunbank House Hotel.** A lesson in traditional style, this early Vic-
★ torian gray-stone mansion in a fine residential area near Perth's Branklyn Gardens provides solid, unpretentious comforts along with great views over the River Tay and the city. The restaurant (£££) specializes in locally raised meats and game, imaginatively prepared Continental style with some Italian overtones. ⊠ *50 Dundee Rd., PH2 7BA,* ☎ *01738/ 624882,* 𝖥𝖠𝖷 *01738/442515,* 𝖶𝖤𝖡 *www.sunbankhouse.com. 9 rooms. Restaurant; no a/c, no-smoking rooms. MC, V.*

Nightlife and the Arts

The Victorian **Perth Repertory Theatre** (⊠ 185 High St., ☎ 01738/ 621031) stages plays and musicals. In the summer it's the main venue for the Perth Festival of the Arts. The **Perth City Hall** (⊠ King Edward St., ☎ 01738/624055) hosts musical performances of all types.

Shopping

CLOTHING

C & C Proudfoot (⊠ 104 South St., ☎ 01738/632483) sells a comprehensive selection of sheepskins, leather jackets, rugs, slippers, and handbags.

GLASS AND CHINA

Perth is an especially popular hunting ground for china and glass. **Caithness Glass** (⊠ Inveralmond, off A9 at northern town boundary, ☎ 01738/492320) sells all types of glassware in its factory shop. **Watson of Perth** (⊠ 163–167 High St., ☎ 01738/639861) has sold exquisite bone china and cut crystal since 1900 and can pack your purchase safely for shipment overseas.

JEWELRY AND ANTIQUES

Perth proffers an unusual buy: Scottish freshwater pearls from the River Tay, in delicate settings, some of which take their theme from Scottish flowers. The Romans coveted these pearls. If you do, too, then you can make your choice at **Cairncross Ltd., Goldsmiths** (⊠ 18 St. John's St., ☎ 01738/624367), where you can also admire a display of some of the more unusual shapes and colors of pearls. Antique jewelry and silver, including a few Scottish items, can be found at **Timothy Hardie** (⊠ 25 St. John's St., ☎ 01738/633127). **Whispers of the Past** (⊠ 15 George St., ☎ 01738/635472) has a collection of jewelry, linens, and other items.

Dunkeld

㉙ *14 mi north of Perth.*

At Dunkeld, Thomas Telford's sturdy river bridge of 1809 carries the road into town. Here, the National Trust for Scotland not only cares for grand mansions and wildlands but also actively restores smaller properties. Its Little Houses project can be seen in the square off the main street, opposite the fish-and-chips shop. All the houses on the square were rebuilt after the 1689 defeat of the Jacobite army here, which occurred after its early victory in the Battle of Killiecrankie.

The ospreys that frequent Speyside's Loch Garten in summer get so much attention from conservation societies that they sometimes overshadow those to be found at **Loch of Lowes,** a Scottish Wildlife Trust reserve near Dunkeld. Here the domestic routines of the osprey, one of Scotland's conservation success stories, can be observed in relative comfort. ⊠ *Off A923, about 2 mi northeast of Dunkeld,* ☎ *01350/ 727337.* ⊗ *Apr.–Sept., daily 10–5.*

Shopping

Dunkeld Antiques (⊠ Tay Terr., ☎ 01350/728832), facing the river as you cross the bridge, stocks mainly 18th- and 19th-century items, from large furniture to ornaments, books, and prints. At the **Jeremy Law of Scotland's Highland Horn and Deerskin Centre** (⊠ City Hall, Atholl St., ☎ 01350/727569), you can purchase stag antlers and cow horns shaped into walking sticks, cutlery, and tableware. Deerskin shoes and moccasins, small leather goods made from deerskin, and a specialty malt-whisky collection of more than 200 different malts are also sold. The center has a worldwide postal service and a tax-free shop.

Pitlochry

㉚ *15 mi north of Dunkeld.*

A typical central Highland resort, always full of leisurely hustle and bustle, Pitlochry has wall-to-wall souvenir and gift shops, large hotels recalling the days when this area was even more laid-back, and a mountainous golf course. Most Scottish dams have salmon passes or ladders of some kind, enabling the fish to swim upstream to their spawning grounds. In Pitlochry, the **Pitlochry Dam and Fish Ladder,** just behind the main street, leads into a glass-paneled pipe that allows the fish to observe the visitors.

If you have a whisky-tasting bent you may want to visit **Edradour Distillery,** which claims to be the smallest single-malt distillery in Scotland (but then, so do others). ✉ *2½ mi east of Pitlochry,* ☎ *01796/472095.* 🎫 *Free.* ⊙ *Tour and tastings Mar.–Oct., Mon.–Sat. 9:30–5, Sun. noon–5; Nov.–Dec., Mon.–Sat. 10–4.*

The **Linn of Tummel** (WEB www.nts.org.uk), a series of marked walks along the river and through tall, mature woodlands, is a little north of Pitlochry. Above the Linn, the A9 rises on stilts and gives an exciting ★ view of the valley. The **Pass of Killiecrankie,** set among the oak woods and rocky river just north of the Linn of Tummel, was a key strategic point in the Central Highlands: a famous battle was won here in the Jacobite rebellion of 1689. The National Trust for Scotland's **visitor center** at Killiecrankie explains the significance of this battle, which was the first attempt to restore the Stewart monarchy. The battle was noted for the death of the central Jacobite leader, John Graham of Claverhouse (1649–89), also known as Bonnie Dundee, who was hit by a stray bullet. The rebellion fizzled after Claverhouse's death. ✉ *Signposted off A9,* ☎ FAX *01796/473233,* WEB *www.nts.org.uk.* 🎫 *£1.* ⊙ *Site year-round, daily; visitor center Apr.–Dec., daily 10–6.*

OFF THE BEATEN PATH

LOCH RANNOCH – With its shoreline of birch trees framed by dark pines, Loch Rannoch is the quintessential Highland loch. Fans of Robert Louis Stevenson (1850–94), especially of *Kidnapped* (1886), will not want to miss the last, lonely section of road. Stevenson describes the setting: "The mist rose and died away, and showed us that country lying as waste as the sea; only the moorfowl and the peewees crying upon it, and far over to the east a herd of deer, moving like dots. Much of it was red with heather, much of the rest broken up with bogs and hags and peaty pools." Apart from the blocks of alien conifer plantings in certain places, little here has changed. To reach this atmospheric locale about 20 mi west of Pitlochry, take the B8019 at the Linn of Tummel north of Pitlochry. Travel west past the Queen's View scenic lookout at the east end of Loch Tummel. At the Tummel Bridge, pick up B846, which travels along the shores of the loch. The road ends at Rannoch, where you meet the West Highland railroad line on its way across Rannoch Moor to Fort William.

Nightlife and the Arts

Pitlochry Festival Theatre (✉ Pitlochry, ☎ 01796/484626 for box office; 01796/484600 for general inquiries, WEB www.pitlochry.org.uk) presents six plays each season and hosts eight Sunday concerts. The theater is open late May–October.

Blair Castle

★ ③ *10 mi north of Pitlochry.*

Thanks to its historic contents and its war-torn past, Blair Castle is one of Scotland's most highly rated sights. The turreted white castle was home to successive dukes of Atholl and their families, the Murrays, until the death of the 10th duke. One of the many fascinating details in the interior is a preserved piece of floor still bearing marks of the red-hot shot fired through the roof during the 1745 Jacobite rebellion—

the last occasion in Scottish history that a castle was besieged. The castle holds not only military artifacts—historically, the duke was allowed to keep a private army, the Atholl Highlanders—but also a fine collection of furniture and paintings. Outside, a Victorian walled garden has been restored, and there are extensive parklands backed by high, rounded hills. ✉ *From Pitlochry take the A9 to Blair Atholl and follow signs,* ☎ *01796/481207,* WEB *www.blair-castle.co.uk.* 🎟 *Castle and grounds £6.25; grounds only, £2.* ☉ *Apr.–late Oct., daily 10–6; last admission at 5.*

Shopping

The **House of Bruar** (✉ On the A9 just north of Blair Atholl, ☎ 01796/483236) is an Aladdin's cave for shopaholics who love top-quality Scottish clothing, crystal and glassware, and decorative items. There's also a good restaurant.

Aberfeldy

15 mi southwest of Pitlochry; 25 mi southwest of Blair Castle.

The sleepy town of Aberfeldy is a popular tourist base. Aberfeldy Bridge (1733), with five arches and a humpback, was designed by William Adam (1689–1748). **Castle Menzies,** a 16th-century fortified tower house, contains the **Clan Menzies' Museum,** which displays many relics of the clan's history. The castle stands west of Aberfeldy, on the opposite bank of the River Tay. ☎ *01887/820982.* 🎟 *£3.50.* ☉ *Apr.–mid-Oct., Mon.–Sat. 10:30–5, Sun. 2–5; last admission at 4:30.*

③③ Glen Lyon, just a few miles away from Aberfeldy, is one of central Scotland's most attractive glens; it has a rushing river, forests, high hills on both sides, prehistoric sites (complete with legendary tales), and the typical *big hoose* (big house) hidden on private grounds. There's even a dam at the head of the loch, a reminder that little of Scotland's scenic beauty is unadulterated. You can reach the glen by a high road from Loch Tay: take the A827 to Fearnan, then turn north to Fortingall. The **Fortingall yew,** in the churchyard near the Fortingall Hotel, wearily rests its great limbs on the ground. This tree is thought to be more than 3,000 years old. Legend has it that Pontius Pilate was born beside it, during the time his father was serving as a Roman legionnaire in Scotland. After viewing the yew, turn west into Glen Lyon.

OFF THE
BEATEN PATH

THE SCOTTISH CRANNOG CENTRE – Here's your chance to travel back 5,000 years to a time when the local inhabitants of this area, in common with others across Scotland and Ireland, started building defensive homesteads, known as *crannogs,* on wooden piles in the water. They were approachable only by narrow bridges that could easily be defended. This practice continued until as late as the 17th century. Archaeologists have found many remains of crannogs in lochs throughout Scotland. One of the best-preserved crannogs (and a mere 2,600 years old!) was found in Loch Tay, off the north shore at Fearnan, and it's now possible to visit an accurate replica here. You can walk across the water to sit within this surprisingly cozy thatched structure, try on some of the clothing from this period, and sample authentic food. The shore-based exhibition gives details about crannog construction and the crannog people and their way of life; don't miss the butter dish, with butter still inside. The Crannog Centre is just west of Aberfeldy, on the southern shore of Loch Tay. ✉ *Kenmore, South Loch Tay,* ☎ *01887/830583,* WEB *www.crannog.co.uk.* 🎟 *£4.25.* ☉ *Mid-Mar.–Oct., daily 10–5:30; Nov., daily 10–4; last entry one hr before closing.*

Outdoor Activities and Sports

Loch Tay Boating Centre (⊠ Pier Rd., Kenmore, ☎ 01887/830291) rents cabin cruisers, fishing boats, and canoes from April through mid-October.

En Route Between Aberfeldy and Killin, take the north-bank road by Loch Tay, the A827, which affords fine views west along Loch Tay toward Ben More and Stobinian and north to Ben Lawers.

Killin

㉞ *24 mi southwest of Aberfeldy, 39 mi north of Stirling, 45 mi west of Perth.*

A village with an almost alpine flavor, known for its modest but surprisingly diverse selection of crafts and woolen wares, Killin is also noted for its scenery. The **Falls of Dochart,** white-water rapids overlooked by a pine-clad islet, are at the west end of the village. The **Breadalbane Folklore Centre** focuses on the area's heritage and folk tales. The most curious of these are the "Healing Stones of St. Fillan"—water-worn stones that have been looked after lovingly for centuries for their supposed curative powers. ⊠ *By the Falls of Dochart,* ☎ 01567/820254. 🔊 *£2.* ☼ *Mar.–May and Oct., daily 10–5; June and Sept., daily 10–6; July–Aug., daily 9:30–6:30.*

Across the River Dochart and near the golf course sit the ruins of **Finlarig Castle,** built by Black Duncan of the Cowl, a notorious Campbell laird. The castle can be visited at any time.

Lodging

£ 🏠 **Lodge House.** Few other guest houses in Scotland can match the mountain views from this 100-year-old property; it's certainly worth the short drive 15 mi west from Killin to Crianlarich. Informal and cozy, the guest house is successful thanks to what the Scots call good "crack"— conviviality, in this case between host and guests. The food is good Scots fare: haggis, salmon, and oatcakes. The bedrooms are plain and unfussy, but more than adequate. You may wish to walk along the riverbank after dinner, or have a wee dram in the tiny bar instead. ⊠ *Crianlarich, Perthshire FK20 8RU,* ☎ 01838/300276, 🌐 *www.lodgehouse.co.uk.* *6 rooms. No a/c, no room phones, no smoking. MC, V.*

Outdoor Activities and Sports

If you want to explore the north end of the Glasgow–Killin cycleway, rent a mountain bike from **Killin Outdoor Centre and Mountain Shop** (⊠ Main St., ☎ 01567/820652, 🌐 www.killinoutdoor.co.uk). Also available are canoes, crampons, skis, and ice axes.

En Route Southwest of Killin the A827 joins the main A85. By turning south over the watershed, you will see fine views of the hill ridges behind Killin. The road leads into Glen Ogle, "amid the wildest and finest scenery we had yet seen . . . putting one in mind of prints of the Khyber Pass," as Queen Victoria (1819–1901) recorded in her diary when she traveled this way in 1842.

Crieff

㉟ *25 mi southwest of Killin.*

The hilly town of Crieff offers walks with Highland views from **Knock Hill** above the town. If you wish to discover the delights of whisky distilling, take a tour of the **Glenturret Distillery.** Also here are two restaurants with Taste of Scotland menus, an audiovisual presentation entitled *The Water of Life,* and the *Spirit of the Glen* exhibition. The distillery is signposted on the west side of the town. ☎ 01764/656565. ☒ £3.50; free in Jan. ☉ Jan., weekdays 11:30–4, last tour at 2:30; Feb.–Dec., Mon.–Sat. 9:30–6, Sun. noon–6, last tour at 4:30.

Just south of Crieff is a paperweight manufacturer, part of a complex called the **Crieff Visitors Centre.** Adjacent to the complex are a small pottery factory, a restaurant, and a shop, where you can purchase Thistle hand-painted pottery and intricate millefiori, among other things. ☒ A822, south of Crieff, ☎ 01764/654014. ☒ Free. ☉ Apr.–Oct., daily 9–5:30; Nov.–Mar., daily 9–5.

Drummond Castle Garden, southwest of Crieff, is a stunning, very large, formal Italian garden—a rarity in Scotland. It's regarded as one of the finest of its kind in Europe, and it even made an appearance in the film Rob Roy. ☒ Off Crieff–Muthill road, ☎ 01764/681257. ☒ £3.50. ☉ Easter weekend and May–Oct., daily 2–6; last admission at 5.

Shopping

Crieff is a center for china and glassware, which you can purchase along with pottery at the **Crieff Visitors Centre. Stuart Crystal** (☒ Muthill Rd., ☎ 01764/654004), a factory shop, sells not only its own Stuart crystal but also Waterford, Dartington, and Wedgwood wares.

Auchterarder

36   11 mi southeast of Crieff.

Famous for the Gleneagles Hotel and nearby golf courses, Auchterarder also has a flock of tony antiques shops to amuse Gleneagles's golf widows and widowers.

Dining and Lodging

££££   ✕☷ **Auchterarder House Hotel.** This secluded and richly furnished
★   Victorian country mansion has a plush, exuberantly styled dining room filled with glittering glassware; it's an appropriate setting for the unusual and creative presentation of local foods. ☒ On B8062 at Auchterarder, 15 mi southwest of Perth, PH3 1DZ, ☎ 01764/663646, FAX 01764/662939, WEB www.auchterarderhouse.com. 15 rooms. Restaurant, golf privileges, croquet; no a/c. AE, DC, MC, V.

££££   ✕☷ **Gleneagles Hotel.** One of Britain's most famous hotels, Gleneagles
★   is the very essence of modern grandeur. Like a vast, secret palace, it stands hidden in breathtaking countryside amid world-famous golf courses. Recreation facilities are nearly endless: three restaurants, a shopping arcade, The Spa, the Gleneagles Equestrian Centre, the Golf Academy, and more, all of which make a stay here a luxurious and unforgettable experience. ☒ Auchterarder, near Perth, PH3 1NF, ☎ 01764/662231, FAX 01764/662134, WEB www.gleneagles.com. 216 rooms. 3 restaurants, golf privileges, 5 tennis courts, indoor pool, sauna, spa, bicycles, horseback riding; no a/c. AE, DC, MC, V.

THE CENTRAL HIGHLANDS A TO Z

To research prices, get advice from other travelers, and book travel arrangements, visit www.fodors.com.

AIR TRAVEL

Perth and Stirling can be reached easily from the Edinburgh and Glasgow airports by train, car, or bus.

BUS TRAVEL

A good network of buses connects with the central belt via Edinburgh and Glasgow. Express services also link the larger towns in the Central Highlands with all main towns and cities in England. For more information contact Scottish Citylink or National Express. The Perth and Kinross Council supplies a map showing all public transport routes in Perthshire, marked with nearby attractions. This map can be obtained from any tourist information center in Perthshire.

The following companies organize reliable service on convenient routes throughout the Central Highlands: First Ltd., Scottish Citylink, and Stagecoach.

➤ Bus Information: **First Ltd** (✉ Goosecroft Rd. bus station, Stirling, ☎ 01324/613777). **National Express** (☎ 08705/808080, WEB www.nationalexpress.co.uk). **Scottish Citylink** (✉ Leonard St. bus station, Perth, ☎ 08705/505050, WEB www.citylink.co.uk). **Stagecoach** (✉ Ruthvenfield Rd., Inveralmond Industrial Estate, Perth, ☎ 01738/629339).

CAR RENTAL

➤ Agencies: **Arnold Clark** (✉ St. Leonard's Bank, Perth, ☎ 01738/638511; ✉ Volvo Complex, Kerse Rd., Stirling, ☎ 01786/478686). **Avis** (✉ Texaco Service Station, Bannockburn Rd., Stirling, ☎ 01786/816828). **Europcar** (✉ 26 Glasgow Rd., Perth, ☎ 01738/636888).

CAR TRAVEL

You'll find easy access to the area from the central belt of Scotland via the motorway network. The M9 runs within sight of the walls of Stirling Castle, and Perth can be reached via the M90 over the Forth Bridge.

There's an adequate network of roads, and the area's proximity to the central belt speeds road communications. Two signed touring routes are useful: the Perthshire Tourist Route, and the Deeside Tourist Route, with a spectacular journey via Blairgowrie and Glenshee to Deeside and Aberdeen. Local tourist information centers can supply maps of these routes.

➤ Information: **Scottish Tourist Board** (✉ 23 Ravelston Terr., Edinburgh EH4 3EU, ☎ 0131/332–2433, FAX 0131/343–1513, WEB www.visitscotland.com).

EMERGENCIES

In case of an emergency, dial **999** to reach an ambulance or the police or fire departments (no coins are needed for emergency calls from phone booths).

If you need to see a doctor or dentist, ask for recommendations from the nearest tourist information center, your hotel receptionist, or B&B host. Late-night pharmacies are found only in the larger towns and cities. In an emergency the police will help you find a pharmacist.

➤ Hospitals: **Perth Royal Infirmary** (✉ Taymount Terr., Perth, ☎ 01738/623311). **Stirling Royal Infirmary** (✉ Livilands Gate, Stirling, ☎ 01786/434000). **Vale of Leven Hospital** (✉ Main St., Alexandria, ☎ 01389/754121).

TOURS

ORIENTATION TOURS

The bus companies listed in the Bus Travel section run a number of general orientation tours. Inquire at the nearest tourist information center, where tour reservations can usually be booked.

PERSONAL TOURS

Many taxi and chauffeur companies arrange tailor-made tours by the day or week; the nearest visitor center is your best source for detailed, up-to-date information. Don't miss the opportunity to take a boat trip on a loch, especially in the Trossachs (Loch Katrine) and Loch Lomond; consult a visitor center for details.

TRAIN TRAVEL

The Central Highlands are linked to Edinburgh and Glasgow by rail, with through routes to England (some direct-service routes from London take fewer than five hours). Several Savers ticket options are available, although in some cases on the ScotRail system, the discount fares must be purchased before your arrival in the United Kingdom. Contact National Rail Enquiries or ScotRail for details.

The West Highland Line runs through the western portion of the area. Services also run to Stirling, Dunblane, Perth, and Gleneagles; destinations on the Inverness–Perth line include Dunkeld, Pitlochry, and Blair Atholl. Contact National Rail Enquiries or ScotRail for details.

➤ TRAIN INFORMATION: **National Rail Enquiries** (☎ 08457/484950). **ScotRail** (☎ 08457/550033, WEB www.scotrail.co.uk).

VISITOR INFORMATION

The tourist offices listed below are open year-round. Seasonal tourist information centers are also open (generally April–October) in the following towns: Aberfoyle, Balloch, Callander, Drymen, Dunblane, Helensburgh, Killin, Pirnhall, Tarbet, and Tyndrum. All are clearly marked with the standard I sign in white on a blue background.

➤ TOURIST INFORMATION: **Aberfeldy** (✉ The Square, ☎ 01887/820276). **Alva** (✉ Mill Trail Visitor Centre, W. Stirling St., ☎ 08707/200605). **Auchterarder** (✉ 90 High St., ☎ 01764/663450). **Blairgowrie** (✉ 26 Wellmeadow, ☎ 01250/872960). **Crieff** (✉ Town Hall, High St., ☎ 01764/652578). **Dumbarton** (✉ A82 north-bound, ☎ 08707/200612). **Dunkeld** (✉ The Cross, ☎ 01350/727688). **Falkirk** (✉ 2/4 Glebe St., ☎ 08707/200614). **Kinross** (✉ Heart of Scotland Visitor Centre, Service Area Junction 6 M90, ☎ 01577/863680). **Perth** (✉ Lower City Mills, W. Mill St., ☎ 01738/450600, WEB www.perthshire.co.uk). **Pitlochry** (✉ 22 Atholl Rd., ☎ 01796/472215). **Stirling** (✉ 41 Dumbarton Rd., ☎ 08707/200620; ✉ Royal Burgh of Stirling Visitor Centre, Castle Esplanade, ☎ 08707/200622, WEB www.visitscottishheartlands.org).

7 ABERDEEN AND THE NORTHEAST

Here, in this granite shoulder of Grampian, are Royal Deeside, the countryside that Queen Victoria made her own; the Castle Country route, where fortresses stand hard against the hills; and the Whisky Trail, where peaty streams embrace the country's greatest concentration of distilleries. The region's gateway is Aberdeen, constructed of granite and now aglitter with new wealth and new blood drawn together by North Sea oil.

By Gilbert
Summers

Updated by
Beth Ingpen

BECAUSE OF ITS ISOLATION, the granite city of Aberdeen has historically been a fairly autonomous place. Even now it's perceived by many U.K. inhabitants as lying almost out of reach in the northeast. In reality, it's only 90 minutes' flying time from London or a little more than two hours by car from Edinburgh. Its magnificent, confident 18th- and early 19th-century city center amply rewards exploration, and there are also many surviving buildings from earlier centuries for you to seek out. Yet even if Aberdeen vanished from the map, an extensive portion of the northeast would still remain at the top of many travelers' wish lists, studded as it is with some of Scotland's most enduring travel icons.

Some credit Sir Walter Scott with having opened up Scotland for tourism through his poems and novels. Others say General Wade did it when he built the Highland roads. But it was probably Queen Victoria who gave Scottish tourism its real momentum when, in 1842, she first came to Scotland and when, in 1847—on orders of a doctor, who thought the relatively dry climate of upper Deeside would suit her—she bought Balmoral. At first sight she described it as "a pretty little castle in the old Scottish style." The pretty little castle was knocked down to make room for a much grander house in full-flown Scottish baronial style, designed, in fact, by her husband, Prince Albert. Before long the entire Deeside and the region north were dotted with handsome country houses and mock-baronial châteaux, as the ambitious rich thought it wise to stake a claim in the neighborhood. The locals, bless 'em, took it all in stride. To this day, the hundreds who line the road when the queen and her family arrive for services at the family's parish church at Crathie are invariably visitors to Deeside—one of Balmoral's great attractions for the monarch has always been the villagers' respect for royal privacy.

Balmoral is merely the most famous castle in the area. Nowhere else in Scotland is there such an eclectic selection of these residences, offering you an opportunity to touch the fabric of Scotland's story. There are so many that in one part of the region a Castle Trail has been established, leading you to such fortresses as the ruined medieval Kildrummy Castle, which once controlled the strategic routes through the valley of the River Don. Later structures, such as Craigievar, a narrow-turreted castle resembling an illustration from a fairy-tale book, reflect the changing times of the 17th century, when defense became less of a priority. Later still, grand mansions such as Haddo House, with its symmetrical facade and elegant interior, surrender any defensive role entirely and instead make statements about their owner's status.

South of Elgin and Banff, where the peaty streams jostle for elbow room on their race down from the Grampian heights to the sea, the glens embrace Scotland's greatest concentration of malt-whisky distilleries. With so many in Morayshire, where the distilling is centered in the valley of the River Spey and its tributaries, there's now a Whisky Trail. Just as the Gironde in France has famous vineyards clustered around it, the Spey has famous single-malt distilleries. Instead of Lafite-Rothschild, Pétrus, and Haut-Brion, there's Glenfiddich, Glen Grant, Tamdhu, or Tamnavulin. As well as being sweeter and less peaty than some of the island malts, eastern or Speyside malts generally have names that are easier to pronounce.

The northeast's chief attraction lies in the gradual transition from high mountain plateau—by a series of gentle steps through hill, forest, and farmland—to the Moray Firth and North Sea coast, where the word *unadulterated* is redefined. Here you'll find some of the United Kingdom's most perfect wild shorelines, both sandy and sheer cliff. The Grampian Mountains, to the west, contain some of the highest ground in the nation, in the area of the Cairngorms. But the Grampian hills also have shaped the character of the folk who live in the northeast. In earlier times the massif made communication with the south somewhat difficult. As a result, native northeasterners still speak the richest Lowland Scottish (*not* Gaelic, which is an entirely different language).

Pleasures and Pastimes

Biking

Northeast Scotland is superb biking country, with networks of minor roads and farm roads crisscrossing rolling fields. You can also ride along former railway track beds that have been converted to bicycle and pedestrian pathways. The Buchan line, from Aberdeen to Fraserburgh and Peterhead, is a good route.

Dining

Partly in response to the demands of spendthrift oilmen, the number of restaurants in Aberdeen has grown during the past several years, and the quality of the food has improved. Elsewhere in the region you're never far from a good pub lunch or a hotel high tea or dinner.

CATEGORY	COST*
££££	over £22
£££	£16–£22
££	£9–£15
£	under £9

per person for a main course at dinner, including VAT

Fishing

With major rivers such as the Dee, Don, Deveron, and Ythan, as well as popular smaller rivers like the Ugie, plus loch and estuary fishing, this is one of Scotland's leading game-fishing areas. You can obtain details of beats, boats, and permit prices from local tourist information centers. Some hotels offer fishing packages or at the least can organize permits. Prices vary widely, depending on the fish and individual river beat.

Golf

The northeast has more than 50 golf clubs, some of which have championship courses. Tourist centers can supply leaflets appropriate to their area. All towns and many villages have their 9- and 18-hole municipal links, where you'll pay from £15 to £20 per round. The more prestigious clubs charge up to £120 a day and expect you to book by letter or to bring a letter of recommendation from a member.

Lodging

The northeast has some splendid country hotels with log fires and rich furnishings, where you can also be sure of eating well. Many Aberdeen hotels offer competitive rates on weekends.

CATEGORY	COST*
££££	over £140
£££	£110–£140
££	£65–£110
£	under £65

All prices are for a standard double room, including service, breakfast, and VAT.

Skiing

The main ski area is at **Glenshee** (☎ 013397/41320), just south of Braemar, though the season can be brief here. Those accustomed to long alpine runs and extensive choices will find the runs here short, unlike the lift lines. The **Lecht** (☎ 01975/651440) lies at a lower altitude than Glenshee and is mainly suitable for beginners. The area at **Cairngorm** (☎ 01479/861261), by Aviemore, is another ski option. There's an artificial "dry" slope at **Alford** (☎ 019755/63024).

Exploring Aberdeen and the Northeast

Once you have spent time in Aberdeen, you may be inclined to venture west into Deeside, with its royal connections and looming mountain backdrop, and then pass over the hills into the Castle Country to the north. You might head farther west to touch on Speyside and the Whisky Trail, before meandering back east and south along the pristine coastline at Scotland's northeasternmost tip.

Numbers in the text correspond to numbers in the margin and on the Royal Deeside, Aberdeen, and the Northeast maps.

Great Itineraries

Although the Grampian area isn't huge, it has many different terrains. To get a real flavor of this most authentic of Scottish regions, sample both the coastline and the mountains.

IF YOU HAVE 3 DAYS

Setting out from **Aberdeen** ①–⑳, follow in the footsteps of Queen Victoria and tour the castles and glens of Royal Deeside. Head for **Crathes Castle** ㉒ and **Banchory** ㉓, with its largely unchanged Victorian High Street. After lunch follow the river upstream to Aboyne, turning north on B9094, then left onto B9119 for 6 mi for a panorama (signposted on B9119) known as the Queen's View, a bit north of Dinnet—this is one of the northeast's most spectacular vistas, stretching across the Howe of Cromar to Lochnagar. Then continue on B9119, dropping gently downhill through the birch woods to A93 and ⛾ **Ballater** ㉖, to the west. The next morning visit Her Majesty's **Balmoral Castle** ㉗ (note that it's open only for three months in the summer)—explore the ballroom and grounds, take a pony ride, and then treat yourself to a walk in nearby Glen Muick. Here you'll find the famous climb of Lochnagar, so beloved by Victoria. Overnight in ⛾ **Braemar.** The next morning set off for Castle Country and some serious castle hopping—**Corgarff Castle** ㉙, **Kildrummy Castle** ㉚, **Craigievar Castle** ㉜, and **Castle Fraser** ㉝—before returning to Aberdeen.

IF YOU HAVE 5 DAYS

Downtown ⛾ **Aberdeen's** ①–⑳ silver granite certainly deserves a little time. Then travel into Speyside for its distilleries: **Dufftown** ㉞, **Craigellachie** ㉟, **Aberlour** ㊱, and ⛾ **Elgin** ㊲. Spend a morning exploring Elgin before moving east along the coast to stay overnight in ⛾ **Fordyce** ㊷. Visit the magnificent Duff House gallery in **Banff** ㊸ before returning to Aberdeen. On the last day see a castle or two: **Drum** ㉑ or **Crathes** ㉒, in Deeside; **Haddo House** ㊺ or **Fyvie Castle** ㊹, northwest of **Ellon** ㊻; or loop northwestward for **Corgarff** ㉙, the ruined castle at ⛾ **Kildrummy** ㉚, fairy-tale **Craigievar** ㉜, or **Castle Fraser** ㉝.

When to Tour Aberdeen and the Northeast

Because the National Trust for Scotland tends to close its properties in winter, many of the northeast's castles are not suitable for off-season travel, though you can always see them from the outside. Duff House, Macduff Marine Aquarium, and some of the distilleries are open much of the year, but May and June are probably the best times to visit.

Royal Deeside

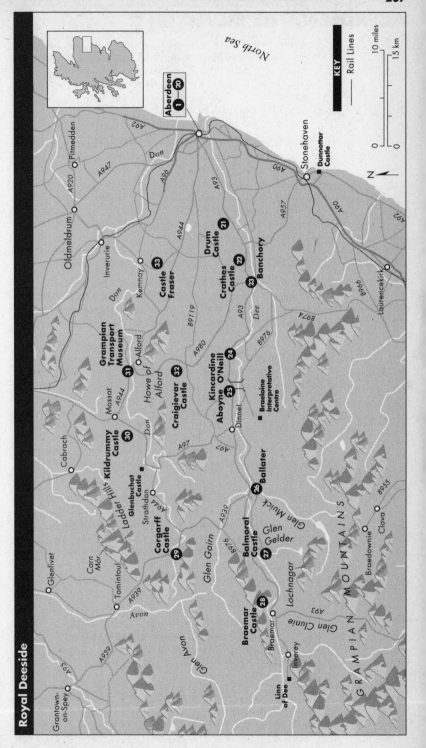

KEY

—— Rail Lines

10 miles

15 km

ABERDEEN, THE SILVER CITY

In the 18th century local granite quarrying produced a durable silver stone that would be used boldly in the glittering blocks, spires, columns, and parapets of Victorian-era Aberdonian structures. The city remains one of the United Kingdom's most distinctive, although some would say it depends on the weather and the brightness of the day. The mica chips embedded in the rock look like a million mirrors in the sunshine. In rain and heavy clouds, however, their sparkle is snuffed out.

The North Sea has always been important to Aberdeen: in the 1850s the city was famed for its sleek, fast clippers that sailed to India for cargoes of tea. In the late 1960s the course of Aberdeen's history was unequivocally altered when oil and gas were discovered offshore. The city seemed destined to become an oil-rich Klondike, and throughout the 1970s it was overcome by new shops, new office blocks, new hotels, new industries, and new attitudes. Some innate local caution, however, has helped the city to retain a sense of perspective.

Exploring Aberdeen

Aberdeen centers on Union Street, with its many fine survivors of the Victorian and Edwardian streetscape. Old Aberdeen is very much a separate area of the city, north of the modern center and clustered around St. Machar's Cathedral and the many fine buildings of the University of Aberdeen.

A Good Tour

Start your walk at the east end of **Union Street** ①. Here within the original old town is the Castlegate. The actual castle once stood somewhere behind the Salvation Army Citadel (1896), an imposing baronial granite tower whose design was inspired by Balmoral Castle. On the north side of Castle Street stands the 17th-century **Tolbooth** ②, a reminder of Aberdeen's earliest days. The impressive **Mercat Cross** ③ is just beyond King Street. Turn north down Broad Street to reach **Marischal College** ④, whose sparkling granite frontage dominates the top end of the street.

A survivor from an earlier Aberdeen can be found opposite Marischal College, beyond the concrete supports of St. Nicholas House (which houses the tourist information center): **Provost Skene's House** ⑤ was once part of a closely packed area of town houses and is now a museum portraying civic life. Just around the corner on Upperkirkgate, at the lowest point, are two modern shopping malls—the St. Nicholas Centre on the left, the Bon-Accord Centre on the right.

Upperkirkgate becomes Schoolhill, where there's a complex of silvertone buildings in front of which stands a statue of General Charles Gordon (1833–85), the military hero of Khartoum (1885). Interestingly, he is not the Gordon for whom **Robert Gordon University** ⑥, behind the statue, was named. The university's next-door neighbor is **Aberdeen Art Gallery** ⑦, which plays an active role in the city's cultural life and is a popular rendezvous for locals.

The silvery and handsome Central Library, St. Mark's Church, and the restored Edwardian His Majesty's Theatre on **Rosemount Viaduct** ⑧ are collectively known to all Aberdonians as Education, Salvation, and Damnation. If you're taking photographs, you can choose an angle that includes the statue of Scotland's first freedom fighter, Sir William Wallace (1270–1305), in the foreground pointing majestically to Damnation. The **Millennium Village** ⑨, great for kids, is off Rosemount Viaduct on Rosemount Place.

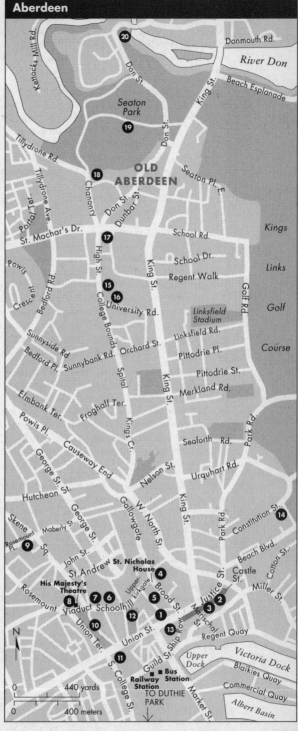

Aberdeen

Union Terrace ⑩, a 19th-century development, runs back toward Union Street. Smug cats decorate **Union Bridge** ⑪, where Union Terrace meets Union Street. Here you can turn left across the bridge and follow Union Street to **St. Nicholas Kirk** ⑫. It's set in a peaceful green churchyard that's screened by a colonnaded facade (1829) and is popular with office workers at lunchtime in summer.

You're now almost back at your starting point. Turn right, opposite Broad Street, and head down Ship Row to enjoy the Aberdeen Maritime Museum, housed partly in **Provost Ross's House** ⑬ and partly in a magnificent modern glass extension. Below Ship Row is the harbor, which contains some fine 18th- and 19th-century architecture. Explore it if time permits and you don't mind the traffic. An essential place to visit if you have children with you is **Satrosphere** ⑭, a hands-on exhibition of science and technology. On Constitution Street, off Justice Street/Park Road beyond the eastern end of Union Street, it's worth the 10-minute walk.

For the second part of your city walk, hop on a bus traveling north from a stop near Marischal College, or up King Street, off the Castlegate, to reach **Old Aberdeen. College Bounds** ⑮ has handsome 18th- and 19th-century houses, cobbled streets, and paved sidewalks. **King's College** ⑯ was founded in 1494 and is now part of the University of Aberdeen. This area has some fine Georgian houses, including the **Town House** ⑰. Behind it the modern intrusion of St. Machar's Drive destroys some of the old-town ambience, but you can recapture it on a stroll along the Chanonry, past the elegant structures that once housed officials connected with the cathedral nearby.

North on the Chanonry is **St. Machar's Cathedral** ⑱. The structure was first built in AD 580, but nothing remains of the original foundation; much of what you see is from the 15th and 16th centuries. Beyond St. Machar's lies **Seaton Park** ⑲, full of daffodils in spring. Until the early 19th century the only way north out of Aberdeen was over the River Don on the **Brig o'Balgownie** ⑳ (constructed in 1314), at the far end of Seaton Park—a 15-minute walk.

TIMING

You can devote a day to each half of this walk, or you can spend a long morning in the center of Aberdeen, then take a bus out to Old Aberdeen after a late lunch, and do the tour in a (long) day.

Sights to See

❼ **Aberdeen Art Gallery.** Locals take great pride and pleasure in this collection—from 18th-century art to contemporary works—of paintings, prints and drawings, sculpture, porcelain, costumes, and much else. It also hosts frequent temporary exhibitions and has a good-value café. ✉ *Schoolhill,* ☎ *01224/523700,* WEB *www.aagm.co.uk.* 🎫 *Free.* ☉ *Mon.–Sat. 10–5, Sun. 2–5.*

⑳ **Brig o'Balgownie.** Until 1827 the only way out of Aberdeen going north was over the River Don on this single-arch bridge. It dates from 1314 and is thought to have been built by Richard Cementarius, Aberdeen's first provost. ✉ *Seaton Park.*

⑮ **College Bounds.** Handsome 18th- and 19th-century houses line this cobbled street, which has paved sidewalks. ✉ *Old Aberdeen.*

OFF THE   **DUTHIE PARK AND WINTER GARDENS –** A great place to feed the ducks,
BEATEN PATH   Duthie Park also has a boating pond and trampolines, carved wooden
                        animals, and playgrounds. In the very attractive (and warm!) Winter
                        Gardens are fish in ponds, free-flying birds, and turtles and terrapins

among the luxuriant foliage and flowers. The park lies close beside Aberdeen's other river, the Dee. ⊠ *Polmuir Rd., Riverside Dr., about 1 mi south from city center.* 🎫 *Free.* ☉ *Gardens daily 10–dusk.*

★ ⓰ **King's College.** Founded in 1494, King's College is now part of the University of Aberdeen. Its **chapel,** which was built around 1500, has an unmistakable flying (or crown) spire. That it has survived at all was because of the zeal of the principal, who defended his church against the destructive fanaticism that swept through Scotland during the Reformation, when the building was less than a century old. Today the renovated chapel plays an important role in university life. The tall oak screen that separates the nave from the choir, the ribbed wooden ceiling, and the stalls constitute the finest medieval wood carvings found anywhere in Scotland. The **King's College Centre** will tell you more about the university. ⊠ *High St.,* ☎ *01224/273702,* WEB *www.abdn. ac.uk/kcc.* ☉ *Weekdays 9:30–5, Sat. 11–4.*

★ ❹ **Marischal College.** Founded in 1593 by the earl of Marischal as a Protestant alternative to the Catholic King's College in Old Aberdeen, Marischal College combined with King's College to form the University of Aberdeen in 1860 (the earls of Marischal held hereditary office as keepers of the king's mares). The original university buildings on this site have undergone extensive renovations, and the current facade was built in 1891. The spectacularly ornate work is set off by the gilded flags, and this turn-of-the-20th-century creation is still the world's second-largest granite building. Only El Escorial, outside Madrid, is larger. The main part of the building, no longer needed by the university, is at present the subject of various plans, one of which would turn it into a hotel. The **Marischal Museum**'s two main galleries house the *Encyclopaedia of the North East,* an A-to-Z look at the northeast's heritage, and *Collecting the World,* the worldwide ethnographic collections of 19th-century northeast travelers. ⊠ *Broad St.,* ☎ *01224/274301,* WEB *www. abdn.ac.uk.* 🎫 *Free.* ☉ *Museum weekdays 10–5, Sun. 2–5.*

❸ **Mercat Cross.** Built in 1686 and restored in 1820, the Mercat Cross, always the symbolic center of a Scottish medieval burgh, stands just beyond King Street. Along its parapet are 12 portrait panels of the Stewart monarchs.

🐾 ❾ **The Millennium Village.** Here you'll find an interactive heritage museum and learning center, based on life in a 2,000-year-old village and today's developing world. The center has costumes, spinning and weaving, mosaic making, puppet plays, and jigsaw puzzles. ⊠ *Rosemount Pl.,* ☎ *01224/648041.* 🎫 *£3.* ☉ *Mon., Wed., and Fri.–Sat. 10–noon; Sun. 2:30–4:30.*

Old Aberdeen. Once an independent burgh near the River Don, but swallowed up by the expanding main city before the end of the 19th century, Old Aberdeen still retains a certain degree of character and integrity. Many of the University of Aberdeen's departments are housed in buildings scattered around Old Aberdeen; there is no university campus, as such. ⊠ *Between King's College and St. Machar's Cathedral.*

★ 🐾 ⓭ **Provost Ross's House.** Dating from 1593, with a striking modern extension, this houses the **Aberdeen Maritime Museum.** Displays here tell the story of the city's involvement with the sea, from early inshore fisheries by way of tea clippers to the North Sea oil boom. It's a fascinating place for grade-schoolers, with its ship models, paintings, and equipment associated with the fishing, shipbuilding, and North Sea oil and gas industries. ⊠ *Ship Row,* ☎ *01224/337701,* WEB *www.aagm.co.uk.* 🎫 *Free.* ☉ *Mon.–Sat. 10–5, Sun. noon–3.*

⑤ Provost Skene's House. *Provost* is Scottish for mayor, and this former mayor's domestic dwelling was once part of a closely packed area of town houses. Steeply gabled and built of rubble, it survives in part from 1545. It is now a museum portraying civic life, with rooms restored and furnished in period style and a painted chapel. ⊠ *Guestrow off Broad St.,* ☎ *01224/641086,* WEB *www.aagm.co.uk.* 🎫 *Free.* ☉ *Mon.– Sat. 10–5, Sun. 1–4.*

⑥ Robert Gordon University. Built in 1731, this was originally called Robert Gordon's Hospital and was used to educate poor boys. It's now an independent school with an associated institute of technology. ⊠ *Schoolhill.* ☉ *View from outside only.*

⑧ Rosemount Viaduct. Three buildings on this bridge are collectively known by all Aberdonians as Education, Salvation, and Damnation. Silvery and handsome, the **Central Library** and **St. Mark's Church** date from the last decade of the 19th century, and **His Majesty's Theatre** (1904–08) has been restored inside to its full Edwardian splendor.

⑱ St. Machar's Cathedral. It's said that St. Machar was sent by St. Columba to build a church on a grassy platform near the sea, where a river flowed in the shape of a shepherd's crook. This spot fit the bill. Founded in AD 580, this cathedral has nothing of its original structure. Much of the existing building dates from the 15th and 16th centuries. The central tower collapsed in 1688, reducing the building to half its original length. The twin octagonal spires on the western towers date from the first half of the 16th century. The nave is thought to have been rebuilt in red sandstone in 1370, but the final renovation was completed in granite by the middle of the 15th century. Along with the nave ceiling, the twin spires were finished in time to take a battering in the Reformation, when the barons of the Mearns stripped the lead off the roof of St. Machar's and stole the bells. The cathedral suffered further mistreatment—including the removal of stone by Oliver Cromwell's (1599–1658) English garrison in the 1650s—until a 19th-century scheme fully restored the church. ⊠ *Chanonry,* ☎ *01224/485988.* ☉ *Daily 9–5.*

⑫ St. Nicholas Kirk. The original burgh church, the Mither Kirk, as this edifice is known, is curiously not within the bounds of the early town settlement; that was located to the east, near the end of present-day Union Street. During the 12th century the port of Aberdeen flourished, and there wasn't room for the church within the settlement. Its earliest features are its pillars—supporting a tower built much later—and its clerestory windows: both date from the 12th century. St. Nicholas was divided into east and west kirks at the Reformation, followed by a substantial amount of renovation from 1741 on. Some early memorials and other works have survived. ⊠ *Union St.* ☉ *Weekdays 10–1, Sun. for services.*

⑭ Satrosphere. The hands-on exhibits at Satrosphere bring science and technology to life. Children (and adults) of even the most unscientific bent love it. ⊠ *179 Constitution St.,* ☎ *01224/640340,* WEB *www.satrosphere. net.* 🎫 *£5.* ☉ *Mon.–Sat. 10–5, Sun. 11:30–5.*

⑲ Seaton Park. With its spring daffodils, tall trees, and boldly colored herbaceous borders, this park is typical of Aberdeen's exceptionally high standards of civic horticulture. The city is a frequent prizewinner in the annual Britain in Bloom contest. ⊠ *Don St., Old Aberdeen.*

② Tolbooth. The city was governed from this 17th-century building for 200 years. It was also the burgh court and jail. ⊠ *Castle St. View from outside only.*

⑰ **Town House.** This Georgian work, plain and handsome, incorporates parts of an earlier building from 1720. ⊠ *High St., Old Aberdeen. View from outside only.*

⑪ **Union Bridge.** Built in the early 19th century, as was much of Union Street, this bridge has a gentle rise—or descent, if you're traveling east— and the street is carried on a series of blind arches. The north side of Union Bridge is the most obvious reminder of the artificial raising of the grand thoroughfare's levels (despite appearances, you'll discover you're not at ground level). Much of the original work remains. ⊠ *Union St.*

① **Union Street.** This great thoroughfare is to Aberdeen what Princes Street is to Edinburgh: the central pivot of the city plan and the product of a wave of enthusiasm to rebuild the city in a contemporary style in the early 19th century.

⑩ **Union Terrace.** In the 19th-century development of Union Terrace stands a statue of Robert Burns (1759–96) addressing a daisy. Behind Burns are the **Union Terrace Gardens,** faintly echoing Edinburgh's Princes Street Gardens in that both separate the older part of the city, to the east, from the 19th-century development to the west. Most buildings around the grand-looking Caledonian Hotel are late Victorian.

OFF THE BEATEN PATH | **DUNNOTTAR CASTLE –** For an afternoon trip out from Aberdeen, it's hard to beat this magnificent cliff-top castle, which straddles a headland overlooking Stonehaven, 15 mi south of Aberdeen. Building began in the 14th century, when Sir William Keith, Marischal of Scotland (i.e., keeper of the king's mares and one of the king's right-hand men), decided to build a tower house as a status symbol to demonstrate his power. Subsequent generations continued to add on to the structure over the centuries, and important visitors included Mary, Queen of Scots. The castle is most famous for holding out for eight months against Oliver Cromwell's army in 1651–2, and thereby saving the Scottish crown jewels, which had been stored here for safekeeping. Reach the castle via the A90; take the Stonehaven turnoff and follow the signs. Wear sensible shoes to allow you to investigate the ruins thoroughly. ⊠ *Stonehaven,* ☎ *01569/762173.* ⊡ *£3.50.* ◷ *Easter–Oct., Mon.–Sat. 9–6, Sun. 2–5.*

Dining and Lodging

££–£££ | ✕ **Silver Darling.** Huge windows afford panoramic views of the harbor at the quayside Silver Darling, one of Aberdeen's most acclaimed restaurants. It specializes, as its name suggests, in fish (a silver darling is a herring). Try the ravioli with langoustine, mushrooms, samphire, and vanilla jus or the macadamia nut–crusted North Sea halibut with a spicy lemongrass-and-coconut emulsion. ⊠ *Pocra Quay, Footdee,* ☎ *01224/576229. Reservations essential. AE, DC, MC, V. Closed Sun. No lunch Sat.*

£ | ✕ **Lascala Ristorante.** Blue and red decor, lit with sparkling chandeliers, and plants everywhere set the scene for a classic Italian restaurant. Veal and fish are prominent on the menu, and the daily specials make the most of fresh produce. Reserve ahead, as the restaurant can get busy. ⊠ *51 Huntly St.,* ☎ *01224/626566. MC, V.*

£££–££££ | ⊞ **Marcliffe at Pitfodels.** This spacious country-house hotel in the West End combines old and new in the individually decorated rooms to impressive effect—some have reproduction antique furnishings, others are more modern. There are two restaurants: an informal conservatory dining area and the Invery, serving international fare with a Scottish flavor. ⊠ *N. Deeside Rd., Pitfodels, AB15 9YA,* ☎ *01224/861000,* FAX

01224/868860, WEB *www.marcliffe.com. 42 rooms. 2 restaurants; no a/c. AE, DC, MC, V.*

££–££££ 🏨 **Thistle Aberdeen Caledonian Hotel.** Well situated and offering pleasant views over city gardens, this is one of the city's larger hotels and is generally considered one of its best. Rooms are decorated in traditional style, and the pleasant restaurant serves tasty dishes from a menu best described as eclectic Scottish. Ask about special deals on the weekend (includes dinner and breakfast) available for two-night stays starting Friday or Saturday. ✉ *10–14 Union Terr., AB10 1WE,* ☎ *01224/640233,* FAX *01224/641627,* WEB *www.thistlehotels.com. 76 rooms. 2 restaurants, bar, coffee shop; no a/c. AE, DC, MC, V.*

££ 🏨 **Atholl Hotel.** The granite Atholl, with its many turrets and gables, is set in a leafy residential area to the west of the city. Rooms are done in rich, dark colors; if space is more important than a view, opt for a room on the first floor. The restaurant prepares such traditional Scottish dishes as lamb cutlets and roasted rib of beef. ✉ *54 Kings Gate, AB15 4YN,* ☎ *01224/323505,* FAX *01224/321555,* WEB *www.atholl-aberdeen.com. 35 rooms. Restaurant; no a/c. AE, DC, MC, V.*

££ 🏨 **Craighaar Hotel.** Perhaps because it's convenient to the airport, the Craighaar is popular with businesspeople. A rustic cinnamon and terra-cotta color scheme and modern teak furnishings decorate the hotel. The gallery suites—split-level rooms—are outstanding. The restaurant's menu has a Scottish slant, with dishes such as lamb with an herb crust, whisky-and-mint sauce, and *skirlie* (oatmeal-stuffed) tomato. ✉ *Waterton Rd., Bankhead, AB21 9HS,* ☎ *01224/712275,* FAX *01224/716362,* WEB *www.craighaar.co.uk. 55 rooms. Restaurant, bar; no a/c. AE, DC, MC, V.*

£–££ 🏨 **Palm Court.** The Palm Court is slightly removed from the city center and is therefore quieter, with high standards of accommodation and service. Rooms, though not especially spacious, are attractively furnished with warm, floral color schemes. Traditional Scottish meals are served in the Conservatory, where your attention may well be distracted from a plate of fresh salmon or roasted chicken by the wealth of decorative artifacts surrounding you. Ask about the special weekend rates. ✉ *81 Seafield Rd., AB15 7YX,* ☎ *01224/310351,* FAX *01224/312707. 24 rooms. Restaurant, bar; no a/c. AE, DC, MC, V.*

Nightlife and the Arts

In part because of the oil-industry boom, Aberdeen has a fairly lively nightlife scene, though much of it revolves around pubs and hotels; theaters, concert halls, arts centers, and cinemas are also well represented. The principal newspapers—the *Press and Journal* and the *Evening Express*—and *Aberdeen Leopard* magazine can fill you in on what's going on anywhere in the northeast. Aberdeen's tourist information center has a monthly publication with an events calendar as well as contact phone numbers.

The Arts

ARTS CENTERS
Aberdeen Arts Centre (✉ 33 King St., ☎ 01224/635208) hosts experimental plays, poetry readings, exhibitions by local and Scottish artists, and many other arts presentations. At **Haddo House** (✉ Off B9005 near Methlick, ☎ 01651/851770), 20 mi north of Aberdeen, the Haddo House Arts Trust runs a mixed-bag of events, from opera and ballet to Shakespeare, Scots-language plays, and puppetry. The **Lemon Tree** (✉ 5 W. North St., ☎ 01224/642230) has an innovative and international program of dance, stand-up comedy, folk, jazz, rock and roll, and art exhibitions.

CONCERT HALL

The **Music Hall** (✉ Union St., ☎ 01224/641122) presents seasonal programs of concerts by the Scottish National Orchestra, the Scottish Chamber Orchestra, and other major groups. Its events also includes folk concerts, crafts fairs, and exhibitions.

DANCE

Many avant-garde dance companies perform at the popular **Aberdeen Arts Centre** (✉ 33 King St., ☎ 01224/635208). **His Majesty's Theatre** (✉ Rosemount Viaduct, ☎ 01224/637788) is a regular venue for classical and modern ballet, as well as musicals.

FESTIVALS

August sees the world-renowned **Aberdeen International Youth Festival** (box office, ✉ Music Hall, Union St., ☎ 01224/641122), which attracts youth orchestras, choirs, dance troupes, and theater companies from many countries. During the festival some companies take their productions to other venues in the northeast.

FILM

The following cinemas show general-release films. **The Belmont** (✉ 49 Belmont St., ☎ 01224/343536). **UGC Cinemas** (✉ Queen's Link Leisure Park, Links Rd., ☎ 0870/155–0502).

OPERA

Haddo House Arts Trust (✉ Off B9005 near Methlick, ☎ 01651/851770) presents an enterprising mix of semiprofessional and professional productions. **His Majesty's Theatre** (✉ Rosemount Viaduct, ☎ 01224/637788) hosts operatic performances once or twice a year.

THEATER

At **His Majesty's Theatre** (✉ Rosemount Viaduct, ☎ 01224/637788), shows are presented throughout the year, many of them in advance of their official opening in London's West End.

Nightlife

CASINO

If you're interested in trying your luck at the gaming tables, you can place bets at the **Gala Casino** (✉ 59 Summer St., ☎ 01224/645273). Membership is granted within 24 hours.

DANCE CLUBS

Most clubs don't allow jeans or sneakers, and it's best to check beforehand that a particular dance club is not closed for a private function. **Cotton Club** (✉ 491 Union St., ☎ 01224/581858), though a bit dingy, is always busy with a young clientele in the 18–30 age range. The popular front bar is cheerfully noisy with karaoke performers. **Franklyn's** (✉ 44 Justice Mill La., ☎ 01224/212817) is popular with a very varied age group, but predominantly the over 21s. The somewhat upscale **G's Nightclub** (✉ 70–78 Chapel St., ☎ 01224/642112) is where professionals 18–30 come to let down their hair. Locals age 20–50 dance the night away at **Hotel Metro** (✉ 17 Market St., ☎ 01224/583275).

MUSIC CLUBS

The **Lemon Tree** (✉ 5 W. North St., ☎ 01224/642230), with a wide-ranging music program, is the main rock venue and stages frequent jazz events. There's live music on Saturday night at the **Masada Bar** (✉ Rosemount Viaduct, ☎ 01224/641587).

Outdoor Activities and Sports

Biking
The tourist information center can provide a leaflet with suggestions for cycle tours. The average rate for a mountain bike is £15 a day. **Alpine Bikes** (⊠ 70 Holburn St., ☎ 01224/211455) rents mountain bikes.

Golf
The following courses in and around Aberdeen are open to visitors. **Auchmill** (☎ 01224/714577): 18 holes, 5,123 yards, SSS 67. **Balgownie, Royal Aberdeen Golf Club** (⊠ Links Rd., Bridge of Don, ☎ 01224/702571): 18 holes, 6,415 yards, SSS 70. **Balnagask** (⊠ St. Fitticks Rd., ☎ 01224/876407): 18 holes, 6,065 yards, SSS 69. **Hazlehead** (☎ 01224/321830): Course 1: 18 holes, 6,204 yards, SSS 70; Course 2: 18 holes, 5,742 yards, SSS 68; Course 3: 9 holes, 2,770 yards, SSS 35. **Kings Links** (☎ 01224/632269): 18 holes, 6,384 yards, SSS 71. **Murcar** (⊠ Bridge of Don, ☎ 01224/704354): 18 holes, 6,241 yards, SSS 71. **Westhill** (☎ 01224/742567): 18 holes, 5,849 yards, SSS 69.

Shopping

Department Stores
You'll find most of the large national department stores in the Bon Accord, St. Nicholas, and Trinity shopping malls or along Union Street.

The spacious **John Lewis** store (⊠ George St., reached via Bon Accord Centre, ☎ 01224/625000; closed Mon.) closely resembles a double-decker sandwich with its filling illuminated. It has clothing, household items, giftware, and much more. **Esslemont & Macintosh** (⊠ 26 Union St., ☎ 01224/647331) is a long-established Aberdeen store. The favorite haunt of well-off ladies who lunch, it has an excellent stock of upscale clothing and accessories, cosmetics, and furniture.

Specialty Shops
There are clusters of small specialty shops in the **Chapel Street–Thistle Street** area at the west end of **Union Street** and on the latter's north side.

ANTIQUES
Colin Wood (⊠ 25 Rose St., ☎ 01224/643019) is the place to go for small antiques, Scottish maps, and prints.

BOOKS
At the **Aberdeen Family History Society Shop** (⊠ 158–164 King St., ☎ 01224/646323) you can browse through publications related to local history and genealogical research. For a small fee the Aberdeen & North East Family History Society will undertake some research on your behalf.

GIFTS
Nova (⊠ 20 Chapel St., ☎ 01224/641270), where the locals go for gifts, stocks major U.K. brand names, such as Neal's Yard, Dartington Glass, and Crabtree and Evelyn, as well as Scottish silver jewelry.

TOYS
The **Early Learning Centre** (⊠ Bon-Accord Centre, George St., ☎ 01224/624188) specializes in toys with educational value. The **Toy Bazaar** (⊠ 45 Schoolhill, ☎ 01224/640021) stocks toys for children preschool age and up.

ROYAL DEESIDE AND CASTLE COUNTRY

Deeside, the valley running west from Aberdeen down which the River Dee flows, earned its "royal" appellation when discovered by Queen Victoria. To this day, where royalty goes, lesser aristocracy and freshly minted millionaires follow. It's still the aspiration of many to own a grand shooting estate in Deeside. In a sense this yearning is understandable because piney hill slope, purple moor, and blue river intermingle tastefully here. Royal Deeside's gradual scenic change adds a growing sense of excitement as you travel deeper into the Grampians.

There are castles along the Dee as well as to the north in Castle Country, a region that also illustrates the gradual geological change in the northeast: uplands lapped by a tide of farms. All the Donside and Deeside castles are picturesquely sited, with most fitted out with tall slender turrets, winding stairs, and crooked chambers that epitomize Scottish baronial. All have tales of ghosts and bloodshed, siege and torture. Many were tidied up and "domesticated" during the 19th century. Although best toured by car, much of this area is accessible either by public transportation or on tours from Aberdeen.

Drum Castle

㉑ *11 mi west of Aberdeen.*

Drum Castle is a foursquare tower that dates from the 13th century, with later additions. Note the tower's rounded corners, said to make battering-ram attacks more difficult. Nearby, fragments of the ancient Forest of Drum still stand, dating from the days when Scotland was covered by great woodlands of oak and pine. The Garden of Historic Roses lays claim to some old-fashioned roses not commonly seen today. ⊠ *Off A93,* ☎ *01330/811204,* 🕸 *www.nts.org.uk.* 🎫 *Castle and garden £7, grounds and garden £1.60.* ⊘ *Castle and garden Apr.–June and Sept.–Oct., daily noon–5; July–Aug., daily 10–6; grounds daily 9:30–dusk.*

Crathes Castle

㉒ *5 mi west of Drum Castle, 16 mi west of Aberdeen.*

Crathes Castle was once the home of the Burnett family. Keepers of the Forest of Drum for generations, the family acquired lands here by marriage and later built a new castle, completed in 1596. Crathes is in the care of the National Trust for Scotland; the trust also looks after the grand gardens, with their calculated symmetry and clipped yew hedges. Sample the tasty home baking in the tearoom. ⊠ *Off A93, 3½ mi east of Banchory,* ☎ *01330/844525,* 🕸 *www.nts.org.uk.* 🎫 *Castle or walled garden £5; castle, garden, and grounds £8.50.* ⊘ *Castle Apr.–Oct., daily 10–5:30, last admission 4:45; visitor center, restaurant, and shop also open late Jan.–Mar. and Nov.–late Dec., Wed.–Sun. 10–5:30; garden and grounds daily 9–dusk.*

Banchory

㉓ *3 mi west of Crathes Castle, 19 mi west of Aberdeen via A93.*

Banchory is an immaculate place with a pinkish tinge to its granite. It's usually bustling with ice-cream-eating strollers, out on a day trip from Aberdeen. If you visit in autumn and have time to spare, drive for a mile along the B974 south of Banchory to the **Brig o'Feuch** (pronounced fyooch, the *ch* as in loch). The area around this bridge is very pleasant: salmon leap in season, and the fall colors and foaming waters make for an attractive scene.

Dining and Lodging

££–£££ ╳⊞ **Banchory Lodge.** With the River Dee running past at the bottom of the garden just a few yards away, tranquil Banchory Lodge is an ideal spot for anglers. This 17th-century country house has retained its period charm. Rooms are individually decorated, though all have bold color schemes and tartan or floral fabrics. The restaurant (££) has high standards for its Scottish cuisine with French overtones; try the fillet of salmon, roasted duckling, or guinea fowl with wild berries. ⊠ *Banchory, Kincardineshire AB31 5HS,* ☎ *01330/822625,* ꜰᴀˣ *01330/ 825019,* ᵂᴱᴮ *www.banchorylodge.co.uk. 22 rooms. Restaurant, fishing, bicycles; no a/c. AE, DC, MC, V.*

Kincardine O'Neill

㉔ *9 mi west of Banchory.*

The ruined kirk in the little village of Kincardine O'Neill was built in 1233 and once sheltered travelers: it was the last hospice before the Mounth, the name given to the massif that shuts off the south side of the Dee Valley. Beyond Banchory (and the B974), no motor roads run south until you reach Braemar (A93), though the Mounth is crossed by a network of tracks once used by Scottish soldiers, invading armies (including the Romans), and cattle drovers. Photography buffs won't want to miss the bridge at Potarch, just to the east.

Aboyne

㉕ *5 mi west of Kincardine O'Neill.*

Aboyne is a pleasant, well-laid-out town, with a village green (unusual for Scotland) that hosts an annual Highland Games. However, there's not a lot to detain you here, except a good coffee shop. The **Braeloine Interpretative Centre,** in Glen Tanar beyond Aboyne, has a natural history display, café, picnic area, and walks. ⊠ *Glen Tanar; cross River Dee, take right on B976, and left into glen,* ☎ *013398/86072.* ☉ *Apr.–Sept., Wed.–Mon. 10–5; Oct.–Mar., Thurs.–Mon. 10–5.*

OFF THE BEATEN PATH **QUEEN'S VIEW –** This is one of the most spectacular vistas in northeast Scotland, stretching across the Howe of Cromar to Lochnagar. From Aboyne, turn due north on B9094, then left onto B9119 for 6 mi.

Dining

£ ╳ **At the Sign of the Blackfaced Sheep.** Filled rolls, soups, salads, steak sandwiches, and delicious home-baked goods are served here, but another good reason to visit is the upscale gifts and paintings that you can buy in this coffee and crafts shop. ⊠ *Ballater Rd.,* ☎ *013398/87311. MC, V.*

En Route   Look for a large granite boulder next to the A93 on which is carved ʏᴏᴜ ᴀʀᴇ ɴᴏᴡ ᴇɴᴛᴇʀɪɴɢ ᴛʜᴇ ʜɪɢʜʟᴀɴᴅs. You may find this piece of information superfluous, given the quality of the scenery.

Ballater

㉖ *12 mi west of Aboyne, 43 mi west of Aberdeen.*

The handsome holiday resort of Ballater, once noted for the curative properties of its local well, has profited from the proximity of the royals, nearby at Balmoral. You might be amused by the array of ʙʏ ʀᴏʏᴀʟ ᴀᴘᴘᴏɪɴᴛᴍᴇɴᴛ signs proudly hanging from many of its various shops (even monarchs need bakers and butchers). Take time to stroll around this well-laid-out community. Note that the railway station now houses the tourist information center and a display on the glories of the Great North of Scotland branch line, closed in the 1960s along with so many others in this country.

★ As long as you have your own car, you can capture the feel of the eastern Highlands yet still be close to town. Start your expedition into **Glen Muick** (Gaelic for pig, pronounced mick) by crossing the River Dee and turning upriver on the south side, shortly after the road forks. The native red deer are quite common throughout the Scottish Highlands, but the flat valley floor here is one of the very best places to see them. Beyond the lower glen, the prospect opens to reveal not only grazing herds but also fine views of the battlement of cliffs edging the mountain called Lochnagar.

Dining and Lodging

£££–££££ ✕🏨 **Hilton Craigendarroch Hotel.** This magnificent country-house hotel, just outside Ballater on a hillside overlooking the River Dee, manages to keep everyone happy. You're cosseted in luxurious surroundings with many facilities. An even better value are the pine lodges set among the trees around the hotel. These self-catering cottages are geared for families and fitted with every kind of labor-saving appliance. Among the on-site restaurants are the Oaks, for modern Scottish à la carte, and the Clubhouse poolside brasserie. ⊠ *Braemar Rd., Ballater AB35 5XA,* ☎ *013397/55858,* ℻ *013397/55447,* 🌐 *www.hilton.com. 39 rooms, 6 suites. 2 restaurants, tennis court, 2 pools, wading pool, gym, hair salón, hot tub, sauna, squash; no a/c. AE, DC, MC, V.*

££–££££ ✕🏨 **Darroch Learg Hotel.** Amid tall trees on a hillside, the Darroch Learg is everything a Victorian Scottish country house should be. Most guest rooms are decorated with mahogany furniture and designer fabrics in rich colors. The Scottish food in the conservatory restaurant (££££) is sophisticated but also substantial, with the rich flavors of local beef and fish. Note that the less expensive rooms are in the neighboring annex, Oak Hall, another handsome Victorian house. ⊠ *Braemar Rd., Ballater, AB35 5UX,* ☎ *013397/55443,* ℻ *013397/55252. 18 rooms. Restaurant; no a/c. AE, DC, MC, V. Closed Jan.*

£££ ✕🏨 **Balgonie Country House.** A tranquil Edwardian country house on 3 acres of gardens overlooking Ballater's golf course, Balgonie delivers top-quality food and accommodations at real value-for-money prices. Bedrooms are individually decorated in soft greens, blues, or pinks, with either antique furniture or, in the attic rooms, modern Swedish-style furniture. The dining room (££££) is a peaceful setting for a four-course meal of classic French cuisine. ⊠ *Braemar Pl., Ballater AB35 5NQ,* ☎ ℻ *013397/55482,* 🌐 *www.royaldeesidehotels. com. 9 rooms. No a/c. AE, DC, MC, V. Closed Jan.–mid-Feb.*

Shopping

At either of **Countrywear**'s shops (⊠ 15 and 35 Bridge St., ☎ 013397/ 55453), you'll find everything you need for Highland country living, including fishing tackle, tweeds, children's clothes, and that flexible garment popular in Scotland between seasons: the body warmer.

Head to the **Clothes Shop** (⊠ 1 Braemar Rd., ☎ 013397/55947) for fleeces and waterproofs to keep you dry on the hills. For a low-cost gift you could always see what's being boiled up at **Dee Valley Confectioners** (⊠ Station Sq., ☎ 013397/55499). The **McEwan Gallery** (⊠ On A939, 1 mi west of Ballater, ☎ 013397/55429) displays fine paintings, watercolors, prints, and books (many with a Scottish or golf theme) in an unusual house built by the Swiss artist Rudolphe Christen in 1902.

Balmoral Castle

 7 mi west of Ballater.

The enormous parking lot is indicative of the popularity of Balmoral Castle, one of Queen Elizabeth II's favorite family retreats. Balmoral is a Victorian fantasy, designed, in fact, for Queen Victoria (1819–1901) by her consort, Prince Albert (1819–61) in 1855. "It seems like a dream to be here in our dear Highland Home again," Queen Victoria wrote. "Every year my heart becomes more fixed in this dear Paradise." Balmoral's visiting hours depend on whether the royals are in residence. In truth, there are more interesting and historic buildings to explore, as the only part of the castle on view is the ballroom, with an exhibition of royal artifacts. The Carriage Hall has displays of commemorative china, carriages, and native wildlife. Perhaps it's just as well that most of the house is closed to the public, for Balmoral suffers from a bad rash of tartanitis. Thanks to Victoria and Albert, stags' heads abounded, the bagpipes wailed incessantly, and the garish Stuart tartan was used for every item of furnishings, from carpets to chair covers. A more somber Duff tartan, black and green to blend with the environment, was later adopted, and from the brief glimpse you may get of Balmoral's interior, it's clear that royal taste is now more restrained. Queen Elizabeth II, however, follows her predecessors' routine in spending a holiday of about six weeks in Deeside, usually from mid-August to the end of September. During this time Balmoral is closed to visitors.

Victoria loved Balmoral more for its setting than its house, so be sure to take in its pleasant gardens. Year by year Victoria and Albert added to the estate, taking over neighboring houses, securing the forest and moorland around it, and developing deer stalking and grouse shooting here. In consequence, Balmoral is now a large property, as the grounds run 12 mi along the Deeside road. Its privacy is protected by belts of pinewood, and the only view of the castle from the A93 is a partial one, from a point near Inver, 2 mi west of the gates. But there's an excellent bird's-eye view of it from an old military road, now the A939, which climbs out of Crathie, northbound for Cockbridge and the Don Valley. This view embraces the summit of Lochnagar (3,786 ft), in whose *corries* (hollows) the snow lies year-round. Around and about Balmoral are some notable spots—Cairn O'Mount, Cambus O'May, and the Cairngorms from the Linn of Dee—and some of them may be seen on pony-trekking expeditions, which use Balmoral stalking ponies and go around the grounds and estate. Note that when the royals are in residence, even the grounds are closed to the public. ⊠ *A93,* ☎ *013397/ 42334,* WEB *www.balmoralcastle.com.* ⊡ *£4.50.* ☉ *Apr.–July, daily 10– 5; last admission at 4.*

En Route As you continue west into Highland scenery, further pine-framed glimpses appear of the "steep frowning glories of dark Lochnagar," as it was described by the poet Lord Byron (1788–1824). Lochnagar (3,786 ft) was made known to an audience wider than hill walkers by the Prince of Wales, who published a children's story, *The Old Man of Lochnagar.*

Braemar

17 mi west of Ballater, 60 mi west of Aberdeen, 51 mi north of Perth via A93.

The village of Braemar is associated with the Braemar Highland Gathering, held every September. Although there are many such gatherings celebrated throughout Scotland, this one is distinguished by the presence of the royal family. You can find out more about the event at the **Braemar Highland Heritage Centre,** in a converted stable block in the middle of town. It tells the history of the village with displays and a film, and it also has a gift shop. ⊠ *The Mews, Mar Rd.,* ☎ *013397/41944.* 🖾 *Free.* ☉ *Daily 9–5, extended hrs in summer; closed for lunch-hr in winter.*

(28) Braemar is dominated by **Braemar Castle** on its outskirts. The castle dates from the 17th century, although its defensive walls, designed in the shape of a pointed star, came later. At Braemar (the *braes,* or slopes, of the district of Mar) the standard, or rebel flag, was first raised at the start of the spectacularly unsuccessful Jacobite Rebellion of 1715. Thirty years later, during the last rebellion, Braemar Castle was strengthened and garrisoned by Hanoverian (government) troops. ⊠ *Braemar,* ☎ *013397/41219,* ⟨WEB⟩ *www.information-britain.co.uk.* 🖾 *£3.50.* ☉ *Apr.–June and Sept.–Oct., Mon.–Thurs., Sat. and Sun. 10–6; July–Aug., daily 10–6.*

OFF THE
BEATEN PATH

LINN OF DEE – Although the main A93 slinks off to the south from Braemar, a little unmarked road will take you farther west into the hilly heartland. In fact, even if you do not have your own car, you can still explore this area by catching the post bus that leaves from the Braemar post office once a day. The road offers views over the winding River Dee and the blue hills before passing through the tiny hamlet of Inverey and crossing a bridge at the Linn of Dee. *Linn* is a Scots word meaning "rocky narrows," and the river's gash here is deep and roaring. Park beyond the bridge and walk back to admire the sylvan setting.

Dining and Lodging

££ ✕🖾 **Invercauld Arms.** This handsome stone Victorian hotel in the center of Braemar makes a good base for exploring Royal Deeside. The entrance lounge, with plush sofas and elegant velvet chairs, leads to beautifully restored public rooms and to comfortable guest rooms with floral drapes and reproduction antique furniture. The restaurant serves international fare with a Scottish touch. Dishes might include Aberdeen Angus steak with tomato and wild-mushroom sauce or chicken with bean sprouts and water chestnuts in oyster sauce. ⊠ *Braemar AB35 5YR,* ☎ *013397/41605,* 𝖥𝖠𝖷 *013397/41428,* ⟨WEB⟩ *www.peelhotels.com. 68 rooms. Restaurant, bar; no a/c. AE, DC, MC, V.*

Outdoor Activities and Sports

Braemar has a tricky 18-hole **golf course** (⊠ Cluny Bank Rd., ☎ 013397/41618) laden with foaming waters. Erratic duffers take note: the compassionate course managers have installed, near the water, poles with little nets on the end for those occasional shots that may go awry.

En Route From Braemar retrace the A93 as far as Balmoral. From Balmoral look for a narrow road going north, signposted B976. Be careful on the first twisting mile through the trees. You'll soon emerge from scattered pines into the open moor in upland Aberdeenshire. Behind is the massif of Lochnagar again, and to the west are snow-tipped domes of the big Cairngorms. Roll down to a bridge and go left on the A939, which comes in from Ballater. Another high moor section follows: as the road leaves the scattered buildings by the bridge, see if you can spot the roadside inscription to the company of soldiers who built the A939 in the 18th century.

Corgarff Castle

㉙ *23 mi northeast of Braemar, 14 mi northwest of Ballater.*

Eighteenth-century soldiers paved a military highway, now the A939, north from Ballater to Corgarff Castle, a lonely tower house with star-shape defensive wall—a curious replica of Braemar Castle. Corgarff was built as a hunting seat for the earls of Mar in the 16th century. After an eventful history that included the wife of a later laird being burned alive in a family dispute, the castle ended its career as a garrison for Hanoverian troops. The troops were responsible for preventing illegal whisky distilling. ✉ *Signposted off A939*, ☎ *0131/668–8800*, 🌐 *www.historic-scotland.gov.uk*. 🎟 *£2.80.* ☼ *Apr.–Sept., daily 9:30–6; Oct.–Mar., Sat. 9:30–4, Sun. 2–4.*

En Route   If you return east from Corgarff Castle to the A939/A944 junction and make a left onto the A944, the thorough castle signposting indicates you are on the **Castle Trail.** The A944 meanders along the River Don to the village of Strathdon, where a great mound by the roadside—on the left—turns out to be a *motte*, or the base of a wooden castle, built in the late 12th century. Although it takes considerable imagination to become enthusiastic about a great grass-covered heap, surviving mottes have contributed greatly to the understanding of the history of Scottish castles. The A944 then joins the A97 (go left), and just a few minutes later a sign points to Glenbuchat Castle, a plain Z-plan tower house.

Kildrummy Castle

★ **㉚** *18 mi northeast of Corgarff, 23 mi north of Ballater, 22 mi north of Aboyne.*

Kildrummy Castle is significant because of its age—it dates to the 13th century—and because it has ties to the mainstream medieval traditions of European castle building. It shares features with Harlech and Caernarfon, in Wales, as well as with Château de Coucy, near Laon, France. Kildrummy underwent several expansions at the hands of England's King Edward I (1239–1307); the castle was back in Scottish hands in 1306, when it was besieged by King Edward I's son. The defenders were betrayed by a certain Osbarn the Smith, who was promised a large amount of gold by the English forces. They gave it to him after the castle fell, pouring it molten down his throat, or so the ghoulish story goes. Kildrummy's prominence ended after the collapse of the 1715 Jacobite uprising. It had been the rebel headquarters and was consequently dismantled. ✉ *A97*, ☎ *0131/668–8800*, 🌐 *www.historic-scotland. gov.uk*. 🎟 *£2.* ☼ *Apr.–Sept., daily 9:30–6.*

Kildrummy Castle Gardens, behind the castle and with a separate entrance from the main road, are built in what was the original quarry for the castle. This sheltered bowl within the woodlands has a broad range of shrubs and alpine plants and a notable water garden. ✉ *A97*, ☎ *019755/71203 or 019755/71277.* 🎟 *£2.50.* ☼ *Apr.–Oct., daily 10–5; call to confirm opening times late in season.*

Dining and Lodging

£££–££££   ✕🏨 **Kildrummy Castle Hotel.** A grand late-Victorian country house, ★ this hotel offers a peaceful stay and attentive service. Oak paneling, beautiful plasterwork, and gentle color schemes create a serene environment, enhanced by the views of Kildrummy Castle Gardens next door. The Scottish cuisine (££–£££) uses local game as well as seafood. ✉ *Kildrummy, by Alford, Aberdeenshire AB33 8RA*, ☎ *019755/ 71288*, FAX *019755/71345*, 🌐 *www.kildrummycastlehotel.co.uk.* 16 rooms. Restaurant, fishing; no a/c. AE, MC, V. Closed Jan.

Alford

9 mi east of Kildrummy, 28 mi west of Aberdeen.

(31) A plain and sturdy settlement in the Howe (Hollow) of Alford, this town gives those who have grown somewhat weary of castle hopping a break: it has a museum instead. The **Grampian Transport Museum** specializes in road-based means of locomotion, backed up by a library and archives. One of its more unusual exhibits is the *Craigievar Express,* a steam-driven creation invented by the local postman to deliver mail more efficiently. ✉ *Alford,* ☎ *019755/62292,* WEB *www.gtm.org.uk.* ⊡ *£4.* ⊙ *Apr.–Oct., daily 10–5.*

Craigievar Castle

★ **(32)** *5 mi south of Alford.*

Craigievar Castle is much as the stonemasons left it in 1626, with its pepper-pot turrets and towers. It was built in relatively peaceful times by William Forbes, a successful merchant in trade with the Baltic Sea ports (hence he was also known as Danzig Willie). Centuries of care and wise stewardship have ensured that the experience is as authentic as possible. ✉ *5 mi south of Alford on A980,* ☎ *013398/83635,* WEB *www. nts.org.uk.* ⊡ *Castle and grounds £8.50, grounds only, £1.* ⊙ *Castle Apr.–Oct., Thurs.–Mon. noon–5; grounds daily 9:30–sunset.*

Castle Fraser

(33) *8 mi southeast of Alford.*

The massive Castle Fraser, southeast of Alford, is the largest of the castles of Mar. Although it shows a variety of styles reflecting the taste of its owners from the 15th through the 19th centuries, its design is typical of the cavalcade of castles that exist here in the northeast, and for good reason, as this—along with many other of the region's castles, including Midmar, Craigievar, Crathes, and Glenbuchat—was designed by a family of master masons called Bell. Castle Fraser has the further advantages of a walled garden, picnic area, and tearoom. ✉ *8 mi southeast of Alford off A944,* ☎ *01330/833463,* WEB *www.nts.org.uk.* ⊡ *£7.* ⊙ *Castle mid-Apr.–June and Sept.–Oct., Thurs.–Mon. noon–5; July–Aug., daily 10–5; gardens daily 9:30–6; grounds daily 9:30–sunset.*

THE NORTHEAST

This route starts inland, traveling toward Speyside—the valley, or strath, of the River Spey—famed for its whisky distilleries, which it promotes in yet another signposted trail. Distilling scotch is not an intrinsically spectacular process. It involves pure water, malted barley, and sometimes peat smoke, then a lot of bubbling and fermentation, all of which cause a number of odd smells. The result is a prestigious product with a fascinating range of flavors that you either enjoy immensely or not at all.

Instead of assiduously following the Whisky Trail, just dip into it and blend it with some other aspects of the lower end of Speyside—the county of Moray. Whisky notwithstanding, Moray's scenic qualities, low rainfall, and other reassuring weather statistics are also worth remembering. The suggested route then allows you to sample the northeastern seaboard, including some of the best but least-known coastal scenery in Scotland.

The Northeast

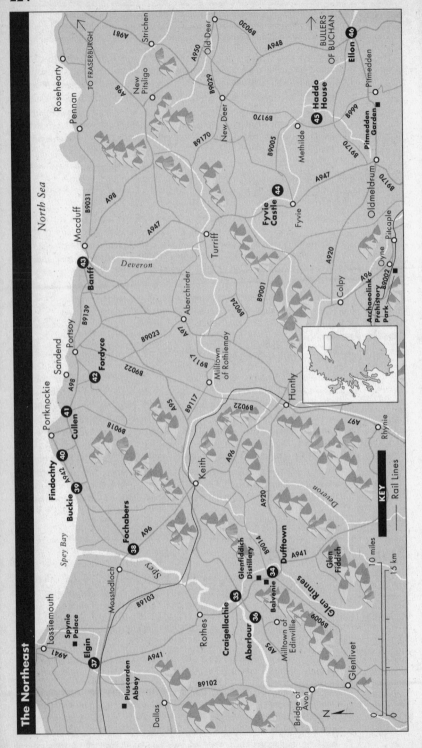

North Sea

Rosehearty
Pennan
TO FRASERBURGH
A98
A981
Strichen
New Pitsligo
A950
Old Deer
B9030
A948
BULLERS OF BUCHAN
Ellon **46**
Pitmedden
A948
B9029
New Deer
B9170
A999
Methlick
B9005
Haddo House **45**
A947
Pitmedden Garden
B9170
Oldmeldrum
B9170
Macduff
A98
B9031
A947
Turriff
Deveron
B9001
Aberchirder
B9025
A947
Fyvie Castle **44**
Fyvie
A920
Colpy
A96
Oyne
B9002
Archaeolink Prehistory Park
Picaple
Banff **43**
Portsoy
B9139
Sandend
B9023
A97
B9117
Milltown of Rothiemay
B9022
Huntly
Rhynie
A97
Fordyce **42**
B9022
A98
A95
B9117
Cullen **41**
Portknockie
B9018
Keith
A96
B9022
Deveron
Findochty **40**
A942
Buckie **39**
Fochabers **38**
A96
Spey Bay
Spey
Mosstodloch
B9103
Lossiemouth
Spynie Palace
A941
Elgin **37**
Pluscarden Abbey
B9102
Dallas
Rothes
A941
Craigellachie **35**
Aberlour **36**
A95
Milltown of Edinville
Glenfiddich Distillery
Dufftown **34**
B9014
Balvenie
A941
Glen Fiddich
Glen Rinnes
B9009
Glenlivet
Bridge of Avon

KEY
Rail Lines

10 miles
15 km

N

Dufftown

★ ㉞ *54 mi from Aberdeen via A96 and A920 (turn west at Huntly).*

On one of the Spey tributaries, Dufftown was planned in 1817 by the earl of Fife. One of the most famous malt whiskies of all is distilled at **Glenfiddich Distillery.** The independent company of William Grant and Sons Limited was the first to realize the tourist potential of the distilling process. It subsequently built an entertaining visitor center in addition to offering tours. If you intend to visit a distillery, it may as well be Glenfiddich. The audiovisual show and displays are as worthwhile as the tour, and the traditional stone-walled premises with the typical pagoda-roof malting buildings are pleasant. You don't have to like whisky to come away feeling you've learned something about a leading Scottish export. ⊠ *North of Dufftown on A941,* ☎ *01340/ 820373.* 🎫 *Free.* ☉ *Easter–mid-Oct., Mon.–Sat. 9:30–4:30, Sun. noon–4:30; mid-Oct.–Easter, weekdays 9:30–4:30.*

On a mound just above the Glenfiddich Distillery is a grim, gray, and squat curtain-walled castle, **Balvenie.** This fortress, which dates from the 13th century, once commanded the glens and passes toward Speyside and Elgin. ⊠ *Dufftown,* ☎ *0131/668–8800.* 🎫 *£1.50.* ☉ *Apr.– Sept., daily 9:30–6.*

In the center of Dufftown, the conspicuous battlemented **clock tower**— the centerpiece of the planned town and a former jail—houses a local museum open in summer. **Mortlach Church,** set in a hollow by the Dullan Water, is thought to be one of Scotland's oldest Christian sites, perhaps founded by St. Moluag, a contemporary of St. Columba, as early as AD 566. Note the weathered Pictish cross in the churchyard and the even older stone under cover in the vestibule, with a strange Pictish elephantlike beast carved on it. Though much of the church was rebuilt after 1876, some early work survives, including three lancet windows from the 13th century and a leper's squint (a hole extended to the outside of the church so that lepers could hear the service but be kept away from the rest of the congregation).

Craigellachie

㉟ *4 mi northwest of Dufftown via A941.*

Renowned as an angling resort, Craigellachie, like so many Speyside settlements, is sometimes enveloped in the malty reek of the local industry. Just before the village you'll notice the huge **Speyside Cooperage and Visitor Centre,** where you can watch craftspeople make and repair barrels. ⊠ *Dufftown Rd.,* ☎ *01340/871108.* 🎫 *£2.95.* ☉ *Jan.– mid-Dec., weekdays 9:30–4:30.*

The Spey itself is crossed by a handsome **suspension bridge,** designed by Thomas Telford (1757–1834) in 1814 and now bypassed by the modern road.

Aberlour

㊱ *2 mi southwest of Craigellachie via A95.*

Aberlour, often listed as Charlestown of Aberlour on maps, is a handsome little burgh, essentially Victorian in style, though actually founded in 1812 by the local landowner. Glenfarclas, Cragganmore, and Aberlour are the names of the noted local whiskies. If you're interested in something nonalcoholic, take a look at the **Village Store.** After the owners retired in 1978, the shop was locked away intact, complete with stock. In the late 1980s new owners discovered they had bought a time capsule—products dating from the early decades of the 20th century—as well as all the paraphernalia, books and ledgers, and notes of a country business. Part of the premises is now a gift shop, but the remainder is preserved for you to enjoy, with stock of a bygone era on the shelves. ⊠ *76 High St.,* ☎ *01340/871243.* 🎟 *Free.* ⊙ *Feb.–Dec., Mon.–Sat. 10–5, Sun. 1:30–5.*

Dining and Lodging

£   ✕ **Old Pantry.** This corner restaurant, overlooking Aberlour's pleasant, tree-shaded central square, serves everything from a cup of coffee with a sticky cake to a three-course spread of soup, roast meat, and traditional pudding. ⊠ *The Square,* ☎ *01340/871617. MC, V.*

£££   ✕🏠 **Minmore House.** Minmore retains a strong private-house feel:
★   faded chintz in the drawing room (where afternoon tea is served) and a paneled library (now housing a bar with more than 80 malt whiskies) are complemented by comfortable guest rooms, with an eclectic mix of antiques. The restaurant (££££) serves exceptional modern Scottish dishes, including fillet of Aberdeen Angus beef. The Speyside Way long-distance footpath passes below the house, and the area is famous for bird-watching. Take the A95 south from Aberlour, then turn left on the B9008 at Bridge of Avon. ⊠ *Glenlivet, Ballindalloch, Banffshire AB37 9DB,* ☎ *01807/590378,* 𝖥𝖠𝖷 *01807/590472. 10 rooms. Restaurant, bar; no a/c, no room TVs. MC, V. Closed Nov. and Feb.*

Elgin

㊲   *16 mi north of Aberlour via A941, 69 mi northwest of Aberdeen, 41 mi east of Inverness via A96.*

As the center of the fertile Laigh (low-lying lands) of Moray, Elgin has been of local importance for centuries. Like Aberdeen, it's self-supporting and previously remote, sheltered by great hills to the south and lying between two major rivers, the Spey and the Findhorn. Beginning in the 13th century, Elgin became an important religious center, a cathedral city with a walled town growing up around the cathedral and adjacent to the original settlement. Left in peace for at least some of its history, Elgin prospered, and by the early 18th century it became a mini-Edinburgh of the north and a place where country gentlemen spent their winters. It even echoed Edinburgh in carrying out wide-scale reconstruction in the early part of the 18th century: much of the old town was swept away in a wave of rebuilding, giving Elgin the fine neoclassical buildings that survive today.

The town's old street plan survived almost intact until the late 20th century, when it succumbed to the modern madness of demolishing great swaths of buildings for the sake of better traffic flow: Elgin suffered from its position on the Aberdeen–Inverness main road. However, the central main-street plan and some of the older little streets and *wynds* (alleyways) remain. You'll also see Elgin's past in the arcaded shop fronts—some of which date from the late 17th century—on the main shopping street.

At the center of Elgin, the most conspicuous structure is **St. Giles Church,** which divides High Street. The grand foursquare building constructed in 1828 exhibits the Greek revival style: note the columns, the pilasters, and the top of the spire, surmounted by a representation of the Lysicrates Monument. Past the arcaded shops at the east end of High Street, you can see the **Little Cross** (17th century), which marked the boundary between the town and the cathedral grounds. The **Elgin Museum,** near the Little Cross, has an especially interesting collection of dinosaur relics. ⊠ *High St.,* ☎ *01343/543675.* ⊙ *Apr.–Oct., weekdays 10–5, Sat. 11–4, Sun. 2–5; Nov.–Mar. by appointment only.*

★ Cooper Park contains a magnificent ruin, the **Elgin Cathedral,** consecrated in 1224. Its eventful story included devastation by fire: a 1390 act of retaliation by Alexander Stewart (circa 1343–1405), the Wolf of Badenoch. The illegitimate-son-turned-bandit of King David II (1324–71) had sought revenge for his excommunication by the bishop of Moray. The cathedral was rebuilt but finally fell into disuse after the Reformation in 1560. By 1567 the highest authority in the land, the regent earl of Moray, had stripped the lead from the roof to pay for his army. Thus ended the career of the religious seat known as the Lamp of the North. Some traces of the cathedral settlement survive— the gateway Pann's Port and the Bishop's Palace—although they've been drastically altered. Cooper Park is a five-minute walk northeast of Elgin Museum, across the modern bypass road. ☎ *0131/668–8800,* WEB *www.historic-scotland.gov.uk.* ⊡ *£2.80; combined admission with Spynie Palace £3.30.* ⊙ *Apr.–Sept., daily 9:30–6; Oct.–Mar., Mon.– Wed. and Sat. 9:30–4, Thurs. 9:30–noon, Sun. 2–4.*

Just north of Elgin is **Spynie Palace,** the impressive 15th-century former headquarters of the bishops of Moray. It has now fallen into ruin, though the top of the tower has good views over the Laigh of Moray. Find it by turning right off the main A941 Elgin–Lossiemouth road. ☎ *0131/668–8800,* WEB *www.historic-scotland.gov.uk.* ⊡ *£2; combined admission with Elgin Cathedral £3.30.* ⊙ *Apr.–Sept., daily 9:30–6; Oct.– Mar., Sat. 9:30–4, Sun. 2–4.*

OFF THE
BEATEN PATH

PLUSCARDEN ABBEY – Given the general destruction caused by the 16th-century upheaval of the Reformation, abbeys in Scotland tend to be ruinous and deserted, but at Pluscarden Abbey the monks' way of life continues. Originally a 13th-century structure, the abbey was abandoned by the religious community after the Reformation. The third marquis of Bute bought the remains in 1897 and initiated a restoration program that continues today. Monks from Prinknash Abbey near Gloucester, England, returned here in 1948, and the abbey is now an active community. ⊠ *6 mi southwest of Elgin, off B9010.* ⊡ *Free.* ⊙ *Daily 5 am–8:30 pm.*

Dining and Lodging

£££–££££ ✕⊞ **Mansion House Hotel.** This Scottish baronial mansion complete with tower is set on the River Lossie. The rooms are individually decorated; all are pleasant and comfortable. The restaurant's (££££) Scottish menu includes a fine loin of venison roasted with juniper berries; the restaurant also serves vegetarian fare. ⊠ *The Haugh, IV30 1AW,* ☎ *01343/548811,* FAX *01343/547916. 23 rooms. Restaurant, pool, gym, hair salon, sauna, bar; no a/c. AE, DC, MC, V.*

Shopping

Gordon and MacPhail (⊠ 58 South St., ☎ 01343/545110), an outstanding delicatessen and wine merchant, also stocks rare malt whiskies. This is a good place to shop for gifts for those foodies among your friends. **Johnstons of Elgin** (⊠ Newmill, ☎ 01343/554099) is a woolen mill with a worldwide reputation for its luxury fabrics, including cashmere. The bold color range is particularly appealing. The large visitor-center shop stocks not only the firm's own products but also top-quality Scottish crafts and giftware. There's also a restaurant. A half mile outside of Elgin on the A96 toward Inverness, you'll find **The Oakwood** (⊠ Forest Rd., Burghead, ☎ 01343/543200), a 1920s Swiss-chalet-style former roadhouse with an excellent antiques center stocking everything from large furniture to lead soldiers. At the restaurant here you can have a delicious bowl of homemade soup and French bread for £2.30. Don't miss the upstairs display area, with its art-nouveau stained-glass windows.

Fochabers

 9 mi east of Elgin.

Once over the Spey Bridge and past the cricket ground (a very unusual sight in Scotland), you'll find that Fochabers has a symmetrical village square, indicative of the mellow lifestyle here. Perhaps this is what attracts the antiques dealers to Fochabers, their wares ranging from kitchenalia to quality 18th- and 19th-century furniture.

Just before reaching Fochabers, you'll see the works of a major local employer, Baxters of Fochabers. From Tokyo to New York, upmarket stores stock their soups, jams, chutneys, and other gourmet products—all of which are made here, close to the River Spey. The **Baxters Visitors Centre** offers a video, *Baxters Experience,* which presents the history of the business; interactive exhibits and cooking demonstrations; a re-creation of the Baxters' first grocery shop; a shop that stocks Baxters' goods, among other products; the Best of Scotland shop, specializing in Scottish goods; and a restaurant serving up an assortment of delectables. ⊠ *1 mi west of Fochabers on the A96,* ☎ *01343/820666,* WEB *www.baxters.com.* ☜ *Free; small charge for cooking demonstrations and other special features.* ☉ *Apr.–Oct., daily 9–6; Nov.–Dec., daily 9–5; Jan.–Mar., daily 10–5; check ahead to ensure all areas are operating in winter months.*

Through one of the antiques shops in Fochabers you can enter the **Fochabers Folk Museum,** a converted church that has a fine exhibit of items relating to past life in the village and surrounding rural area. Displays range from carts and carriages to farm implements and Victorian toys. ⊠ *Behind Pringle Antiques,* ☎ *01343/821204.* ☜ *Free.* ☉ *Easter–Oct., daily 9:30–1 and 2–5.*

One of the village's lesser-known treasures is the **Gordon Chapel** (⊠ Duke St., just off the Square), which has an exceptional set of stained-glass windows by Pre-Raphaelite artist Sir Edward Burne-Jones.

Consider diverting onto the road that runs south directly opposite the Fochabers Folk Museum. Leaving the houses behind for well-hedged country lanes, you will discover a Forestry Commission sign to the **Earth Pillars.** These curious eroded sandstone pillars are framed by tall-trunk pines and overlook a wide prospect of the lower Spey Valley.

Shopping

Antiques (Fochabers) (⊠ Hadlow House, The Square, ☎ 01343/820838) carries quirky old kitchenware, stripped pine, china, pictures, jewelry, and antique furniture. Take a break from all the white elephants by stopping into **Balance Natural Health** (⊠ 59 High St., ☎ 01343/821443), which stocks homeopathic remedies, potpourris, and the like. If you're interested in modern art, some by local artists, head to **Just Art** (⊠ 64 High St., ☎ 01343/820500), a fine gallery with high-quality ceramics and paintings. **Pringle Antiques** (⊠ High St., ☎ 01343/820362) is a good place to shop for small furniture, pottery, glassware, silver, and jewelry. At **The Quaich** (⊠ 85 High St., ☎ 01343/820981) you can stock up on cards and small gifts, then sit with a cup of tea and a home-baked snack. **Elements** (⊠ 48 High St., ☎ 01343/829076) gift shop stocks cards, soft toys, prints, glassware, ornaments, and more. **Watts Antiques** (⊠ 45 High St., ☎ 01343/820077) has small collectibles, jewelry, ornaments, and china.

Buckie

39   *8 mi east of Fochabers via A98 and A942.*

The fishing port of Buckie and its satellite villages are gray and workaday, with plenty of Victorian architecture added to the original fishermen's cottages, which sit almost on the sea. The **Buckie Drifter Maritime Heritage Centre,** housed in premises reminiscent of an old fishing drifter (a fishing vessel with sails), is a hands-on visitor center that tells the story of the herring industry and of Buckie's development as a port. Upstairs, you enter a 1920s quayside scene, with a replica steam drifter that you can board and barrels you can pack with herring. ⊠ *Freuchny Rd. off Commercial Rd.,* ☎ *01542/834646,* WEB *www.moray.org.* 🖾 *£3.* ☉ *Apr.–Oct., Mon.–Sat. 10–5, Sun. noon–5.*

The **Peter Anson Gallery** displays a selection of watercolor works related to the development of the fishing industry. The gallery is housed in a room accessed through a library. ⊠ *Cluny Pl.,* ☎ *01542/832121.* 🖾 *Free.* ☉ *Weekdays 10–8, Sat. 10–noon.*

Dining

££   ✕ **Old Monastery.** On a broad, wooded slope set back from the coast
★   near Buckie, with westward views as far as the hills of Wester Ross, sits the Old Monastery, once a Victorian religious establishment. This theme carries through to the restrained decor of the Cloisters Bar and the Chapel Restaurant, with its hand stenciling. Local specialties—the freshest fish, venison, and Aberdeen Angus beef—make up the Scottish menu. There's a no-smoking dining room. ⊠ *Drybridge, Buckie,* ☎ *01542/832660. AE, MC, V. Closed Sun., except 1st Sun. of month for lunch, Mon., and 3 wks in Jan.*

En Route   Driving east you'll pass a string of salty little fishing villages. They paint a colorful scene with their gabled houses and fishing nets set out to dry amid the rocky shoreline.

Findochty

40   *2 mi east of Buckie on A942.*

The residents of Findochty are known for their fastidiousness and creativity in painting their houses, taking the art of house painting to a new level. Some residents even paint the mortar between the stonework a different color from the exterior. The harbor here has a faint echo of the Mediterranean about it.

Cullen

★   **41**   *3 mi east of Findochty.*

Look for some wonderfully painted homes at Cullen, in the old fishermen's town below the railway viaduct. But the real attractions of this little resort are its white-sand beach and the fine view west toward the aptly named Bowfiddle Rock. A stroll along the beach reveals the shape of the fishing settlement below and the planned town above. Cullen and its shops are far enough away from major town superstores to survive on local, intermittent trade. Most unusual for a town of its size, Cullen has numerous specialty shops—antiques and gift stores, butchers, an ironmonger, a baker, a pharmacy, and a locally famous ice cream shop among them—as well as several hotels and cafés.

Dining and Lodging

£–££   ✕🏨 **The Seafield Hotel.** A former coaching inn built in 1822, this hotel has high standards in every area: service, decor, and food. Deep, rich colors prevail, and comfort and friendliness are key. The restaurant, with its deep blue walls and tartan carpet, has an extensive à la carte Scottish menu with seafood, game, beef, and lamb. ⊠ *Seafield St., Cullen AB56 4SG,* ☎ *01542/840791,* FAX *01542/840736,* WEB *www. theseafieldhotel.com. 20 rooms. Restaurant, bar; no a/c. AE, MC, V.*

Fordyce

㊷ *5 mi east of Cullen.*

The conservation village of Fordyce lies among the barley fields of Banffshire like a small slice of rural England gone far adrift. You can stroll by the churchyard, picnic on the old bleaching green (a notice board explains everything), or visit a restored 19th-century carpenter's workshop, where musical instruments are made.

Lodging

£ ▣ **Academy House.** This bed-and-breakfast offers accommodations in
★ what was once the headmaster's house for the local secondary school. Well-chosen antiques decorate the spacious rooms. Evening meals are served on request. ⊠ *School Rd., Fordyce AB45 2SJ,* ☎ *01261/842743,* WEB *www.fordyceaccommodation.com. 2 rooms. No a/c, no room phones. No credit cards.*

Banff

㊸ *36 mi east of Elgin, 47 mi north of Aberdeen.*

Midway along the northeast coast, overlooking Moray Firth and the estuary of the River Deveron, Banff is a fishing town of considerable elegance that feels as though it's a million miles from tartan-clad Scotland. Part Georgian, like Edinburgh's New Town, and part 16th-century small burgh, like Culross, Banff is an exemplary east-coast salty town, with its tiny harbor and fine architecture. It's also within easy reach of plenty of unspoiled coastline—cliff and rock to the east, at Gardenstown (known as Gamrie) and Pennan, or beautiful little sandy beaches westward toward Sandend and Cullen.

The jewel in Banff's crown is the grand mansion of **Duff House,** a splendid William Adam–designed (1689–1748) baroque mansion that has been restored as an outstation of the National Galleries of Scotland. Many fine paintings are displayed in rooms furnished to reflect the days when the house was occupied by the dukes of Fife. A good tearoom and a shop are in the basement. ⊠ *Off the A98,* ☎ *01261/818181.* ⊡ *£4.* ☉ *Apr.–Oct., daily 11–5; Nov.–Mar., Thurs.–Sun. 11–4.*

Across the river in Banff's twin town, Macduff, on the shore east of
Ⓒ the harbor, stands **Macduff Marine Aquarium.** A 250,000-gallon central tank and many smaller display areas and touch pools show the sea life of the Moray Firth and North Atlantic. ⊠ *High Shore,* ☎ *01261/833369.* ⊡ *£3.90.* ☉ *Daily 10–5.*

Fyvie Castle

㊹ *18 mi south of Banff, 18 mi northwest of Ellon.*

In an area rife with castles, Fyvie Castle stands out as the most complex. Five great towers built by five successive powerful families turned a 13th-century foursquare castle into an opulent Edwardian statement of wealth. There are some superb paintings on view, including 12 Raeburns, as well as myriad sumptuous interiors and many walks on the castle grounds. Fyvie is impressive for its sheer impact—if you like your castles oppressive and gloomy. ⊠ *Off A947 between Oldmeldrum and Turriff,* ☎ *01651/891266,* WEB *www.nts.org.uk.* ⊡ *£6.* ☉ *Castle Apr.–*

June and Sept.–Oct., Sat.–Wed. noon–5; July–Aug., daily 10–5; grounds daily 9:30–dusk.

Haddo House

45 *12 mi southeast of Fyvie Castle.*

Created as the home of the earls and marquesses of Aberdeen, Haddo House—designed by William Adam—is now cared for by the National Trust for Scotland. Built in 1732, the elegant mansion has a light and graceful design, with curving wings on either side of a harmonious, symmetrical facade. The chapel has a Pre-Raphaelite stained-glass window by Sir Edward Burne-Jones. ⊠ *Off B999, 8 mi northwest of Ellon,* ☎ *01651/851440,* WEB *www.nts.org.uk.* ⊠ *£7.* ☉ *House July–Aug., daily 10–5, shop and tearoom Apr.–Sept., daily 10–5; Oct., weekends 10–5. Garden and park daily, 9:30–dusk.*

Ellon

46 *8 mi southeast of Haddo House, 32 mi southwest of Banff.*

Formerly a market center on what was then the lowest bridging point of the River Ythan, Ellon, a bedroom suburb of Aberdeen, is a small town at the center of a rural hinterland. It's also well placed for visiting several of Castle Country's splendid properties.

Five miles west of Ellon, at Pitmedden, is a unique re-creation by the National Trust for Scotland of a 17th-century garden. **Pitmedden Garden** is best visited in high summer, from July onward, when annual bedding plants form intricate formal patterns. The 100-acre estate also has woodland and farmland walks, as well as the Museum of Farming Life. ☎ *01651/842352,* WEB *www.nts.org.uk.* ⊠ *£5.* ☉ *Garden, visitor center, museum, and tearoom May–Sept., daily 10–5; grounds, daily 10–5.*

OFF THE
BEATEN PATH

ARCHAEOLINK PREHISTORY PARK – A strange grass-covered dome rises from the hillside halfway between Huntly and Aberdeen. This example of modern architecture houses an exhibition about far older structures: the many stone circles, symbol stones, and other prehistoric monuments scattered all over this part of the northeast. Dedicated to the "exploration of life before history," Archaeolink also includes open-air exhibits, such as a replica of an Iron Age farm. ⊠ *Off A96 at Oyne, 20 mi west of Ellon,* ☎ *01464/851500.* ⊠ *£4.* ☉ *Apr.–Oct., daily 10–5.*

ABERDEEN AND THE NORTHEAST A TO Z

To research prices, get advice from other travelers, and book travel arrangements, visit www.fodors.com.

AIR TRAVEL

CARRIERS

Airlines linking Aberdeen with Europe include KLM U.K., with flights to Amsterdam (the Netherlands), to Bergen and Stavanger (Norway), and within the United Kingdom; SAS (Scandinavian Airlines), serving Stavanger; British Airways, serving Paris via Manchester and offering domestic flights as well; and British Midland, with flights to Esbjerg (Denmark) and within the United Kingdom. In addition to British Airways, British Midland, and KLM U.K., domestic service between Aberdeen and most major U.K. airports is offered by Brymon, a British Airways subsidiary, and easyJet.

The direct Amsterdam–Aberdeen link enables transatlantic passengers to visit Scotland's northeast by first flying from the United States to Amsterdam and then flying on to Aberdeen with KLM U.K.; this can actually be faster than traveling to Aberdeen from other parts of Scotland or England.

➤ AIRLINES AND CONTACTS: **British Airways** (☎ 08457/733377, WEB www.britishairways.co.uk). **British Midland** (☎ 0870/607–0555, WEB www.flybmi.com). **Brymon** (☎ 01224/770596). **easyJet** (☎ 0870/600–0000, WEB www.easyjet.com). **KLM U.K.** (☎ 0870/507–4074, WEB www.klmuk.com). **SAS** (Scandinavian Airlines; ☎ 0845/6072772, WEB www.scandinavian.net).

AIRPORTS
Aberdeen Airport—serving both international and domestic flights—is in Dyce, 7 mi west of the city center on the A96 (Inverness). The terminal building is modern and generally uncrowded.

➤ AIRPORT INFORMATION: **Aberdeen Airport** (☎ 01224/722331).

AIRPORT TRANSFERS
First Aberdeen Bus 27 operates between the airport terminal and Union Street in the center of Aberdeen. Buses (£1.45) run frequently at peak times, less often at midday and in the evening; the journey time is approximately 40 minutes.

The drive to the center of Aberdeen is easy via the A96 (which can be busy during rush hour).

Dyce is on ScotRail's Inverness–Aberdeen route. The rail station is a short taxi ride from the terminal building. The ride takes 12 minutes, and trains run approximately every two hours. If you intend to visit the western region first, you can travel northwest, from Aberdeen, by rail, direct to Elgin via Inverurie, Insch, Huntly, and Keith. For information contact National Rail Enquiries.

➤ INFORMATION: **First Aberdeen** (☎ 01224/650000). **National Rail Enquiries** (☎ 08457/484950).

BOAT AND FERRY TRAVEL
There's ferry service between Aberdeen, Lerwick (Shetland), and Kirkwall (Orkney) operated by Northlink Ferries. From Lerwick, you can catch the Smyril Line ferry to Bergen (Norway); this ferry runs between May and September.

➤ BOAT AND FERRY INFORMATION: **Northlink Ferries** (✉ The New Harbour Building, Ferry Rd., Stromness, Orkney, KW16 3BH, ☎ 01856/851144, FAX 01856/851155, WEB www.northlinkferries.co.uk). **Smyril Line** (✉ Holmsgarth Terminal, Lerwick, ZE1 0PR, ☎ 01595/690845, WEB www.smyril-line.com).

BUS TRAVEL
Long-distance buses run to and from most parts of Scotland, England, and Wales. Contact National Express for bus connections with English towns. Contact Scottish Citylink for bus connections with Scottish towns.

First Aberdeen operates services within the city of Aberdeen. There is an inquiry kiosk on St. Nicholas Street, outside a Marks & Spencers department store, and timetables are available at the kiosk or from the tourist information center at nearby St. Nicholas House.

➤ BUS INFORMATION: **First Aberdeen** (☎ 01224/650000). **National Express** (☎ 08705/808080). **Scottish Citylink** (☎ 08705/505050).

CAR RENTAL
➤ AGENCIES: **Alamo National Car Rental** (✉ At Skean Dhu Hotel, Dyce, ☎ 01224/770955; ✉ 46 Summer St., ☎ 01224/626955). **Avis** (✉ Ab-

erdeen Airport, ☎ 01224/722282). **Arnold Clark** (✉ Citroen Garage, Girdleness Rd., ☎ 01224/249159). **Budget Rent-a-Car** (✉ Wellheads Dr. and Aberdeen Airport, ☎ 0800/181181). **Enterprise Rentacar** (✉ 80 Skene Sq., ☎ 01224/642642). **Europcar** (✉ Aberdeen Airport, ☎ 01224/770770; ✉ 121 Causeway End, ☎ 01224/631199). **Hertz** (✉ Aberdeen Airport, ☎ 01224/722373).

CAR TRAVEL

You can travel from Glasgow and Edinburgh to Aberdeen on a continuous stretch of the A90/M90, a fairly scenic route that runs up Strathmore, with a fine hill view to the west. The coastal route, the A92, is a more leisurely alternative, with its interesting resorts and fishing villages. The most scenic route, however, is the A93 from Perth, north to Blairgowrie and into Glen Shee. The A93 then goes over the Cairnwell Pass, the highest main road in the United Kingdom. (This route isn't recommended in the winter months, when snow can make driving over high ground difficult.)

Aberdeen is a compact city with good signage. Its center is Union Street, the main thoroughfare running east–west, which tends to get crowded with traffic. Anderson Drive is an efficient ring road on the city's west side; be extra careful on its many traffic circles. In general, road signs are clear and legible, and parking near the center of Aberdeen is no worse than in any other U.K. city. It's best to leave your car in one of the parking garages (arrive early to get a space) and walk around, or use the convenient park-and-ride scheme at the Bridge of Don, north of the city. Street maps are available from the tourist information center, newsdealers, and booksellers.

Around the northeast roads are generally not busy, but speeding and erratic driving can be a problem on the main A roads. The rural side roads are a pleasure to drive.

EMERGENCIES

Dial **999** in case of an emergency to reach an ambulance, or the fire, coast guard, or police departments (no coins are needed for emergency calls made from public phone booths). For a doctor or dentist, consult your hotel receptionist, B&B proprietor, or the yellow pages.

There's a lost-property office at the Grampian Police headquarters.

Notices on pharmacy doors will guide you to the nearest open pharmacy at any given time. The police can provide assistance in an emergency. Anderson Pharmacy (open Monday–Saturday, 9–6) and Boots the Chemists Ltd. (open Monday–Friday 8:30–5, Saturday 8:30–6, Sunday noon–5), both in Aberdeen, keep longer hours than most. There's an in-store pharmacist at Safeway Food Store (open Monday–Friday 8–10, Saturday 8–8, Sunday 9–9), also in Aberdeen.

➤ EMERGENCY CONTACT: **Grampian Police** (✉ Force Headquarters, Queen St., Aberdeen, ☎ 01224/386000).

➤ HOSPITALS: **Aberdeen Royal Infirmary** (✉ Accident and Emergency Department, Foresterhill, Aberdeen, ☎ 01224/681818). **Dr. Gray's Hospital, Elgin** (✉ Accident and Emergency Department, at end of High St. on A96, ☎ 01343/543131).

➤ LATE-NIGHT PHARMACIES: **Anderson Pharmacy** (✉ 34 Holburn St., ☎ 01224/587148). **Boots the Chemists Ltd.** (✉ Bon Accord Centre, George St., ☎ 01224/626080). **Safeway Food Store** (✉ 215 King St., ☎ 01224/624398).

LODGING

CAMPING

Most population centers in the area have campsites; contact tourist offices for information. You can camp on private land, but you must obtain the permission of the landowner first. Except for the more remote upland areas, "wildland" camping is better pursued farther west.

TAXIS

You'll find taxi stands throughout the center of Aberdeen: along Union Street, at the railway station at Guild Street, at Back Wynd, and at Regent Quay. Taxis (metered) are mostly black, though cabs painted with variations in beige, maroon, or white exist.

TOURS

BUS TOURS

First Bus (operated by First Aberdeen) conducts city tours, available on most days between July and mid-September. Grampian Coaches (operated by First Aberdeen) run tours encompassing the northeast coastline and countryside. Some tours are based on one of the area's various trails: Malt Whisky, Coastal, Castle, or Royal. Whyte's Coaches offers tours throughout the northeast and beyond.
➤ CONTACTS: **First Bus** (☎ 01224/650000). **Grampian Coaches** (☎ 01224/650024). **Whyte's Coaches** (☎ 01651/862211).

PRIVATE GUIDES

The Scottish Tourist Guides Association can supply experienced personal guides, including foreign-language-speaking guides if necessary.
➤ CONTACT: **Scottish Tourist Guides Association** (✉ Wendy Simpson, Howemill Cottage, Craigievar, Aberdeenshire AB33 8JD, ☎ FAX 019755/81335, WEB www.grampianlanguage.com).

WALKING TOURS

The Scottish Tourist Guides Association conducts an Old Aberdeen walk by request.
➤ CONTACT: **Scottish Tourist Guides Association** (✉ Wendy Simpson, Howemill Cottage, Craigievar, Aberdeenshire AB33 8JD, ☎ FAX 019755/81335, WEB www.grampianlanguage.com).

TRAIN TRAVEL

You can reach Aberdeen directly from Edinburgh (2½ hours), Glasgow (3 hours), and Inverness (2½ hours). Get a ScotRail timetable for full details, or call National Rail Enquiries. There are also London–Aberdeen routes that go through Edinburgh and the east-coast main line.
➤ TRAIN INFORMATION: **National Rail Enquiries** (☎ 08457/484950). **ScotRail** (☎ 08457/550033, WEB www.scotrail.co.uk).

VISITOR INFORMATION

The tourist information center in Aberdeen has a currency exchange and supplies information on all of Scotland's northeast. There are also year-round tourist information offices in Braemar and Elgin.

In summer, also look for tourist information centers in Alford, Banchory, Banff, Crathie, Dufftown, Forres, Fraserburgh, Huntly, Stonehaven, and Tomintoul.
➤ TOURIST INFORMATION: **Aberdeen** (✉ Ship Row, Aberdeen, ☎ 01224/288828, WEB www.castlesandwhisky.com). **Ballater** (✉ The Old Royal Station, Station Sq., Ballater, ☎ 013397/55306). **Braemar** (✉ The Mews, Mar Rd., ☎ 013397/41600). **Elgin** (✉ 17 High St., ☎ 01343/542666). **Inverurie** (✉ 18 High St., Inverurie, ☎ 01467/625800).

8 ARGYLL AND THE ISLES

With long sea lochs carved into its hilly, wooded interior, and its mossy terrain richly nourished by rainy Atlantic weather, Argyll is a beguiling interweaving of water and land. The Kintyre Peninsula is a wonderland of sea views and ancient monuments, and the neighboring isles are at once microcosms of Scotland and distinct communities. Arran has long been the Scots' outdoor playground; scenic Islay is synonymous with whisky; Iona was an early Christian sanctuary; and Tobermory, a town of brightly painted houses on the Isle of Mull, has a Mediterranean air.

By Gilbert
Summers

Updated by
Beth Ingpen

D IVIDED IN TWO by the long peninsula of Kintyre, western Scotland is characterized by a complicated, splintered seaboard. The west is an aesthetic delight, though it does catch those moist (yes, that's a euphemism) Atlantic weather systems. But the occasional wet foray is a small price to pay for the glittering freshness of oak woods and bracken-covered hillsides and for the bright interplay of sea, loch, and rugged green peninsula. Only a few decades ago the Clyde estuary was a coastal playground for people living in Glasgow and along Clydeside: their annual holiday was a steamer trip to any one of a number of Clyde resorts, known as going *doon the watter.*

Some impressive castles gaze out over this luxuriant landscape. Ruined Dunstaffnage and Kilchurn castles once guarded the western seaboard; turreted Inveraray Castle and magnificent Brodick, on the Isle of Arran, now guard their own historic interiors, with hundreds of antiques and portraits. The Kilmartin area has stone circles, carved stones, and burial mounds from the Bronze Age and earlier, taking imaginative travelers thousands of years back in time. Gardens are another Argyll specialty thanks to the temperate west-coast climate—Crarae Gardens, south of Inveraray, invites you down winding paths through plantings of magnolias and azaleas that reach their colorful peaks in late spring. The Brodick Castle grounds have fine azalea plantings, and Ardkinglas Woodland Garden adds an outstanding conifer collection.

Kintyre separates the islands of the Firth of Clyde (including Arran) from the islands of the Inner Hebrides. These isles are essentially microcosms of Scotland: each has its jagged cliffs or tongues of rock, its smiling sands and fertile pastures, its grim and ghostly fortress, and its tale of clan outrage or mythical beast. The pace of life is gentle out here, and the roads narrow and tortuous—not designed for heavy vehicles (beware pilgrim buses to Iona in summer, as they can cause major delays on the south-side routes). Arran is the place for hill walking on Goat Fell, the mountain that gives the island its distinctive profile. On Islay you can hunt down peaty, iodine-scented malt whisky: each of the island's distilleries makes a subtly different malt, and the process of choosing your favorite makes for a pleasant evening in the island's friendly pubs and hotels. Mull and Iona (just off Mull's western tip) are different again: Mull has yet more castles, a short stretch of narrow-gauge railway, some demanding walks along the rocky coastline of the Burg, and the pretty port of Tobermory, with its brightly painted houses. Iona is famous as an early seat of Christianity in Scotland and the burial place of Scottish kings in the Dark Ages. You could spend all your time in this region touring these larger islands, but keep in mind that plenty of small islands are just as rich.

Pleasures and Pastimes

Biking

As both a vacation destination and a ferry gateway, Oban gets a lot of bike traffic. The main routes into and out of town are busy, and there are few side roads. Arran is popular for cycling, with a large number of bike-rental shops. Many roads here have one lane only, so wear high-visibility clothing, especially in the busy summer months—and, above all, bring rain gear.

Dining

This part of Scotland is not a great gastronomic center, but it does have some restaurants of distinction, and local ingredients are high in quality: the seafood, fresh from the sparkling lochs and sea, could hardly be better. Beef, lamb, and game are also common. In rural districts it's prudent to choose a hotel or guest house that serves a decent evening meal as well as breakfast.

CATEGORY	COST*
££££	over £22
£££	£16–£22
££	£9–£15
£	under £9

*per person for a main course at dinner, including VAT

Fishing
Local fishing literature, available in tourist offices, identifies at least 50 loch and river sites for game fishing and at least 20 coastal settlements suited to sea angling.

Golf
This area has about two dozen golf courses, notably some fine coastal links. Machrihanish, near Campbeltown, is the best known (☞ Chapter 12).

Lodging
Accommodations in Argyll and the isles range from châteaulike hotels to modest inns. Many traditional provincial hotels and small coastal resorts have been equipped with modern conveniences yet retain their personalized service and historic charm. Apart from these, however, your choices are limited; the best overnight option is usually a simple guest house offering bed, breakfast, and an evening meal.

CATEGORY	COST*
££££	over £140
£££	£110–£140
££	£65–£110
£	under £65

*All prices are for a standard double room, including service, breakfast, and VAT.

Exploring Argyll and the Isles

Loch Fyne tends to get in the way of a breezy mainland tour: it's a long haul around the end of this fjordlike sea loch to Inveraray. Ferry services allow all kinds of interisland tours and can shorten mainland trips as well.

Numbers in the text correspond to numbers in the margin and on the Argyll and the Isles map.

Great Itineraries
You could easily spend a week exploring the islands alone, so consider spending at least a few nights in this region.

IF YOU HAVE 2 DAYS

From Glasgow make your way to **Inveraray** ③ via Loch Lomond (A82) and the Rest and Be Thankful Pass (A83). Continue south via the **Crarae Gardens** ⑤, then south to Lochgilphead, where you take A816 north to the **Crinan Canal** ⑦. Continue north on A816 and stay overnight in 🛏 **Oban** ①. The next day follow A85 east to see **Dunstaffnage Castle** and **Kilchurn Castle** ② before returning to the Loch Lomond/Glasgow area.

IF YOU HAVE 4 DAYS

Starting from Ardrossan, in Ayrshire, take the ferry to 🛏 **Brodick** and stay overnight on the island of Arran, visiting **Brodick Castle and Country Park** ⑫. Cross to Kintyre Peninsula by taking the ferry from **Lochran-**

Argyll and the Isles

Ben Nevis

Fort William

A82

Glen Coe

Kinlochleven

A82

Ardgour

Corran

Ballachulish

A861

Inversanda

Ardgour

A828

Bacaldine Forest

Strontian

A861

Sunart

A884

Loch Sunart

Morvern

Ardnamurchan

B8007

Sanna

Glenborrodale

Ardnamurchan

Isle of Eriska

Port Appin

Connel Barcaldine
Bridge

A85

Taynuilt

Ben Cruachan

Loch Etive

2 **Kilchurn**
Castle

Dalmally

Lochawe

A85

Loch Awe

A819

3 **Inveraray**

Rest and
Be Thankful
Pass

A83

A815

Strachur

A819

A83

A886

Loch Fyne

4 **Auchindrain**
Museum

A819

A816

Loch Awe

5 **Crarae**
Gardens

Kilninver

B844

1 **Dunstaffnage**
Castle

Oban

Rudha an
Ridire

Loch Linnhe

A884

Lochaline

Loch
Don

Seil

A816

Kilmartin
Museum

Carnasserie
Castle

Kinuachdrach

8 **Dunadd**
Fort

7

Crinan Canal

Scarba

Gulf of Corryvreckan

Easdale
Island

Lealt

Firth of Lorne

24

25
Torosay Castle
Duart Castle

Loch
Spelve

Craignure

Fishnish
Pier

Sound of Mull

Aros

B849

A848

Salen

B8035

A849

Ardmeanach

Ben More

Loch na Keal

Isle of Mull

B8073

28 **Tobermory**

27 **Dervaig**

Calgary
Bay

Glenborrodale

Ulva

The Burg

Staffa

Treshnish
Isles

Loch Scridain

Bunessan

Ross of Mull

Fionnphort

26 **Iona**

Sound
of Iona

Carsaig

Carsaig
Arches

Colonsay

Scalasaig

INNER HEBRIDES

Coll

Arinagour

Scarinish

Tiree

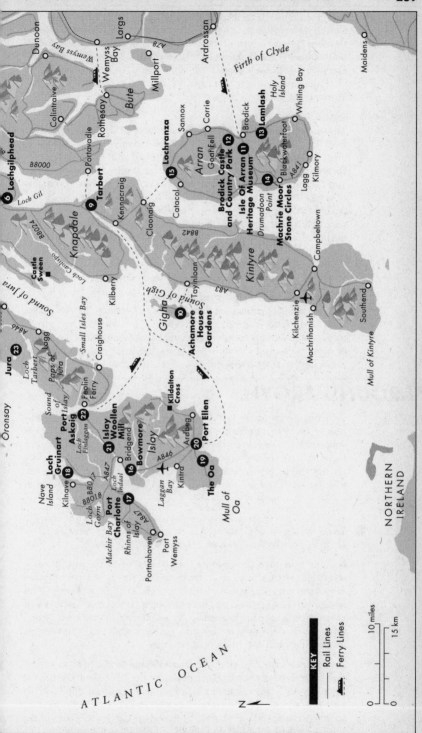

Largs
Dunoon
Wemyss Bay
Wemyss Bay
A78
Ardrossan
Firth of Clyde
Maidens
Colintraive
Rothesay
Millport
Bute
Portavadie
6 Lochgilphead
B8000
Tarbert 9
Loch Gil
B8024
Kennacraig
Knapdale
Kilberry
Castle Sween
Loch Caolisport
Sound of Jura
Lochranza 15
Sannox
Corrie
Goat Fell
Arran
Brodick 12
13 Lamlash
Holy Island
Whiting Bay
Isle Of Arran
Heritage Museum 11
Blackwaterfoot
A841
Kilmory
Lagg
Catacol
Brodick Castle
and Country Park
14
Machrie Moor
Stone Circles
Claonaig
B842
Drumadoon
Point
Kintyre
A83
Campbeltown
Tayinloan
Sound of Gigha
Gigha
Achamore
House Gardens 10
Southend
Kilchenzie
Machrihanish
Mull of Kintyre
Jura 23
Lagg
Oronsay
Paps of Jura
Loch Tarbert
A846
Small Isles Bay
Craighouse
Feolin Ferry
Sound of Islay
Port Askaig 22
Loch Finlaggan
Kildalton Cross
Islay
Woollen
Mill 21
Bridgend
Ardbeg
Port Ellen 20
Bowmore 16
A846
Loch Gruinart 18
Kilnave
Nave Island
A847
B8017
B8018
Laggan
Bay
Kintra
19 The Oa
Mull of Oa
Loch Indaal
Loch Gorm
Machir Bay
Port Charlotte 17
Rhinns of Islay
A847
Portnahaven
Port Wemyss
NORTHERN IRELAND
ATLANTIC OCEAN

KEY
Rail Lines
Ferry Lines

10 miles
15 km

N

za ⑮ for Claonaig; then cross the peninsula itself to Kennacraig. For a lovely day trip head south to the Isle of Gigha and its **Achamore House Gardens** ⑩; then return north to the ☆ **Crinan** area. The next day go up to **Oban** ① and make an excursion to Mull for **Iona** ㉖, ☆ **Tobermory** ㉘, and **Torosay Castle** ㉔. Finally, return to Oban *or* leave Mull via Fishnish Pier, where you can take a ferry to Lochaline and travel north on the mainland from there.

IF YOU HAVE 7 DAYS

This noncircular route provides a good flavor of the islands. Starting from Ardrossan, take the ferry to ☆ **Brodick** and stay overnight on Arran, visiting **Brodick Castle and Country Park** ⑫. Take the ferry from **Lochranza** ⑮ to Claonaig, cross the Kintyre Peninsula to Kennacraig, and continue west to the island of ☆ **Islay** ⑯–㉒, staying two nights to sample its wildlife preserves, coastal scenery, and malt whisky and perhaps to take the short ferry trip to **Jura** ㉓ to enjoy its wilder terrain. Return to the mainland to explore the area around Knapdale, staying in the ☆ **Crinan** area for at least one night. Go north to ☆ **Oban** ① and take the ferry to Mull to see **Iona** ㉖, ☆ **Tobermory** ㉘, and **Torosay Castle** ㉔, staying two nights. Finally, return to Oban and head east on A85 to see **Dunstaffnage Castle** and **Kilchurn Castle** ②.

When to Tour Argyll and the Isles

This part of the mainland is close enough to Glasgow that it's convenient year-round. You can take advantage of quiet roads and plentiful accommodations in early spring and late autumn. Avoid the islands in winter, however, when howling gales and frigid temperatures may prove unpleasantly distracting.

AROUND ARGYLL

Take time to get to know the mixture of topographical grandeur and lush greenery that make this part of Argyll special. Try to take to the water at least once, even if your time is limited. The sea and the sea lochs have played a vital role in the history of western Scotland since the time of the war galleys of the clans. Oban is the major ferry gateway and transport hub, with a main road leading south into Kintyre.

Oban

❶ *96 mi northwest of Glasgow, 125 mi northwest of Edinburgh, 50 mi south of Fort William, 118 mi southwest of Inverness.*

It's almost impossible to avoid Oban when touring the west. Luckily it has a waterfront with some character and serves as a launch point for several ferry excursions. A traditional Scottish resort town, Oban has *ceilidhs* (song, music, and dance festivals) and tartan kitsch as well as late-night revelry in pubs and hotel bars. There's an inescapable sense, however, that just over the horizon, on the islands or down Kintyre, lie more peaceful and traditional environs.

Four miles north of Oban stands **Dunstaffnage Castle,** once an important stronghold of the MacDougall clan in the 13th century. From the ramparts you have outstanding views across the **Sound of Mull** and the **Firth of Lorne,** a nautical crossroads of sorts, once watched over by Dunstaffnage Castle and commanded by the galleys (*birlinn* in Gaelic) of the Lords of the Isles. ✉ *Off A85,* ☎ *0131/668–8800,* ⓦⒺⒷ *www.historic-scotland.gov.uk.* 💷 *£2.20.* ⊘ *Apr.–Sept., daily 9:30–6; Oct.–Mar., daily 9:30–4.*

From Dunstaffnage Castle you should be able to see **Connel Bridge,** less than a mile to the east. This elegant structure once carried a branch railway along the coast, but it has since surrendered to the all-conquering automobile. Below the bridge, in the shadow of the girders, foam the **Falls of Lora,** given the right tidal conditions. Upstream is fjordlike **Loch Etive** (with cruises from Oban); the water leaving this deep, narrow loch foams and fights with the incoming tides, creating turbulence and curious cascades under the bridge.

OFF THE
BEATEN PATH

SCOTTISH SEALIFE SANCTUARY – Kids (as well as adults) love this outstanding display of marine life, including shoals of herring, sharks, rays, catfish, otters, and seals. There's even a children's adventure playground and, of course, a gift shop. The restaurant serves morning coffee with homemade scones; a full lunch menu, which might include homemade soup, fish pie, or baked potatoes with various fillings; and afternoon tea. To get here drive north from Oban for 10 mi on A828. ⊠ *Barcaldine, Connel,* ☎ *01631/720386,* WEB *www.sealsanctuary.co.uk.* 🎫 *£6.95.* ⊙ *July–Aug., daily 9–6; Mar.–June and Sept.–Dec., daily 10–5; Jan.–mid-Feb., weekends 10–4; mid-Feb.–late Feb., daily 10–4.*

Dining and Lodging

££££ ✕⊡ **Isle of Eriska.** A severe, baronial-style granite facade belies the luxurious welcome within this hotel, set on its own island 10 mi north of Oban and accessible by a bridge from the mainland. Every detail in the spacious rooms has been carefully chosen for your comfort. The restaurant serves innovative Scottish cuisine made with local ingredients: try the scallop and zucchini timbale with lobsters, artichoke, and champagne butter sauce. You can take a stroll to watch seals and otters offshore or herons and badgers on the grounds. ⊠ *Ledaig, by Oban, Argyll PA37 1SD,* ☎ *01631/720371,* FAX *01631/720531,* WEB *www.eriska-hotel.co.uk. 17 rooms. Restaurant, 6-hole golf course, tennis court, pool, health club; no a/c. AE, MC, V. Closed Jan.–mid-Feb.*

£–££ ⊡ **Kilchrenan House.** A fully refurbished Victorian house just a few minutes' walk from the town center, this is a high-grade bed-and-breakfast. Guest rooms overlook the sea and the islands. ⊠ *Corran Esplanade, Oban, Argyll PA34 5AQ,* ☎ FAX *01631/562663. 10 rooms. No a/c. MC, V. Closed Jan.*

£–££ ⊡ **Manor House Hotel.** On the shore just outside Oban, this 1780 stone house, once the home of the duke of Argyll, has wonderful sea views. The public areas are furnished with antiques, the bedrooms with reproductions. The restaurant (££££) serves Scottish and French dishes, including lots of local seafood and game in season, complemented by a carefully selected wine list. The house is within walking distance of downtown Oban and the bus, train, and ferry terminals. ⊠ *Gallanach Rd., Oban, Argyll PA34 4LS,* ☎ *01631/562087,* FAX *01631/563053. 11 rooms. Restaurant; no a/c. AE, MC, V.*

£ ⊡ **Dungrianach.** Aptly named with a word meaning "the sunny house
★ on the hill," this B&B is set high in woodland with superb views of the ocean and islands. Yet it's only a few minutes' walk from Oban's ferry piers and town center. Antique and reproduction furniture fill the guest rooms of this late-Victorian house. ⊠ *Pulpit Hill, Oban, Argyll PA34 4LU,* ☎ FAX *01631/562840,* WEB *www.dungrianach.com. 2 rooms. No a/c, no room phones. No credit cards. Closed Oct.–Mar.*

£ ⊡ **Ronebhal Guest House.** You can see Loch Etive and the mountains beyond from this stone house east of Oban, set back within its own grounds. It offers B&B accommodations in spacious surroundings. ⊠ *Connel, Argyll PA37 1PJ,* ☎ FAX *01631/710310,* WEB *www.ronebhal.co.uk. 5 rooms, 4 with bath. No a/c, no room phones, no smoking. MC, V. Closed Dec.–Jan.*

Nightlife and the Arts

The **Highland Theatre** (⌗ George St., ☎ 01631/562444) shows feature films and has a separate theater for plays.

Biking

You can rent bicycles from **Oban Cycles** (⌗ 29 Lochside St., ☎ 01631/566996).

Shopping

The factory store **Caithness Glass Oban** (⌗ Railway Pier, ☎ FAX 01631/563386) is a good place to buy a memento of Scotland. The paperweights with swirling colored patterns are particularly lovely.

Lochawe

18 mi east of Oban.

Lochawe is a loch-side community squeezed between the broad shoulder of Ben Cruachan and Loch Awe itself. The road gets busy in peak season, filled with people trying to park by Lochawe Station.

★ ❷ **Kilchurn Castle,** a ruined fortress at the east end of Loch Awe, was built in the 15th century by Sir Colin Campbell (d. 1493) of Glenorchy (the Campbells had their original power base in this area), and rebuilt in the 17th century. Airy vantage points amid the towers have fine panoramas of the surrounding highlands and loch. ⌗ *1 mi northeast of Lochawe on A85,* ☎ *0131/668–8800,* WEB *www.historic-scotland.gov.uk.* ⌐ *Free.* ⊙ *Daily 24 hrs.*

The **Duncan Ban Macintyre Monument** was erected in honor of this Gaelic poet (1724–1812), sometimes referred to as the Robert Burns of the Highlands. The view from here is one of the finest in Argyll, taking in Ben Cruachan and the other peaks nearby, as well as Loch Awe and its scattering of islands. To find the monument from Dalmally, just east of Lochawe, follow an old road running southwest toward the banks of Loch Awe—you'll see the round, granite structure from the road's highest point, often called Monument Hill.

En Route The A819 south to Inveraray initially runs alongside Loch Awe, the longest loch in Scotland, but soon leaves these pleasant banks to turn east and join the A83, which carries traffic from Glasgow and Loch Lomond by way of the high Rest and Be Thankful pass. (Many travelers come up Loch Lomond and head west by the A83.) The Rest and Be Thankful is perhaps the road's most scenic point; aptly named, it's a quasi-alpine pass among high green slopes and gray rocks.

Inveraray

★ ❸ *21 mi south of Lochawe, 61 mi north of Glasgow, 29 mi west of Loch Lomond.*

On the approaches to Inveraray, note the ornate 18th-century bridge-work that carries the road along the loch side. This is your first sign that Inveraray is not just a jumbled assembly of houses; in fact, much of it was designed as a planned town for the third duke of Argyll in the mid-18th century. The current seat of the Campbell duke is **Inveraray Castle,** a smart, grayish-green turreted stone house with a self-satisfied air, visible through trees from the town itself. Like the well-disciplined town, the castle was built around 1743. Tours of the interior convey the history of the powerful Campbell family. ☎ *01499/302203,* WEB *www.inveraray-castle.com.* ⌐ *£5.50.* ⊙ *July–Aug., Mon.–Sat. 10–5:45, Sun. 1–5:45; Apr.–June and Sept.–mid-Oct., Mon.–Thurs. and Sat. 10–1 and 2–5:45, Sun. 1–5:45.*

The **Inveraray Jail** is one of the latest generation of visitor centers. The old town jail and courtroom now house realistic courtroom scenes, period cells, and other paraphernalia that give you a glimpse of life behind bars in Victorian times—and today. The site includes a Scottish crafts shop. ⊠ *Inveraray,* ☎ *01499/302381.* 🎫 *£4.95.* ⊘ *Apr.–Oct., daily 9:30–6; Nov.–Mar., daily 10–5; last admission 1 hr before closing.*

The 1911 lightship **Arctic Penguin** is a rare example of a riveted iron vessel. It now houses exhibits and displays on the maritime heritage of the River Clyde and Scotland's west coast. ☎ *01499/302213.* 🎫 *£3.60.* ⊘ *Apr.–Oct., daily 10–6; Nov.–Mar., daily 10–5.*

Ardkinglas Woodland Garden has one of Britain's finest collections of conifers, set off by rhododendron blossoms in early summer. You'll find it around the head of Loch Fyne, about 4 mi east of Inveraray. ⊠ *A83, Cairndow,* ☎ *01499/600261.* 🎫 *£3.* ⊘ *Daily dawn–dusk.*

At **Loch Fyne Oysters,** about 11 mi northeast of Inveraray, you can purchase these delicious shellfish to go, order them to be shipped, or sit down and consume a dozen with a glass of white wine. ⊠ *A83, Clachan Farm, Cairndow,* ☎ *01499/600236.* ⊘ *Daily 9–8.*

Dining and Lodging

££–£££ ✕🏨 **Creggans Inn.** This traditional inn overlooking Loch Fyne from its eastern shore, 21 mi southeast of Inveraray, dates from the 17th century. At mealtimes you can eat an appetizing lunch or supper in the bar, or sit down to a more formal dinner in the cozy dining room. The menu highlights local produce and seafood, including Loch Fyne oysters. Each guest room is individually decorated, and the staff is friendly and hospitable. ⊠ *Strachur, Argyll PA27 8BX,* ☎ *01369/860279,* 🅵🅰🆇 *01369/860637,* 🆆🅴🅱 *www.creggans-inn.co.uk. 14 rooms. Restaurant; no a/c. MC, V.*

Auchindrain Museum

★ ❹ *5 mi south of Inveraray.*

Step a few centuries back in time at the Auchindrain Museum. Once a communal tenancy farm, this 18th-century cooperative venture has been restored. The old bracken-thatch and iron-roof buildings give you a feel for early farming life in the Highlands, and the interpretation center explains it all. ⊠ *A83,* ☎ *01499/500235.* 🎫 *£4.* ⊘ *Apr.–Sept., daily 10–5.*

Crarae Gardens

★ ❺ *10 mi southwest of Inveraray.*

Well worth a visit for plant lovers are the Crarae Gardens, where magnolias and azaleas flourish in the moist and lush environment. The flowers and trees attract several different species of birds and butterflies. ⊠ *Off A83, about 10 mi southwest of Inveraray,* ☎ *01546/886614,* 🆆🅴🅱 *www.crarae-gardens.org.* 🎫 *£2.50.* ⊘ *Gardens daily 9–6, reduced to daylight hrs in winter; visitor center Easter–Oct., seasonal hrs, call ahead.*

Lochgilphead

❻ *26 mi south of Inveraray.*

Lochgilphead, the largest town in this region, looks best when the tide is in, as Loch Gilp (really a bite out of Loch Fyne) reveals a muddy shoreline at low tide. With a series of well-kept, colorful buildings along its main street, this neat little town is worth a look.

OFF THE
BEATEN PATH
CARNASSERIE CASTLE – This tower house has the distinction of having belonged to the writer of the first book printed in Gaelic. The writer, John Carswell, bishop of the isles, translated a text by the Scottish reformer John Knox into Gaelic and published it in 1567. *Off A816, 9 mi north of Lochgilphead,* ☎ *0131/668–8800,* WEB *www.historic-scotland.gov.uk.* ✉ *Free.* ☉ *Daily 24 hrs.*

Horseback Riding

From **Castle Riding Centre and Argyll Trail Riding** (✉ Brenfield, Ardrishaig, Argyll, ☎ 01546/603274, WEB www.brenfield.co.uk), south of Lochgilphead, highly qualified trail guides lead riders along routes throughout Argyll and farther afield into the West Highlands.

Shopping

The factory shop at the **Highbank Collection** (✉ Highbank Industrial Estate, ☎ 01546/602044) sells glassware made on-site, model wooden boats, hand-painted pottery, and ceramic giftware.

Crinan

1 mi north of Lochgilphead.

Crinan is synonymous with its canal, the reason for this tiny community's existence and its mainstay. The narrow road beside the Crinan Hotel bustles with yachting types waiting to pass through the locks, bringing a surprisingly cosmopolitan feel to such an out-of-the-way corner of Scotland. To reach Crinan, take the A816 Oban road north from Lochgilphead for about a mile, then turn left.

❼ The **Crinan Canal** was opened in 1801 to enable fishing vessels to reach the Hebridean fishing grounds without making the long haul south around the Kintyre Peninsula. At its west end the canal drops to the sea in a series of locks. This area gets busy at times, with yachting enthusiasts strolling around and drinking coffee at the shop beside the Crinan Hotel.

★ ❽ For an exceptional encounter with early Scottish history, visit the **Kilmartin House Museum** at Kilmartin, about 8 mi north of Crinan on the A816. The museum, housed in a former manse, explores the stone circles and avenues, burial mounds, and carved stones dating from the Bronze Age and earlier that are scattered thickly around this neighborhood. Nearby **Dunadd Fort**, a rocky hump rising out of the level ground between Crinan and Kilmartin, was once the capital of the early kingdom of Dalriada, founded by the first wave of Scots who migrated from Ireland around AD 500. Clamber up the rock to see a basin, a footprint, and an outline of a boar carved on the smooth upper face of the knoll. ✉ *At Kilmartin, on A816,* ☎ *01546/510278,* WEB *www.kilmartin.org.* ✉ *£4.50.* ☉ *Daily 10–5:30.*

OFF THE
BEATEN PATH
CASTLE SWEEN – The oldest stone castle on the Scottish mainland, dating from the 12th century, sits on a rocky bit of coast about 12 mi south of Crinan. You can reach it by an unclassified road from Crinan that grants outstanding views of the Paps of Jura (the mountains on Jura), across the sound. There are some temptingly deserted white-sand beaches here.

Dining and Lodging

£££–££££   ✗⊡ **Crinan Hotel.** This turn-of-the-20th-century property overlooks
★   the picturesque Crinan Canal and the Sound of Jura. One of the owners, the friendly and helpful Frances Macdonald, is an artist, and her talents are evident in the hotel's interior design. Two restaurants serve Scottish cuisine and the freshest local seafood: the Westward Room

serves dinner in a luxurious country-mansion setting that surrounds you with antiques and flowers, and the rooftop Lock 16 (open May through September only) has a nautical theme, with superb sunsets to accompany the fine seafood. ⊠ *Crinan, PA31 8SR,* ☎ *01546/830261,* FAX *01546/830292,* WEB *www.crinanhotel.com. 22 rooms. 2 restaurants, coffee shop, boating, fishing; no a/c. AE, MC, V.*

Kintyre Peninsula

52 mi (to Campbeltown) south of Lochgilphead.

9 Rivers and streams crisscross this long, narrow strip of green pasturelands and hills stretching south from Lochgilphead. **Tarbert,** a name that appears throughout the Highlands, is the Gaelic word for "place of portage," and a glance at the map tells you why it was given to this little town with a workaday waterfront: Tarbert sits on the narrow neck of land between East and West Loch Tarbert, where long ago boats were actually carried across the land to avoid looping all the way around the peninsula. The **TairbeartHeritage Centre,** just south of the village, will tell you more about the area's history. ⊠ *Tarbert,* ☎ *01880/821116.* 🔲 *Free.* ☉ *Mid-Mar.–Dec., daily 10–sunset.*

The **Isle of Gigha** is a delectable Hebridean island, barely 5 mi long, sheltered in a frost-free, sea-warmed climate between Kintyre and Islay. The island was long favored by British aristocrats as a summer destination. One relic of the Isle of Gigha's aristocratic legacy is the **10** **Achamore House Gardens,** which produce lush shrubberies with spectacular azalea displays in late spring. For a nimble day trip, take the 20-minute ferry to Gigha from Tayinloan and walk right over to the gardens. You may not want to take your car, as the walk is fairly easy. ☎ *01583/505267,* WEB *www.isle-of-gigha.co.uk.* 🔲 *Gardens £2; ferry £4.75 per person plus £17.90 per car, or £20.85 for a car and 4 passengers on a day-saver ticket.* ☉ *Gardens daily dawn–dusk. Ferry May–mid-Oct., daily 9–6, hourly; mid-Oct.–Apr., daily 9–4, hourly.*

ARRAN

Many Scots, especially those from Glasgow and the west, are well disposed toward Arran, as it reminds them of unhurried childhood holidays. Today the Scottish masses go to Spain, but, like other parts of the Clyde, the island of Arran has long been associated with the healthy outdoor life.

To get to Arran, take the ferry from Ardrossan, on the mainland. (It's also possible to take the ferry from Claonaig on the Kintyre Peninsula in summer.) You'll see a number of fellow travelers wearing hiking boots: they're ready for the delights of Goat Fell, the impressive peak (2,868 ft) that gives Arran one of the most distinctive profiles of any island in Scotland. As the ferry approaches Brodick, you'll see Goat Fell's cone, its satellites forming an eye-catching backdrop to the northwest. Arran's southern half is less mountainous; the Highland Boundary Fault crosses just to the north of Brodick Bay. Exploring the island is easy, as the A841 road neatly circles it.

Brodick

1 hr by ferry from Ardrossan.

11 The largest township on Arran, Brodick is really just a village, its frontage set spaciously back from a promenade and beach. The **Isle of Arran Heritage Museum** documents the life of the island from ancient times to the present. Several buildings, including a cottage and *smiddy* (smithy), have period furnishings as well as displays on prehistoric life, geology, farming, fishing, and other aspects of the island's social history. ⊠ *Rosaburn, Brodick,* ☎ *01770/302636.* ⊡ *£2.25.* ⊙ *Apr.–Oct., daily 10:30–4:30.*

In **Glen Rosa** you can stroll through a long glen that affords a glimpse of the wild ridges that beckon so many outdoors enthusiasts; to get here from Brodick, pass the Isle of Arran Heritage Museum and find the junction where the String Road cuts across the island. Drive a short way up the String Road and turn right at the signpost into the glen. The road soon becomes undrivable; park the car and wander on foot.

★ ⑫ Arran's biggest cultural draw is **Brodick Castle and Country Park,** on the north side of Brodick Bay, its red sandstone cosseted by trees and parkland. Several rooms are open to the public—the castle's furniture, paintings, and silver are opulent in their own right—but the real attraction is the garden, where brilliantly colored rhododendrons bloom, particularly in late spring and early summer. There are many unusual varieties here, though the ordinary yellow kind is unmatched for its scent: your first encounter with these is like hitting a wall of perfume. Save time to visit the Servants' Hall, where an excellent restaurant serves morning coffee (with hot scones—try the date-and-walnut variety), a full lunch menu that changes daily, and afternoon teas with home-baked goods. If the weather is fine, you may want to eat on the terrace and watch the chaffinches clamoring for crumbs. ⊠ *1 mi north of Brodick Pier,* ☎ *01770/302202,* WEB *www.nts.org.uk.* ⊡ *Castle and gardens £7; gardens only, £3.50.* ⊙ *Castle and gardens Apr.–Oct., daily 10–5. Reception center and restaurant Apr.–Oct., daily 10–5; Nov.–Dec., Fri.–Sun. 10–5. Country park daily 9:30–dusk.*

Dining and Lodging

£££–££££ ✕⊞ **Kilmichael Country House Hotel.** Built by the Fullerton family on
★ land granted to them by Robert the Bruce, this 300-year-old mansion sits at the head of Glen Cloy, just outside Brodick. Sunny colors, Georgian oak antiques, and Sanderson fabrics fill this outstanding hotel. The exceptional cuisine weds fresh Scottish produce and international flair: dishes might include fresh beetroot ravioli filled with four Italian cheeses, chestnut and roasted-garlic soup, or rack of Scottish lamb on red cabbage with rosemary and red-currant sauce. ⊠ *Brodick, Isle of Arran, KA27 8BY,* ☎ *01770/302219,* FAX *01770/302068,* WEB *www.kilmichael.com. 3 rooms, 4 suites. Restaurant; no a/c, no kids under 12. MC, V. Closed Nov.–Mar.*

Shopping

Arran's shops are well stocked with island-produced goods. The Home Farm is a popular shopping area with a small restaurant. The **Duchess Court Shops** (⊠ The Home Farm, ☎ 01770/302831) include Bear Necessities, with everything bearly; the Nature Shop, with nature-oriented books and gifts; the Home Farm Kitchen Shop for locally made preserves and kitchenware. **The Island Cheese Company,** (⊠ The Home Farm, ☎ 01770/302788) stocks such Arran specialties as blue cheese and a wide selection of other handmade British cheeses.

Lamlash

⑬ *4 mi south of Brodick.*

With views offshore to Holy Island, which is flanked by steep cliffs, Lamlash has a breezy seaside-holiday atmosphere. To reach the highest point accessible by car, go through the village and turn right beside the bridge onto Ross Road, which climbs steeply from a thickly planted valley, **Glen Scorrodale,** and yields fine views of Lamlash Bay. From

When you pack your MCI Calling Card, it's like packing your loved ones along too.

Your MCI Calling Card is the easy way to stay in touch when you travel. Use it to call to and from over 125 countries. Plus, every time you call, you can earn frequent flier miles. So wherever your travels take you, call home with your MCI Calling Card. It's even easy to get one. Just visit **www.mci.com/worldphone** or **www.mci.com/partners**.

EASY TO CALL WORLDWIDE

1. Just enter the WorldPhone® access number of the country you're calling from.

2. Enter or give the operator your MCI Calling Card number.

3. Enter or give the number you're calling.

Austria ◆	0800-200-235
Belgium ◆	0800-10012
Czech Republic ◆	00-42-000112
Denmark ◆	8001-0022
Estonia ★	0800-1122
Finland ◆	08001-102-80
France ◆	0-800-99-0019
Germany	0800-888-8000
Greece ◆	00-800-1211
Hungary ◆	06 ▼800-01411
Ireland	1-800-55-1001
Italy ◆	800-17-2401
Luxembourg	8002-0112
Netherlands ◆	0800-022-91-22
Norway ◆	800-19912
Poland ∻	00-800-111-21-22
Portugal ∻∻	800-800-123
Romania ∻	01-800-1800
Russia ◆ ∻	747-3322
Spain	900-99-0014
Sweden ◆	020-795-922
Switzerland ◆	0800-89-0222
Ukraine ∻	8 ▼10-013
United Kingdom	0800-89-0222
Vatican City	172-1022

◆ Public phones may require deposit of coin or phone card for dial tone. ★ Not available from public pay phones.
▼ Wait for second dial tone. ∻ Limited availability.

EARN FREQUENT FLIER MILES

Find America *with a Compass*

Alaska
Written by John Murray and Nick Jans

Arizona
Written by Lawrence Cheek

Gulf South
Louisiana, Southern Mississippi, and Alabama's Gulf Coast
Written by residents Barbara Sewell Buchanan, Malin Boyd, and Stanley Dry

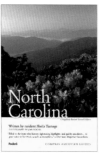

North Carolina
Written by resident Sheila Turnage

San Francisco
Written by resident Barry Parr

Vermont
Written by Don Mitchell

Written by local authors and illustrated throughout
with spectacular color images, Compass American
Guides reveal the character and culture of more than
40 of America's most fascinating destinations. Perfect
for residents who want to explore their own backyards
and for visitors who want an insider's perspective
on the history, heritage, and all there is to see and do.

Fodor's COMPASS AMERICAN GUIDES

At bookstores everywhere.

Lamlash you can explore the southern part of Arran: 10 mi southwest is the little community of **Lagg**, sitting peacefully by the banks of the Kilmory Water, and **Whiting Bay** has a waterfront string of hotels and well-kept properties.

Biking

Rent bicycles at **Whiting Bay Cycle Hire** (⊠ Elim, Silverhill, Whiting Bay, ☎ 01770/700382), open May through September.

Shopping

Patterson Arran Ltd. (⊠ The Old Mill, Lamlash, ☎ 01770/600606) is famous for its mustards, preserves, and marmalades.

Machrie

11 mi north of Lagg.

The area surrounding Machrie, which has scattered homesteads and a popular beach, is littered with prehistoric sites: chambered cairns, hut circles, and standing stones dating from the Bronze Age. From Machrie, a well-surfaced track takes you to a grassy moor by a ruined **14** farm, where you can see the **Machrie Moor Stone Circles:** small, rounded granite-boulder circles and much taller, eerie red-sandstone monoliths. Out on the bare moor, the lost and lonely stones are very evocative, well worth a walk to see if you like the feeling of solitude. The stones are about a mile outside of Machrie; just follow the HISTORIC SCOTLAND sign pointing the way.

Horseback Riding

Even novices can enjoy a guided ride on a mount from **Cairnhouse Riding Centre** (⊠ Blackwaterfoot, 2 mi south of Machrie on A84, ☎ 01770/860466).

Shopping

The **Old Byre Showroom** (⊠ Auchencar Farm, 2 mi north of Machrie on A841, ☎ 01770/840227, WEB www.oldbyre.co.uk) sells sheepskin goods, hand-knit sweaters, designer knitwear, leather goods, and rugs.

En Route Continuing to Blackwaterfoot, you can return to Brodick via the String Road: turn left by the Kinloch Hotel, up the hill. As you drive, there are more fine views of the granite complexities of Arran's hills: gray notched ridges beyond brown moors and, past the watershed, a vista of Brodick Bay. From this high point the road rolls down to Brodick.

Lochranza

15 *14 mi north of Brodick.*

North of Brodick is Lochranza, a crafts community sheltered by the Bay of Loch Ranza, which spills in shallows up the flat-bottom glacial glen. The village is set off by a picturesque ruin, **Lochranza Castle,** set on a low sand spit. This is said to have been the landing place of Robert the Bruce when he returned from Rathlin Island in 1307 to start the campaign that won Scotland's independence. ☎ 0131/668–8800, WEB *www.historic-scotland.gov.uk.* ⊠ *Free.* ☉ *Apr.–Sept., daily 9:30–6; Oct.– Mar, Mon.–Sat. 9:30–4, Sun. 2–4.*

En Route South of Lochranza, there are fine views across the Kilbrannan Sound to the long rolling horizon of Kintyre.

ISLAY AND JURA

Islay has a character distinct from that of the rest of the Hebrides. In contrast to areas where most residents live on crofts (generally worked by someone who has another job, i.e., fisherman, teacher, postman), Islay's western half in particular has large self-sustaining farms. Many of the island's best beaches, wildlife preserves, and historical sites are also on its western half, whereas the southeast is mainly an extension of Jura's inhospitable quartzite hills. Islay is particularly known for its wildlife, especially its birds, including the rare chough (a crow with red legs and beak) and, in winter, its barnacle geese.

Several distilleries—source of the island's delectable malt whiskies— provide jobs for the locals. Islay's sheer number of distilleries will spoil you for choice. A peaty taste characterizes the island's malt whiskies, which are available in local pubs, off-license shops, and distillery shops. Though not all have shops, most distilleries welcome visitors by appointment; some charge a small fee for a tour, which you can redeem against a purchase of whisky.

Although it's possible to meet an Islay native in a local pub, such an event is statistically less likely on Jura, with its one road, one distillery, one hotel, and six sporting estates. In fact, you have a better chance of bumping into one of the island's red deer, which outnumber the human population by at least 20 to 1. The island has a much more rugged look than Islay, with its profiles of the Paps of Jura, a hill range at its most impressive when basking in the rays of a west-coast sunset.

Bowmore

⑯ *11 mi north of Port Ellen.*

Compact Bowmore is about the same size (population 1,000) as Port Ellen, but it works slightly better as a base for touring because it's central to the island's main routes. Sharing its name with the whisky made in the distillery by the shore (founded 1779), Bowmore is a tidy town, its grid pattern having been laid out in 1768 by the local landowner Daniel Campbell, of Shawfield. Main Street stretches from the pier head to the commanding parish church, built in 1767 in an unusual circular design—so the devil could not hide in a corner.

Dining and Lodging

££ ✕🏠 **Harbour Inn.** The cheerfully noisy bar is frequented by locals and off-duty distillery workers, who are happy to rub elbows with travelers and exchange island gossip. The superb restaurant serves morning coffee, lunch, and dinner, and both the bistro-style lunch menu and the "modern Scottish" dinner menu are also available at the bar. Both menus highlight local lobster, crab, prawns, and island lamb and beef. A different theme decorates each of the guest rooms—Victorian Garden, Seaside, Tartan, Captain's Cabin. ✉ *Main St., Bowmore, Islay, Argyll, PA43 7JR,* ☎ *01496/810330,* 𝖥𝖠𝖷 *01496/810990,* 𝖶𝖤𝖡 *www.harbour-inn.com. 7 rooms. Restaurant; no a/c. AE, MC, V.*

Shopping

You can purchase whisky and take a tour at **Bowmore distillery** (✉ School St., ☎ 01496/810671).

En Route   Traveling north out of Bowmore (past a sign for Bridgend), the road skirts the sand flats at the head of Loch Indaal. To reach Port Charlotte, follow the loch shores all the way past Bruichladdich, which, like Bowmore, produces a malt whisky with the same name.

Port Charlotte

⑰ *11 mi west of Bowmore via A846/A847.*

Above the road on the north side in a converted kirk (church) is the **Museum of Islay Life,** a haphazard but authentic and informative display of times past. ⊠ *A847,* ☎ *01496/850358.* 🎟 *£2.* ☉ *Apr.–Oct., Mon.–Sat. 10–5, Sun. 2–5; Nov.–Mar., Mon. and Sat. 10–4.*

South of Port Charlotte, a loop road lets you explore the wild landscapes of the **Rhinns of Islay.** At the south end of the Rhinns are the scattered cottages of **Portnahaven** and its twin, **Port Wemyss.** Take the A847 to the villages, then return by the bleak, unclassified road that loops north and east, passing by the recumbent stone circle at Coultoon and the chapel at Kilchiaran.

En Route For a glimpse of Islay's peerless western seascapes, turn left onto the B8018 north of Bruichladdich. After about 2 mi turn left again onto a little road that meanders past Loch Gorm and ends near Machir Bay, with its superb (and usually deserted) sandy beach. Soon after you turn around to go back, turn right to see the derelict kirk of Kilchoman. The kirkyard holds some interesting grave slabs and two late-medieval stone crosses from the Iona school of carving (as opposed to the Kintyre school). From Kilchoman turn right and then left to circle Loch Gorm, pausing as the road all but touches the coast at Saligo. It's worth a stroll (beyond the former wartime camp) to absorb the fine sea views, especially if westerly breezes are piling high breakers onto the rocky ridges. Heading east from here, turn right at the B8018, then left on the B8017, and take a left at Aoradh Farm onto the minor road that runs north along the west side of Loch Gruinart.

Loch Gruinart

⑱ *7 mi northeast of Port Charlotte, 8 mi north of Bowmore.*

You may feel yourself magnetically pulled toward the long reaches of Loch Gruinart. Dunes flank its outlet to the sea, and pale beaches rise from the falling tides. Traveling north up the loch's western shore, the road soon brings you to **Cill Naoimh** (Kilnave). The ruined chapel here carries a dark tale of a group of Maclean clansmen defeated in a nearby battle with the Macdonalds in 1598: the Macleans sought sanctuary in the chapel, but their pursuers set its roof aflame, and the clansmen perished within. There's a weathered 8th-century carved cross in the graveyard.

If you're into wide skies, crashing waves, and lonely stretches of coast, the best view of Loch Gruinart is to the north up its eastern shore. From the far dunes of the headland, held together with marram grass, you can see the islands of **Colonsay** and **Oronsay** across Hebridean waters, on which plumes and fans of white spray rise from hidden reefs. The priory on the island of Oronsay, with its famous carved cross, is barely distinguishable. To witness this peerless scenery, return to the B8017 from Kilnave, cross the flats at the head of the loch, then turn left up its eastern shore. Park in front of the gate, where the road deteriorates, and continue on foot.

The Oa

⑲ *13 mi south of Bowmore.*

The southern Oa peninsula is a region of caves that's rich in smuggling lore. At its tip, the Mull of Oa, is a monument recalling the 650 men who lost their lives in 1918 when the troopships *Tuscania* and *Otranto*

WHISKY, THE WATER OF LIFE

CONJURED FROM AN INNOCUOUS MIX of malted barley, water, yeast, and possibly peat smoke, malt whisky is for many synonymous with Scotland. The Gaelic-speaking clans produced whisky for hundreds, possibly even thousands, of years before it emerged as Scotland's national drink and major export. Today those centuries of expertise result in a sublimely subtle drink with many different layers of flavor. Each distillery produces a malt with—to the expert—instantly identifiable, predominant notes peculiarly its own.

There are two types of whisky: malt and grain. Malt whisky, generally acknowledged to have a more sophisticated bouquet and flavor, is made with malted barley—barley that is soaked in water until the grains germinate and then dried to halt the germination, all of which adds extra flavor and a touch of sweetness to the brew. Grain whisky also contains malted barley, but with the addition of unmalted barley and maize. Blended whiskies, which make up many of the leading brands, usually balance malt and grain whisky distillations; deluxe blends contain a higher percentage of malts. Blends that contain several malt whiskies are called "vatted malts." Whisky connoisseurs often prefer to taste the single malts: the unblended whisky from a single distillery. In simple terms, malt whiskies may be classified into "eastern" and "western" in style, with the whisky made in the east of Scotland, for example in Speyside, being lighter and sweeter than the products of the western isles, especially those from Islay, which often have a taste of peat smoke or even iodine.

The production process is, by comparison, relatively straightforward: just malt your barley, mash it, ferment it and distill it, then mature to perfection. To find out the details, join one of the many distillery tours on offer, especially in Speyside or Islay, and be rewarded with a dram.

went down nearby. To get here, drive south on the A846: before you reach Port Ellen, go straight ahead; when the A846 turns to a minor road to Imeraval, make a right at the junction, then a left.

Port Ellen

 11 mi south of Bowmore.

The sturdy community of Port Ellen was founded in the 1820s, and much of its architecture dates from the 19th century. It has a harbor, a few shops, and some inns, but not enough commercial development to mortgage its personality.

The road east from Port Ellen passes communities bearing names—such as Lagavulin—that will be familiar to the malt-whisky connoisseur. You can purchase the whisky with the strongest iodine scent of all the island malts and take a tour at the **Lagavulin Distillery.** Tours are free but you must call ahead to reserve a spot. ⊠ *Port Ellen,* ☎ *01496/302400.* ⊡ *Free.* ☉ *Tours weekdays at 10, 11:30, and 2:30.*

The whisky of the **Laphroaig Distillery,** which offers tours, is one of the most distinctive local whiskies, with a tangy, peaty seaweed-and-iodine flavor. The distillery is a little less than a mile along the road to Ardbeg. ☎ *01496/302418.* ✉ *Free.* ☉ *Tours by appointment.*

About 8 mi northeast of Port Ellen is one of the highlights of Scotland's Celtic heritage. After passing through a pleasantly rolling, partly wooded landscape, take a narrow road (it's signposted KILDALTON CROSS) from Ardbeg. This leads to a ruined chapel with surrounding kirkyard, in which stands the finest carved cross anywhere in Scotland:
★ the 8th-century **Kildalton Cross.** Carved from a single slab of epidiorite rock, the ringed cross is encrusted on both sides with elaborate designs in the style of the Iona school. The surrounding grave slabs date as far back as the 12th and 13th centuries.

Horseback Riding

Ballivicar Pony Trekking (✉ Ballivicar Farm, ☎ 01496/302251) leads trips on nearby beaches and into the surrounding countryside.

Islay Woollen Mill

★ ㉑ *3 mi north of Bowmore via A846; follow signs for Port Askaig.*

The mill, set in a wooded hollow by the river, has a fascinating array of working machinery; the proud owner will take you around. The shop here sells high-quality products that were woven on-site. Beyond the usual tweed, there's a distinctive selection of hats, caps, and clothing made from the mill's own cloth. All the tartans and tweeds worn in the film *Braveheart* originated here. Look for the sign for the mill on the main road about a mile east beyond the tiny community of Bridgend. ✉ *Off A846,* ☎ *01496/810563,* WEB *www.islaywoollenmill.co.uk.* ✉ *Free.* ☉ *Mon.–Sat. 10–5.*

Port Askaig

㉒ *3 mi northeast of Loch Finlaggan via A846.*

Serving as the ferry port for Jura, Port Askaig is nothing more than a cluster of cottages by the pier. Uphill, just outside the village, a side road travels along the coast, giving impressive views of Jura on the way. At road's end, the **Bunnahabhain Distillery** (☎ 01496/840646) sits on the shore. Call ahead for tour times.

You can take a tour and purchase whisky at the **Caol Ila Distillery** (☎ 01496/840207). Call ahead for tour times.

Dining and Lodging

££ ✕▥ **Port Askaig Hotel.** The hotel grounds extend all the way to the shore at this modernized roadside drovers' inn overlooking the Sound of Islay and the island of Jura and convenient to the ferry terminal. Accommodations are comfortable without being luxurious, and the traditional Scottish food (£) is well prepared using homegrown produce. ✉ *Port Askaig, Isle of Islay, Argyll PA46 7RD,* ☎ *01496/840245,* FAX *01496/840295,* WEB *www.portaskaig.co.uk. 8 rooms, 6 with bath. Restaurant, 2 bars; no a/c, no room phones. MC, V.*

Jura

㉓ *5 mins by ferry from Port Askaig.*

The rugged, mountainous landscape of Jura, home to deer and not much else, looms immediately east of Port Askaig. Having crossed the Sound of Islay from Port Askaig, you will find it easy to choose which road to take—Jura has only one, starting at Feolin, the ferry pier. Apart from the initial stretch it's all single-lane. The A846 starts off below one of the many raised beaches, then climbs across moorland, providing scenic views across the Sound of Jura. The ruined Claig Castle, on an island just offshore, was built by the Lords of the Isles to control the sound.

Beyond the farm buildings of Ardfin, and Jura House (with gardens occasionally open to the public), the road turns northward across open moorland with scattered forestry blocks and the faint evidence, in the shape of parallel ridges, of the original inhabitants' lazy beds or strip cultivation. The original settlements were cleared with the other parts of the Highlands when the island became more of a sheep pasture and deer forest. The community of Craighouse has the island's only distillery, the **Isle of Jura Distillery** (⊠ A846, ☎ 01496/820240), producing malt whisky. Phone ahead to reserve your place on a tour.

The aptly named **Small Isles Bay** has a superb strip of beach to the north of Craighouse. As the road climbs away from the bay it passes a little cottage above the creek, a reminder of the history of this island: the cottage is the only survivor of a village with a population of 56 that was destroyed in Highland Clearances in 1841. The Clearances came about when landowners, realizing that raising sheep would be more profitable than leasing land to crofters, forced tenants—often by burning down their cottages—off potential grazing land. The crofters were forced to scrape a living on the poorer land along the shoreline, or in many cases, to emigrate overseas. A sheep *fank* (fold) farther up the creek shows what became of the stones of the demolished cottages. Although the landscapes of Jura seem devoid of life, they are, in fact, populated with many ghosts.

Beyond the River Corran the road climbs, offering austere views of the Paps, with their long quartzite screes, and of the fine, though usually deserted, anchorage in the scoop of **Lowlandman's Bay.** The next section of road is more hemmed in and runs to **Lagg**, formerly a ferry-crossing point on the old cattle-driving road between here and Feolin. Beyond Lagg the sea views are blocked by conifer plantings.

Views of fjordlike **Loch Tarbert** are at their best next to the forestry plantation a little farther on from Lagg. At this point the road leads through a stretch of rough, uninhabited landscape. A gate and cattle grid by **Ardlussa**, north of Lagg, mark the start of a Site of Special Scientific Interest—a government-agency designation for rare plants and/or insects—in a shady oak wood. The coast here is rocky and unspoiled. Yellow flag (a Scottish iris), bracken, strands of crisp seaweed on the salty grass, and background birdsong from the mossy woods make this an idyllic stretch when the sun shines. Choose your own picnic site but be sure to park sensibly—the road is very narrow. Try not to be too loud so as not to distract the area's resident otter population.

At **Lealt,** where you'll see the last house as you travel north, you can cross the river. Shortly beyond this point the tarmac ends rather abruptly, with a turning space cut into the hill. Ordinary cars should not be driven any farther on the remainder of this trail, though jeeps, Rovers, and other high-clearance vehicles can make it through. With an ordinary car you have no choice but to retrace your route to the ferry pier at Feolin.

The settlement of **Kinuachdrach** once served as a crossing point to Scarba and the mainland. To get to Kinuachdrach after crossing the river at Lealt, follow the track beyond the surface road for 5 mi. The coastal footpath to Corryvreckan lies beyond, over the bare moors. This area has two enticements: the first, for fans of George Orwell (1903–50), is the house of **Barnhill** (not open to the public), where the author wrote *1984*; the second, for wilderness enthusiasts, is the whirlpool of the **Corryvreckan** and the unspoiled coastal scenery.

Dining and Lodging

££ ╳🍽️ **Jura Hotel.** In spite of its monopoly, this hotel set in pleasant gardens genuinely welcomes its guests and can be relied on for high-quality accommodations and good, simple food cooked using local ingredients. ✉ *Craighouse, Isle of Jura, PA60 7XU,* ☎ *01496/820243,* FAX *01496/820249,* WEB *www.stay.at/jurahotel. 17 rooms, 11 with bath. Restaurant; no a/c, no room phones. AE, DC, MC, V.*

IONA AND THE ISLE OF MULL

Though Mull certainly has an indigenous population, the island is often called the Officers' Mess because of its popularity with retired military personnel. Across from the Ross of Mull is the island of Iona, cradle of Scottish Christianity and ancient burial site of the kings of Scotland.

Craignure

40-min ferry crossing from Oban, 15-min ferry crossing to Fishnish (5 mi northwest of Craignure) from Lochaline.

Craignure, little more than a pier and some houses, is close to Mull's two best-known castles, Torosay and Duart. Reservations for the year-round ferry trip from Oban to Craignure are advisable in summer. The ferry from Lochaline to Fishnish, just northwest of here, runs only in summer and accepts no reservations.

★ ㉔ A trip to **Torosay Castle** can include the novelty of steam-and-diesel service on a narrow-gauge railway, which takes 20 minutes to run from the pier at Craignure to the grounds of Torosay (about ½ mi). Scottish baronial in style, the turreted mid-19th-century castle has a friendly air. Between Easter and October you have the run of much of the house, which is full of intrigue and humor by way of idiosyncratic information boards and informal family albums. The main feature of the castle's gardens—a gentle blend of formal and informal elements—is its Italian statue walk. ✉ *Off the A849, about 1 mi southeast of Craignure,* ☎ *01680/812421,* WEB *www.torosay.com.* 🎫 *Castle and gardens £5; train £2.50.* ☉ *Castle: Easter–Oct., daily 10:30–5:30; last admission at 5. Gardens; Easter–Oct., daily 9–7; Nov.–Easter, daily dawn–dusk. Train departs between 4 and 8 times a day when castle is open.*

㉕ The 13th-century **Duart Castle,** the ancient Maclean seat, was ruined by the Campbells in 1691, but was purchased and restored by Sir Fitzroy Maclean in 1911. Inside, one display depicts the wreck of the *Swan,* a Cromwellian vessel sunk offshore in the mid-17th century and excavated in the 1990s by marine archaeologists. Outside, you can visit nearby **Millennium Wood,** planted with groups of Mull's indigenous trees. If you're an enthusiastic hiker you can walk 4 mi along the shore from Torosay to Duart Castle.; if you have less energy, you can drive (or walk) the 3 mi from Craignure. To reach Duart by car, take the A849 and turn left around the shore of Duart Bay. ✉ *3 mi southeast of Craignure,* ☎ *01680/812309,* WEB *www.duartcastle.com.* 🎫 *£4.* ☉ *Apr., Sun.–Fri. 11–4; May–mid-Oct., daily 10:30–6.*

Lodging

£ 🏨 **Inverlussa.** Idyllically set beside a stream near Loch Spelve, this warm, friendly, modern guest house makes a good base for exploring. Pine furniture, an open fire in the lounge, and tranquil green, blue, or cream color schemes in the guest rooms create a relaxing environment, and you have your pick of several nearby restaurants and pubs for evening meals. ✉ *By Craignure, Isle of Mull, Argyll PA65 6BD,* ☎ FAX *01680/*

812436. 3 rooms, 1 with bath. No a/c, no room phones. No credit cards. Closed Nov.–Mar.

En Route Between Craignure and Fionnphort at the end of the Ross of Mull the double-lane road narrows as it heads southwest, touched by sea inlets at Lochs Don and Spelve. Inland, vivid grass and high rock faces in Glen More make gray and green the prevalent hues. These stepped-rock faces, the by-product of ancient lava flows, reach their highest point in Ben More, the only island *munro* outside Skye (a munro is a Scottish mountain more than 3,000 ft high). Its high, bald slopes are prominent by the time you reach the road junction at the head of Loch Scridain. Stay on the A849 for a pleasant drive the length of the Ross of Mull, a wide promontory with scattered settlements. There are good views to the right of the dramatic cliff ramparts of Ardmeanach, the stubbier promontory to the north. The National Trust for Scotland cares for the rugged stretch of coast, known as The Burg and home to a 40-million-year-old fossil tree (at the end of a long walk from the B8035, signposted west off the A849). The A849 continues through the village of Bunessan and eventually ends in a long parking lot opposite the houses of Fionnphort. The vast parking space is a testament to the popularity of the nearby island of Iona, which does not allow cars. Ferry service is frequent in the summer.

Iona

★ 26 *5 mins by ferry from Fionnphort, which is 36 mi west of Craignure.*

No less a travel writer than Dr. Samuel Johnson (1709–84) wrote, "We were now treading that illustrious Island which was once the luminary of the Caledonian regions." The fiery and argumentative Irish monk Columba (circa 521–97) chose Iona for the site of a monastery in 563 because it was the first landing place from which he could *not* see Ireland. Christianity had been brought to Scotland (Galloway) by St. Ninian (circa 360–432) in 397, but until St. Columba's church was founded, the word had not spread widely among the ancient northerners, the Picts.

As the most important Christian site in the land, Iona was the burial place of the kings of Scotland until the 11th century, so many Dark Age kings, 48 of them Scottish (others were Pictish and Celtic), are interred here, not to mention princes and bishops. The tombstones that are still visible are near the abbey. Many carved slabs also commemorate clan chiefs.

Columba's monastery survived repeated Norse sackings but finally fell into disuse around the time of the Reformation. Restoration work began at the turn of the 20th century, and in 1938 the **Iona Community** was founded. Today the restored buildings, including the abbey, serve as a spiritual center under the jurisdiction of the Church of Scotland. Beyond the ancient cloisters, the island's most delightful aspect is its almost mystical tranquillity—enhanced by the fact that most visitors make only the short walk from the ferry pier to the abbey (by way of the nunnery), rather than press on to the island's farther reaches. ☎ 01681/700793, WEB *www.historic-scotland.gov.uk.* ⌑ £2.80. ◷ Apr.–Sept., daily 9:30–6; Oct.–Mar., daily 9:30–4. Guided tours every ½ hr in summer and on demand in winter.

Shopping

Iona has a few pleasant surprises for shoppers, the biggest of which is the **Old Printing Press Bookshop** (✉ Beside St. Columba Hotel), an excellent antiquarian and secondhand bookstore. The **Iona Community Shop** (☎ 01681/700404), across the road from the abbey itself, carries a nice selection of Celtic-inspired gift items, plus locally made crafts, sheet music and songbooks, and CDs and tapes.

En Route Back on Mull, turn west onto the B8035 at Loch Scridain: the road rises away from the loch to the conifer plantations and green slopes of Gleann Seilisdeir. The main road through the glen breaches the stepped cliffs and drops to the shore, revealing inspiring views of the island of Ulva guarding Loch na Keal. This stretch of the B8035 feels remote, with splinters of rock from the heights strewn across it in places. High ledges eventually give way to vistas of the screes of Ben More. Continue to skirt the coast on the B8073, and you'll take in a succession of fine coastal views with Ulva in the foreground. Beyond Calgary Bay the landscape is gentler as you approach the village of Dervaig.

Dervaig

㉗ *60 mi north of Fionnphort, 27 mi northwest of Craignure.*

At the **Old Byre Heritage Centre,** an audiovisual presentation on the history of Mull plays hourly on the half hour; there's also a crafts shop. The restaurant's wholesome fare, particularly the thick, hearty home-made soup, is a boon to weary travelers. Driving on the B8073 you'll see signs for the center just before the village of Dervaig. ⊠ *Dervaig,* ☎ *01688/400229.* 🖼 *£3.* ☉ *Easter–Oct., daily 10:30–6:30; last admission at 5:30.*

Dining and Lodging

£££–££££ ✕🏠 **Druimard Country House.** From this handsome Victorian house on the village outskirts, you have both loch and glen views over the River Bellart. The room rate includes breakfast and dinner, and the elegant restaurant has an original menu (with several vegetarian options); two popular dishes are roast loin of venison on a bed of red cabbage with game sauce, and medallions of local monkfish topped with Provençal bread crumbs and served in a pool of two pepper sauces. Antique Victorian oak and mahogany furniture and floral wallpaper and fabrics fill the guest rooms. ⊠ *Dervaig, Isle of Mull, Argyll PA75 6QW,* ☎ FAX *01688/400345,* WEB *www.druimard.co.uk. 7 rooms. Restaurant; no a/c. MC, V. Closed Nov.–Mar.*

Nightlife and the Arts

With just 43 seats the aptly named **Mull Little Theatre** (☎ 01688/302828) has the not-insignificant distinction of being the smallest professional theater in the United Kingdom. The theater stages a varied program of plays throughout the summer.

Tobermory

㉘ *5 mi northeast of Dervaig.*

Founded as a fishing station, Tobermory gradually declined, hastened by the arrival of railroad service in Oban. Still, the brightly painted crescent of 18th-century buildings around the harbor—now a popular mooring for yachtsmen—gives Tobermory a Mediterranean look.

Dining and Lodging

££–££££ ✕🏠 **Western Isles Hotel.** Many of the spacious rooms in this traditional resort hotel set high above town have superb views of Tobermory Bay and the Sound of Mull. Floral fabrics, grand bed canopies, and touches of tartan decorate the guest rooms. The terra-cotta lounge and airy conservatory bar are comfortable and relaxing. The restaurant (££) serves local fish, seafood, game, and lamb. ⊠ *Tobermory, Isle of Mull, Argyll PA75 6PR,* ☎ *01688/302012,* FAX *01688/302297,* WEB *www.mullhotel.com. 28 rooms. Restaurant, bar; no a/c. AE, MC, V.*

Biking

On Yer Bike (✉ Salen, Aros, ☎ 01680/300501) rents bicycles.

En Route   To reach the ferry at Fishnish to leave the Isle of Mull, drive south from Tobermory on the A848, which yields pleasant, if unspectacular, views across to the mountainous region of Morvern, on the mainland. On the coast just beyond Aros, across the river flats, stands the ruined 13th-century **Aros Castle.** The road runs through Salen to Fishnish (for the ferry to Lochaline) and then continues onto Craignure (for the ferry to Oban).

ARGYLL AND THE ISLES A TO Z

To research prices, get advice from other travelers, and book travel arrangements, visit www.fodors.com.

AIR TRAVEL

The nearest full-service airport is in Glasgow, but there are two small airports in this region: British Airways Express flies from Glasgow to Campbeltown (on the Kintyre Peninsula) and the island of Islay.

➤ AIRLINES INFORMATION: **British Airways Express** (☎ 08457/733377, WEB www.britishairways.com).

BOAT AND FERRY TRAVEL

Caledonian MacBrayne (CalMac) operates car-ferry service to and from the main islands. An Island Hopscotch ticket reduces the cost of island-hopping. Serco Denholm Ltd. operates the Islay–Jura ferry. *See* Car Travel for route information.

➤ BOAT AND FERRY INFORMATION: **Caledonian MacBrayne** (main office, ✉ Ferry Terminal, Gourock, ☎ 01475/650100 for schedules; 08705/650000 for reservations, WEB www.calmac.co.uk). **Serco Denholm Ltd.** (☎ 01475/731540).

BUS TRAVEL

Scottish Citylink runs daily bus service from Glasgow's Buchanan Street station to the mid-Argyll region and Kintyre. The other companies listed below provide local service within the region.

➤ BUS INFORMATION: **Alex Dunuachie** (✉ Jura, ☎ 01496/820314 or 01496/820221). **B. Mundell Ltd.** (✉ Islay, ☎ 01496/840273). **Bowmans Coaches** (✉ Mull, ☎ 01680/812313). **Oban & District Buses** (✉ Oban and Lorne, ☎ 01631/562856). **Scottish Citylink** (☎ 08705/505050, WEB www.citylink.co.uk). **Stagecoach Western Buses** (✉ Arran, ☎ 01770/302000). **West Coast Motor Service** (✉ Mid-Argyll and Kintyre, ☎ 01586/552319).

CAR TRAVEL

Negotiating this area is easy except in July and August, when the roads around Oban may be congested. There are some single-lane roads, especially on the east side of the Kintyre Peninsula and on the islands.

You'll probably have to board a ferry at some point; all ferries take cars as well as pedestrians. The A85 takes you to Oban, the main ferry terminal for Mull. The A83 rounds Loch Fyne and heads down Kintyre to Kennacraig, the ferry terminal for Islay. Farther down the A83 is Tayinloan, the ferry port for Gigha. You can reach Brodick on Arran by ferry from Ardrossan, on the Clyde coast (A8/A78 from Glasgow), or, in summer, you can travel to Lochranza from Claonaig on the Kintyre Peninsula. *See* Boat and Ferry Travel for more information.

EMERGENCIES

Dial 999 in case of an emergency to reach an ambulance, coast guard, or the fire or police departments (no coins are needed for emergency calls made from public phone booths). Lorne and Islands District General Hospital has an emergency room.

If you need medical or dental care, inquire at your hotel, the local tourist office, the police station, or look under "Doctors" or "Dentists" in the local yellow pages.

➤ HOSPITAL: **Lorne and Islands District General Hospital** (✉ Glengallen Rd., Oban, ☎ 01631/567500).

TOURS
BOAT TOURS
Gordon Grant Tours leads a Three Isles ferry excursion to Mull, Iona, and Staffa and leaves Mull on other trips to Treshnish Isles and Staffa. From Taynuilt, near Oban, boat trips are available from Loch Etive Cruises. Sea Life Surveys offers four- and six-hour whale-watching and wildlife day trips from Tobermory, on the Isle of Mull. Turas Mara runs daily excursions in summer from Oban and Mull to Staffa, Iona, and the Treshnish Isles and specializes in wildlife tours.

➤ CONTACT: **Gordon Grant Tours** (✉ Waterfront, Railway Pier, Oban, ☎ 01631/562842). **Loch Etive Cruises** (✉ Taynuilt, ☎ 01866/822430; or call Oban tourist office). **Sea Life Surveys** (✉ Torrbreac, Dervaig, Mull, ☎ 01688/400223). **Turas Mara** (✉ Penmore Mill, Dervaig, Mull, ☎ FAX 01688/400242).

BUS TOURS
Many of the bus companies listed in Bus Travel arrange general sightseeing tours. Bowmans Tours runs trips from Oban to Mull, Staffa, and Iona between March and October.

➤ CONTACT: **Bowmans Tours** (✉ Scallastle Farm, Craignure, Mull, ☎ 01680/812313, FAX 01631/563221).

TRAIN TRAVEL
Oban and Ardrossan are the main rail stations. For information call National Rail Enquiries. All trains connect with ferries.

Aside from the main line to Oban—with stops at Dalmally, Loch Awe, Falls of Cruachan (on request), Taynuilt, and Connel Ferry—there's no train service to this part of Scotland. A narrow-gauge railway takes ferry passengers from the pier head at Craignure (Mull) to Torosay Castle, a distance of about half a mile.

➤ TRAIN INFORMATION: **National Rail Enquiries** (☎ 08457/484950).

VISITOR INFORMATION
The tourist offices in Lochgilphead, Tarbert, and Tobermory (Mull) are open April through October only; the rest are open year-round.

➤ TOURIST INFORMATION: **Bowmore, Islay** (✉ The Square, ☎ 08707/200617). **Brodick, Arran** (✉ The Pier, ☎ 01770/302140, FAX 01770/302395, www.ayrshire-arran.com). **Campbeltown** (✉ Mackinnon House, The Pier, ☎ 08707/200609). **Craignure, Mull** (✉ The Pierhead, ☎ 08707/200610). **Dunoon** (✉ 7 Alexandra Parade, ☎ 08707/200629). **Inveraray** (✉ Front St., ☎ 08707/200616). **Lochgilphead** (✉ Lochnell St., ☎ 08707/200618). **Oban** (✉ Argyll Square, ☎ 08707/200630, www.visitscottishheartlands.org). **Tarbert, Loch Fyne** (✉ Harbour St., ☎ 08707/200624). **Tobermory, Mull** (✉ Main St., ☎ 08707/200625).

9 AROUND THE GREAT GLEN

INVERNESS, LOCH NESS,
CAWDOR CASTLE, FORT WILLIAM

Sooner or later, all feet march in the direction of mythical Brigadoon, toward those splendid heath-clad mountain slopes and shimmering lochs so typical of the southern Highlands. Here, where the Great Glen runs from Inverness to Fort William— two of the Highlands' best areas for lodging and shopping—is Ben Nevis, Britain's highest peak. Here, too, is Loch Ness, supposedly home to Nessie, everyone's favorite monster and charter member of the local chamber of commerce.

By Gilbert
Summers

Updated by
Beth Ingpen

T HE **ANCIENT RIFT VALLEY** of the Great Glen is a dramatic feature on the map of Scotland, giving the impression that the top half of the country has slid southwest. Geologists confirm that this actually occurred, after matching granite from Strontian, in Morvern, west of Fort William, with the same type of rock found at Foyers, on the east side of Loch Ness, some 65 mi away. The Great Glen, with its sense of openness, lacks the grandeur of Glencoe or the mountains of the Torridons, but the highest mountain in the United Kingdom, Ben Nevis (4,406 ft), looms over its southern portals, and spectacular scenery lies within a short distance of the main glen. A map of Scotland gives a hint of the grandeur and beauty to be found here: fingers of inland lochs, craggy and steep-sided mountains, rugged promontories, and deep inlets. But no map can convey the area's brilliant purple and emerald moorland, its forests and astonishingly varied wildlife (mountain hares, red deer, golden eagles, ospreys), or the courtesy of its soft-spoken inhabitants and the depth of their ancestral memory and clan mythology.

Though it's the capital of the Highlands, Inverness has the flavor of a Lowland town, its winds blowing in a sea-salt air from the Moray Firth. Inverness is also home to one of the world's most famous monster myths: in 1933, during a quiet news week, the editor of a local paper decided to run a story about a strange sighting of something splashing about in Loch Ness. Seventy years later the story lives on, and the dubious Loch Ness phenomenon continues to keep cameras trained on the deep waters.

Fort William, without a monster on its doorstep, makes do with Ben Nevis and the Road to the Isles, a title sometimes applied to the breathtaking scenic route to Mallaig. This is best seen by rail, since the road to Mallaig is still narrow, winding, and single track in places, and meeting an oncoming bus can be alarming—especially if you are distracted by the view. On the way, road and rail routes pass Loch Morar, the country's deepest body of water, which lays claim to its own monster, Morag. Away from the Great Glen to the north lie the heartlands of Scotland, a bare backbone of remote mountains.

The great hills that loom to the south can be seen clearly on either side of Strathspey, the broad valley of the River Spey, an area also commonly known as Speyside. This is one of Scotland's main whisky-distilling areas, with the industry's distinctive kilns, bonded stores, and pungent reek to be found all across the countryside. Speyside malt whiskies are generally sweeter in taste, with much less of the peaty, iodinelike tang of the western, island malts, which you may have encountered on Islay.

Impressive and historic castles are also on the agenda in the Great Glen, perhaps one of the best known of which is Urquhart Castle, a favorite haunt of Nessie-watchers because of its location halfway down Loch Ness. It was once a great royal base and dates to the 13th and 14th centuries, though it's largely in ruins now. To the east are two top-of-the-list castles that are still inhabited: Cawdor Castle, with its happy marriage of different furnishings—modern and ancient, mellow and brightly colored—and Brodie Castle, with its magnificent library and a collection of paintings that extend well into the 20th century.

Pleasures and Pastimes

Biking

The Great Glen itself has a very busy main road, not recommended for cyclists, along the northwest bank of Loch Ness via Drumnadrochit. The B862/B852, which runs by the southeast side of Loch Ness,

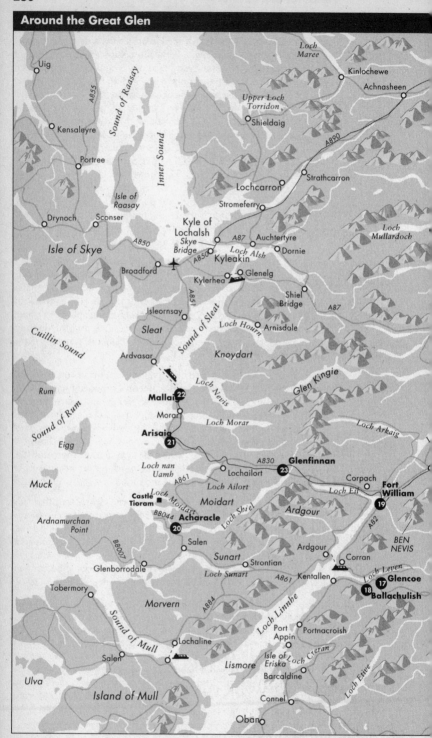

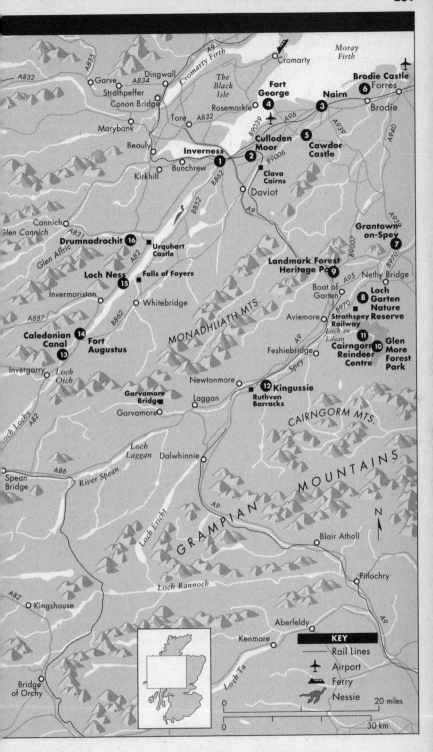

A832

A832

A833

A834

Dingwall

Garve

Strathpeffer

Conon Bridge

Marybank

Beauly

Kirkhill

Cannich

Glen Cannich

Glen Affric

A831

A82

Invermoriston

A887

Invergarry

Spean Bridge

Kingshouse

Bridge of Orchy

Cromarty Firth

The Black Isle

Rosemarkie

Tore

A832

Bunchrew

B862

B852

B862

A9

Whitebridge

Loch Oich

Loch Lochy

A82

River Spean

A86

Loch Laggan

Loch Eight

Loch Rannoch

Loch Ta

Kenmore

Moray Firth

Cromarty

Fort George

4

Culloden Moor

2

Clava Cairns

Daviot

A9

B9039

B9006

A96

Nairn

3

Brodie Castle

6

Forres

Brodie

A939

A940

Cawdor Castle

5

Inverness

1

A9

Drumnadrochit **16**

Urquhart Castle

Loch Ness **15**

Falls of Foyers

Caledonian Canal **14**

13

Fort Augustus

Grantown-on-Spey **7**

A938

B9007

B970

Landmark Forest Heritage Park **9**

A95

Nethy Bridge

Boat of Garten

Loch Garten Nature Reserve **8**

Aviemore

B970

Strathspey Railway

Loch an Eilean

11

Cairngorm Reindeer Centre

10

Glen More Forest Park

MONADHLIATH MTS.

Feshiebridge

Spey

Newtonmore

Garvamore Bridge

Laggan

Garvamore

Kingussie **12**

Ruthven Barracks

CAIRNGORM MTS.

Dalwhinnie

GRAMPIAN MOUNTAINS

A9

Blair Atholl

N

Pitlochry

A9

Aberfeldy

KEY

—— Rail Lines

✈ Airport

⛴ Ferry

🦕 Nessie

20 miles

0

0

30 km

has less traffic and is a better bet for cyclists. A dedicated cycle path runs from Fort William to Inverness: local tourist information centers can provide details. To the east, there is a good network of back roads around Inverness and toward Nairn. The A9, however, on either side of Aviemore, is not recommended for cyclists.

Dining

There is a wealth of country-house hotels serving superb meals from which to choose, as well as an excellent seafood restaurant in Fort William. Inverness and Fort William, the main population centers for the area, have lots of fast-food outlets and restaurants where you can grab a quick bite.

CATEGORY	COST*
££££	over £22
£££	£16–£22
££	£9–£15
£	under £9

*per person for a main course at dinner, including VAT

Fishing

The Great Glen is laced with rivers and lochs where you can fly-fish for salmon and trout. The fishing seasons are as follows: salmon, from early February through September or early October (depending on the area); brown trout, from March 15 to September 30; sea trout, from May through September or early October; rainbow trout, no statutory-close season. Sea angling from shore or boat is also possible. Tourist centers can provide information on locations, permits, and fishing rights (which differ from those in England and Wales).

Lodging

The main centers—Inverness, Fort William, and Aviemore—have plenty of accommodations in all price ranges. Because this is an established vacation area, you should have no trouble finding a room for a night. However, the area is quite busy in peak season.

CATEGORY	COST*
££££	over £140
£££	£110–£140
££	£65–£110
£	under £65

*All prices are for a standard double room, including service, breakfast, and VAT.

Walking

The Great Glen area is renowned for its hill walking, but if you head for the hills, you should be fit and properly outfitted. Remember that on Ben Nevis, a popular route even for inexperienced hikers, it can snow on the summit plateau at any time of the year—this is a large and often dangerous mountain because weather conditions can change very rapidly and unpredictably.

Exploring the Great Glen

The first possible route centers on Inverness, moving east into Speyside, then west down the Great Glen. The second route, originating in Fort William, takes in the unique qualities of the birch-knoll and blue-island West Highland views. There are many romantic and historic associations with this area. It was here that the rash adventurer Prince Charles Edward Stuart (1720–88) arrived for the final Jacobite Rebellion, of 1745–46, and it was from here that he departed after the last battle.

Numbers in the text correspond to numbers in the margin and on the Around the Great Glen map.

Great Itineraries

The road between Fort William and Mallaig, though narrow and winding, is one of the classic routes of Scottish touring and is popularly known as the Road to the Isles. Similarly, the Great Glen road is a vital coast-to-coast link.

IF YOU HAVE 2 DAYS

Both ⌂ **Inverness** ① and ⌂ **Fort William** ⑲ have a choice of loops running from them. Base yourself anywhere around Fort William so that you can take in the spectacular scenery of **Glencoe** ⑰ and Glen Nevis and also get a glimpse of the western seaboard toward **Mallaig** ㉒.

IF YOU HAVE 4 DAYS

Spend two days at one of two bases at each end of the Great Glen, say, ⌂ **Inverness** ① or ⌂ **Nairn** ③, at the north end, and ⌂ **Fort William** ⑲ or ⌂ **Ballachulish** ⑱, at the south end. This will give you adequate time to see this chunk of Scotland. On the first day travel to Nairn from Inverness, and from Nairn go southward via **Cawdor Castle** ⑤ and/or **Brodie Castle** ⑥ to **Grantown-on-Spey** ⑦. Then follow the Spey as far as you like via **Boat of Garten,** with its ospreys in spring and early summer; **Aviemore** and its mountain scenery; and **Kingussie** ⑫, where the Highland Folk Museum does a good job of explaining what life was really like before modern domestic and agricultural equipment made things easy. The next day explore **Loch Ness** ⑮, traveling down the eastern bank as far as **Fort Augustus** ⑭ and returning up the western bank via **Drumnadrochit** ⑯; if you have time on a long summer evening, divert northward at Drumnadrochit to discover the beautiful glens Affric and Cannich, before returning to Inverness. On the third day travel to ⌂ **Fort William** ⑲, taking in the **Caledonian Canal** ⑬. Spend a day doing the suggested loop to **Mallaig** ㉒ and go back through **Glenfinnan** ㉓ to Fort William, or go straight to **Arisaig** ㉑ and take an unforgettable day cruise among the Small Isles.

IF YOU HAVE 7 DAYS

Seven days will give you plenty of time to visit all the highlights of the Great Glen area. Base yourself at ⌂ **Inverness** ① or ⌂ **Nairn** ③ for two nights, then spend a night at ⌂ **Kingussie** ⑫ and a night at ⌂ **Drumnadrochit** ⑯. Moving west to the Fort William area, either stay in ⌂ **Fort William** ⑲ itself, or go farther west and spend two nights in the excellent accommodations of ⌂ **Arisaig** ㉑ for two nights. Either base will allow for exploration of the suggested circular route, a day at sea among the Small Isles, and a half day or day amid the grandeur of **Glencoe** ⑰ or Glen Nevis, behind Fort William. You may also want to make excursions farther north and west.

When to Tour the Great Glen

This is a spring and autumn kind of area—summer contends with pesky midges, and winter brings raw chill. However, in summer, if the weather is settled, it can be very pleasant in the far west, perhaps on the Road to the Isles, toward Mallaig. Early spring is a good time to sample Scottish skiing at Nevis Range or Glencoe.

SPEYSIDE AND LOCH NESS

Because Jacobite tales are interwoven with landmarks throughout this entire area, you should first learn something about this thorny but colorful period of Scottish history in which the Jacobites tried to restore the exiled Stuarts to the British monarchy. One of the best places to do this is at Culloden, just east of Inverness, where a major battle ended in final, catastrophic defeat for the Jacobites. Inverness itself is not really a town in which to linger, unless you need to do some shopping. Other areas to concentrate on are the inner Moray Firth moving down into Speyside, before moving west into the Great Glen. Loch Ness is just one of the attractions hereabouts. In the Great Glen and Speyside, the best sights are often hidden from the main road, an excellent reason to favor peaceful rural byways and to avoid as far as possible the busy A82 (down Loch Ness's western shore), as well as the A96 and A9, which carry much of the eastern traffic in the area.

Inverness

❶ *176 mi north of Glasgow, 109 mi northwest of Aberdeen, 161 mi northwest of Edinburgh.*

Inverness seems designed for the tourist, with its banks, souvenirs, high-quality woolens, and well-equipped visitor center. Compared with other Scottish towns, however, Inverness has less to offer visitors who have a keen interest in Scottish history. Throughout its past, Inverness was burned and ravaged by one or another of the restive Highland clans competing for dominance in the region. Thus, a decorative wall panel here and a fragment of tower there are all that remain amid the modern shopping facilities and 19th-century downtown developments. This does make a good base, however, for exploring the northern end of the Great Glen.

One of Inverness's few historic landmarks is the **castle** (the local Sheriff Court), nestled above the river. The current structure is Victorian, built after a former fort was blown up by the Jacobites in the 1745 campaign. The excellent, although small, **Inverness Museum and Art Gallery** (⊠ Castle Wynd, ☎ 01463/237114) covers archaeology, art, local history, and the natural environment in its lively displays.

Dining and Lodging

£££–££££ ✕🏠 **Dunain Park Hotel.** You'll receive individual attention in this 18th-century mansion set amid 6 acres of wooded gardens. An open fire awaits you in the living room, a good place to sip a drink and browse through books and magazines. Antiques and traditional decor make the bedrooms equally cozy and attractive. The restaurant serves French-influenced Scottish dishes such as Shetland salmon baked in sea salt or medallions of venison rolled in oatmeal with a claret and crème de cassis sauces. ⊠ *Dunain, 2½ mi southwest of Inverness on A82, IV3 8JN,* ☎ *01463/230512,* 𝖥𝖠𝖷 *01463/224532,* 𝖶𝖤𝖡 *www.dunainparkhotel. co.uk. 13 rooms. Restaurant, pool, sauna; no a/c. AE, MC, V.*

£££–££££ ✕🏠 **Inverness Marriott Hotel.** Families appreciate this central rambling mansion set among 4 acres of gardens on the edge of a golf course: kids under 14 stay free, and the heated indoor pool and extensive leisure facilities—including privileges at the golf course next door—offer plenty to do. The bedrooms are spacious, comfortable, and well equipped, if a bit characterless. Six two-bedroom, two-bathroom apartments (each with kitchen) are a good value. The restaurant serves well-prepared and reliable steaks, seafood tagliatelle, and game pâté. ⊠ *Culcabock Rd., IV2 3LP,* ☎ *01463/237166,* 𝖥𝖠𝖷 *01463/712984,* 𝖶𝖤𝖡 *www.marriotthotels.com/invkm. 76 rooms, 6 apartments. Restaurant, golf privileges, pool, health club; no a/c. AE, DC, MC, V.*

££   🏠 **Ballifeary House.** The particularly helpful proprietors at this well-maintained Victorian bed-and-breakfast offer high standards of comfort and service. Rooms are individually decorated with modern furnishings, and the common areas have reproduction antiques. Baillifeary House is within easy reach of downtown Inverness. ⊠ *10 Ballifeary Rd., IV3 5PJ,* ☎ *01463/235572,* FAX *01463/717583,* WEB *www.ballifearyhousehotel.co.uk. 5 rooms. No a/c, no room phones, no children under 15, no smoking. MC, V. Closed Nov.–Mar.*

££ 🖭 **Culduthel Lodge.** Overlooking the River Ness sits an elegant 1840s stone villa, its white-pillared portico inviting you into a relaxing country-house environment: crackling log fires, flowers, sherry, luxury toiletries, and even a complimentary newspaper are all part of the deal. You can enjoy good Scottish cuisine in the dining room, with a menu that changes daily. ⊠ *14 Culduthel Rd., IV2 4AG,* ☎ FAX *01463/240089, www.culduthel.com. 12 rooms. Restaurant; no a/c. MC, V.*

£ 🖭 **Atholdene House.** A family-run 19th-century stone villa serves as a B&B with a friendly welcome and modern accommodations. Rooms are simple, with lots of pastel colors. Note that two of the rooms share a bath. The bus and railway stations are a short walk away. ⊠ *20 Southside Rd., IV2 3BG,* ☎ *01463/233565,* FAX *01463/729101,* WEB *www.atholdenehouse.com. 9 rooms. No a/c, no room phones. MC, V.*

£ 🖭 **Clach Mhuilinn.** This modern family home sits in a pretty garden in
★   a residential area. Floral fabrics and a mahogany bed are in one bedroom; the other has pinewood and tartan. ⊠ *7 Harris Rd., IV2 3LS,* ☎ *01463/237059,* FAX *01463/242092,* WEB *www.ness.co.uk. 2 rooms. No a/c, no room phones, no smoking. MC, V. Closed Nov.–Feb.*

£ 🖭 **Daviot Mains Farm.** Built in Highland-lodge style and 5 mi south
★   of Inverness on the A9, Daviot Mains Farm provides the perfect setting for home comforts and traditional Scottish cooking (for guests only); lucky ones may find wild salmon on the menu in the dining room. The master bedroom has a four-poster bed and bay windows. ⊠ *Daviot Mains, Inverness IV2 5ER,* ☎ *01463/772215,* FAX *01463/772099,* WEB *www.daviotmainsfarm.co.uk. 6 rooms. Restaurant, in-room data ports; no a/c, no smoking. MC, V.*

Nightlife and the Arts

BARS AND LOUNGES

Blackfriars Pub (⊠ Academy St., ☎ 01463/233881) prides itself on its cask-conditioned ales, which can be enjoyed to the accompaniment of regular live entertainment. **The Gellion's Bar** (⊠ 14 Bridge St., ☎ 01463/233648) claims to be Inverness's oldest pub, dating from 1841, and hosts live music nightly, with *ceilidhs* (a mix of country dancing, music, and song; pronounced *kay*-lees) on Saturday afternoons (4–7 PM). **The Harlequin** (⊠ 1 View Pl., ☎ 01463/718178) has castle and river views and a welcoming beer garden, along with live music.

CABARET

June through September, **Scottish Showtime** (⊠ Spectrum Theatre, Faraline Park Bus Station, ☎ 0800/015–8001 for details and bookings) presents Scottish cabaret of the tartan-clad-dancer and bagpipe/accordion variety.

THEATER

Eden Court Theatre (⊠ Bishops Rd., ☎ 01463/234234) offers not only drama but also a program of music, film, and light entertainment, plus an art gallery and an excellent café.

Outdoor Activities and Sports

Inverness Golf Club (⊠ Culcabock Rd., ☎ FAX 01463/239882, WEB www.invernessgolfclub.co.uk) welcomes visitors to its par-69 parkland course 1 mi from downtown. **Torvean Golf Course** (⊠ Glenurquhart Rd., ☎ 01463/711434) is a par-69 municipal course with one of the longest par-5s in the north of Scotland (565 yards).

Shopping

Although Inverness has the usual indoor shopping malls and department stores—including Marks and Spencer—the most interesting goods are to be found in the specialty outlets in and around town. Don't miss the atmospheric indoor **Victorian Market** (✉ Academy St.), built in 1870, which houses more than 40 privately owned specialist shops.

FINE ART AND ARTS AND CRAFTS

art.tm (✉ 20 Bank St., ☎ 01463/712240) aims to present the best of contemporary arts and crafts. The **Castle Gallery** (✉ 43 Castle St., ☎ 01463/729512) displays contemporary British painting, sculpture, prints, and crafts by British artists. The **Riverside Gallery** (✉ 11 Bank St., ☎ 01463/224781) sells paintings, etchings, and prints of Highland landscapes, and contemporary work by Highland artists.

SCOTTISH SPECIALTIES

Highland Wineries (✉ Moniack Castle, Kirkhill, ☎ 01463/831283) creates wines from Scottish ingredients, such as birch sap, and also makes jams, marmalade, and other preserves.

Made in Scotland (✉ Station Rd., Beauly, IV4 7EH, ☎ 01463/782821) is well worth a 14-mi drive west from Inverness (on Route A862) to see one of the biggest and best selections of Scottish-made gifts, textiles, and crafts. (There's a restaurant here, too, to recover in after your spending spree.)

Duncan Chisholm and Sons (✉ 47–51 Castle St., ☎ 01463/234599, WEB www.kilts.co.uk) specializes in Highland dress, tartans, and Scottish crafts. Mail-order and made-to-measure services are available. **Hector Russell Kiltmakers** (✉ 4–9 Huntly St., ☎ 01463/222781, WEB www.hector-russell.com) explains the history of the kilt, shows them being made, and then gives you the opportunity to buy from a huge selection or have a kilt made to measure. The firm offers overseas mail order. **James Pringle Ltd.** (✉ Holm Woollen Mills, Dores Rd., ☎ 01463/223311) stocks a vast selection of cashmere, lamb's-wool, and Shetland knitwear, tartans, and tweeds; a weaving exhibit and an exhibit on the history of tartan are also on-site. You can watch cloth being made here and, for a £3 charge, have a go on a loom yourself.

Midway between Inverness and Nairn on the A96 is the **Taste of Moray** (✉ Gollanfield, ☎ 01667/462340, WEB www.tasteofmoray.co.uk), well worth a stop for its restaurant, but especially for the Food Hall, which stocks a huge selection of Scottish, and especially Morayshire, produce. There's an excellent selection of gift items and household wares.

Culloden Moor

❷ *5 mi east of Inverness via B9006.*

Culloden Moor was the scene of the last major battle fought on British soil—to this day considered one of the most infamous and tragic in all of warfare. Here, on a cold April day in 1746, the outnumbered Jacobite forces of Bonnie Prince Charlie were destroyed by the superior firepower of George II's army. The victorious commander, the duke of Cumberland (George II's son), earned the name of "Butcher" Cumberland for the bloody reprisals carried out by his men on Highland families, Jacobite or not, caught in the vicinity. In the battle itself, the duke's army—greatly outnumbering the Scots—killed more than 1,000 soldiers. The National Trust for Scotland has re-created a slightly eerie version of the battlefield as it looked in 1746. The uneasy silence of the open moor overshadows the merry clatter from the visitor center's coffee shop and the tinkle of cash registers. ⊠ *B9006,* ☎ *01463/ 790607,* WEB *www.nts.org.uk.* ⬚ *£5.* ⊙ *Site daily, 24 hrs; visitor center Apr.–Oct., daily 9–6; Nov.–Dec. and mid-Jan.–Mar., daily 10–4; last entry 30 mins before closing.*

Not far from Culloden, on a narrow road southeast of the battlefield, are the **Clava Cairns,** dating from the Bronze Age. In a cluster among the trees, these stones and monuments form a large ring with passage graves, which consist of a central chamber below a cairn, reached via a tunnel. Placards explain the graves' significance.

Nairn

❸ *12 mi east of Culloden Moor, 17 mi east of Inverness via B9006/ B9091; 92 mi west of Aberdeen.*

Although Nairn has the air of a Lowland town, it's actually part of the Highlands. A once-prosperous fishing village, Nairn has something of a split personality. King James VI (1566–1625) once boasted of a town so large the residents in either end spoke different languages. This was a reference to Nairn, whose fisherfolk, living by the sea, spoke Lowland Scots, whereas its uptown farmers and crofters spoke Gaelic.

The fishing boats have moved to larger ports, but Nairn's historic flavor has been preserved at the **Nairn Museum** in Viewfield House, a handsome Georgian building in the center of town. Exhibits emphasize artifacts, photographs, and model boats relating to Nairn's fishing past. A genealogy service is also offered. A library in the same building has a strong local-history section. ⊠ *Viewfield House, Viewfield Drive,* ☎ *01667/456791.* ⬚ *£1.50.* ⊙ *May–Sept., Mon.–Sat. 10–4:30.*

Dining and Lodging

££££ ✕⬚ **Boath House.** Two surprises await inside this stunning 1820s
★ mansion set on 20 acres: an Aveda health and beauty spa in the basement, and spacious rooms with handsome 19th-century furniture and contemporary Highland art. The restaurant uses local produce, game in season, and fish and seafood delivered fresh daily by the fisherfolk themselves. ⊠ *Auldearn, near Nairn, IV12 5TE,* ☎ *01667/454896,* FAX *01667/455469,* WEB *www.boath-house.com. 6 rooms, 1 cottage. Restaurant, spa; no a/c. AE, MC, V. Closed 2 wks in Jan.*

££ ✕⬚ **Clifton House.** Original works of art cover the walls of this unique
★ hotel, antique furniture graces its rooms, and antique silver gleams in the dining room. The hotel is also licensed as a theater, and each year (September through April) you can enjoy excellent theatrical and musical performances. The restaurant is famous for its classic Scottish cuisine—the lamb cutlets and the duck à l'orange are particularly good—and the wine list is probably the longest in the area. ⊠ *Viewfield St., IV12 4HW,* ☎ *01667/453119,* FAX *01667/452836,* WEB *www.clifton-hotel. co.uk. 12 rooms. 2 restaurants; no a/c, no room phones, no room TVs. AE, DC, MC, V. Closed Dec.–Jan.*

££ ⬚ **Carnach House Hotel.** An overnight at this elegant stone mansion on 7 acres of lawns and woodland is an experience, thanks to the pleasant setting, nice rooms, good food, and caring service. ⊠ *Delnies, IV12 5NT,* ☎ *01667/452094,* FAX *01667/452994. 8 rooms. Restaurant, bar; no a/c, no room phones. AE, MC, V.*

Nightlife and the Arts
Clifton House (⊠ Viewfield St., ☎ 01667/453119) runs a program of concerts, recitals, and plays from September through April.

Outdoor Activities and Sports

GOLF

Nairn's courses are highly regarded by golfers and are very popular, so be sure to book far in advance. **Nairn Golf Club** (⊠ Seabank Rd., ☎ 01667/453208) hosted the 1999 Walker Cup on its par-72 Championship Course, a traditional 18-hole Scottish coastal golf links with what are claimed to be the finest greens in Scotland. **Nairn Dunbar Golf Club** (⊠ Lochloy Rd., ☎ 01667/452741) is a highly rated 18-hole Scottish Championship course, with gorse framing the sea views.

Shopping

At **Auldearn Antiques** (⊠ Dalmore Manse, Auldearn, near Nairn, ☎ 01667/453087) it's easy to spend an hour or more wandering around the old church—filled with furniture, fireplaces, architectural antiques, and linens—and the converted farmsteads, with their tempting antique (or just old) chinaware and textiles. Visit **Brodie Country Fare** (⊠ Brodie, east of Nairn, ☎ 01309/641555) only if you are feeling flush: you may covet the unusual knitwear, quality designer clothing and shoes, gifts, and toys, but they are *not* cheap. You'll also find a food store and delicatessen and an excellent and inexpensive restaurant. Not surprisingly, this establishment is extremely popular with the locals. **Nairn Antiques** (⊠ St. Ninian Pl., near the traffic circle, ☎ 01667/453303) carries a wide selection of antique jewelry, silver, glassware, furniture, pottery, prints, and some unusual giftware.

Fort George

★ ❹ *10 mi west of Nairn.*

As a direct result of the battle at Culloden, the nervous government in London ordered the construction of a large fort on a promontory reaching into the Moray Firth: Fort George was started in 1748 and completed some 20 years later. It survives today as perhaps the best-preserved 18th-century military fortification in Europe. A visitor center and tableaux at the fort portray the 18th-century Scottish soldier's way of life, as does the **Regimental Museum of the Queen's Own Highlanders.** To get here take the B9092 north from A96 west of Nairn. ⊠ *Ardersier,* ☎ *0131/668–8800,* WEB *www.historic-scotland.gov.uk.* 🎫 *Fort £5, museum free.* ☉ *Apr.–Sept., daily 9:30–6; Oct.–Mar., Mon.–Sat. 9:30–4, Sun. 2–4; last admission 45 mins before closing.*

Cawdor Castle

★ ❺ *5 mi southwest of Nairn.*

Shakespeare's (1564–1616) Macbeth was Thane of Cawdor, but the sense of history that exists within the turreted walls of Cawdor Castle is more than fictional. Cawdor is a lived-in castle, not an abandoned, decaying structure. The earliest part of the castle is the 14th-century central tower; the rooms contain family portraits, tapestries, fine furniture, and paraphernalia reflecting 600 years of history. Outside the castle walls are sheltered gardens and woodland walks. ⊠ *Cawdor, off B9090, 5 mi southwest of Nairn,* ☎ *01667/404615,* WEB *www.cawdorcastle.com.* 🎫 *Castle £6.10, garden and grounds £3.20.* ☉ *May–mid-Oct., daily 10–5.*

Brodie Castle

★ ❻ *8 mi east of Nairn.*

The original medieval castle here was rebuilt and extended in the 17th and 19th centuries. Fine examples of late-17th-century plasterwork are preserved in the Dining Room and Blue Sitting Room; an impressive library and a superb collection of pictures extend into the 20th century. Brodie Castle is in the care of the National Trust for Scotland. ⊠ *Off A96, Brodie, by Nairn,* ☎ *01309/641371,* WEB *www.nts.org.uk.* 🎫 *Castle £5; grounds only, £1 (honesty box).* ☉ *Castle Apr.–Sept., Thurs.–Mon. 11–6; grounds year-round, daily 9:30–sunset.*

Grantown-on-Spey

❼ *24 mi south of Nairn via A939.*

The sturdy settlement of Grantown-on-Spey, set amid tall pines that flank the River Spey, is a classic Scottish planned town. This means it's a community that was planned and laid out by the local landowner, in this case Sir James Grant in 1776. It has handsome buildings in silver granite and some good shopping for Scottish gifts.

Shopping

Ewe and Me (⊠ 82 High St., ☎ 01479/872911) is a well-stocked, high-quality gift shop with Scottish silver jewelry, glassware, Highland Stoneware platters and jugs, stuffed toys, and a large selection of greetings cards. **Speyside Heather Centre** (⊠ Skye of Curr, ☎ 01479/851359) has 200–300 varieties of heather for sale. The company can supply heather plants by mail order (United Kingdom only). A crafts shop, floral-art sundries, an antiques shop, and a tearoom are also here.

Boat of Garten

11 mi southwest of Grantown via B970.

In the peaceful village of Boat of Garten, the scent of pine trees mingles with an equally evocative smell—that of steam trains. Boat of Garten is the terminus of the **Strathspey Steam Railway** (☎ 01479/810725), and the oily scent of smoke and steam hangs faintly in the air near the authentically preserved train station. From here you can take a 5-mi train trip to Aviemore, offering a chance to wallow in nostalgia and enjoy superb views of the high and often white domes of the Cairngorm Mountains.

❽ The **Loch Garten Nature Reserve** achieved fame when the osprey, a bird that was facing extinction in the early part of the 20th century, returned to breed here. Instead of cordoning off the nest site, conservation officials encouraged visitors by constructing a blind for bird-watching. Now thousands of bird lovers visit annually to get a glimpse of the domestic arrangements of this fish-eating bird, which has since bred in many other parts of the Highlands. The sanctuary, which is about 1 mi east of Boat of Garten via the B970, is administered by the Royal Society for the Protection of Birds (RSPB). ☎ *01479/831694 or 01463/715000.* 🎫 *£2.50.* ☉ *Osprey observation post Apr.–Aug., daily 10–6; other areas of reserve year-round, daily.*

🖐 ❾ **Landmark Forest Heritage Park** has a working steam-powered sawmill and a Clydesdale horse to haul the logs; a forestry workshop, where you can try out skills such as crosscut sawing; a bookstore; and a restaurant. Outdoors you'll find nature trails, a treetop trail, and a giant, climbable fire tower. Diversions for children include a Wild Forest Maze, terrifying Wild Water coasters (incredibly steep water slides), and an adventure playground. Reach Carrbridge on the quiet B9153—keep off the A9. ⊠ *Carrbridge, 3 mi north of Boat of Garten,* ☎ *01479/841613,* WEB *www.landmark-centre.co.uk.* 🎫 *£2.60–£7.15.* ☉ *Apr.–mid-July, daily 10–6; mid-July–Aug., daily 10–7; Sept.–Oct., daily 10–5:30; Nov.–Mar., daily 10–5; last admission 1 hr before closing.*

Aviemore

6 mi southwest of Boat of Garten via B970.

Once a quiet junction on the Highland Railway, Aviemore now has all the brashness and concrete boxiness of a year-round holiday resort. The Aviemore area is a versatile walking base, but you must be dressed properly and carry emergency safety gear for high-level excursions onto the near-arctic plateau. For skiing and rugged hiking follow the B970 **⑩** from Aviemore, through **Glen More Forest Park,** past Loch Morlich to the high parking lots on the exposed shoulders of the Cairngorm Mountains. There are dozens of trails here, and the park is also good for cycling, bird-watching, and any number of outdoor activities. The **CairnGorm Mountain Railway,** a funicular railway to the top of Cairn Gorm (the mountain that gives its name to the Cairngorms), operates both during and after the ski season and affords extensive views of the broad valley of the Spey. At the top is an interpretation center and restaurant. Be forewarned: it can get very cold above 3,000 ft, and weather conditions can change rapidly, even in the middle of summer. ☒ *Off B9152,* ☎ *01479/861261,* WEB *www.cairngormmountain.com.* ☒ *£6 for funicular railway.* ⊙ *Daily; call for funicular schedule.*

On the high slopes of the Cairngorms, you may see the reindeer herd **⑪** that was introduced here in the 1950s. You can inquire at the **Cairngorm Reindeer Centre,** by Loch Morlich, about accompanying the herders on their daily rounds. The reindeer are surprisingly docile creatures and seem to enjoy human company. Be sure to wear waterproof gear, as conditions can be wet and muddy. ☒ *Loch Morlich, Glen More Forest Park,* ☎ FAX *01479/861228,* WEB *www.reindeer-company. demon.co.uk.* ☒ *Reindeer Centre £6; paddocks £1.50, £3 Oct.–Christmas.* ⊙ *Reindeer Centre Mar.–Dec., daily 10–5 or dusk; rounds Apr.–Sept., daily at 11 and 2:30; Oct.–Mar., daily at 11 (subject to weather conditions). Paddocks closed Jan.–Easter.*

★ The place that best sums up Speyside's piney ambience is probably **Loch an Eilean** (signs guide you to it from Aviemore). On the **Rothiemurchus Estate** (☎ 01479/810858, WEB www.rothiemurchus.net), a converted cottage beside Loch an Eilean is a visitor center (the area is a National Nature Reserve). The estate also offers several diversions, including fly-fishing for salmon and trout, guided walks, safari tours, off-road driving, clay-pigeon shooting, and farm-shop tastings of estate-produced beef, venison, and trout.

Kingussie

⑫ *13 mi southwest of Aviemore, via A9 and A86.*

The village of Kingussie (pronounced Kin-*yoo*-see) is of interest primarily for its **Highland Folk Museum.** The interior exhibits are in what was an 18th-century shooting lodge, its paneled and varnished ambience still apparent. Displays include 18th-century furniture, clothing, and implements. Outside, various types of Highland buildings have been reconstructed. The museum also maintains a Victorian schoolhouse in nearby Newtonmore. ☒ *Kingussie,* ☎ *01540/661307,* WEB *www.highlandfolk. com.* ☒ *Kingussie £1, Newtonmore £5.* ⊙ *Kingussie Apr.–Sept., Mon.–Sat. 9–5; Oct., weekdays 9:30–4; Nov.–Mar., weekdays, guided tours only, at 11 and 1. Newtonmore Apr.–Aug., daily 10:30–5:30; Sept., daily 11–4:30; Oct., weekdays 11–4:30.*

Ruthven Barracks, which from a distance looks like a ruined castle on a mound, is redolent with tales of the '45 (as the last Jacobite Rebellion is often called). The defeated Jacobite forces rallied here after the battle at Culloden, but then abandoned and blew up the government outpost they had earlier captured. You'll see it as you approach Kingussie. ☒ *B970, ½ mi south of Kingussie,* ☎ *0131/668–8800,* 🕸 *www.historic-scotland.gov.uk.* 🖼 *Free.* ☉ *Daily, 24 hrs.*

Dining and Lodging

££££ ★ ✕🖬 **The Cross.** Meals are superb and the wine list extensive at this "restaurant with rooms." Dinner, which could be fillet of local venison with port and red currants or pike mousse with a prawn sauce, is included in the price of your room. Bedrooms—all with king-size beds—are individually decorated and may have a balcony, canopy bed, or antique dressing table. ☒ *Tweed Mill Brae, Inverness-shire PH21 1TC,* ☎ *01540/661166,* 🇫🇦🇽 *01540/661080,* 🕸 *www.thecross.co.uk. 9 rooms. Restaurant; no a/c. MC, V. Closed Dec.–Feb. No dinner Tues.*

£ ✕🖬 **Osprey Hotel.** This friendly hotel is an ideal base for skiing and hiking. Rooms are all individually decorated, with antique furniture. An impressive wine list complements the much praised cuisine, which might include breast of duck with grape and red wine sauce or monkfish with Bloody Mary sauce. ☒ *Ruthven Rd., Inverness-shire PH21 1EN,* ☎ 🇫🇦🇽 *01540/661510,* 🕸 *www.ospreyhotel.co.uk. 8 rooms. Restaurant; no a/c, no room phones. AE, MC, V.*

En Route Eleven miles southwest of Kingussie on the A86 at Laggan Bridge, where the main road crosses the River Spey, an unnamed road runs west up the glen to Garvamore. If you're not pressed for time, it's worth taking this road to view the **Garvamore Bridge** (about 6 mi north of the junction, at the south side of Corrieyairack Pass). This dual-arched bridge was built in 1735 by General Wade (1673–1748), who had been ordered to improve Scotland's roads by a British government concerned that its troops would not be able to travel the Highlands quickly enough to quell an uprising.

A stretch of the **A86,** quite narrow in some places, hugs the western shore of Loch Laggan. It has superb views of the mountainous heartlands to the north, and, over the silvery spine of hills known as the Grey Corries, culminating with views of Ben Nevis to the south.

Caledonian Canal

⓭ *40 mi west of Kingussie.*

Traveling north up the Great Glen takes you parallel to Loch Lochy (on the eastern shore) and over the Caledonian Canal at Laggan Locks. From this beautiful spot, which offers stunning vistas of lochs, mountains, and glens in all directions, you can look back on the impressive profile of Ben Nevis. The canal, which links the lochs of the Great Glen—Loch Lochy, Loch Oich, and Loch Ness—owes its origins to a combination of military as well as political pressures that emerged at the time of the Napoleonic Wars with France: for the most part, the British needed a better and faster way to get naval vessels from one side of Scotland to the other. The great Scottish engineer Thomas Telford (1757–1834) surveyed the route in 1803. The canal, which took 19 years to complete, has 29 locks and 42 gates. Telford ingeniously took advantage of the three lochs that lie in the Great Glen, which have a combined length of 45 mi, so that only 22 mi of canal had to be constructed to connect the lochs and complete the waterway from coast to coast.

Dining and Lodging

££–£££ ✕🖬 **Glengarry Castle Hotel.** This rambling, pleasantly old-fashioned mansion makes a good touring base; Invergarry is just south of Loch Ness and within easy reach of the Great Glen's best sights. Rooms have traditional Victorian decor; some have superb views over Loch Oich. The food is traditional Scottish fare. Try the poached salmon with hollandaise or the loin of lamb with rosemary. The grounds include the ruins of Glengarry Castle, a seat of the MacDonnell clan. The hotel entrance is south of the A82–A87 road junction. ⊠ *Invergarry, Inverness-shire PH35 4HW,* ☎ *01809/501254,* FAX *01809/501207,* WEB *www.glengarry. net. 26 rooms. Restaurant, tennis court, fishing; no a/c. MC, V. Closed Nov.–Mar.*

Fort Augustus and Loch Ness

53 mi north of Laggan.

⑭ The best place to see the locks of the Caledonian Canal in action is at **Fort Augustus,** at the southern tip of Loch Ness. In the village center considerable canal activity takes place at a series of locks that rise from Loch Ness. Fort Augustus itself was captured by the Jacobite clans during the 1745 Rebellion. Later the fort was rebuilt as a Benedictine abbey, but monks no longer live here. The **Caledonian Canal Heritage Centre** (⊠ Ardchattan House, Canalside, Fort Augustus, ☎ 01320/366493), in a converted lockkeeper's cottage, gives the history of the canal and its uses over the years.

⑮ From the B862, just east of Fort Augustus, you'll get your first good long view of the formidable and famous **Loch Ness,** which has a greater volume of water than any other Scottish loch, a maximum depth of more than 800 ft, and its own monster—at least according to popular myth. Early travelers who passed this way included English lexicographer Dr. Samuel Johnson (1709–84) and his guide and biographer, James Boswell (1740–95), who were on their way to the Hebrides in 1783. They remarked at the time about the condition of the population and the squalor of their homes. Another early travel writer and naturalist, Thomas Pennant (1726–98), noted that the loch kept the locality frost-free in winter. Even General Wade came here, his troops blasting and digging a road up much of the eastern shore. None of these observant early travelers ever made mention of a monster. Clearly, they had not read the local guidebooks.

En Route   A more leisurely alternative to the fast-moving traffic on the busy A82 to Inverness, and one that combines monster-watching with peaceful road touring, is to take the B862 from Fort Augustus and follow the east bank of Loch Ness; join the B852 just beyond Whitebridge and take the opportunity to view the waterfalls at Foyers. The B862 runs around the end of Loch Ness, then climbs into moorland and forestry plantation. Fine views of Fort Augustus can be seen by climbing a few yards up and to the right, onto the moor; here you'll be able to see above the conifer spikes. The half-hidden track beside the road is a remnant of the military road built by General Wade. Loch Ness quickly drops out of sight but is soon replaced by the peaceful, reedy Loch Tarff.

Drumnadrochit

⑯ *21 mi north of Fort Augustus via A82.*

If you're in search of the infamous beast Nessie, head to Drumnadrochit: here you'll find the **Official Loch Ness Monster Exhibition Centre,** which presents the facts and the fakes, the photographs, the unexplained sonar contacts, and the sincere testimony of eyewitnesses. You'll have to make up your own mind on Nessie. All that's really known is that Loch Ness's huge volume of water has a warming effect on the local weather, making the lake conducive to mirages in still, warm conditions. These are often the circumstances in which the "monster" appears. Whether or not the *bestia aquatilis* lurks in the depths—more than ever in doubt since 1994, when the man who took one of the most convincing photos of Nessie confessed on his deathbed that it was a fake—plenty of camera-toting, sonar-wielding, and submarine-traveling scientists and curiosity seekers haunt the lake. ⊠ *Off the A82, Drumnadrochit,* ☎ *01456/450573 or 01456/450218,* WEB *www.loch-ness-scotland.com.* ⊡ *£5.95.* ☉ *Easter–May, daily 9:30–5; June–Sept., daily 9–6; Oct., daily 9:30–5:30; Nov.–Easter, daily 10–3:30; last admission 30 mins before closing.*

Urquhart Castle, near Drumnadrochit, is a favorite Loch Ness monster-watching spot. This weary fortress stands on a promontory overlooking the loch, as it has since the Middle Ages. Because of its central and strategic position in the Great Glen line of communication, the castle has a complex history involving military offense and defense, as well as its own destruction and renovation. The castle was begun in the 13th century and was destroyed before the end of the 17th century to prevent its use by the Jacobites. The ruins of what was one of the largest castles in Scotland were then plundered for building material. A visitor center relates these events and gives an idea of what life was like here in medieval times. Today swarms of bus tours pass through after investigating the Loch Ness phenomenon. ⊠ *2 mi southeast of Drumnadrochit on A82,* ☎ *0131/668–8800,* WEB *www.historic-scotland. gov.uk.* ⊡ *£5.* ☉ *Apr.–Sept., daily 9:30–6; Oct.–Mar., daily 9:30–4; last admission 45 mins before closing.*

Dining and Lodging

£££ ✕🏠 **Polmaily House.** This country house amid lovely parkland is on
★ the northern edge of Loch Ness; sailing on the loch is even possible. Books, log fires, and a helpful staff contribute to an atmosphere that is warmer and more personal than that found at grander, more expensive hotels, and families are sincerely welcomed. The restaurant is noted for its traditional British cuisine using fresh Highland produce. Tay salmon in pastry with dill sauce, roast rack of lamb with rosemary, and cold smoked venison with melon are examples of some flavorful dishes. ⊠ *Drumnadrochit IV63 6XT,* ☎ *01456/450343,* FAX *01456/450813,* WEB *www.polmaily.co.uk. 9 rooms, 5 suites. Restaurant, tennis court, pool, boating, fishing, croquet, horseback riding; no a/c. MC, V.*

TOWARD THE SMALL ISLES

Fort William has enough points of interest—a museum, exhibits, and shopping—to compensate for its less-than-picturesque setting. The town's primary purpose is to serve the west Highland hinterland; its role as a tourist stop is secondary. Because this is a relatively wet part of Scotland and because Fort William itself can always be explored if it rains, strike west toward the coast if the weather looks clear: on a sunny day the Small Isles—Rum, Eigg, Canna, and Muck—look as blue as the sea and sky together. From here you can also visit Skye via the ferry at Mallaig, or take a day cruise from Arisaig to the Small Isles for a glimpse of traffic-free island life. South of Fort William, Ballachulish and Glencoe are within easy striking distance.

Glencoe

❶⑦ *92 mi north of Glasgow, 44 mi northwest of Edinburgh.*

Glencoe, where great craggy buttresses loom darkly over the road, has a special place in the folk memory of Scotland: it was the site of an infamous massacre in 1692, still remembered in the Highlands for the treachery with which soldiers of the Campbell clan, acting as a government militia, treated their hosts, the MacDonalds. According to Highland code, in his own home a clansman should give shelter even to his sworn enemy. In the face of bitter weather, the Campbells were accepted as guests by the MacDonalds. Apparently acting on orders from the British government, the Campbells turned on their hosts, committing murder "under trust." **The National Trust for Scotland's Visitor Center** at Glencoe (at the west end of the glen) tells the story of the massacre and also has an excellent display on mountaineering. ☎ 01855/811307. ✉ £3.50. ☺ May–Oct., daily 10–6.

Outdoor Activities and Sports

The **Glencoe Ski Centre** (✉ Kingshouse, Glencoe, ☎ 01855/851226, WEB www.ski-glencoe.co.uk), at the east end of the glen, has challenging black runs, well-maintained beginner and intermediate runs on the lower plateau, and snowboarding facilities. There's also a good restaurant.

Ballachulish

⑱ *1 mi west of Glencoe, 15 mi south of Fort William, 39 mi north of Oban.*

Ballachulish, once a slate-quarrying community, acts as gateway to the western approaches to Glencoe (though there is a Glencoe village as well). With several dining and lodging options, the town serves as a good base for exploring the area.

Dining and Lodging

££££ ✕🏠 **Airds Hotel.** This former ferry inn, dating to the 17th century, has some of the finest views in all of Scotland. Set in a peaceful village midway between Ballachulish and Oban, the long white building, backed by trees, has a congenial air to it. Quilted bedspreads and family mementos make you feel at home. Fishing trips can be arranged. The restaurant serves Scottish cuisine, including venison and grouse. ✉ *Port Appin, Argyll PA38 4DF,* ☎ *01631/730236,* FAX *01631/730535,* WEB *www.airds-hotel.com. 12 rooms. Restaurant, fishing; no a/c. MC, V.*

£££ ✕🏠 **Isles of Glencoe Hotel.** An excellent base for families, this hotel
★ has its own leisure facilities including a toy corner. Everything from food to staff attitude makes children welcome, but adults won't feel neglected. The interior is modern, with streamlined, fitted furniture in the bedrooms and plenty of original landscape paintings. Though neither original nor inventive, the cuisine—a choice of well-cooked beef, chicken, fish, and game dishes—is satisfying after a hard day's sightseeing. In keeping with its youth-friendly environment, there is also a separate children's menu. ✉ *Ballachulish PA39 4HL,* ☎ *01855/ 821582,* FAX *01855/821463,* WEB *www.freedomglen.co.uk. 59 rooms. Restaurant, pool, sauna, playground; no a/c. MC, V.*

Fort William

⑲ *15 mi north of Ballachulish, 69 mi southwest of Inverness, 108 mi northwest of Glasgow, 138 mi northwest of Edinburgh.*

As its name suggests, Fort William originated as a military outpost, first established by Oliver Cromwell's (1599–1658) General Monk in 1655 and refortified by George I (1660–1727) in 1715 to help combat an uprising by the turbulent Jacobite clans. It remains the southern gateway to the Great Glen and the far west, and it's a bustling, tourist-oriented place. The **West Highland Museum,** in the town center, explores the history of Prince Charles Edward Stuart and the 1745

Rebellion. Included in the museum's folk exhibits are a costume and tartan display and a famous collection of Jacobite relics. ⊠ *Cameron Sq.,* ☏ *01397/702169.* ⌷ *£2.* ☉ *June and Sept., Mon.–Sat. 10–5; July–Aug., Mon.–Sat. 10–5 and Sun. 2–5; Oct.–May, Mon.–Sat. 10–4.*

Britain's highest mountain, the 4,406-ft **Ben Nevis,** looms over Fort William less than 4 mi from Loch Linnhe, an inlet of the sea. A trek to its summit is a rewarding experience, but you should be fit and well prepared—food and water, compass, first-aid kit, whistle, hat, gloves, and warm clothing (yes, even in summer) for starters—as the unpredictable weather can make it a hazardous hike. Ask advice at the local tourist office before you begin.

A huge collection of gemstones, crystals, and fossils, including a 26-pound uncut emerald, are displayed at **Treasures of the Earth,** in a converted church near Fort William. ⊠ *A830, Corpach,* ☏ *01397/772283.* ⌷ *£3.* ☉ *July–Sept., daily 9:30–7; Oct.–Dec. and Feb.–June, daily 10–5.*

Dining and Lodging

££ ✕ **Crannog Seafood Restaurant.** Set conspicuously on a small pier jut-
★ ting out over the waters of Loch Linnhe, the Crannog has transformed Fort William dining. The sight of a fishing boat drawing up to the pier to take its catch straight to the kitchen says it all about the freshness of the seafood. The chef's capable touch ensures the fresh flavors are not overwhelmed. From the window seats you can watch the sun setting behind the steep hills on the far side of the loch. ⊠ *Town Pier,* ☏ *01397/705589. MC, V.*

££££ ✕🏠 **Inverlochy Castle.** A red-granite Victorian castle, Inverlochy stands on 50 acres of woodlands in the shadow of Ben Nevis, with striking Highland landscape on every side. Dating from 1863, the hotel retains all the splendor of its period, with a fine fresco ceiling, crystal chandeliers, a handsome staircase in the Great Hall, and plush, comfortable bedrooms. The restaurant is exceptional—many specialties use local ingredients, such as roast saddle of roe deer or wood-pigeon consommé, with orange soufflé as the final touch. ⊠ *Torlundy, 3 mi northeast of Fort William on A82, PH33 6SN,* ☏ *01397/702177,* ℻ *01397/702953,* 🖳 *www.inverlochy.co.uk. 17 rooms. Restaurant, tennis court, fishing, billiards, croquet; no a/c. AE, MC, V. Closed Jan.–Feb.*

££ 🏠 **Ashburn House.** A Victorian house with its own grounds that's only a five-minute walk from downtown offers luxury at B&B prices. Chintz-draped bedrooms in shades of pink and blue are furnished with huge beds—they are 6 ft wide and have no footboard. The conservatory lounge affords stunning loch views, and a breakfast that includes home-baked scones is served in a delightful Victorian-corniced dining room. ⊠ *Achintore Rd., PH33 6RQ,* ☏ *01397/706000,* ℻ *01397/702024,* 🖳 *www.highland5star.co.uk. 7 rooms. No a/c, no room phones, no smoking. AE, MC, V. Closed Dec.*

££ 🏠 **Crolinnhe.** An elegant Victorian house with colorful gardens, over-
★ looking Loch Linnhe yet only a 10-minute walk from town, Crolinnhe is an exceptionally comfortable B&B. Antique and high-quality reproduction furniture is set off by pastel walls and bold-tone curtains. The breakfasts are among the best served in any establishment in Scotland. ⊠ *Grange Rd., PH33 6JF,* ☏ *01397/702709,* ℻ *01397/700506,* 🖳 *www.crolinnhe.co.uk. 3 rooms. No a/c, no room phones, no smoking. No credit cards. Closed Nov.–Mar.*

££ 🏠 **The Grange.** A delightful, white-frosted confection of a Victorian villa stands in pretty gardens a 10-minute walk from downtown. Antiques, flowers, log fires, and views of Loch Linneh await in these deluxe

B&B accommodations. ✉ *Grange Road, Fort William PH33 6JF,* ☎
01397/705516, FAX *01397/701595,* WEB *www.thegrange-scotland.co.uk.*
4 rooms. No a/c, no room phones. No credit cards. Closed Dec.–Feb.

Outdoor Activities and Sports

BIKING

An unusual but recommended option is the downhill mountain bike
track (available between May and September) at the Nevis Range: up
via the gondola, then a thrilling 2000-ft descent by bike. Bicycles can
be rented for this and other excursions from **Off Beat Bikes** (✉ 117
High St., ☎ 01397/704008, WEB www.offbeatbikes.co.uk).

GOLF

The 18-hole, par-72 heathland golf course at **Fort William** (✉ Torlundy,
Fort William, ☎ 01397/704464) has spectacular views of Ben Nevis
and welcomes visitors.

HIKING

This area—especially around Glen Nevis, Glencoe, and Ben Nevis—
is very popular with hikers, but you should try it only if fit and properly outfitted. The tourist information center can offer guidance on
low-level routes. Several excellent guides are available locally; they can
and should be consulted for high-altitude routes. Keep in mind that
Ben Nevis is a large and dangerous mountain, where snow can fall on
the summit plateau any time of the year.

SKIING

Nevis Range (☎ 01397/705825, WEB www.nevis-range.co.uk), is a
modern development on the flanks of Aonach Mor, 7 mi north of Fort
William, has good and varied skiing, as well as views of Ben Nevis.
There are runs for all ability levels and a gondola system.

Shopping

The majority of shops here are along High Street, which in summer
attracts ever-present, bustling crowds intent on stocking up for excursions
to the west. The **Ben Nevis Woollen Mill** (✉ Belford Rd., ☎ 01397/
704244), at the north end of town, is a major supplier of tartans, woolens,
and tweeds and has a restaurant. The **Granite House** (✉ 74 High St.,
☎ 01397/703651) stocks Scottish contemporary jewelry, china and crystal giftware, wildlife sculptures, folk music CDs, ethnic clothing, musical instruments, toys and collectibles, and cards. The **Scottish Crafts
and Whisky Centre** (✉ 135–139 High St., ☎ 01397/704406) has the
usual souvenirs, but it also sells homemade chocolates and a vast range
of malt whiskies, including miniatures and limited-edition bottlings.
Treasures of the Earth (✉ Corpach, ☎ 01397/772283) stocks an
Aladdin's cave assortment of gemstone jewelry, crystal ornaments,
mineral specimens, polished stones, fossils, and books on related
subjects. It's a trove of unusual gifts. Note that the shop is closed in
January.

En Route   Travel down the east side of Loch Linnhe to Corran, where a frequent
ferry shuttles cars and foot passengers across the loch to Ardgour. (You
can avoid the ferry by driving around the head of Loch Eil, but it's not
a particularly scenic route.) From Ardgour the two-lane A861 runs south
along Loch Linnhe before heading into Glen Sanda, crossing the watershed, and running down to the long shores of **Loch Sunart.** This is a
typical western Highlands sea loch: orange kelp marks the tide lines,
and herons stand muffled and miserable, wondering if it's worth risk-
ing a free meal at the local fish farm. As for the fish farms themselves,
you'll grow accustomed to their floats and cages turning up in the fore-

ground of every sea-loch view. The farms created jobs and were originally hailed as the savior of the Highland economy, but questions are now being raised about their environmental impact, at the same time that the market for their product is threatened by Scandinavian imports.

At the little village of Salen, either turn north immediately or divert to the westernmost point of mainland Scotland, at **Ardnamurchan Point,** reached along a narrow road with blind curves, in part through thickets of rhododendrons. The Ardnamurchan Peninsula is a must-see if you love unspoiled coastal scenery. Here you'll find small farming communities and vacation homes.

Acharacle

★ ⑳ *3 mi north of Salen.*

On the way north to Acharacle (pronounced ach-*ar*-ra-kle with a Scots *ch*), you'll pass through deep-green plantations and moorland lily ponds. This spread-out settlement, backed by the hills of Moidart, lies at the shallow and reedy west end of **Loch Shiel;** the north end is more dramatic and sits deep within the rugged hills.

En Route Traveling between Acharacle and Arisaig, you'll reach the upper sandy shores of Loch Moidart by climbing on the A861 over a high moorland pass. On the next ascent, from Loch Moidart, you'll be greeted by stunning sea views. You can reach the sea coast by the mouth of **Loch Ailort** (pronounced *eye*-ort), and there are plenty of places to pull off among the boulders and birch scrub and sort out the view of the islands. In the distance you'll be able to spot Eigg, a low island marked by the dramatic black peak of An Sgurr. Beyond Eigg is the larger Rum, with its range of hills and the Norse-named, cloud-capped Rum Coullin looming over the island. Loch Ailort itself is another picturesque inlet, now cluttered with the garish floats of fish cages. You'll meet the main road again at the junction with the A830, the main route from Fort William to Mallaig. Turn left here. The breathtaking seaward views should continue to distract you from the road beside **Loch nan Uamh** (from Gaelic, meaning "cave" and pronounced *oo*-am). This loch is associated with Prince Charles Edward Stuart's nine-month stay on the mainland, during which he gathered a small army, marched as far south as Derby in England, alarmed the king, retreated to unavoidable defeat at Culloden in the spring, and then spent a few months as a fugitive in the Highlands. A cairn by the shore marks the spot where the prince was picked up by a French ship; he never returned to Scotland.

Arisaig

㉑ *27 mi north of Acharacle.*

Considering its small size, Arisaig, gateway to the Small Isles, offers a surprising choice of high-quality options for dining and lodging. To the north of Arisaig, the road cuts across a headland to reach a stretch of coastline where silver sands glitter with the mica in the local rock; clear water, blue sky, and white sand lend a tropical flavor to the beaches—when the sun is shining.

From Arisaig try to visit at least a couple of the **Small Isles: Rum, Eigg, Muck,** and **Canna,** each very small and different in feel. Rum is a wildlife reserve. Contact **Arisaig Marine Ltd.** (✉ Arisaig Harbour, Arisaig, Inverness-shire PH39 4NH, ☎ 01687/450224), which runs a service from the harbor at Arisaig daily at 11 April through October. The MV *Shearwater,* a former naval inshore minesweeper, delivers supplies and mail as well as visitors to the diminutive island communities. What sets this operation apart from the tourism-oriented excursions is that it affords a glimpse of island life from a working vessel going about its summer routine.

Dining and Lodging

££££ ✕📷 **Arisaig House Hotel.** This secluded and grand Victorian mansion offers tranquillity and some marvelous scenery, including views of Loch nan Uamh. The bedrooms are plush and restful, with soft pastels, original moldings, and antique furniture. The cuisine showcases fresh local ingredients: try the poached fillet of turbot with crushed potatoes and chilled oyster cream, or the roast loin of spring lamb with potato-and-herb *galette* (round, flat cake), broad beans, and a rosemary jus. A 9-hole golf course is at Traigh, 6 mi to the north. ✉ *Beasdale, by Arisaig, 13 mi south of Mallaig on A830, west of Glenfinnan, PH39 4NR,* ☎ *01687/450622,* FAX *01687/450626,* WEB *www.arisaighouse. co.uk. 12 rooms. Restaurant, billiards, croquet, library; no a/c. MC, V. Closed Dec.–Feb.*

££ ✕📷 **Old Library Lodge and Restaurant.** A barn on the waterfront has been converted into a guest house and a fine restaurant with reasonable prices. Local produce is prepared in a French-bistro style and served in a whitewashed, airy dining room. The bedrooms are very comfortable, with flowery duvets and cozy armchairs. ✉ *Arisaig PH39 4NH,* ☎ *01687/450651,* FAX *01687/450219,* WEB *www.oldlibrary.co.uk. 6 rooms. Restaurant; no a/c. MC, V. Closed Nov.–Mar.*

£–££ ✕📷 **Arisaig Hotel.** An old coaching inn close to the water, this hotel has magnificent views of the Small Isles. The inn has retained its provinciality with simple furnishings and home cooking (££–£££). High-quality local ingredients are used to good advantage; lobster, langoustines, and crayfish are specialties, as are "proper" puddings, such as fruit crumbles. ✉ *Arisaig PH39 4NH,* ☎ *01687/450210,* FAX *01687/ 450310,* WEB *www.arisaighotel.co.uk. 13 rooms. Restaurant, recreation room; no a/c. MC, V.*

Mallaig

㉒ *8 mi north of Arisaig, 44 mi northwest of Fort William.*

After the approach along the coast, the workaday fishing port of Mallaig itself is anticlimactic. It has a few shops, and there is some bustle by the quayside when fishing boats unload or the Skye ferry departs: this is the departure point for the southern ferry connection to the Isle of Skye, the largest island of the Inner Hebrides. Mallaig is also the starting point for day cruises up the Sound of Sleat, which separates Skye from the mainland. The sound offers views into the rugged Knoydart region and its long, fjordlike sea lochs, Lochs Nevis and Hourn. The area to the immediate north and west beyond Loch Nevis, one of the most remote in Scotland, is often referred to as the Rough Bounds of Knoydart. For cruises to Loch Nevis, which operate all year, contact **Bruce Watt Sea Cruises** (✉ Western Isles Guest House, East Bay, Mallaig, PH41 4QG, ☎ 01687/462320).

The **Heritage Centre** of Mallaig has exhibits, films, photographs, and models on all aspects of the local history. ✉ *Station Rd.,* ☎ *01687/ 462085,* WEB *www.mallaigheritage.org.uk.* 🎟 *£1.80.* ⊙ *Apr.–Oct., Mon.–Sat. 9:30–4:30, Sun. 12:30–4:30.*

Beside the harbor, **Mallaig Marine World** shows you what goes on beneath the surface of the Sound of Sleat: live fish and shellfish and a display on the local fishing traditions are among the attractions here.

✉ *The Harbour,* ☎ *01687/462292.* 🎫 *£3.* ◷ *Daily 9:30–5:30; call to confirm hrs.*

A small, unnamed side road just south of Mallaig leads east to an even smaller road that will bring you to **Loch Morar,** the deepest of all the Scottish lochs (more than 1,000 ft); the next deepest point is miles out into the Atlantic, beyond the continental shelf. The loch is said to have its own resident monster, Morag, who undoubtedly gets less recognition than its famous cousin Nessie. Apart from this short public road, the area around the loch is all but roadless.

Glenfinnan

㉓ *26 mi southeast of Mallaig.*

Glenfinnan, perhaps the most visitor-oriented stop on the route between Mallaig and Fort William, has much to offer if you're interested in Scottish history. Here the National Trust for Scotland has capitalized on the romance surrounding the story of the Jacobites and their intention of returning a Stuart monarch and the Roman Catholic religion to a country that had become staunchly Protestant. In Glenfinnan in 1745, the sometimes-reluctant clans joined forces and rallied to Prince Charles Edward Stuart's cause.

The raising of the prince's standard is commemorated by the **Glenfinnan Monument,** an unusual tower on the banks of Loch Shiel; the story of his campaign is told in the nearby visitor center. Note that the figure at the top of the monument is of a Highlander, not the prince. The view down Loch Shiel from the Glenfinnan Monument is one of the most photographed views in Scotland. ✉ *A830,* ☎ *01397/722250,* 🌐 *www.nts.org.uk.* 🎫 *£2.* ◷ *Visitor center Apr.–Oct., daily 10–6.*

As impressive as the Glenfinnan Monument (especially if you've tired of the Jacobite "Will He No Come Back Again" sentiment) is the curving railway viaduct that stretches across the green slopes behind the monument. The **Glenfinnan Viaduct,** 21 spans and 1,248 ft long, was in its time the wonder of the Highlands. The railway's contractor, Robert MacAlpine, known as Concrete Bob by the locals, pioneered the use of mass concrete for viaducts and bridges when his company built the Mallaig extension, which opened in 1901. Now the viaduct is famous again, this time for its appearance in the "Harry Potter" films.

The train is the most relaxing way to take in the landscape of birch- and bracken-covered wild slopes; diesel **rail services** (☎ 08457/484950) run all year on the stretch of line between Fort William and Mallaig. But the best train of all is a steam train, the **Jacobite Steam Train** (☎ 01463/239026), which runs between July and September.

AROUND THE GREAT GLEN A TO Z

To research prices, get advice from other travelers, and book travel arrangements, visit www.fodors.com.

AIR TRAVEL

Inverness Airport has flights from London, Edinburgh, and Glasgow. Domestic flights covering the Highlands and islands are operated by British Airways, Servisair, and easyJet. Fort William has bus and train connections with Glasgow, so Glasgow Airport can be an appropriate access point.

➤ AIRLINES: **British Airways** (☎ 08457/733377, WEB www.britishairways. com). **easyJet** (☎ 0870/600–0000, WEB www.easyjet.com). **Servisair** (☎ 01667/464040).

➤ AIRPORT INFORMATION: **Glasgow Airport** (☎ 0141/887–1111). **Inverness Airport** (✉ Dalcross, ☎ 01667/464000).

BUS TRAVEL

A long-distance Scottish Citylink service connects Glasgow and Fort William. Inverness is also well served from the central belt of Scotland; for information call the Inverness coach station.

There is limited service available within the Great Glen area and some local service running from Fort William. Highland Country Buses operates buses down the Great Glen and around Fort William. A number of postbus services will help get you to the more remote corners of the area. A timetable is available from the Royal Mail.

➤ BUS INFORMATION: **Highland Country Buses** (☎ 01397/702373). **Inverness coach station** (☎ 01463/233371). **Royal Mail Post Buses** (✉ 7 Strothers La., Inverness IV1 1AA, ☎ 01463/256273). **Scottish Citylink** (☎ 08705/505050, WEB www.citylink.co.uk).

CAR RENTAL

➤ AGENCIES: **Avis** (✉ Dalcross Airport, Inverness, ☎ 01667/464070). **Budget** (✉ Burns Cottage, Railway Terr., Inverness, ☎ 0800/181181). **Europcar Ltd.** (✉ Friar's Bridge Service Station, Telford St., Inverness, ☎ 01463/235337). **Hertz** (✉ Dalcross Airport, Inverness, ☎ 01667/462652).

CAR TRAVEL

The fast A9 brings you to Inverness in roughly three hours from Glasgow or Edinburgh, even if you take your time.

As in all areas of rural Scotland, a car is a great asset for exploring the Great Glen and Speyside, especially since the best of the area is away from the main roads. You can use the main A82 from Inverness to Fort William to explore this area, or use the smaller B862/B852 roads (former military roads) to explore the much quieter east side of Loch Ness. The same applies to Speyside, where several options open up away from the A9, especially through the pinewoods by Coylumbridge and Feshiebridge, east of the main road. Mallaig, west of Fort William, has improving road connections, but the road is still narrow and winding in many places, and rail remains the most enjoyable way to experience the rugged hills and loch scenery between these two places. In Morvern, the area across Loch Linnhe southwest of Fort William, you may encounter single-lane roads, which require slower speeds and concentration.

EMERGENCIES

In case of any emergency, dial **999** for an ambulance, the police, the coast guard, or the fire department (no coins are needed for emergency calls from phone booths).

Pharmacies are not common away from the larger towns, and doctors often dispense medicines in very rural areas. In an emergency, the police will assist you in locating a pharmacist. In Fort William, Boots the Chemist is open weekdays 8:45–6, Saturday 8:45–5:30. In Inverness, Kinmylies Pharmacy is open weekdays until 6 and Saturdays until 5:30. The pharmacy at the Scottish Co-Op superstore is open Monday–Wednesday 9–8, Thursday and Friday 9–9, Saturday 9–6, and Sunday 10–6.

➤ HOSPITALS: **Belford Hospital** (✉ Belford Rd., Fort William, ☎ 01397/702481). **Raigmore Hospital** (✉ Old Perth Rd., Inverness,

☎ 01463/704000). **Town and County Hospital** (✉ Cawdor Rd., Nairn, ☎ 01667/452101).

➤ Late-Night Pharmacies: **Boots the Chemist** (✉ High St., Fort William, ☎ 01397/705143). **Kinmylies Pharmacy** (✉ 1 Charleston Ct., Kinmylies Inverness, ☎ 01463/221094). **Scottish Co-Op** (✉ Milton of Inshes, Perth Rd., outside Inverness, ☎ 01463/712188).

TOURS
BOAT TOURS

Arisaig Marine operates highly recommended Hebridean day cruises for whale-, seal-, and bird-watching. Your vessel is the MV *Shearwater*, which travels to the Small Isles at Easter and daily from May through September, when charter trips also go to Skye. Also available for charter from Arisaig Marine is a fast twin-engine motor yacht, which can take up to 12 passengers around the Small Isles and farther afield. Caledonian MacBrayne runs scheduled service and cruises from Mallaig to Skye, the Small Isles, and Mull.

Jacobite Cruises Ltd. runs morning and afternoon cruises on Loch Ness to Urquhart Castle and boat and coach excursions to the Monster Exhibition in Drumnadrochit.

An unusual option from Inverness is a day trip to Orkney: John o'-Groats Ferries runs day tours from Inverness to Orkney, daily from June through August. Moray Firth Cruises provides trips by boat from Inverness harbour into the Moray Firth, offering you the chance to see dolphins in their breeding area.

➤ Fees and Schedules: **Arisaig Marine** (☎ 01687/450224). **Caledonian MacBrayne** (☎ 01475/650100). **Jacobite Cruises Ltd.** (☎ 01463/233999). **John o'Groats Ferries** (☎ 01955/611353). **Moray Firth Cruises** (☎ 01463/717900).

PERSONAL GUIDES

James Johnstone is based in Inverness but will drive you anywhere; he has a particularly good knowledge of the Highlands and islands, including the Outer Isles.

➤ Fees and Schedules: **James Johnstone** (☎ 01463/798372, FAX 01463/790179, WEB www.jajcd.com).

TRAIN TOURS

From Fort William, ScotRail runs services on the outstandingly beautiful West Highland Line to Mallaig. The Jacobite Steam Train is an exciting summer (July to September) option on the same route.

➤ Fees and Schedules: **Jacobite Steam Train** (☎ 01463/239026). **ScotRail** (☎ 08457/550033, WEB www.scotrail.co.uk).

TRAIN TRAVEL

There are connections from London to Inverness and Fort William (including overnight sleeper service), as well as reliable links from Glasgow and Edinburgh. For information call National Rail Enquiries.

Though there is no rail connection among towns within the Great Glen, this area has the West Highland line, which links Fort William to Mallaig; a trip on this scenic line is recommended (steam trains are a bonus in the summer months). There's train service between Glasgow (Queen Street) and Inverness, via Aviemore, which gives access to the heart of Speyside. For information call National Rail Enquiries.

➤ Train Information: **National Rail Enquiries** (☎ 08457/484950). **Jacobite Steam Train** (☎ 01463/239026 for bookings). **ScotRail** (☎ 08457/550033, WEB www.scotrail.co.uk).

VISITOR INFORMATION

Aviemore, Fort William, and Inverness have year-round tourist offices. Other tourist information centers, open seasonally, include those at Ballachulish, Fort Augustus, Grantown-on-Spey, Kingussie, Mallaig, Nairn, and Strontian. The Web site for the whole area is www.host.co.uk.
➤ TOURIST INFORMATION: **Aviemore** (✉ Grampian Rd., ☎ 01479/810363). **Fort William** (✉ Cameron Centre, Cameron Sq., ☎ 01397/703781). **Inverness** (✉ Castle Wynd, ☎ 01463/234353, WEB www.host.co.uk).

10 THE NORTHERN HIGHLANDS

SUTHERLAND, ISLE OF SKYE,
OUTER HEBRIDES

If you haven't visited the "real" Highlands, you haven't seen Scotland. In this region is concentrated much of the romance of "Caledonia stern and wild"—the glamour of the clans, the red deer and golden eagles, the Celtic mists and legends, and a mixture of splendor and tranquillity found hardly anywhere else in the world. Here is Eilean Donan—the most romantic of all Scottish castles—the land's end at John o'Groats, and Skye, the mysterious island immortalized by the exploits of Bonnie Prince Charlie.

By Gilbert
Summers

Updated by
Beth Ingpen

T HE OLD COUNTIES OF ROSS AND CROMARTY (sometimes called
Easter and Wester Ross), Sutherland, and Caithness constitute
the most northern portion of mainland Scotland. The population
is sparse, mountains and moorland limit the choice of touring routes,
and distances are less important than whether the winding, hilly roads
you sometimes encounter are two lanes or one. On a map, this area may
seem far from major urban centers, but it's easy to reach. Inverness has
an airport with direct links to London, Edinburgh, Glasgow, and even
Amsterdam, and you can reach destinations such as the fishing town
of Ullapool in an hour by car from Inverness. In fact, much of the western seaboard is easily accessible from the Northern Highlands.

And accessible it should be, for this area contains some of Scotland's
most intriguing scenery. Much of Sutherland and Wester Ross, for example, is made up of a rocky platform of Lewisian gneiss, certainly
the oldest rocks in Britain, scoured and hollowed by glacial action into
numerous lochs. On top of this rolling, wet moorland landscape sit
strangely shaped quartzite-capped sandstone mountains, eroded and
pinnacled. Take a walk here, and the Ice Age doesn't seem so far away.
One of the region's leitmotivs is the sea lochs that thrust salty fingers
into the loneliest landscapes in Scotland, carrying the Atlantic's salty
tang among the moors and deep forests. Strange, solitary peaks rear
up out of the heather, and if you're lucky, you may sight a golden eagle
soaring overhead in search of rabbits.

Many place-names in this region reflect its early links with Scandinavia.
Sutherland, the most northern portion of mainland Scotland, was once
the southernmost land belonging to the Vikings. Scotland's most northern point, Cape Wrath, got its name from the Viking word *hvarth* (turning point), and Laxford, Suilven, and dozens of other names in the area
have Norse rather than Gaelic derivations.

The islands of Skye and especially the Outer Hebrides, which are now
often referred to as the Western Isles, are the stronghold of the Gaelic
language. Skye, famous for its misty mountains, called the Cuillins, has
a surprisingly wide variety of landscape, considering its relatively small
size. The south of the island is generally flatter; its coastline is the place
to hunt out hidden beaches, perhaps overlooked by a ruined castle, and
its interior moorlands are dotted with lochans (small lakes). As you
travel northward, however, the landscape becomes increasingly mountainous, with green pastures surrounding the scattered crofting (farming) communities and sea inlets strewn with jewel-like islets, miniature
versions of Skye itself. Both sides of the island have their own distinctive
character, and both offer much to enjoy, so don't hurry north from the
Mallaig-Armadale ferry terminal or the bridge to Skye. Instead, take
time to divert down side roads for an exhilarating autumn trip through
the glowing gold, silver, russet, and copper of southern Skye—birch,
bracken, heather, and peat bog all playing their part in nature's rich
tapestry. Leave plenty of time for some excellent shopping, then travel
on northward to explore Trotternish, Flora Macdonald's home base;
Waternish, with some excellent restaurants; Dunvegan, with a castle
and more good restaurants; or Glendale, its winding road threaded with
a profusion of crafts and heritage sites.

Pleasures and Pastimes

Biking
The landscapes are great, but the open and rugged terrain has not favored the development of a network of rural back roads. Be prepared

to meet holiday traffic at peak season, especially on the mainland. Some side roads (and even some main roads, especially on the islands) are single lane and narrow, meaning there will be traffic coming the other way between passing places. High-visibility clothing is advised.

Dining

Dining options are more limited here than in other parts of Scotland; the exception is Skye, which has several restaurants of very high standard. Reliable country houses and inns serving hearty, traditional Highland fare can be found throughout the region.

CATEGORY	COST*
££££	over £22
£££	£16–£22
££	£9–£15
£	under £9

*per person for a main course at dinner, including VAT

Fishing

The possibilities for fishing are endless here, as a glance at the loch-covered map of Sutherland suggests. Trout-fishing permits for several hill lochans are available at local post offices, shops, and hotels. Inquire at your lodging or at the nearest tourist information center.

Lodging

This region of Scotland has some good modern hotels and charming inns but not many establishments in the more expensive categories, except in the more popular areas such as Skye. You'll often find that the most enjoyable accommodations are low-cost guest houses, often family run, providing a bed and breakfast. Dining rooms of country-house lodgings frequently reach the standard of top-quality restaurants.

CATEGORY	COST*
££££	over £140
£££	£110–£140
££	£65–£110
£	under £65

*All prices are for a standard double room, including service, breakfast, and VAT.

Exploring the Northern Highlands

From Inverness, the gateway to the Northern Highlands, roads fan out like the spokes of a wheel to join the coastal route around the rim of mainland Scotland. Many roads here are single lane, requiring you to pause at passing places to allow ongoing traffic to pass: do not underestimate driving times, especially when driving on minor roads or on the islands. There are simply no roads into the wilder areas, and few roads at all—so you're bound to be sharing the roads with heavy trucks and buses. Ferry services are generally very reliable, weather permitting.

Numbers in the text correspond to numbers in the margin and on the Northern Highlands and Skye and the Outer Hebrides maps.

Great Itineraries

The quality of the northern light and the sheer beauty of the landscapes add to the adventure. Above all, don't rush things. And take a good look at how multiple-journey ferry tickets—the Island Hopscotch, for example—can help you stay flexible.

IF YOU HAVE 2 DAYS

If you only have two days, head to the fabled isle of Skye, whose mists shroud so many legends. Stay in towns with remarkable hotels, such

The Northern Highlands and Skye

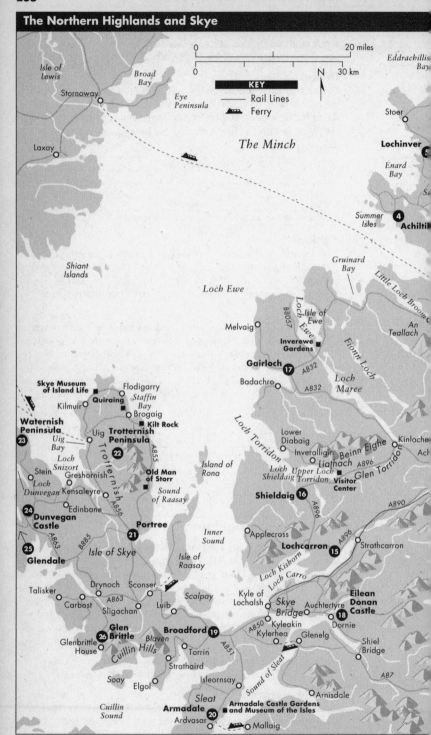

0 ____ 20 miles
0 ____ 30 km
N

Isle of Lewis
Broad Bay
Eddrachillis Bay
Stornoway
Eye Peninsula
Stoer
The Minch
Lochinver
Laxay
Enard Bay
Achiltibuie 4
Summer Isles
Shiant Islands
Gruinard Bay
Little Loch Broom
An Teallach
Loch Ewe
Isle of Ewe
B8057
Melvaig
Fionn Loch
Inverewe Gardens
Gairloch 17
A832
Badachro
A832
Loch Maree
Skye Museum of Island Life
Flodigarry
Staffin Bay
Quiraing
Brogaig
Kilmuir
Kilt Rock
Waternish Peninsula 23
Uig
Loch Torridon
Kinlochewe
Lower Diabaig
Beinn Eighe
Ach
Inverallligin
Liathach
Uig Bay
Trotternish Peninsula 22
Loch Snizort
A855
Loch Shieldaig
Upper Loch Torridon
A896
Glen Torridon
Greshornish
Old Man of Storr
Visitor Center
Stein
Kensaleyre
Island of Rona
Shieldaig 16
Loch Dunvegan
Edinbane
A856
Sound of Raasay
A896
Dunvegan Castle 24
A890
Portree 21
Applecross
Lochcarron 15
Strathcarron
Glendale 25
A863
B885
Inner Sound
Isle of Skye
Isle of Raasay
A896
Loch Kishorn
Loch Carro
Talisker
Drynoch
Sconser
Scalpay
Eilean Donan Castle
Carbost
A863
Luib
Kyle of Lochalsh
Skye Bridge
Auchtertyre 18
Sligachan
Glen Brittle 26
Broadford 19
Kyleakin
Dornie
Glenbrittle House
Blaven
Torrin
A850
Kylerhea
Glenelg
Shiel Bridge
Cuillin Hills
Strathaird
A851
Sound of Sleat
A87
Soay
Elgol
Isleornsay
Arnisdale
Cuillin Sound
Armadale 20
Sleat
Armadale Castle Gardens and Museum of the Isles
Ardvasar
Mallaig

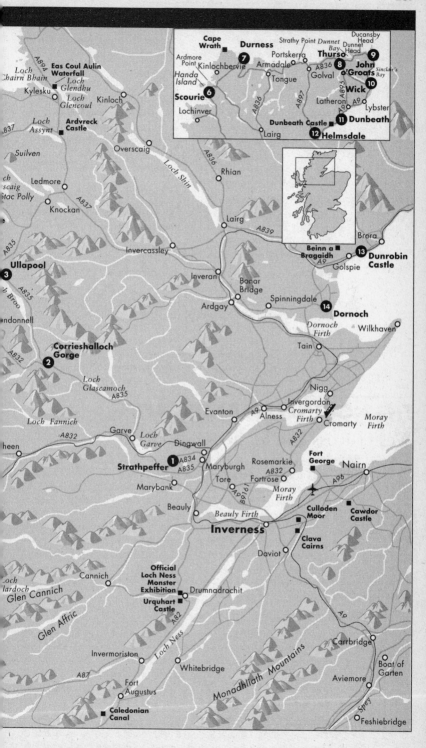

as 🏠 **Broadford** ⑲ or 🏠 **Armadale** ⑳, then tour the spectacular countryside, including the celebrated Cuillin ridges near **Glen Brittle** ㉖. Be sure to detour to see Scotland's most romantic castle, **Eilean Donan** ⑱, once you're back on the mainland.

IF YOU HAVE 5 DAYS

If the weather looks settled, head for Skye, basing yourself at 🏠 **Portree** ㉑. You could then hop over from Uig, in the north of Skye, to 🏠 **Tarbert** ㉛, in the Western Isles, for **Calanais Standing Stones** ㉚, the **Arnol Black House** ㉙, and some deserted beaches, returning to 🏠 **Ullapool** ③, in the north, and traveling to Inverness via **Strathpeffer** ①. Otherwise, stick to the mainland and do the entire loop of the north of Scotland, staying overnight at 🏠 **Ullapool** ③, 🏠 **Scourie** ⑥, 🏠 **Thurso** ⑧, 🏠 **Wick** ⑩, or 🏠 **Dornoch** ⑭.

IF YOU HAVE 8 DAYS

Tackle the coastal loop of the north of Scotland counterclockwise, taking the ferry at 🏠 **Ullapool** ③ for 🏠 **Stornoway** ㉗ and the Western Isles, and returning to the mainland via the ferry from 🏠 **Tarbert** ㉛ to Uig on Skye, then go over the Skye Bridge.

When to Tour the Northern Highlands

The Northern Highlands and islands are best seen in late spring, summer, and early autumn. The earlier in the spring or later in the autumn you go, the greater the chances of your encountering the elements in their extreme form, and the fewer attractions and accommodations you will find open; even tourist-friendly Skye closes down almost completely by the end of October. As a final deciding factor, you may not want to take a western sea passage in a gale, a frequent occurrence in the winter months.

THE NORTHERN LANDSCAPES

Wester Ross and Sutherland

The northern landscapes have some of the most distinctive mountain profiles in all of Scotland, although the coastal rim roads are more interesting than the cross-country routes. The essence of Caithness, the area at the top of Scotland, is space, big skies, and distant blue hills beyond endless rolling moors (although "tax-break" conifer planting has encroached on the views in some areas). There's a surprising amount to see and do on the east coast beyond Inverness—so make sure you allow enough time to take in the visitor centers and croft houses open to view.

Strathpeffer

❶ *19 mi northwest of Inverness via A9, A835, and A834.*

At the former Victorian spa town of Strathpeffer you can take a walk to admire Victorian "holiday houses" and a Pictish stone carved with a lifelike eagle, or enjoy a toy museum in the former railway station. Not far from Strathpeffer are the tumbling **Falls of Rogie** (signposted off the A835), where an interestingly bouncy suspension bridge presents you with a fine view of the splashing waters below.

Lodging

£ 🏠 **Craigvar.** Host Margaret Scott is a delight and stocks plenty of tourist
★ leaflets to keep you busy at this pretty Georgian bed-and-breakfast. The so-called Beige Room is actually white and cream, with a swag of dried hydrangea above the bed. Idiosyncratic pictures—from 18th-century portraits to Japanese-style still lifes—hang on the walls. The Blue

CLANS AND TARTANS

WHATEVER THE ORIGINS of the clans—some with Norman roots, intermarried into Celtic society; some of Norse origin, the product of Viking raids on Scotland; others traceable to the monastic system; yet others possibly descended from Pictish tribes—by the 13th century the clan system was at the heart of Gaelic tribal culture. By the 15th century the clan chiefs of the Scottish Highlands were a threat even to the authority of the Stewart monarchs.

The word clann means "family" or "children" in Gaelic, and it was the custom for clan chiefs to board out their sons among nearby families, a practice that helped to bond the clan unit and create strong allegiances: the chief became "father" of the tribe and was owed loyalty by lesser chiefs and ordinary clansmen.

The clan chiefs' need for strong men-at-arms, fast-running messengers, and bards for entertainment and the preservation of clan genealogy was the probable origin of the Highland Games, still celebrated in many Highland communities each year, and which are an otherwise rather inexplicable mix of sports, music, and dance.

Gradually, by the 18th century, increasing knowledge of Lowland agricultural improvements, and better roads into the Highlands that improved communication of ideas and "southern" ways, began to weaken the clan system: fine clothes, French wines, and even a Lowland education became more common in chiefly households. Even before Culloden, where Bonnie Prince Charles, supported by some of the clans, was defeated by George II's army, the clan system had lost its tight grip on the Highlands. After Culloden, as more modern economic influences took hold, those on the "wrong" side lost all; many chiefs lost their lands, tartan was banned, and clan culture withered.

Tartan's own origins as a part of the clan system are disputed; the Gaelic word for striped cloth is breacan—piebald or spotted—so even the word itself is not Highland. However, it is indisputable that in the days before mass manufacture, when cloth was locally spun, woven, and dyed using plant derivatives, each neighborhood would have different dyestuffs—bilberry, iris, bramble, water lily—and therefore different colors available. In this way, particular combinations of colors and favorite patterns of the local weavers could become associated with a particular area and therefore clan, but were not in any sense a clan's "own by exclusive right."

Between 1746 and 1782 the wearing of tartan was generally prohibited. By the time the ban was lifted, many recipes for dyes and weaving patterns had been forgotten. In addition, some neighborhoods stopped making and coloring their own cloth because of the mechanization and use of chemical dyes in cloth production.

It took the influence of Sir Walter Scott, with his romantic, and fashionable, view of Highland history, to create the "modern myth" of clans and tartan. Sir Walter engineered George IV's visit to Scotland in 1822, which turned into a tartan extravaganza. The idea of one tartan or group of tartans "belonging" to one particular clan was created at this time—literally created, with new patterns and color ways dreamed up and "assigned" to particular clans. Queen Victoria and Prince Albert, with their passion for all things Scottish and for tartan in particular at Balmoral, reinforced the tartan culture later in the century, and it persists on and off to this day.

It is considered more "proper" in some circles to wear the "right" tartan, that is, that of your clan. You may be able to find a clan connection with the help of expertise such as that available at **Scotland's Clan Tartan Centre** (✉ 70–74 Bangor Rd., Leith, Edinburgh, ☎ 0131/553–5100).

Room has a four-poster bed and Victorian bath. ⊠ *The Square, Strath-peffer, Ross-shire IV14 9DL,* ☏ *01997/421622,* ⅁ᴬˣ *01997/421796,* ᵂᴱᴮ *www.craigvar.com. 3 rooms. No a/c, no smoking. MC, V.*

Corrieshalloch Gorge

★ ❷   *39 mi northwest of Strathpeffer.*

For a thrilling touch of vertigo, don't miss Corrieshalloch Gorge. A creek draining the high moors plunges 150 ft into a 200-ft-deep, thickly wooded gorge. There's a suspension-bridge viewpoint and a heady atmosphere of romantic grandeur, like an old Scottish print come to life.

Ullapool

❸   *5 mi northwest of Corrieshalloch Gorge, 238 mi north of Glasgow.*

By the shores of salty **Loch Broom,** Ullapool was founded in 1788 as a fishing station to exploit the local herring stocks. The town has a cosmopolitan air and comes to life when the Lewis ferry docks and departs.

Dining and Lodging

£–£££   ✕⌾ **Ceilidh Place.** You can borrow one of the many books scattered throughout this comfortable house and while away the hours on deep, luxurious sofas in the sitting room, which overlooks the bay. Rooms have cream bedspreads and rich, warm color schemes. The inn's restaurant (££) specializes in seafood and vegetarian food; try the rocket pancakes with wild mushrooms. *Ceilidhs* (country dancing, music, and song; pronounced *kay*-lees) and concerts of chamber music, folk music, and opera are held frequently during summer. The bunkhouse across the road is an inexpensive alternative, with access to the hotel's facilities. ⊠ *W. Argyle St., IV26 2TY,* ☏ *01854/612103,* ⅁ᴬˣ *01854/612886. 26 rooms, 10 with bath. Restaurant; no a/c, no phones in some rooms, no room TVs. AE, DC, MC, V.*

En Route   Drive north of Ullapool and you'll enter into a different kind of landscape. Here you won't find the broad flanks of great hills that hem you in, as you would in the Great Glen or Glen Coe. Instead, in Wester Ross the mountains rear out of the hummocky terrain and seem to shift their position, hiding behind one another in bewitching ways. Even their names seem different from those of the *bens* (mountain peaks or high hills) elsewhere: Cul Mor, Cul Beag, Stac Polly, Canisp, Suilven. Some owe their origins to Norse words rather than to undiluted Gaelic—a reminder that Vikings used to sail this northern seaboard. Much of this area lies within the Inverpolly National Nature Reserve.

Achiltibuie

❹   *25 mi northwest of Ullapool.*

A spread-out line of crofts, many now owned by newcomers, marks the approach to Achiltibuie. Offshore are the **Summer Isles,** romantic enough in theory, but in reality bleak and austere.

At the **Achiltibuie Smokehouse,** Summer Isles Foods smokes all sorts of fish—salmon, haddock, eel, and trout—that can be purchased in the small shop; mail order is also available. ⊠ *Altandhu,* ☏ *01854/ 622353,* ⌖ *Easter–mid-Oct., Mon.–Sat. 9:30–5.*

The **Hydroponicum** hydroponically produces luscious fruit and vegetables year-round, which would otherwise be impossible in the harsh winter climate. ☏ *01854/622202,* ⬛ *£4.75 for guided tour.* ⌖ *Apr.–Sept., daily 10–6; Oct., weekdays 11:30–3.*

En Route A single-lane unclassified road winds north from Achiltibuie through a wild though harmonious landscape of bracken and birch trees, heather and humped-hill horizons, with outstanding sea views on the second half of the route. Don't fall victim to the breathtaking landscape views, however; the road has several blind curves that demand extreme care. Just before Inverkirkaig is a parking lot next to the River Kirkaig, and a short stroll away is Achins Book and Craft Shop—perhaps Scotland's most remote bookstore.

Lochinver

❺ *18 mi north of Achiltibuie via unclassified road, 38 mi north of Ullapool via A835/A837.*

Lochinver is a bustling shoreside community of whitewashed cottages, with a busy harbor used by the west coast fishing fleet, and a few dining and lodging options. Behind the town the mountain Suilven rises abruptly. This unusual monolith is best seen from across the water, however. Take the cul-de-sac, **Baddidarroch Road,** for the finest photo opportunity.

Bold souls spending time at Lochinver may enjoy the interesting single-lane B869 **Drumbeg loop** to the north of Lochinver—it has several challenging hairpin turns along with breathtaking views. (The junction is just north of the River Inver bridge on the outskirts of the village, signposted as STOER and CLASHNESSIE.) Just beyond the scattered community of Stoer, a road leads west to **Stoer Point Lighthouse.** If you're an energetic walker, you can hike across the short turf and heather along the cliff top for fine views east toward the profiles of the northwest mountains. There's also a red-sandstone sea stack: the **Old Man of Stoer.** This makes a pleasant excursion on a long summer evening. If you stay on the Drumbeg section, there's a particularly tricky hairpin turn in a steep dip, which may force you to take your eyes off the fine view of Quinag, yet another of Sutherland's shapely mountains.

OFF THE
BEATEN PATH
ARDVRECK CASTLE – Beside Loch Assynt, on the A837 11 mi east of Lochinver, stand the abandoned ruins of Ardvreck Castle, a clan MacLeod stronghold, built in the 15th century.

EAS COUL AULIN WATERFALL – This is the longest waterfall in the United Kingdom, with a drop of 685 ft. A rugged hike leads to the falls, which are at the head of Loch Glencoul; in summer, cruises offer a less taxing alternative. The falls are 3 mi southeast of the Kylesku Bridge off the A894; contact the tourist center in Ullapool or Lochinver for more information.

Dining and Lodging

£££ ✕🏠 **Inver Lodge Hotel.** On a hillside above Lochinver, this modern hotel has stunning views of the sea from all its bedrooms. Floral fabrics and traditional mahogany furniture decorate the smart guest rooms. The restaurant (££££) makes the most of fresh, local seafood on its Scottish menu; try the lobster, straight from the sea the day you dine. Anglers feel especially at home here, with three salmon rivers and many trout lochs within easy reach. ⊠ *Iolaire Rd., Sutherland, IV27 4LU,* ☎ *01571/844496,* FAX *01571/844395,* WEB *www.inverlodge.com. 20 rooms. Restaurant, room service, sauna, fishing, recreation room; no kids under 7. AE, DC, MC, V. Closed Nov.–Easter.*

£ 🏠 **Davar.** Rooms are light-filled, airy, and simple at this modern, comfortable B&B with views over Lochinver Bay. Green carpets set off pastel walls, and the bedrooms are spacious. The owners provide just what happy guests require. ⊠ *Lochinver, Sutherland, IV27 4LS,* ☎ *01571/*

844501. 3 rooms. No a/c, no room phones, no smoking. No credit cards. Closed Dec.–Mar.

£ 🏠 **Polcraig Guest House.** This quiet detached house with views toward Lochinver Bay has high-quality B&B accommodations. Rooms are Victorian in style, with pine furniture and a green, blue, or pink color scheme. ✉ Cruamer, Sutherland, IV27 4LD, ☎ FAX 01571/844429. 5 rooms. No a/c, no room phones, no-smoking rooms. No credit cards.

£ 🏠 **Tigh-Na-Sith.** Convenient for shops and restaurants, this central B&B has ground-floor bedrooms and panoramic harbor views from the lounge. The interior is modern, with bright colors. ✉ Cruamer, Sutherland, IV27 4LD, ☎ 01571/844740. 2 rooms. No a/c, no room phones, no room TVs, no smoking. No credit cards. Closed Nov.–Mar.

Shopping

Highland Stoneware (✉ Baddidarroch, ☎ 01571/844376) manufactures tableware and decorative items with hand-painted designs of Highland wildflowers, animals, and landscapes. In the showroom you can browse and purchase wares.

At Inverkirkaig, just south of Lochinver, don't miss **Achins Book and Craft Shop** (✉ Inverkirkaig, ☎ 01571/844262). It's a great place for Scottish books on natural history, hill walking, fishing, and crafts. It also sells well-chosen craft items—knitwear, tweeds, and pottery—along with artwork and traditional music. The shop is open daily from 9:30 to 6 between Easter and October (phone ahead in winter to check opening times), and its pleasant coffee shop is open from Easter through October, daily 10 to 5.

Scourie

❻ *28 mi north of Lochinver.*

Scourie is a small settlement catering to visitors—fisherfolk especially—with a choice of local accommodations. It also makes a good base for a trip to the bird sanctuary on the island of Handa.

OFF THE   **HANDA ISLAND –** Just off the coast of Scourie is a bird sanctuary that
BEATEN PATH   shelters huge seabird colonies, especially impressive at nesting time in spring and early summer. It's administered by the Scottish Wildlife Trust. In spring and summer only, Handa can be reached by a small open boat from Tarbet; contact the tourist information center in Lochinver or Durness for details.

Dining and Lodging

££ ✕🏠 **Eddrachilles Hotel.** This long-established, traditional inn has one of the best views of any hotel in Scotland—across the islands of Eddrachillis Bay (which can be explored by boat from the hotel). The hotel sits on 320 acres of private moorland and is just south of the Handa Island bird sanctuary. The bedrooms are modern and comfortable, each equipped with tea- and coffeemaking facilities. The chef uses local produce to prepare meals in straightforward Scottish style, with the emphasis on fish and game; try the saddle of venison or the poached salmon. ✉ Badcall Bay, IV27 4TH, ☎ 01971/502080, FAX 01971/502477, WEB www.eddrachilles.com. 11 rooms. Restaurant, bar; no a/c. MC, V. Closed Nov.–Feb.

En Route From Scourie northward, the A894/A838 traverses the most northerly landscapes, with the empty quarter below Cape Wrath on its west side. You can sample this wild landscape by hiking to Sandwood Bay, at the end of the B801, beyond the fishing port of Kinlochbervie. Sandwood has rock stacks, a white beach, and its own ghost, said to frequent a cottage (or *bothy*) near the shore; so this is a truly haunting area in all senses of the word.

Durness

❼ *27 mi north of Scourie, 55 mi north of Lochinver.*

The sudden patches of green at Durness, on the north coast, are caused by the richer limestone outcrops among the acid moorlands. The limestone's most spectacular feature is **Smoo Cave,** a cave system hollowed out of the limestone by water action. Boat tours run daily from April through September; reservations are advised because there's a limit of six per 20-minute tour. The seasonal **tourist information center** (⌧ Durine, Durness IV27 4PN, ☎ 01971/511259) has complete information.

Craftspeople and artists sell pottery, leatherwork, weaving, paintings, and more from their studios at **Balnakeil Craft Village** (☎ 01971/511777). The village, on an unnamed road but clearly signed from Durness, is open April through October. Hours at the studios vary, but most places stay open daily from 10 to 5, and even later on summer evenings.

If you've made it this far north, you'll probably want to go all the way to **Cape Wrath,** at the northwest tip of Scotland. You can't drive your own vehicle. May through September, a small boat (☎ 01971/511376) ferries people (no cars) across the Kyle of Durness, a sea inlet, from Keoldale; a minibus (☎ 01971/511287) will then take you to the lighthouse. The highest mainland cliffs in Scotland lie between the Kyle and Cape Wrath—the 800-ft **Cleit Dubh.** The name is Gaelic for "black cleft"—the cliffs, which face north, are always in the shade—and comes from the Old Norse *klettr* (crag).

En Route   The north-coast road along the top of Scotland is both attractive and severe. It runs, for example, around the head of Loch Eriboll, which was a World War II convoy assembly point and was usually referred to as "Loch 'orrible" by the crews. Yet it has its own desolate charm. There are little beaches and settlements to explore along this road, and the landscape gradually softens as you journey east.

Thurso

❽ *74 mi east of Durness.*

The town of Thurso, which is quite substantial for a community so far north, is hard to categorize. Since the 1950s its development has been related to the atomic reactor (Britain's first) along the coast at Dounreay—presumably situated there to be as far as possible from the seat of government, in London. There's not much to see in the town itself, though there are fine beaches, particularly to the east, at Dunnet Bay. And with restaurants and hotels, Thurso is one of the few towns that makes a good base for exploring the far north. Many people make the trip to the northernmost point of mainland Britain, which is at **Dunnet Head,** with its fine views to Orkney.

Dining and Lodging

££ ✕🔟 **Forss Country House Hotel.** Despite its stark, gray exterior, this 1810 house surrounded by woodland provides a welcoming environment as a base for fishing (guide service and instruction provided) or touring. Restrained decor with plain, soft-tone walls and spare, dark-wood antique and reproduction furniture, along with log fires and sturdy Scottish cuisine make for a charming place to stay. The restaurant (££££) serves such dishes as haggis-stuffed sirloin with Glenmorangie whisky sauce. ⌧ *Forss, about 4 mi west of Thurso, KW14 7XY,* ☎ *01847/*

861201, FAX *01847/861301,* WEB *www.forsscountryhouse.co.uk. 14
rooms. Restaurant, golf privileges, fishing; no a/c. AE, MC, V.*

£ ⌂ **Murray House.** This Victorian town house in the center of Thurso
is a B&B of a very high standard, and it's convenient to the Orkney
ferry. ⊠ *1 Campbell St., Thurso KW14 7HD,* ☎ *01847/895759,* WEB
www.murrayhousebb.com. 4 rooms. No a/c. No credit cards.

Outdoor Activities and Sports

Bikes can be rented from **Wheels Cycle Shop** (⊠ 35 High St., ☎ FAX
01847/896124); the staff here is also happy to advise on routes.

John o'Groats

❾ *21 mi east of Thurso via A836.*

The windswept little outpost of John o'Groats is usually taken to be
the most northern community in the Scottish mainland, though that
is not strictly accurate, as an exploration of the little network of roads
between Dunnet Head and John o'Groats will confirm. However, John
o'Groats, with some high-quality crafts shops, warrants a visit if you
have the time. Go east to **Duncansby Head** for spectacular views of cliffs
and sea stacks by the lighthouse—and puffins, too.

Nightlife and the Arts

The **Lyth Arts Centre** (⊠ Lyth, 4 mi off A9, ☎ 01955/641270), between
Wick and John o'Groats, is in an old country school. From April
through November each year, it hosts performances by professional
touring music and theater companies, as well as exhibitions of contemporary fine art. At this writing (autumn 2002) the center was un-
dergoing renovations, but was expected to reopen completely by
summer 2003. Check local papers or tourist information centers for
opening times, schedules, and fees.

Outdoor Activities and Sports

John o'Groats Ferries (☎ 01955/611353) operates wildlife cruises
from John o'Groats Harbor. The 1½-hour trip takes you past spectacular cliff scenery and bird life into the Pentland Firth, to Duncansby
Stacks, and to the island of Stroma. Cruises cost £12 and are available
daily from mid-June through August, at 2:30.

Wick

❿ *17 mi south of John o'Groats, 22 mi southeast of Thurso via A882.*

Wick is a substantial town that was built on its fishing industry. The
gaunt, bleak ruins of **Castle Sinclair** and **Castle Girnigoe** teeter on a cliff
top to the north of the town.

To learn how this town grew, visit the **Wick Heritage Centre**—it's run
by local people in part for the local community, and they're real enthusiasts. ⊠ *18 Bank Row,* ☎ *01955/605393 or 01955/603385.* ▭
£3. ☉ *June–Sept., Mon.–Sat. 10–5; last admission at 3:45.*

The **Northlands Viking Centre,** which highlights the role of Scandinavian settlers in this area, has models of the Viking settlement at Freswick
and of a Viking long ship, as well as coins and other artifacts. ⊠ *The
Old School, Auckengill, Keiss, 10 mi north of Wick via A9,* ☎ *01847/
805518.* ▭ *£1.40.* ☉ *June–Sept., daily 10–4.*

Lodging

£ ⌂ **Greenvoe.** This B&B is a well-appointed modern house, fresh and
beautifully maintained, with unfussy, functional, and comfortable bedrooms. A delicious, generous breakfast is included in the room rate,
and late-night snacks are a hospitable touch. ⊠ *George St., Caithness*

KW1 4DE, ☎ 01955/603942. 3 rooms share bath. No a/c, no room phones, no smoking. No credit cards. Closed last 2 wks Dec.

Shopping

Perhaps the best-known purveyor of crafts in the area is **Caithness Glass** (✉ Airport Industrial Estate, Wick Airport, ☎ 01955/602286). Producing a distinctive style of glassware and paperweights—most of the better gift shops stock Caithness Glass—the factory has tours of the glassblowing workshops and a shop with the full product range.

En Route Signposted west off the A9 about 10 mi south of Wick are the extraordinary **Grey Cairns of Camster,** two Neolithic chambered cairns, dating from 4000 to 3000 BC, that are among the best preserved in Britain. **Camster Round Cairn** is 20 yards in diameter and 13 yards high, and **Camster Long Cairn** reaches nearly 77 yards in length. Nineteenth-century excavations revealed skeletons, pottery, and flint tools in the round cairn's internal chamber. If you don't mind dirty knees, you can crawl into the chambers in both cairns.

Dunbeath

⑪ *21 mi south of Wick.*

As the moors of Caithness roll down to the sea at Dunbeath, you find the **Dunbeath Heritage Centre,** an old school that the local community, interested in recording its past, turned into a museum. It displays photographs and domestic and crofting artifacts that relay the area's history from the Bronze Age to the oil age. It's particularly helpful to those researching family histories. ✉ *Off A9,* ☎ *01593/731233.* ⊡ *£2.* ☉ *Apr.–Oct., daily 10–5; phone for winter hrs.*

The **Laidhay Croft Museum,** just north of Dunbeath, feels more like a private home than a museum. It was built around 1842, comprises a longhouse and barn—animals and people lived under the same long roof—and is furnished as it would have been during its working life. ✉ *Off A9,* ☎ *01593/731244.* ⊡ *£1.* ☉ *Easter–Oct., daily 10–6.*

Helmsdale

⑫ *15 mi south of Dunbeath.*

The **Timespan Heritage Centre,** a thought-provoking mix of displays, artifacts, and audiovisual materials, portrays the history of the area, from the Stone Age to the 1869 gold rush in the Strath of Kildonan. The complex also includes a café and an art gallery, with changing exhibitions that cover the whole breadth of the arts. ✉ *Helmsdale,* ☎ *01431/821327,* WEB *www.timespan.org.uk.* ⊡ *£3.50.* ☉ *Apr.–Oct., Mon.–Sat. 9:30–5, Sun. 2–5; last admission 1 hr before closing.*

Golspie

18 mi south of Helmsdale.

Golspie is a little coastal town with a number of shops and accommodations, though it has the air of a place that visitors merely pass ⑬ through. The Scottish home of the dukes of Sutherland is **Dunrobin Castle,** an ancient seat developed by the first duke into a 19th-century flamboyant white-turreted behemoth. Trains so fascinated the duke that he built his own railroad in the park and staffed it with his servants. This duke, who also owned one of the largest palaces in London, was in good part responsible for the Sutherland Clearances of 1810–20, which devastated this region in the 19th century. Thousands of native Gaels were shamefully evicted from settlements in the interior and forced to emigrate or settle at sites on the coast. Traveling south on the A9, you'll see the controversial statue of the duke, in which he looks like some Eastern Bloc despot, on Beinn a Bragaidh (Ben Braggie), the hilltop to the west. Many people strongly feel that it should be removed, as the "improvement" policies of the duke were ultimately responsible for the brutality associated with the Clearances. ⊠ *A9,* ☎ *01408/ 633177.* ⛴ *£6.25.* ⊙ *Apr.–May and early Oct., daily 10:30–4; June– Sept., daily 10:30–5; last entry 30 mins before closing.*

Shopping

The **Orcadian Stone Company** (⊠ Main St., ☎ 01408/633483) makes stone products, including giftware crafted from local Caithness slate, jewelry, incised plaques, and prepared mineral specimens. There's also a geological exhibit.

Dornoch

⑭   *10 mi south of Golspie, 40 mi north of Inverness.*

A town of sandstone, tiny rose-filled gardens, and a 13th-century cathedral with stunning traditional and modern stained-glass windows, Dornoch is also noted for its golf. You may hear it referred to as the St. Andrews of the North, but because of the town's location so far north, the courses here are delightfully uncrowded. Royal Dornoch is the jewel in its crown, praised by the world's top golfers.

Dining and Lodging

£–££   ✕ ⛽ **Dornoch Castle Hotel.** A genuine late-15th-century castle, once the
★   palace of the bishops of Caithness, this hotel blends the very old and the more modern, with some rooms in the 1974 wing. The lounge is a relaxing Adamesque room of soft green and cream, and bedrooms wear pastel stripes and floral fabrics. This is not a luxury hotel, but it's clean and comfortable, with friendly staff and satisfying, well-cooked Scottish food in the restaurant (££££): try the roast haunch of venison with juniper-and-cranberry sauce. ⊠ *Dornoch, Sutherland, IV25 3SD,* ☎ *01862/810216,* fax *01862/810981,* web *www.dornochcastlehotel. com. 18 rooms. Restaurant, room service; no a/c. AE, MC, V.*

£   ⛽ **Highfield House.** On its own grounds on the edge of town, the Highfield delivers deluxe B&B accommodations in a modern family home. Rooms are light and airy, with pastel colors and natural-wood furnishings. ⊠ *Evelix Rd., IV25 3HR,* ☎ *01862/810909,* fax *01862/ 811605,* web *www.highfieldhouse.co.uk. 3 rooms. No a/c, no room phones, no smoking. V.*

Outdoor Activities and Sports

Were it not for its remote northern location, **Royal Dornoch** (☎ 01862/ 810219) would undoubtedly be a candidate for the British Open Championship. It's a superb, breezy, and challenging links course, offering 18 holes, with par 70. For more information *see* Chapter 12.

En Route   If you're driving south toward Inverness on the A9, consider detouring first to Tain (look for signs to the town), with its excellent **Tain through Time,** which explores Tain's history as an important pilgrimage center, thanks to the shrine of St. Duthus, in the late 15th-century. King James IV (1473–1513) was a frequent pilgrim here. The center consists of a museum, the Collegiate Church, and the Pilgrimage Centre. ⊠ *Tower St.,* ☎ *01862/894089.* ⛴ *£3.50.* ⊙ *Mid-Mar.–Oct., daily 10–6.*

Cromarty has handsome Georgian town houses as well as the Church Street cottage that was the birthplace of famous Scottish geologist Hugh Miller (1802–56). To get here from Tain, head a couple of miles south on the A9 and detour via Route B9175 to Nigg. A short ferry crossing (summer only; ☎ 01862/851324 or 0790/999–6416) will take you to Cromarty. A pleasant 20-mi drive westward on Route A832 will return you, via the farming lands of the Black Isle, to Route A9 just north of Inverness.

THE TORRIDONS

The Torridons have a grand, rugged, and wild air that feels especially remote, yet it doesn't take much more than an hour from Inverness before you reach Kinlochewe, at the east end of Glen Torridon. The western side is equally spectacular. Opportunities abound to enjoy mountain panoramas as well as walks and trails.

The A890, which runs from the A832 into the heart of the Torridons, is a single-lane road in some stretches, with plenty of open vistas across the deserted heart of northern Scotland.

Lochcarron

⑮ *66 mi west of Inverness via A9/A835/A832/A890.*

Lochcarron, a village strung along the shore, functions as a local hub for shopping, garage facilities, and so on. **The Smithy Heritage Centre,** in a restored blacksmith's forge, will tell you all about the area, and also arranges woodland walks. ⊠ *Ribhuachan, by Lochcarron,* ☎ *01520/722246.* ⊗ *Apr.–Oct., Mon.–Sat. 10–5.*

Shopping
The premises of **Lochcarron Weavers** (⊠ Mid Strome, ☎ 01520/722212) are open to the public: you can observe a weaver at work, producing pure-wool worsted tartans that can be bought on-site or at the firm's other outlets in the area.

En Route Driving north by the A896, you pass **Rassal Ash Wood,** on your right. The lushness of the fenced-in area within this small nature reserve is a reminder of what Scotland might have been had sheep and deer not been kept here in such high numbers. The combined nibbling of these animals ensures that Scotland's natural tree cover does not regenerate without human intervention.

Shieldaig

⑯ *16 mi northwest of Lochcarron.*

Just west of the southern coast of Upper Loch Torridon is Shieldaig, a village that sits in an attractive crescent overlooking a loch of its own, **Loch Shieldaig.** For an atmospheric evening foray, walk north toward Loch Torridon, at the northern end of the village by the church. The path is fairly well made, though hiking shoes are recommended. Exquisite views and tiny rocky beaches await you.

★ The scenic spectacle of **Glen Torridon** lies east of Shieldaig. Some say that Glen Torridon has the finest mountain scenery in Scotland. It consists mainly of the long gray quartzite flanks of **Beinn Eighe** (rhymes with *say*), which make up Scotland's oldest national nature reserve, and **Liathach** (*leea*-gach), with its distinct ridge profile that looks like the keel of an upturned boat. At the end of the glen the National Trust for Scotland operates a **visitor center** that explains the ecology and geology of the area. ☎ *01445/791221.* ⊡ *Audiovisual display and deer museum £2.* ⊗ *Countryside center May–Sept., daily 10–6; estate, deer park, and deer museum year-round, daily 9–5.*

OFF THE
BEATEN PATH

APPLECROSS – The tame way to reach this small community facing Skye is by a coastal road from near Shieldaig; the exciting route turns west off the A896 a few miles farther south. A series of hairpin turns corkscrews up the steep wall at the head of a corrie (a glacier-cut mountain valley), over the **Bealach na Ba** (Pass of the Cattle). There are spectacular views of Skye from the bare plateau on top, and you can brag afterward that you've been on what is probably Scotland's highest drivable road. The village of Applecross itself is pleasant but not riveting.

Dining and Lodging

£££ ✕🖬 **Loch Torridon Hotel.** Forest and mountains make up the impressive backdrop for this former shooting lodge, now a hotel where you'll receive a real Highland welcome, on the shore of Loch Torridon. Log fires, handsome plasterwork ceilings, mounted stag heads, and traditional furnishings set the mood downstairs, and bedrooms are decorated in restrained pastel shades with antique mahogany furniture. The restaurant (££££) makes elaborate use of local seafood, salmon, beef, lamb, and game, and the cellar has many fine wines. ✉ *Torridon, by Achnasheen, Wester Ross, IV22 2EY,* ☎ *01445/791242,* 🖷 *01445/791296,* WEB *www.lochtorridonhotel.com. 20 rooms. Restaurant, fishing, library; no a/c. AE, DC, MC, V.*

Gairloch

⓱ *38 mi north of Shieldaig.*

This region's main center, with some shops and accommodations, Gairloch has one further advantage: lying just a short way from the mountains of the interior, this small oasis often escapes the rain clouds that sometimes cling to the high summits. You can enjoy a game of golf here and perhaps stay dry, even when the nearby Torridon hills are deluged. In the village is the **Gairloch Heritage Museum,** with exhibitions covering prehistoric times to the present. The staff is helpful in dealing with family-history inquiries. ✉ *Junction of A832 and B8031,* ☎ *01445/712287,* WEB *www.gairlochheritagemuseum.org.uk.* 🎫 *£2.50.* ⊙ *Apr.–Sept., Mon.–Sat. 10–5; Oct., weekdays 10–1:30; Nov.–Mar. by appointment.*

Southeast of Gairloch stretches one of Scotland's most scenic lochs,
★ **Loch Maree.** The harmonious environs of the loch, with its tall Scots pines and the mountain Slioch looming as a backdrop, witnessed the destruction of much of the tree cover in the 18th century. Iron ore was shipped in and smelted using local oak to feed the furnaces. Oak now grows here only on the northern limits of the range. Scottish Natural Heritage has an **information center** and nature trails by the loch side. Red deer sightings are virtually guaranteed; locals say the best place to spot another local denizen, the pine marten, is around the trash containers in the parking turnoffs.

★ The highlight of this area is **Inverewe Gardens,** 6 mi northeast of Gairloch. The main attraction lies in the contrast between the bleak coastal headlands and thin-soiled moors and the lush plantings of the garden behind its dense shelterbelts. These are proof of the efficacy of the warm North Atlantic Drift, part of the Gulf Stream, which takes the edge off winter frosts. Inverewe is sometimes described as subtropical, but this is an inaccuracy that irritates the head gardener; do not expect coconuts and palm trees here. ✉ *A832, Poolewe,* ☎ *01445/781200,* WEB *www.nts.org.uk.* 🎫 *£5.* ⊙ *Gardens Apr.–Oct., daily 9–9; Nov.–Mar., daily 9:30–5. Visitor center, shop, and restaurant Apr.–Oct., daily 10–5. Guided walks Apr.–Sept., weekdays at 1:30.*

Dining and Lodging

£££ ✕🖭 **Dundonnell Hotel.** This excellent family-run hotel, set on the roadside by Little Loch Broom, east of Gairloch, has cultivated a solid reputation for its hospitality and cuisine. Light floral curtains and bedspreads and contemporary furnishings fill the fresh, modern bedrooms. Many of the guest rooms and public rooms have stunning views of pristine hills and lochs. The restaurant serves homemade soups and fresh seafood, as well as desserts well worth leaving room for. ✉ *Dundonnell, near Garve, Ross-shire, IV23 2QR,* ☎ *01854/633204,* 🖷 *01854/633366,* 🕸 *www.dundonnellhotel.com. 30 rooms. Restaurant, bar; no a/c. AE, MC, V.*

Outdoor Activities and Sports

Gairloch Golf Club (☎ 01445/712407, 9 holes, 1,942 yards, SSS 62) is one of the few on this stretch of coast.

En Route   The road between Gairloch and the Corrieshalloch Gorge initially affords coastal scenery with views of Gruinard Bay and its white beaches, then woodlands around Dundonnell and Loch Broom. Soon the route traverses wild country: the toothed ramparts of the mountain An Teallach (pronounced *tyel*-lach, with Scots *ch*, of course) are visible on the horizon. The moorland route you travel is known chillingly as Destitution Road. It was commissioned in 1851 to give the local folk (long vanished from the area) some way of earning a living after the failure of the potato crop; it's said the workers were paid only in food. At Corrieshalloch the A832 joins the A835 for Inverness.

SKYE, THE MISTY ISLAND

Skye ranks near the top of most visitors' priority lists: the romance of Prince Charles Edward Stuart (1720–88), known as Bonnie Prince Charlie, combined with the misty Cuillin Hills and their proximity to the mainland all contribute to its popularity. Today Skye remains fey, mysterious, and mountainous, an island of sunsets that linger brilliantly until late at night and of beautiful, soft mists. Much photographed are the really old crofts, one or two of which are still inhabited, with their thick stone walls and thatch roofs. Much written about is the story known as the Adventure—the sad history of the "prince in the heather" and pretender to the British throne, Bonnie Prince Charlie. At the disastrous Battle of Culloden, George II's army outnumbered and destroyed the Jacobite forces of Prince Charles Edward Stuart. After the battle Bonnie Prince Charlie wandered over the Highlands, a passive object, handed like a bale of contraband from one smuggler to another, numbed with constant applications of whisky—the beginnings of the alcoholism that finally killed him. He then escaped to the isles of Harris and South Uist, where he met Flora Macdonald (1722–90), the woman who took him, disguised as her maid, "over the sea to Skye" and then back to the mainland. His Scottish exploits were the stuff of legend. *Will ye no' come back again . . . Speed, bonnie boat . . . Charlie is my darling . . .* the tunes and lyrics of Lady Nairn, jaunty or mournful, composed long after the events, are as good an epitaph as any adventurer could wish for.

To reach Skye these days, you can cross over the bridge spanning the narrow channel of Kyle Akin, between Kyle of Lochalsh and Kyleakin, or take the (more romantic) ferry options between Mallaig and Armadale or between Glenelg and Kylerea. You can tour comfortably around the island in two or three days. Orientation is easy: follow the only roads around the loops on the northern part of the island and enjoy the road running the length of the Sleat Peninsula in southern Skye, taking the loop roads that exit to the north and south as you please. There are some stretches of single-lane road, but none poses a problem.

Kyle of Lochalsh

55 mi west of Inverness, 120 mi northwest of Glasgow.

This little town is the mainland gateway to Skye. Time used to mean nothing in this part of Scotland—so many other things were of greater importance. But the area has seen great changes as the Skye Bridge has transformed not only travel to Skye but the very seascape itself. The most noticeable attraction, though (in fact, almost a cliché), is not in Kyle at all, but 8 mi farther east at Dornie—Eilean Donan Castle.

★ ⑱ Guarding the confluence of lochs Long, Alsh, and Duich stands that most picturesque of all Scottish castles, **Eilean Donan Castle,** perched on a little islet connected to the mainland by a stone-arched bridge. Dating from the 14th century, this romantic icon has all the massive stone walls, timber ceilings, and winding stairs that you could ask for. Empty and neglected for years after being bombarded by frigates of the Royal Navy during an abortive Spanish-Jacobite landing in 1719, it was almost entirely rebuilt from a ruin in the early 20th century. Now the hero of travel brochures, Eilean Donan has appeared in many Hollywood movies and TV series. ⊠ *Off A97, Dornie,* ☎ FAX *01599/ 555202.* 🖃 *£3.75.* ☉ *Apr.–Nov., daily 9–6.*

Broadford

⑲ *8 mi west of Kyle of Lochalsh via Skye Bridge.*

One of the larger of Skye's settlements, Broadford lies along the shore of Broadford Bay, which has on occasion welcomed whales to its sheltered waters. You can observe and handle snakes, frogs, lizards, and tortoises at the **Serpentarium,** in the town center. ⊠ *The Old Mill, Harrapool,* ☎ *01471/822209.* 🖃 *£2.50.* ☉ *Easter–Oct., Mon.–Sat. 10–5.*

An unlikely but worthwhile stop is **Sutherlands** (⊠ A850, ☎ 01471/ 822225), where the Esso gas station offers a lot more than gasoline: 24-hour car rental (with pickup service at Armadale Pier or Kyle of Lochalsh), a bureau de change, Internet access, a launderette, a well-stocked gift and book shop, and fresh foods and ready-made snacks.

OFF THE BEATEN PATH | **THE ROAD TO ELGOL –** The B8083 leads from Broadford to one of the finest views in Scotland. This road passes through **Strath Suardal** and little **Loch Cill Chriosd** (Kilchrist) by a ruined church. If there are cattle wading in the loch and the light is soft—typical of Skye—then this place takes on the air of a romantic oil painting. Skye marble, with its attractive green veining, was produced from the marble quarry at **Torrin.**

You can appreciate breathtaking views of the mountain called **Blaven** as the A881 continues to Elgol, a gathering of crofts along this road that descends to a pier. Admire the heart-stopping profile of the Cuillin peaks from the shore, or at a point about halfway down the hill, you can find the path that goes toward them across the rough grasslands.

For even better views, take a boat trip on the **Bella Jane** (⊠ Elgol Jetty, ☎ 0800/731–3089, WEB www.bellajane.co.uk) from Elgol jetty toward Loch Coruisk; you'll be able to land and walk up to the loch itself, as well as see seals during your boat trip. The boat excursion is available from April through October, daily, and advance booking is essential (ticket price is £15).

Lodging

£ ⊡ ★ **Ptarmigan.** This top-of-the-range B&B is run by a couple that knows Skye inside out and can help with planning your route (whether driving or hiking), bird-watching, crafts shopping, or anything else. The three bedrooms, all with sea views, have modern dark-wood furnishings, neutral wall coverings, and sophisticated green-and-purple tartan drapes. Large-scale maps of the island line the walls of the cozy sitting room, which has a window looking right onto the water's edge, ideal for spotting birds, otters, and the occasional whale. There's also a separate cottage with cooking facilities. ⊠ *Broadford, Isle of Skye, IV49 9AQ,* ☎ *01471/822744,* FAX *01471/822745,* WEB *www.ptarmigan-cottage.com. 3 rooms, 1 cottage. No a/c, no smoking. AE, MC, V.*

Outdoor Activities and Sports

FairwindsBicycle Hire (⊠ Fairwinds, Elgol Rd., ☎ 01471/822270) rents bicycles year-round.

Shopping

Craft Encounters (⊠ A850, ☎ 01471/822754) stocks Skye crafts, including pottery and jewelry.

Armadale

⓴ *17 mi south of Broadford, 43 mi south of Portree, 5 mi (ferry crossing) west of Mallaig.*

Rolling interior moorlands, scattered with rivers and lochans, give way to enchanting hidden coves and scattered waterside communities here in **Sleat,** the southernmost part of Skye. Sleat well rewards a day or two spent exploring its side roads and its many craft outlets. For most visitors, Armadale is the first town to visit.

The popular **Armadale Castle Gardens and the Museum of the Isles,** including the Clan Donald Centre, tell the story of the Macdonalds and their proud title—the Lords of the Isles—with the help of an excellent audiovisual presentation. In the 15th century the clan was powerful enough to threaten the authority of the Stuart monarchs of Scotland. There are extensive gardens and nature trails, a large and well-chosen selection in the gift shop, a restaurant, a library, and an archive facility. Also on the grounds are high-quality accommodations in seven cottages with kitchen facilities. ⊠ *½ mi north of Armadale Pier,* ☎ *01471/ 844305 or 01471/844275,* WEB *www.highlandconnection.org.* 🖃 *£4.* ☉ *Clan Donald Centre Apr.–Oct., daily 9:30–5:30, last entry at 5; gardens year-round, daily 24 hrs.*

Dining and Lodging

££££ ✕⊡ **Kinloch Lodge.** This country-house hotel, run by Lord and Lady Macdonald with flair and considerable professionalism, serves up elegant comfort on the edge of the world. Antiques, chintz fabrics, bookcases, and family photographs fill the warm, restful lounges, and the snug bedrooms are individually decorated with quilted bedspreads and pastel wallpaper. Lady Macdonald conducts cooking demonstrations and short courses (reserve ahead). The dinner menu might include Skye langoustines with salad made from local produce, Highland lamb with a peppercorn and pinhead-oatmeal crust, and "dark-chocolate nemesis" for dessert. ⊠ *Off A851, Sleat, Isle of Skye, IV43 8QY,* ☎ *01471/833214,* FAX *01471/833277,* WEB *www.kinloch-lodge.co.uk. 14 rooms. Restaurant, fishing, helipad; no a/c. AE, MC, V.*

£££–££££ ✕⊡ ★ **Hotel Eilean Iarmain.** The Isle Ornsay Hotel (as it is also more pronounceably known) sits beside the shore and is an enchanting collection of wood paneling, chintz, antiques, and soft country-house-style color schemes. Each room is an atmospheric individual: try the Tower

Room, with its nooks and crannies, or the room with the canopy bed from Armadale Castle. The menu in the dining room changes daily but might include such dishes as seared venison with juniper and rowan, or steamed mussels with cream and whisky. ⊠ *Isleornsay, Sleat, Isle of Skye, IV43 8QR,* ☎ *01471/833332,* FAX *01471/833275,* WEB *www. eileaniarmain.co.uk. 12 rooms, 4 suites. Restaurant, fishing, helipad; no a/c, no room TVs. AE, MC, V.*

Outdoor Activities and Sports

The Skye Ferry Filling Station (⊠ Ardvasar, ☎ 01471/844249) rents bicycles in summer.

Shopping

Local designer Chryssy Gibbs creates colorful wool sweaters and sells them at **Harlequin Knitwear** (⊠ Off A851, Duisdale, Sleat, ☎ 01471/ 833321). She works from her home, which is up a rather bumpy, steep track. It's worth the trek because once you arrive (and after being greeted by the family cats), you will find distinctive sweaters—with descriptive names such as Stained Glass, Mosaic, and Tudor—of Shetland wool, mohair, or chenille in colors that reflect the tones of the Skye landscape.

Ragamuffin (⊠ Armadale Pier, ☎ 01471/844217) specializes in designer knitwear and clothing. Once inside, you'll find a huge array of styles, and the friendly staff will be happy to make you a cup of coffee while you browse, then mail your purchases back home for you.

Portree

㉑ *43 mi north of Armadale.*

Portree, the population center of the island, is not overburdened by historical features, but it's a pleasant center clustered around a small and sheltered bay, and it makes a good touring base. On the outskirts of town is **Tigh na Coille: The Aros Experience** (*Tigh na Coille* is Gaelic for "house of the forest," and *Aros* means "home" or "homestead"), where the story of Skye, told via tableaux and a taped guide, continues where the Armadale Castle audiovisual tour left off; together the two provide an excellent account of Skye's often turbulent history over the centuries. You'll also find a gift shop, restaurant, and cinema, which also hosts musical events. Forest walks can be enjoyed in the surrounding woodlands: discover the link between the Gaelic alphabet and tree names. ⊠ *Viewfield Rd.,* ☎ *01478/613649.* ☞ *£3 for taped guide.* ☉ *Daily 10–5.*

Dining and Lodging

£££ ✕ 🏨 **Cuillin Hills Hotel.** Just outside Portree, this gabled hotel has many rooms with outstanding views over Portree Bay toward the Cuillin Hills. Bold floral patterns decorate the bedrooms. The seafood dishes in the restaurant (££££) are especially good: try the local prawns, lobster, or scallops, or the glazed ham carved from the bone. ⊠ *Isle of Skye, IV51 9QU,* ☎ *01478/612003,* FAX *01478/613092,* WEB *www.cuillinhills. demon.co.uk. 30 rooms. Restaurant, bar; no a/c. AE, MC, V.*

££ ✕ 🏨 **Bosville Hotel.** Wood furniture and tartan and floral fabrics fill the traditional-style guest rooms, most of which have harbor views, at this comfortable, family-run hotel. You have an excellent choice of eating options (£–££): fine cuisine in the Chandlery Seafood Restaurant, or a more homey bar supper of Scottish fare in the lounge bar. ⊠ *Bosville Terrace, IV51 9DG,* ☎ *01478/612846,* FAX *01478/613434,* WEB *www. macleodhotels.co.uk/bosville. 15 rooms. Restaurant, bar, lounge; no a/c. AE, DC, MC, V.*

££ ✕ 🏨 **Rosedale Hotel.** Converted 19th-century buildings right on the harbor house modern accommodations and a restaurant serving delicious

Scottish cooking. The menu (£££) might include breast of duck with cranberries and parsnip puree, or pasta rolls with smoked haddock and lemon butter. ⊠ *Beaumont Crescent, Isle of Skye, IV51 9DB,* ☎ *01478/613131,* 𝔽𝔸𝕏 *01478/612531,* ᵂᴱᴮ *www.rosedalehotelskye.co.uk. 23 rooms. Restaurant; no a/c. MC, V. Closed Dec.–Mar.*

Shopping

An Tuireann Arts Centre (⊠ Struan Rd., ☎ 01478/613306) is a showcase for locally made crafts and is a good place to look for unusual gifts or greetings cards. **Croft Comforts Antiques** (⊠ 2 Wentworth St., ☎ 𝔽𝔸𝕏 01478/613762) has an enviable selection of silver, porcelain, antique and modern jewelry, and pottery, as well as larger items. In addition, it provides a mine of information about Skye: just ask David or Fiona Middleton for advice on places to eat, attractions to visit, or hidden coves to enjoy, and you won't be disappointed. **Skye Batiks** (⊠ The Green, ☎ 01478/613331) stocks unique Celtic-influenced batik clothing, cushion covers, and wall hangings; chunky handwoven cotton smocks, jackets, and skirts; silver jewelry; wood carvings; and much more. **Skye Original Prints** (⊠ 1 Wentworth St., ☎ 01478/612544) sells original prints by local artist Tom Mackenzie.

Trotternish Peninsula

㉒ *16 mi north of Portree via A855.*

As the road (A855) goes north from Portree, cliffs rise to the left. They're actually the edge of an ancient lava flow, set back from the road and running for miles as your rugged companion. In some places the hardened lava has created spectacular features, including a curious pinnacle called the **Old Man of Storr.** The A855 travels past neat white croft houses and forestry plantings to **Kilt Rock.** Everyone on the Skye tour circuit stops here to peep over the cliffs (there is a safe viewing platform) for a look at the geology of the cliff edge: bands of two types (and colors) of rock create a folded, pleated effect, just like a kilt.

The spectacular **Quiraing** dominates the horizon 5 mi past Kilt Rock. For a closer view of the strange pinnacles and rock forms, make a left onto a small road at Brogaig by Staffin Bay. There's a parking lot near the point where this road breaches the ever-present cliff line, though you will have to be physically fit to walk back toward the Quiraing itself, where the rock formations and cliffs are most dramatic. The trail is on uneven, stony ground, and it's a steep scramble up to the rock formations. In ages past, stolen cattle were hidden deep within the Quiraing's rocky jaws.

The main A855 reaches around the top end of Trotternish, to the **Skye Museum of Island Life** at Kilmuir, where you can see the old farming ways brought to life. Included in the displays and exhibits are documents and photographs, reconstructed interiors, and implements. Flora Macdonald, helpmate of Bonnie Prince Charlie, is buried nearby. ⊠ *Kilmuir,* ☎ 𝔽𝔸𝕏 *01470/552206.* 🎟 *£2.* ☉ *Easter–Oct., Mon.–Sat. 9:30–5:30.*

Dining and Lodging

£££–££££ ✕🏠 **Flodigarry Country House Hotel.** Close links with Flora Macdonald, Prince Charles Edward Stuart's helpmate, are not the least of the attractions at this country-house hotel, which is well placed for exploring the north and west of Skye. Yes, you can actually have a room in Flora's own cottage, adjacent to the hotel, where six of her children were born. The main hotel is a bit grander but just as comfortable, and excellent seafood is a feature of the restaurant's menu. ⊠ *Staffin, Isle of Skye, IV51 9HZ,* ☎ *01470/552203,* 𝔽𝔸𝕏 *01470/552301,* ᵂᴱᴮ *www. flodigarry.co.uk. 19 rooms. Restaurant, bar; no a/c. MC, V.*

Waternish Peninsula

㉓ *20 mi northwest of Portree via A850.*

The northwest corner of Skye has scattered crofting communities, magnificent coastal views, and two good restaurants, well worth the trip in themselves. In the Hallin area look westward for an islet-scattered sea loch with miniature cliffs rising from the water—and looking like miniature models of full-size islands. Just above the village of Stein, on the left side of the road, is a restored and inhabited "black house"—a thatched cottage blackened over time because a hole in its roof stood in for a chimney—today a rare sight on Skye and, in any event, now painted white.

Stoneware pottery is fired in a wood-fired kiln at the **Edinbane Pottery, Workshop and Gallery,** in southern Waternish. You can visit the workshops to watch the potters, then buy from the showroom. ⊠ *Edinbane,* ☏ 01470/582234, ⓦⓔⓑ *www.edinbane-pottery.co.uk.* ☉ *Easter–Oct., daily 9–6; Nov.–Easter, weekdays 9–6.*

Dining and Lodging

££–££££ ✕ **Loch Bay Seafood Restaurant.** Down on the waterfront at Stein stands
★ a distinctive black-and-white-painted restaurant known as the place where the island's top chefs eat on their nights off. The atmosphere is laid-back, the fish and seafood freshly caught and simply prepared; top-quality ingredients are allowed to speak for themselves without being overwhelmed by extraneous sauces. ⊠ *Near fishing jetty, Stein,* ☏ ⒻⒶⓍ 01470/592235. MC, V. Closed weekends (although it may open some Sat. nights in summer; phone for details) and late Oct.–wk before Easter.

££–£££ ✕🏨 **Greshornish House.** The best reason to come here is the restaurant (£££), where mahogany tables are laid with damask, crystal, and candelabra. The menu might include scallops poached in white wine with flakes of smoked haddock and cream, freshly caught local lobster or king prawns with salad and mayonnaise, or Skye lamb cutlets with heather honey and ginger, served with wild Skye berries. Greshornish is a quirky hotel with spacious, if rather eclectically furnished, public rooms and bedrooms of all shapes and sizes. ⊠ *Greshornish, Isle of Skye, IV51 9PN,* ☏ 01470/582266, ⒻⒶⓍ 01470/582345, ⓦⓔⓑ *www. greshornishhotel.co.uk. 8 rooms. Restaurant, tennis court, fishing, croquet; no a/c, no room phones, no room TVs. MC, V.*

Dunvegan Castle

㉔ *22 mi west of Portree.*

In a commanding position above a sea loch, Dunvegan Castle has been the seat of the chiefs of Clan MacLeod for more than 700 years. Though the structure has been greatly changed over the centuries, a gloomy ambience prevails, and there's plenty of family history on display, notably the Fairy Flag—a silk banner, thought to be originally from Rhodes or Syria and believed to have magically saved the clan from danger. The banner's powers are said to suffice for only one more use. Make time to visit the gardens, with their water garden and falls, fern house, a walled garden, and viewing points. Dunvegan Sea Cruises runs a boat trip from the castle to the nearby seal colony. ⊠ *At junction of A850 and A863, Dunvegan,* ☏ 01470/521206, ⓦⓔⓑ *www. dunvegancastle.com.* 🎫 *Garden only £4; castle and garden £6; boat trips to see the seals £4.* ☉ *Mid-Mar.–Oct., daily 10–5:30, last admission at 5; Nov.–mid-Mar., daily 11–4, last entry at 3:30.*

Dining and Lodging

££ ✕⌂ **Roskhill House.** A white 19th-century croft house, which once housed the local post office in the dining room, Roskhill is more of a home away from home than a country-house hotel. Bold colors decorate the bedrooms, and the lounge has books and games. Stone walls, dark stick-back chairs, and a scarlet carpet lend the dining room a publike air; old favorites appear on the menu, such as Lancashire hot pot; pork Haslet with bacon, onion, and mustard sauce; and raspberry trifle. ✉ *Roskhill, by Dunvegan, Isle of Skye, IV55 8ZD,* ☎ *01470/ 521317,* FAX *01470/521761,* WEB *www.roskhill.demon.co.uk. 4 rooms. No a/c, no room phones, no room TVs. MC, V.*

Glendale

㉕ *2 mi south of Dunvegan.*

The Glendale Visitor Route, a signed driving trail off the A863 through the westernmost area of northwest Skye, leads past crafts outlets, museums, and other attractions. With its bears, dolls, trains, puzzles and games, books, and puppets, the **Toy Museum** lets you relive your childhood. ✉ *Glendale,* ☎ *01470/511240.* ▱ *£2.50.* ☉ *Mon.–Sat. 10–6.*

Borreraig Park has a fascinating museum of island life—rightly described by the owner as "a unique gallimaufry for your delight and edification"—that includes a detailed series of panels on the making of bagpipes and on the history of the MacCrimmons, hereditary pipers to the Clan MacLeod. A superb gift shop stocks unique island-made sweaters (the exact sheep can be named), wool, bagpipes, Celtic silver and gold jewelry, and CDs of traditional music. ✉ *Borreraig Park, by Dunvegan,* ☎ *01470/511311.* ▱ *£2.* ☉ *Daily 10–6.*

Dining and Lodging

££££ ✕⌂ **Three Chimneys Restaurant with Rooms.** One of Skye's top-notch
★ restaurants, Shirley Spear's shoreside cottage might be small on space, but it's big on flavor: fresh local seafood, beef, lamb, and game are transformed into dishes such as prawn and lobster bisque, or grilled loin of Skye lamb with honey-roasted root vegetables and sherried button-mushroom sauce. Skye soft fruits—raspberries, strawberries, black currants—may follow. Adjacent to the restaurant are luxury accommodations in a courtyard wing, with magnificent sea views from all the rooms. ✉ *B884, Colbost, by Dunvegan, Isle of Skye, IV55 8ZT,* ☎ *01470/511258,* FAX *01470/511358,* WEB *www.threechimneys.co.uk. 6 rooms. No a/c. AE, MC, V. No lunch Sun.*

Shopping

Skye Silver (✉ The Old School, Colbost, Glendale, ☎ 01470/511263), west of Dunvegan, designs gold and silver jewelry with a Celtic theme and also has more unusual pieces that reflect the natural forms of the seashore and countryside: silver-coral earrings, silver-leaf pendants, and starfish and cockleshell earrings.

Glen Brittle

★ ㉖ *28 mi southeast of Glendale.*

You can safely enjoy spectacular mountain scenery in Glen Brittle, with some fine views of the Cuillin ridges (which are not for the casual walker, as there are many dangerous ridges and steep faces). Glen Brittle extends off the A863/B8009 on the west side of the island.

OUTER HEBRIDES (WESTERN ISLES)

The Outer Hebrides—the Western Isles in common parlance—stretch about 130 mi from end to end and lie about 50 mi from the Scottish mainland. This splintered archipelago extends from the Butt of Lewis in the north to the 600-ft Barra Head on Berneray in the south, whose lighthouse has the greatest arc of visibility in the world. The Isle of Lewis and Harris is the northernmost and largest of the group. The island's only major town, Stornoway, is on a nearly landlocked harbor on the east coast of Lewis; it's probably the most convenient starting point for a driving tour of the islands if you're approaching the Western Isles from the Northern Highlands.

Just south of the Sound of Harris is North Uist, rich in monoliths, chambered cairns, and other reminders of a prehistoric past. Though it is one of the smaller islands in the chain, Benbecula, sandwiched between North and South Uist and sometimes referred to as the Hill of the Fords, is in fact less bare and neglected looking than its bigger neighbors to the north. South Uist, once a refuge of the old Catholic faith, is dotted with ruined forts and chapels; in summer its wild gardens burst with alpine and rock plants. Eriskay and a scattering of islets almost block the 6-mi strait between South Uist and Barra, the southernmost major formation in the Outer Hebrides, an isle you can walk across in an hour.

Harris tweed is available at many outlets on the islands, including some of the weavers' homes; keep an eye out for signs directing you to weavers' workshops. Sunday on the islands is strictly observed as a day of rest, and nearly all shops and visitor attractions are closed.

Stornoway

㉗ *2½-hr ferry trip from Ullapool.*

The port capital for the Outer Hebrides is Stornoway, the only major town on Lewis. In the Town Hall, the **An Lanntair Gallery** has exhibitions of contemporary and traditional art that change monthly, as well as a coffee and gift shop and frequent traditional Gaelic musical and theatrical events. ⊠ *Town Hall, S. Beach St.,* ☎ *01851/703307.* ☞ *Free.* ⊙ *Mon.–Sat. 10–5:30.*

Lodging

£   🏠 **27 Springfield Road.** A quiet residential area backing onto open fields is the setting for this modern detached house with very comfortable accommodations. Modern furniture fills the rooms: one is done in blue and pink florals; another uses navy and beige geometric prints. Immaculate gardens surround the house, which is just a short walk from downtown. ⊠ *27 Springfield Rd., Stornoway, Isle of Lewis, HS1 2PS,* ☎ *01851/703254,* WEB *www.davinamacdonald.co.uk. 3 rooms. No a/c, no room phones, no smoking. No credit cards.*

Outdoor Activities and Sports

Alex Dan Cycle Centre (⊠ 67 Kenneth St., ☎ 01851/704025) rents bicycles.

En Route   The best road to use to explore the territory north of Stornoway is the A857, which runs first across the island to the northwest and then to the northeast all the way to Port of Ness (about 30 mi).

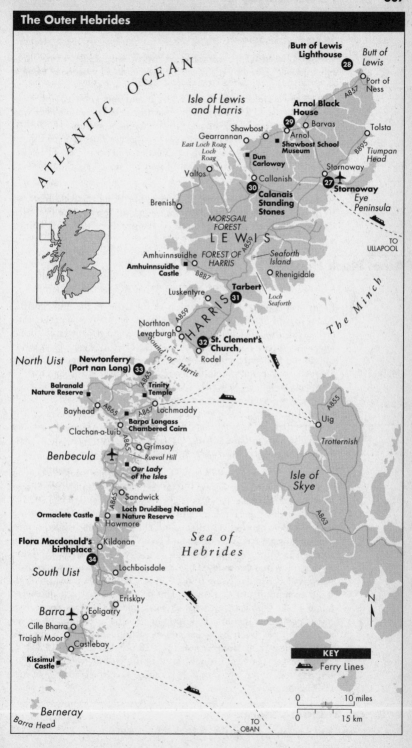

Port of Ness

30 mi north of Stornoway.

The stark, windswept community of Port of Ness cradles a small harbor squeezed in among the rocks and overlooked by **Harbour View**, a small gallery and café. At the northernmost point of Lewis stands the **28 Butt of Lewis Lighthouse**, designed by David and Thomas Stevenson (of the prominent engineering family whose best-known member was not an engineer at all: the novelist Robert Louis Stevenson [1850–94]). The lighthouse was first lit in 1862. The adjacent cliffs provide a good vantage point for viewing seabirds, whales, and porpoises. The lighthouse is a few minutes northwest of Port of Ness along the B8014.

Shopping

At **Borgh Pottery** (⊠ Fivepenny House, Borve, on the road to Ness, ☎ 01851/850345, WEB www.borghpottery.com) you can buy attractive hand-thrown studio pottery made on the premises, including lamps, vases, mugs, and dishes.

Arnol Black House

29 *21 mi southwest of Port of Ness, 16 mi northwest of Stornoway.*

In the small community of Arnol, look for signs off the A858 for the Arnol Black House, a well-preserved example of an increasingly rare type of traditional Hebridean home. Once common throughout the islands—as recently as 50 years ago—these dwellings were built without mortar and thatched on a timber framework without eaves. Other characteristic features include an open central peat hearth and the absence of a chimney—hence the soot and the designation *black*. On display inside are many of the house's original furnishings. To reach Arnol from Port of Ness, go back south on the A857 and pick up the A858 at Barvas. ⊠ *Off the A858, Arnol,* ☎ *0131/668–8800,* WEB *www.historic-scotland.gov.uk.* 🎫 *£2.80.* ☉ *Apr.–Sept., Mon.–Sat. 9:30–6; Oct.–Mar., Mon.–Sat. 9:30–4.*

En Route   The journey along the A857 to the Calanais Standing Stones takes you past several interesting sights. The rather dusty but illuminating **Shawbost School Museum** (⊠ Off A857, Shawbost, ☎ 01851/710212) survives from the Highland Village Competition in 1970, during which students gathered artifacts and contributed to displays aimed at illustrating a past way of life in Lewis. The museum is open April through October, Monday through Saturday 10 to 5, with admission by donation. **Dun Carloway** (Off A857), one of the best-preserved Iron Age *brochs* (circular stone towers) in Scotland, dominates the scattered community of Carloway. The mysterious circular defensive tower of the Dun Carloway broch was built 2,000 years ago, possibly as protection against seaborne raiders. The interpretative center explains more about the broch and its setting. Up a side road north from Carloway at **Gearrannan** (☎ 01851/643416) an old blackhouse village has been brought back to life with a museum, live interpretation, and guided tours explaining the old island way of life. Call for hours.

Calanais Standing Stones

★ **30** *22 mi southeast of Arnol.*

At Calanais (Callanish) are the Calanais Standing Stones, lines of megaliths reminiscent of those in Stonehenge, in England. Probably positioned in several stages between 3000 and 1500 BC, this grouping consists of an avenue of 19 monoliths extending northward from a circle of 13 stones, with other rows leading south, east, and west. It's believed they may have been used for astronomical observations. The site is accessible at any time. The **visitor center** has an exhibit on the stones, a shop, and a tearoom. ⊠ *Off A858, Calanais,* ☎ *01851/ 621422.* ⌹ *Exhibit £1.75.* ⊙ *Visitor center Apr.–Sept., Mon.–Sat. 10–6, tearoom closes at 5:30; Oct.–Mar., Wed.–Sat. 10–4, tearoom closes at 3:30.*

The restored black house next to the gate leading to the Calanais Standing Stones is the site of the **Callanish Stones Tearoom** (☎ 01851/ 621373), an interesting spot in which to take refreshment or browse among the crafts on display.

Tarbert

❸❶ *47 mi south of Calanais.*

Tarbert is the main port of Harris, with one or two shops and accommodations. **Traigh Luskentyre,** roughly 5 mi southwest of Tarbert, is a spectacular example of Harris's tidy selection of beaches—2 mi of yellow sands adjacent to **Traigh Seilebost** beach, with superb views northward to the hills of the Forest of Harris. Turreted **Amhuinnsuidhe Castle** (pronounced avun-*shooee*) was built in the 1860s by the earls of Dunmore as a base for fishing and hunting in the North Harris deer forest. The castle stands about 10 mi northwest of Tarbert on the B887, and you can view it from the outside only.

Lodging

£££ ⊡ **Ardvourlie Castle.** Ardvourlie, a former Victorian hunting lodge, sits
★ in splendid isolation amid the dramatic mountain scenery of Harris, an ideal habitat for hill walking. The decor is bold, idiosyncratic, and entirely in keeping with the High Victorian atmosphere of the castle. A well-stocked library and roaring fires complement the country-house hospitality. The cooking (for guests only) is along traditional lines and of a high standard, favoring fresh local produce and, often, wild game. ⊠ *Isle of Harris, 15 mi north of Tarbert, signed off the A859, HS3 3AB,* ☎ *01859/502307,* 🅵🅰🆇 *01859/502348. 4 rooms. Restaurant, library; no a/c, no room phones. MC, V. Closed Nov.–Mar.*

Northton

16 mi south of Tarbert.

The little community of Northton has two attractions. The **McGillivray Centre** focuses on the life and work of William McGillivray, a noted naturalist with strong links to Harris. ⊠ *Off A859,* ☎ *01859/502011.* ⌹ *Donation.* ⊙ *Mon.–Sat. 9–9.*

The **Seallam! Visitor Centre and Co Leis Thu? Genealogical Research Centre** has exhibitions on the people and landscape of Harris. The owners organize guided walks and cultural evenings weekly between May and September. There's also a family-history resource center with a genealogical research service. ⊠ *Off A859,* ☎ *01859/520258,* 🆆🅴🅱 *www.seallam.com.* ⌹ *£2.50 for exhibitions.* ⊙ *Mon.–Sat. 9–6.*

St. Clement's Church

❸❷ *20 mi south of Tarbert.*

At the southernmost point of Harris is the community of Rodel, where you'll find St. Clement's Church, a cruciform church standing on a hillock. This is the most impressive pre-Reformation church in the Outer Hebrides; it was built around 1500 and contains the magnificently sculptured tomb (1528) of the church's builder, Alasdair Crotach, MacLeod chief of Dunvegan Castle. An arched recess has sculpted panels showing, among other scenes, St. Michael and Satan weighing souls. There are also other effigies and carvings within the building.

North Uist

8 mi south of Rodel via ferry from Leverburgh, Harris.

The island of North Uist is particularly known for its prehistoric remains. At **Newtonferry (Port nan Long),** by Otternish and the ferry pier for the Leverburgh (Harris) ferry service, stand the remains of what was reputed to be the last inhabited broch in North Uist, **Dun an Sticar.** This defensive tower, reached by a causeway over the loch, was home to Hugh Macdonald, a descendant of MacDonald of Sleat, until 1602.

You can see the ruins of **Trinity Temple (Teampull na Trionaid),** a medieval college and monastery said to have been founded in the 13th century by Beathag, daughter of Somerled, the progenitor of the Clan Donald. The ruins stand 8 mi southwest of Lochmaddy, off the A865.

The **Barpa Langass Chambered Cairn,** dating from the 3rd millennium BC, is the only chambered cairn in the Western Isles known to have retained its inner chamber fully intact. It sits very close to the A867 on the stretch between Lochmaddy and Clachan.

The **Balranald Nature Reserve** (⊠ Visitor center at Goular, ☎ 01876/560287 or 01463/715000), administered by the Royal Society for the Protection of Birds (RSPB), shelters large numbers of waders and seabirds, including red-necked phalaropes, living in a varied habitat of loch, marsh, *machair* (grasslands just behind the beach), and sandy and rocky shore. The reserve can be viewed anytime (guided walks by an RSPB warden May–August), but you are asked to keep to the paths during breeding season (April–June) so as not to disturb the birds. It's on the west side of North Uist, about 3 mi northwest of Bayhead, which you can reach via the A865.

Horseback Riding

Uist Community Riding School (⊠ The Stables, Balivanich, Isle of Benbecula, ☎ 01870/604283) offers daily tuition for all levels and rides out into the countryside.

South Uist

34 mi south of Newtonferry via Grimsay, Benbecula, and 3 causeways.

Carpets of wildflowers in spring and early summer, superb deserted west-coast beaches, and historical connections to Flora Macdonald and Bonnie Prince Charlie head the list of reasons to visit South Uist. You can travel the length of South Uist along Route A865, making short treks off this main road on your way to Lochboisdale, on the southeast coast of the island. At Lochboisdale you can catch ferries to Barra, the southernmost principal island of the Outer Hebrides, or to Oban, on the mainland.

About 5 mi south of the causeway from Grimsay to Benbecula, atop Rueval Hill, stands the 125-ft-high statue of the Madonna and Child known as *Our Lady of the Isles.* The local Catholic community erected the statue, the work of sculptor Hew Lorimer, in 1957. One of only two remaining British native—that is, nonmigrating—populations of greylag geese make their home at **Loch Druidibeg National Nature Reserve** in a fresh and brackish loch environment. This is a few miles south of Reuval Hill, to the west of A865; stop at the warden's office for information about access.

A few miles south of Howmore, just west of A865, stand the ruins of **Ormaclete Castle,** built in 1708 for the chief of the Clan Ranald but accidentally destroyed by fire in 1715 on the eve of the Battle of Sheriffmuir, during which the chief was killed.

Kildonan Museum and Heritage Centre focuses on local history, archaeology, and culture and has a crafts shop and tearoom. ⊠ *A865, Kildonan,* ☎ *01878/710343.* ⌦ *£1.50.* ☉ *Easter–Oct., Mon.–Sat. 10–5, Sun. 2–5.*

㉞ At Gearraidh Bhailteas (just west of A865 near Milton), you can see the ruins of **Flora Macdonald's birthplace.** South Uist's most famous daughter, Flora helped the Young Pretender, Prince Charles Edward Stuart, avoid capture and was feted as a heroine afterward.

Shopping
Hebridean Jewelry (⊠ Garrieganichy, Lochdar, ☎ 01870/610288) sells decorative jewelry and framed pictures; the owners also run a crafts shop on the premises.

THE NORTHERN HIGHLANDS A TO Z

To research prices, get advice from other travelers, and book travel arrangements, visit www.fodors.com.

AIR TRAVEL
The main airports for the Northern Highlands are Inverness and Wick (both on the mainland). There's direct air service from Edinburgh and Glasgow to Inverness and from Edinburgh to Wick. Contact British Airways. You can fly from London's Luton Airport to Inverness on one of the daily easyJet flights.

British Regional Airways/Loganair operates flights among the islands of Barra, Benbecula, and Stornoway, in the Outer Hebrides (weekdays only).
➤ CARRIERS: **British Airways** (☎ 08457/733377, WEB www.britishairways. com). **British Regional Airways/Loganair** (☎ 08457/733377, WEB www.loganair.co.uk). **easyJet** (☎ 0870/600–0000, WEB www.easyjet. com).
➤ AIRPORT INFORMATION: **Inverness Airport** (☎ 01667/464000).

BOAT AND FERRY TRAVEL
The fastest route to this area is the A9 to the gateway town of Inverness. The ferry services—run by Caledonian MacBrayne, called Cal-Mac—link the Outer Hebrides. Ferries run from Ullapool to Stornoway, from Oban to Castlebay and Lochboisdale, and from Uig, on the Isle of Skye, to Tarbert and Lochmaddy. Causeways link North Uist, Benbecula, and South Uist.

The Island Hopscotch planned-route ticket and the Island Rover pass, both offered by CalMac, give considerable reductions on interisland ferry fares; for details contact Caledonian MacBrayne.
➤ BOAT AND FERRY LINES: **Caledonian MacBrayne** (⊠ Ferry Terminal, Gourock PA19 1QP, ☎ 01475/650100, WEB www.calmac.co.uk). **Oban to Castlebay and Lochboisdale ferry** (☎ 01631/566688). **Ullapool to**

Stornoway ferry (☎ 01854/612358). **Uig to Tarbert and Lochmaddy ferry** (☎ 01470/542219).

BUS TRAVEL

Scottish Citylink and National Express run buses from England to Inverness, Ullapool, Thurso, Scrabster, and Wick. There are also coach connections between the ferry ports of Tarbert and Stornoway; consult the local tourist information center for details.

Highland Country Buses provides bus service in the Highlands area. On the Outer Hebrides several small operators run regular routes to most towns and villages. The post-bus service—which also delivers mail—becomes increasingly important in remote areas; it supplements the regular bus service, which runs only a few times per week. A full timetable of services for the Northern Highlands (and the rest of Scotland) is available from the Royal Mail.

➤ Bus Lines: **Highland Country Buses** (in the mainland and Skye, ☎ 01463/222244). **National Express** (☎ 08705/808080, WEB www.nationalexpress.co.uk). **Royal Mail Post Buses** (✉ 7 Strothers La., Inverness, IV1 1AA, ☎ 01463/256273). **Scottish Citylink** (☎ 08705/505050, WEB www.citylink.co.uk).

CAR RENTAL

➤ Agencies: **Avis** (✉ Inverness Airport, ☎ 01667/464070). **Budget Rent-a-Car** (✉ Burns Cottage, Railway Terrace, Inverness, ☎ 0800/181181). **Europcar Ltd.** (✉ Friar's Bridge Service Station, Telford St., Inverness, ☎ 01463/235337). **Hertz** (✉ Inverness Airport, Inverness, ☎ 01667/462652).

CAR TRAVEL

Because of the infrequent bus services and sparse railway stations, a car is definitely the best way to explore this region. The twisting, winding single-lane roads demand a degree of driving dexterity. Local rules of the road require that when two cars meet, whichever driver reaches a passing place first must stop in it or opposite it and allow the oncoming car to continue. Small cars tend to yield to large commercial vehicles. Never park in passing places, and remember that these sections of the road can also allow traffic behind you to pass. Don't hold up a vehicle trying to pass you.

Note that in this sparsely populated area, distances between gas stations can be considerable. Although getting around is easy, even on single-lane roads, the choice of routes is restricted by the rugged terrain.

DISCOUNTS AND DEALS

It is in the Highlands and islands that the Freedom of Scotland Travelpass really becomes useful, saving you money on ferries, trains, and some buses (☞ Train Travel *in* Smart Travel Tips A to Z).

EMERGENCIES

Dial 999 in an emergency for an ambulance, the police, the fire department, or the coast guard (no coins are needed for emergency calls from public phone booths).

Pharmacies are not found in rural areas. Pharmacies in the main towns—Thurso, Wick, Stornoway—keep normal shop hours. In an emergency the police will provide assistance in locating a pharmacist. General practitioners may also dispense medicines in rural areas.

TOURS

BOAT TOURS

Several small firms run boat cruises along the spectacular west-coast seaboard. On Skye there's also a broad selection of mountain guides. Contact the local tourist information center for details about local operators.

Dunvegan Sea Cruises, at Dunvegan Castle, Skye, runs a boat trip to the nearby seal colony for £4. John o'Groats Ferries operates wildlife cruises from John o'Groats harbor daily from mid-June through August. The trip takes passengers into the Pentland Firth, to Duncansby Stacks, and the island of Stroma, passing by spectacular cliff scenery and bird life. John o'Groats Ferries also runs day tours to Orkney from Inverness (with a guided tour of the islands), daily June through early September.

➤ CONTACT: **Dunvegan Sea Cruises** (☎ 01470/521206). **John o'Groats Ferries** (☎ 01955/611353).

SPECIAL-INTEREST TOURS

Highland Heritage Tours will take you on a minibus day trip to the Isle of Skye from Inverness. James Johnstone will drive you anywhere and knows a lot about the Highlands and islands, including the Outer Hebrides. Puffin Express runs unusual "Wildlife and Stone Age" day tours from Inverness between Easter and October, with limited tours in the winter (when the owner goes wolf-watching in Poland).

Raasay Outdoor Centre organizes courses in kayaking, sailing, windsurfing, climbing, rappeling, archery, walking, and navigation skills.

➤ CONTACT: **Highland Heritage Tours** (☎ 01463/798618, WEB www.highlandheritagetours.com). **James Johnstone** (☎ 01463/798372, FAX 01463/790179). **Puffin Express** (☎ 01463/717181; FAX 01463/717188, WEB www.puffinexpress.co.uk). **Raasay Outdoor Centre** (☎ 01478/660266, WEB www.raasayoutdoorcentre.co.uk).

TRAIN TRAVEL

Main railway stations in the area include Oban (for Barra and the Uists) and Kyle of Lochalsh (for Skye), on the west coast, or Inverness (for points north to Thurso and Wick). There's direct service from London to Inverness and connecting service from Edinburgh and Glasgow. For information contact National Rail Enquiries.

Stations on the northern lines (Inverness to Thurso–Wick and Inverness to Kyle of Lochalsh) include Beauly, Muir of Ord, and Dingwall; on the Thurso–Wick line, Alness, Invergordon, Fearn, Tain, Ardgay, Culrain, Invershin, Lairg, Rogart, Golspie, Brora, Helmsdale, Kildonan, Kinbrace, Forsinard, Altnabreac, Scotscalder, and Georgemas Junction; and on the Kyle line, Garve, Lochluichart, Achanalt, Achnasheen, Achnashellach, Strathcarron, Attadale, Stromeferry, Duncraig, Plockton, and Duirinish.

➤ TRAIN INFORMATION: **National Rail Enquiries** (☎ 08457/484950). **ScotRail** (☎ 08457/550033, WEB www.scotrail.co.uk).

VISITOR INFORMATION

The tourist information centers at Dornoch, Dunvegan, Durness, Portree, Stornoway, Tarbert, Ullapool, and Wick are open year-round, with limited winter hours at Dunvegan, Durness, Ullapool, and Wick.

Seasonal tourist information centers are at Bettyhill, Broadford (Skye), Castlebay (Barra, Outer Hebrides), Gairloch, Helmsdale, John o'Groats, Kyle of Lochalsh, Lairg, Lochboisdale (South Uist, Outer Hebrides), Lochcarron, Lochinver, Lochmaddy (North Uist,

Outer Hebrides), North Kessock, Shiel Bridge, Strathpeffer, Thurso,
and Uig.

➤ TOURIST INFORMATION: **Dornoch** (✉ The Square, Dornoch IV25 3SD,
☎ 01862/810400). **Dunvegan,** Isle of Skye (✉ 2 Lochside, Dunvegan
IV55 8WB, ☎ 01470/521581). **Durness** (✉ Durine, Durness IV27 4PN,
☎ 01971/511259). **Portree,** Isle of Skye (✉ Bayfield House, Bayfield
Rd., Portree, Isle of Skye, IV51 9EL, ☎ 01478/612137). **Stornoway,**
Isle of Lewis and Harris (✉ 26 Cromwell St., HS1 2DD, ☎ 01851/
703088, WEB www.witb.co.uk). **Tarbert,** Isle of Lewis and Harris (✉
Pier Rd., Tarbert, ☎ 01859/502011). **Ullapool** (✉ Argyll St., Ullapool
IV26 2UB, ☎ 01854/612135). **Wick** (✉ Whitechapel Rd. off High St.,
Wick KW1 4EA, ☎ 01955/602596).

11 THE NORTHERN ISLES

ORKNEY, SHETLAND

Wind, frequent mists, and severe exposure make the northern islands a challenge as much as an adventure. Orkney—a cluster of almost 70 islands, 20 of which are inhabited—has the greatest concentration of prehistoric sites in all of Scotland. And to many, the Shetland islands, with their epic cliffs, dramatic fissurelike sea inlets, and barren moors in the interior, don't feel "British" at all.

By Gilbert
Summers

Updated by
Beth Ingpen

BOTH ORKNEY AND SHETLAND possess a Scandinavian heritage that gives their collective 200 islets an ambience different from any other region of Scotland. For mainland Scots, visiting this archipelago is a little like traveling abroad without having to worry about a different language or currency. Both Orkney and Shetland are essentially bleak and austere, but have awe-inspiring seascapes and genuinely warm, friendly people. Neither has yet been overrun by tourism.

An Orcadian has been defined as a farmer with a boat, whereas a Shetlander has been called a fisherman with a croft (small farm). Orkney is the greener archipelago and is rich with artifacts that testify to the many centuries of continuous settlement here: stone circles, burial chambers, ancient settlements, and fortifications. Shetland, with its ocean views and sparse landscapes—trees are a rarity because of ever-present wind—is endowed with a more remote air than neighboring Orkney. However, don't let Shetland's desolate countryside fool you: it has a wealth of historic interest and is far from being a backwater island. Oil money from its mineral resources and its position as a crossroads in the northern seas for centuries have helped make Shetland a cosmopolitan place.

Pleasures and Pastimes

Boating

There are good anchorages among Orkney's many islands. Contact the tourist information centers for details. There are also sailboats available on Shetland. Details may be obtained from the Lerwick Boating Club, which can be contacted through the tourist information center.

Dining

Seafood is first class and so is Orkney's malt whisky. Meals are usually of the stick-to-your-ribs variety, as vegetable gardeners do face some extra challenges from the northerly latitude. For local tastes, try Orkney *bere bannocks* (bere is a kind of primitive barley, bannock a kind of oatcake), Orkney-brewed ales, and local cheeses.

CATEGORY	COST*
££££	over £22
£££	£16–£22
££	£9–£15
£	under £9

per person for a main course at dinner, including VAT

Diving

Orkney, especially the former wartime anchorage of Scapa Flow on Hoy, claims to have the best dive sites in Britain. Part of the attraction lies in the remains of German navy ships that were scuttled here in 1919. Many boat-rental companies arrange diving charters; contact the tourist information centers. Shetland also has exceptional underwater visibility, perfect for viewing the wrecks and abundant marine life.

Festivals

Shetland has quite a strong cultural identity, thanks to its Scandinavian heritage. There are, for instance, books of local dialect verse, a whole folklore contained in knitting patterns, and a strong tradition of fiddle playing. In the middle of the long winter, at the end of January, the Shetlanders celebrate their Viking culture with the Up-Helly-Aa Festival, which involves much merrymaking, dressing up, and the burning of a replica of a Viking long ship. The Shetland Folk Festival, held in April, and October's Shetland Accordion and Fiddle Festival both attract large numbers of visitors. Orkney's St. Magnus Festival, a musical celebration, is based in Kirkwall and usually held the third week in June. Orkney also hosts a jazz festival in April, an annual folk festival at the end of May, the unique Boys' Ploughing Match in mid-August, and The Ba' (ball; street rugby-football played by the Uppies and Doonies residents of Kirkwall) on Christmas and New Year's Day.

Fishing

Sea fishing is such a popular sport in Orkney that the local tourist board advises anglers to book early. Several companies rent sea-angling boats, with fishing rods available in most cases. Loch angling in Orkney is also popular; Loch of Harray and Loch of Stenness are the best-known spots. Contact the Orkney visitor center for information. Shetland, also renowned for sea angling, holds several competitions throughout the year. Contact the Shetland Association of Sea Anglers via the tourist information center.

Lodging

Accommodations in the Northern Isles are on par with mainland Scotland. However, to experience a simpler lifestyle, check out the unique "camping bods" in Shetland—old cottages providing inexpensive, basic accommodation (log fires, cold water, and sometimes no electricity). For details, contact the Shetland visitor center. Unless otherwise indicated, all rooms listed below have private baths.

CATEGORY	COST*
££££	over £140
£££	£110–£140
££	£65–£110
£	under £65

*All prices are for a standard double room, including service, breakfast, and VAT.

Exploring the Northern Isles

Both island groupings require at least a couple of days if you are to do more than just scratch the surface. The extra effort necessary to get to Shetland means you'll probably want to invest four or five days here. In any case, the Northern Isles generate their own laid-back approach to life, and once here, you may want to take it slowly.

Numbers in the text correspond to numbers in the margin and on the Shetland Islands and the Orkney Islands maps.

Great Itineraries

Getting around is quite straightforward—the roads are good on both Shetland and Orkney. A fast and frequent interisland passenger and car ferry service makes island-hopping perfectly practical. Only at peak season are reservations advisable.

IF YOU HAVE 1 DAY
From Inverness take a day trip to Orkney—though it will be a long one—by bus and ferry, to see some of Orkney's top historic sites. A trip to Shetland is not realistic for such a short length of time.

IF YOU HAVE 4 DAYS
Get a good taste of Orkney by taking in the main sights—St. Magnus Cathedral, Earl Patrick's Palace, and the Bishop's Palace on ☎ **Kirkwall** ⑱—then go out to **Skara Brae** ⑭, **Maes Howe** ⑬, and the **Ring of Brogar** ⑫. You could also see a bit of Shetland in this length of time, provided you get a good night's sleep on the direct Orkney–Shetland

ferry, leaving you a full day as soon as you arrive to take in the south of the island: **Shetland Croft House Museum** ③, **Jarlshof** ④, Sumburgh Head, and **St. Ninian's Isle** ⑤. Stay overnight in ⊞ **Lerwick** ① on your fourth day and make a quick exploration of Lerwick itself and **Scalloway** ⑥; then make a trip up to Esha Ness to get the flavor of the north of Mainland. In theory, in this length of time it's possible to get out to the very end of Scotland at Muckle Flugga, but Shetland is such an extraordinary place that it merits more time.

IF YOU HAVE 8 DAYS

This is enough time in the Northern Isles for you to see all the main sights on Orkney and then catch a midweek ferry to Shetland, with enough time to get to the far north of Shetland as well.

When to Tour the Northern Isles

Go in the early summer when the bird colonies are at their most spectacular and the long northern daylight hours give you plenty of sightseeing time.

AROUND SHETLAND

The Shetland coastline is an incredible 900 mi because of all the indentations, and there isn't a point on the island farther than 3 mi from the sea. Settlements away from Lerwick, the primary town, are small and scattered—ask the friendly locals for directions.

Lerwick

❶ *14 hrs by ferry from Aberdeen.*

Take the time to explore some of Lerwick's nearby diversions before venturing beyond it. The town was founded by Dutch fishermen in the 17th century. Handsome stone buildings front Lerwick's twisting flagstone lanes and harbor, which is still a very active port. **Fort Charlotte**, a 17th-century Cromwellian stronghold, was built to protect the Sound of Bressay. ⊠ *Market St.,* ☎ *0131/668–8800.* ⊡ *Free.* ☉ *Daily.*

The **Shetland Museum** gives an interesting account of the development of the town, with displays on archaeology, art and textiles, shipping, and folk life. ⊠ *Lower Hillhead,* ☎ *01595/695057,* WEB *www. shetland-museum.org.uk.* ⊡ *Free.* ☉ *Mon., Wed., and Fri. 10–7; Tues., Thurs., and Sat. 10–5.*

Clickhimin Broch, on the site of what was originally an Iron Age fortification, makes a good introduction to these mysterious Pictish structures (a *broch* is a circular stone structure), possibly intended as a place of retreat and protection in the event of attack. South of the broch are vivid views of the cliffs at the south end of the island of Bressay, which shelters Lerwick Harbor. ⊠ *1 mi south of Lerwick off A970,* ☎ *0131/668–8800.* ⊡ *Free.* ☉ *Daily.*

Dining and Lodging

££ ✕⊞ **Shetland Hotel.** Modern and well-appointed—a result of the oil boom in the area and the needs of high-flying oil executives—the Shetland is done up in an attractive blend of burgundy and blue color schemes. The food is rich and filling, with sometimes wildly clashing flavors. One entrée consists of saddle of Shetland lamb filled with haggis forcemeat stuffing, sliced and served with a rich Orkney malt whisky and rosemary jus—enough of a meal to sink the Shetland ferry! The hotel sits directly opposite the ferry terminal. ⊠ *Holmsgarth Rd., ZE1 0PW,* ☎ *01595/695515,* FAX *01595/695828,* WEB *www.shetlandhotels. com. 63 rooms. 2 restaurants, 2 bars; no a/c. AE, DC, MC, V.*

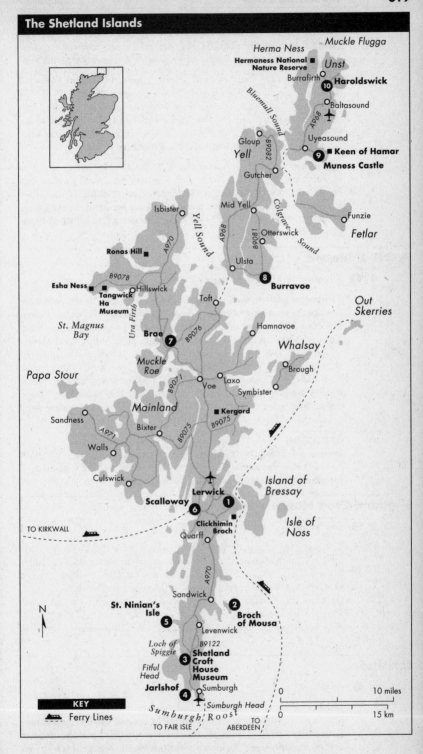

The Shetland Islands

Muckle Flugga

Herma Ness

Hermaness National
Nature Reserve

Unst

Burrafirth

(10) Haroldswick

Baltasound

A968

Gloup

Uyeasound

(9) ■ Keen of Hamar

Muness Castle

Yell

B9082

Gutcher

Isbister

Mid Yell

Funzie

A968

Yell Sound

A970

Otterswick

Fetlar

Ronas Hill ■

Colgrave Sound

B9081

Ulsta

B9078

Esha Ness ■

Hillswick

(8) Burravoe

**Tangwick
Ha
Museum**

Toft

Out
Skerries

St. Magnus
Bay

Hamnavoe

B907b

Ura Firth

Brae (7)

Whalsay

Muckle
Roe

Brough

Papa Stour

Voe   Laxo

B9071

Symbister

Mainland

■ Kergord

Sandness

Bixter

B9075

B9075

A971

Walls

Culswick

Lerwick

Island of
Bressay

Scalloway (6)   **(1)**

Clickhimin
Broch

Isle of
Noss

TO KIRKWALL

Quarff

Sandwick

N

St. Ninian's
Isle

(2)

(5)

Levenwick

**Broch
of Mousa**

Loch of
Spiggie

B9122

**(3) Shetland
Croft
House
Museum**

Fitful
Head

Jarlshof

(4) Sumburgh

Sumburgh Head

KEY

Sumburgh Roos

0 ___ 10 miles

⚓ Ferry Lines

TO FAIR ISLE

TO
ABERDEEN

0 ___ 15 km

Bicycling

Bicycles can be rented from **Eric Brown Cycles** (⊠ Grantfield Garage, North Rd., ☎ 01595/692709).

Shopping

Several shops sell knitwear and woolen goods in Lerwick. **Anderson & Co.** (⊠ Shetland Warehouse, 60–62 Commercial St., ☎ 01595/693714) carries handmade knitwear and has a small stock of machine-made items and souvenirs. **The Spider's Web** (⊠ 45 Commercial St., ☎ 01595/695246, ☉ Mon.–Sat. 9–5) sells hand-spun and hand-knitted goods in both traditional and contemporary styles.

Hjaltasteyn (⊠ 161 Commercial St., ☎ 01595/696224) handcrafts gems and jewelry in gold and silver. **J. G. Rae Limited** (⊠ 92 Commercial St., ☎ 01595/693686) stocks Shetland silvercraft and gold and silver jewelry with Norse and Celtic motifs. **Shetland Jewelry** (⊠ Sound Side, Weisdale, ☎ 01595/830275) sells gold and silver Celtic-inspired jewelry.

Broch of Mousa

★ ❷ *14 mi south of Lerwick via A970.*

The community of Sandwick is the departure point for the passenger ferry to the tiny isle of Mousa, where you can see the Broch of Mousa, the most fully extant of all the broch towers remaining in Scotland. The broch's towering walls give a real sense of enclosure and security, which must have been reassuring for islanders subject to attacks from ship-borne raiders. ⊠ *Mousa,* ☎ *0131/668–8800; 01950/431367 ferry,* WEB *www.historic-scotland.gov.uk.* 🖾 *Broch free, ferry £8 round-trip.* ☉ *Broch year-round; ferry departs mid-Apr.–mid-Sept., Mon.–Thurs. and Sat. at 2, Fri. and Sun. at 12:30 and 2, weather permitting in all cases.*

Shopping

Lawrence J. Smith Ltd. (⊠ Hoswick, 2 mi west of Sandwick, ☎ 01950/431215) sells Shetland knitwear—both handmade and machine-made—for all ages in a wide selection of colors.

Shetland Croft House Museum

★ ❸ *7 mi south of Sandwick.*

The scattered village of Voe (one of several with this name on Shetland; *voe* means "coastal inlet") is the home of the Shetland Croft House Museum. This 19th-century thatched house contains a broad range of artifacts that depict the former way of life of the rural Shetlander, which the museum attendant will be delighted to discuss with you. ⊠ *South Voe, Dunrossness, unclassified road east of A970,* ☎ *01595/695057,* WEB *www.shetland-museum.org.uk.* 🖾 *Free.* ☉ *May–Sept., daily 10–1 and 2–5.*

Jarlshof

★ ❹ *4 mi south of Voe.*

Jarlshof, a centuries-old site, includes the extensive remains of Norse buildings, as well as prehistoric wheelhouses and earth houses representing thousands of years of continuous settlement. The site also has a 17th-century laird's (landowner's) house built on the ruins of a medieval farmstead. Excavations at nearby Old Scatness, under the auspices of the Shetland Amenity Trust, uncovered a broch and an Iron

Age village with one building still in possession of its roof. ⊠ *Sumburgh Head*, ☎ *0131/668–8800*, WEB *www.historic-scotland.gov.uk*. ⊠ *£3.* ⏱ *Apr.–Sept., daily 9:30–6.*

St. Ninian's Isle

❺ *8 mi north of Sumburgh via A970 and B9122; turn left at Skelberry.*

It was on St. Ninian's Isle—actually a tombolo, a spit of sand that moors an island to the mainland—that archaeologists in the 1950s uncovered the St. Ninian treasure, a collection of 28 silver objects from the 8th century. While excavating the site of a 12th-century church, archaeologists discovered under the nave the remains of an earlier chapel dating to the 8th century and the silver objects, including a sword, torque (neck collar), bowls, and spoons. This Celtic silver is now in the Museum of Scotland in Edinburgh, though good replicas are on view in the Shetland Museum in Lerwick. Though the silver has been removed, this is still a lovely, scenic spot with a sense of history.

Scalloway

❻ *21 mi north of St. Ninian's Isle, 6 mi west of Lerwick.*

On the west coast of Mainland Island is Scalloway, which preceded Lerwick as capital of the islands and still has a very active harbor. During World War II, Scalloway was the port for the "Shetland Bus," a boat operation to and from Norway. The boats would carry British agents to Norway to perform acts of sabotage against Germany. On the return trips, the boats would carry escaped British prisoners of war back to Shetland. Look for the information board just off the main road (A970), which overlooks the settlement and its castle. **Scalloway Castle** was built in 1600 by Patrick Stewart, earl of Orkney, who coerced the locals to build it for him. He was executed in 1615 for his cruelty and misdeeds, and the castle was never used again. ⊠ *Scalloway,* ☎ *0131/668–8800,* WEB *www.historic-scotland.gov.uk.* ⊠ *Free.* ⏱ *Daily, 24 hrs.*

OFF THE
BEATEN PATH

KERGORD VALLEY – Take the B9075 east off the A970, at the head of a narrow sea inlet. This leads into this unexpectedly green valley, noted for its woodland. This would be unremarkable farther south, but here it is a novelty.

Shopping

The **Shetland Woollen Company** (⊠ Castle St., ☎ 01595/880243) is one of many purveyors in Scalloway with a selection of Shetland knitwear.

Brae

❼ *24 mi north of Scalloway.*

Brae is the home of the Busta House Hotel, one of the best hotels on the island. Beyond Brae the main road meanders past **Mavis Grind,** a strip of land so narrow you can throw a stone—if you are strong—from the Atlantic, in one inlet, to the North Sea, in another.

OFF THE
BEATEN PATH

ESHA NESS AND RONAS HILL – For outstanding views of the rugged, forbidding cliffs around Esha Ness, drive north, then turn left onto the B9078. On the way, look for the sandstone stacks in the bay that resemble a Viking galley under sail. After viewing the cliffs at Esha Ness, and calling in at Tangwick Haa Museum (⊠ off the B9078, Tangwick, ☎ 01806/503389), a former laird's house, return to join the A970 at Hillswick and follow an ancillary road from the head of Ura Firth. This road provides vistas of rounded, bare Ronas Hill, the highest hill in Shetland. Though only 1,468 ft high, it's noted for its arctic-alpine flora growing at low levels.

Dining and Lodging

££ ✕⊡ **Busta House.** Busta House dates in part from the 16th century and ★ is surrounded by terraced grounds. Bedrooms are well furnished in traditional style, with floral chintzes and antique furniture. The 16th-century Long Room is a delightful place to sample the hotel's selection of malt whiskies while sitting beside a peat fire. On the Taste of Scotland menu, Shetland salmon and lamb are usually available. ⊠ *Brae, Shetland, ZE2 9QN,* ☎ *01806/522506,* FAX *01806/522588,* WEB *www.bustahouse. com. 20 rooms. Restaurant, bar; no a/c. AE, DC, MC, V.*

Yell

11 mi northeast of Brae, 31 mi north of Lerwick via A970, A968, or B9076, and ferry from Toft.

There's not a lot to say about the blanket bog that cloaks two-thirds of the island of Yell, but the Old Haa building here is worth visiting, and you have to pass through Yell to get to Unst. To get here, catch ⑧ the ferry from Toft to Ulsta and take the B9081 east to **Burravoe.** The **Old Haa** (hall) of Burravoe, the oldest building on the island, is architecturally interesting. White and with crow-stepped gables, this is a typical example of an early 18th-century Shetland merchant's house. One of the displays in the upstairs museum tells the story of the wrecking of the German sail ship, the *Bohus,* in 1924. A copy of the ship's figurehead is displayed outside the Old Haa itself; the original is at the shipwreck site, overlooking Otterswick along the coast on the B9081. The Old Haa serves light meals with home-baked buns, cakes, and other goodies and also acts as a kind of unofficial information point. The staff is friendly and gives advice to sightseers. There's also a crafts shop on the premises. ⊠ *Burravoe,* ☎ *01957/722339.* ☜ *Free.* ☾ *Late Apr.– Sept., Tues.–Thurs. and Sat. 10–4, Sun. 2–5.*

Unst

49 mi north of Lerwick via ferry from Gutcher.

The ferry (take the main A968 at Mid Yell to Gutcher) crosses the Bluemull Sound to Unst, the northernmost inhabited island in Scotland.

⑨ **Muness Castle** (WEB www.historic-scotland.gov.uk), Scotland's northernmost castle, was built just before the end of the 16th century. Admission is free; just ask for the key keeper. To get here from the A968, turn right onto the B9084. Just to the north of Muness Castle is the **Keen of Hamar** national nature reserve, with subarctic flora and arctic terns.

⑩ In the far north of Unst is **Haroldswick,** with its post office, proud of its status as the most northerly one, and heritage center. Also here is **Unst Boat Haven,** displaying a collection of traditional small fishing and sailing boats reflecting Shetland's maritime heritage. ☎ *01957/ 711528.* ☜ *£2.* ☾ *May–Sept., daily 2–5.*

Hermaness National Nature Reserve, a bleak and open bird-watching territory, is replete with diving skuas—single-minded sky pirates that attack anything that strays near their nest sites. Gannets, puffins, and other seabirds nest in spectacular profusion by the cliffs on the left as you look out to sea. A visitor center here has more information on the birds. To get here from Haroldswick, follow the B9086 around the head of Burra Firth, a sea inlet. ⊠ *Shore Station, Burrafirth,* ☎ *01957/711278.* ⌨ *Free.* ☉ *Reserve daily, 24 hrs; visitor center mid-Apr.–mid-Sept., daily 9–5.*

A path in the Hermaness National Nature Reserve meanders across moorland and climbs up a gentle hill, from which you can see **Muckle Flugga,** to the north, a series of tilting offshore rocks; the largest of these sea-battered protrusions has a lighthouse. This is the northern-most point in Scotland—the sea rolls out on three sides, and no land lies beyond.

AROUND ORKNEY

Most of Orkney's many prehistoric sites are open to view, providing an insight into the life of bygone eras. At Maes Howe, for example, it becomes evident that graffiti is not solely an expression of today's youths: the Vikings left their marks here way back in the 12th century.

Stromness

⓫ *1¼ hrs north of Thurso via ferry from Scrabster.*

Stromness makes a good base for visiting the northern and western parts of Orkney, and the town holds two points of interest. The **Pier Arts Centre,** a former Stromness merchant's house (circa 1800), has adjoining buildings that now serve as a gallery with a permanent collection of 20th-century paintings and sculptures. ⊠ *Victoria St.,* ☎ *01856/ 850209.* ⌨ *Free.* ☉ *Tues.–Sat. 10:30–12:30 and 1:30–5.*

The **Stromness Museum** displays a varied collection of local natural-history material. Also here are ship models, a feature on the German fleet that was scuttled on Scapa Flow in 1919, and exhibits on fishing, shipping, whaling, and the Hudson Bay Company, which recruited work-ers in Stromness between the late 18th and 19th centuries. ⊠ *Alfred St.,* ☎ *01856/850025.* ⌨ *£2.50.* ☉ *May–Sept., daily 10–5; Oct.– Apr., Mon.–Sat. 10:30–12:30 and 1:30–5.*

Lodging

£ ⌂ **Mill of Eyrland.** White-painted stone walls, country antiques, and the rippling sound of the mill stream running beneath the windows make for a pleasant stay at this 1861 water mill that has been converted into a bed-and-breakfast. The mill's old machinery can still be seen, and attractive gardens surround the house. Evening meals are available on request. This makes a good base for visiting the main archaeological sites on Orkney. ⊠ *Stenness, KW16 3HA,* ☎ *01856/850136,* ℻ *01856/851633,* ⓦⒺⒷ *www.orknet.co.uk/mill. 4 rooms, 2 with bath. No a/c, no room phones, no smoking. No credit cards.*

Ring of Brogar

★ ⓬ *5 mi northeast of Stromness.*

The Ring of Brogar is a magnificent circle of 36 Neolithic stones (orig-inally 60) surrounded by a deep ditch. When the fog descends over the stones—a frequent occurrence—their looming shapes seem to come alive. Though their original use is uncertain, it's not hard to imagine strange rituals taking place here in the misty past. The stones stand between

The Orkney Islands

N

| 0 | 10 miles |
| 0 | 15 km |

KEY
Ferry Lines

ATLANTIC OCEAN

Seal Skerry
North Ronaldsay

Hollandstoun

North Ronaldsay
Firth

Knap of Howar ■
Holland

Papa
Westray

Pierowall

The North
Sound

Northwall
Burness

Westray

Rapness

Sanday

Kettletoft

Calfsound

Braeswick

Westray Firth

Sanday Sound

Rousay

Brough Head

Wasbister

Eday

Whitehall

**Earl's
Palace**

Birsay ○ 16

A966

Brinyan

Backaland

Aith ○

Stronsay

**Gurness
Broch** 17

**Marwick Head
Nature Reserve** 15

B9056

Dounby

Stronsay Firth

Marwick
Bay

A986

Skara Brae 14

Mainland

Unstan
Chambered
Tomb

Balfour

Shapinsay

Finstown ■

Ring of Brogar 12 13
**Maes
Howe**

A965

TO
SCALLOWAY

Stromness 11

A964

18 **Kirkwall**

**Orphir
Church** ○

A960

Skaill

Moness ○

Orphir ○

A961

St. Mary's ○

**Old Man
of Hoy** ■

Scapa Flow

Copinsay

Rackwick

**Italian
Chapel** ■

**Scapa Flow
Visitor Centre**

B9047

Lambholm

Lyness 19

St. Margaret's
Hope

Hoy

South Ronaldsay

Burwick ○

Pentland Firth

Old Head ○

Pentland
Skerries

Gills ○

Scrabster ○

A836

John o'
Groats

Thurso ○

Loch of Harray and Loch of Stenness, 5 mi northeast of Stromness. ⊠ *Off the A965,* ☎ *0131/668–8800,* WEB *www.historic-scotland.gov.uk.* ⬛ *Free.* ⊙ *Year-round.*

Maes Howe

★ ⑬ *1 mi north of Ring of Brogar on the A965.*

The huge burial mound of Maes Howe (circa 2500 BC) measures 115 ft in diameter and contains an enormous burial chamber. It was raided by Vikings in the 12th century, and Norse crusaders found shelter here, leaving a rich collection of runic inscriptions. Maes Howe is 1 mi northeast of the Ring of Brogar on the A965. ☎ *0131/668–8800,* WEB *www.historic-scotland.gov.uk.* ⬛ *£2.80.* ⊙ *Apr.–Sept., daily 9:30–6; Oct.–Mar., Mon.–Sat. 9:30–4, Sun. 2–4.*

Skara Brae

★ ⑭ *8 mi north of Stromness.*

At the Neolithic village of Skara Brae you'll find houses, joined by covered passages, with stone beds, fireplaces, and cupboards that have survived since the village was first occupied around 3000 BC. The site was preserved in sand until it was uncovered in 1850. It can be found 8 mi north of Stromness off the A967/B9056. ☎ *0131/668–8800,* WEB *www.historic-scotland.gov.uk.* ⬛ *£4.50, £3.50 in winter.* ⊙ *Apr.–Sept., daily 9:30–6; Oct.–Mar., Mon.–Sat. 9:30–4, Sun. 2–4.*

Marwick Head Nature Reserve

⑮ *5 mi north of Skara Brae.*

The Royal Society for the Protection of Birds tends the Marwick Head Nature Reserve, with its spectacular seabird cliffs. The Kitchener Memorial, which recalls the 1916 sinking of the cruiser HMS *Hampshire* with Lord Kitchener aboard, can also be seen in the reserve, on a cliff-top site. The reserve, which is unstaffed, lies to the north of Skara Brae, up the B9056; access to the reserve is along a path north from Marwick Bay. Take care near cliff edges. ☎ *01856/850176.* ⬛ *Free.* ⊙ *Daily, 24 hrs.*

Birsay

12 mi north of Stromness, 25 mi northwest of Kirkwall.

⑯ At Birsay is **Earl's Palace,** the impressive remains of a 16th-century palace built by the earls of Orkney. The **Brough of Birsay** and the remains of a Romanesque church and a Norse settlement stand close to Birsay on an island accessible only at low tide. To ensure you won't be swept away, check the tide tables before setting out.

⑰ **Gurness Broch** is an Iron Age tower standing more than 10 ft high, surrounded by stone huts. It's off the A966, about 8 mi from Birsay along Orkney's northern coast. ⊠ *Aikerness,* ☎ *0131/668–8800,* WEB *www.historic-scotland.gov.uk.* ⬛ *£2.80.* ⊙ *Apr.–Sept., daily 9:30–6.*

Kirkwall

⑱ *16 mi east of Stromness.*

In bustling Kirkwall, the main town on Orkney, there's plenty to see in the narrow, winding streets extending from the harbor, which retain a strong medieval feel. **Earl Patrick's Palace,** built in 1607, is perhaps the best surviving example of Renaissance architecture in Scotland. ✉ *Kirkwall,* ☎ *0131/668–8800.* 🎫 *£2, includes Bishop's Palace.* ⊙ *Apr.–Sept., daily 9:30–6.*

The **Bishop's Palace,** near Earl Patrick's Palace, dates to the 12th century. It was rebuilt in the late 15th century, and its round tower was added in the 16th century. ✉ *Kirkwall,* ☎ *0131/668–8800.* 🎫 *£2, includes Earl Patrick's Palace.* ⊙ *Apr.–Sept., daily 9:30–6.*

★ Founded by Jarl Rognvald in 1137 and dedicated to his uncle St. Magnus, **St. Magnus Cathedral,** in Kirkwall, was built between 1137 and 1200; however, additional work was carried out during the following 300 years. The cathedral is still in use and contains some of the best examples of Norman architecture in Scotland. The ornamentation on some of the tombstones is particularly striking. ⊙ *Mon.–Sat. 9–1 and 2–6; Sun. for services and 2–6.*

The **Orkney Wireless Museum** tells the story of wartime communications at Scapa Flow. Thousands of servicemen and -women were stationed here and used the equipment displayed in the museum to protect the Home Fleet. The museum also contains many handsome 1930s wireless radios and examples of the handicrafts produced by Italian prisoners of war. ✉ *Kiln Corner, Junction Rd.,* ☎ *01856/871400.* 🎫 *£2.* ⊙ *Apr.–Sept.; check with tourist information center for hrs.*

The **Unstan Chambered Tomb** is a 5,000-year-old cairn containing a chambered tomb. Pottery found within the tomb is now known as Unstan ware. The tomb is midway between Kirkwall and Stromness, roughly 3½ mi from each. ☎ *0131/668–8800.* 🎫 *Free.* ⊙ *Daily, 24 hrs.*

OFF THE
BEATEN PATH

ITALIAN CHAPEL – Created from a corrugated-iron hut by Italian prisoners of war during World War II, this beautiful and inspiring chapel has interior frescoes that were painted with whatever came to hand—bits of metal, colorful stones, leftover paints. It can be found in Lambholm, on the A961, 7 mi south of Kirkwall and just across from the first of the Churchill Barriers. 🎫 *Free.* ⊙ *Daily.*

ORKNEYINGA SAGA CENTRE– This makes a good starting point for exploration of Orkney's Norse heritage. Exhibits include the remains of the 12th-century **Orphir Church,** Scotland's only circular medieval church, and also the outline of a Viking drinking hall. The center is off the A964, 8 mi southwest of Kirkwall. ☎ *01856/811319.* 🎫 *Free.* ⊙ *Daily 9–5.*

Dining and Lodging

££ ✕🖼 **Foveran Hotel.** Thirty-four acres of grounds surround this comfortable hotel just outside Kirkwall and overlooking Scapa Flow. The Foveran has an attractive light-wood, Scandinavian-style dining room and an open fire in its sitting room. The Taste of Scotland menu includes homemade soups, pâtés, and seafood. ✉ *St. Ola, KW15 1SF,* ☎ *01856/872389,* FAX *01856/876430,* WEB *www.foveranhotel.co.uk. 8 rooms. Restaurant, lounge; no a/c. MC, V.*

£–££ ✕🖼 **Creel Inn.** Right on the waterfront, this outstanding small "restaurant with rooms" affords magnificent sea views from all three of its guest rooms, which are decorated in a simple, country style. The kitchen (££££) prepares imaginative modern Scottish cuisine using the freshest Orcadian seafood, meat, and locally grown vegetables. The Creel is well worth the 13-mi drive south from Kirkwall. ✉ *Front Rd.,*

St. Margaret's Hope, South Ronaldsay, KW17 2SL, ☎ *01856/831311,* WEB *www.thecreel.co.uk. 3 rooms. Restaurant; no a/c, no room phones. MC, V. Closed Oct.–Nov. and Jan.–Feb.*

£–££ 🏨 **Merkister Hotel.** On the edge of Loch Harray, this hotel is an angler's dream, with a great location, rental equipment and boats, instruction for novices, and experienced gillies (guides). The comfortable, traditional-style bedrooms encourage a good night's sleep after a hard day on the water. The restaurant serves Scottish cuisine. Even if you're not interested in fishing, the Merkister makes a good base for touring the region. ⊠ *Harray Loch, Harray, KW17 2LF,* ☎ *01856/771366,* FAX *01856/771515,* WEB *www.smoothhound.co.uk/hotels/merkister.html. 14 rooms. Restaurant, fishing; no a/c. AE, MC, V.*

£ 🏨 **Polrudden Guest House.** This modern guest house sits in a quiet area, yet it's close to the town center and public parks. It offers a high standard of lodging for the price. Multicolor matching curtains and quilt covers complement the cream-color rooms and pine furnishings. ⊠ *Peerie Sea Loan, KW15 1UH,* ☎ *01856/874761,* FAX *01856/870950,* WEB *www. polrudden.com. 7 rooms. No room phones, no a/c. MC, V.*

Nightlife and the Arts

Orkney's cultural highlight is the **St. Magnus Festival** (☎ 01856/ 871445, WEB www.stmagnusfestival.com), a music festival based in Kirkwall and usually held the third week in June. Orkney also hosts an annual folk festival at the end of May.

Bicycling

Bicycles can be rented from **Bobby's Cycle Centre** (⊠ Tankerness La., ☎ FAX 01856/875777).

Shopping

Kirkwall is Orkney's main shopping hub. At **Judith Glue** (⊠ 25 Broad St., ☎ 01856/874225) you can purchase designer knitwear with traditional patterns, as well as Orkney-made crafts and hampers of Orkney produce. Don't miss **Ola Gorrie at the Longship** (⊠ 7–15 Broad St., ☎ 01856/888790), which sells gold and silver jewelry with Celtic and Norse themes, including a delightful representation of a dragon originally drawn on the wall of the burial chamber at Maes Howe. **Ortak Jewelry** (⊠ Hatston, ☎ 01856/872224), a visitor center and shop, stocks Celtic-theme jewelry and has exhibits and jewelry-making demonstrations.

After all your shopping, you will have earned a dram of the local single malt at the **Highland Park Distillery** (⊠ Halm Rd., ☎ 01856/ 874619, WEB www.highlandpark.co.uk). Highland Park is a mellow whisky, less sweet than the Speyside malts, yet without the peat or iodine tinge of the western malts. It can be purchased all over Orkney (and farther afield), as well as from the distillery itself, which has a visitor center and shop.

Scapa Flow Visitor Centre

❶❾ *On Hoy, 14 mi southwest of Kirkwall, 6 mi south of Stromness via ferry.*

The **Scapa Flow Visitor Centre,** on Hoy, portrays the strategic role of the sheltered anchorage of Scapa Flow—said to be Britain's best diving site—in two world wars. Note that if you want to take your car over to Hoy, you will need to book well in advance with Orkney Ferries, as this is a very popular route and space is limited. ⊠ *Lyness, off the B9047, a short walk from the ferry terminal,* ☎ *01856/791300* *center; 01856/872044 ferry.* ✉ *Free.* ⊙ *June–Sept., Mon.–Sat. 9–4, Sun. 10–4; Oct.–May, weekdays 9–4.*

THE NORTHERN ISLES A TO Z

To research prices, get advice from other travelers, and book travel arrangements, visit www.fodors.com.

AIR TRAVEL

British Airways provides regular service to Lerwick (Shetland) and Kirkwall (Orkney) from Edinburgh, Glasgow, Aberdeen, and Inverness.

Because of the isolation of Orkney and Shetland there's a network of interisland flights. Tourist information centers can provide details, or call Loganair for more information.

➤ CARRIERS: **British Airways** (☎ 08457/733377, WEB www.britishairways. com). **Loganair** (☎ 08457/733377; 01856/872494 in Orkney, WEB www.loganair.co.uk).

BOAT AND FERRY TRAVEL

To get to Lerwick, Shetland, take the ferry from the port in Aberdeen. To reach Stromness, Orkney, take the ferry from the port in Scrabster. Contact Northlink Ferries for reservations for trips to both Lerwick and Stromness. Northlink also runs longer sea voyages from Aberdeen to Orkney.

As an alternative, you can take the ferry from John o'Groats to Burwick, Orkney, operated by John o'Groats Ferries, with up to four sailings daily from May through September. Another alternative is the ferry from Gill's Bay, Caithness, to St. Margaret's Hope, Orkney, operated by Pentland Ferries and with three sailings a day.

Both Orkney and Shetland are part of a network of islands with interconnecting ferries that are heavily subsidized. Book ferry tickets in advance. In Shetland, for ferry information, contact the tourist information center or call Northlink Orkney and Shetland Ferries if you are visiting during peak season. If you want to get to Orkney from Shetland you can do so by way of ferry from Lerwick to Stromness.

In Orkney, for details of ferry services operated interisland, call Orkney Ferries.

➤ BOAT AND FERRY INFORMATION: **John o'Groats Ferries** (☎ 01955/611353, WEB www.jogferry.co.uk). **Orkney Ferries** (☎ 01856/872044). **Northlink Orkney and Shetland Ferries** (☎ 01856/851144, FAX 01856/851155, WEB www.northlinkferries.co.uk). **Pentland Ferries** (☎ 01856/831226, FAX 01856/831614, WEB www.pentlandferries.co.uk).

BUS TRAVEL

Aberdeen and Thurso, one of the closest towns on the mainland to the Northern Isles, have two reliable bus links to and from each other and all over Scotland and the rest of Britain: Scottish Citylink and National Express. John o'Groats Ferries operates the Orkney Bus, a direct express coach from Inverness to Kirkwall (via ferry) that runs daily from May to early September. The same company runs a day tour from Inverness to Orkney daily from June through August.

The main bus services on Orkney are operated by James D. Peace & Co., Causeway Coaches, and Orkney Coaches; on Shetland, by Shalder Coaches and J. Leask.

➤ BUS INFORMATION: **Causeway Coaches** (☎ 01856/831444). **James D. Peace & Co.** (☎ 01856/872866). **John o'Groats Ferries** (☎ 01955/

611353). **J. Leask** (☎ 01595/693162). **National Express** (☎ 08705/808080, WEB www.nationalexpress.co.uk). **Orkney Coaches** (☎ 01856/870555). **Scottish Citylink** (☎ 08705/505050, WEB www.citylink.co.uk). **Shalder Coaches** (☎ 01595/880217).

CAR RENTAL
You can take your car from Aberdeen by sea, but generally, for fewer than five days, it's cheaper to rent a car from one of Shetland's many car-rental agencies. Most rental companies are based in Lerwick; they include Star Rent-a-Car and Bolts Car and Minibus Hire. On Orkney, try James D. Peace & Co. or W. R. Tullock.
➤ AGENCIES: **Bolts Car and Minibus Hire** (✉ 26 North Rd., Lerwick, ☎ 01595/693636). **James D. Peace & Co.** (✉ Junction Rd., Kirkwall, ☎ 01856/872866, WEB www.orkneycarhire.co.uk). **Star Rent-a-Car** (✉ 22 Commercial Rd., Lerwick, ☎ 01595/692075, WEB www.starrentacar.co.uk). **W. R. Tullock** (✉ Terminal Building, Kirkwall Airport, Kirkwall, ☎ 01856/875500, WEB www.orkneycarrental.co.uk).

CAR TRAVEL
Because of its oil wealth, the roads on Shetland are in very good shape. Orkney has causeways connecting some of the islands, but in some cases using these roads will take you on fairly roundabout routes.

DISCOUNTS AND DEALS
A joint entry ticket to all of Historic Scotland's Orkney sites is available from the sites themselves. The ticket lasts until you've seen all the sites and costs £11 (£10 in October and November).

EMERGENCIES
Dial **999** in an emergency for the police, fire department, or an ambulance (no coins are needed for emergency calls from public phone booths).

Most general practitioners will see visitor patients by appointment or immediately in case of emergency. Your hotel or local tourist information center can advise you accordingly. You can also consult the yellow pages of the telephone directory, under "Doctor" or "Dentist."
➤ HOSPITALS: **Balfour Hospital** (✉ New Scapa Rd., Kirkwall, Orkney, ☎ 01856/885400). **Gilbert Bain Hospital** (✉ South Rd., Lerwick, Shetland, ☎ 01595/695678).

OUTDOORS AND SPORTS
The Merkister Hotel, on Orkney, arranges fishing packages, with all equipment, including boats, available to rent.
➤ CONTACTS: **Merkister Hotel** (✉ Harray, Orkney, ☎ 01856/771366).

TOURS
Orkney Coaches runs general tours as well as special-interest tours of Orkney. J. Leask and Shalder Coaches arrange tours of Shetland. These companies can also tailor tours to your interests.

Michael Hartley, an accredited tour guide in Orkney, runs Wildabout; phone for details on minibus tours that combine sightseeing of archaeological sites and the folklore, flora, and fauna of the islands. In Shetland several companies tour the spectacular Noss Bird Sanctuary, a national nature reserve, in summer, weather permitting. The tourist information center can provide details and take reservations.
➤ FEES AND SCHEDULES: **J. Leask** (☎ 01595/693162). **Orkney Coaches** (☎ 01856/870555). **Shalder Coaches** (☎ 01595/880217). **Wildabout** (☎ 01856/851011, WEB www.norsecom.co.uk/wildabout).

TRAIN TRAVEL

There are no trains on Orkney or Shetland, although Aberdeen, which has a ferry to Shetland, is well served by train, and Thurso is the terminus of the far-north line. For information contact National Rail Enquiries. From Thurso a bus connects to Scrabster for Orkney.

➤ TRAIN INFORMATION: **National Rail Enquiries** (☎ 08457/484950).

VISITOR INFORMATION

The following tourist centers are open year-round.

➤ TOURIST INFORMATION: **Kirkwall, Orkney** (✉ 6 Broad St., Kirkwall, Orkney KW15 1NX, ☎ 01856/872856, WEB www.visitorkney.com). **Lerwick, Shetland** (✉ Market Cross, Lerwick, Shetland ZE1 0LU, ☎ 01595/693434, WEB www.visitshetland.com). **Stromness, Orkney** (✉ Ferry Terminal Bldg., ☎ 01856/850716).

12 SCOTLAND: THE HOME OF GOLF

GOLFING THROUGHOUT THE COUNTRY

By John
Hutchinson

Updated by
Beth Ingpen

THERE ARE MORE THAN 400 GOLF COURSES in Scotland and only 5 million residents, so the country has probably the highest ratio of courses to people anywhere in the world. Some of these courses are renowned venues for major championships, and if you're a golfer coming to Scotland, you'll probably want to play the "famous names" sometime in your career. Telling your friends in the clubhouse back home that you got a birdie at the Road Hole on the Old Course in St. Andrews, where Lyle, Faldo, and Jacklin have played, somehow conveys more prestige than an excellent round at a delightful but obscure course.

So, by all means, play the championship courses and impress your friends, but remember they *are* championship courses and therefore difficult; you may enjoy the game itself much more at a less challenging, albeit lesser known, course. Remember, too, that everyone else wants to play them, so booking can be a problem, particularly at peak times in summer. Book early, or if you're staying in a hotel attached to a course, get them to book for you.

There has always been considerable debate as to who invented golf, but there's no doubt that its development into one of the most popular games in the world stems from Scotland. Like many other games that involve hitting a ball with a stick, golf evolved in the countries that border the North Sea during the Middle Ages and gradually took on its present form in the last 200 years.

The first written reference to golf, variously spelled as "gowf" or "goff," was as long ago as 1457, when James II (1430–60) of Scotland declared that both golf and football (soccer) should be *"utterly cryit doune and nocht usit"* (publicly criticized and prohibited) because they were distracting his subjects from their archery practice. Mary, Queen of Scots (1542–87), it seems, was fond of golf. When in Edinburgh in 1567, she played on Leith Links and on Bruntsfield Links. When in Fife, she played at Falkland, near the palace, and at St. Andrews itself.

Golf must surely rank as one of Scotland's earliest cultural exports. In 1603, when James VI (1566–1625) of Scotland also became James I of England, he moved his court to London. With him went his golf-loving friends, and they set up a course on Blackheath Common, then on the outskirts of London.

Golf clubs (i.e., organizations) first arose in the middle of the 18th century. Written evidence attests to the founding of the Honourable Company of Edinburgh Golfers, now residing at Muirfield, in 1744, and to the Royal & Ancient at St. Andrews, which began in 1754. From then on, clubs sprang up all over Scotland: Royal Aberdeen (1780), Crail Golfing Society (1786), Dunbar (1794), and the Royal Perth Golfing Society (1824).

By the early 19th century, clubs had been set up in England, and the game was being carried all over the world by enthusiastic Scots. These golf missionaries spread their knowledge not only of the sport, but also of the courses. Large parts of the Scottish coast are natural golf courses; indeed, the origins of bunkers and the word *links* (courses) are found in the sand dunes of Scotland's shores. In countries where such natural terrain didn't exist, courses had to be designed and created. Willie Park of Musselburgh (who laid out Sunningdale), James Braid, and C. K. Hutchison (whose crowning glory is at Gleneagles Hotel) are some of the best known of Scotland's golf-course architects.

Golf has always had a peculiar classlessness in Scotland. It's a game
for everyone, and for centuries Scottish towns and cities have maintained golf courses for the enjoyment of their citizens. The snobbish-
ness and exclusivity of golf clubs in some parts of the world have few
echoes here. Admittedly, there are at least a few clubs that have always
been noted for their exclusive air, and newer golf courses are emerg-
ing as part of exclusive leisure complexes. These are exceptions to the
long tradition of recreation for all. Golf here is usually a democratic
game, played by ordinary folk as well as the rich and carefree. (Signs
saying NO GOLF can be seen on grassy areas around the public housing projects in parts of Edinburgh and Glasgow; some children prefer
a golf club and ball even to a football.)

Many of the important changes in the design and construction of balls
and clubs were pioneered by the professional players who lived and
worked around the town courses and who made the balls and clubs
themselves. The original balls, called *featheries,* were leather bags
stuffed with boiled feathers. Often they lasted only one round. When,
in 1848, the gutta-percha ball, called a *guttie,* was introduced, there
was considerable friction, particularly in St. Andrews, between the makers of the two rival types of ball. The gutta-percha proved superior and
was in general use until the invention of the rubber-core ball in 1901.

Clubs were traditionally made of wood: shafts were of ash, later hick-
ory, and heads were of thorn or some other hardwood such as apple
or pear. Heads were spliced, then bound to the shaft with twine. Players generally managed with far fewer clubs than today. About 1628
the marquis of Montrose, a golf enthusiast, had a set of clubs made
for him in St. Andrews that illustrates the range of clubs used in Stuart times: "Bonker clubis, a irone club, and twa play clubs."

Caddies—the word comes from the French *cadet* (young boy) and was
used, particularly in Edinburgh, to refer to anyone who ran mes-
sages—carried the players' clubs around, usually under the arm. Golf
carts didn't come into fashion in Britain until the 1950s, and some people still considered them to be potentially injurious to the national health
and moral fiber.

The technology of golf may change, but its addictive qualities are
timeless. Toward the end of the 18th century, an Edinburgh golfer named
Alexander McKellar regularly played golf all day and refused to stop
even when it grew dark. One night his wife carried his dinner and night-
cap onto Bruntsfield Links, where he was playing, in an attempt to shame
him into changing his ways. She failed.

And the addiction continues.

Where to Play

There are courses everywhere in Scotland except for the far northern Highlands and some of the islands. Most courses welcome visitors with a minimum of formalities, and some at surprisingly low cost. Off-season, a
few clubs still use the "honesty box," into which you drop your fees.

Just three pieces of advice, particularly for North Americans: 1) In Scotland the game is usually played fairly quickly, so don't dawdle if others
are waiting; 2) caddy carts are hand-pulled carts for your clubs; driven
golf carts are rarely available in Scotland (most courses charge from
£1.30 to £2 per round for use of caddy carts); and 3) when they say
"rough," they really mean "rough."

Unless specified otherwise below, course playing hours are generally
9 AM to sundown, which in June can be as late as 10 PM. Note that

SSS indicates the "standard scratch score," or average score. For a complete list of courses, contact local tourist offices, and for more regional information, *see* Outdoor Activities and Sports *in* individual chapters.

The Stewartry

At the very southern border, the Stewartry is a delightful part of Scotland set in the rich farmlands around Dumfries, a golfing vacation area since Victorian times. Powfoot and Southerness are enjoyable links courses along the shores of the Solway Firth, and inland, Dumfries and Moffat have long-established courses that provide superb golf in a clean, invigorating environment. There are also several fine 9-hole courses in the area.

Powfoot. A pleasant mix of links and parkland holes (9 of each) and views south over the Solway Firth to distract you make this lesser known British Championship course a pleasure to play. ⊠ *Powfoot Golf Club, Cummertrees, Annan,* ☎ FAX *01461/700276. 18 holes. Yardage 6,266. SSS 71.* ⊞ *£25 per round, £33 per day.* ☉ *Weekdays and Sun. after 1. Caddy carts, catering.*

Southerness. Mackenzie Ross designed this, the first course built in Scotland after World War II, in 1947. Southerness is a long course, played over extensive links with fine views southward over the Solway Firth. The greens are hard and fast, and the frequent winds make for some testing golf. ⊠ *Southerness Golf Club, Southerness,* ☎ *01387/880677. 18 holes. Yardage 6,566. Par 69.* ⊞ *Weekdays £35 per day; weekends £45 per day.* ☉ *Daily. Reservations essential. Caddy carts, catering.*

Ayrshire and the Clyde Coast

An hour south of Glasgow by car or train, Ayrshire and the Clyde Coast have been a holiday area for Glaswegians for generations. Few golfers need an introduction to the names of Turnberry, Royal Troon, Prestwick, or Western Gailes—all challenging links courses along this coast. There are at least 20 other courses in the area within an hour's drive. Remember, too, that at major areas, such as Turnberry, Troon, and Ayr, there are several different courses to play from the same base.

Girvan. This is an old, established course with play along a narrow coastal strip and a more lush inland section next to the Water of Girvan—a river that constitutes a particular hazard at the 15th, unless you are a big hitter. The course is scenic, with good views of Ailsa Craig and the Clyde Estuary. ⊠ *40 Golf Course Rd., Girvan,* ☎ *01465/714346. 18 holes. Yardage 4,590. Par 64.* ⊞ *Weekdays £13 per round, £21 per day; weekends £16.50 per round, £29 per day.* ☉ *Daily. Caddy carts, catering.*

Prestwick. Tom Morris was involved in designing this challenging Ayrshire coastal links course, which saw the birth of the British Open Championship in 1860. Prestwick has excellent, fast rail links with Glasgow. ⊠ *2 Links Rd., Prestwick,* ☎ *01292/477404. 18 holes. Yardage 6,544. Par 71.* ⊞ *Weekdays £85 per round, £125 per day.* ☉ *Weekdays only. Caddy carts, catering.*

Royal Troon. Of the two courses at Royal Troon, it's the Old Course—a traditional links course with superb sea views—that is used for the British Open Championship. You can buy a day ticket for one round on each course, a good value, as the ticket includes an excellent lunch. ⊠ *Craigend Rd., Troon,* ☎ *01292/311555. Old Course: 18 holes, yardage 7,107, SSS 74. Portland Course: 18 holes, yardage 6,289, SSS 70.* ⊞ *£150 daily ticket, 1 round on each course, lunch included.* ☉ *Mon., Tues., and Thurs. Caddy carts, catering.*

Turnberry. The Ailsa Course at Turnberry is perhaps the most famous links course in Scotland. Right on the seashore, the course is open to the elements, and the 9th hole requires you to hit the ball over the open sea. The British Open was staged here in 1977, 1986, and 1994. A second course, the Kintyre, is more compact than the Ailsa, with tricky sloped greens providing a real challenge. Five of the holes on this course have sea views; the remaining holes are more inland. ✉ *Turnberry Hotel, Golf Courses and Spa, Turnberry,* ☎ *01655/331000. Ailsa Course: 18 holes, yardage 6,976, SSS 72. Kintyre Course: 18 holes, yardage 6,853, SSS 72.* ✉ *Ailsa Course: weekdays £105 per round for hotel guest, £130 per round for nonguest; weekends £105 per round for hotel guest, £175 per round for nonguest. Kintyre Course: £90 per round for hotel guest, £105 per round for nonguest, weekdays and weekends.* ⊙ *Daily. Caddies, caddy carts, catering.*

Western Gailes. Known as the finest natural links course in Scotland, Western Gailes is entirely nature-made, and the greens are kept in truly magnificent condition. This is the final qualifying course when the British Open is held at Troon or Turnberry. Tom Watson lists the par-5 sixth as one of his favorite holes. ✉ *Gailes, Irvine,* ☎ *01294/311357. 18 holes. Yardage 6,639. Par 71.* ✉ *Weekdays £85 per round, £115 per day; Sun. afternoon £90 per round; all fees include a meal, except on Sunday.* ⊙ *Mon., Wed., Fri., and Sun. afternoon. Caddies, caddy carts, catering.*

Glasgow

As Scotland's industrial and commercial hub, Glasgow is well known for its shopping, nightlife, art galleries, theaters, and restaurants. Less well known are the parks and gardens, affectionately called the "dear green places," that breathe life into the city. Most of the old golf courses have now moved out to the suburbs, but you can tee off from at least 30 different courses less than an hour from the city center. And remember: in addition to these, all the Ayrshire courses are just down the road.

Douglas Park. North of the city near Milngavie (pronounced mul-*gai*), Douglas Park is a long, attractive course set among birch and pine trees with masses of rhododendrons blooming in early summer. The Campsie Fells form a pleasant backdrop. ✉ *Hillfoot, Bearsden,* ☎ *0141/942–0985. 18 holes. Yardage 5,962. Par 69.* ✉ *£23 per round, £31 per day.* ⊙ *Wed. and Thurs., by appointment only. Caddy carts, catering.*

Killermont and Gailes, The Glasgow Golf Club. This was originally the club played on Glasgow Green in the heart of the ancient city center, but as the pressure for space grew, it moved north to the leafy suburb of Bearsden, on the road to Loch Lomond. The Killermont course was laid out by Tom Morris (1904) in beautiful parkland with ancient trees, fine greens, and an elegant clubhouse. Visitors cannot play at Killermont, but you can use the facilities of the club's other course at Gailes, near Irvine on the Firth of Clyde. The Glasgow Club's Tennant Cup, in June, is the oldest open amateur tournament in the world. ✉ *Glasgow Golf Club, Gailes, Irvine,* ☎ *0141/942–2011. 18 holes. Yardage 6,537. SSS 72.* ✉ *Weekdays £45 per round, £60 per day; weekends £58 per round.* ⊙ *Weekdays 9:30–4:30, weekends after 2:30. Practice area, caddy carts, catering.*

East Lothian

The sand dunes that stretch eastward from Edinburgh along the southern shore of the Firth of Forth made an ideal location for some of the world's earliest golf courses. Muirfield is perhaps the most famous course in the area, but around it are more than a dozen others, at Gullane,

North Berwick, Dunbar, and Aberlady and, nearer Edinburgh, at Long-niddry, Prestonpans, and Musselburgh. All are links courses, many with views to the islands of the Firth of Forth and northward to Fife. If you weary of the East Lothian courses, try one of the nearly 30 courses within the city of Edinburgh, just 20 mi or so to the west.

Dunbar. This ancient golfing site by the sea even has a lighthouse at the ninth hole. It's a good choice for a typical east-coast links course in a seaside town but within easy reach of Edinburgh. ⊠ *East Links, Dunbar,* ☎ *01368/862086. 18 holes. Yardage 6,404. Par 71.* ▧ *Weekdays £32 per round, £45 per day; weekends £37 per round, £50 per day.* ☉ *Fri.–Wed. after 9:30. Reservations essential. Practice area, caddies (by reservation), electric caddy carts, golf carts, catering.*

Muirfield. The championship course at Muirfield is one of the best known links courses in the world, so be prepared to pay the price of fame with expensive green fees and severe limitations on when you can play. But it may be worth the expense and hassle to be able to walk in the footsteps of some of the greatest names in golf. ⊠ *Muirfield, Gullane,* ☎ *01620/842123. 18 holes. Yardage 6,601. Par 70.* ▧ *£90 per round, £120 per day.* ☉ *Visitors Tues. and Thur., tee off between 8:30 and 10:10. Reservations essential. Handicap certificate required (18 or less for men, 24 or less for women) and membership in a recognized golf club. Caddies (by reservation), golf carts, catering.*

Edinburgh

Edinburgh is best known as Scotland's capital and home to the Edinburgh International Festival, the largest of its kind in the world. The city also has nearly 30 golf courses within its boundaries. Most are parkland courses, though along the shores of the Firth of Forth they take on the characteristics of traditional links. Some are used by private clubs and offer visitors limited access; others that belong to the city are more accessible and have much lower fees.

Barnton, Royal Burgess Golfing Society. Dating to 1735, this is one of the world's oldest golf clubs. Its members originally played on Bruntsfield Links; now they and their guests play on elegantly manicured parkland in the city's northwestern suburbs. It's a long course with fine greens. ⊠ *181 Whitehouse Rd., Barnton,* ☎ *0131/339–2075. 18 holes. Yardage 6,111. Par 68.* ▧ *Weekdays £42 per round, £55 per day.* ☉ *Weekdays. Reservations essential. Caddy carts, golf carts (£5 per round), catering.*

Braids. Braids Number 1 and Braids Number 2 (no connection with James Braid) are beautifully laid out over a rugged range of small hills in the southern suburbs. The views to the south and the Pentland Hills and north toward the Edinburgh skyline are worth a visit in themselves. The city built these courses as urban development nearly 90 years ago, forcing golfers out of the city center. ⊠ *The Braids, Braids Hill Rd.,* ☎ *0131/447–6666. No. 1: 18 holes, yardage 5,865, par 70. No. 2: 18 holes, yardage 4,744, par 65.* ▧ *Weekdays £12 per round, weekends £14 per round.* ☉ *Daily. Reservations essential. Caddy carts.*

Bruntsfield Links. The British Seniors and several other championship games are held at this Willie Park–designed 1898 course 3 mi west of the city. The course meanders among 155 acres of mature parkland and has fine views over the Firth of Forth to Fife. Bruntsfield takes its name from one of the oldest golf links in Scotland, in the center of Edinburgh—now just a 9-hole pitch-and-put course—where the club used to play. ⊠ *32 Barnton Ave., Davidson's Mains,* ☎ *0131/336–1479. 18 holes. Yardage 6,407. Par 71.* ▧ *Weekdays £42 per round,*

£60 per day; weekends £47 per round, £65 per day. ☉ *Daily. Reservations essential. Caddy carts, golf carts, catering.*

Fife

Few would dispute the claim of St. Andrews to be the home of golf, holding as it does the Royal & Ancient, the organization that governs the sport worldwide. Golf has been played here since the game's inception, and to play in Fife is for most golfers a cherished ambition. St. Andrews itself has several full 18-hole courses in addition to the famous 15th-century Old Course. Along the north shores of the Firth of Forth is a string of ancient villages, each with its harbor, ancient red-roof buildings, and golf course. In all, there are about 30 courses in the area.

Ladybank. Fife is known for its coastal courses, but this one has an interesting inland contrast: although Ladybank, designed by Tom Morris in 1876, is laid out on fairly level ground, the fir woods, birches, and heathery rough give it a Highland flavor among the gentle Lowland fields. Qualifying rounds of the British Open are played here when the main championship is played at St. Andrews. ✉ *Annsmuir, Ladybank,* ☎ *01337/830814. 18 holes. Yardage 6,601. Par 71.* ⊞ *Apr.–Oct., weekdays £35 per round, £45 per day; weekends £40 per round. Nov.–Mar., weekdays £10 per round, £15 per day; weekends £10 per round.* ☉ *Daily. Reservations essential. Practice area, caddy carts, golf carts (£20 per round), catering.*

Leven. A fine Fife course used as a British Open qualifier, this one, a links course, feels like the more famous St. Andrews, with hummocky terrain and a tang of salt in the air. The 1st and 18th share the same fairway, and the 18th green has a creek running by it. ✉ *The Promenade, Leven,* ☎ *01333/428859. 18 holes. Yardage 6,436. Par 71.* ⊞ *Weekdays £30 per round, £40 per day; Sun. £35 per round, £50 per day.* ☉ *Sun.–Fri. Reservations essential. Caddy carts, catering.*

Perthshire

Perthshire has several attractive country courses developed specifically for visiting golfers. Gleneagles Hotel is, with its outstanding facilities, the most famous of these golf resorts. But several courses in the area, set on the edges of beautiful Highland scenery, will delight any golfer. Crieff, Taymouth, and other courses are in the mountains; Blairgowrie and Perth sit amid the rich farmlands nearer the sea.

Callander. Callander was designed by Tom Morris (1913) and has a scenic upland feel in a town well prepared for visitors. Pine and birch woods and hilly fairways afford fine views, especially toward Ben Ledi, and the tricky moorland layout demands accurate hitting off the tee. ✉ *Callander Golf Club, Aveland Rd., Callander,* ☎ *01877/330090. 18 holes. Yardage 5,151. Par 66.* ⊞ *Weekdays £18 per round, £26 per day; weekends £26 per round, £31 per day.* ☉ *Daily. Practice area, caddy carts, catering.*

Killin. A scenic course, Killin is typically Highland, with a roaring river, woodland birdsong, and a backdrop of high green hills. There are a few surprises, including two blind shots to reach the green at the fourth. The attractive village of Killin has an almost alpine feel, especially in spring, when the hilltops may still be white. ✉ *Killin Golf Club, Aberfeldy Rd., Killin,* ☎ *01567/820312. 9 holes. Yardage 2,508. Par 65.* ⊞ *£12 per round, £15 per day.* ☉ *Apr.–Oct., daily. Caddy carts, club rental, catering.*

Rosemount, Blairgowrie Golf Club. Well known to native golfers looking for a challenge, Rosemount's 18 (James Braid, 1934) are laid out on rolling land in the pine, birch, and fir woods, which bring a wild air to the scene. You may encounter a browsing roe deer if you stray too far. There are, however, wide fairways and at least some large greens. If you can't manage a game on Rosemount itself, you can play on Lansdowne, another 18-hole course, or Wee, a 9-hole course. A handicap certificate is required to play here. ⊠ *Golf Course Rd., Blairgowrie,* ☎ *01250/872622. Rosemount course: 18 holes, yardage 6,590, par 72. Lansdowne course: 18 holes, yardage 6,802, par 72. Wee course: 9 holes, yardage 2,327, par 32.* ▩ *£50 per round (Rosemount), £40 per round (Lansdowne), £20 per round (Wee); £70 per day (1 round on Rosemount, 1 on Lansdowne); £60 per day (1 round on Lansdowne, 1 on Wee).* ⊙ *Daily, some restrictions. Practice area, caddies, golf carts (£20), trolleys (£2.50 per round, £4 per day), catering.*

Angus
East of Perthshire, north of the city of Dundee, lies a string of demanding courses along the shores of the North Sea and inland into the foothills of the Grampian Mountains. The most famous course in Angus is probably Carnoustie, one of several British Open Championship venues in Scotland, but there are many more along the same stretch of coast from Dundee northward as far as Stonehaven. Golfers who excel in windy conditions particularly enjoy the sea breezes blowing eastward from the sea. Inland Edzell, Forfar, Brechin, and Kirriemuir all have courses nestling in the Strathmore farmlands.

Carnoustie. The venue for the British Open Championship in 1999, the extensive coastal links around Carnoustie have been played since at least 1527. Open winners here have included Armour, Hogan, Cotton, Player, and Watson. Carnoustie was also once a training ground for coaches, many of whom went to the United States. The choice municipal course here is full of historical snippets and local color, as well as being tough and interesting. ⊠ *Carnoustie Golf Links, Links Parade, Carnoustie,* ☎ *01241/853789. Championship Course: 18 holes, yardage 6,941, par 75.* ▩ *May–Oct. £80 per round; Nov.–Apr. £40 per round.* ⊙ *Weekdays 9–3:50, Sat. after 2, Sun. after 12:30. Reservations essential. Caddies, caddy carts.*

Aberdeenshire
Aberdeen, Scotland's third-largest city, is known for its sparkling granite buildings and the amazing displays of roses each summer. It also has a good selection of courses. Aberdeen itself has six courses, and to the north, as far as Fraserburgh and Peterhead, there are five others, including the popular Cruden Bay. Royal Deeside has three, and in the rich farmlands to the north are three more with at least six 9-hole courses.

Balgownie, Royal Aberdeen Golf Club. This old club (1780) is the archetypal Scottish links course: long and testing over uneven ground, with the frequently added hazard of a sea breeze. Prickly gorse is inclined to close in and form an additional hurdle. The two courses are tucked behind the rough, grassy sand dunes, and there are surprisingly few views of the sea. One historical note: in 1783 this club originated the five-minute-search rule for a lost ball. ⊠ *Balgownie Links, Links Rd., Bridge of Don, Aberdeen,* ☎ *01224/702571. Balgownie Course: 18 holes, yardage 6,415, par 70. Silverburn Course: 18 holes, yardage 4,021, SSS 61.* ▩ *Weekdays £65 per round (Balgownie), £32.50 per round (Silverburn), £90 per day; weekends £75 per round (Balgownie), £37.50 per round (Silverburn), £120 per day.* ⊙ *Balgownie: tee off weekdays 10–11:30 and 2–3:30; weekends after 3:30. Silverburn: daily. Balgownie: Handicap limit 24; handicap certificate or letter of introduction required from home club. Reservations essential. Practice area, caddies, caddy carts, catering.*

Ballater. The mountains of Royal Deeside surround this course laid out along the sandy flats of the River Dee. Ideal for a relaxing round of golf, the course makes maximum use of the fine setting between river and woods. The club, originally opened in 1906, has a holiday atmosphere, and the shops and pleasant walks in nearby Ballater make this a good place for nongolfing partners. ⊠ *Victoria Rd., Ballater,* ☎ *013397/55567. 18 holes. Yardage 6,112. Par 70.* ▨ *Weekdays £18 per round, £22 per day; weekends £19 per round, £28 per day.* ☉ *Daily. Reservations advised. Practice area, caddy carts, golf carts (£15 per round), catering.*

Cruden Bay. An east-coast Lowland course sheltered behind extensive sand hills, Cruden Bay offers a typical Scottish golf experience. Runnels and valleys, among other hazards, on the challenging fairways ensure plenty of excitement, and some of the holes are rated among the country's finest. Like Gleneagles and Turnberry, this course owes its origins to an association with the grand railway hotels that were built in the heyday of steam. Unlike the other two, however, Cruden Bay's railway hotel and the railway itself have gone, but the course remains in fine shape. ⊠ *Aulton Rd., Cruden Bay, Peterhead,* ☎ *01779/812285. 18 holes. Yardage 6,395. Par 70.* ▨ *Weekdays £50 per round, £70 per day; weekends £60 per round, restricted access.* ☉ *Daily. Reservations essential. Practice area, covered driving range, caddy carts, catering.*

Speyside

On the main A9 road an hour south of Inverness amid the Cairngorm Mountains, the valley of the River Spey is one of Scotland's most attractive all-year sports centers, with winter skiing and, in summer, sailing and canoeing, pony trekking, fishing, and some fine golf. The area's main courses are Newtonmore, Grantown-on-Spey, and Boat of Garten, all fine inland courses with wonderful views of the surrounding mountains and challenging golf provided by the springy turf and the heather. For a change of pace, head an hour's drive away to the links courses along the coastline of the Moray Firth, with their seaside attractions.

Boat of Garten. This is possibly one of Scotland's greatest "undiscovered" courses. Boat of Garten, which dates to the late 19th century, was redesigned and extended by famous golf architect James Braid in 1932, and each of its 18 holes is individual: some cut through birch wood and heathery rough; most have long views to the Cairngorms and a strong Highland air. An unusual feature is the preserved steam railway that runs along part of the course. The occasional puffing locomotive can hardly be considered a hazard. ⊠ *Village center,* ☎ *01479/831282. 18 holes. Yardage 5,866. Par 69.* ▨ *Weekdays £25 per round, £30 per day; weekends £30 per round, £35 per day.* ☉ *Daily. Starting sheet used. Reservations essential. Caddies on request, caddy carts, catering.*

Moray Coast

No one can say that the Lowlands have a monopoly on Scotland's fine seaside golf courses. The Moray Coast, stretching eastward from Inverness, has some spectacular sand dunes that have been adapted to create stimulating and exciting links courses. The two courses at Nairn have long been known to golfers both famous and unknown. Charlie Chaplin regularly played here. But in addition there are a dozen courses looking out over the sea from Inverness as far along as Banff, Macduff, and Fraserburgh and several inland amid the fertile Moray farmland.

Banff, Duff House Royal Golf Club. Just moments away from the sea, this club combines a coastal course with a parkland setting. It lies only minutes from Banff center, within the parkland grounds of Duff House, a country-house art gallery in a William Adam–designed mansion. The club has inherited the ancient traditions of seaside play (golf records here go back to the 17th century). Mature trees and gentle slopes create a pleasant playing environment. ⊠ *The Barnyards, Banff,* ☎ *01261/812075. 18 holes. Yardage 6,161. Par 70.* ⌦ *Weekdays £18 per round, £24 per day; weekends £25 per round, £30 per day; all fees halved Oct.–Mar.* ☉ *Daily. Reservations essential. Practice area, caddy carts, catering.*

Fraserburgh. This northeast fishing town has extensive links and dunes that seem to have grown up around the course rather than the other way around. Be prepared for a hill climb and a tough finish. ⊠ *Philorth, Fraserburgh, at the eastern end of town,* ☎ *01346/518287. 18 holes, 9 additional for warm-up. Yardage 6,200. Par 70.* ⌦ *Weekdays £16 per round, £19 per day; weekends £22 per round, £27 per day.* ☉ *Daily. Practice area, caddy carts, catering.*

Lossiemouth, Moray Golf Club. Discover the mild airs of what's called the Moray Riviera, as Tom Morris did in 1889 when he was inspired by the lay of the natural links. There are two courses plus a 6-hole minicourse. There's lots of atmosphere here, with golfing memorabilia in the clubhouse, as well as the tale of the pre–World War I British prime minister Asquith, who took a vacation in this out-of-the-way spot yet still managed to be attacked by a crowd of suffragettes at the 17th. All other hazards on these testing courses are entirely natural, with the 18th hole providing a memorable finish. ⊠ *Stotfield Rd., Lossiemouth,* ☎ *01343/813330. Old Course: 18 holes, yardage 6,617, par 71. New Course: 18 holes, yardage 6,004, par 69.* ⌦ *Old Course: weekdays £35 per round, £50 per day; weekends £45 per round, £65 per day. New Course: weekdays £25 per round, £35 per day; weekends £30 per round, £40 per day. Joint ticket (1 round on each course) £45 weekdays, £55 weekends.* ☉ *Daily. Practice area, caddy carts, catering.*

Nairn. Widely regarded in golfing circles as a truly great course, Nairn dates from 1887 and is the regular home of Scotland's Northern Open. Huge greens, aggressive gorse, a beach hazard for five of the holes, a steady prevailing wind, and distracting views across the Moray Firth to the northern hills make play here unforgettable. The course hosted the 37th Walker Cup in 1999. ⊠ *Seabank Rd., Nairn,* ☎ *01667/453208. 18 holes. Yardage 6,705. Par 72.* ⌦ *£70 per round.* ☉ *Daily. Reservations essential. Practice area, caddies available on request, caddy carts, catering.*

Dornoch Firth

The east coast north of Inverness is deeply indented with firths (the word is linked to the Norwegian *fjord*) that border some excellent, relatively unknown golf courses. Knowledgeable golfers have been making the northern pilgrimage to these courses for well over 100 years. There are half a dozen enjoyable links courses around Dornoch, and inland, another Victorian golfing holiday center, Strathpeffer, preserves much of the atmosphere those of a past age set out to achieve.

Royal Dornoch. This course, laid out by Tom Morris in 1886 on a sort of coastal shelf behind the shore, has matured to become one of the world's finest. Its location in the north of Scotland, though less than an hour's drive from Inverness Airport, means it's far from overrun even in peak season. It may not have the fame of a Gleneagles or a St. Andrews, but Royal Dornoch is memorable. The little town of Dornoch, behind the course, is sleepy and timeless. ⊠ *Golf Rd., Dornoch,* ☎ *01862/810219. 18 holes. Yardage 6,514. Par 70.* ⌦ *Weekdays £60* *per round; Sun. £70 per round; day ticket (weekdays and weekends) £100. ☽ Sun.–Fri., and occasionally Sat. Handicap limit: men 24, women 39. Reservations essential. Practice area, caddies, caddy carts, catering.*

Argyll

The lochs and glens of Argyll in the west of Scotland have provided the scenic backdrop for family outings for generations. Wherever Scots take their holidays, golf courses are soon developed, so the string of courses north from the Mull of Kintyre all offer golf in a relaxed environment, with sea, beach, and hills not far away.

Machrihanish, by Campbeltown. Many enthusiasts discuss this course in hushed tones—it's a kind of out-of-the-way golfers' Shangri-la. It was laid out in 1876 by Tom Morris on the links around the sandy Machrihanish Bay. The drive off the first tee is across the beach to reach the green—an intimidating start to a memorable series of individual holes. If you're short on time, consider flying from Glasgow to nearby Campbeltown, the last town on the long peninsula of Kintyre. ✉ *Machrihanish, Campbeltown,* ☎ *01586/810277. 18 holes. Yardage 6,225. Par 70. ✉ Weekdays and Sun. £30 per round, £50 per day; Sat. £40 per round, £60 per day. ☽ Daily. Reservations essential. Practice area, caddy carts, catering.*

13 BACKGROUND AND ESSENTIALS

Books and Movies

Chronology

BOOKS AND MOVIES

Books

Scotland has always been a land with a love and respect for books and learning, for poetry and song. From the love poems of Robert Burns, which reflect his Ayrshire roots, to the "bothy ballads" of the northeast, with which the farmhands entertained each other after a hard day's work, from Sir Walter Scott's Borders sagas to Mairi Hedderwick's Katie Morag children's stories set in the Western Isles—all share the strong visual thread of their own Scottish landscapes. Whether written 200 or 2 years ago, these books and poems have much to tell visitors about the character of Scotland's hugely varied countryside and of the resilient, soft-hearted, yet outwardly often dour Scottish people. Wherever you intend to travel in Scotland, there are books to read to set the scene beforehand.

Edinburgh has inspired many writers. Muriel Spark's *The Prime of Miss Jean Brodie* was written in 1961 yet still has much to say about the Edinburgh phenomenon of private schools and their importance in the city's business and social life. Even today, having attended one of the "right" schools certainly oils the wheels in business. Children's author Aileen Paterson affectionately and amusingly highlights the importance of such external factors, sometimes at the expense of more worthwhile internal qualities (at its extreme, summed up in the apt expression "She's all fur coat and nae knickers"), in her Maisie series. The books, set in the archetypally "fur coat" Edinburgh suburb of Morningside and full of closely observed characters and illustrations, tell the story of Maisie, a kitten sent to live with her grandmother in a typical Edinburgh tenement building. Maisie also visits many Scottish landmarks, such as the Royal Museum of Scotland in Edinburgh and Loch Ness.

The darker side of Edinburgh appears in Ian Rankin's excellent Inspector Rebus crime thrillers, which cunningly exploit the contrasts between the architecture of the Old and New towns, between the wealth of the professional community and the poverty of the public-housing schemes' occupants, and of the dangers of relying on appearances. Some of Rankin's popular titles are *Let It Bleed, Mortal Causes,* and *Black and Blue.* Even harder-hitting is *Trainspotting,* by Irvine Welsh, with its depiction of disaffected Edinburgh youth and the city's drug scene. Neither will impinge on the average visitor, however.

The novels of Lewis Grassic Gibbon (pseudonym of James Leslie Mitchell, 1901–35) are set in the bleak farmlands of northeast Scotland, in the area known as the Howe of Mearns, south of Stonehaven, where he grew up. His trilogy *A Scots Quair* (*Sunset Song, Cloud Howe,* and *Grey Granite*) incorporates the rhythms and cadences of speech in the northeast; you can still hear this distinctive dialect today. The unremitting harshness of farming life in this part of Scotland, described in *A Scots Quair,* is still to some extent valid today, despite the advent of modern machinery and farming practices: this is not the lush, warm countryside of southern England. Nonetheless, the spare beauty of the landscape—with its patchwork of fields rising to higher ground and a spectacular coastline with towering cliffs, puffins, dolphins, and white-sand beaches—rewards those who visit the northeast. While in this part of Scotland, travel west to Cawdor, near Nairn, to visit beautiful Cawdor Castle, fictional home of Shakespeare's Macbeth, Thane of Cawdor, but with 600 years of real-life furniture, paintings, and artifacts contained within its walls.

From the far north, another writer and poet whose work is intimately related to his environment is George Mackay Brown, born in 1921 in Stromness, Orkney. His work reflects Orkney's rich heritage of prehistoric sites, its farming and fishing communities, and its religious history. Brown's *Greenvoe* vividly describes life in an imaginary Orkney village; you may also want to read *Fishermen with Ploughs* or any of Brown's other books of poems.

Brown was greatly influenced by the 13th-century *Orkneyinga Saga,* which tells of Magnus, Orkney's own saint, and of the earls of Orkney. The glowing, reddish-stone St. Magnus Cathedral is still a center of worship in Kirkwall and well worth a visit for its warmly enclosed, ancient atmosphere and the carvings on its grave slabs. Also open to visitors are the ruins of Earl Patrick's Palace, in Kirkwall, and Earl's Palace at Birsay; both date from the 16th century, testifying to the continuing status and wealth of the earls of Orkney over the centuries.

Over to the west coast, now, and to Ayrshire, home of Scotland's most famous poet and champion of the underdog, Robert Burns. His poems and songs will never be far away during your Scottish visit. The Burns Heritage Trail takes you to Alloway, where you can visit the poet's birthplace; to Auld Alloway Kirk, where Tam o'Shanter saw the witches; and to the Tam o'Shanter Experience, which brings the poem to life. Burns Night is still a fixture on the Scottish calendar, with readings of "Ode to a Haggis" and "Selkirk Grace" the highlights. But familiarity will not breed contempt; Burns's work is strongly rooted in the countryside he loved, and the poems gain an extra dimension from being read in the land of their birth.

For a taste of life in the Scottish Hebridean islands before you arrive, get a hold of Mairi Hedderwick's delightful Katie Morag children's stories, set on a Hebridean island. Children's stories they may be, but for insights into life on the islands—positive and negative—they are hard to equal. Many teenagers on the islands still dream of their eventual escape to Glasgow or Edinburgh, just as they did 50 or 100 years ago, and Katie Morag's day-to-day life perhaps shows why: the islands are not rich in dance clubs, sports and entertainment centers, fashion boutiques, or Internet cafés. But they are rich in community spirit, tradition and music, and beauty of land and seascape, all of which comes across vividly both in Mairi Hedderwick's text and in the superb, amusingly detailed illustrations. *Kaite Morag and the Big Boy Cousins* is a good title to start with.

Historical novels are a painless way to absorb some of Scotland's history. Mollie Hunter's work is geared toward teenagers; *Escape from Loch Leven* deals with Mary, Queen of Scots, and *The Ghosts of Glencoe* covers the infamous Glencoe massacre. Eric Linklater's *The Prince in the Heather* tells of Bonnie Prince Charlie's efforts to escape after the failure of the 1745 Jacobite rebellion. D. K. Broster's *The Flight of the Heron* and its sequel, *The Dark Mile,* deal with the changes to the clan system effected by the defeat of the Jacobites at Culloden in the mid-18th century. If you want your history fiction-free, try T. C. Smout's *A History of the Scottish People, 1560–1830,* one of the best guides to Scotland's complex past.

And then, of course, there are those quintessentially Scottish books that you are told to read (but few, even Scottish people, seem to get around to reading). The novels and narrative poems of Sir Walter Scott don't seem very user-friendly these days—with their melodramatic plots, overpowering wealth of historical detail, and stately language. But Scott tells a great story, and his settings among the hills and river valleys of southern Scotland are not so very different today: try reading *Rob Roy* or *The Lady of the Lake* when traveling in the Trossachs west of Stirling.

Also a top storyteller was Robert Louis Stevenson, born in Edinburgh though destined to spend much of his life outside Scotland. Read *Kidnapped* and shiver amid the bleak expanse of Rannoch Moor. Then go and gaze across that very moor—its gray, brown, and watery wastes so accurately described by Stevenson—and imagine being a fugitive among its hummocks and pools.

The *Oxford Literary Guide to the British Isles,* edited by Dorothy Eagle and Hilary Carnell, and *Scotland: A Literary Guide,* by Alan Bold, can direct you to other literary landscapes in addition to those mentioned above.

And what about essential reference books to take around with you as you explore Scotland? The series of guides to Scotland's regional architecture produced by the RIAS (Royal Incorporation of Architects in Scotland) are well illustrated, easy to read, and compact enough to keep in the car glove compartment or a handbag. If you enjoy walking, the Official Guides produced for the West Highland Way, the Southern Upland Way, and the Speyside Way are invaluable, and can be purchased locally or before you arrive. There are also several walking guides available locally, including *Walk Loch Lomond and the Trossachs* and *Walk Perthshire.*

Movies

The quintessential "kilt movies" are *Rob Roy* (1995), with Liam Neeson and Jessica Lange—shot at and around Glen Nevis and Glencoe, the gardens of Drummond Castle, and Crichton Castle—and Mel Gibson's *Braveheart* (1995), the story of Scotland's first freedom fighter, Sir William Wallace (circa 1270–1305), which also uses the spectacular craggy scenery of Glen Nevis. Both films are great on atmosphere, not so hot on accurate historical detail, but give a fine preview of Scotland's varied scenery. *Highlander* (1986), with Christopher Lambert and Sean Connery, also used the spectacular crags of Glencoe, along with the prototypical Scottish castle Eilean Donan—almost a visual cliché in Scottish terms. Mel Gibson's *Hamlet* (1990) was filmed at the far more dramatic ruins of cliff-top Dunnottar Castle, Stonehaven, on the northeast coast south of Aberdeen.

The movie of the Scottish classic tale by Muriel Spark, *The Prime of Miss Jean Brodie* (1969), starring Maggie Smith, was filmed in several locations around Edinburgh (as well as in London). In stark contrast, *Trainspotting* (1996), starring Ewan McGregor and based on the book by Irvine Welsh, is a commentary on heroin addicts in an economically depressed Edinburgh. *Small Faces* (1995), written and directed by Gillies MacKinnon, sketches a gritty picture of Glasgow and its gangland violence in the 1960s.

On a more off-beat (and upbeat) note, try to get hold of *Local Hero* (1983), with Burt Lancaster and Peter Riegert. Set in the northeast of Scotland but incorporating a west-coast white-sand beach, the film portrays the best of the east and the west coasts. In the movie the village of Pennan, an hour's drive north of Aberdeen, which huddles below spectacular cliffs, became Ferness, a village threatened by oil development. The village phone box (telephone booth), which played an important part in the film's story, has been carefully preserved. (And, yes, you can see the aurora borealis [the northern lights] from it—sometimes.)

For more information on movies filmed in Scotland, visit the Scotland the Movie Guide Web site (www.scotlandthemovieguide.com).

SCOTLAND AT A GLANCE: A CHRONOLOGY

ca. 3000 BC Neolithic migration from Mediterranean: "chambered cairn" people in north (such as the Grey Cairns of Camster), "beaker people" in southeast.

ca. 300 BC Iron Age: infusion of Celtic peoples from the south and from Ireland; "Gallic forts," "brochs" built.

79–89 Julius Agricola (AD 40–93), Roman governor of Britain, invades Scotland; Scots tribes defeated at the battle of Mons Graupius (thought to be somewhere in the Grampians). Roman forts built at Inchtuthil and Ardoch.

142 Emperor Antoninus Pius (86–161) orders the defensive Antonine Wall built between the Firths of Forth and Clyde.

185 Antonine Wall abandoned.

367 Massive invasion of Britain by Picts, Scots, Saxons, and Franks.

392 Ninian's (ca. 360–432) mission to Picts: first Christian chapel at Whitehorn.

400–1000 Era of the Four Peoples: redheaded Picts in the north, Gaelic-speaking Scots and Britons in the west and south, Germanic Angles in the east. Origins of Arthurian legend (Arthur's Seat, Ben Arthur). Picts, with bloodline through mothers, eventually dominate.

563 Columba (ca. 521–97) establishes monastery at Iona.

780–1065 Scandinavian invasions; Hebrides remain Norse until 1263, Orkney and Shetland until 1472.

1005–34 Malcolm II (ca. 953–1034) unifies Scotland and (temporarily) repels the English.

1040 Malcolm's heir, Duncan (d. 1040), is slain by his rival, Macbeth (d. 1057), whose wife has a claim to the throne.

House of Canmore

1057 Malcolm III (ca. 1031–93), known as Canmore (Big Head), murders Macbeth and assumes the throne.

1093 Death of Malcolm's queen, St. Margaret (1046–93), founder of modern Edinburgh.

1124–53 David I (ca. 1082–1153), *soir sanct* (sore saint), builds the abbeys of Jedburgh (1118), Kelso (1128), Melrose (1136), and Dryburgh (1150) and brings Norman culture to Scotland.

1290 The first of many attempts to unite Scotland peacefully with England fails when the Scots queen Margaret (1283–90), the Maid of Norway, dies on the way to her wedding to Edward (1284–1327), son of Edward I (1239–1307) of England. The Scots naively ask Edward I (subsequently known as the Hammer of the Scots) to arbitrate between the remaining 13 claimants to the throne. Edward's choice, John Balliol (1249–1315), is known as Toom Tabard (Empty Coat).

1295 Under continued threat from England, Scotland signs its first treaty of the "auld alliance" with France. Wine trade flourishes.

1297 Revolutionary William Wallace (ca. 1270–1305), immortalized by Burns, leads the Scots against the English.

1305 Wallace captured by the English and executed.

1306–29 Reign of Robert the Bruce (1274–1329), King Robert I. Defeats Edward II (1284–1327) at Bannockburn, 1314; Treaty of Northampton, 1328, recognizes Scottish sovereignty.

1368 Edinburgh Castle rebuilt.

House of Stewart

1371 Robert II (1316–90), son of Robert the Bruce's daughter Marjorie and Walter the Steward, is crowned. Struggle (dramatized in Scott's novels) between the crown and the barony ensues for the next century, punctuated by sporadic warfare with England.

1411 University of St. Andrews founded.

1451 University of Glasgow founded.

1488–1513 Reign of James IV (1473–1513). The Renaissance reaches Scotland. The Golden Age of Scots poetry includes Robert Henryson (ca. 1425–1508), William Dunbar (ca. 1460–1530), Gavin Douglas (1474–1522), and the king himself.

1495 University of Aberdeen founded.

1507 Andrew Myllar and Walter Chapman set up first Scots printing press in Edinburgh.

1513 At war against the English, James IV is slain at Flodden.

1542 Henry VIII (1491–1547) defeats James V (1512–42) at Solway Moss; the dying James, hearing of the birth of his daughter, Mary, declares: "It came with a lass [Marjorie Bruce] and it will pass with a lass."

1542–67 Reign of Mary, Queen of Scots (1542–87). Romantic, Catholic, and with an excellent claim to the English throne, Mary proved to be no match for her barons, John Knox (1513–72), or her cousin Elizabeth I (1533–1603) of England.

1560 Mary returns to Scotland from her childhood in France at the same time that Catholicism is abolished in favor of Knox's Calvinism.

1565 Mary marries Lord Darnley (1545–67), a Catholic.

1567 Darnley is murdered at Kirk o' Field; Mary marries one of the conspirators, the earl of Bothwell (ca. 1535–78). Driven from Scotland, she appeals to Elizabeth, who imprisons her. Mary's son, James (1566–1625), is crowned James VI of Scotland.

1582 University of Edinburgh is founded.

1587 Elizabeth orders the execution of Mary.

1603 Elizabeth dies without issue; James VI is crowned James I of England. Parliaments remain separate for another century.

1638 National Covenant challenges Charles I's personal rule.

1639–41 Crisis. The Scots and then the English parliaments revolt against Charles I (1600–49).

1643 Solemn League and Covenant establishes Presbyterianism as the Church of Scotland (the Kirk). Civil War in England.

1649 Charles I beheaded. Oliver Cromwell (1599–1658) made Protector.

1650–52 Cromwell roots out Scots royalists.

1658 First Edinburgh–London coach: the journey took two weeks.

1660 Restoration of Charles II (1630–85). Episcopalianism reestablished in Scotland; Covenanters persecuted.

1688–89 Glorious Revolution; James VII and II (1633–1701; the first title is Scottish, the second English), a Catholic, deposed in favor of his daughter Mary (1662–94) and her husband, William of Orange (1650–1702). Supporters of James (known as Jacobites) defeated at Killiecrankie. Presbyterianism reestablished.

1692 Highlanders who were late in taking oath to William and Mary massacred at Glencoe.

1698–1700 Attempted Scottish colony at Darien fails. Many of the Scottish nobility face bankruptcy, and are therefore open to overtures from an English government anxious to unite the Scottish and English parliaments.

1707 Union of English and Scots parliaments under Queen Anne (1665–1714); deprived of French wine trade, Scots turn to whisky.

House of Hanover

1714 Queen Anne dies; George I (1660–1727) of Hanover, descended from a daughter of James VI and I, crowned.

1715 First Jacobite Rebellion. Earl of Mar (1675–1732) defeated.

1730–90 Scottish Enlightenment. The Edinburgh Medical School is the best in Europe; David Hume (1711–76) and Adam Smith (1723–90) redefine philosophy and economics. In the arts, Allan Ramsay the elder (1686–1758) and Robert Burns (1759–96) refine Scottish poetry; Allan Ramsay the younger (1713–84) and Henry Raeburn (1756–1823) rank among the finest painters of the era. Edinburgh's New Town, begun in the 1770s by the brothers Adam (Robert, 1728–92; brother James, 1730–94; father William 1689–1748), provides a fitting setting.

1745–46 Last Jacobite Rebellion. Bonnie Prince Charlie (1720–88), grandson of James VII and II, is defeated at Culloden; wearing of the kilt is forbidden until 1782. James Watt (1736–1819) of Glasgow is granted a patent for his steam engine.

1771 Birth of Walter Scott (1771–1832), Romantic novelist.

1778 First cotton mill, at Rothesay.

1788 Death of Bonnie Prince Charlie.

1790 Forth and Clyde Canal opened.

1800–50 Highland Clearances: overpopulation, increased rents, and conversion of farms to sheep pasture lead to mass migration, sometimes forced, to North America and elsewhere. Meanwhile, the Lowlands industrialize; Catholic Irish immigrate to factories of southwest.

1828 Execution of Burke and Hare, who sold their murder victims to an Edinburgh anatomist, a lucrative trade.

1832 Parliamentary Reform Act expands the franchise, redistributes seats.

1837 Victoria (1819–1901) ascends to the British throne.

1842 Edinburgh–Glasgow railroad opened.

1846 Edinburgh–London railroad opened.

1848 Queen Victoria buys estate at Balmoral as her Scottish residence. Andrew Carnegie emigrates from Dunfermline to Pittsburgh.

1884–85 Gladstone's Reform Act establishes manhood suffrage. Office of Secretary for Scotland authorized.

1886 Scottish Home Rule Association founded.

1901 Death of Queen Victoria.

House of Windsor

1928 Equal Franchise Act gives the vote to women. Scottish Office established as governmental department in Edinburgh. Scottish National Party founded.

1931 Depression hits industrialized Scotland severely.

1945 Two Scottish Nationalists elected to parliament.

1959 Finnart Oil Terminal, Chapelcross Nuclear Power Station, and Dounreay Fast Breeder Reactor opened.

1964 Forth Road Bridge opened.

1970 British Petroleum strikes oil in the North Sea; revives economy of northeast.

1973 Britain becomes a member of the European Economic Community (known as the Common Market).

1974 Eleven Scottish Nationalists elected as members of parliament. Old counties reorganized and renamed as new regions.

1979 Referendum on devolution—the creation of a separate Scotland: 33% for, 31% against; 36% don't vote.

1981 Europe's largest oil terminal opens at Sullom Voe, Shetland.

1988 Revival of Scots nationalism under banner of "Scotland in Europe," anticipating 1992 economic union.

1992 Increasing attention focused on Scotland's dissatisfaction with rule from London. Poll shows 50% of Scots want independence.

1995 In the face of a Tory government increasingly looking like a lame duck and divided on the issue of Europe, Scotland continues to argue its own way forward. The Labour Party promises a Scottish parliament but wants to keep Scotland within the United Kingdom; the Scottish National Party still wants independence and sees Labour's Scottish parliament as a stepping-stone to full autonomy.

1997 The Labour Party wins the general election in May. A referendum held in Scotland votes in favor of the establishment of a Scottish parliament (with restricted powers) by 2000.

2000 At the start of the new millennium, Scotland celebrates its new parliament, elected in May 1999—the first to serve on Scottish soil in more than two centuries.

2003 Parliament is scheduled to move into its own government building at the foot of the Royal Mile in Edinburgh.

INDEX

Icons and Symbols

★ Our special recommendations
✕ Restaurant
🏨 Lodging establishment
✕🏨 Lodging establishment whose restaurant warrants a special trip
🐤 Good for kids (rubber duck)
☞ Sends you to another section of the guide for more information
✉ Address
☎ Telephone number
🕐 Opening and closing times
💷 Admission prices

Numbers in white and black circles ③ ❸ that appear on the maps, in the margins, and within the tours correspond to one another.